Mario and Janet,

With great affection,

over many years.

John

CASES AND MATERIALS

SOCIAL SCIENCE IN LAW

SEVENTH EDITION

by

JOHN MONAHAN

John S. Shannon Distinguished Professor of Law and
Horace W. Goldsmith Research Professor
University of Virginia

LAURENS WALKER

T. Munford Boyd Professor of Law
University of Virginia

FOUNDATION PRESS
2010

THOMSON REUTERS™

© 1985, 1990, 1994, 1998, 2002 FOUNDATION PRESS
© 2006 THOMSON REUTERS/FOUNDATION PRESS
© 2010 By THOMSON REUTERS/FOUNDATION PRESS
          195 Broadway, 9th Floor
          New York, NY 10007
          Phone Toll Free 1–877–888–1330
          Fax (212) 367–6799
          foundation–press.com
Printed in the United States of America

ISBN 978–1–59941–669–4

Mat #40853366

To Linda, Kate, and John (J.M.)

To Sharon (L.W.)

PREFACE TO SEVENTH EDITION

The seventh edition of this book, like the first six, is conceived as a traditional law school casebook, albeit on a non-traditional topic and with an effort to make it accessible to social scientists. The purpose of the book should be clear at the outset: to apprise the reader of the actual and potential uses of social science in the American legal process and how those uses might be evaluated. We here view social science as an analytic tool in the law, familiarity with which will heighten the lawyer's professional effectiveness and sharpen the legal scholar's insights. The principal alternative to this "inside" perspective on the relationship of social science to law is the "law and society" or "sociology of law" approach which seeks to understand the functioning of "law" as a social system. See, for example, S. Macaulay, L. Friedman, and J. Stookey, Law & Society: Readings on the Social Study of Law (1995); R. Abel, The Law and Society Reader (1995). In choosing an orientation from within the legal system rather than that of the law and society observer, we mean no disparagement of the latter. Indeed, we hope that the materials will be found stimulating to those within the law and society tradition. See Monahan and Walker, Teaching Social Science in Law: An Alternative to "Law and Society," 35 Journal of Legal Education 478 (1985).

We have adopted as our particular objectives in this book the analysis of four subtopics, all part of the larger involvement of social science in law: (1) substantive law, meaning the legal rules which make the involvement relevant; (2) legal method, referring to the process of managing the involvement; (3) social science findings, meaning the relevant research results, and (4) social science method, referring to the techniques of carrying out and analyzing that research. These objectives can be restated as an analytic or heuristic framework within which social science in law is viewed as a matrix or table consisting, on one dimension, of issues that are primarily "legal" as compared with issues that are primarily "social science" in nature, and, on the other dimension, of issues that focus on "substantive" matters as compared with issues that focus on "methodological" ones. The matrix could be diagramed as follows:

	Law	**Social Science**
Substance	Substantive Law	Social Science Findings
Method	Legal Method	Social Science Method

Issues pertaining to the nature of a legal doctrine under consideration (e.g., why is social science relevant to the legal determination of obscenity or segregation?) would be Substantive Law. Questions regarding the means by which courts apprise themselves of social science information (e.g., should a study have been introduced at trial rather than on appeal?) would be questions of Legal Method. The results of social science research pertinent to a given legal issue (e.g., does the death penalty deter crime?) would be Social Science Findings. Finally, the methods of data collection and analysis that generated the social science findings (e.g., did the studies eliminate all rival hypotheses that could account for the results?) would be Social Science Method.

The first two chapters of the book build the foundation necessary for appreciating the uses that have been found for social science in American law. The first chapter, Jurisprudential Origins of Social Science in Law, considers the development and ramifications of Legal Realism as the jurisprudential movement that gave legitimacy to empirical inquiry. The second chapter, A Primer of Legal and Social Science Methods, offers a short introduction to fundamental concepts in scientific evidence and in social science research. With this jurisprudential and methodological background, we turn to the legal topics upon which social science has been brought to bear.

Rather than organize the substance of the book according to conventional legal categories (e.g., Constitutional Law, Criminal Law, Civil Procedure) or traditional social science disciplines (e.g., Sociology, Psychology, Anthropology), we have chosen a more theoretical scheme, one that has potential for uncovering relationships that span many different legal categories.

The substance of the book identifies four major uses of social science in law. In chapter three, Social Science Used to Determine Facts, we consider the first of these legal applications, the use of social science to determine factual issues specific to a particular case. In chapter four, Social Science Used to Make Law, we go on to consider the use of social research by courts to establish legal rules that will not only determine the outcome of a particular case, but will also govern a broad category of future cases. In the next chapter, Social Science Used to Provide Context, we consider a use of social science by courts that falls somewhere between the uses identified in chapters three and four: the use of general social science research to provide a context or background for the determination of a factual issue important only in a particular case. In the last chapter, Social Science Used to Plan the Litigation of a Case, we consider the efforts of attorneys to employ social science to prepare for trial.

In each of these chapters our objective is to encourage the development of new insights about the future of social science in law. In this comparatively new field of endeavor, there is much to be learned about the best way to involve social research in the legal process. We provide our own thoughts about this topic with the hope that these views will provoke criticism and discussion. If both teachers and students are encouraged by our presentation to participate in this creative process, our hopes for this book will be fully realized.

While the chapters include material from all of the social sciences, less emphasis is placed on economics and psychiatry, since the relationship of these disciplines to the law has developed to the point that specialized case-books are already available. See, e.g., R. Cooter and T. Ulen, Law and Economics (5th. ed, 2008); R. Reisner, C. Slobogin, and A. Rai, Law and the Mental Health System: Civil and Criminal Aspects (5th ed., 2009).

When taking our course in Social Science in Law, law students frequently asked how to find social science materials on a legal topic not covered in the book or how to update what was included. When graduate and undergraduate students in the social sciences enrolled in the course, they asked how to read legal citations. We have included Appendices, originally drafted by David Faigman and thoroughly revised and updated for this edition by Kent Olson, to help answer both questions. Also compiled in an Appendix are the Federal Rules of Evidence most relevant to the involvement of social science in law.

We appreciate the advice of a number of colleagues on revisions for the seventh edition: Shari Diamond, Phoebe Ellsworth, David Faigman, Michael Saks, and Christopher Slobogin. We are grateful for the excellent work of our student assistants for the seventh edition, Mary Niemann, Elizabeth Kade, and Katherine Foster.

A word is necessary on several editorial conventions we have adopted. Many citations and footnotes that we considered non-essential in the reprinted material have been omitted without indication. Where footnotes are retained, they bear their original numbering. Omissions in the text of the cases and materials, except at the beginning of an excerpt, are indicated by bracketing the first letter of the succeeding word, rather than by a series of dots or asterisks. All extended quotations begin as a new paragraph. Finally, we would like to thank those authors and publishers who gave us permission to reprint in this edition from their works. They are as follows:

Excerpts from ABA Standards for Criminal Justice, Second Edition, copyright © 1980 by American Bar Association; reprinted by permission of the American Bar Association.

Excerpts from The Practice of Social Research, Seventh Edition by Earl Babbie, copyright © 1995 by Wadsworth Publishing Co.; reprinted by permission of the publisher.

Baldus, Woodworth, and Pulaski, Law and Statistics in Conflict: Reflections on McCleskey v. Kemp, in Handbook of Psychology and Law, 265–69 (Kagehiro and Laufer eds. 1992), reprinted with kind permission of Springer Science and Business Media.

Bazelon, Morality of the Criminal Law, 49 Southern California Law Review 1269 (1976); reprinted with the permission of the Southern California Law Review.

Belli, Melvin M., Modern Trials (2d ed. 1982); reprinted with the permission of the author.

Frederick, Jeffrey T., The Psychology of the American Jury (1987); reprinted with the permission of the Michie Company.

Gerard, Harold B., School Desegregation: The Social Science Role, 38 American Psychologist 869 (1983). Copyright © 1983 by the American Psychological Association. Reprinted by permission.

Gross, Samuel R., Overruled: Jury Neutrality in Capital Cases; reprinted from Stanford Lawyer, Vol. 21, No. 1 (Fall 1986). Copyright © 1986 by the Board of Trustees of the Leland Stanford Junior University. Reprinted with permission of the Stanford Lawyer and the author.

Haney, Banks, and Zimbardo, International Dynamics in a Simulated Prison, 1 International Journal of Criminology and Penology 69 (1973). Copyright © 1973 by Academic Press, Inc. (London) Limited; reprinted with the permission of the authors.

Specified Excerpt from Simple Justice by Richard Kluger. Copyright © 1975 by Richard Kluger. Reprinted by permission of Alfred A. Knopf, Inc.

Lawrence, Robert, The Allure of Increased Conviction Rates: The Admissibility of Expert Testimony on Rape Trauma Syndrome in Criminal Proceedings, 70 Virginia Law Review 1657 (1984); reprinted with the permission of the Virginia Law Review and Fred B. Rothman & Co.

Linz, Daniel, S.D. Penrod, and E. Donnerstein, The Attorney General's Commission on Pornography: The Gaps Between Findings and "Facts", 1987 American Bar Foundation Research Journal 713. This material was first published in the American Bar Foundation Research Journal, Number 4, Fall 1987.

Llewellyn, Some Realism About Realism—Responding to Dean Pound, 44 Harvard Law Review 1222 (1931), copyright © 1931 by The Harvard Law Review Association. Reprinted with permission.

Loftus, Elizabeth F., Eyewitness Testimony, excerpts, reprinted by permission of the publisher from EYEWITNESS TESTIMONY, by Elizabeth F. Loftus, Cambridge, Mass.: Harvard University Press, copyright © 1979 by the President and Fellows of Harvard College.

McCarthy, J. Thomas, Trademarks and Unfair Competition (4th ed. 1996); reprinted with permission of the copyright holder, Clark Boardman Callaghan, a division of Thomson Information Services Inc.

McConahay, Mullin, and Frederick, The Use of Social Science in Trials with Political and Racial Overtones: The Trial of Joan Little, 41 Law and Contemporary Problems 205 (1977), copyright © 1977, Duke University School of Law. Reprinted with permission of Duke University School of Law and the authors.

Monahan, John and Laurens Walker, Social Authority: Obtaining, Evaluating, and Establishing Social Science in Law, 134 University of Pennsylvania Law Review; reprinted with permissions of the University of Pennsylvania Law Review and William S. Hein & Co.

Walker and Monahan, Social Facts: Scientific Methodology and Legal Precedent, 76 California Law Review No. 4, July 1988, 877, 877–896. Copyright © 1988 by California Law Review, Inc. Reprinted with permission.

Walker and Monahan, Social Frameworks: A New Use of Social Science in Law, 73 Virginia Law Review 559 (1987); reprinted with the permission of the Virginia Law Review Association and Fred B. Rothman & Co.

White, From Sociological Jurisprudence to Realism: Jurisprudence and Social Change in Early Twentieth Century America, 58 Virginia Law Review 999 (1972); reprinted with permission of the Virginia Law Review Association and Fred B. Rothman & Co.

J.M.
L.W.

Charlottesville, Virginia
September, 2009

SUMMARY OF CONTENTS

TABLE OF CONTENTS

CHAPTER FIVE.   Social Science Used to Provide Context ---- 396

TABLE OF CASES

Principal cases are in bold type. Non-principal cases are in roman type. References are to Pages.

TABLE OF MATERIALS

References are to Pages.

CASES AND MATERIALS

SOCIAL SCIENCE IN LAW

CHAPTER ONE

JURISPRUDENTIAL ORIGINS OF SOCIAL SCIENCE IN LAW

The origins of social science in law are to be found in the jurispruden-tial revolution that took place in the latter part of the 19th and early part of the 20th centuries. American law until this period had been dominated by the belief that a single, correct legal solution could be reached in every case by the application of rules of logic to a set of natural and self-evident principles. Judges constantly sought to ascertain and to follow these immutable principles, and the decision of a particular case was often incidental to the proper statement of the applicable doctrine. This classical jurisprudence has been correctly described as formal or mechanical, since the process of deciding cases was understood as purely rational and deductive, with the results largely inevitable. As the court put it in Green v. Hudson River Railroad Co., 28 Barb. 9, 22 (N.Y.1858), "I have no alternative but to administer the law as I find it—no dispensation from its injunctions to stand by its ancient landmarks."

Two examples of this classical legal thought in action are commonly cited. In United States v. E.C. Knight Co., 156 U.S. 1, 15 S.Ct. 249, 39 L.Ed. 325 (1895), the Supreme Court considered whether a virtual monopo-ly in the manufacture of sugar could be suppressed under the Sherman Act, which prohibited the monopolization of any part of "commerce" in the United States. Though recognizing that there was an "indirect" relation-ship between the production and marketing of sugar, the court nevertheless held that there was a sufficient semantic distinction between "manufactur-ing" and "commerce" to prevent the government from halting monopoliza-tion by the defendants. In a later case, Ives v. South Buffalo Railway Co., 201 N.Y. 271, 94 N.E. 431 (1911), the highest court of New York state invalidated state workmen's compensation legislation as contrary to both the federal and New York constitutions. The court expressly refused to consider a substantial body of social information which a legislative com-mission had collected. It held that "courts must regard all economic, philosophical and moral theories, attractive and desirable though they may be, as subordinate to the primary question [of] whether they can be molded into statutes without infringing upon the letter or spirit of our written Constitutions." Id. at 287, 94 N.E. at 437.

The classical view, however, was not completely dominant; and impor-tant criticisms had emerged as early as the 1880's. Gradually, dissatisfac-tion became widespread, and the established view underwent changes. In general, these changes in legal philosophy reflected a loss of confidence in

1

natural law theories and an increasing tendency to view law as a means of establishing social policy. The classical belief that the application of logic could determine a single, correct solution for every case gave way to the view that the answer to legal problems varies according to the social context. The decision process changed from an exclusively deductive one to a process that incorporated inductive elements. Hence, the discovery and review of information about the functioning of society became more important, and the rational analysis of doctrine began to play a lesser role. Compare Alschuler, Rediscovering Blackstone, 145 University of Pennsylvania Law Review 1 (1996).

The materials that follow present a brief survey of these developments. Their objective is to establish an intellectual background sufficient to provide insight into the topical issues that are the principal subject of this book. Section I examines developments between the late 1800's and about 1930, when the new jurisprudence came to be called "legal realism." Section II focuses on realism and the relationship between this point of view about law and the origins of social science in law.

SECTION I.   EARLY DEVELOPMENTS

Three great figures of American law, Holmes, Brandeis, and Pound, offered early criticism of classical jurisprudence. Their views eventually became instrumental in changing the national consensus about the nature of law and the work of lawyers. Their criticisms undermined the typically formal and mechanical method of classical jurisprudence and supported the notion that law should, at least in part, be concerned with making public policy. The change was dramatic, and its implications still arouse debate. Holmes laid the intellectual foundations for this change by arguing that the essence of law was not logic, but experience. Brandeis demonstrated the practical implications of these new views by using them to win cases. He gained judicial acceptance for the practice of incorporating social science materials in briefs. Pound communicated these ideas prolifically during the period when they were known as "sociological jurisprudence." He generated interest and debate concerning this new paradigm. The materials that follow first sample the contributions of Holmes, Brandeis, and Pound and then indicate how changes in American society eventually led to the reformulation of their early criticism into the "school" of legal realism.

———

THE COMMON LAW (1881)

Oliver Wendell Holmes, Jr.

The object of this book is to present a general view of the Common Law. To accomplish the task, other tools are needed besides logic. It is something to show that the consistency of a system requires a particular result, but it is not all. The life of the law has not been logic: it has been experience. The felt necessities of the time, the prevalent moral and political theories, intuitions of public policy, avowed or unconscious, even the prejudices which judges share with their fellow-men, have had a good deal more to do than the syllogism in determining the rules by which men should be governed. The law embodies the story of a nation's development through many centuries, and it cannot be dealt with as if it contained only the axioms and corollaries of a book of mathematics. In order to know what it is, we must know what it has been, and what it tends to become. We must alternately consult history and existing theories of legislation. But the most difficult labor will be to understand the combination of the two into new products at every stage. The substance of the law at any given time pretty nearly corresponds, so far as it goes, with what is then understood to be convenient; but its form and machinery, and the degree to which it is able to work out desired results, depend very much upon its past.

[There is a] paradox of form and substance in the development of law. In form its growth is logical. The official theory is that each new decision follows syllogistically from existing precedents. But just as the clavicle in the cat only tells of the existence of some earlier creature to which a collarbone was useful, precedents survive in the law long after the use they once served is at an end and the reason for them has been forgotten. The result of following them must often be failure and confusion from the merely logical point of view.

On the other hand, in substance the growth of the law is legislative. And this in a deeper sense than that what the courts declare to have always been the law is in fact new. It is legislative in its grounds. The very considerations which judges most rarely mention, and always with an apology, are the secret root from which the law draws all the juices of life. I mean, of course, considerations of what is expedient for the community concerned. Every important principle which is developed by litigation is in fact and at bottom the result of more or less definitely understood views of public policy; most generally, to be sure, under our practice and traditions, the unconscious result of instinctive preferences and inarticulate convictions, but none the less traceable to views of public policy in the last analysis. And as the law is administered by able and experienced men, who know too much to sacrifice good sense to a syllogism, it will be found that, when ancient rules maintain themselves, [n]ew reasons more fitted to the time have been found for them, and that they gradually receive a new content, and at last a new form, from the grounds to which they have been transplanted.

But hitherto this process has been largely unconscious. It is important, on that account, to bring to mind what the actual course of events has been. If it were only to insist on a more conscious recognition of the legislative function of the courts, as just explained, it would be useful.

[W]hat has been said will explain the failure of all theories which consider the law only from its formal side, whether they attempt to deduce the *corpus* from *a priori* postulates, or fall into the humbler error of supposing the science of the law to reside in the *elegantia juris,* or logical cohesion of part with part. The truth is, that the law is always approaching, and never reaching, consistency. It is forever adopting new principles from life at one end, and it always retains old ones from history at the other, which have not yet been absorbed or sloughed off. It will become entirely consistent only when it ceases to grow.

———

NOTES

1. The Role of the Judiciary. Holmes' statement that "the growth of the law is legislative" should not be misunderstood as a call for judicial activism. Indeed, Holmes was a noted advocate of judicial restraint and practiced this conservative philosophy during his many years on the Supreme Judicial Court of Massachusetts and the United States Supreme Court. He believed that judges should be cautious and should not initiate change measurably ahead of public acceptance. For Holmes, making major shifts in legal doctrine was a task for elected legislators, and their judgments should command substantial judicial deference. See Kaplan, Encounters With O.W. Holmes, Jr., 96 Harvard Law Review 1828, 1847 (1983). Holmes' statement about the development of common law should be considered in light of his distaste for classical legal thought and its emphasis on the role of deduction from principle in deciding cases. He thought that the policy preferences of judges determined judicial decision making, a process he called "legislative." But he thought that this "legislative" function of courts should be as subservient as possible to the "legislative" function of the legislature.

2. The Role of Social Science. In The Path of the Law, 10 Harvard Law Review 457, 469 (1897), published sixteen years after The Common Law, Holmes asserted that, "For the rational study of the law the black-letter man may be the man of the present, but the man of the future is the man of statistics and the master of economics." Thus it appears that Holmes linked the jurisprudence described in The Common Law with use of the methods and theories that are today generally included under the rubric of the "social sciences." Holmes identified a wide range of social issues that must be investigated if the law is to be reformed. Consider, for example, Holmes' statement, Id. at 470:

> What have we better than a blind guess to show that the criminal law in its present form does more good than harm? I do not stop to refer to the effect which it has had in degrading prisoners and in plunging them further into crime, or to the question whether fine and imprisonment do not fall more heavily on a criminal's wife and children than on himself. I have in mind more far-reaching questions. Does punishment deter? Do we deal with criminals on proper principles?

———

BRIEF FOR THE DEFENDANT IN ERROR MULLER v. OREGON

Supreme Court of the United States, 1907.
208 U.S. 412, 28 S.Ct. 324, 52 L.Ed. 551.

Louis D. Brandeis, Counsel for the State of Oregon.

[In 1903, the Oregon legislature enacted a statute which limited the work day of any female employed in a factory or a laundry to ten hours. In 1905, the Oregon Supreme Court affirmed the conviction of laundry owner Curt Muller, who had violated this statute. Muller appealed.]

The experience of manufacturing countries has illustrated the evil effect of overwork upon the general welfare. Deterioration of any large portion of the population inevitably lowers the entire community physically, mentally, and morally. When the health of women has been injured by long hours, not only is the working efficiency of the community impaired, but the deterioration is handed down to succeeding generations. Infant mortality rises, while the children of married working-women, who survive, are injured by inevitable neglect. The overwork of future mothers thus directly attacks the welfare of the nation.

(1) The State's Need of Protecting Woman

Report of the Massachusetts State Board of Health, 1873. Edward Jarvis, M.D.

All additions to the physical, moral, or intellectual power of individuals—in any individual are, to that extent, additions to the energy and the productive force—the effectiveness of the State; and on the contrary, all deductions from these forces, whether of mind or body—every sickness, and injury or disability, every impairment of energy—take so much from the mental force, the safe administration of the body politic. . . .

The State thus has an interest not only in the prosperity, but also in the health and strength and effective power of each one of its members. . . .

The first and largest interest of the State lies in the great agency of human power—the health of the people.

Report of the Massachusetts Bureau of Labor Statistics, 1871.

It is claimed that legislation on this subject is an interference between labor and capital. . . . But legislation has interfered with capital and labor both, in the demand for public safety and the public good. Now public safety and public good, the wealth of the commonwealth, centered, as such wealth is, in the well-being of its common people, demands that the State should interfere by special act in favor of . . . working-women, and working children, by enacting a ten-hour law, to be enforced by a system of efficient inspection.

International Conference in Relation to Labor Legislation. Berlin, 1890.

It is the idea of the German Emperor that the industrial question demands the attention of all the civilized nations. ...

The quest of a solution becomes not only a humanitarian duty, but it is exacted also by governmental wisdom, which should at once look out for the well-being of all its citizens and the preservation of the inestimable benefits of civilization.

Proceedings of the French Senate. Session of July 7, 1891. M. Jules Simon.

It is impossible for me not to tell the Senate what I think of the position of women in industry, and that I may gain your favor, gentlemen, I ask permission to tell you that for at least forty years I have applied myself to this question.

When I ask, when we ask, for a lessening of the daily toil of women, it is not only of the women that we think; it is not principally of the women, it is of the whole human race. It is of the father, it is of the child, it is of society, which we wish to re-establish on its foundation, from which we believe it has perhaps swerved a little.

Report of the New York Bureau of Labor Statistics.

The family furnishes the really fundamental education of the growing generation—the education of character; and the family life thus really determines the quality of the rising generation as efficient or non-efficient wealth producers. If a reduction in the hours of labor does promote the growth of a purer and better family life, it will unquestionably result in the production of greater material wealth on the part of the generation trained under its influence; nothing else in fact will so effectively diminish the vast number of criminals, paupers, and idlers, who, in the present generation, consume the people's substance. When one or both parents are away from home for twelve or thirteen hours (the necessary period for those who work ten hours) a day, the children receive comparatively little attention. What was said in the opening paragraph of this section in discussing the importance of a good family life in the training of character needs repeated emphasis, for it is the fundamental argument for a shorter working day.

Hygiene of Occupations. Dr. Theodore Weyl. Jena, 1904.

Women bear the following generation whose health is essentially influenced by that of the mothers, and the State has a vital interest in securing for itself future generations capable of living and maintaining it.

The Working Hours of Female Factory Hands. From reports of the Factory Inspectors collated by the Imperial Home Office. Berlin, 1905.

The reports from Marseburg, Erfurt, Breslau, Hanover, Wurtemberg, and Offenbach dwell upon the dependence of future generations—their total efficiency and value—upon the protection of working women and girls.

President Roosevelt's Annual Message delivered to Second Session of 59th Congress. December 4, 1906.

More and more our people are growing to recognize the fact that the questions which are not merely of industrial but of social importance outweigh all others; and these two questions (labor of women and children) most emphatically come in the category of those which affect in the most far-reaching way the home life of the Nation.

Legislative Control of Women's Work. By S.P. Breckinridge. Journal of Political Economy. Vol. XIV. 1906.

The assumption of control over the conditions under which industrial women are employed is one of the most significant features of recent legislative policy. In many of the advanced industrial communities the State not only undertakes to prescribe a minimum of decency, safety, and healthfulness, below which its wage-earners may not be asked to go, but takes cognizance in several ways of sex differences and sex relationships. ... In the third place, the State sometimes takes cognizance of the peculiarly close relationship which exists between the health of its women citizens and the physical vigor of future generations. ... It has been declared a matter of public concern that no group of its women workers should be allowed to unfit themselves by excessive hours of work, by standing, or other physical strain, for the burden of motherhood which each of them should be able to assume.

The object of such control is the protection of the physical well-being of the community by setting a limit to the exploitation of the improvident, unworkmanlike, unorganized women who are yet the mothers, actual or prospective, of the coming generation.

Conclusion

[W]e submit that in view of the facts above set forth and of legislative action extending over a period of more than sixty years in the leading countries of Europe, and in twenty of our States, it cannot be said that the Legislature of Oregon had no reasonable ground for believing that the public health, safety, or welfare did not require a legal limitation on women's work in manufacturing and mechanical establishments and laundries to ten hours in one day.

———

NOTES

1. Development of the Brief. The National Consumers' League, a progressive citizen's group, became involved in Muller v. Oregon when the case reached the United States Supreme Court. Progressivism was an early 20th century political movement that sought to remedy a number of problems associated with industrialization. The enactment of legislation regulating wages, hours, and child labor was a key aspect of the progressive agenda.

In 1905, the Supreme Court decided Lochner v. New York, 198 U.S. 45, 25 S.Ct. 539, 49 L.Ed. 937, which invalidated a New York statute limiting the work week of bakers to 60 hours. The court held that the New York statute was not a legitimate exercise of state police powers, but rather an encroachment on freedom of contract as established by the Fourteenth Amendment. Apparently the leaders of the Consumers' League saw in *Muller* an opportunity to narrow the effect of the *Lochner* case, a decision that had cast doubt on much of the progressive program. Two League members, Florence Kelley and Josephine Goldmark, persuaded the Oregon Attorney General to invite Boston attorney Louis Brandeis to serve as counsel in the case. Brandeis already had a national reputation as a progressive advocate.

The need to avoid the *Lochner* precedent dictated the specific focus of the Brandeis brief. One possible way to avoid *Lochner* was to argue that women workers required special protection by the state. Obviously this argument infringed on efforts, already then underway, to secure equal treatment for women in other areas (e.g., the right to vote), but apparently the leaders of the Consumers' League believed that the pragmatic benefits of obtaining protection for women from exploitation in the workplace outweighed the risk of damaging other efforts toward equality.

Goldmark directed the research for the brief. She supervised a team of eleven investigators who searched the Columbia University Library for material concerning the impact of long working hours on working women. The results of their work filled most of Brandeis' 113 page brief. See Collins and Friesen, Looking Back on Muller v. Oregon, 69 American Bar Association Journal 294 (1983).

2. Quality of the Research. Ironically, although Brandeis' brief in Muller v. Oregon initiated the use of social science materials in American courts, today its contents would not be accepted as social science evidence. As the above excerpt reveals, the brief was a collection of broad, value-laden statements supported largely by casual observation and opinion. This was typical of social science scholarship at that time. During the next several decades, however, social science became more positivistic and naturalistic, reflecting new beliefs that knowledge about people and society should be gathered "scientifically," through experimental and empirical means.

————

MULLER v. OREGON

Supreme Court of the United States, 1907.
208 U.S. 412, 28 S.Ct. 324, 52 L.Ed. 551.

■ MR. JUSTICE BREWER delivered the opinion of the Court.

We held in Lochner v. New York, 198 U.S. 45, 49 L.Ed. 937, 25 Sup.Ct.Rep. 539, that a law providing that no laborer shall be required or permitted to work in a bakery more than sixty hours in a week or ten hours in a day was not as to men a legitimate exercise of the police power of the State, but an unreasonable, unnecessary and arbitrary interference with the right and liberty of the individual to contract in relation to his labor, and as such was in conflict with, and void under, the Federal Constitution. That decision is invoked by plaintiff in error as decisive of the question before us. But this assumes that the difference between the sexes does not justify a different rule respecting a restriction of the hours of labor.

In patent cases counsel are apt to open the argument with a discussion of the state of the art. It may not be amiss, in the present case, before examining the constitutional question, to notice the course of legislation as well as expressions of opinion from other than judicial sources. In the brief filed by Mr. Louis D. Brandeis, for the defendant in error, is a very copious collection of all these matters, an epitome of which is found in the margin.[1]

[T]he legislation and opinions referred to in the margin may not be, technically speaking, authorities, and in them is little or no discussion of the constitutional question presented to us for determination, yet they are significant of a widespread belief that woman's physical structure, and the functions she performs in consequence thereof, justify special legislation restricting or qualifying the conditions under which she should be permitted to toil. Constitutional questions, it is true, are not settled by even a consensus of present public opinion, for it is the peculiar value of a written constitution that it places in unchanging form limitations upon legislative action, and thus gives a permanence and stability to popular government which otherwise would be lacking. At the same time, when a question of fact is debated and debatable, and the extent to which a special constitutional limitation goes is affected by the truth in respect to that fact, a widespread and long continued belief concerning it is worthy of consideration. We take judicial cognizance of all matters of general knowledge.

It is undoubtedly true, as more than once declared by this court, that the general right to contract in relation to one's business is part of the liberty of the individual, protected by the Fourteenth Amendment to the Federal Constitution; yet it is equally well settled that this liberty is not

---

1. The following legislation of the States impose restrictions in some form or another upon the hours of labor that may be required of women: [Nineteen state statutes are cited.]

In foreign legislation Mr. Brandeis calls attention to these statutes: [Statutes from six foreign countries are cited.] Then follow extracts from over ninety reports of committees, bureaus of statistics, commissioners of hygiene, inspectors of factories, both in this country and in Europe, to the effect that long hours of labor are dangerous for women, primarily because of their special physical organization. The matter is discussed in these reports in different aspects, but all agree as to the danger. It would of course take too much space to give these reports in detail. Following them are extracts from similar reports discussing the general benefits of short hours from an economic aspect of the question. In many of these reports individual instances are given tending to support the general conclusion. Perhaps the general scope and character of all these reports may be summed up in what an inspector for Hanover says: "The reasons for the reduction of the working day to ten hours—(a) the physical organization of women, (b) her maternal functions, (c) the rearing and education of the children, (d) the maintenance of the home—are all so important and so far reaching that the need for such reduction need hardly be discussed."

absolute and extending to all contracts, and that a State may, without conflicting with the provisions of the Fourteenth Amendment, restrict in many respects the individual's power of contract.

[T]hat woman's physical structure and the performance of maternal functions place her at a disadvantage in the struggle for subsistence is obvious. This is especially true when the burdens of motherhood are upon her. Even when they are not, by abundant testimony of the medical fraternity continuance for a long time on her feet at work, repeating this from day to day, tends to injurious effects upon the body, and as healthy mothers are essential to vigorous offspring, the physical well-being of woman becomes an object of public interest and care in order to preserve the strength and vigor of the race.

[T]he judgment of the Supreme Court of Oregon is affirmed.

————

NOTES

1.   Rationality Review. The outcome in Muller v. Oregon was an exception to the Supreme Court's common practice, from 1897 to 1937, of invalidating state and federal legislation that the court viewed as interfering with private economic transactions. Acting under the Fifth and Fourteenth Amendments, the court vigorously investigated the substantive wisdom of legislation using a test requiring that there be a reasonable relation between legislation and some legitimate state interest. This practice commenced with Allgeyer v. Louisiana, 165 U.S. 578, 17 S.Ct. 427, 41 L.Ed. 832 (1897), which invalidated a statute regulating insurance companies, and only waned as the onset of the Depression in the 1930's created a demand for government economic intervention. The era of widespread substantive review ended with West Coast Hotel Co. v. Parrish, 300 U.S. 379, 57 S.Ct. 578, 81 L.Ed. 703 (1937), which upheld minimum wage legislation, and NLRB v. Jones & Laughlin Steel Corp., 301 U.S. 1, 57 S.Ct. 615, 81 L.Ed. 893 (1937), which approved the National Labor Relations Act. The basic justification for judicial intervention under *Lochner* was that courts were restoring the "natural" order which legislative action had disrupted. The growing perception that there was no natural economic order to disrupt (or restore) contributed to the end of "Lochnerizing," as the practice was labeled. See, L. Tribe, American Constitutional Law 1332, 1343–1346 (3rd ed., 2000). Application of the reasonable relation test in *Muller* meant that the brief filed by Brandeis did not, theoretically, need to demonstrate the truth of the proposition concerning the harmful effect of long working hours on women, but only needed to show that a respectable body of opinion supported such views.

The rational relationship test, in principle, still limits all legislation, but since 1937 its application has been tantamount to finding legislation constitutional; the court has found virtually any proposed reason sufficient to sustain a statute. In recent years the Supreme Court has developed other tests which apply only in narrowly defined situations, but which constitute more demanding standards concerning legislative action. The court will strictly scrutinize legislation when a fundamental right, such as freedom of speech, is affected or a suspect classification, such as race, is used by a legislative body. A state must demonstrate some compelling interest if the legislation is to be upheld. Also, the court has used an intermediate test to examine marginally suspect classifications such as gender. That test requires that an important state interest be shown, apparently a stricter requirement than the reasonable relation test, but less strict than the compelling state interest standard.

2.   Subsequent Cases. The brief filed in Muller v. Oregon proved to be the first of several similar briefs filed in support of legislation establishing maximum hours for workers. For example, Brandeis and Goldmark filed a 610 page brief in W.C. Ritchie & Co. v. Wayman, 244 Ill. 509, 91 N.E. 695 (1910), where the court decided that an Illinois statute which generally limited the working hours of women to ten per day did not violate the Illinois Constitution. The series culminated in Bunting v. Oregon, 243 U.S. 426, 37 S.Ct. 435, 61 L.Ed. 830 (1917), for which Brandeis, Goldmark, and a new member of their team, Felix Frankfurter, prepared a 1,021 page brief in support of Oregon legislation limiting the working hours of both men and women to ten per day. Unlike the *Muller* and *Ritchie* briefs, the *Bunting* brief did not mention physical differences between men and women. Instead, it emphasized work-related fatigue and its ill effects. Notwithstanding *Lochner* (and without mentioning that case), a majority of the justices upheld the statute. By the time *Bunting* was decided, Brandeis himself had become a justice of the Supreme Court. He did not participate in the decision. See Friesen and Collins, Looking Back on Muller v. Oregon, 69 American Bar Association Journal 472 (1983).

————

THE SCOPE AND PURPOSE OF SOCIOLOGICAL JURISPRUDENCE

Roscoe Pound.
25 Harvard Law Review 489 (1912).

The main problem to which sociological jurists are addressing themselves today is to enable and to compel law-making, and also interpretation and application of legal rules, to take more account, and more intelligent account, of the social facts upon which law must proceed and to which it is to be applied. More specifically, they insist upon six points:

(1) The first is study of the actual social effects of legal institutions and legal doctrines.

(2) The second is sociological study in connection with legal study in preparation for legislation. The accepted scientific method has been to study other legislation analytically. Comparative legislation has been taken to be the best foundation for wise lawmaking. But it is not enough to compare the laws themselves. It is much more important to study their

social operation and the effects which they produce, if any, when put in action.

(3) The third is study of the means of making legal rules effective. This has been neglected almost entirely in the past. We have studied the making of law sedulously. It seems to have been assumed that, when made, law will enforce itself. This is true not only of legislation but also of that more important part of our law which rests in the reports. Almost the whole energy of our judicial system is employed in working out a consistent, logical, minutely precise body of precedents. The important part of our system is not the trial judge who dispenses justice to litigants but the judge of the appellate court who uses the litigation as a means of developing the law; and we judge the system by the output of written opinions and not by the actual results *inter partes* in concrete causes. But the life of the law is in its enforcement. Serious scientific study of how to make our huge annual output of legislation and judicial interpretation effective is imperative.

(4) A means toward the end last considered is a sociological legal history; that is, study not merely of how doctrines have evolved and developed, considered solely as jural materials, but of what social effects the doctrines of the law have produced in the past and how they have produced them. Accordingly Kantorowicz calls for a legal history which shall not deal with rules and doctrines apart from the economic and social history of their time, as if the causes of change in the law were always to be found in the legal phenomena of the past; a legal history that shall not try to show that the law of the past can give us an answer to every question, by systematic deduction, as if it were a system without hiatus and without antinomies. Instead it is to show us how the law of the past grew out of social, economic, and psychological conditions, how it accorded with or accommodated itself to them, and how far we can proceed upon that law as a basis, or in disregard of it, with well-grounded expectations of producing the results desired.

(5) Another point is the importance of reasonable and just solutions of individual causes, too often sacrificed in the immediate past to the attempt to bring about an impossible degree of certainty. A whole literature has grown up in recent years upon this subject. In general the sociological jurists stand for what has been called equitable application of law; that is, they conceive of the legal rule as a general guide to the judge, leading him toward the just result, but insist that within wide limits he should be free to deal with the individual case, so as to meet the demands of justice between the parties and accord with the general reason of ordinary men.

(6) Finally, the end, toward which the foregoing points are but some of the means, is to make effort more effective in achieving the purposes of law.

Summarily stated, the sociological jurist pursues a comparative study of legal systems, legal doctrines, and legal institutions as social phenomena, and criticizes them with respect to their relation to social conditions and social progress. Comparing sociological jurists with jurists of the other schools, we may say:

    1.   They look more to the working of the law than to its abstract content.

    2.   They regard law as a social institution which may be improved by intelligent human effort, and hold it their duty to discover the best means of furthering and directing such effort.

    3.   They lay stress upon the social purposes which law subserves rather than upon sanction.

    4.   They urge that legal precepts are to be regarded more as guides to results which are socially just and less as inflexible molds.

    5.   Their philosophical views are very diverse. Beginning as positivists, recently they have adhered to some one of the groups of the social philosophical school, from which, indeed, the sociological school, on many essential points, is not easily distinguishable. While Professor Moore tells us that the time has come "in the development of the pragmatic movement for systematic and detailed applications of pragmatic conceptions and methods to specific problems, rather than further discussion of general principles,"[103] unhappily discussion of general principles goes on and a pragmatist philosophy of law is yet to come. When it is promulgated it may expect many adherents from the sociological jurists.

NOTES

1. Law In Action. Many of Pound's views have become so widely accepted that today they are regarded as commonplace. For example, it is now well understood that the actual operation of any legal system diverges significantly from the formally stated specification of that system. This important insight can be traced directly to a single, early article written by Pound, Law In Books and Law In Action, 44 American Law Review, 12 (1910), in which he pointed out numerous then-current examples of divergence between doctrine and practice. Pound concluded, Id. at 35–36:

> Let us look the facts of human conduct in the face. Let us look to economics and sociology and philosophy, and cease to assume that jurisprudence is self-sufficient. It is the work of lawyers to make the law in action conform to the law in the books, not by futile thunderings against popular lawlessness, nor eloquent exhortations to obedience of the written law, but by making law in the books such that the law in action can conform to it, and providing a speedy, cheap and efficient legal mode of applying it.

103. Pragmatism and its Critics, Preface.

2. Cardozo. In addition to Pound, Benjamin Cardozo is also recognized as an important American advocate of sociological jurisprudence. In his book, The Nature of the Judicial Process 112–13 (1922), Cardozo both acknowledged the value of logic and precedent and urged that the interests of society be taken into account. He wrote:

> Analysis of the judicial process comes then to this, and little more: logic, and history, and custom, and utility, and the accepted standards of right conduct, are the forces which singly or in combination shape the progress of the law. Which of these forces shall dominate in any case, must depend largely upon the comparative importance or value of the social interests that will be thereby promoted or impaired. One of the most fundamental social interests is that law shall be uniform and impartial. There must be nothing in its action that savors of prejudice or favor or even arbitrary whim or fitfulness. Therefore in the main there shall be adherence to precedent. There shall be symmetrical development, consistently with history or custom when history or custom has been the motive force, or the chief one, in giving shape to existing rules, and with logic or philosophy when the motive power has been theirs. But symmetrical development may be bought at too high a price. Uniformity ceases to be a good when it becomes uniformity of oppression. The social interest served by symmetry or certainty must then be balanced against the social interest served by equity and fairness or other elements of social welfare. These may enjoin upon the judge the duty of drawing the line at another angle, of staking the path along new courses, of marking a new point of departure from which others who come after him will set out upon their journey.

————

FROM SOCIOLOGICAL JURISPRUDENCE TO REALISM: JURISPRUDENCE AND SOCIAL CHANGE IN EARLY TWENTIETH CENTURY AMERICA

G. Edward White.
58 Virginia Law Review 999 (1972).

A stimulus to the emergence of Realism was the changed face of Progressivism in the 1920's. The movement did not, as historians once thought, disappear in that decade. The federal administrative apparatus Progressivism had erected, including the Federal Trade Commission and the Federal Reserve Board, remained intact; states continued to pass welfare legislation; the most popular political figure of the time, Herbert Hoover, called himself a Progressive and promoted the respected Progressive values of efficiency, honesty, morality, and social engineering. But the sense of optimism and cheerfulness about the eventual destiny of man that had pervaded America prior to World War I had vanished with that experience. Progressivism rested, finally, on the concept of progress, a composite of the inherent perfectibility of man and the permanently dynamic quality of society. The First World War made progress a hollow belief.

Morality too, in its old-fashioned form, seemed vanished with the war. A reexamination of traditional standards of morality had been stimulated by Progressivism itself; as its adherents became more impressed with the notion of social change and the impermanence of ideas and institutions, they came to question the inviolability of their own moral principles. Divorce rates rose sharply in the early twentieth century; traditional definitions of sex roles were challenged. The war, with its images of holocaust and meaningless death and its mood of social instability, accelerated this process. Earnestness, a favorite state of the prewar years, was replaced by cynicism; social responsibility gave way to alienation, virtuousness appeared as hypocrisy.

In keeping with this shift in attitudes was a growing interest in the behavioral sciences, with their emphasis on sexuality and their relativistic view of human nature and morality. [T]he primary impact of the behavioral sciences was their suggestion that the personalities of humans and even nations or cultures could be studied empirically. Once the human psyche had been explained, enthusiasts felt, its impact on the institutions and artifacts of society could be better understood.

[T]he thrust of behavioral science research was that human behavior was idiosyncratic and often irrational and that external sanctions on personal actions were actually products of an individual's own psyche. This insight was subversive of collective behavior standards based on external phenomena, such as religious or moral beliefs. All these beliefs were indistinguishable from one's superego, and their permanency was questionable. This appeared to suggest that collective moral values, on which the Progressives had placed such faith, were ephemeral and perhaps even nonexistent.

[T]he year 1930 marked the full scale emergence of a new theory of American jurisprudence which contained within it an alternative to Pound's view of adjudication. That year witnessed a selective gathering of strands from Sociological Jurisprudence and the behavioral sciences into a loose theoretical patchwork termed "the realist movement," "realist jurisprudence," or, most commonly, Realism. The principal collectors, Karl Llewellyn and Jerome Frank, may be considered the primary exponents of Realism not because their views were most representative of the movement (most of the individuals who considered themselves Realists were disinclined to allow their colleagues' views to represent their own), but because they were the most anxious of their peers to see themselves as members of a jurisprudential "school," to attempt to state its canons, and to criticize other schools. Consequently, of all the Realists, Llewellyn's and Frank's views received the most attention within the legal community; critics of Realism continually assumed that these two men were its leading exponents and often based their attacks on the movement exclusively on a reading of their work.

———

NOTE

1. Jurisprudence and Politics. In other parts of his article, Professor White noted that the advocates of sociological jurisprudence were often identified with the progressive political movement, while leading realists were almost always advocates of President Franklin Roosevelt's New Deal programs, which had been proposed in response to the problems of the Depression. White suggests that the differences between the two jurisprudential schools were analogous to the differences between the political movements. The progressives and the sociological jurisprudes maintained a core belief in traditional principles and moral values. The New Dealers and the realists discounted the worth of many traditional values and expressed a preference for pragmatic experimentation.

SELECTED BIBLIOGRAPHY

A. Alschuler, Law Without Values: The Life, Work, and Legacy of Oliver Wendell Holmes (2000).

S. Burton, The Path of the Law and its Influences: The Legacy of Oliver Wendell Holmes, Jr. (2007).

Collins & Friesen, Looking Back on Muller v. Oregon, 69 American Bar Association Journal 294 (1983).

J. De Haas, Louis D. Brandeis (2007).

Friesen and Collins, Looking Back on Muller v. Oregon, 69 American Bar Association Journal 472 (1983).

Galanter, In The Winter of Our Discontent: Law, Anti–Law, and Social Science, 2 Annual Review of Law and Social Science 1 (2006).

N. Hull, Roscoe Pound and Karl Llewellyn: Searching for an American Jurisprudence (1997).

The Role of Social Science in Law (E. Mertz ed, 2008).

Nelson, Judicial Review of Legislative Purpose, 83 New York University Law Review 1784 (2008).

E. Purcell, Brandeis and the Progressive Constitution: Erie, the Judicial Power, and the Politics of the Federal Courts in Twentieth–Century America (2000).

P. Sayre, The Life of Roscoe Pound (2008).

SECTION II.   THE REALIST MOVEMENT

The early criticism of classical jurisprudence eventually led to a truly radical revolt against formalism. A clear sign of this change was the publication by Llewellyn of A Realistic Jurisprudence—The Next Step, 30 Columbia Law Review 431 (1930). Though the views expressed in the article were plainly tentative, it was the first self-conscious claim that a decisive break with the past had occurred. The young leaders of this movement insisted that a new school of jurisprudence was forming, and over the next few years they undertook to define—and defend—a "realistic" jurisprudence. The realist movement was a logical elaboration and extension of the views proposed by Holmes nearly half a century before, and was clearly influenced by the beliefs of Brandeis, Pound, and other sociological jurisprudes. Yet, as White points out above, there were important differences between the early critics of classical jurisprudence and the realists, primarily concerning the role of values and rules in a legal system. Perhaps the most significant difference, however, was the fervor of the realists. They advocated their views with such zeal that realist jurisprudence, at least in modified form, became a core assumption, a starting point in thinking about American law. As a consequence, the empiricism of realist thinking has become an inherent aspect of current American legal thought. The following materials briefly trace the surge of realism and indicate its ultimate scope and impact.

SOME REALISM ABOUT REALISM—RESPONDING TO DEAN POUND

Karl N. Llewellyn.
44 Harvard Law Review 1222 (1931).

I speak for myself of that movement which in its sum is realism; I do not speak of "the realists"; still less do I speak *for* the participants or any of them. And I shall endeavor to keep in mind as I go that the justification for grouping these men together lies not in that they are *alike* in belief or work, but in that from certain common points of departure they have branched into lines of work which seem to be building themselves into a whole, a whole planned by none, foreseen by none, and (it may well be) not yet adequately grasped by any.

The common points of departure are several.

(1) The conception of law in flux, of moving law, and of judicial creation of law.

(2) The conception of law as a means to social ends and not as an end in itself; so that any part needs constantly to be examined for its purpose, and for its effect, and to be judged in the light of both and of their relation to each other.

(3) The conception of society in flux, and in flux typically faster than the law, so that the probability is always given that any portion of law needs re-examination to determine how far it fits the society it purports to serve.

(4) The *temporary* divorce of Is and Ought for purposes of study. By this I mean that whereas value judgments must always be appealed to in order to set objectives for inquiry, yet during the inquiry itself into what Is, the observation, the description, and the establishment of relations between the things described are to remain *as largely as possible* uncontami-

nated by the desires of the observer or by what he wishes might be or thinks ought (ethically) to be. More particularly, this involves during the study of what courts are doing the effort to disregard the question what they ought to do. Such divorce of Is and Ought is, of course, not conceived as permanent. To men who begin with a suspicion that change is needed, a permanent divorce would be impossible. The argument is simply that no judgment of what Ought to be done in the future with respect to any part of law can be intelligently made without knowing objectively, as far as possible, what that part of law is now doing. And realists believe that experience shows the intrusion of Ought-spectacles *during the investigation of the facts* to make it very difficult to see what is being done. On the Ought side this means an insistence on informed evaluations instead of armchair speculations.

(5) Distrust of traditional legal rules and concepts insofar as they purport to *describe* what either courts or people are actually doing. Hence the constant emphasis on rules as "generalized predictions of what courts will do." This is much more widespread as yet than its counterpart: the careful severance of rules *for* doing (precepts) from rules *of* doing (practices).

(6) Hand in hand with this distrust of traditional rules (on the descriptive side) goes a distrust of the theory that traditional prescriptive rule-formulations are *the* heavily operative factor in producing court decisions. This involves the tentative adoption of the theory of rationalization for the study of opinions. It will be noted that "distrust" in this and the preceding point is not at all equivalent to "negation in any given instance."

(7) The belief in the worthwhileness of grouping cases and legal situations into narrower categories than has been the practice in the past. This is connected with the distrust of verbally simple rules—which so often cover dissimilar and non-simple fact situations (dissimilarity being tested partly by the way cases come out, and partly by the observer's judgment as to how they ought to come out; but a realist tries to indicate explicitly which criterion he is applying).

(8) An insistence on evaluation of any part of law in terms of its effects, and an insistence on the worthwhileness of trying to find these effects.

(9) Insistence on *sustained and programmatic attack* on the problems of law along any of these lines. None of the ideas set forth in this list is new. Each can be matched from somewhere; each can be matched from recent orthodox work in law. New twists and combinations do appear here and there. What is as novel as it is vital is for a goodly number of men to pick up ideas which have been expressed and dropped, used for an hour and dropped, played with from time to time and dropped—to pick up such ideas and set about *consistently, persistently, insistently to carry them through.* Grant that the idea or point of view is familiar—the results of steady, sustained, systematic work with it are not familiar. Not hit-or-miss stuff, not the insight which flashes and is forgotten, but sustained effort to force an old insight into its full bearing, to exploit it to the point where it laps

over upon an apparently inconsistent insight, to explore their bearing on each other by the test of fact. This urge, in law, is quite new enough over the last decades to excuse a touch of frenzy among the locust-eaters.

The first, second, third and fifth of the above items, while common to the workers of the newer movement, are not peculiar to them. But the other items (4, 6, 7, 8 and 9) are to me the characteristic marks of the movement. Men or work fitting those specifications are to me "realistic" whatever label they may wear.

NOTES

1.   Values in Law. Llewellyn's article was written, as the title indicates, in response to a major critique of the emerging realist movement offered by Pound in The Call for a Realist Jurisprudence, 44 Harvard Law Review 697 (1931). By this time, Pound had become Dean of Harvard Law School, and he continued to publish prolifically. The realists were willing to claim Pound as one of their own, but he stated his disagreement with them concerning such matters as the function of rules and the place of value and ideals. Pound argued that the realists made too much of the subjective world of the judge, and not enough of the certainty rules offered. He contended that a legal system must recognize ideals and values. As to this last point, note that Llewellyn argued only for the *"temporary* divorce of Is and Ought" and wrote that empirical research should remain *"as largely as possible"* value free.

2.   Realism and Pragmatism. The influence of Holmes, Brandeis, and Pound on the realist movement is clear. In W.E. Rumble, American Legal Realism 4–8 (1968), the author suggested that the influence of philosopher-psychologists William James and John Dewey was equally significant. According to Rumble, the realists inherited from the founders of pragmatism a dislike for formalism, deduction, and abstraction. The emphasis of both James and Dewey on evolution and change was also a part of the realist view. Finally, according to Rumble, the realist interest in reform could be linked to Dewey and his conviction that scientific methods must be applied to the study of social problems, Id. at 8:

> When Dewey claimed that "the reconstructive work to be done by philosophy" is "to undertake to do for the development of inquiry into human affairs ... what the philosophers of the last few centuries did for promotion of scientific inquiry in physical and physiological conditions and aspects of human life," he defined very well how the realists viewed the reconstructive work to be done by legal study.

3.   Law Schools. Most of the major realists were members of either the Columbia or Yale law school faculties. See L. Kalman, Legal Realism at Yale 67–97 (1986). Llewellyn, for example, was first a member of the Yale faculty, then moved to Columbia in 1925. The relevance of social science to law and the need for empirical research received particular emphasis at

Yale, in part because of the support of Robert Hutchins, who became dean at Yale in 1927. Hutchins apparently saw in empirical research the opportunity to establish a unique identity for Yale Law School. Among those who participated in empirical projects at Yale were Charles Clark, who followed Hutchins as dean and later became a judge on the United States Court of Appeals for the Second Circuit, William O. Douglas, later a United States Supreme Court justice, and Underhill Moore. Clark investigated court administration and Douglas studied bankruptcy. Moore studied the banking system and compliance with traffic rules. His controversial work is described in Schlegel, American Legal Realism and Empirical Social Science: The Singular Case of Underhill Moore, 29 Buffalo Law Review 195 (1980).

After only a few years, this high degree of activity at Yale declined. One reason for this decline was the onset of the Depression, which made obtaining research support difficult. Another probable reason was the departure of Hutchins to become the president of the University of Chicago. A third reason had to do with the nature of the empirical research enterprise. Some of the Yale researchers wished to harness the enterprise to solve short term reform objectives. The empirical work, however, proved to be expensive and time consuming: the median time for studies undertaken at Yale during this period was five years. In addition, the results did not always lend support to the policy preferences of the researcher. Law professors learned that they needed to develop technical skills in order to do work that had at first seemed simple. See Schlegel, American Legal Realism and Empirical Social Science: From The Yale Experience, 28 Buffalo Law Review 459 (1979).

———

MR. JUSTICE HOLMES AND NON–EUCLIDEAN LEGAL THINKING

Jerome Frank.
17 Cornell Law Quarterly 568 (1932).

As an experiment, let us examine briefly one set of axioms of the traditional jurisprudence which reads thus:

In our judicial system the personality of the judge—his peculiar set of individual reactions—has a relatively small effect upon legal rights; our system has reduced those effects to a minimum. The prejudices, passions and weaknesses of the judge are enormously diminished in their effects by the fact that a judge is required to and does center his attention on a body of impersonal legal rules. These rules prevent cases from being decided by "the private mind of the judge unguarded against his predilections". Decisions are the product of those rules applied by the judge to the facts of cases.

This is a paraphrased summary of a passage from Dickinson.[31]

A related package of axioms reads thus: A judge is required to set forth publicly the reasons for his decision *in terms of legal rules;* this requirement secures the public "against the well-meant ignorance of the weak judge" and is a "mainstay against improper motives" on the part of the crooked judge.

This is a paraphrase of a passage from Dean Pound.[32]

Now let us note that Dickinson and Pound advance no proof of the factual truth of these propositions. They do not show that they are based upon observation of what actually happens in court-rooms. They do not show, on the other hand, that, if you begin with these postulates, you can work out deductions which will jibe with observation of what actually happens (or can be made to happen) in court.

Suppose, now, we abandon those postulates and tentatively substitute the following assumptions:

The human element in the administration of justice by judges is irrepressible. A judicial decision is a decision by a human being called a judge.[33] The more you try to conceal the fact that judges are swayed by human prejudices, passions and weaknesses, the more likely you are to augment those prejudices, passions and weaknesses. Our legal system has been built up about the beliefs that (1) a judge centers his attention on impersonal so-called legal rules; (2) that his decision is the product of his application of those rules to the facts of the case; and (3) as a consequence, the human element in decision-making is reduced to a minimum. These beliefs, and the attending requirement that judges should write opinions explaining their decisions in accord with this belief, enhance the evil effects of the judges' prejudices, passions and weaknesses. For, as a result, self-scrutiny by judges of their own thought-ways is often blocked and it has become compulsory and respectable for judges to give explanations of their decisions in so artificial a manner as to insure, to the maximum, the concealment from the judges and others of judicial biases and predilections, and from others of judicial laziness, ignorance, or crookedness (when such unfortunate factors exist).

A variety of influences affect judicial decisions (i.e., court judgments, orders and decrees). Among those influences are the so-called legal rules. Sometimes those rules have considerable influence, sometimes little. How much effect those rules will have is unknown; it may always be unknowable; it varies with the judge and with the particular case, especially if the case is "contested" (i.e., involves conflicting testimony on a critical fact-issue). Knowledge of all the legal rules now in existence will not enable anyone to define most legal rights and duties with any high degree of

31. [Dickinson, Administrative Justice and the Supremacy of the Law, 141 (1927)].

32. Justice According to Law (1913) 13 Col.L.Rev. 696 at 710.

33. This discussion neglects jury trials. With respect to jury trials the traditional postulates are almost self-evidently erroneous. See Frank, Law and The Modern Mind (1930) 170–185, 302–309.

accuracy. For those legal rights and duties mean merely what a judge will decide in specific cases. And most future specific decisions are not predictable with any high degree of accuracy because no one can prophesy whether any particular future lawsuit will be "contested" (i.e. whether questions of fact will be raised and conflicting testimony introduced), and, if so, what witnesses will be believed, what the judge will guess as to the facts of the case, and what his reactions to that guess will be. For judges behave substantially like the human beings who are not judges.

The core of this package of substitute postulates is that the human element in the judicial determination of legal rights and obligations is irrepressible, and that a system like ours which seeks to repress and conceal that human element makes for the operation of the judges' failings in their most evil form.

Note that the writer does not dogmatically say that the suggested alternative postulates *are* or *must be* true. He says: "Try them out. See if they are not more accurate, more adequately adjusted to what exists, to what occurs every day in court houses. If they are, or as far as they are, they are true. Perhaps they are false, or partly false. Perhaps there needs to be inserted in those postulates such words as 'sometimes' or 'more often than not', or the like. They are suggested assumptions, tentatively formulated. If they are more serviceable than the old assumptions, good; if not, then away with them."

Now go back to the Pound–Dickinson axioms. Examine them carefully and you will find that they are sophisticated restatements of very ancient axioms. In more naive form they are discoverable in Blackstone's axiom that the judge is a mere passive oracle or mouthpiece of a somewhat called Law, a sort of a speaking-tube through which Law talks to the laity. And Blackstone's axiom is in turn traceable to the axiom that society must, can, and does have a government of laws and not of men.

And if we keep on pushing back we come to the early period in social development when private armed conflicts are in process of yielding to some sort of judicial procedure. We then come close to the genesis of these axioms: They are born of fear of human judgment, of a demand for a magical or Divine source of decisions. The early modes of trial (the ordeal, the judicial duel, the oath, the compurgators) are substitutes for private war. But these substituted arbitraments are considered to involve no human element. The judgment is the judgment of the supernatural, or "the judgment of God". The appeal is to magic or to Heaven. The decision is the infallible decision of the superhuman power. *Decision-making is deemed impersonal, non-human. Slowly, oh so slowly, there emerges a tolerance of a human being as the proper decider of the issues. Legal history might be written in terms of the increase of that tolerance. But, while in practice the human decider becomes more and more apparent, in theory the old fear, the old intolerance remains.* The old axioms become more and more out of line with actual events; as a consequence, there develops much tinkering with the old axioms in the hope that it can be adjusted sufficiently to square with the facts. *And so, at last, we reach Pound and Dickinson, whose axioms do not mesh with observable occurrences in the legal world. The only value of the Pound–Dickinson axioms is the doubtful one that they mesh with ancient fears and antiquated hopes.*

———

NOTES

1.   Gender and Judging. On the issue of judges bringing their backgrounds to the bench, a study of all Title VII sexual harassment and sex discrimination cases decided between 1999 and 2001 addressed how the presence of female judges on three-judge federal appellate panels affected the panels' decisions. Peresie, Note: Female Judges Matter: Gender and Collegial Decisionmaking in the Federal Appellate Courts, 114 Yale Law Journal 1759 (2005). The author concluded:

> Wise old men and wise old women sometimes reach different conclusions. Although plaintiffs lost in the majority of cases in my data set, they were significantly more likely to win when a female judge was on the bench. This effect was independent of judicial ideology—the presence of both liberal and conservative female judges increased the probability that plaintiffs prevailed on panels of varying ideological composition. The gender impact I observed is significant. Panels with at least one female judge decided cases for the plaintiff more than twice as often as did all-male panels. Assuming the gender impact illustrated in this Note persists, increasing the gender diversity of the federal appellate bench—as all recent presidents beginning with President Carter have done—will have important substantive implications. If, for instance, the number of panels with at least one female judge doubled, then approximately eight more Title VII sexual harassment and sex discrimination cases out of every hundred would be decided for plaintiffs. Id. at 1787.

2.   Politics, Race, and Judging. The effects of a judge's race on his or her decision making has also been the subject of recent research. For example, Section 2 of the Voting Rights Act of 1982 (42 U.S.C. § 1973(a) (2000)) requires plaintiffs to show that minority voters "have less opportunity than other [voters] to participate in the political process and to elect representatives of their choice." Adam Cox and Thomas Miles, Judging the Voting Rights Act, 108 Columbia Law Review 1 (2008) studied all 341 decisions on Section 2 issued by federal district and circuit courts between 1982 and 2004. Individual judges' votes in these cases in favor or against liability for violating Section 2 were analyzed in relation to publically-available demographic and biographical information on each judge available on the Federal Judicial Center's website.

> First, we find that a judge's partisan affiliation relates closely to the likelihood that she will vote in favor of liability under section 2 of the Voting Rights Act. Democratic appointees are, on average, about 15 percentage points more likely than Republican appointees to find a violation—which makes them nearly 50% more likely to rule for the

minority plaintiffs in these cases. Moreover, a judge's partisan affiliation affects the votes of her colleagues when they review section 2 cases on appellate panels. The partisan composition of panels has the largest impact when a judge sits on a politically homogenous panel. Second, we find that a judge's race exerts even more influence than his partisan affiliation. African–American judges are, on average, more than twice as likely as white judges to find that minority citizens' voting rights were violated under section 2. African–American judges vote in favor of liability more than half the time, while judges who are not African–American do so only about one-quarter of the time. Moreover, a judge's race substantially affects the votes of his colleagues on a panel. Both Republican and Democratic appointees are substantially more likely to vote in favor of liability when they sit with an African–American judge than when they do not. Id. at 48–49.

THE CRISIS OF DEMOCRATIC THEORY (1973)

Edward A. Purcell, Jr.

Morris Cohen and Mortimer Adler criticized the realists from the viewpoint of philosophy, insisting on the need for objective standards of judgment beyond mere empirical facts. The realists, Cohen argued, "do away altogether with the normative point of view in law."[66] He insisted that legal science had the obligation to be normative, and that the realists had overlooked that fundamental difference between legal and physical science. Adler charged that the new critics were ignorant of the values of deductive logic and argued that there was a rational "law in discourse," which men could know with certainty and use as a standard to judge the practical "law as official action." Frank drew his special condemnation as "a splendid illustration" of the weakness of American jurisprudence.[67]

Though most of the criticism directed at legal realism before 1935 was discriminating and often technical, such scholars as Pound, Adler, and Morris Cohen pointed to the challenge the new movement posed for traditional democratic ideas. By excluding ethical considerations and reverting to a philosophical nominalism, some suggested, the realists were necessarily destroying the ethical basis of democracy and making force the only meaningful arbiter of human affairs. Explaining the source and character of natural law, the Reverend Charles C. Miltner of Notre Dame claimed that its principles could determine the intrinsic ethical quality of all human actions. "This basis of moral judgment is objective," he declared, "and therefore free from the inevitable variations and inconsistencies of purely subjective standards."[68] Such an objective norm was necessary, he

---

66. Morris R. Cohen, "Justice Holmes and the Nature of Law," Columbia Law Review, 31 (March 1931), 357.

67. Mortimer Adler, "Legal Certainty," Part II of "Law and the Modern Mind: A Symposium," Columbia Law Review, 31 (January 1931), 108.

68. Charles C. Miltner, "Law and Morals," Notre Dame Lawyer, 10 (November, 1934), 8.

suggested, to provide the moral foundation and justification for democratic government.

To harm the cause of democratic government was the last thing the realists wished to do. In attacking traditional abstractions and nonempirical concepts of justice, they were usually assailing what they considered the practical injustices of American society. Abstraction in economics and politics, as in the law, they believed, had been one of the biggest obstacles to the attainment of a truly democratic society. Frank, Oliphant, Clark, Arnold, Douglas, and Felix Cohen all became ardent New Dealers, sharing a strong hostility to the method of juristic reasoning that struck down social welfare laws and wrought what they considered great human injustices. Most of the other realists expressed equally strong disapproval of the social and economic situation in the thirties, and they viewed themselves as fighting to extend democratic social values. The new criticism was thus not intentionally hostile toward the idea of democratic government. As early as 1931 Frank defended the realists against charges that they excluded ethical considerations from the law. "The point is," he retorted, *"that the rational and ethical factors are thwarted in their operations by the conventional tendency to ignore the non-rational and non-ethical factors."*[69] The problem was not whether there was something abstract called justice, but rather how human relations could be made more just in practice. Though the theoretical problems the realists raised left them open to bitter and telling attack, the obtuse formalism of American constitutional interpretation throughout the first third of the twentieth century helped drive them to their extreme positions. The manifest human needs created by the depression further convinced them of the necessity for a more realistic and flexible legal theory.

Like most of the philosophers and social scientists who shared the same basic assumptions, the realists were driven by the twin motives of intellectual discovery and social improvement. They hoped to understand the legal process in a new and more useful manner, and they hoped to see both political and legal reform flow from their discoveries. They readily recognized the fundamental importance of moral ideals and values in human society and consciously hoped to see them reach greater practical fulfillment. "It is no evidence that a student of law is deficient in moral sense," Oliphant declared, "if he merely observes and records the uniformities of social behavior with which the law is concerned."[71]

As with their colleagues in philosophy and the social sciences, however, the realists' motives could not explain away the intellectual problems they generated. Intentionally or not, their theoretical position raised two basic questions about traditional democratic theory. First, how could the idea of the subjectivity of judicial decision be squared with the doctrine that free men should be subject only to known and established law, one of the hallmarks of republican as opposed to despotic government? Second, if the

69. Jerome Frank, review of The Bramble Bush by Karl N. Llewellyn, Yale Law Journal, 40 (May, 1931), 1121, note.

71. Herman Oliphant, "Facts, Opinions, and Value–Judgments," Texas Law Review, 10 (February, 1932), 137.

acts of government officials were the only real law, on what basis could anyone evaluate or criticize those acts? What, in other words, was the moral basis of the legal system in particular and of democratic government in general? Most revealingly, Felix Cohen, who alone among the realists attempted an elaborate analysis of ethical theory, admitted that his conclusions remained "in the shadow" of doubt and bordered on failure.[72] That was an unsatisfactory solution to almost everyone after the middle thirties.

———

NOTE

1. Post–Realism. American legal realism had lost its force and identity as a discrete social movement by the early 1950's. There were many reasons for this development, including the distraction and disruption of World War II, difficulties of principle posed by vivid examples of totalitarian governments, disappointment with some research products of the movement, and simple personal and professional restlessness—the human tendency to turn to new endeavors. But perhaps the dominant reason for the end of the realist movement was simply its success, for in a broad, jurisprudential sense legal realism won a substantial victory. According to Dawson, Legal Realism and Legal Scholarship, 33 Journal of Legal Education 406 (1983), the ultimate fate of the realists "was to merge into the general environment as their messages came to be understood and accepted, I would say, everywhere."

The proposition that law should be seen in a larger social context became a virtual truism, and it is commonly and correctly said about both academic and practicing lawyers, "We are all realists now." For example, no one is any longer surprised when in certain cases, the rulings of judges appointed by conservatives differ from those of judges appointed by liberals. We find the observation trivial. It is trivial only because we have accepted the basic realist premises. In most law schools the analysis of difficult issues both in the classroom and on examinations often turns on a statement (or assumption) about public policy. The realists' influence is pervasive.

At least three comparatively recent developments stem from this triumph of realist jurisprudence. They include jurisprudential focus on "neutral principles" of legal process, the study of law and economics, and social science in law. It is a remarkable tribute to the realists that this list includes most of the significant phenomena in current legal practice and scholarship.

The legal process movement was an important response to the problems discussed above by Purcell. The movement was fashioned by a group of scholars who argued that the dangers of tyranny could be avoided by recognizing certain immutable principles of process. For example, judges must state reasons for decisions, rules must be promulgated, public officials

---

72. Felix S. Cohen, Ethical Systems and Legal Ideals: An Essay on the Founda-   tions of Legal Criticism (New York, 1933), 227.

must be subject to law. Herbert Wechsler's article, Toward Neutral Principles of Constitutional Law, 73 Harvard Law Review 1 (1959), is an important statement of this point of view, as is Lon Fuller's book, The Morality of Law (1964). This "process jurisprudence" was also central to two very influential books prepared for use in law school courses, H.M. Hart and H. Wechsler, The Federal Courts and the Federal System (1953) and H. Hart and A. Sacks, The Legal Process (1958; W. Eskridge and P. Frickey eds. 1994). The key principles of the legal process were said to be "neutral" because they could be recognized and enforced without favoring one substantive outcome or another. These desirable conditions of decision-making afforded protection against tyranny because they were not relativistic and hence, theoretically, were not subject to change because of change in political authority. Essentially, these idealists contended that there was something more to law than policy making.

A second important post-realist development was the rapid growth of interest in law and economics. According to Kitch, The Fire of Truth: A Remembrance of Law and Economics at Chicago, 1932–70, 26 Journal of Law and Economics 163 (1983), legal realism created an environment that was receptive to the introduction of economics into the law school curriculum. "It is clear that legal realism made people in law schools open to the social sciences, indeed to any and all social science: psychology, economics, sociology, political science, anthropology. No one was sure which if any of the social sciences might prove helpful, but there was a willingness to try any of them." Id. at 165. Economics quickly proved to be helpful and to date has made a more significant contribution to legal analysis than any other social science discipline. See R. Cooter and T. Ulen, Law and Economics (4th ed., 2004).

Finally, legal realism is the origin of social science in law. Widespread acceptance of the view that law is at least in part concerned with policy making, coupled with realist enthusiasm for empiricism has resulted in increasing use of social science materials in resolving many legal problems. This development is the principal subject of this book, and we examine its details and implications in chapters 3 through 6. Social science in law is related to the law and economics movement, and there is now a burgeoning integration between law and economics scholarship—which in the past has been heavily theoretical and relatively non-empirical—and social science in law scholarship—which in the past has been heavily empirical and relatively non-theoretical. See C. Sunstein, Behavioral Law and Economics (2000).

———

CONFIRMATION HEARING ON THE NOMINATION OF JOHN G. ROBERTS, JR., TO BE CHIEF JUSTICE OF THE UNITED STATES: HEARING BEFORE THE SENATE COMMITTEE ON THE JUDICIARY, 109TH CONGRESS (2005)

JUDGE ROBERTS: Judges are like umpires. Umpires don't make the rules, they apply them. The role of an umpire and a judge is critical. They make sure everybody plays by the rules. But it is a limited role. Nobody ever went to a ballgame to see the umpire.... And I will remember that it's my job to call balls and strikes, and not to pitch or bat.

SENATOR CORNYN: One of these blogs [that I read last night] said that your comparison of a judge to a baseball umpire reminded him of an old story about three different modes of judicial reasoning built on the same analogy.

First, was the umpire that says some are balls and some are strikes, and I call them the way they are.

The second umpire says some are balls and some are strikes, and I call them the way I see them.

The third said: Some are balls and some are strikes, but they ain't nothing till I call them.

Well, I don't know whether it's a fair question to ask you which of those three types of umpires represents your preferred mode of judicial reasoning. But I wonder if you have any comment about that.

JUDGE ROBERTS: It's not the last, because they are balls and strikes regardless, and if I call them one and they're the other, that doesn't change what they are, it just means that I got it wrong.

I guess I liked the one in the middle, because I do think there are right answers. I know that it's fashionable in some places to suggest that there are no right answers and that the judges are motivated by a constellation of different considerations and, because of that, it should affect how we approach certain other issues. That's not the view of the law that I subscribe to.

I think when you folks legislate, you do have something in mind in particular and you put it into words and you expect judges not to put in their own preferences, not to substitute their judgment for you, but to implement your view of what you are accomplishing in that statute. I think, when the framers framed the Constitution, it was the same thing.

SENATOR KOHL: Judge Roberts, yesterday you described your role as a judge as just an umpire, as you called it, calling balls and strikes. And that's an interesting analogy for me, as I have, more than most, some personal experience with umpires and referees. But as all of us with any involvement in sports knows, no two umpires or no two referees have the same strike zone or call the same kind of a basketball game. And ballplayers and basketball players understand that depending upon who the umpire is and who the referee is, the game can be called entirely differently.

When we look at real legal cases, I wonder whether or not your analogy works. For example, in our private conversation, I asked you whether the words of the Constitution must always be interpreted in the same way as the authors originally intended.

For example, the Fourteenth Amendment which guarantees equal protection under the laws to all citizens, was written at a time when schools were in fact segregated based on race.

And yet, in *Brown v. Board of Education*, the equal protection clause was interpreted to find segregated schools unconstitutional. And you, of course, have endorsed that decision.

No one disagrees with that conclusion today, but would a neutral umpire, as you described yourself yesterday, have decided back in 1954 to expand the words of the Constitution outside of the strike zone? Would a neutral umpire have overturned a 58–year–old Supreme Court precedent and gone against the understanding of the authors of the Fourteenth Amendment and also the views of almost half of the state legislatures at that time in making the decision that they made?

JUDGE ROBERTS: Well, Senator, I think the answer to your question is yes. The research into the original understanding of the drafters of the Fourteenth Amendment has expanded and changed quite a bit ... They chose broad language and they should be held to their word. And I think it is perfectly consistent with an original understanding to argue and to conclude that their original understanding meant that segregated schools were unconstitutional—not just in 1954, but at the time they enacted the amendment.

I think a strong case can be made there. And what was interesting about the *Brown* case—maybe it's my own perspective—but if you look at the arguments in that case, yes, John W. Davis arguing for the Board was arguing on the basis of precedent in *Plessy v. Ferguson*, saying this is the established law, but so is Thurgood Marshall.

He went in and he was arguing on the basis of more recent precedent, *Sweatt v. Painter*, a more recent decision of the court about law school, separate but equal. And he was saying: You need to build on that more recent precedent in addressing this case.

So the court was not changing the strike zone. That wasn't the way Marshall presented his argument. And it wasn't necessary for them to say, "We're changing the rules of the game."

What was necessary for them to do—and what Marshall was urging them to do—was to get it right when they had gotten it wrong in *Plessy*.

SENATOR KOHL: Judge, back in 1954, clearly the Supreme Court justices were willing to step outside the box, to break new ground, to do something that no one, no court, no legislature, no president had done before and strike out in an entirely new and positive direction for this country.

They were not umpires simply calling balls and strikes. They were breaking new ground. And they did so in the best interests of our country, didn't they?

JUDGE ROBERTS: Of course it was a dramatic shift. And the overruling of *Plessy v. Ferguson* was exactly that.

My point is simply that, if you look at the *Brown* decision, it is more consistent with the Fourteenth Amendment and the original understanding of the Fourteenth Amendment than *Plessy v. Ferguson*. And it's based on the conclusion that the separation of the races in the schools was itself a violation of equal protection.

SENATOR KOHL: One more observation, Judge, about your analogy of the judge as an umpire, neutral umpire. You're 50 years old, you bring great life experience to the bench, Judge, and don't you and all judges bring their own life experiences, their philosophies to the bench in deciding cases. Or would you have us believe [t]hat judges merely operate as automatons?

JUDGE ROBERTS: Not automatons, no, Senator. I appreciate that, that judges don't. And of course we all bring our life experiences to the bench.

But I will say this, that the ideal in the American justice system is epitomized by the fact that judges, justices do wear the black robes, and that is meant to symbolize the fact that they're not individuals promoting their own particular views, but they are supposed to be doing their best to interpret the law, to interpret the Constitution according to the rule of law, not their own preferences, not their own personal beliefs. That's the ideal.

————

NOTE

1. Baseball and Judging. Professor James Ryan, Does It Take a Theory? Originalism, Active Liberty, and Minimalism, 58 Stanford Law Review 1623 (2006) commented upon the above testimony as follows:

> Chief Justice Roberts used a baseball analogy in his confirmation hearings, comparing judges to umpires calling balls and strikes. But this isn't right. If baseball umpires were like most Supreme Court Justices, they would be able to decide who wins a baseball game by considering a number of "sources," including runs, hits, errors, strikes, balls, double plays, and steals. Umpires would throw all of these sources into the mix and not feel obliged from one game to the next to consider any of them in the same order or to assign them the same weight. This would undoubtedly increase the power of umpires but likely diminish the integrity of the game. To be clear, I am not arguing that Supreme Court Justices can or should act just like umpires, or that umpires should act more like Supreme Court Justices (though the latter would be a humorous, short-lived experiment). I am simply suggesting that an accurate contrast between the two highlights what is sometimes frustrating about Supreme Court decisionmaking. Id. at 1646.

————

CONFIRMATION HEARING ON THE NOMINATION OF SONIA SOTOMAYOR TO BE ASSOCIATE JUSTICE OF THE UNITED STATES: HEARING BEFORE THE SENATE COMMITTEE ON THE JUDICIARY, 111TH CONGRESS (2009)

SEN. SESSIONS: Judge, [y]ou spoke about your approach to rendering opinions and said, "I seek to strengthen both the rule of law and faith in the impartiality of the justice system,'' and I would agree. But you have previously said this: I am willing to "accept that we who judge must not deny ... differences resulting from experiences and heritage, but attempt [c]ontinuously to judge when those opinions, sympathies and prejudices are appropriate."

JUDGE SOTOMAYOR: What I was talking about was the obligation of judges to examine what they are feeling as they're adjudicating a case, and to ensure that that's not influencing the outcome.

Life experiences have to influence you. We're not robots who listen to evidence and don't have feelings. We have to recognize those feelings, and put them aside.

SEN. SESSIONS: You also said that your decisions have always been made to serve the larger interests of impartial justice. [B]ut in the past, you've repeatedly said this: "I wonder whether achieving the goal of impartiality is possible at all, in even most cases. And I wonder whether by ignoring our differences as women, men or people of color we do a disservice to both the law and society." Aren't you saying there that you expect your background and heritage to influence your decision-making?

JUDGE SOTOMAYOR: What I was speaking about in that speech was [that] life experiences do influence us, in good ways. That's why we seek the enrichment of our legal system from life experiences. That can affect what we see or how we feel, but that's not what drives a result.

SEN. SESSIONS: You said [t]hat "in each case ... I've applied the law to the facts at hand." But you've repeatedly made this statement: "I accept the proposition that a difference there will be by the presence of women and people of color on a bench," and that "my experiences affect the facts I choose to see as a judge."

First, that's troubling to me as a lawyer. When I present evidence, I expect a judge to hear and see all the evidence that gets presented. How is it appropriate for a judge ever to say that they will choose to see some facts and not others?

JUDGE SOTOMAYOR: It's not a question of choosing to see some facts or another, Senator. I didn't intend to suggest that. And in the wider context, [t]he point I was making was that our life experiences do permit us to see some facts and understand them more easily than others.

But in the end, you're absolutely right, that's why we have appellate [courts] that are more than one judge, because each of us, from our life experiences, will more easily see different perspectives argued by parties.

SEN. KYL: I don't want to be misunderstood here as disagreeing with a general look [i]nto the question of whether people's gender, ethnicity or background in some way affects their judging. I suspect you can make a very good case that that is true in some cases. [I]'m not questioning whether the studies [of the effect of judges' backgrounds on their decision making] are not valuable. In fact, I would agree with you that it's important for us to be able to know these things so that we are on guard to set aside prejudices that we may not even know that we have.

Let me just ask you one last question here: [h]ave you ever seen a case where—to use your example—the wise Latina made a better decision than non-Latina judges?

JUDGE SOTOMAYOR: No.

[I] think that's what Justice Alito was referring to when he was asked questions by this Committee. He said, you know, when I decide a case, I think about my Italian ancestors and their experiences coming to this country. I don't think anybody thought that he was saying that commanded the result in the case.

SEN. GRAHAM: Now, Legal Realism, are you familiar with that term?

JUDGE SOTOMAYOR: I am. [B]ut I don't apply that label to myself at all. I look at law and precedent and discern its principles and apply it to the situations before me.

SEN. GRAHAM: So you would not be a disciple of the Legal Realism School?

JUDGE SOTOMAYOR: No.

SEN. CORNYN: Do you believe that judges ever change the law?

JUDGE SOTOMAYOR: We can't change law. We're not lawmakers. But we change our view of how to interpret certain laws based on new facts, new developments of doctrinal theory, considerations of [w]hat the reliance of society may be in an old rule. We think about whether a rule of law has proven workable.

SEN. CORNYN: In [a] speech in 1996, you celebrated the uncertainty of the law. You wrote that the law is always in a "necessary state of flux." You wrote that the law judges declare is not "a definitive, capital 'L' law that [m]any would like to think exist[s]." And "that the public fails to appreciate the importance of the indefiniteness in the law."

Can you explain those statements? And why do you think indefiniteness is so important to the law?

JUDGE SOTOMAYOR: It's not that it's important to the law as much as it is that it's what legal cases are about. People bring cases to courts because they believe that precedents don't clearly answer the fact situation that they're presenting in their individual case.

That creates uncertainty. That's why people bring cases. And they say, "Look, the law says this, but I'm entitled to that. I have this set of facts that entitle me to relief under the law." It's the entire process of law. If law was always clear, we wouldn't have judges.

SELECTED BIBLIOGRAPHY

Danzig, Justice Frankfurter's Opinions in the Flag Salute Cases: Blending Logic and Psychologic in Constitutional Decision Making, 36 Stanford Law Review 675 (1984).

W. de Been, Legal Realism Regained: Saving Realism from Critical Acclaim (2008).

Edwards and Livermore, Pitfalls of Empirical Studies that Attempt to Understand the Factors Affecting Appellate Decisionmaking, 58 Duke Law Journal 1895 (2009).

Ellsworth, Legal Reasoning, in Cambridge Handbook of Thinking and Reasoning (K. Loyoak and R. Morrison eds. 2005).

D. Faigman, Constitutional Fictions: A Unified Theory of Constitutional Facts (2008).

R. Feldman, The Role of Science in Law (2009).

Furgeson, Babcock, and Shane, Do a Law's Policy Implications Affect Beliefs About Its Constitutionality? An Experimental Test, 32 Law and Human Behavior 219 (2008).

Guthrie, Rachlinski, and Wistrich, Blinking on the Bench: How Judges Decide Cases, 93 Cornell Law Review 1 (2007).

Haack, Irreconcilable Differences? The Troubled Marriage of Science and Law, 72 Law and Contemporary Problems 1 (2009).

L. Kalman, Legal Realism at Yale, 1927–1960 (1986).

Katz and Baldwin, Why Counting Votes Doesn't Add Up: A Response to Cox and Miles' *Judging the Voting Rights Act*, 108 Columbia Law Review Sidebar 23 (2008).

D. Klein and G. Mitchell (eds), The Psychology of Judicial Decision Making (in press).

S. Macaulay, L. Friedman, and E. Mertz, Law in Action A Social–Legal Reader (2007).

Merlino, Richardson, Chamberlain, and Springer, Science in the Law School Curriculum: A Snapshot of the Legal Education Landscape, 58 Journal of Legal Education 190 (2008).

Mertz, Inside the Law School Classroom: Toward a New Realist Pedagogy, 60 Vanderbilt Law Review 483 (2007).

Miles and Sunstein, The New Legal Realism, 75 University of Chicago Law Review 831 (2008).

Posner, Does Political Bias in the Judiciary Matter? Implications of Judicial Bias Studies for Legal and Constitutional Reform, 75 University of Chicago Law Review 853 (2008).

Ramji–Nogales, Schoenholtz, and Schrag, Refugee Roulette: Disparities in Asylum Adjudication, 60 Stanford Law Review 295 (2007).

Schlegel, American Legal Realism and Empirical Social Science: From the Yale Experience, 28 Buffalo Law Review 459 (1979).

J. Schlegel, American Legal Realism and Empirical Social Science (1995).

Simon, A Third View of the Black Box: Coherence in Legal Decision Making, 71 The University of Chicago Law Review 511 (2004).

Tamanaha, Understanding Legal Realism, 87 Texas Law Review 731 (2009).

Tamanaha, The Distorting Slant of Quantitative Studies of Judging, 50 Boston College Law Review 685 (2009).

Wilkins, Legal Realism for Lawyers, 104 Harvard Law Review 468 (1990).

CHAPTER TWO

A PRIMER OF LEGAL AND SOCIAL SCIENCE METHODS

The previous chapter considered the jurisprudential roots of social science in law. This chapter addresses courts' use of social science research at a more pragmatic, working level. We consider two related topics: by what legal methods do courts obtain social science evidence, and by what scientific methods do courts evaluate the evidence they have obtained? With this chapter's introduction to legal and scientific methods, the reader will be prepared for the specific uses of social science research in law that are the focus of the succeeding chapters of this book.

SECTION I. LEGAL METHODS

One party offers in evidence the testimony of a scientific expert witness. The other party objects. Does the expert get to testify? In many federal and state courts, the answer to that question had been "does the testimony pass the *Frye* test of being generally accepted in the scientific discipline?" In some of these federal and state courts, the answer changed with the adoption of the Federal Rules of Evidence, which stated that scientific evidence should be admitted if it "assists the trier of fact" (FRE 702). Since the Commentary to the Federal Rules did not make clear whether Rule 702 was meant to replace the *Frye* test or merely to augment it, debates over the merits of *Frye* versus the Federal Rules as the better test for the admissibility of scientific evidence became a staple of law review articles and notes. In 1993, those debates were ended—for the federal courts, at least—by the United States Supreme Court's decision in the case of Daubert v. Merrill Dow Pharmaceuticals that the Federal Rules did indeed supplant the *Frye* test. While some state courts have decided to remain with *Frye*, much of the enormous amount of activity in this area since 1993 has consisted of federal and state courts trying to elaborate the precise meaning of the Supreme Court's *Daubert* case. In 2000, Rule 702 was amended in response to *Daubert* and to the many federal cases applying *Daubert*.

———

FRYE v. UNITED STATES

Court of Appeals of District of Columbia, 1923.
54 App.D.C. 46, 293 Fed. 1013.

■ VAN ORSDEL, Associate Justice.

Appellant, defendant below, was convicted of the crime of murder in the second degree, and from the judgment prosecutes this appeal.

A single assignment of error is presented for our consideration. In the course of the trial counsel for defendant offered an expert witness to testify to the result of a deception test made upon defendant. The test is described as the systolic blood pressure deception test. It is asserted that blood pressure is influenced by change in the emotions of the witness, and that the systolic blood pressure rises are brought about by nervous impulses sent to the sympathetic branch of the autonomic nervous system. Scientific experiments, it is claimed, have demonstrated that fear, rage, and pain always produce a rise of systolic blood pressure, and that conscious deception or falsehood, concealment of facts, or guilt of crime, accompanied by fear of detection when the person is under examination, raises the systolic blood pressure in a curve, which corresponds exactly to the struggle going on in the subject's mind, between fear and attempted control of that fear, as the examination touches the vital points in respect of which he is attempting to deceive the examiner.

[P]rior to the trial defendant was subjected to this deception test, and counsel offered the scientist who conducted the test as an expert to testify to the results obtained. The offer was objected to by counsel for the government, and the court sustained the objection. Counsel for defendant then offered to have the proffered witness conduct a test in the presence of the jury. This also was denied.

Counsel for defendant, in their able presentation of the novel question involved, correctly state in their brief that no cases directly in point have been found. The broad ground, however, upon which they plant their case, is succinctly stated in their brief as follows:

> "The rule is that the opinions of experts or skilled witnesses are admissible in evidence in those cases in which the matter of inquiry is such that inexperienced persons are unlikely to prove capable of forming a correct judgment upon it, for the reason that the subject-matter so far partakes of a science, art, or trade as to require a previous habit or experience or study in it, in order to acquire a knowledge of it. When the question involved does not lie within the range of common experience or common knowledge, but requires special experience or special knowledge, then the opinions of witnesses skilled in that particular science, art, or trade to which the question relates are admissible in evidence."

Numerous cases are cited in support of this rule. Just when a scientific principle or discovery crosses the line between the experimental and demonstrable stages is difficult to define. Somewhere in this twilight zone the evidential force of the principle must be recognized, and while courts will go a long way in admitting expert testimony deduced from a well-recognized scientific principle or discovery, the thing from which the deduction is made must be sufficiently established to have gained general acceptance in the particular field in which it belongs.

We think the systolic blood pressure deception test has not yet gained such standing and scientific recognition among physiological and psychological authorities as would justify the courts in admitting expert testimony deduced from the discovery, development, and experiments thus far made.

The judgment is affirmed.

FEDERAL RULES OF EVIDENCE

Rule 702. Testimony by Experts[1]

If scientific, technical, or other specialized knowledge will assist the trier of fact to understand the evidence or to determine a fact in issue, a witness qualified as an expert by knowledge, skill, experience, training, or education, may testify thereto in the form of an opinion or otherwise.

DAUBERT v. MERRELL DOW PHARMACEUTICALS

Supreme Court of the United States, 1993.
509 U.S. 579, 113 S.Ct. 2786, 125 L.Ed.2d 469.

■ JUSTICE BLACKMUN delivered the opinion of the Court.

In this case we are called upon to determine the standard for admitting expert scientific testimony in a federal trial.

Petitioners Jason Daubert and Eric Schuller are minor children born with serious birth defects. They and their parents sued respondent [a]lleging that the birth defects had been caused by the mothers' ingestion of Bendectin, a prescription anti-nausea drug marketed by respondent.

[A]fter extensive discovery, respondent moved for summary judgment, contending that Bendectin does not cause birth defects in humans and that petitioners would be unable to come forward with any admissible evidence that it does. In support of its motion, respondent submitted an affidavit of Steven H. Lamm, physician and epidemiologist, who is a well-credentialed expert on the risks from exposure to various chemical substances. Doctor Lamm stated that he had reviewed all the literature on Bendectin and human birth defects—more than 30 published studies involving over 130,-000 patients. No study had found Bendectin to be a human teratogen (i.e., a substance capable of causing malformations in fetuses).

---

1. [Ed. Note: This version of Rule 702 was in force when the next three principal cases were decided. Rule 702 was amended in 2000. See p. 52 infra.]

[P]etitioners [r]esponded to respondent's motion with the testimony of eight experts of their own, each of whom also possessed impressive credentials. These experts had concluded that Bendectin can cause birth defects. Their conclusions were based upon "in vitro" (test tube) and "in vivo" (live) animal studies that found a link between Bendectin and malformations; pharmacological studies of the chemical structure of Bendectin that purported to show similarities between the structure of the drug and that of other substances known to cause birth defects; and the "reanalysis" of previously published epidemiological (human statistical) studies.

The District Court granted respondent's motion for summary judgment. The court stated that scientific evidence is admissible only if the principle upon which it is based is " 'sufficiently established to have general acceptance in the field to which it belongs.' " 727 F.Supp. 570, 572 (S.D.Cal.1989), quoting United States v. Kilgus, 571 F.2d 508, 510 (C.A.9 1978). The court concluded that petitioners' evidence did not meet this standard. Given the vast body of epidemiological data concerning Bendectin, the court held, expert opinion which is not based on epidemiological evidence is not admissible to establish causation. 727 F.Supp., at 575. Thus, the animal-cell studies, live-animal studies, and chemical-structure analyses on which petitioners had relied could not raise by themselves a reasonably disputable jury issue regarding causation. Ibid. Petitioners' epidemiological analyses, based as they were on recalculations of data in previously published studies that had found no causal link between the drug and birth defects, were ruled to be inadmissible because they had not been published or subjected to peer review. Ibid.

The United States Court of Appeals for the Ninth Circuit affirmed. 951 F.2d 1128 (1991). Citing Frye v. United States, 54 App./D.C. 46, 47, 293 F. 1013, 1014 (1923), the court stated that expert opinion based on a scientific technique is inadmissible unless the technique is "generally accepted" as reliable in the relevant scientific community. 951 F.2d, at 1129–1130.

[I]n the 70 years since its formulation in the *Frye* case, the "general acceptance" test has been the dominant standard for determining the admissibility of novel scientific evidence at trial. Although under increasing attack of late, the rule continues to be followed by a majority of courts.

[T]he *Frye* test has its origin in a short and citation-free 1923 decision concerning the admissibility of evidence derived from a systolic blood pressure deception test, a crude precursor to the polygraph machine. In what has become a famous (perhaps infamous) passage, the then Court of Appeals for the District of Columbia described the device and its operation and declared: "Just when a scientific principle or discovery crosses the line between the experimental and demonstrable stages is difficult to define. Somewhere in this twilight zone the evidential force of the principle must be recognized, and while courts will go a long way in admitting expert testimony deduced from a well-recognized scientific principle or discovery, the thing from which the deduction is made must be sufficiently established to have gained general acceptance in the particular field in which it belongs." 54 App.D.C., at 47, 293 F., at 1014 (emphasis added).

[T]he merits of the *Frye* test have been much debated, and scholarship on its proper scope and application is legion. Petitioners' primary attack, however, is not on the content but on the continuing authority of the rule. They contend that the *Frye* test was superseded by the adoption of the Federal Rules of Evidence. We agree. [R]ule 702, governing expert testimony, provides: "If scientific, technical, or other specialized knowledge will assist the trier of fact to understand the evidence or to determine a fact in issue, a witness qualified as an expert by knowledge, skill, experience, training, or education, may testify thereto in the form of an opinion or otherwise." Nothing in the text of this Rule establishes "general acceptance" as an absolute prerequisite to admissibility. Nor does respondent present any clear indication that Rule 702 or the Rules as a whole were intended to incorporate a "general acceptance" standard. The drafting history makes no mention of *Frye,* and a rigid "general acceptance" requirement would be at odds with the "liberal thrust" of the Federal Rules and their "general approach of relaxing the traditional barriers to 'opinion' testimony." Beech Aircraft Corp. v. Rainey, 488 U.S., at 169 (citing Rules 701 to 705). Given the Rules' permissive backdrop and their inclusion of a specific rule on expert testimony that does not mention "general acceptance," the assertion that the Rules somehow assimilated *Frye* is unconvincing. *Frye* made "general acceptance" the exclusive test for admitting expert scientific testimony. That austere standard, absent from and incompatible with the Federal Rules of Evidence, should not be applied in federal trials.

That the *Frye* test was displaced by the Rules of Evidence does not mean, however, that the Rules themselves place no limits on the admissibility of purportedly scientific evidence. Nor is the trial judge disabled from screening such evidence. To the contrary, under the Rules the trial judge must ensure that any and all scientific testimony or evidence admitted is not only relevant, but reliable.

The primary locus of this obligation is Rule 702, which clearly contemplates some degree of regulation of the subjects and theories about which an expert may testify. [T]he subject of an expert's testimony must be "scientific ... knowledge." The adjective "scientific" implies a grounding in the methods and procedures of science. Similarly, the word "knowledge" connotes more than subjective belief or unsupported speculation. The term "applies to any body of known facts or to any body of ideas inferred from such facts or accepted as truths on good grounds." Webster's Third New International Dictionary 1252 (1986). Of course, it would be unreasonable to conclude that the subject of scientific testimony must be "known" to a certainty; arguably, there are no certainties in science. But, in order to qualify as "scientific knowledge," an inference or assertion must be derived by the scientific method. Proposed testimony must be supported by appropriate validation—i.e., "good grounds," based on what is known. In short, the requirement that an expert's testimony pertain to "scientific knowledge" establishes a standard of evidentiary reliability.[9]

9. We note that scientists typically distinguish between "validity" (does the principle support what it purports to show?) and "reliability" (does application of the principle

Rule 702 further requires that the evidence or testimony "assist the trier of fact to understand the evidence or to determine a fact in issue." This condition goes primarily to relevance. "Expert testimony which does not relate to any issue in the case is not relevant and, ergo, non-helpful." 3 Weinstein & Berger P 702[02], p. 702–18. [R]ule 702's "helpfulness" standard requires a valid scientific connection to the pertinent inquiry as a precondition to admissibility.

[F]aced with a proffer of expert scientific testimony, then, the trial judge must determine at the outset, pursuant to Rule 104(a), whether the expert is proposing to testify to (1) scientific knowledge that (2) will assist the trier of fact to understand or determine a fact in issue.[11] This entails a preliminary assessment of whether the reasoning or methodology underlying the testimony is scientifically valid and of whether that reasoning or methodology properly can be applied to the facts in issue. We are confident that federal judges possess the capacity to undertake this review. Many factors will bear on the inquiry, and we do not presume to set out a definitive checklist or test. But some general observations are appropriate.

Ordinarily, a key question to be answered in determining whether a theory or technique is scientific knowledge that will assist the trier of fact will be whether it can be (and has been) tested. "Scientific methodology today is based on generating hypotheses and testing them to see if they can be falsified; indeed, this methodology is what distinguishes science from other fields of human inquiry." Green, [Expert Witnesses and Sufficiency of Evidence in Toxic Substances Litigation: The Legacy of Agent Orange and Bendectin Litigation, 86 Nw.U.L.Rev. 643 (1992)] at 645.

Another pertinent consideration is whether the theory or technique has been subjected to peer review and publication. Publication (which is but one element of peer review) is not a sine qua non of admissibility; it does not necessarily correlate with reliability, and in some instances well-grounded but innovative theories will not have been published. Some propositions, moreover, are too particular, too new, or of too limited interest to be published. But submission to the scrutiny of the scientific community is a component of "good science," in part because it increases the likelihood that substantive flaws in methodology will be detected. The fact of publication (or lack thereof) in a peer-reviewed journal thus will be a relevant, though not dispositive, consideration in assessing the scientific

produce consistent results?). [O]ur reference here is to evidentiary reliability—that is, trustworthiness. [I]n a case involving scientific evidence, evidentiary reliability will be based upon scientific validity.

11. Although the *Frye* decision itself focused exclusively on "novel" scientific techniques, we do not read the requirements of Rule 702 to apply specially or exclusively to unconventional evidence. Of course, well-established propositions are less likely to be challenged than those that are novel, and they are more handily defended. Indeed, theories that are so firmly established as to have attained the status of scientific law, such as the laws of thermodynamics, properly are subject to judicial notice under Fed. Rule Evid. 201.

validity of a particular technique or methodology on which an opinion is premised.

Additionally, in the case of a particular scientific technique, the court ordinarily should consider the known or potential rate of error, and the existence and maintenance of standards controlling the technique's operation.

Finally, "general acceptance" can yet have a bearing on the inquiry. A "reliability assessment does not require although it does permit, explicit identification of a relevant scientific community and an express determination of a particular degree of acceptance within that community." United States v. Downing, 753 F.2d, at 1238. Widespread acceptance can be an important factor in ruling particular evidence admissible, and "a known technique that has been able to attract only minimal support within the community," Downing, supra, at 1238, may properly be viewed with skepticism.

The inquiry envisioned by Rule 702 is, we emphasize, a flexible one. Its overarching subject is the scientific validity—and thus the evidentiary relevance and reliability—of the principles that underlie a proposed submission. The focus, of course, must be solely on principles and methodology, not on the conclusions that they generate.

[T]o summarize: "general acceptance" is not a necessary precondition to the admissibility of scientific evidence under the Federal Rules of Evidence, but the Rules of Evidence—especially Rule 702—do assign to the trial judge the task of ensuring that an expert's testimony both rests on a reliable foundation and is relevant to the task at hand. Pertinent evidence based on scientifically valid principles will satisfy those demands.

The inquiries of the District Court and the Court of Appeals focused almost exclusively on "general acceptance," as gauged by publication and the decisions of other courts. Accordingly, the judgment of the Court of Appeals is vacated and the case is remanded for further proceedings consistent with this opinion.

■ CHIEF JUSTICE REHNQUIST, with whom JUSTICE STEVENS joins, concurring in part and dissenting in part.

The Court speaks of its confidence that federal judges can make a "preliminary assessment of whether the reasoning or methodology underlying the testimony is scientifically valid and of whether that reasoning or methodology properly can be applied to the facts in issue." The Court then states that a "key question" to be answered in deciding whether something is "scientific knowledge" "will be whether it can be (and has been) tested." Following this sentence are three quotations from treatises, which speak not only of empirical testing, but one of which states that "the criterion of the scientific status of a theory is its falsifiability, or refutability, or testability."

I defer to no one in my confidence in federal judges; but I am at a loss to know what is meant when it is said that the scientific status of a theory depends on its "falsifiability," and I suspect some of them will be, too.

I do not doubt that Rule 702 confides to the judge some gatekeeping responsibility in deciding questions of the admissibility of proffered expert testimony. But I do not think it imposes on them either the obligation or the authority to become amateur scientists in order to perform that role. I think the Court would be far better advised in this case to decide only the questions presented, and to leave the further development of this important area of the law to future cases.

———

DAUBERT v. MERRELL DOW PHARMACEUTICALS

United States Court of Appeals, Ninth Circuit, 1995.
43 F.3d 1311.

■ KOZINSKI, Circuit Judge.

On remand from the United States Supreme Court, we undertake "the task of ensuring that an expert's testimony both rests on a reliable foundation and is relevant to the task at hand." Daubert v. Merrell Dow Pharmaceuticals, Inc., 509 U.S. 579, 597, 113 S.Ct. 2786, 2799, 125 L.Ed.2d 469 (1993).

[A].   Brave New World

Federal judges ruling on the admissibility of expert scientific testimony face a far more complex and daunting task in a post-Daubert world than before. The judge's task under Frye is relatively simple: to determine whether the method employed by the experts is generally accepted in the scientific community. Solomon, 753 F.2d at 1526. Under Daubert, we must engage in a difficult, two-part analysis. First, we must determine nothing less than whether the experts' testimony reflects "scientific knowledge," whether their findings are "derived by the scientific method," and whether their work product amounts to "good science." 509 U.S. at 589, 593, 113 S.Ct. at 2795, 2797. Second, we must ensure that the proposed expert testimony is "relevant to the task at hand," id. at 593, 113 S.Ct. at 2797, i.e., that it logically advances a material aspect of the proposing party's case. The Supreme Court referred to this second prong of the analysis as the "fit" requirement. Id. at 591, 113 S.Ct. at 2796.

The first prong of Daubert puts federal judges in an uncomfortable position. The question of admissibility only arises if it is first established that the individuals whose testimony is being proffered are experts in a particular scientific field; here, for example, the Supreme Court waxed eloquent on the impressive qualifications of plaintiffs' experts. Id. at 580 n. 2, 113 S.Ct. at 2791 n. 2. Yet something doesn't become "scientific knowledge" just because it's uttered by a scientist; nor can an expert's self-serving assertion that his conclusions were "derived by the scientific method" be deemed conclusive, else the Supreme Court's opinion could have ended with footnote two. As we read the Supreme Court's teaching in Daubert, therefore, though we are largely untrained in science and certainly no match for any of the witnesses whose testimony we are reviewing, it is our responsibility to determine whether those experts' proposed testimony amounts to "scientific knowledge," constitutes "good science," and was "derived by the scientific method."

The task before us is more daunting still when the dispute concerns matters at the very cutting edge of scientific research, where fact meets theory and certainty dissolves into probability. As the record in this case illustrates, scientists often have vigorous and sincere disagreements as to what research methodology is proper, what should be accepted as sufficient proof for the existence of a "fact," and whether information derived by a particular method can tell us anything useful about the subject under study.

Our responsibility, then, unless we badly misread the Supreme Court's opinion, is to resolve disputes among respected, well-credentialed scientists about matters squarely within their expertise, in areas where there is no scientific consensus as to what is and what is not "good science," and occasionally to reject such expert testimony because it was not "derived by the scientific method." Mindful of our position in the hierarchy of the federal judiciary, we take a deep breath and proceed with this heady task.

[B].   Deus ex Machina

The Supreme Court's opinion in Daubert focuses closely on the language of Fed.R.Evid. 702, which permits opinion testimony by experts as to matters amounting to "scientific ... knowledge." The Court recognized, however, that knowledge in this context does not mean absolute certainty. 509 U.S. at 589, 113 S.Ct. at 2795. Rather, the Court said, "in order to qualify as 'scientific knowledge,' an inference or assertion must be derived by the scientific method." Id. Elsewhere in its opinion, the Court noted that Rule 702 is satisfied where the proffered testimony is "based on scientifically valid principles." Id. at 597, 113 S.Ct. at 2799. Our task, then, is to analyze not what the experts say, but what basis they have for saying it.

Which raises the question: How do we figure out whether scientists have derived their findings through the scientific method or whether their testimony is based on scientifically valid principles? Each expert proffered by the plaintiffs assures us that he has "utiliz[ed] the type of data that is generally and reasonably relied upon by scientists" in the relevant field, see, e.g., Newman Aff. at 5, and that he has "utilized the methods and methodology that would generally and reasonably be accepted" by people who deal in these matters, see, e.g., Gross Aff. at 5. The Court held, however, that federal judges perform a "gatekeeping role," Daubert, 509 U.S. at 595, 113 S.Ct. at 2798; to do so they must satisfy themselves that scientific evidence meets a certain standard of reliability before it is admitted. This means that the expert's bald assurance of validity is not enough. Rather, the party presenting the expert must show that the expert's findings are based on sound science, and this will require some objective, independent validation of the expert's methodology.

While declining to set forth a "definitive checklist or test," id. at 591, 113 S.Ct. at 2796, the Court did list several factors federal judges can consider in determining whether to admit expert scientific testimony under Fed.R.Evid. 702: whether the theory or technique employed by the expert is generally accepted in the scientific community; whether it's been subjected to peer review and publication; whether it can be and has been tested; and whether the known or potential rate of error is acceptable. Id. at 591–593, 113 S.Ct. at 2796–97. We read these factors as illustrative rather than exhaustive; similarly, we do not deem each of them to be equally applicable (or applicable at all) in every case. Rather, we read the Supreme Court as instructing us to determine whether the analysis undergirding the experts' testimony falls within the range of accepted standards governing how scientists conduct their research and reach their conclusions.

One very significant fact to be considered is whether the experts are proposing to testify about matters growing naturally and directly out of research they have conducted independent of the litigation, or whether they have developed their opinions expressly for purposes of testifying. That an expert testifies for money does not necessarily cast doubt on the reliability of his testimony, as few experts appear in court merely as an eleemosynary gesture. But in determining whether proposed expert testimony amounts to good science, we may not ignore the fact that a scientist's normal workplace is the lab or the field, not the courtroom or the lawyer's office.[5]

That an expert testifies based on research he has conducted independent of the litigation provides important, objective proof that the research comports with the dictates of good science. See Peter W. Huber, Galileo's Revenge: Junk Science in the Courtroom 206–09 (1991) (describing how the prevalent practice of expert-shopping leads to bad science). For one thing, experts whose findings flow from existing research are less likely to have been biased toward a particular conclusion by the promise of remuneration; when an expert prepares reports and findings before being hired as a witness, that record will limit the degree to which he can tailor his testimony to serve a party's interests. Then, too, independent research carries its own indicia of reliability, as it is conducted, so to speak, in the usual course of business and must normally satisfy a variety of standards to attract funding and institutional support. Finally, there is usually a limited number of scientists actively conducting research on the very subject that is germane to a particular case, which provides a natural constraint on parties' ability to shop for experts who will come to the desired conclusion. That the testimony proffered by an expert is based directly on legitimate, preexisting research unrelated to the litigation provides the most persua-

---

5. There are, of course, exceptions. Fingerprint analysis, voice recognition, DNA fingerprinting and a variety of other scientific endeavors closely tied to law enforcement may indeed have the courtroom as a principal theatre of operations. As to such disciplines, the fact that the expert has developed an expertise principally for purposes of litigation will obviously not be a substantial consideration.

sive basis for concluding that the opinions he expresses were "derived by the scientific method."

We have examined carefully the affidavits proffered by plaintiffs' experts, as well as the testimony from prior trials that plaintiffs have introduced in support of that testimony, and find that none of the experts based his testimony on preexisting or independent research. While plaintiffs' scientists are all experts in their respective fields, none claims to have studied the effect of Bendectin on limb reduction defects before being hired to testify in this or related cases.

If the proffered expert testimony is not based on independent research, the party proffering it must come forward with other objective, verifiable evidence that the testimony is based on "scientifically valid principles." One means of showing this is by proof that the research and analysis supporting the proffered conclusions have been subjected to normal scientific scrutiny through peer review and publication. Huber, Galileo's Revenge at 209 (suggesting that "[t]he ultimate test of [a scientific expert's] integrity is her readiness to publish and be damned").

Peer review and publication do not, of course, guarantee that the conclusions reached are correct; much published scientific research is greeted with intense skepticism and is not borne out by further research. But the test under Daubert is not the correctness of the expert's conclusions but the soundness of his methodology. See n. 11 infra. That the research is accepted for publication in a reputable scientific journal after being subjected to the usual rigors of peer review is a significant indication that it is taken seriously by other scientists, i.e., that it meets at least the minimal criteria of good science. Daubert, 509 U.S. at 593, 113 S.Ct. at 2797 ("[S]crutiny of the scientific community is a component of 'good science.'"). If nothing else, peer review and publication "increase the likelihood that substantive flaws in methodology will be detected." Daubert, 509 U.S. at 593, 113 S.Ct. at 2797.

Bendectin litigation has been pending in the courts for over a decade, yet the only review the plaintiffs' experts' work has received has been by judges and juries, and the only place their theories and studies have been published is in the pages of federal and state reporters. None of the plaintiffs' experts has published his work on Bendectin in a scientific journal or solicited formal review by his colleagues. Despite the many years the controversy has been brewing, no one in the scientific community— except defendant's experts—has deemed these studies worthy of verification, refutation or even comment. It's as if there were a tacit understanding within the scientific community that what's going on here is not science at all, but litigation.

Establishing that an expert's proffered testimony grows out of pre-litigation research or that the expert's research has been subjected to peer review are the two principal ways the proponent of expert testimony can show that the evidence satisfies the first prong of Rule 702. Where such evidence is unavailable, the proponent of expert scientific testimony may attempt to satisfy its burden through the testimony of its own experts. For such a showing to be sufficient, the experts must explain precisely how they went about reaching their conclusions and point to some objective source— a learned treatise, the policy statement of a professional association, a published article in a reputable scientific journal or the like—to show that they have followed the scientific method, as it is practiced by (at least) a recognized minority of scientists in their field. See United States v. Rincon, 28 F.3d 921, 924 (9th Cir.1994) (research must be described "in sufficient detail that the district court [can] determine if the research was scientifically valid").[11]

Plaintiffs have made no such showing. As noted above, plaintiffs rely entirely on the experts' unadorned assertions that the methodology they employed comports with standard scientific procedures. In support of these assertions, plaintiffs offer only the trial and deposition testimony of these experts in other cases. While these materials indicate that plaintiffs' experts have relied on animal studies, chemical structure analyses and epidemiological data, they neither explain the methodology the experts followed to reach their conclusions nor point to any external source to validate that methodology. We've been presented with only the experts' qualifications, their conclusions and their assurances of reliability. Under Daubert, that's not enough.

[C].   No Visible Means of Support

In elucidating the second requirement of Rule 702, Daubert stressed the importance of the "fit" between the testimony and an issue in the case: "Rule 702's 'helpfulness' standard requires a valid scientific connection to the pertinent inquiry as a precondition to admissibility." 509 U.S. at 591, 113 S.Ct. at 2796. Here, the pertinent inquiry is causation. In assessing whether the proffered expert testimony "will assist the trier of fact" in resolving this issue, we must look to the governing substantive standard, which in this case is supplied by California tort law. [C]alifornia tort law requires plaintiffs to show not merely that Bendectin increased the likelihood of injury, but that it more likely than not caused their injuries.[17]

---

11. This underscores the difference between Daubert and Frye. Under Frye, the party proffering scientific evidence had to show it was based on the method generally accepted in the scientific community. The focus under Daubert is on the reliability of the methodology, and in addressing that question the court and the parties are not limited to what is generally accepted; methods accepted by a minority in the scientific community may well be sufficient. However, the party proffering the evidence must explain the expert's methodology and demonstrate in some objectively verifiable way that the expert has both chosen a reliable scientific method and followed it faithfully. Of course, the fact that one party's experts use a methodology accepted by only a minority of

scientists would be a proper basis for impeachment at trial.

17. The Supreme Court recognized that the "fit" requirement "goes primarily to relevance," Daubert, 509 U.S. at 591, 113 S.Ct. at 2795, but it obviously did not intend the second prong of Rule 702 to be merely a reiteration of the general relevancy requirement of Rule 402. In elucidating the "fit" requirement, the Supreme Court noted that scientific expert testimony carries special dangers to the fact-finding process because it " 'can be both powerful and quite misleading because of the difficulty in evaluating it.' " Id. at 595, 113 S.Ct. at 2798 (quoting Weinstein, Rule 702 of the Federal Rules of Evidence Is Sound; It Should Not Be Amended,

[A]s the district court properly found below, "the strongest inference to be drawn for plaintiffs based on the epidemiological evidence is that Bendectin could possibly have caused plaintiffs' injuries." 727 F.Supp. at 576. The same is true of the other testimony derived from animal studies and chemical structure analyses—these experts "testify to a possibility rather than a probability." Turpin, 959 F.2d at 1360. Plaintiffs do not quantify this possibility, or otherwise indicate how their conclusions about causation should be weighted, even though the substantive legal standard has always required proof of causation by a preponderance of the evidence.

[T]he district court's grant of summary judgment is AFFIRMED.

GENERAL ELECTRIC COMPANY v. JOINER

Supreme Court of the United States, 1997.
522 U.S. 136, 118 S.Ct. 512, 139 L.Ed.2d 508.

■ CHIEF JUSTICE REHNQUIST delivered the opinion of the Court.

We granted certiorari in this case to determine what standard an appellate court should apply in reviewing a trial court's decision to admit or exclude expert testimony under Daubert v. Merrell Dow Pharmaceuticals, Inc., 509 U.S. 579, 113 S.Ct. 2786, 125 L.Ed.2d 469 (1993).

[R]espondent Robert Joiner began work as an electrician in the Water & Light Department of Thomasville, Georgia (City) in 1973. This job required him to work with and around the City's electrical transformers, which used a mineral-based dielectric fluid as a coolant. Joiner often had to stick his hands and arms into the fluid to make repairs. The fluid would sometimes splash onto him, occasionally getting into his eyes and mouth. In 1983 the City discovered that the fluid in some of the transformers was contaminated with polychlorinated biphenyls (PCBs). PCBs are widely considered to be hazardous to human health. [J]oiner was diagnosed with small cell lung cancer in 1991.

[T]he District Court [g]ranted summary judgment for petitioners because [t]he testimony of Joiner's experts had failed to show that there was a link between exposure to PCBs and small cell lung cancer. The court believed that the testimony of respondent's experts to the contrary did not rise above "subjective belief or unsupported speculation." 864 F.Supp. 1310, 1326 (N.D.Ga.1994). Their testimony was therefore inadmissible. The Court of Appeals for the Eleventh Circuit reversed. 78 F.3d 524 (1996). It held that "[b]ecause the Federal Rules of Evidence governing expert testimony display a preference for admissibility, we apply a particularly stringent standard of review to the trial judge's exclusion of expert testimony." Id. at 529. Applying that standard, the Court of Appeals held that the District Court had erred in excluding the testimony of Joiner's expert

138 F.R.D. 631, 632 (1991)). Federal judges must therefore exclude proffered scientific evidence under Rules 702 and 403 unless they are convinced that it speaks clearly and directly to an issue in dispute in the case, and that it will not mislead the jury.

witnesses. The District Court [e]xcluded the experts' testimony because it "drew different conclusions from the research than did each of the experts." The Court of Appeals opined that a district court should limit its role to determining the "legal reliability of proffered expert testimony, leaving the jury to decide the correctness of competing expert opinions." Id. at 533.

[R]espondent points to Daubert's language that the "focus, of course, must be solely on principles and methodology, not on the conclusions that they generate." 509 U.S., at 595, 113 S.Ct., at 2797. He claims that because the District Court's disagreement was with the conclusion that the experts drew from the studies, the District Court committed legal error and was properly reversed by the Court of Appeals. But conclusions and methodology are not entirely distinct from one another. Trained experts commonly extrapolate from existing data. But nothing in either Daubert or the Federal Rules of Evidence requires a district court to admit opinion evidence which is connected to existing data only by the ipse dixit of the expert. A court may conclude that there is simply too great an analytical gap between the data and the opinion proffered. That is what the District Court did here, and we hold that it did not abuse its discretion in so doing. We hold, therefore, that abuse of discretion is the proper standard by which to review a district court's decision to admit or exclude scientific evidence. We further hold that, because it was within the District Court's discretion to conclude that the studies upon which the experts relied were not sufficient, whether individually or in combination, to support their conclusions that Joiner's exposure to PCBs contributed to his cancer, the District Court did not abuse its discretion in excluding their testimony. [W]e accordingly reverse the judgment of the Court of Appeals and remand this case for proceedings consistent with this opinion. It is so ordered.

■ JUSTICE BREYER, concurring.

The Court's opinion, which I join, emphasizes Daubert's statement that a trial judge, acting as "gatekeeper," must " 'ensure that any and all scientific testimony or evidence admitted is not only relevant, but reliable.' " Ante, at 517 (quoting Daubert v. Merrell Dow Pharmaceuticals, Inc., 509 U.S. 579, 589, 113 S.Ct. 2786, 2795, 125 L.Ed.2d 469 (1993)). This requirement will sometimes ask judges to make subtle and sophisticated determinations about scientific methodology and its relation to the conclusions an expert witness seeks to offer—particularly when a case arises in an area where the science itself is tentative or uncertain, or where testimony about general risk levels in human beings or animals is offered to prove individual causation. Yet, as amici have pointed out, judges are not scientists and do not have the scientific training that can facilitate the making of such decisions. See, e.g., Brief for Trial Lawyers for Public Justice as Amicus Curiae 15; Brief for The New England Journal of Medicine et al. as Amici Curiae 2 ("Judges . . . are generally not trained scientists"). Of course, neither the difficulty of the task nor any comparative lack of expertise can excuse the judge from exercising the "gatekeeper" duties that the Federal Rules impose—determining, for example, whether particular expert testimony is reliable and "will assist the trier of fact," Fed. Rule Evid. 702, or whether the "probative value" of testimony is substantially outweighed by risks of prejudice, confusion or waste of time. Fed. Rule Evid. 403. To the contrary, when law and science intersect, those duties often must be exercised with special care.

[I]t is, thus, essential in this science-related area that the courts administer the Federal Rules of Evidence in order to achieve the "end[s]" that the Rules themselves set forth, not only so that proceedings may be "justly determined," but also so "that the truth may be ascertained." Fed. Rule Evid. 102. I therefore want specially to note that, as cases presenting significant science-related issues have increased in number, see Judicial Conference of the United States, Report of the Federal Courts Study Committee 97 (Apr. 2, 1990) ("Economic, statistical, technological, and natural and social scientific data are becoming increasingly important in both routine and complex litigation"), judges have increasingly found in the Rules of Evidence and Civil Procedure ways to help them overcome the inherent difficulty of making determinations about complicated scientific or otherwise technical evidence. Among these techniques are an increased use of Rule 16's pretrial conference authority to narrow the scientific issues in dispute, pretrial hearings where potential experts are subject to examination by the court, and the appointment of special masters and specially trained law clerks. See J. Cecil & T. Willging, Court–Appointed Experts: Defining the Role of Experts Appointed Under Federal Rule of Evidence 706, pp. 83–88 (1993); J. Weinstein, Individual Justice in Mass Tort Litigation 107–110 (1995); cf. Kaysen, In Memoriam: Charles E. Wyzanski, Jr., 100 Harv.L.Rev. 713, 713–715 (1987) (discussing a judge's use of an economist as a law clerk in United States v. United Shoe Machinery Corp., 110 *521 F.Supp. 295 (D.Mass.1953), aff'd, 347 U.S. 521, 74 S.Ct. 699, 98 L.Ed. 910 (1954)). In the present case, the New England Journal of Medicine has filed an amici brief "in support of neither petitioners nor respondents" in which the Journal writes:

> "[A] judge could better fulfill this gatekeeper function if he or she had help from scientists. Judges should be strongly encouraged to make greater use of their inherent authority ... to appoint experts. ... Reputable experts could be recommended to courts by established scientific organizations, such as the National Academy of Sciences or the American Association for the Advancement of Science."

Brief for The New England Journal of Medicine 18–19; cf. Fed. Rule Evid. 706 (court may "on its own motion or on the motion of any party" appoint an expert to serve on behalf of the court, and this expert may be selected as "agreed upon by the parties" or chosen by the court); see also Weinstein, supra, at 116 (a court should sometimes "go beyond the experts proffered by the parties" and "utilize its powers to appoint independent experts under Rule 706 of the Federal Rules of Evidence"). Given this kind of offer of cooperative effort, from the scientific to the legal community, and given the various Rules-authorized methods for facilitating the courts' task, it seems to me that Daubert's gatekeeping requirement will not prove inordinately difficult to implement; and that it will help secure the basic objectives of the Federal Rules of Evidence; which are, to repeat, the ascertainment of truth and the just determination of proceedings. Fed. Rule Evid. 102.

———

KUMHO TIRE COMPANY v. CARMICHAEL

Supreme Court of the United States, 1999.
526 U.S. 137, 119 S.Ct. 1167, 143 L.Ed.2d 238.

■ JUSTICE BREYER delivered the opinion of the Court.

This case requires us to decide how Daubert applies to the testimony of engineers and other experts who are not scientists. [I]n Daubert, this Court held that Federal Rule of Evidence 702 imposes a special obligation upon a trial judge to "ensure that any and all scientific testimony ... is not only relevant, but reliable." 509 U.S. at 589. The initial question before us is whether this basic gatekeeping obligation applies only to "scientific" testimony or to all expert testimony. We, like the parties, believe that it applies to all expert testimony.

For one thing, Rule 702 itself says:

"If scientific, technical, or other specialized knowledge will assist the trier of fact to understand the evidence or to determine a fact in issue, a witness qualified as an expert by knowledge, skill, experience, training, or education, may testify thereto in the form of an opinion or otherwise."

This language makes no relevant distinction between "scientific" knowledge and "technical" or "other specialized" knowledge. It makes clear that any such knowledge might become the subject of expert testimony.

[N]either is the evidentiary rationale that underlay the Court's basic Daubert "gatekeeping" determination limited to "scientific" knowledge. Daubert pointed out that Federal Rules 702 and 703 grant expert witnesses testimonial latitude unavailable to other witnesses on the "assumption that the expert's opinion will have a reliable basis in the knowledge and experience of his discipline." The Rules grant that latitude to all experts, not just to "scientific" ones.

Finally, it would prove difficult, if not impossible, for judges to administer evidentiary rules under which a gatekeeping obligation depended upon a distinction between "scientific" knowledge and "technical" or "other specialized" knowledge. There is no clear line that divides the one from the others. Disciplines such as engineering rest upon scientific knowledge. Pure scientific theory itself may depend for its development upon observation and properly engineered machinery. And conceptual efforts to distinguish the two are unlikely to produce clear legal lines capable of application in particular cases.

[T]he petitioners ask more specifically whether a trial judge determining the "admissibility of an engineering expert's testimony" may consider several more specific factors that Daubert said might "bear on" a judge's gate-keeping determination. These factors include:

— Whether a "theory or technique . . . can be (and has been) tested";

— Whether it "has been subjected to peer review and publication";

— Whether, in respect to a particular technique, there is a high "known or potential rate of error" and whether there are "standards controlling the technique's operation"; and

— Whether the theory or technique enjoys "general acceptance" within a "relevant scientific community." *509 U.S. at 592–594.*

Emphasizing the word "may" in the question, we answer that question yes.

Engineering testimony rests upon scientific foundations, the reliability of which will be at issue in some cases. In other cases, the relevant reliability concerns may focus upon personal knowledge or experience. As the Solicitor General points out, there are many different kinds of experts, and many different kinds of expertise. See Brief for United States as Amicus Curiae 18–19, and n. 5 (citing cases involving experts in drug terms, handwriting analysis, criminal modus operandi, land valuation, agricultural practices, railroad procedures, attorney's fee valuation, and others). Our emphasis on the word "may" thus reflects Daubert's description of the Rule 702 inquiry as "a flexible one." *509 U.S. at 594.* Daubert makes clear that the factors it mentions do not constitute a "definitive checklist or test." *Id. at 593.* [I]ndeed, those factors do not all necessarily apply even in every instance in which the reliability of scientific testimony is challenged. It might not be surprising in a particular case, for example, that a claim made by a scientific witness has never been the subject of peer review, for the particular application at issue may never previously have interested any scientist. Nor, on the other hand, does the presence of Daubert's general acceptance factor help show that an expert's testimony is reliable where the discipline itself lacks reliability, as, for example, do theories grounded in any so-called generally accepted principles of astrology or necromancy.

At the same time, [s]ome of Daubert's questions can help to evaluate the reliability even of experience-based testimony. In certain cases, it will be appropriate for the trial judge to ask, for example, how often an engineering expert's experience-based methodology has produced erroneous results, or whether such a method is generally accepted in the relevant engineering community. Likewise, it will at times be useful to ask even of a witness whose expertise is based purely on experience, say, a perfume tester able to distinguish among 140 odors at a sniff, whether his preparation is of a kind that others in the field would recognize as acceptable.

[W]e do not believe that Rule 702 creates a schematism that segregates expertise by type while mapping certain kinds of questions to certain kinds of experts. Life and the legal cases that it generates are too complex to warrant so definitive a match.

To say this is not to deny the importance of Daubert's gatekeeping requirement. The objective of that requirement is to ensure the reliability and relevancy of expert testimony. It is to make certain that an expert, whether basing testimony upon professional studies or personal experience, employs in the courtroom the same level of intellectual rigor that characterizes the practice of an expert in the relevant field. Nor do we deny that, as stated in Daubert, the particular questions that it mentioned will often be appropriate for use in determining the reliability of challenged expert testimony. Rather, we conclude that the trial judge must have considerable leeway in deciding in a particular case how to go about determining whether particular expert testimony is reliable. That is to say, a trial court should consider the specific factors identified in Daubert where they are reasonable measures of the reliability of expert testimony.

The trial court must have the same kind of latitude in deciding how to test an expert's reliability, and to decide whether or when special briefing or other proceedings are needed to investigate reliability, as it enjoys when it decides whether that expert's relevant testimony is reliable. Our opinion in Joiner makes clear that a court of appeals is to apply an abuse-of-discretion standard when it "reviews a trial court's decision to admit or exclude expert testimony." *522 U.S. at 138–139.* That standard applies as much to the trial court's decisions about how to determine reliability as to its ultimate conclusion. Otherwise, the trial judge would lack the discretionary authority needed both to avoid unnecessary "reliability" proceedings in ordinary cases where the reliability of an expert's methods is properly taken for granted, and to require appropriate proceedings in the less usual or more complex cases where cause for questioning the expert's reliability arises.

FEDERAL RULES OF EVIDENCE

Rule 702. Testimony by Experts

If scientific, technical, or other specialized knowledge will assist the trier of fact to understand the evidence or to determine a fact in issue, a witness qualified as an expert by knowledge, skill, experience, training, or education, may testify thereto in the form of an opinion or otherwise, if (1) the testimony is based upon sufficient facts or data, (2) the testimony is the product of reliable principles and methods, and (3) the witness has applied the principles and methods reliably to the facts of the case.

Committee Note

Rule 702 has been amended in response to *Daubert v. Merrell Dow Pharmaceuticals, Inc.,* 509 U.S. 579, 113 S.Ct. 2786, 125 L.Ed.2d 469 (1993), and to the many cases applying *Daubert,* including *Kumho Tire Co.*

v. Carmichael, 526 U.S. 137, 119 S.Ct. 1167, 143 L.Ed.2d 238 (1999). In *Daubert* the Court charged trial judges with the responsibility of acting as gatekeepers to exclude unreliable expert testimony, and the Court in *Kumho* clarified that this gatekeeper function applies to all expert testimony, not just testimony based in science. *See also Kumho*, 119 S.Ct. at 1178 (citing the Committee Note to the proposed amendment to Rule 702, which had been released for public comment before the date of the *Kumho* decision). The amendment affirms the trial court's role as gatekeeper and provides some general standards that the trial court must use to assess the reliability and helpfulness of proffered expert testimony. Consistently with *Kumho*, the Rule as amended provides that all types of expert testimony present questions of admissibility for the trial court in deciding whether the evidence is reliable and helpful.

———

NOTES

1. *Daubert* and State Courts. The reception of *Daubert* in state courts is reviewed in D. Faigman, D. Kaye, M. Saks, J. Sanders, and E. Cheng, Modern Scientific Evidence: The Law and Science of Expert Testimony, 2008–2009 ed (2008) (citations omitted) at 20–21:

> First, 25 states have accepted the essential principles of *Daubert*, either because they were persuaded by the Supreme Court's reasoning or they already adhered to a substantially similar test. Second, four states have stated their openness to reconsidering the rule they apply to expert testimony. Third, 10 states have rejected the *Daubert* standard, at least for the time being, preferring to remain with the *Frye* test or an alternative state formulation of general acceptance and relevancy. Fourth, eight states and the District of Columbia follow their own state version of a relevance/reliability determination, usually based on the respective state code of evidence. Fifth, four states apply some combination of *Frye* or *Daubert*.

2. Recent Developments in Scientific Evidence. A landmark report on the use of forensic science evidence in litigation has recently been released by the research arm of the National Academy of Sciences. National Research Council, Strengthening Forensic Science in the United States: A Path Forward (2009). While the report focuses on physical and biological evidence such as DNA and fingerprints, it may have significant implications for social science evidence as well:

> The simple reality is that the interpretation of forensic evidence is not always based on scientific studies to determine its validity. This is a serious problem. Although research has been done in some disciplines, there is a notable dearth of peer-reviewed, published studies establishing the scientific bases and validity of many forensic methods.[T]he law's greatest dilemma in its heavy reliance on forensic evidence [c]oncerns the question of whether—and to what extent—there is science in any given forensic science discipline.

Two very important questions should underlie the law's admission of and reliance upon forensic evidence in criminal trials: (1) the extent to which a particular forensic discipline is founded on a reliable scientific methodology that gives it the capacity to accurately analyze evidence and report findings and (2) the extent to which practitioners in a particular forensic discipline rely on human interpretation that could be tainted by error, the threat of bias, or the absence of sound operational procedures and robust performance standards. Id. at 8–9.

The full report is available at http://www.nap.edu/catalog.php?record_id=12589.

The report has already been cited by the United States Supreme Court. In his opinion for the 5–4 majority in Melendez–Diaz v. Massachusetts, 129 S.Ct. 2527 (2009), Justice Scalia wrote:

[It is not] evident that what respondent calls "neutral scientific testing" is as neutral or as reliable as respondent suggests. Forensic evidence is not uniquely immune from the risk of manipulation. According to a recent study conducted under the auspices of the National Academy of Sciences, "[t]he majority of [laboratories producing forensic evidence] are administered by law enforcement agencies, such as police departments, where the laboratory administrator reports to the head of the agency." National Research Council of the National Academies, Strengthening Forensic Science in the United States: A Path Forward 6–1 (Prepublication Copy Feb. 2009) (hereinafter National Academy Report). And "[b]ecause forensic scientists often are driven in their work by a need to answer a particular question related to the issues of a particular case, they sometimes face pressure to sacrifice appropriate methodology for the sake of expediency." Id., at S–17. A forensic analyst responding to a request from a law enforcement official may feel pressure-or have an incentive-to alter the evidence in a manner favorable to the prosecution.

[C]onfrontation is designed to weed out not only the fraudulent analyst, but the incompetent one as well. Serious deficiencies have been found in the forensic evidence used in criminal trials. [O]ne study of cases in which exonerating evidence resulted in the overturning of criminal convictions concluded that invalid forensic testimony contributed to the convictions in 60% of the cases. Garrett & Neufeld, Invalid Forensic Science Testimony and Wrongful Convictions, 95 Va. L.Rev. 1, 14 (2009). And the National Academy Report concluded:

> *"The forensic science system, encompassing both research and practice, has serious problems that can only be addressed by a national commitment to overhaul the current structure that supports the forensic science community in this country."* National Academy Report P–1 (emphasis in original).

3. Reference Manual. The Reference Manual on Scientific Evidence (2d 2000) is available from the Federal Judicial Center at http://www.fjc.gov/

public/pdf.nsf/lookup/sciman00.pdf/$file/sciman00.pdf. A third edition is planned for publication in 2011.

SELECTED BIBLIOGRAPHY

E. Beecher–Monas, Evaluating Scientific Evidence: An Interdisciplinary Framework for Intellectual Due Process (2007).

Bernstein, Expert Witnesses, Adversarial Bias, and the (Partial) Failure of the *Daubert* Revolution, 93 Iowa Law Review 451 (2008).

Cheng, Independent Judicial Research in the *Daubert* Age, 56 Duke Law Journal 1263 (2007).

Cole, Where the Rubber Meets the Road: Thinking About Expert Evidence as Expert Testimony, 52 Villanova Law Review 803 (2007).

D. Faigman, Laboratory of Justice: The Supreme Court's 200–Year Struggle to Integrate Science and the Law (2004).

Faigman and Monahan, Psychological Evidence at the Dawn of the Law's Scientific Age, 56 Annual Review of Psychology 631 (2005).

Faigman and Monahan, Standards of Legal Admissibility and Their Implications for Psychological Science, in Psychological Science in the Courtroom: Controversies and Consensus (J. Skeem, K. Douglas, and S. Lilienfeld eds. 2009).

Gatowski, Dobbin, Richardson, Ginsburg, Merlino, and Dahir, Asking the Gatekeepers: A National Survey of Judges on Judging Expert Evidence in a Post–*Daubert* World, 25 Law and Human Behavior 433 (2001).

T. Golan, Laws of Men and Laws of Nature: The History of Scientific Expert Testimony in England and America (2004).

Groscup, Penrod, Studebaker, Huss, and O'Neil, The Effects of *Daubert* on the Admissibility of Expert Testimony in State and Federal Criminal Cases, 8 Psychology, Public Policy, and Law 339 (2002).

Haack, What's Wrong With Litigation–Driven Science? An Essay on Legal Epistemology, 38 Seton Hall Law Review 1053 (2008).

Helland and Klick, Does Anyone Get Stopped at the Gate? An Empirical Assessment of the *Daubert* Trilogy in the States (2009). Available at http:/ssrn.com/abstract=1370518.

Jasanoff, Law's Knowledge: Science for Justice in Legal Settings, 95 American Journal of Public Health S49 (2005).

Kaye, On "Falsification" and "Falsifiability": The First *Daubert* Factor and the Philosophy of Science, 45 Jurimetrics Journal 473 (2005).

Kritzer, *Daubert* in the Law Office: Routinizing Procedural Change, 5 Journal of Empirical Legal Studies 109 (2008).

Levett and Kovera, The Effectiveness of Opposing Expert Witnesses for Educating Jurors about Unreliable Expert Evidence, 32 Law and Human Behavior 363 (2008).

McAuliff and Groscup, *Daubert* and Psychological Science in Court: Judging Validity from the Bench, Bar, and Jury Box, in Psychological Science in the Courtroom: Controversies and Consensus (J. Skeem, K. Douglas, and S. Lilienfeld eds. 2009).

McQuiston–Surrett and Saks, The Testimony of Forensic Identification Science: What Expert Witnesses Say and What Factfinders Hear, Law and Human Behavior (in press).

Merlino, Murray, and Richardson, Judicial Gatekeeping and the Social Construction of Admissibility of Expert Testimony, 26 Behavioral Sciences and the Law 187 (2008).

Redding, How Common-sense Psychology Can Inform Law and Psycholegal Research, 5 University of Chicago Law School Roundtable 107 (1998).

Redding, Reconstructing Science Through Law, 23 Southern Illinois Law Journal 585 (1999).

Redding and Murrie, Judicial Decision Making about Forensic Mental Health Evidence, in Forensic Psychology: Emerging Topics and Expanding Roles (A. Goldstein ed. 2007).

Risinger, The Irrelevance, and Central Relevance, of the Boundary Between Science and Non–Science in the Evaluation of Expert Witness Reliability, 52 Villanova Law Review 679 (2007).

Risinger, Saks, Thompson, and Rosenthal, The *Daubert/Kumho* Implications of Observer Effects in Forensic Science: Hidden Problems of Expectation and Suggestion, 90 California Law Review 1 (2002).

Saks, Banishing *Ipse Dixit*: The Impact of *Kumho Tire* on Forensic Identification Science, 57 Washington and Lee Law Review 879 (2000).

Saks, The Aftermath of *Daubert*: An Evolving Jurisprudence of Expert Evidence, 40 Jurimetrics 229 (2000).

Saks and Faigman, Expert Evidence after *Daubert*, 1 Annual Review of Law and Social Science 105 (2005).

Saks and Faigman, Failed Forensics: How Forensic Science Lost Its Way and How It Might Yet Find It, 4 Annual Review of Law and Social Science 149 (2008).

M. Saks, D. Faigman, D. Kaye, and J. Sanders, Second Annotated Reference Manual on Scientific Evidence (2004).

Sanders, Diamond, and Vidmar, Legal Perceptions of Science and Expert Knowledge, 8 Psychology, Public Policy, and Law 139 (2002).

Schweitzer and Saks, The Gatekeeper Effect: The Impact of Judges' Admissibility Decisions on the Persuasiveness of Expert Testimony, 15 Psychology, Public Policy, and Law 1 (2009).

Slobogin, Doubts About *Daubert*: Psychiatric Anecdata as a Case Study, 57 Washington and Lee Law Review 919 (2000).

Vidmar, The Origin and Outcome of an Amicus Brief in *Kumho Tire v. Carmichael* (1999), 24 Law and Human Behavior 383 (2000).

Walker and Monahan, *Daubert* and the *Reference Manual*: An Essay on the Future of Science in Law, 82 Virginia Law Review 837 (1996).

SECTION II.   SOCIAL SCIENCE METHODS

The succeeding chapters of this book describe and analyze the roles that social science has come to play in contemporary American law, with a particular emphasis on post-*Daubert* developments. In order to understand the cases and materials presented and to critique them intelligently, however, one must first have at least a rudimentary appreciation of how social science works, that is, of the methods by which social scientists pursue their interests. This section introduces those methods. Our objective here is frankly pragmatic. We consider social science methods not for their own sake and certainly not comprehensively or with attention to technical detail. Rather, we consider them because even a limited introduction to "how to think like a social scientist" will make reading the principal chapters of the book much more profitable. This section anticipates each aspect of social science method that appears later in legal context. For those with a solid background in social science this chapter will serve primarily as a refresher. For those new to the field, these primer-level materials should be adequate preparation for dealing intelligently with the applications to come.

Perhaps the most straightforward way to unpack the topic of methodology is to look first at how social scientists go about asking questions, then to consider the various methods social scientists use to gather information relevant to the questions posed, and finally to examine the strategies they use to interpret information that their research has generated.

A.   METHODS OF ASKING QUESTIONS

Asking the right question is the necessary first step in any form of useful social inquiry. To a social scientist, some questions the law poses are clear and answerable, e.g., "What percentage of consumers confuse one product with another?" Other questions require a great deal of rephrasing before the social scientist can deal with them, e.g., "Is pornography harmful?" Still other questions are so far removed from the kind of discourse in which social scientists engage that the questions are best referred elsewhere, e.g., "Is retribution just?" Evaluation of any example of social science in law should begin with consideration of whether the right question was asked.

To have meaning to a social scientist, a question must refer to some aspect of the empirical world, i.e., to something we can observe with our senses. Often, the question would call also for an explanation of what caused the state of the world to be as we observe it, rather than being some other way. Finally, the question would be put in such a manner that answering it necessarily would involve measuring or quantifying in some way what is observed. Thus, the empirical approach, causal explanation, and measurement, seem to be the three components of asking the right question in social science.

1.   THE EMPIRICAL APPROACH

It is useful, at the outset, to characterize in general terms the factors that make "scientific" questions distinctive. Terms such as "objective," "observable," "verifiable," or what *Daubert* referred to as "falsifiable" are often used to describe what has come to be known as "the empirical approach" to asking questions.

———

APPROACHES TO SOCIAL RESEARCH (4TH ED. 2005)*

Royce A. Singleton, Jr., and Bruce C. Straits.

Scientists limit themselves to problems and issues that can be resolved by making observations. This means that scientific inquiry is based on *empiricism*. Empiricism is a way of knowing or understanding the world that relies directly or indirectly on what we experience through our senses: sight, hearing, taste, smell, and touch. In other words, information or data are acceptable in science only insofar as they can be observed or "sensed" in some way under specifiable conditions by people possessing the normal sensory apparatus, intelligence, and skills. Claire Selltiz, Lawrence Wrightsman, and Stuart Cook ([Research Methods in Social Relations, 3d ed.] 1976:22), for example, point out that whereas people can see a baseball, they cannot see a neutron. "But people can see neutrons indirectly, by observing photographic representations of paths neutrons leave. Under no normal conditions can people regularly observe ghosts. Nor do ghosts leave any other observable or tangible manifestations. Thus, we can have scientific theories about baseballs and neutrons but not about ghosts." To say that science is based upon empiricism, therefore, is to say that the only admissible evidence for or against a scientific hypothesis or theory must be observable, directly or indirectly, through some tangible manifestation.

This statement implies that appeals to authority, tradition, revelation, intuition, or other nonempirical ways of knowing, which may be acceptable in other endeavors (such as theology and philosophy), cannot be used as scientific evidence. Scientists do not accept a statement or generalization about the world simply because an authority or expert says it is true, or because tradition and common sense say it is so, or because it seems intuitively plausible.

———

* From APPROACHES TO SOCIAL RE-SEARCH, FOURTH EDITION by Royce A. Singleton, Jr. and Bruce C. Straits, copyright © 2005 by Oxford University Press, Inc. Used by permission of Oxford University Press, Inc.

NOTE

1. Distinctions Among the Sciences. Singleton and Straits addressed characteristics common to all sciences. While the essence of the scientific method remains the same regardless of the context in which it is applied, distinctions among various types of science are well known.

This book deals with what is variously referred to as social science or behavioral science. While the terms are often used synonymously, behavioral science could be viewed as the study of all influences upon behavior, including biological factors (e.g., genetics). Since our focus here does not extend to the uses of biology in the law, we refer to our subject matter throughout as social science. Compare L. Friedman and S. Macaulay, Law and the Behavioral Sciences (2d ed. 1977).

The social sciences themselves can be further subdivided. Some of the social sciences are defined by virtue of their level of analysis. Thus, psychology typically takes the individual human being as its level of study while sociology focuses primarily on the group. Other social sciences are defined by reference to the units used in their research. History, for example, emphasizes time and economics often emphasizes money as the principal unit in the explanations they provide. Still other social sciences are defined in terms of the specific problems they address, regardless of the level or unit of analysis they use. Thus, criminology is the study of crime and political science is the study of politics, whether done with methods traditionally associated with psychology, sociology, history, or economics.

It is important not to take distinctions among the social sciences too seriously, for the degree of overlap among them is great. Much of the disciplines of psychology and sociology, for example, deal with the *relationship* between the individual and the group, and offer theories that necessarily involve both individual factors, such as beliefs and expectancies, as well as group factors, such as social class. Courses titled "Social Psychology" are found in both the psychology and the sociology departments of every university. Often, distinctions among the social sciences are purely arbitrary and result from historical accident in the development of the disciplines. At best, the distinctions represent the characteristic *emphases* of a given field, rather than rigid criteria for classifying approaches to knowledge.

2. CAUSAL EXPLANATION

The phrase "empirical approach" characterizes the general orientation of social scientists to asking questions. More specifically, the empirical approach subsumes three generic goals that social scientists work toward in asking questions about some aspect of the world: they wish to predict when the event being studied will occur; they wish to have the ability to control whether the event occurs; and they wish to understand what causes the event to occur.

———

SCIENCE AND BEHAVIOR: AN INTRODUCTION TO METHODS OF PSYCHOLOGICAL RESEARCH (4TH ED. 1995)*

Robert M. Liebert and Lynn Langenbach Liebert.

The search for causal relationships in nature is rarely straightforward. For one thing, there are a number of different types of causal relationships. Moreover, these different types can operate in various combinations to influence a given phenomenon.

[F]our broad types of causal relationships can be identified: necessary and sufficient relationships, necessary but not sufficient relationships, sufficient but not necessary relationships, and contributory relationships.

A *necessary and sufficient causal relationship* is one in which some factor or condition, X, is required to produce an effect, and will invariably do so. A specific genetic anomaly is necessary and sufficient to cause some hereditary diseases, such as Tay–Sachs disease. In psychology it is rare to find important causal relationships that are both necessary and sufficient.

The world is filled with causal relationships in which some specifiable factor, X, is *necessary but not sufficient* for Y to occur. For example, a writing instrument is necessary but not sufficient to compose a book; possession of a loaded gun is necessary but not sufficient for a shooting to occur.

Sufficient but not necessary causal relationships are those in which X is one of many causes that can independently produce Y. For most people, the sight of an angry bear is not a necessary condition to keep out of a mountain cave. A host of other factors will dissuade people from entering a dark cave, even if no bears are around to assert a territorial claim. Because most behavioral phenomena can be caused by many different factors and circumstances, all that can usually be done in psychological research is to identify sufficient but not necessary causes.

Contributory causal relationships are those in which X is neither necessary nor sufficient to cause Y, but can nonetheless contribute to (that is, change the likelihood of) Y's occurrence. Annoying experiences during the day are often contributory causes to the arguments that couples have during the evening. A "bad day at the office" may not be sufficient or necessary to cause a domestic scuffle; but if a person has had a bad day, this factor may contribute (combine with other factors) to cause a fight at home in the evening.

Several more complicated varieties of causal relationships have been discussed in recent years. Our previous example of a contributory causal relationship implied that X (a bad day at the office) → Y (an argument at home). But an argument at home in the evening, in turn, may contribute to having a bad day at the office the next day. So our causal model becomes complicated: Y⇌X. X is still a cause of Y, but Y can now also be a cause of X. The mutual influence of X and Y on each other is an example of a *feedback loop*.

Another recent idea is the *causal chain*: X→Y→Z. Here X causes Y and Y, in turn, causes Z. For example, poor social skills (X) may cause a person to receive little social reinforcement (Y), which then leads to depression (Z). In this case, poor social skills (X) would be regarded as an indirect cause of depression (Z).

Because many different patterns of causal relationships might underlie and explain any phenomenon, the unguided empirical search for causes can be a clumsy or even an impossible strategy.

For this reason, investigators in both the social and physical sciences typically begin with some *theoretical model*. This permits them to structure and conceptualize the phenomenon of interest and its possible causes.

[T]he suggestion or possibility that changes in one variable (X) cause changes in another variable (Y) may be considered an *hypothesis*. Hypotheses may be derived from many sources, including formal theories, informal observation, or even hunches. It is useful to think of the search for causal relationships as *hypothesis testing*.

Hypothesis testing involves formulating an explicit claim about the relationship between two (or more) variables, choosing a design or plan for making relevant observations or gathering relevant data, and then analyzing the data to see if they support or fail to support the hypothesis. The goal of the researcher is always to reach a valid ("true" or "correct") conclusion from the data. The problem, therefore, is to avoid erroneous or unjustified conclusions.

———

NOTES

1. "Hypotheses" in Science and in Law. Epstein and King, The Rules of Inference, 69 University of Chicago Law Review 1, 9 (2002) have observed that scientists and lawyers approach their hypotheses in very different ways:

> While a Ph.D. is taught to subject his or her favored hypothesis to every conceivable test and data source, seeking out all possible evidence *against* his or her theory, an attorney is taught to amass all the evidence *for* his or her hypothesis and distract attention from anything that might be seen as contradictory information. An attorney who treats a client like a hypothesis would be disbarred; a Ph.D. who advocates a hypothesis like a client would be ignored.

2. The Nature of "Control." Control is one of the goals of social science. It refers to the knowledge of how to change something and has no implications as to whether something should be changed. While the term "social control" often evokes repressive images, it is important to separate (at least provisionally) the scientific question of how to control from the moral and policy (and often legal) question of whether to control.

3.   Prediction and Control Without Understanding. Predicting and controlling a phenomenon usually requires understanding it. However, there are numerous historical illustrations where prediction and control have been achieved without understanding. An actuary in the British navy, for example, noticed that sailors on ships that had been well stocked with limes and other citrus fruits tended not to get scurvy. Scurvy was then controlled by placing fresh fruit on all ships, despite the fact that no one, at the time, understood why eating fresh fruits prevented this disease. G. Caplan, Principles of Preventive Psychiatry (1964).

3.   MEASUREMENT

Social science, we have asserted, involves asking questions regarding the prediction, control, and understanding of human behavior. However, other methods of inquiry attempt similar objectives. Philosophy and religion, for example, also seek to increase understanding. One additional characteristic of social science more sharply distinguishes it from other approaches to asking questions: the answer to social science questions always involves *measurement* of some sort. The three principal components of this concept of measurement are variables, operational definition, and reliability and validity.

(a) Variables

To specify when a relationship between two things will change, it is necessary to study things that are capable of changing, that is, things that can vary. Implicit in the framing of a social science question is the choice of "variables" whose change will be measured.

———

BASIC RESEARCH METHODS IN SOCIAL SCIENCE (3D ED. 1985)*

Julian L. Simon and Paul Burstein.

A variable is not just "some quantity that varies." A variable is a quantity *in which you are interested* that varies in the course of the research or that has different values for different samples in your study. Everything changes sooner or later. But a variable is a factor whose change or difference you study.

[T]he researchers choose their variables on the basis of their interests and their ideas about what would be especially important or valuable to investigate. For example, it is entirely a decision of the researcher to study

* Julian Simon and Paul Burstein, Research Methods in Social Science, Copyright © 1969, 1978, 1985 by Random House, Inc., reproduced with permission of McGraw–Hill Book Co.

the effects of broken homes on juvenile delinquency rather than the relationship between neurosis and juvenile delinquency. Both choices may be good ones, and the choice is not forced by the nature of reality. Of course, the good researcher does not choose his variables at random or casually; rather, he or she chooses them with extreme care, for such choices are among the crucial ones he must make. Poorly-chosen variables yield useless results.

The Dependent Variable

The dependent variable (actually there may be several dependent variables, but that is unusual) is that quantity or aspect of nature whose *change or different states* the researcher wants to understand or explain or predict. In cause-and-effect investigations, the effect variable is the dependent variable. If you wish to investigate whether there is any relationship between the mother's smoking cigarettes and the weight of the baby, then cigarette smoking is an independent variable.

The Independent Variable

The best definition of an independent variable is a variable *whose effect upon the dependent variable you are trying to understand*. There may be several independent variables. You may simultaneously investigate the effect of the mother's cigarette smoking, the mother's exercise, parents' weights, and other variables upon the weight of the baby.

In some kinds of research one cannot label the variables as dependent and independent. In descriptive studies, you may only wish to show how a population is distributed on some variables; the U.S. Census tells, for example, how many people live in each county in the United States. But in studies dealing with complex processes and many variables, a variable may be independent in one part of the study and dependent in another part. When trying to analyze the determinants of economic success, for instance, one may first use education as an independent variable to predict income level, and then treat education as a dependent variable predicted by such variables as father's occupation, in order to map the multistage process leading to success.

———

NOTE

1. Scales of Measurement. There are several types of variables that can be chosen in framing a social science question. Variables that are qualitative in nature are called nominal measures or measures that are placed on a nominal scale. If numbers are assigned to them, the numbers are purely arbitrary and have no inherent meaning. Variables that can be rank-ordered are called ordinal measures. These do connote "more than" or "less than" but do not say how much more than or how much less than. Variables that do say how much more or less one value is than another value are called interval measures.

For example, consider the variables that could be chosen in asking questions about a hypothetical employment discrimination case filed under Title VII of the Civil Rights Act of 1964. The allegations are that employees who are women are promoted from worker to supervisor and from supervisor to management positions less frequently than employees who are men, and that within each position, women are paid less than men who have the same number of years of experience. In this example, gender is a *nominal* variable. It makes no difference in the analysis whether one scores "female" as 1 and "male" as 2 or vice versa, as long as the scoring is consistent. Position in the company is an *ordinal* variable. Being in a management position is "better than" being in a supervisor position, which in turn is "better than" being in a worker position. But it is not clear that the difference between being a worker and being a supervisor is exactly the same as the difference between being a supervisor and being in management. Salary and years of experience are *interval* measures. The difference between being paid $50,000 per year and being paid $40,000 per year is (monetarily) the same as the difference between being paid $40,000 per year and being paid $30,000 per year. The difference between 8 years experience and 6 years experience is the same as the difference between 6 years experience and 4 years experience.

These distinctions have importance for the mathematical computations that can be performed on the various scales. For example, one cannot take averages of nominal measures. It would make no sense to speak of the "average phone number" of a group of people.

(b) Operational Definition

Social scientists ask questions by choosing variables to measure. But two different social scientists interested in the same variables may define those variables in different ways. To be sure that each person knows exactly what the other person is talking about when he or she reports the results of social science research, it is necessary to define the variables being studied clearly and precisely. This greatly facilitates communication among social scientists. The universally accepted way to define variables in the social sciences is to specify the procedures or operations used to measure them.

THE PRACTICE OF SOCIAL RESEARCH (11TH ED. 2007)*

Earl Babbie.

The specification of concepts in scientific inquiry depends [o]n nominal and operational definitions. A *nominal definition* is one that is simply

* From The Practice of Social Research (with CD–ROM and Info Trac) 11th edition by BABBIE. © 2007. Reprinted with permission of Wadsworth, a division of Thomson Learning: www.thomsonrights.com. Fax 800 730–2215.

assigned to a term without any claim that the definition represents a "real" entity. [A]n *operational definition* [s]pecifies precisely how a concept will be measured—that is, the operations we'll perform. [I]n the midst of disagreement and confusion over what a term "really" means, we can specify a working definition for the purposes of an inquiry. Wishing to examine socioeconomic status (SES) in a study, for example, we may simply specify that we are going to treat SES as a combination of income and educational attainment. In this decision, we rule out other possible aspects of SES: occupational status, money in the bank, property, lineage, lifestyle, and so forth.

[T]hough specifying nominal definitions focuses our observational strategy, it does not allow us to observe. As a next step we must specify exactly what we are going to observe, how we will do it, and what interpretations we are going to place on various possible observations. All these further specifications make up the operational definition of the concept.

In the example of socioeconomic status, we might decide to ask survey respondents two questions, corresponding to the decision to measure SES in terms of income and educational attainment:

1. What was your total family income during the past twelve months?

2. What is the highest level of school you completed?

To organize our data, we'd probably want to specify a system for categorizing the answers people give us. For income, we might use categories such as "under $5,000," "$5,000 to $10,000," and so on. Educational attainment might be similarly grouped in categories: less than high school, high school, college, graduate degree. Finally, we would specify the way a person's responses to these two questions would be combined in creating a measure of SES.

In this way, we would create a working and workable definition of SES. Although others might disagree with our conceptualization and operationalization, the definition would have one essential scientific virtue: It would be absolutely specific and unambiguous. Even if someone disagreed with our definition, that person would have a good idea how to interpret our research results, because what we meant by SES—reflected in our analyses and conclusions—would be precise and clear.

Here is a diagram showing the progression of measurement steps from our vague sense of what a term means to specific measurements in a fully structured scientific study:

Conceptualization

↓

Nominal Definition

↓

Operational Definition

↓

Measurements in the Real World

NOTE

1. Making "Performance" Operational. To pose a question concerning whether performance in law school predicted later performance as an associate in a law firm, both the independent variable (performance as a law student) and the dependent variable (performance as an associate) would have to be operationally defined. This could be done in many ways. "Grade point average," "class rank," or "law review membership" would be among the possible operational definitions of performance as a law student. "Billable hours per year" or "probability of making partner" (perhaps as rated by the partnership committee of a firm) would be among the operational definitions of performance as an associate.

(c) Reliability and Validity

In order to ask questions appropriately in the social sciences, one must choose relevant variables and operationally define them. But not all operational definitions are alike. While there can be legitimate differences of opinion about the operations that should define a given variable, any operationally defined variable must have two characteristics. It must yield consistent (or reliable) measurements, and those measurements must truly (or validly) reflect the phenomenon in which one is interested. Only to the extent that they are reliable and valid will operational definitions produce useful answers to social science questions.

REFERENCE GUIDE ON STATISTICS

David H. Kaye and David A. Freeman.
In Reference Manual on Scientific Evidence (2d Ed. 2000).

1. Is the Measurement Process Reliable?

In science, reliability refers to reproducibility of results. A reliable measuring instrument returns consistent measurements of the same quantity. A scale, for example, is reliable if it reports the same weight for the same object time and again. It may not be accurate—it may always report a weight that is too high or one that is too low—but the perfectly reliable scale always reports the same weight for the same object. Its errors, if any, are systematic; they always point in the same direction.

Reliability can be ascertained by measuring the same quantity several times. For instance, one method of DNA identification requires a laboratory to determine the lengths of fragments of DNA. By making duplicate measurements of DNA fragments, a laboratory can determine the likelihood that two measurements will differ by specified amounts. Such results are needed when deciding whether an observed discrepancy between a crime sample and a suspect sample is sufficient to exclude the suspect.

In many studies, descriptive information is obtained on the subjects. For statistical purposes, the information may have to be reduced to numbers, a process called "coding." The reliability of the coding process should be considered. For instance, in a study of death sentencing in Georgia, legally trained evaluators examined short summaries of cases and ranked them according to the defendant's culpability. Two different aspects of reliability are worth considering. First, the "within-observer" variability of judgments should be small—the same evaluator should rate essentially identical cases the same way. Second, the "between-observer" variability should be small—different evaluators should rate the same cases the same way.

2.   Is the Measurement Process Valid?

Reliability is necessary, but not sufficient, to ensure accuracy. In addition to reliability, "validity" is needed. A valid measuring instrument measures what it is supposed to. Thus, a polygraph measures certain physiological responses to stimuli. It may accomplish this task reliably. Nevertheless, it is not valid as a lie detector unless increases in pulse rate, blood pressure, and the like are well correlated with conscious deception.

[W]hen an independent and reasonably accurate way of measuring the variable of interest is available, it may be used to validate the measuring system in question. Breathalyzer readings may be validated against alcohol levels found in blood samples. Employment test scores may be validated against job performance. A common measure of validity is the correlation coefficient between the criterion (job performance) and the predictor (the test score).

———

NOTE

1.   **Illustrations of Reliability.** Between-observer (or "inter-rater") reliability means that different people measuring the same variable will arrive at the same value. Some variables used in the law have high between-observer reliability. In a study of the extent to which age related to the

ability to perform a given job, the variable of "age" probably would be very reliable. Looking at a birth certificate, we could all agree on the age of a person. The between-observer reliability of other variables may be much poorer. If, in the example in the previous Note, the dependent variable of "performance on the job" is operationally defined by having supervisors rate the person on a 5–point scale from (1) "very poor performance" to (5) "very good performance," the scoring of this variable would probably be much less reliable than the scoring of the person's age. To the extent that different supervisors would give different ratings of job performance, the variable of job performance would be unreliable.

SELECTED BIBLIOGRAPHY

Diamond, Empirical Marine Life in Legal Waters: Clams, Dolphins, and Plankton, 2002 University of Illinois Law Review 803 (2002).

Federal Judicial Center, Experimentation in the Law: Report of the Federal Judicial Center, Advisory Committee on Experimentation in the Law (1981).

Mitchell, Case Studies, Counterfactuals, and Causal Explanations, 152 University of Pennsylvania Law Review 1517 (2004).

Mitchell, Empirical Legal Scholarship as Scientific Dialogue, 83 North Carolina Law Review 167 (2004).

R. Schutt, Investigating the Social World (4th ed. 2003).

B.   METHODS OF GATHERING INFORMATION

When a social scientist has framed a question properly—that is, when the question is empirical and the variables presumed to be causally related have been operationally defined in a reliable and valid way—the next task is to gather relevant information. The way that social scientists gather this information or data is referred to as research design. Before one can appreciate the strengths and limits of various research designs as applied in the law, however, it is necessary to consider the methodological problems that the research designs must avoid. These are called threats to validity.

1.   THREATS TO VALIDITY

The term "validity" is used in two related senses in social science. As we have previously seen, a variable is said to be valid to the extent that it truly or accurately measures what it is supposed to measure. In a more general sense, the inferences drawn from an entire research project are said to be valid to the extent that they give true or accurate answers to the question that was asked.

Validity in this larger sense has two components. The first component considers the research on its own terms and looks to whether the methods and analyses employed were sound enough to justify the inferences drawn by the researcher. This is referred to as internal validity. The second component deals with whether the inferences drawn from the study can be applied to groups beyond those actually studied. This is referred to as external validity.

For example, assume that a study seeking to answer the question of whether videotaped witnesses have the same effect as live witnesses upon jurors at trial used college undergraduates as "jurors." If all the videotaped witnesses used in the study were men and all the live witnesses were women, the issue of internal validity would arise. Any differences found could be a function of gender differences rather than differences in the medium of presenting the witnesses. This internal validity problem could be rectified by making sure that men and women were equally represented as videotaped and as live witnesses. The issue of external validity, however, would remain as to the question of ultimate interest: can one apply findings drawn from a study of college undergraduates to the behavior of "real" jurors?

(a) Internal Validity

Social science research progresses through the process of elimination. The researcher begins with a *hypothesis,* preferably derived from a theory, about how two or more variables relate. For example, one might hypothesize based upon a theory of deterrence that increasing the fine for speeding (the independent variable) will reduce the frequency with which speeding tickets are given (the dependent variable). The researcher then tries to think of any *other* hypotheses—called "plausible rival hypotheses"—that also could account for or explain a decrease in the frequency of speeding tickets being issued (e.g., an increase in the price of fuel that made people drive less often, a reduction in the number of state troopers issuing tickets). Finally, the researcher attempts to design a study that would allow him or her to eliminate as many of these hypotheses as possible. Whatever hypothesis cannot be eliminated or disconfirmed may be the true one.

Some hypotheses are plausible rivals to nearly any hypothesis the researcher may investigate. They have come to be referred to as "threats" to the internal validity of research. The researcher must design his or her research to eliminate them. Success at eliminating these threats is a major consideration in evaluating any proposed application of social science findings to the legal system.

QUASI–EXPERIMENTATION: DESIGN AND ANALYSIS ISSUES FOR FIELD SETTINGS (1979)

Thomas D. Cook and Donald T. Campbell.

History

"History" is a threat when an observed effect might be due to an event which takes place between the pretest and the posttest, when this event is not the treatment of research interest. In much laboratory research the threat is controlled by *insulating* respondents from outside influences (e.g., in a quiet laboratory) or by *choosing dependent variables* that could not plausibly have been affected by outside forces (e.g., the learning of nonsense syllables). Unfortunately, these techniques are rarely available to the field researcher.

Maturation

This is a threat when an observed effect might be due to the respondent's growing older, wiser, stronger, more experienced, and the like between pretest and posttest and when this maturation is not the treatment of research interest.

Testing

This is a threat when an effect might be due to the number of times particular responses are measured. In particular, familiarity with a test can sometimes enhance performance because items and error responses are more likely to be remembered at later testing sessions.

Instrumentation

This is a threat when an effect might be due to a change in the measuring instrument between pretest and posttest and not to the treatment's differential impact at each time interval. Thus, instrumentation is involved when human observers become more experienced between a pretest and posttest or when a test shifts in metric at different points. The latter can happen, for instance, if intervals are narrower at the ends of a scale than at the midpoint, resulting in so-called ceiling or basement effects. (Basement effects are also called "floor" effects.)

Statistical Regression

This is a threat when an effect might be due to respondents' being classified into experimental groups at, say, the pretest on the basis of pretest scores or correlates of pretest scores. When this happens and measures are unreliable, high pretest scorers will score relatively lower at the posttest and low pretest scorers will score higher. It would be wrong to attribute such differential "change" to a treatment because it might be due to statistical regression.

Statistical regression is not an easy concept to grasp intuitively. It might help you understand it if you think of your own academic test taking. You may sometimes have surprised yourself by doing worse than you expected, perhaps because you didn't sleep well the night before, you read the questions too quickly and misunderstood them, there may have been someone with an infuriating cough in front of you, or because the test just happened to have had a disproportionately high number of items from a part of the curriculum that you had not studied in detail. Any or all of these factors could have depressed your scores, and they can be conceptualized as error factors that do not reflect true ability. Consequently, the next time you took a test on the same or similar subject matter your scores would probably be higher and would more accurately reflect your ability.

This is because, all things being equal, you will be less likely to have been deprived of sleep, less likely to have read the questions too quickly, less likely to have had someone with a cough sit in front of you, and less likely to have received questions from parts of the curriculum that you had studied the least.

Viewed more generally, statistical regression (1) operates to increase obtained pretest-posttest gain scores among low pretest scores, since this group's pretest scores are more likely to have been depressed by error; (2) operates to decrease obtained change scores among persons with high pretest scores since their pretest scores are likely to have been inflated by error; and (3) does not affect obtained change scores among scorers at the center of the pretest distribution since the group is likely to contain as many units whose pretest scores are inflated by error as units whose pretest scores are deflated by it. Regression is always to the population mean of a group.

[S]election

This is a threat when an effect may be due to the difference between the kinds of people in one experimental group as opposed to another. Selection is therefore pervasive in quasi-experimental research, which is defined in terms of different groups receiving different treatments as opposed to probabilistically equivalent groups receiving treatments as in the randomized experiment.

Mortality

This is a threat when an effect may be due to the different kinds of persons who dropped out of a particular treatment group during the course of an experiment. This results in a selection artifact, since the experimental groups are then composed of different kinds of persons at the posttest.

NOTE

1. Legal Illustrations. Legally-relevant examples can be found for each of the threats to internal validity.

A study of the effects of court-ordered busing that found that the proportion of white students in the affected school district decreased in the five-year period after the court order would have to contend with *history* as a threat to the inference that the court order resulted in "white flight." One would want to ascertain what *else* took place during the five-year period (e.g., an increase in property taxes, or a long-term trend toward the suburbanization of whites) that might plausibly account for the results.

If a seven-year prison treatment program that found that offenders committed fewer crimes during the year after they left the program than during the year before they went to prison, *maturation* would be a threat to the validity of the inference that the program was a success. The results could be due solely to the fact that the offenders were seven years older when the program ended than they were when it began.

Consider a study that took a randomly chosen group of people who had taken the LSAT without first having completed a test-preparation course, put these people through a test-preparation course, and then had them take the LSAT again. This study would be subject to the threat of *testing* if it found that the scores increased and attempted to attribute the cause of the increase to the test-preparation course. The scores may have risen simply because it was the second time the people had taken the test.

A study finding that law students who scheduled their moot court arguments for the end of the semester received poorer grades than those who scheduled their arguments for the beginning of the semester would be subject to the threat of *instrumentation* if it concluded that the better students signed up for the earlier time slots. It could be that the judges in the moot court exercises became progressively bored or modified their grading standards as the semester progressed.

In the LSAT example above, assume that the subjects for the study were not randomly chosen but instead were chosen because they did poorly on the LSAT the first time they took it. If they were then put through the test-preparation course and their scores improved, the results could have been due to *statistical regression* (in addition to the threat of testing). That is, since the subjects were chosen precisely because of their extreme (in this case, low) scores, and since extreme scores may be due to chance factors that are unlikely to repeat themselves (e.g., feeling ill on the day of the test), it is possible that the results merely reflect the tendency for extreme scores to become less extreme over time, rather than the effects of the test-preparation course.

A study that assessed the effects of a new pre-trial conference procedure by comparing the settlement rate in 10 courts that volunteered for the new procedure with the settlement rate in 10 courts that did not volunteer would be open to the threat of *selection*. Any differences between the two groups could be due to pre-existing differences between them, e.g., higher motivation on the part of the volunteers, rather than the new procedure.

Assume that in an evaluation of the impact of a job training program on the arrest rate of delinquents, half the delinquents dropped out of the program before it was completed. If one compared the arrest rate of those who remained in the program with the arrest rate of a randomly chosen control group, *mortality* would threaten the validity of any conclusions drawn. It may be that the half that dropped out were better (or worse) than the half that remained and that the results of the study would have been very different had the drop-outs figured in the final comparison.

(b) External Validity

Internal validity refers to the truth or accuracy of the inferences drawn from a study as applied to the circumstances of that particular study. External validity refers to the extent to which the findings of the study can be generalized, e.g., can they be generalized from the circumstances of the particular study to the circumstances in which one is most interested?

The principal dimensions on which one can question the external validity of social science research are generalization across *persons* (i.e., do the findings apply to people other than the particular people who were in the study?), generalization across *settings* (i.e., do the findings apply to settings or places other than the particular setting or place in which the study was done?), and generalization over *time* (i.e., do the findings from a study done at one particular time apply to other times?).

———

QUASI–EXPERIMENTATION: DESIGN AND ANALYSIS ISSUES FOR FIELD SETTINGS (1979)

Thomas D. Cook and Donald T. Campbell.

[Generalization Across Persons]

In which categories of persons can a cause-effect relationship be generalized? Can it be generalized beyond the groups used to establish the initial relationship—to various racial, social, geographical, age, sex, or personality groups? Even when respondents belong to a target class of interest, systematic recruitment factors lead to findings that are only applicable to volunteers, exhibitionists, hypochondriacs, scientific do-gooders, those who have nothing else to do, and so forth. One feasible way of reducing this bias is to make cooperation in the experiment as convenient as possible. For example, volunteers in a television-radio audience experiment who have to come downtown to participate are much more likely to be atypical than are volunteers in an experiment carried door-to-door. An experiment involving executives is more likely to be ungeneralizable if it takes a day's time than if it takes only ten minutes, for only the latter experiment is likely to include those people who have little free time.

[Generalization Across Settings]

Can a causal relationship obtained in a factory be obtained in a bureaucracy, in a military camp, or on a university campus? The solution here is to vary settings and to analyze for a causal relationship within each. This threat is of particular relevance to organizational psychology since its settings are on such disparate levels as the organization, the small group, and the individual. When can we generalize from any one of these units to the others? The threat is also relevant because of the volunteer bias as to which organizations cooperate. The refusal rate in getting the cooperation of industrial organizations, school systems, and the like must be nearer 75% than 25%, especially if we include those that were never contacted because it was considered certain they would refuse. The volunteering organizations will often be the most progressive, proud, and institutionally exhibitionist. For example, [one researcher] although working with Office of Naval Research funds, could not get access to destroyer crews and had to settle for high-morale submarine crews. Can we extrapolate from such situations to those where morale, exhibitionism, pride, or self-improvement needs are lower?

[Generalization Over Time]

To which periods in the past and future can a particular causal relationship be generalized? Sometimes an experiment takes place on a very special day (e.g., when a president dies), and the researcher is left wondering whether he would have obtained the same cause-effect relationship under more mundane circumstances. Even when circumstances are relatively more mundane, we still cannot logically extrapolate findings from the present to the future. Yet, while logic can never be satisfied, "common-sense" solutions for short-term historical effects lie either in replicating the experiment at different times or in conducting a literature review to see if prior evidence exists which does not refute the causal relationship.

––––––

NOTES

1. Different People. Research involving trial simulations using undergraduates as subjects is often criticized on the ground that the findings may not be generalizable to "real" jurors. Research conducted in the field is also subject to criticism on the ground of external validity when the subjects of the study comprise only a selected subset of the group to which one wishes to generalize. Research concluding that a given treatment is effective in reducing recidivism among male (or young, or white) prisoners may not be generalizable to female (or older, or African–American) prisoners. Note that the results *may* be generalizable, but that it would take additional research to demonstrate this.

2. Different Places. A study finding that the political leanings of state trial judges affected their rulings would raise external validity issues if it attempted to generalize its findings to federal trial judges, or state appellate judges. Attempts to apply the results of prison rehabilitation programs in Scandinavian countries to U.S. prisons frequently meet with external validity objections: what works for them may not work for us (and vice versa).

3. Different Times. At some point, many social research findings—no matter how valid at the time they were obtained—can be criticized as being outdated or "stale." They no longer reflect the current situation. A study finding massive discrimination against women in law schools in the 1950's, for example, may not be generalizable as evidence in a Title VII suit against a law school in the 2000's.

4. Trade–Offs Between Internal and External Validity. Often a research strategy that yields results high in internal validity does so at the cost of leaving external validity questions unanswered, and vice versa. A study randomly assigning collegiate "jurors" to deliberate in groups of either six or 12 would have high internal validity as a test of the effects of jury size, but would be open to the external validity issue of generalization across persons (college students versus real jurors). A study of "naturally" occurring instances in which real juries have consisted of six as compared with 12 jurors would have high external validity, but would leave many internal validity questions (e.g., how were the cases tried before each group selected?). The choice of which type of validity to maximize and which to sacrifice is a hotly debated issue in the social sciences. Usually, researchers reach some sort of pragmatic compromise. They trade-off a bit of internal validity to achieve a higher level of external validity, and vice versa.

2. RESEARCH DESIGN

In answering a legal question, a social scientist gathers information in such a way as to avoid or at least to minimize threats to the internal and external validity of the inferences that he or she wishes to draw. According to J. Simon, Basic Research Methods in Social Science 4 (1978), "There is never a single, standard, correct method of carrying out a piece of research. [A] research method for a given problem is not like the solution to a problem in algebra. It is more like a recipe for beef stroganoff; there is no one best recipe."

Among the most frequently used social science recipes in the law are case studies, correlational studies, true experiments, and quasi-experiments.

(a) Case Studies

The case study, a detailed description of a single instance of the phenomenon of interest, is the most familiar method of studying human behavior. Biography and investigative journalism rely almost exclusively on the analysis of the single case. The social sciences also include case studies among their methods of investigation.

———

BASIC RESEARCH METHODS IN SOCIAL SCIENCE (3D ED. 1985)*

Julian L. Simon and Paul Burstein.

In the beginning, there is description. When one does not know anything at all about a problem, one must understand it in a *general* way before beginning to make specific inquiries about specific aspects of the subject. For example, the early explorer in a new land writes a general description of the appearance of the country, its geography, climate, people, flora, fauna, and much else. [T]he early explorer chooses to describe what he or she thinks is important and interesting, without any rigid rules of scientific evidence. This first description is important because it serves to focus subsequent studies. Geologists later come to study the peculiar stone formations mentioned in the explorer's report. And anthropologists rush to study with great objectivity the extraordinary patterns of mating with foreigners only hinted at therein.

Detailed, descriptive case studies are usually the jumping-off point for the study of new areas in the social sciences. Freud's case history "Observation 1—Miss Anna O." and similar histories of other patients laid the foundation for modern clinical and personality psychologies. Since Freud's original descriptive explorations, there have appeared many other types of studies of the original theories, including observational and questionnaire surveys and experiments. As Freud put it, "the true beginning of scientific activity consists . . . in describing phenomena and [only] then in proceeding to group, classify and correlate them . . ." [quoted in A. Kaplan, The Conduct of Inquiry 78 (1964).]

Much anthropological research is descriptive, deliberately setting out to create a rounded picture of an entire culture or some broad aspect of it. In economics the industry case study continues to be done long after economics has left its infancy.

[S]ome scientists regard descriptive research as only an early stage of research. There is something to this point of view. Descriptive research does not create laws and conclusions that apply beyond the subject matter described. Rather, it provides *clues* for subsequent research to pin down and generalize.

———

NOTE

1. Selection Bias. Case studies perform valuable functions in social science. They provide concrete illustrations that give form to more abstract theories. Most importantly, case studies are a source of hypotheses for systematic testing by more rigorous research methods. When used to test hypotheses, however, case studies have severe limitations because they are subject to so many threats to internal validity. The most salient of these threats is *selection*. When one case is selected for description out of a large number of possible cases, one never knows how typical or representative the chosen case is of the larger group. There is the possibility that, if another case had been chosen, the results would have been entirely different. This is a severe threat to the validity of any inferences drawn from the investigation, and it places the case study among the most problematic designs for social science research.

(b) Correlational Studies

Much and perhaps most social science research in law examines the relationship between two variables by seeing how they relate to one another in the natural environment. When the values of one variable increase, do the values of the other variable increase, decrease, or remain unchanged? These are correlational questions.

For example, survey research in which persons are asked their opinions about a political issue is sometimes purely descriptive in nature, e.g., concluding that "X% of registered voters support the death penalty." However, when two or more variables in the survey are related to one another—as would be the case in a finding that "support for the death penalty increased with the age of the respondents"—the study would be correlational.

Archival studies that derive data from official records are most often correlational in design, as would be true of a study finding that the crime rate increased as the unemployment rate increased.

SCIENCE AND BEHAVIOR: AN INTRODUCTION TO METHODS OF PSYCHOLOGICAL RESEARCH (4TH ED. 1995)*

Robert M. Liebert and Lynn Langenbach Liebert.

The goal of science is almost always to go beyond description and into the realm of explanation. The scientist wants to know not only *that* a given percentage of the population is aggressive or conservative or obese; he or she also wants to know *why* these relationships occur. Answers to "Why?" questions involve bridging the gap between associations and correlations on the one hand, and inferences about cause and effect on the other. Such inferences must be made very carefully. There are many serious pitfalls for researchers who too readily infer the existence of a causal relationship.

[W]hen a psychologist observes a naturally occurring correlation between two variables, X and Y, it is often tempting to assume that the relationship is causal in nature, that is, X→ Y. This assumption is unsound. Often the observed relationship can be explained in other ways.

Plausible Rival Hypotheses

Causal inferences require research designs that can control for *plausible rival hypotheses*. [W]hen X and Y are associated, there are two major rival hypotheses to the inference that X→ Y:

(1) that instead Y→ X

(2) that some third variable (arbitrarily called "Z") is the cause of both X and Y.

* Liebert, Robert M.; Liebert, Lynn L., Science and Behavior: An Introduction to Methods of Psychological Research, 4th Edition, © 1995. Reprinted by permission of Pearson Education, Inc., Upper Saddle River, NJ.

These rival hypotheses are referred to as the *directionality problem* and the *third variable problem*, respectively.

The Directionality Problem

A simple correlation between two variables tells us only that they are related, or tend to vary together. It does *not* tell us whether one is caused by the other. For example, there is a positive correlation between grades and attendance in class. One possible interpretation of this relationship is that greater attendance in class increases the amount learned and thus causes higher grades. A second and equally plausible hypothesis is that good grades lead students who obtain them to enjoy class and therefore to attend more often. Hence the oft-cited dictum: "Correlation does not imply causation."

But the directionality of the relationship is not always impossible to determine. Some relationships can be conceptualized only in one direction. For example, suppose a new car dealer finds a relationship between the income of car shoppers and the likelihood that they will actually buy a new car. Suppose, too, that the relationship is positive; the wealthier a potential customer is, the more likely he or she is to actually make a purchase. How can the dealer explain the relationship?

It is extremely unlikely that buying a new car will increase a person's income, but a greater income might enable a person to buy a new car. Here, the assumed causal relationship might lead the dealer to predict the circumstances (for example, a booming vs. a troubled economy) in which sales volume can be expected to increase or decrease.

Although simple "passive" correlations do not usually allow statements about causation, they may contribute to the *dis*confirmation of causal hypotheses. *Causation usually implies correlation.*

Consider the claim that cigarette smoking causes lung cancer. This claim implies that lung cancer and cigarette smoking will be positively related. If a correlation between smoking and lung cancer were *not* obtained, our confidence in the hypothesis should be reduced. But the presence of a correlation between smoking and lung cancer still does not permit a causal inference, because the nature of the relationship has not been established. Specifically, the relationship could be due to a *third variable*.

The Third Variable Problem

The *third variable problem* refers to the possibility that neither of the two variables involved in a correlation produces the other. Rather, some unspecified third variable or process has produced the observed relationship. For example, there is a high positive correlation between the number of places of worship in a city and the number of crimes committed in that city. The more places of worship a city has, the more crimes are committed in it. Does this mean that religion fosters crime or that crime fosters religion? It means neither. The relationship is due to a third variable—population. The higher the population of a community, the greater are (1) the number of places or worship and (2) the frequency of criminal activities.

As a second example, consider the high positive correlation between the number of drownings on a particular day and the consumption of ice cream on that day. The drownings do not cause depressed people to comfort themselves by consuming large amounts of ice cream, nor does eating ice cream cause drowning. Instead, warm temperatures cause both. The warmer the weather, the more people are likely to be swimming (which is directly related to the frequency of drowning). And more ice cream is sold and eaten on warm days.

The fact that we cannot infer causation from simple passive correlations does not necessarily mean that a cause and effect relationship does not exist. It merely means that it is often impossible to obtain enough information to be sure of the specific nature and direction of this causal relationship.

———

NOTES

1. Directionality. Correlational research that finds that when the punishment for crime becomes less severe, the crime rate increases, is commonly explained in terms of deterrence. The inference is that punishment deters crime, and therefore when the level of punishment is lowered, the crime rate rises. Yet it is possible that the causal relationship actually operates in the opposite direction. As the National Academy of Sciences, Deterrence and Incapacitation: Estimating the Effects of Criminal Sanctions on Crime Rates 25 (A. Blumstein, J. Cohen, and D. Nagin eds. 1978) put it:

> Any negative association between crimes and sanctions could also be interpreted as reflecting an inverse causal effect: jurisdictions impose lower sanctions because they have higher crime rates. Such an inverse causal effect of crimes on sanctions may arise because the criminal justice system resources (e.g., police, prosecutors, prisons) become overburdened in dealing with an increased amount of crime and hence less effective in pursuing offenders. Another explanation of such an inverse effect is that an increased tolerance for criminality may develop in those jurisdictions where crime is more common, as reflected, for example, by a reduction in the average sanctions imposed for a particular type of crime.

2. Third Variables. Continuing with the same example, the National Academy of Sciences noted that "a negative association between crimes and sanctions might be produced by some common third cause that influences crimes and sanctions in opposite directions. It may be, for example, that juveniles have appreciably higher crime rates than adults and are also treated more leniently by the courts." Id. at 23. If this is so and if the proportion of juveniles in the population increases—as was the case in the

1960's when the post-World War II "baby boom" infants reached adolescence—then any inverse relationship between the variables of crime and punishment found in research could be explained by reference to the third variable of age. Frequently, the existence of a third causal variable is referred to as a "confound," e.g., the relationship between crime and punishment in deterrence studies could be said to be confounded by a change in the average age of the population.

3.   Correlation and Causality. The Surgeon General's report, Smoking and Health (1964), concluded that a causal relationship existed between cigarette smoking and lung cancer. It did so on the basis of reviewing correlational studies. The report commented upon the factors that have to be taken into consideration in assessing the causal implications of an observed correlation. Id. at 182:

> The causal significance of an association is a matter of judgment which goes beyond any statement of statistical probability. To judge or evaluate the causal significance of the association between cigarette smoking and lung cancer a number of criteria must be utilized, no one of which, by itself, is pathognomonic or a sine qua non for judgment. These criteria include: (a) the consistency of the association; (b) the strength of the association; (c) the specificity of the association; (d) the temporal relationship of the association; and (e) the coherence of the association.

By *consistency*, the report means that diverse methods of studying the correlation lead to the same basic conclusions. In the Surgeon General's report, 29 retrospective studies and 7 prospective ones all led to the same finding. By *strength* of association, the report means the ratio of pathology rates between the groups of interest. In this case, lung cancer was nine to ten times more prevalent in cigarette smokers than in nonsmokers. *Specificity* refers to the precision with which knowledge of one component can be used to predict other components. Of the total amount of lung cancer in males, about 90 percent was found to be associated with cigarette smoking. *Temporal relationship* means that exposure to the presumed agent must precede the disease. The early exposure to tobacco smoke and later manifestation of lung cancer fulfill this condition. *Coherence* refers to the fact that the correlation should agree with known facts about the natural history of the disease. For example, the dose-response relationship between cigarette smoking and lung cancer supports causality: the amount of smoking and the duration of smoking positively correlate with the probability of cancer.

4.   Sampling. The correlational survey is by far the most frequent research technique used in social science studies of law, accounting for more than half of all research in the area. See Diamond, Problems of Method in the Empirical Study of Law, in Handbook of Law and Social Science (L. Lipson, ed. 1987). Rarely, however, does a social scientist actually question all the people in whose views or behavior he or she is interested. Instead, the researcher takes a subset or *sample* of the larger population about which he or she wishes to make inferences. (This is true not only of surveys but of all other research designs as well.) The critical aspect of a sample is that it be representative of the population from which it is drawn. A sample that is non-representative is called a biased sample. The most famous illustration of a survey based on a biased sample is the 1936 Literary Digest poll that predicted Alfred M. Landon to defeat Franklin D. Roosevelt by a landslide. The magazine had drawn its sample of prospective voters from telephone directories and automobile registration lists. In the Depression-era election of 1936, however, an unprecedented number of poor people came to the polls, people who did not have telephones and automobiles and whose views were not accurately represented in a sample of those who did.

Modern scientific surveys typically employ probability sampling, meaning that every person in the population has a specifiable likelihood or probability of being included in the sample. There are two major forms of probability sampling. In simple random sampling, each person has an equal probability of being included in the sample. For example, in a lottery a simple random sample of 10 winners may be picked from a drum containing a population of 1000 entries. Each entrant has the same probability (1 in 100) of being included in the sample of winners. In the other form of probability sampling, stratified random sampling, the population is divided into two or more groups (or strata), and the researcher then randomly samples from each stratum. For example, to be sure that his or her sample was representative of the population of interest on the characteristic of age, the researcher could divide the population into five age groups and then randomly sample from each age group.

Probability sampling of either form is to be distinguished from non-probability sampling, in which every person in the population does not have a specifiable likelihood or probability of being included in the sample. "People on the street" surveys, often done by news reporters, in which the first 10 or 100 people encountered become the sample for questioning, are illustrations of non-probability sampling. The difficulty with non-probability sampling is that it is unlikely to produce a sample that is representative of the population about which one wishes to make inferences. The first 10 or 100 people on a given street corner in a certain area of a city may give answers that do not accurately reflect the views of people on other street corners (or at home) in other areas of the city.

(c) True Experiments

For many purposes, the "ideal" research design in social science is the "true" experiment. The true experiment is defined by the random assignment of subjects either to an experimental (or treatment) group or to one or more comparison (or control) groups that do not receive the treatment under investigation. Random assignment means that each subject has an equal probability of being assigned to each group. In other words, in a true experiment, the researcher controls the independent variable and deliberately creates variation within it, rather than measuring variation that occurs naturally (as in correlational designs).

———

METHODS FOR EMPIRICAL EVALUATION OF INNOVATIONS IN THE JUSTICE SYSTEM

E. Allan Lind, John E. Shapard, and Joe S. Cecil.
In Experimentation in the Law: Report of the Federal Judicial Center Advisory Committee on Experimentation in the Law (1981).

[S]uppose that an administrator in the federal prison system wants to test a program of special, intensive training in job skills for inmates who are about to be paroled. Suppose further that the program, *if successful*, is expected to increase the prospects of regular employment among parolees and to result in lower rates of recidivism. And suppose that the program is expensive and the administrator has decided that clear evidence of its effectiveness is necessary before such training will be made a permanent and widespread feature of federal prisons.

Simple Randomized Experiment

Consider the following strategy for evaluating the hypothetical job skills program. Suppose we select 200 inmates from the group of potential participants in the program, twice as many as we intend to place in the program. A lottery randomly assigns half of these individuals to the program; the remaining half are given the normal, or status quo, treatment. Suppose further that we monitor, for a set period of time, both the 100 parolees assigned to the program and the 100 assigned the status quo treatment. Upon completion of this data collection period, we compare the percentage of program participants who hold regular employment and the percentage who have been convicted of a subsequent offense to the corresponding percentages in the group that did not participate in the program.

The random lottery is the crucial element distinguishing this class of designs from all others, and the implications of its use in the study are great. The assignment of any particular person to one group or the other is the result of a purely random process, and not the result of any characteristic of the person. If the groups are sufficiently large, the laws of probability assure us that it is very unlikely there will be any substantial difference between the group exposed to the program and the group not exposed to the program. The "all else being equal" criterion has been achieved, at least at the time the lottery is conducted, and if the only difference in how the groups are subsequently treated is the job skills program, we can confidently attribute to the program any differences we later observe between the groups.

[I]n the simple randomized experiment described above, we would be able, if we found statistically significant differences in employment and recidivism rates favoring the experimental group, to conclude that the program had caused these differences. Testing the strength of the design by adopting a skeptical approach reveals few alternative explanations and shows the randomized experiment to be relatively unambiguous. The results could not be due to preexisting differences between the groups, because the lottery has eliminated such differences. Nor could the results be readily ascribed to such factors as the economic climate in which employment is sought, because both the experimental and control groups are subject to the same situation in that regard.

In the randomized experiment, sound conclusions hinge on various assumptions. We must assume that assignment to the two groups was indeed random. If those in charge of the assignment have deviated from the use of a truly random procedure, the logic of the randomized experiment cannot be applied. Deviations from random assignment might occur, for example, if those assigning inmates to the job skills program thought that they should occasionally determine who was most in need of the program, a practice that would subvert the intended assignment scheme. Even if an apparently arbitrary, but not truly random process, such as assigning every other inmate on a list to one group, is used, the experiment would be suspect because, for example, the assignment scheme might be detected and manipulated. If such deviations did occur, the experimental group and the control group could not be assumed to be equivalent, because systematic differences other than exposure to the program might have been introduced.

All designs, randomized or not, suffer potential weaknesses aside from those that may arise from preexisting systematic differences in the groups compared. If there are differences other than the program in the postrandomization treatment or environment of the experimental and control groups, a randomized experimental design may lead to erroneous conclusions. If, for example, the prison officials charged with administering the experiment felt that the control group inmates were being deprived by not being afforded the job skills training and tried to "make it up to them" in other ways, the desired comparison between the program and the status quo treatment would not be produced. Similarly, if the control group inmates knew of the program and felt that they were being unjustly deprived of it, they might behave in a different fashion, and the comparison would be invalid.

[C]onsiderations such as these show that the randomized experiment is not an infallible technique for evaluation; there are certainly situations in which it can lead to erroneous conclusions. The crucial issue in deciding the methodological attractiveness of a research design, however, turns on whether it is less fallible than available alternatives.

Although we have been discussing random assignment of individual persons to experimental and control groups, it should be noted that other entities can be randomly assigned and many of the logical qualities of the randomized experiment retained. It is possible to randomly assign cases, courts, or institutions, if enough are available to afford some reasonable expectation that the lottery will eliminate preexisting differences. For example, if twenty federal prisons were available for a test of the job skills program, ten could be randomly assigned to an experimental group, with all eligible inmates receiving the program, and ten could be assigned to a control group, without the program. Although, strictly speaking, the statistical analyses would have to be conducted using prisons as the "subjects" of the analysis, few methodologists would quarrel with application of the findings to inferences about the effects of the program for individual parolees. The use of random assignment of entities larger than the individual person or case is preferable when the potential effects of the program involve characteristics of the larger entity. If an evaluation seeks to determine whether a new program leads to increased civil filings in district court, for example, a design that included random assignments of courts to the experimental and control groups would be preferable to a design that randomly assigned cases.

———

NOTES

1. Use of the Term "Experimental." It is important to contrast the precise social science use of the term "experimental" with its more colloquial use as a synonym for "innovative" or "new." For example, in Experimentation in the Law: Report of the Federal Judicial Center Advisory Committee on Experimentation in the Law 2, n. 2 (1981), a committee appointed by Chief Justice Warren E. Burger stated that "the term 'experiment' is used throughout this report in its general, popular meaning to refer to a test of a new concept or program. This report does not generally use the term 'experiment' in its narrower technical sense, which is synonymous with 'randomized experimental design.' " See Farrington, Randomized Experiments on Crime and Justice, in Crime and Justice: An Annual Review of Research 266 (M. Tonry and N. Morris eds. 1983).

2. Randomization and the Law. The essence of true experimentation is that some people are treated differently than other people and that randomization determines who gets which treatment. This has sometimes been thought to conflict directly with the Fourteenth Amendment's guarantee of equal protection. However, virtually all scholarly analysis and case law has concluded that "if the proposed research is not otherwise constitutionally impermissible, random assignment of research subjects, with limited exceptions, should not be considered to violate equal protection." Winick, A Preliminary Analysis of Legal Limitations on Rehabilitative Alternatives in Corrections and Correctional Research, in New Directions in the Rehabilitation of Criminal Offenders 359 (S. Martin, L. Sechrest, and R. Redner eds. 1981). See, e.g., Department of Motor Vehicles v. Superior Court, 58 Cal.App.3d 936, 130 Cal.Rptr. 311 (1976). Proponents of true experiments in the law are fond of citing Justice Brandeis' dissent in New State Ice Co. v. Liebmann, 285 U.S. 262, 52 S.Ct. 371, 76 L.Ed. 747 (1932). He stated, 285 U.S. at 310, 311, 52 S.Ct. at 386, 387:

> [A]dvances in the exact sciences and the achievements in invention [i]n large measure [h]ave been due to experimentation. [I]t is one of the happy incidents of the federal system that a single courageous state may, if its citizens choose, serve as a laboratory; and try novel social and economic experiments without risk to the rest of the country. This Court has the power to prevent an experiment. [B]ut in the exercise of

this high power we must be ever on our guard, lest we erect our prejudices into legal principles. If we would guide by the light of reason, we must let our minds be bold.

3. **Alternatives to Randomization.** In reviewing the field of research design, Shadish and Cook, The Renaissance of Field Experimentation in Evaluating Interventions, 60 Annual Review of Psychology 607, 623 (2008), recently concluded:

> Randomized experiments remain the method of choice, all things being equal and when they are feasible and ethical, for their strong statistical warrant has no peer among the nonrandomized alternatives. The conditions under which those nonrandomized alternatives seem to produce accurate results are only tentatively understood and place demands on the researcher for good measurement and careful attention to design that cannot be routinely assumed to occur in practice.

(d) Quasi–Experiments

Case studies may be the source of interesting hypotheses, but they cannot test whether those hypotheses are true. Correlational studies may establish an association between two variables, but they have difficulty demonstrating the direction of causality and eliminating the possibility that a third variable is responsible for the results. True experiments may establish causal relationships, but they are sometimes unethical or impractical to do. There is one final category of research design that resembles the true experiment in that it compares two or more conditions, but it differs from the true experiment in that it does not randomly assign subjects to the various conditions. This type of design is called a quasi-experiment.

METHODS FOR EMPIRICAL EVALUATION OF INNOVATIONS IN THE JUSTICE SYSTEM

E. Allan Lind, John E. Shapard, and Joe S. Cecil.
In Experimentation in the Law: Report of the Federal Judicial Center Advisory Committee on Experimentation in the Law (1981).

Quasi–Experimental Designs

Quasi-experimental designs are those that focus on some "comparison" group of subjects not exposed to the innovative treatment, or that employ observations before exposure to the treatment, in order to infer what would have happened in the absence of the innovation. The comparison group, however, is always in some way systematically different from the "treatment" group, in the sense that there is *some* identifiable difference between the groups other than the fact that one group receives the treatment and the other does not. These designs may yield ambiguous results whenever this systematic difference suggests a credible alternative explanation for apparent effects of the innovation.

Before–After Design on Individuals

An apparently straightforward, but actually quite problematic, design for evaluating programs that offer potential for some change involves constituting a single group of program participants, measuring the characteristics of interest, exposing the participants to the program, and then measuring the characteristics again.

In our hypothetical example involving the job skills program [in the previous reading], one might use this design by recording for each participant whether he or she was employed during some period prior to the current conviction, and by observing the participant for an equal period of time after completion of the program and granting of parole. From this example, though, some of the problems associated with the design become apparent, if one adopts the skeptical approach required to test the strength of a research design. Suppose that it is found that parolees are indeed more likely to be employed following the job skills program than they were prior to their last conviction, and consider the alternative explanations that might be advanced. It is, of course, possible that the program has achieved its goal. But it is also possible that the greater likelihood of employment is simply due to the fact that the participants are older than they were at the time they were convicted and that older workers are more likely to find employment. It also might be the case that simply having been incarcerated has motivated the participants to seek employment. Or it might be that the increase is due simply to the normal monitoring of parolees, which might encourage them to find work. Another rival hypothesis, which would be especially credible if economic conditions had improved during the time of imprisonment, is that the job market has so improved that, with or without skills training, any parolee is now more likely to find employment. The capacity of the design to test the effects of the program is weakened to the extent that such alternative explanations are credible.

In general, before-after designs on individuals are subject to ambiguity whenever it is conceivable that changes would have occurred naturally in the characteristics of the individual, as the result of aging for example, or whenever it is conceivable that the results of the study might be due to changes in external circumstances between the time of the "before" observations and the time of the "after" observations.

[S]imple Comparison Group Design

A second quasi-experimental design involves a comparison between two groups, as does the simple randomized experimental design, but uses groups that are known to differ in some systematic fashion other than exposure to the program. For example, the job skills program might be made available to eligible inmates at one prison and the results compared to those seen with a similar group of inmates at a prison without the program.

Suppose that a group of soon-to-be-paroled inmates at Prison A is given the job skills training and a similar group at Prison B is not. Suppose further that it is subsequently found that the Prison A treatment group is more likely to be regularly employed and less likely to recidivate than the Prison B comparison group. These results would provide some basis for inferring that the program caused increased employment and decreased recidivism, but only if any potent alternative hypotheses could be dismissed. There is no assurance, for example, that inmates at Prison A do not normally find employment and avoid recidivism at a better rate than do those at Prison B. This might occur if the systematic difference that we know exists between the treatment and comparison groups is such that it affects employment and recidivism. It might be that differences in the nature of the inmate population, in the other programs provided at the two prisons, or in employment opportunities in the geographic areas to which the prisoners are released could explain the results of the study without reference to the job skills program.

This example points to the most troublesome aspect of comparison group designs: the possibility that differences existing before the program is instituted have caused or contributed to any differences that are subsequently observed. An evaluator may attempt to select a comparison group in such a way as to eliminate the most obvious differences between the comparison and treatment groups, but there is always the possibility that remaining differences might provide a viable alternative explanation of the results. For example, if a variety of prisons are available for study, two might be selected that are similar in terms of inmate populations and programs other than the one under study, but there remains the possibility that some factor—for example, attitudes toward hiring parolees in the area to which most are released—could account for the results of the study.

[S]imple Time–Series Design

A popular quasi-experimental design that might be used to evaluate the job skills program is the "simple time-series design." One might observe for several years the recidivism rate of paroled inmates who would be eligible for the program if it existed, then institute the program and observe the recidivism rates of the participants during several years of operation of the program. If recidivism rates were constant or increased or decreased at a steady rate during the several years prior to the start of the program and if a sudden drop were seen when the program began and then the steady pattern continued at a lower level, the inference that the program reduced recidivism might be reasonable. For example, if 60 percent, 55 percent, and 50 percent, respectively, of the inmates released during the three years prior to the program recidivated within eighteen months of release and if 35 percent, 30 percent, and 25 percent, respectively, of the inmates released after the program commenced recidivated within eighteen months of release, there would be strong evidence that the program was effective.

[T]he greatest benefit of the simple time-series design is that, unlike designs employing single "before" and "after" observations, it permits the identification of some time-based changes that might affect the characteristics under study and allows the consequences of these changes to be removed from the effects that might be attributed to the program. If only a single "before" and a single "after" observation had been made, it would be uncertain whether the drop from a 50 percent to a 35 percent recidivism rate were due to the program or to some general time-based change. The multiple "before" observations used in the time-series design, in contrast, make it clear that the change in recidivism rate is considerably more than would be expected from the general trend toward lower rates of recidivism. The multiple "after" observations make it clear that the drop in recidivism is not a temporary phenomenon.

———

NOTES

1.   Before–After Designs. Studies attempting to assess the effects of the law school experience upon student values are frequently before-after designs. For example, an instrument designed to measure attitudes toward public interest work is given at the beginning of the first year of law school and at the end of the third year of law school. Typically, a "conservative" effect of legal education is reported: students leaving law school are less favorably disposed toward public interest work, and more favorably disposed toward servicing corporate clients, than they were when they entered it. See, e.g., Kubey, Three Years of Adjustment: Where Your Ideals Go, 6 Juris Doctor 34 (1976).

2.   Simple Comparison Group Designs. A frequent strategy for evaluating the effects of prison treatment programs is to report the re-arrest rate of program participants and to compare this figure with published statistics on the re-arrest rate of persons released from prisons across the country. Such a comparison may be misleading, however, if the prisoners who volunteered for the treatment are more motivated than the average prisoner.

3.   Time Series Designs. The superiority of a time series design over a simple before-and-after design is dramatically illustrated by using both to evaluate the effects of the Community Mental Health Centers Act of 1963, which had as one of its goals the reduction of state mental hospitalization. In 1963, the year the act was passed, the resident population of state and county mental hospitals in the United States was approximately 500,000. In 2009, it was approximately 50,000. These before-after figures have been used to persuade Congress of the effectiveness of the act. When a time-series with more than one measurement before the passage of the act is used, however, the results seem quite different. A time-series shows the population of state mental hospitals to have increased each year from early in the century until 1955, and decreased each year thereafter, with no noticeable acceleration in the rate of decrease in 1963, the year the act was passed. In this light, the most plausible hypothesis is that the factor causing the population decrease began in the mid–1950's, and not in the mid–1960's. Many now view the introduction of psychotropic medication as the principal method of treating mental patients, which indeed began in

1955, as the most plausible hypothesis to account for the "deinstitutionalization" of mental hospitals. While the time-series makes this hypothesis more plausible than the community mental health center hypothesis, it does not preclude other rival hypotheses. For example, A. Scull, Decarceration–Community Treatment and the Deviant: A Radical View (1977), made a strong case that with the unionization of state hospital employees in the mid–1950's, it became too expensive for states to fund large hospitals, and consequently they began to discharge patients simply as a way to cut costs, regardless of whether the patients received medication.

4. Websites. A Judge's Deskbook on the Basic Philosophies and Methods of Science, by S. Dobbin and S. Gatowski, can be found at http://www.unr.edu/justicestudies/About/JudgesDeskbook.pdf.

SELECTED BIBLIOGRAPHY

Bornstein, The Ecological Validity of Jury Simulations: Is the Jury Still Out?, 21 Law and Human Behavior 75 (1999).

Diamond, Methods for the Empirical Study of Law, in Law and the Social Sciences (L. Lipson and S. Wheeler eds. 1987).

Federal Judicial Center, Experimentation in the Law: Report of the Federal Judicial Center Advisory Committee on Experimentation in the Law (1981).

G. Kranzler and J. Moursund, Statistics for the Terrified (3d ed. 1999).

National Research Council, Strengthening Forensic Science in the United States: A Path Forward (2009).

Samaha. Randomization in Adjudication (2009). Available at: http://works.bepress.com/adam_samaha/1.

Squire, Why the 1936 Literary Digest Poll Failed, 52 Public Opinion Quarterly 125 (1988).

H. Zeisel and D. Kaye, Prove It With Figures: Empirical Methods in Law and Litigation (1997).

C. METHODS OF INTERPRETING INFORMATION

After appropriate questions have been asked and the information required to answer them has been gathered, the task of making sense of that information remains. While case studies are often interpreted without recourse to arithmetic computation, other research designs almost inevitably require the assistance of statistics to transform "raw" data into more palatable form. The two generic uses of statistics in this context are to describe the data collected and to make inferences from the data collected from the sample groups to larger populations of interest.

1. THE DESCRIPTION OF RESULTS

The first use of statistics in social science research is to describe or summarize the data that has been gathered. One may wonder why it is necessary to use statistics for such a seemingly elementary task. Why not simply look at the data? There are, indeed, occasions when "eyeballing" is all that is needed. For example, the "semester grade point average" may not be a very useful statistic to describe college performance, since it may average only 4 or 5 course grades, and it may be just as easy to remember the 4 or 5 grades themselves. But as soon as the data become more complex, some way to summarize them becomes essential. No one asking the question, "How did you do in college?" wants a credit-by-credit answer.

The three most common categories of descriptive or summary statistics are central tendency, variability, and association.

(a) Measures of Central Tendency

The first thing a person usually wishes to know of some set of data is the "typical" value or score on the variable being measured. When all the scores are not the same—which is to say, when the scores are "distributed" over a range of values—one usually wants to get an idea of where the middle or center of the distribution of scores lies. This is what measures of central tendency provide. They are the most popularly known form of statistics.

———

REFERENCE GUIDE ON STATISTICS

David H. Kaye and David A. Freeman.
In Reference Manual on Scientific Evidence (2d Ed. 2000).

Is an Appropriate Measure Used for the Center of the Distribution?

Perhaps the most familiar descriptive statistic is the mean (or the "arithmetic mean"). The mean can be found by adding up all the numbers and dividing by how many there are. By comparison, the median is defined so that half the numbers are bigger than the median, and half are smaller. Yet a third statistic is the mode, which is the most common number in the data set. These statistics are different, although they are not always clearly distinguished. The mean takes account of all the data—it involves the total of all the numbers; however, particularly with small data sets, a few unusually large or small observations may have too much influence on the mean. The median is resistant to such outliers.

To illustrate the distinction between the mean and the median, consider a report that the "average" award in malpractice cases skyrocketed from $220,000 in 1975 to more than $1 million in 1985. The median award almost certainly was far less than $1 million, and the apparently explosive growth may result from a few very large awards. Still, if the issue is whether insurers were experiencing more costs from jury verdicts, the mean is the more appropriate statistic: The total of the awards is related directly to the mean, not to the median.

———

NOTE

1. Choice of a Measure of Central Tendency. A survey of lawyers' views about a courtroom innovation that wanted to describe the lawyers' annual income would probably report the median income. Mean income, in this case, might be misleading, since a few extreme scores, e.g., a few million dollar per year partners in large law firms or a few unemployed lawyers, could greatly affect the mean. The mean is used whenever one wants to take into account all the scores, even the extreme ones. The grade point average, i.e., the mean of one's grade points, is therefore the preferred statistic to summarize educational performance. One wants the extreme scores, the A's and the D's, to figure in.

Unfortunately, the choice of which measure of central tendency to report is not always an innocent one, particularly when the person doing the reporting has a vested interest in the outcome of the report. For example, the mayor of a city with a high mean income (due to the existence of a few wealthy neighborhoods) and a lower median income may report the mean income to developers ("Move your business here, we're rich") and the median income to the federal government ("We need aid, we're poor").

(b) Measures of Variability

The initial question one asks of a set of data usually is, "What is the typical score?" i.e., what is the central tendency of the scores. The second question usually is, "How typical is this typical score?" i.e., how similar or dissimilar are the scores to one another. For example, assume that in a study comparing the effects of two different forms of pre-trial conference on the length of 30 subsequent trials, both types of conference resulted in a mean length of 10 trial days. It would still make a great deal of difference if it turned out that for one group all 30 trials were completed in 10 days while for the other group half the trials were completed in 1 day and half took 19 days. While the mean is the same in both cases, the variability among the scores is much greater in the latter group than in the former.

READING STATISTICS AND RESEARCH (5TH ED. 2008)*

Schuyler W. Huck.

Most groups of scores possess some degree of variability. That is, at least some of the scores differ (vary) from one another. A *measure of variability* simply indicates the degree of this *dispersion* among the scores. If the scores are very similar, there is little dispersion and little variability. If the scores are very dissimilar, there is a high degree of dispersion

* From Huck, Schuyler W., Reading Statistics and Research, 5e. Published by Allyn and Bacon, Boston, MA. Copyright © 2008 by Pearson Education. Reprinted/adapted by permission of the publisher.

(variability). In short, a measure of variability does nothing more than indicate how spread out the scores are.

The term *variability* can also be used to pinpoint where a group of scores might fall on an imaginary homogeneous-heterogeneous continuum. If the scores are similar, they are *homogeneous* (and have low variability). If the scores are dissimilar, they are *heterogeneous* (and have high variability).

Even though a measure of central tendency provides a numerical index of the average score in a group, we need to know the variability of the scores to better understand the entire group of scores. For example, consider the following two groups of IQ scores:

Group I	*Group II*
102	128
99	78
103	93
96	101

In both groups the mean IQ is equal to 100. Although the two groups have the same mean score, their variability is obviously different. While the scores in the first group are very homogeneous (low variability), the scores in the second group are far more heterogeneous (high variability).

The specific measures of variability that we will now consider are similar in that the numerical index will be zero if all of the scores in the data set are identical, a small positive number if the scores vary to a small degree, or a large positive number if there is a great deal of dispersion among the scores. (No measure of variability, no matter how computed, can ever turn out equal to a negative value.)

The *range* is the simplest measure of variability. It is the difference between the lowest and highest scores. For example, in Group I of the example just considered, the range is equal to 103–96, or 7. The range is usually reported by citing the extreme scores, but sometimes it is reported as the difference between the high and low scores.

[T]wo additional indices of dispersion, the *standard deviation* and the *variance*, are usually better indices of dispersion than [the range]. This is due to the fact that the standard deviation and variance are each based on all of the scores in a group (and not just the high and low scores). [T]he standard deviation is determined by (1) figuring how much each score deviates from the mean and (2) putting these deviation scores into a computational formula. The variance is found by squaring the value of the standard deviation.

In reporting their standard deviations, authors may employ the abbreviation *SD*, utilize the symbols *s* or **s**, or simply write out the word *sigma*. Occasionally, authors will report the standard deviation using a "plus-and-minus" format—for example, 14.83 ± 2.51, where the first number (14.83) stands for the mean and the second number (2.51) stands for the standard deviation. The variance, being the square of the standard deviation, is symbolized as s^2 or σ^2.

———

NOTES

1. The Range. Since the range focuses solely on the two most extreme scores, it can give a deceptive picture of the amount of variability in the data. For example, studies of judicial sentencing disparity often give the same information concerning conviction offense and the same probation report to judges and ask them what sentence they would impose on the offender. Assume that in such a study of 100 judges, one judge responded "one year," one judge responded "twenty years" and ninety-eight judges responded "six years." It would be true but misleading to describe the data by reporting, "In response to the same case, the judges' sentences varied from 1 to 20 years." It would be true because indeed one judge gave a 1 year sentence and one gave a 20 year sentence. But it would be misleading because it does not reflect the fact that there was no variation at all among 98 of the judges.

2. The Variance. At first glance, the best way to measure the degree of variability in any set of data might seem to be to take the amount each score differs from the mean score, add these differences together, and take their average. The problem with doing this is that the result is always zero. (To illustrate, take the scores, 3, 4, 5, 6, and 7. The mean is 5. Subtracting the mean from each score yields: $3 - 5 = -2$; $4 - 5 = -1$; $5 - 5 = 0$; $6 - 5 = +1$; $7 - 5 = +2$. Add together -2, -1, 0, $+1$ and $+2$ and you get 0. Zero divided by anything is zero.) The way around this problem is to get rid of the minus signs. This is done by squaring the differences between each score and the mean, adding these squared differences together, and dividing by the number of scores. The resulting number is called the variance of the sample. The formula for the sample variance, therefore, is:

$$\text{Variance} = \frac{\text{Sum of (difference between each score and the mean)}^2}{\text{number of scores}}$$

To compute the variance of the sample of data given above, one would (a) subtract the mean from each score (i.e., -2, -1, 0, $+1$ and $+2$); (b) square each result (i.e., 4, 1, 0, 1 and 4); (c) add them together (i.e., $4 + 1 + 0 + 1 + 4 = 10$); and (d) divide by the number of scores (i.e., $10/5 = 2$). The variance of the sample, therefore, is 2.

3. Standard Deviation. There is one problem with the variance. Having squared the deviations from the mean in order to avoid always coming up with zero, what is left is a measure of variability that is in terms of the original units of measurement squared. For example, if in the example given above the data were being measured in dollars, the variance would be in "squared dollars," which would not make much sense. Since it is often useful to have the measure of variability in the same units as the original measurement, researchers frequently use another statistic, the standard deviation, as the preferred measure of variability. It is simply the square root of the variance. So in the example given in which the variance was 2, the standard deviation would be the square root of 2, or 1.4.

4.   The Normal Distribution. While a detailed discussion of statistical models of variability is clearly beyond our scope here, it is important to note that a great many things have means that vary according to a "normal distribution." The normal distribution is the well-known bell-shaped curve. A few scores are at either end (or "tail") and most are in the middle. The height and weight of adults in the population, for example, will fall along a normal curve: relatively few people are very short or very thin, relatively few people are very tall or very heavy, and most of us are somewhere in between.

For this reason, as well as for more technical statistical reasons, the normal curve plays an important role in statistical theory. The important point here is that in a normal distribution, if one knows the mean and the standard deviation, one also knows how many scores fall within given distances from the mean. This is presented graphically below, with standard deviation being abbreviated "SD."

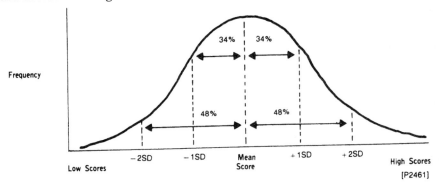

Approximately 34 percent of the scores in a normal distribution fall within 1 standard deviation below the mean and approximately 34 percent within 1 standard deviation above the mean. Approximately 68 percent of the scores, therefore, fall within 1 standard deviation above or below the mean. Approximately 48 percent of the scores fall within 2 standard deviations below the mean and approximately 48 percent within 2 standard deviations above it. Approximately 96 percent of the scores, therefore, are within 2 standard deviations above or below the mean.

If, for example, a study of the speed at which people drive on the highway after a police crackdown reported that the mean speed was 55 miles per hour with a standard deviation of 3, one would know that 68 percent of the cars drove between 52 and 58 (that is 55 ± 3) miles per hour, and 96 percent drove between 49 and 61 miles per hour (that is 55 ± 6).

(c) Measures of Association

In describing a set of data, a measure of central tendency gives us the most typical or representative score on the variable being measured, and a measure of variability tells us just how typical or representative of the other scores that number is. Often in social research, however, more than one variable will be measured. When that is so, the researcher may want to know, in addition to the central tendency and variability of each variable, whether the two variables "go together." When scores on one variable go up, for example, do scores on the other variable tend to go up as well? Or, do they tend to go down or to remain unchanged? Measuring the extent to which two variables are associated is what a correlation does.

STATISTICAL EVIDENCE IN LITIGATION: METHODOLOGY, PROCEDURE, AND PRACTICE (1986)*

David W. Barnes and John M. Conley.

The *correlation coefficient* is a measure of the consistency with which the values of two variables change in the same direction. If two variables are *correlated*, knowing the value of one helps us to predict the value of the other: knowing the circumference of someone's head, for instance, helps one to infer hat size, and knowing someone's age helps one to predict remaining life expectancy.

When an increase in the value of one variable, e.g., head circumference, leads us to expect an increase in the value of the other, e.g., hat size, we say that there is a *positive correlation* between the two or that the variables are *directly related*. When an increase in the value of one variable, e.g., age, leads us to expect a decrease in the value of the other, e.g., remaining life expectancy, there is a *negative correlation* between the two variables, an *inverse relationship*.

Head circumference and hat size have an almost perfect positive correlation, because when head circumference in inches is divided by 3.14, that is the corresponding hat size as it is customarily measured. Age and remaining life expectancy are negatively correlated but not perfectly so, because there are other factors that determine life expectancy, such as health, family history, evil habits, and occupation.

[T]he correlation coefficient always takes a value between -1 (for perfect negative correlations) and $+1$ (for perfect [positive] correlations). If the value of one variable, such as [employment] exam score, is totally unrelated to the measurement of the other, such as [job] performance score, the coefficient equals zero.

———

NOTE

1. Illustrative Correlations. Two variables have a correlation of -1.0 when every time one of them increases in value, the other decreases by a proportional amount and vice versa. The correlation between the height of the ends of a child's see-saw would be -1.0. Two variables have a correlation of $+1.0$ when every time one of them increases in value, the other also increases by a proportional amount. The correlation between the distance traveled by one's left foot and the distance traveled by one's right foot when walking in a straight line would be $+1.0$. As Professors Kaye and Freeman state in the Reference Guide on Statistics in the Federal Judicial Center's Reference Manual on Scientific Evidence (2d ed. 2000, at 136):

> Moderate associations are the general rule in the social sciences; correlations larger than, say, 0.7 are quite unusual in many fields. For example, the correlation between college grades and first-year law school grades is under 0.3 at most law schools, while the correlation between LSAT scores and first-year law school grades is generally about 0.4. The correlation between heights of fraternal twins is about 0.5, while the correlation between heights of identical twins is about 0.95.

2. THE INFERENCES DRAWN FROM RESULTS

Describing or summarizing the "raw" data in hand is the first step in interpreting the information obtained through social science research. The second step is making inferences from the data about the groups in which one is interested.

As discussed above, rarely in social science does a researcher ever study all of the people or events about which he or she would like to draw conclusions. This group of all the people or events of interest is called the population. Instead of studying the population (which would often take unlimited time and resources), social scientists study a sample drawn from the population. For example, when one is interested in the recidivism rate of all of the thousands of parolees from a state prison system (the population), one might study the recidivism rate of a random group of 500 parolees (the sample).

The problem then is that one has studied (i.e., measured) only a sample while one is interested in making statements about the population. Inferential statistics allow a researcher to make inferences about an entire population based on a limited sample of that population.

———

RESEARCH METHODS IN SOCIAL RELATIONS (3D ED. 1976)

Claire Selltiz, Lawrence S. Wrightsman, and Stuart W. Cook.

Let us suppose that we have asked a thousand people, who have been selected as a sample of the adult population of England, a series of questions to gather information about their movie-going habits. Assume that we have developed a number of sets of categories and have coded the responses of each individual. The coding may be considered a method of summarizing the responses of each individual; if we were concerned only about each individual, this might be as far as we would go in the analysis. However, the purposes of our research are broader than this. We wish to know more than that a given government clerk in London goes to the movies four times a month and that an innkeeper in Yarmouth goes only once a month. Our inquiry is directed toward providing information about the adult population of England.

[S]uppose that we have studied samples of people living either in rural or urban England and that our results show differences between the two samples. One may ask whether the differences that have been obtained reflect true differences between rural and urban English citizens, or whether the two samples might have differed to this extent by chance even though the total rural and urban populations are alike in their movie-going habits. Through statistical procedures, one is able to answer such a question in terms of a statement of probability.

When we are contrasting samples or studying the differences between experimental and control groups, we usually wish to test some hypothesis about the nature of the true difference between the larger populations represented by the samples. Most commonly, in the social sciences, we are still concerned with relatively crude hypotheses (for example, that urban residents go to the movies more often than rural residents); we are usually not in a position to consider more specific hypotheses (for example, that they go to the movies *twice* as often). Suppose our data show that our sample of urban English adults attend an average of three motion pictures a month and that our sample of rural English adults attend an average of only two motion pictures. Clearly, the findings within our samples are in line with the hypothesis: urban residents attend the movies more often than rural residents. But we know that the findings based on our samples are not very likely to be exactly the same as the findings we would obtain if we had interviewed all the adults in England. Now we want to estimate whether, if we had interviewed the total population, we would still have found more frequent movie attendance on the part of urban residents. This, we do, ordinarily, by testing the *null hypothesis*—in this case, the hypothesis that in the English population as a whole, rural and urban residents do *not* differ in frequency of movie going. Various statistical techniques (called statistical *tests of significance*) have been devised, which tell us the likelihood that our two samples might have differed as much as they do by chance even if there were *no* difference between urban and rural English adults as a whole.

[I]f we are comparing two groups, there are obviously two possibilities: either the two populations are alike, or they are different. Suppose that our *samples* from the two populations are different on a particular measure or attribute. Clearly, this would be likely to happen if the two populations from which the samples are drawn do in fact differ on that attribute. However, it does not in itself constitute evidence that they *do* differ, since there is always the possibility that the samples do not correspond exactly to the populations they are intended to represent. We must consider the possibility that the element of chance which is involved in the selection of a sample may have given us samples which differ from each other even if the two populations do not differ. Thus the crucial question is: Is it likely that we would have come up with samples that differ to this extent if the two populations were actually alike? This is the question the test of the null hypothesis answers; it tells us what the chances are that two samples differing to this extent would have been drawn from two populations that are in fact alike. Only if the statistical test indicates that it is improbable that two samples differing to this extent could have been drawn from similar populations can we conclude that the two populations probably differ from each other.

Suppose, however, that our findings show no difference between the two samples; let us say that in our samples, both rural and urban English adults attend the movies, on an average, two and one-half times a month. Can we then conclude that the total populations of rural and urban English adults are alike in frequency of movie going? Not with any certainty. Just as there is the possibility that samples may *differ* when the populations are alike, so there is the possibility that samples may be *alike* when in fact the populations differ. Thus, if our two samples are alike, all we can conclude is that we have no evidence that the populations differ—in other words, the idea that the two populations are alike is tenable.

But to go back to the case where the two samples differ. We can affirm that the two populations they represent probably differ if we can reject the null hypothesis—that is, if we can show that the obtained difference between the two samples would be unlikely to appear if the two populations were in fact the same. It is, however, in the nature of probability that even highly improbable events can sometimes happen. Thus, we can never be absolutely certain of our generalizations to the total population. Whenever we reject the null hypothesis, there is some chance that we are wrong in doing so.

However, since we are always dealing with inferences and probabilities, there is always some chance that if we accept the null hypothesis, we are wrong in doing so. That is, even if our statistical test indicates that the sample differences might easily have arisen by chance even if the two populations are alike, it may nevertheless be true that the populations differ.

In other words, we are always confronted with the risk of making one of two types of error. We can reject the null hypothesis when, in fact, it is true; that is, we may conclude that there is a difference between the two populations when, in fact, they are alike. This is commonly referred to as the *Type I error*. Or, on the other hand, we can accept the null hypothesis as tenable when, in fact, it is false; that is, we may conclude that the two populations are alike when, in fact, they are different. This is referred to as the *Type II error*.

The risk of making the Type I error is determined by the *level of significance* we accept in our statistical testing. Thus, if we decide that we will conclude that the populations truly differ whenever a test of significance shows that the obtained difference between two samples would be expected to occur by chance not more than five times in one hundred if the two populations were in fact alike, we are accepting five chances in one hundred that we will be wrong in rejecting the null hypothesis. We can reduce the risk of a Type I error by making our criterion for rejecting the null hypothesis more extreme; for example, by rejecting the null hypothesis only if the statistical test indicates that the sample difference might have appeared by chance only once in one hundred times, or once in one thousand times, or once in ten thousand times. Unfortunately, however, the chances of making Type I and Type II errors are inversely related. The more we protect ourselves against the risk of making a Type I error (that is, the less likely we are to conclude that two populations differ when in fact they do not), the more likely we are to make a Type II error (that is, to fail to recognize population differences which actually exist). Once we have determined the degree of Type I risk we are willing to run, the only way of reducing the possibility of Type II error is to take larger samples and/or to use statistical tests that make the maximum use of available relevant information.

The inverse relationship of the risks of the two types of errors makes it necessary to strike a reasonable balance. In the social sciences, it is more or less conventional to reject the null hypothesis when the statistical analysis indicates that the observed difference would not occur more than five times out of one hundred by chance alone. If the statistical analysis indicates that the difference between the two samples might have appeared by chance more than five times out of one hundred, the null hypothesis is not rejected. But these conventions are useful only when there is no other reasonable guide. The decision as to just how the balance between the two kinds of error should be struck must be made by the investigator. In some instances, it is obviously more important to be sure of rejecting a hypothesis when it is false than to fail to accept it when it is true. In other cases, the reverse may be true.

————

RESEARCH METHODS IN SOCIAL RELATIONS (7TH ED. 2002)*

Rick H. Hoyle, Monica J. Harris, and Charles M. Judd.

It probably seems odd that when we are interested in one hypothesis (that two variables are associated), we start with its opposite (that they are unassociated). But the logic behind this curious approach is not difficult to follow. There is a direct analogy with criminal trials. A jury must decide whether a defendant is guilty of the crime of which he or she is accused. Before the trial begins and any arguments are heard, the defendant is entitled in the U.S. legal system to a "presumption of innocence," that the defendant did not commit the crime. The prosecutor would like the hypothesis of guilty to be confirmed by the jury, but the prosecutor must provide enough evidence to overrule this presumption of innocence beyond a reasonable doubt. Our legal system recognizes that it is not possible to prove the lack of innocence, or guilt, of a defendant conclusively, without any doubts whatsoever. So the requirement is that the prosecution must disprove innocence beyond a reasonable doubt.

Social scientists are engaged in a task quite analogous to that of the prosecutor. When they collect data from a sample, they wish to conclude that the hypothesis that motivated the research is correct (i.e., that two variables are associated). So they start out with the presumption that their hypothesis is not true—the null hypothesis. They must then demonstrate, based on their sample of data, that this presumption is unlikely to be true in the population. Only then can they have reasonable confidence that their research hypothesis is potentially true in the population.

————

NOTES

1. A Legal Illustration. Consider a hypothetical case brought under the Equal Protection Clause of the 14th Amendment alleging that a county discriminated against Mexican–Americans in selecting jurors. As one element of its case, the plaintiff wishes to establish that the percentage of persons on the jury rolls who are Mexican–American is less than the percentage of the population eligible for jury duty that is Mexican–American, and that this difference is unlikely to have occurred by chance. How would this be done? As follows:

(1) State the Null Hypothesis. In this example, the null hypothesis would be that there is no difference between the percentage of Mexican–Americans on the jury rolls and the percentage of Mexican–Americans in the jury-eligible population.

* From *EMTX:RESRCH METH IN SOCIAL RELATIONS 7E 7th edition by HOYLE. © 2002. Reprinted with permission of Wadsworth, a division of Thomson Learning: www.thomsonrights.com. FAX 800 730-2215.

(2) Choose a Significance Level. According to social science convention, the .05 level of significance might be chosen. This means that one would reject the null hypothesis if the chance of its being true was five in one hundred or less.

(3) Gather the Sample Data. Assume that a random sample of people on the jury rolls was drawn and that 9 percent of these people were Mexican–American, and that a random sample of the jury-eligible population was drawn and that 12 percent of these people were Mexican–American.

(4) Enter the Sample Data into a Formula. There are a large number of tests of statistical significance, from the very simple to the very complex. For a discussion of the appropriate test to use, see any of the books excerpted in the previous sections of this chapter. The formulae all ultimately yield an estimate of the probability that the null hypothesis can be rejected.

(5) Reject or Fail to Reject the Null Hypothesis. Given that the .05 level of significance has been chosen, if the probability that one could find by chance a difference as large as the one actually found (i.e., a difference of 12% − 9% = 3%) is 5 in 100 or less, reject the null hypothesis (i.e., state that the null hypothesis is *not* true). In other words, state that there is a "statistically significant difference" between the percentage of Mexican–Americans on the jury rolls and the percentage of Mexican–Americans in the jury-eligible population in the county.

Alternatively, if the probability that one could find by chance a difference as large as the one actually found is greater than 5 in 100, state that the null hypothesis cannot be rejected. In other words, state that there is "no significant difference" between the percentage of Mexican–Americans on the jury rolls and the percentage of Mexican–Americans in the jury-eligible population.

2.   Statistical Significance and Legal Significance. It is important to realize that the conclusion asserting a "statistically significant difference" between two groups simply means that the difference between the two groups is sufficiently large that it is unlikely to have occurred by chance. That is, it means that there is probably a "real" difference between the two populations from which the samples were drawn. It does *not* necessarily mean that the difference between the two populations is sufficiently large that the difference attains some sort of legal or social "significance." This point is particularly germane when very large sample sizes are used in the research. With a large enough sample size, any "real" difference between two populations, no matter how small or trivial, will be statistically significant. For example, a "real" difference in the recidivism rate of two groups of parolees of one half of one percent will be statistically significant if the groups studied are large enough. Yet it is hard to think of any legal decision or social policy that would find a one-half of one percent difference in recidivism sufficient to rely upon. Given this fact, one must first ascertain through statistical tests whether an obtained difference between two groups is statistically significant and then, if—and only if—it is, decide whether the difference is of sufficient magnitude to be of "significance" in making a legal decision.

3. Proof and Probability. It should be clear by now that social science research (or, indeed, research in any other area of science, including physics) never "proves" anything in the sense of concluding that any assertion is absolutely true or absolutely false. Rather, it assigns a probability to the truth or falsity of assertions that are tested. When the statement is made that the null hypothesis of no difference between the populations is rejected at the .05 level of significance, this means that the probability that one could get a difference as large as the one found in the research if the null hypothesis were really true is 5 in 100. In other words, 5 out of 100 times that one says there *is* a difference between the populations, there in fact is *no* difference, only chance variation. At times, however, the differences between two groups is sufficiently improbable as to convince all but the obstinate. One social scientist, for example, who was called as an expert witness in a discrimination case, calculated that the probability that a difference between the percentage of African–Americans on the jury rolls and the percentage of African–Americans in the jury-eligible population as large as that found could have occurred by chance was "a decimal point followed by 195 zeros and a 4." That was, he translated, the same as the probability in a poker game of being dealt 30 consecutive royal flushes. The trial judge commented that he would "start shooting" on the third consecutive royal flush. De Cani, Statistical Evidence in Jury Discrimination Cases, 65 Journal of Criminal Law and Criminology 234 (1974).

Courts sometimes do not appreciate the probabilistic reasoning of the social sciences. Berk and Oppenheim reported another case challenging the racial composition of a jury pool. A social scientist testified that the chances of obtaining the observed proportion of African–Americans in the jury pool, given the proportion of African–Americans in the jury-eligible population, were approximately 4 in 10,000. Doing Good Well: The Use of Quantitative Social Science Data in Advocacy Proceedings, 1 Law and Policy Quarterly 123, 129 (1979). They described the court's response as follows:

> The scientific validity of this statement was never seriously challenged in court, but nevertheless the court ruled against quashing the venire. The Judge argued by anecdote that from time to time he, too, had been worried about the underrepresentation of blacks on particular jury panels, but just about the time he became especially concerned, he would notice a panel in which blacks were "over-represented." Thus, there was in this case no cause for alarm. He claimed to understand the laws of probability to suggest that you win some and lose some and that in this instance the plaintiffs had simply lost.

SELECTED BIBLIOGRAPHY

Blumenthal, Meta–Analysis: A Primer for Legal Scholars, 80 Temple Law Review 201 (2007).

Epstein, Martin, and Boyd, On the Effective Communication of the Results of Empirical Studies, Part II, 60 Vanderbilt Law Review 801 (2007).

Epstein, Martin, and Schneider, On the Effective Communication of the Results of Empirical Studies, Part I, 59 Vanderbilt Law Review 1811 (2006).

Faigman, Is Science Different for Lawyers? 197 Science 339 (2002).

M. Finkelstein, Basic Concepts of Probability and Statistics in the Law (2009).

M. Finkelstein and B. Levin, Statistics for Lawyers (2007).

G. Gigerenzer, Rationality for Mortals: How People Cope with Uncertainty (2008).

J. Kadane, Statistics in the Law: A Practitioner's Guide, Cases, and Materials (2008).

T. Knapp, Learning Statistics Through Playing Cards (1996).

Koehler, Probabilities in the Courtroom: An Evaluation of Objections and Policies, in Handbook of Psychology and Law (D. Kagehiro and W. Laufer eds. 1992).

Koehler, Misconceptions about Statistics and Statistical Evidence, in Handbook of Trial Consulting: A Psychological Perspective (R. Wiener and B. Bornstein eds. in press).

Lempert, The Significance of Statistical Significance, 34 Law and Social Inquiry 225 (2009).

Redding and Reppucci, Effects of Lawyers' Socio–Political Attitudes on Their Judgments of Social Science in Legal Decision Making, 23 Law and Human Behavior 31 (1999).

D. Rowntree, Statistics Without Tears: A Primer for Non–Mathematicians (2004).

N. Salkind, Statistics for People Who (Think They) Hate Statistics (2d ed. 2004).

T. Urdan, Statistics in Plain English (2001).

Zou, DeTora, Haker, and Mulkern, Revisiting the *P*-value: A Comparison of Statistical Evidence in Clinical and Legal Medical Decision Making, Law, Probability and Risk (in press). Available at http://lpr.oxford journals.org/cgi/reprint/mgp004v1.

CHAPTER THREE

SOCIAL SCIENCE USED TO DETERMINE FACTS

In this chapter, we begin our examination of the uses of social science in law. We take as our point of departure the most straightforward and least controversial legal application of social science: its use to determine what Professor Kenneth Culp Davis called "adjudicative facts." Davis defined adjudicative facts as follows:

> When an agency [or court] finds facts concerning immediate parties— what the parties did, what the circumstances were, what the background conditions were—the agency [or court] is performing an adjudicative function, and the facts may conveniently be called adjudicative facts.

Davis, An Approach to Problems of Evidence in the Administrative Process, 55 Harvard Law Review 364, 402 (1942).

Adjudicative facts, in other words, are facts that apply only to the particular parties before the court. They are used to determine (or "adjudicate") what happened in a specific case, and not for some larger purpose, such as to argue that a law should be changed. What Davis called an adjudicative fact has been referred to by other commentators, e.g., T. Marvell, Appellate Courts and Lawyers (1978), as a "case fact," and by one court as "a plain, garden-variety fact." Bowling v. Department of Ins., 394 So.2d 165, 174 (Fla.Dist.Ct.App.1981).

The three areas we have chosen to explore the use of social science to determine adjudicative or case-specific facts involve trademarks, obscenity and damages.

SECTION I. TRADEMARKS

Trademarks identify products and producers. More precisely, the Trademark Act of 1946, known as the Lanham Act, as amended by the Trademark Law Revision Act of 1988, 15 U.S.C. § 1127, defines a trademark as follows:

> The term "trademark" includes any word, name, symbol, or device, or any combination thereof—
>
> (1) used by a person, or

(2) which a person has a bona fide intention to use in commerce and applies to register on the principal register established by this Act,

to identify and distinguish his or her goods, including a unique product, from those manufactured or sold by others and to indicate the source of the goods, even if that source is unknown.

Thus, both "COKE" and the distinctive shape of the Coca–Cola bottle are trademarks of the Coca–Cola Company.

Trademarks can serve several valuable functions. First, they can serve an identifying function, indicating the source of the goods. This would facilitate determining the manufacturer if the product turned out to be defective. Second, trademarks can have a quality assurance function. Consumers who are impressed with the quality of a particular manufacturer's products may come to expect that repeat purchases from this manufacturer will be of similar quality. Finally, trademarks can have an advertising function. Repetition of the trademark through advertising may attract customers and create demand for the product. Thus, trademarks are an unusual form of property right in which the validity of the property interest depends on the reaction of third parties (i.e., consumers) rather than on the traditional indices of ownership such as possession. See E. Kitch and H. Perlman, Legal Regulation of the Competitive Process (5th ed. 1998).

Trademarks are often confused with two other forms of "intellectual property" rights, patents and copyrights, which together form much of the law prohibiting "unfair competition" in commerce. Patents, however, apply only to new inventions and copyrights apply only to original writings (or other forms of tangible expression, such as plays or films). In the case of a word processor, for example, the interior hardware may be protected by a patent, the instruction manual and software programs may be protected by a copyright, and the name of the word processor may be protected by a trademark. Unlike patents and copyrights, which confer a monopoly only for time-limited periods (20 years in the case of patents, and the life of the author plus 70 years, in the case of copyrights), trademarks can confer a perpetual monopoly.

We focus here on only one issue in trademark law: "consumer confusion." The federal Patent and Trademark Office will refuse to register a new trademark if it so resembles a trademark already registered to another person "as to be likely, when used on or in connection with the goods of the applicant, to cause confusion or to cause mistake, or to deceive." 15 U.S.C. § 1052(d). A person who sells a product that is likely to cause confusion with an already trademarked product is liable for trademark infringement. If the plaintiff—the party with the existing trademark—can prove by a preponderance of the evidence that the defendant has caused consumers to be confused, an injunction can be issued by the court ordering the defendant to cease using the product designation in question, and civil damages can be awarded.

Before examining the ways that social science research has been used as evidence of consumer confusion, we first consider the rule of evidence that for many years barred the introduction of social science research in trademark cases: the "hearsay" rule.

A.   Social Science Evidence and the Hearsay Rule

Rule 801(c) of the Federal Rules of Evidence defines "hearsay" as "a statement, other than one made by the declarant while testifying at the trial or hearing, offered in evidence to prove the truth of the matter asserted." Rule 802—the "hearsay rule"—states that "[h]earsay is not admissible" in court. Rule 803 states several exceptions to the hearsay rule. See Appendix A for the text of these rules.

When empirical data in the form of surveys first began to be introduced as evidence of consumer confusion in trademark cases, courts often rejected it as violating the hearsay rule: the subjects (or "respondents") in the surveys were seen as offering "statements" in evidence, despite the fact that they were not present at trial to testify and be cross-examined on the truth of those statements.

————

ELGIN NATIONAL WATCH CO. v. ELGIN CLOCK CO.

United States District Court, District of Delaware, 1928.
26 F.2d 376.

■ Morris, District Judge.

In this suit, instituted by the Elgin National Watch Company against the Elgin Clock Company to obtain a decree enjoining and restraining the defendant, which manufactures or assembles clocks for automobiles, from using [a]ny corporate name or business style of which the word "Elgin" forms a part, the plaintiff [h]as presented its petition praying for an order granting it leave to file an affidavit of Arthur L. Lynn and the exhibits thereto annexed. The affidavit, submitted with the petition, purports to be that of an expert witness with respect to the meaning of the word "Elgin," as understood by the public when used in connection with timepieces, their manufacture or sale. [T]he affidavit reads thus:

"Arthur L. Lynn, being duly sworn, upon oath states as follows:

"I am a member of the advertising firm of Lennen & Mitchell, Inc. [I]n order to ascertain whether or not the word 'Elgin,' as applied to timepieces, means to retail jewelers the products of any particular concern, our company, under my supervision, mailed to representative retail jewelers throughout the United States a questionnaire which embraced the following questions:

"[1]. In connection with clocks and watches, does the name 'Elgin' mean to you and your customers the products of any particular concern or not? If so, whose?

"[2]. If you saw the name Elgin Clock Company on an automobile clock or watch, who would you think made it?

"[3]. Who would your customers think made such a clock or watch?

"[F]rom a careful examination of these questionnaires, I am of the opinion that the name 'Elgin,' used in connection with timepieces, means the Elgin National Watch Company, and that the name 'Elgin,' used in connection with the manufacture and sale of timepieces, would be taken by the public to mean the products of the Elgin National Watch Company."

[A]bout 2,000 returned questionnaires were submitted as exhibits with the affidavit.

The plaintiff concedes that its petition presents a case of first impression. It has found no judicial construction [t]o reveal or define the character of testimony which [m]ight be properly considered expert testimony in trademark cases.

[J. Cutler, On Passing Off (1904)] asserts that the plaintiff has to prove that to a considerable portion of the trade or of the public the trade-name means the plaintiff's goods and nothing else, and that such evidence can and ought to be given by traders and by members of the purchasing public. The author then says: "Of course, to call one such witness would be insufficient, as no court would place much, if any, reliance upon the evidence of one such witness. But then how many such witnesses ought the plaintiff to call? It may be stated that he ought to be prepared with from 20 to 30 such witnesses. * * * In selecting his 20 or 30 witnesses, the plaintiff must not take them all from one locality, but from different parts of the country, and in particular he ought to have some from the locality where the defendant's trade is carried on."

The plaintiff [proposes] to eliminate the necessity of calling, in cases of this character, numerous witnesses from all the different parts of the United States, and that apparently only by the procedure adopted by the plaintiff can such result be accomplished. While recognizing the practical difficulties presented in establishing, by satisfactory proof, what a trade-name nationally known denotes to the trade and to the public, I am not convinced [t]o make the innovation with respect to such proof that is here suggested by the plaintiff.

Were plaintiff's position sound, [there would be] a nullification of the long-established proposition that the rule against hearsay evidence finds no exception in the case of expert witnesses.

[T]he affidavit submitted for filing is one based, not upon personal knowledge of the affiant nor upon facts admitted in evidence, but, on the contrary, is predicated solely upon the unverified statements or opinions of persons not called as witnesses.

[I] am constrained to conclude that the prayer of plaintiff's petition must be denied, for the reason that a proper basis is wanting for the judgment or opinion of the affiant.

————

TRIANGLE PUBLICATIONS v. ROHRLICH

United States Court of Appeals, Second Circuit, 1948.
167 F.2d 969.

■ FRANK, CIRCUIT JUDGE, Dissenting.

[The plaintiff, Triangle Publications, published a magazine titled "Seventeen." The defendants, Joseph Rohrlich and others, began to produce girdles labeled "Miss Seventeen." A majority of the Court of Appeals affirmed the District Court's finding of trademark infringement based on likelihood of confusion.]

The [trial] judge's finding as to what was "likely" [to confuse] is nothing but a surmise, a conjecture, a guess. We are not bound by such a finding. We can guess as well as the trial judge.

I think that we should not pioneer in amplifying the trade-name doctrine on the basis of the shaky kind of guess in which the trial judge indulged. Like the trial judge's, our surmise must here rest on "judicial notice." As neither the trial judge nor any member of this court is (or resembles) a teen-age girl or the mother or sister of such a girl, our judicial notice apparatus will not work well unless we feed it with information directly obtained from "teen-agers" or from their female relatives accustomed to shop for them. Competently to inform ourselves, we should have a staff of investigators like those supplied to administrative agencies. As we have no such staff, I have questioned some adolescent girls and their mothers and sisters, persons I have chosen at random. I have been told uniformly by my questionees that no one could reasonably believe that any relation existed between plaintiff's magazine and defendants' girdles.

I admit that my method of obtaining such data is not satisfactory. But it does serve better than anything in this record to illuminate the pivotal fact. It convinces me that the plaintiff should bear a very heavy burden of proving that confusion is likely, a burden plaintiff did not discharge. For instance, plaintiff or the trial judge might have utilized, but did not, "laboratory" tests, of a sort now familiar, to ascertain whether numerous girls and women, seeing both plaintiff's magazine and defendants' advertisements, would believe them to be in some way associated.

NOTE

1. Judicial Notice. In his dissent in Triangle Publications v. Rohrlich, Judge Frank relied on an early form of the doctrine of "judicial notice" in conducting his "survey" of adolescent girls and their mothers and sisters. See Federal Rule of Evidence 201, "Judicial Notice of Adjudicative Facts," in Appendix A. This Rule—which was adopted in its current form in 1975, almost thirty years after the *Triangle* case—would seem to clearly bar independent judicial investigations of the type conducted by Judge Frank, since the degree to which consumers are confused between two products is not "generally known within the territorial jurisdiction of the trial court" and is not "capable of accurate and ready determination by resort to sources whose accuracy cannot reasonably be questioned."

———

ONEIDA v. NATIONAL SILVER

Supreme Court of New York, Madison County, 1940.
25 N.Y.S.2d 271.

■ DAVIS, JUSTICE.

The cause of action alleged by the plaintiff is one [f]or unfair competition. Its claim is that it being in the business of manufacturing silver plate and having originated a pattern or design called "Coronation," which had met with an extraordinary sale, the defendant, seeking to take advantage of the extensive advertising, sale and popularity of this particular pattern, copied or simulated the pattern, and sold in the market in competition with plaintiff, a pattern of its own called, "Princess Royal," thereby injuring unlawfully the plaintiff in its good will, its sales and profits. An injunction restraining these alleged unlawful acts, and an accounting are sought.

[F]ive [y]oung ladies [w]ere employed [t]o make what was called a "survey." They were given a book of fifty sheets upon each of which there were three questions. On the cover was one of the articles of the Princess Royal pattern with the backstamp concealed. These witnesses separately visited homes of what may be called the middle class of people, sought an interview with the housewife, explained that they had nothing to sell but were simply making a survey, showed the pattern and asked the housewife to identify it and to write and sign the answers. Two of the questions were in the following form: (1) Who do you think puts out this silverware? (2) If you wanted to buy a set of this silverware how would you ask for it? [T]hey interviewed 1,000 women and received a variety of answers, a considerable portion of which identified the article as that of plaintiff; and in only one instance was identification made as Princess Royal. More than one-third did not know the manufacturer or pattern.

When this evidence was offered I had doubts as to its competency, but took it subject to motion to strike out, or eventually to disregard it. I think that the evidence was competent. These persons, though not customers of a store, were members of the public and may be regarded as potential purchasers.

[T]he plaintiff did not rest alone upon this survey. From the housewives who had in the questionnaire identified the pattern as one of plaintiff or its manufacture, twenty-four women were called as witnesses who gave their reasons for being confused or deceived in identifying the Princess Royal pattern shown them. They were familiar with advertisements of silverware patterns. Such evidence has greater weight than that obtained in the "survey."

[I] reach the conclusion that the defendant, by [t]he fact that persons were readily confused and deceived, was engaged in acts of recognized unfair competition.

————

ZIPPO MANUFACTURING CO. v. ROGERS IMPORTS, INC.

United States District Court, Southern District of New York, 1963.
216 F.Supp. 670.

■ FEINBERG, DISTRICT JUDGE.

This case involves the attempt of a manufacturer of a popular cigarette lighter to keep others from imitating the lighters shape and appearance. Plaintiff Zippo Manufacturing Company ("Zippo"), a Pennsylvania corporation, alleges [t]rademark infringement [o]n the part of Rogers, Inc. ("Rogers"), a New York corporation, by reason of Rogers' sale of pocket lighters closely resembling Zippo's.

[P]laintiff has relied heavily on a consumer study to prove the elements of its case. [T]he purpose of the study was to determine [w]hether the similar physical attributes of the Rogers' lighters cause public confusion.

[T]he "universe" to be studied consisted of all smokers aged eighteen years and older residing in the continental United States, which the research project indicated was approximately 115,000,000 ("the smoking population"). All percentage results in the surveys represent projected percentages of the smoking population.

The three separate surveys were conducted across a national probability sample of smokers, with a sample size of approximately 500 for each survey. The samples were chosen on the basis of data obtained from the Bureau of Census.

[D]efendant objects to the admission of the surveys into evidence. It first contends that the surveys are hearsay. The weight of case authority, the consensus of legal writers, and reasoned policy considerations all indicate that the hearsay rule should not bar the admission of properly conducted public surveys. Although courts were at first reluctant to accept survey evidence or to give it weight, the more recent trend is clearly contrary. Surveys are now admitted over the hearsay objection on two technically distinct bases. Some cases hold that surveys are not hearsay at all; other cases hold that surveys are hearsay but are admissible because they are within the recognized exception to the hearsay rule for statements of present state of mind, attitude, or belief. Still other cases admit surveys without stating the ground on which they are admitted.

The cases holding that surveys are not hearsay do so on the basis that the surveys are not offered to prove the truth of what respondents said and, therefore, do not fall within the classic definition of hearsay.

[R]egardless of whether the surveys in this case could be admitted under the non-hearsay approach, they are admissible because the answers of respondents are expressions of presently existing state of mind, attitude, or belief. There is a recognized exception to the hearsay rule for such statements, and under it the statements are admissible to prove the truth of the matter contained therein.

———

NOTE

1. Non–Hearsay and Exceptions to the Hearsay Rule. Judge Feinberg gave two alternate grounds for admitting surveys as evidence. One was that surveys are not hearsay because they are not "offered in evidence to prove the truth of the matter asserted." Federal Rule of Evidence 801(c). That is, the fact that respondents confused Rogers lighters with Zippo lighters was not being offered to prove that Rogers, Inc., actually manufactured Zippos. The other ground for admitting surveys was that, even if they are hearsay, one of the exceptions to the hearsay rule is the "present sense impression," which allows the introduction of a statement "describing or explaining an event or condition made while the declarant was perceiving the event or condition, or immediately thereafter." Federal Rule of Evidence 803(1). See Appendix A.

B. SOCIAL SCIENCE EVIDENCE OF CONSUMER CONFUSION

Zippo effectively marked the end of the hearsay objection to the introduction of survey evidence in trademark cases. *Zippo* also marked the beginning of the modern trend in trademark litigation in which the introduction of survey evidence has become the normal method of proving consumer confusion. In the following cases, we examine the range of methodologies that have been used by social scientists and accepted by courts to demonstrate that consumers are confused between two products or two producers.

———

ZIPPO MANUFACTURING CO. v. ROGERS IMPORTS, INC.

United States District Court, Southern District of New York, 1963.
216 F.Supp. 670.

■ FEINBERG, DISTRICT JUDGE.

[The allegations of the parties and descriptions of the survey sample are contained in the previous excerpt from this case.]

Defendant's [o]bjection to the surveys is that they should not have been conducted in respondents' homes but in stores, the actual places of purchase. While it may be that in general the store is the best place to measure the state of mind at the time of purchase, it would be virtually impossible to obtain a representative national sample if stores were used. An interview at a respondent's home is probative of his state of mind at the time of purchase, although the deviation from the actual purchase situation should be considered in weighing the force of this evidence. Therefore, the surveys are not inadmissible merely because they were conducted in homes.

[T]he [key] element of plaintiff's case is that the Rogers lighter is likely to cause prospective purchasers to regard it as a Zippo lighter. Plaintiff claims that this likelihood of confusion is established for the standard model principally by Survey C. [I]n Survey C, respondents were handed a standard Rogers lighter with all of its identifying marks, including the name on the bottom, and asked to identify its brand. 34.7 percent of respondents thought it was a Zippo lighter, and only 14.3 percent identified it as a Rogers. This would indicate that a substantial number of persons might confuse the Zippo and Rogers standard lighters because of their physical attributes, despite the appearance of the brand name on the lighters. Defendant's objections to the weight of this evidence must, of course, be seriously regarded, particularly its argument that no such confusion would exist in the store at the time of purchase because Rogers lighters are sold from display cards bearing the name "Rogers." This contention is buttressed by the fact that almost all of those who did correctly identify the Rogers lighter did so because they saw the brand name on the bottom, and the brand name would be more conspicuous on the display card. However, it is difficult to get away from the fact that the number of confused respondents was almost two and one-half times greater than those who recognized a Rogers as a Rogers, and a good portion of the confusion was due to the shape and style of the Rogers lighter.

[O]n all the evidence then, I find that plaintiff has established the likelihood of confusion—indeed actual confusion—between the Zippo and Rogers standard lighters.

―――――

AMSTAR CORPORATION v. DOMINO'S PIZZA

United States Court of Appeals, Fifth Circuit, 1980.
615 F.2d 252.

■ AINSWORTH, CIRCUIT JUDGE.

Amstar Corporation brought this suit asserting trademark infringement and unfair competition against Domino's Pizza, Inc. and several of its franchisees to enjoin their use of Amstar's federal registration of the "Domino" trademark. The complaint is based on allegations that defendants' use of the mark "Domino's Pizza" in connection with the sale of fast-food delivered hot pizza pies constitutes trademark infringement and a false designation of origin or representation in violation of the Trademark Act of 1946, 15 U.S.C.A. § 1051 et seq. [T]he district court ruled in favor of plaintiff, dismissed defendants' counterclaim, and permanently enjoined defendants use of the names "Domino" or "Domino's Pizza." Defendants then filed this appeal.

Standard of Review

[I]nitially, we must determine the appropriate standard of review applicable to the district court's finding of likelihood of confusion. [T]his circuit has held that likelihood of confusion is a question of fact which can only be set aside if clearly erroneous. The record in the present case indicates that the district court's finding of likelihood of confusion is clearly erroneous.

Likelihood of Confusion

[I]nfringement of a registered mark is governed by the provisions of 15 U.S.C.A. § 1114(1), which imposes liability against "use ... likely to cause confusion, or to cause mistake, or to deceive." [P]laintiff's claims against defendants, [t]herefore, turn on the determination of whether defendants' use of the mark "Domino's Pizza" is likely to cause confusion, mistake, or deception.

[D]issimilarities between the retail outlets for and the predominant consumers of plaintiff's and defendants' goods lessen the possibility of confusion, mistake, or deception. The dissimilarities here are substantial.

Plaintiff's "Domino" sugar products are distributed to the public primarily through grocery stores; defendants' pizzas and soft drinks are distributed exclusively through fast-food outlets specializing in home delivery or customer pickup, but offering no facilities for sit-down service.

[T]here are substantial dissimilarities between the predominant purchasers of plaintiff's and defendants' products. According to surveys presented at trial, "Domino's Pizza" patrons are primarily young (85.6% under 35 years of age), single (61%) males (63.3%). This coincides with the fact that 75% of the "Domino's Pizza" stores throughout the country are situated in college campus towns or around military bases where the advertising for "Domino's Pizza" is directed to the 18- to 34–year–old single male. In contrast, "Domino" sugar purchasers are predominantly middle-aged housewives.

[A]t trial, both parties introduced survey evidence on the issue of likelihood of confusion. The trial court characterized the defendants' survey as "about as contrived a survey as I have ever run across," but found plaintiff's survey "properly conducted and fair." Our own examination of the survey evidence convinces us that both surveys are substantially defective.

Plaintiff's survey was made by Dr. Russ Haley, Professor of Marketing at the University of New Hampshire. It was conducted in ten cities among female heads of household primarily responsible for making food purchases. Each participant was shown, in her own home, a "Domino's Pizza" box and was asked if she believed the company that made the pizza made any other product. If she answered yes, she was asked, "What products other than pizza do you think are made by the company that makes Domino's Pizza?" Seventy-one percent of those asked the second question answered "sugar."

While the possible confusion level shown by the Haley study is high, there are several defects in the survey which significantly reduce its probative value. First, one of the most important factors in assessing the validity of an opinion poll is the adequacy of the "survey universe," that is, the persons interviewed must adequately represent the opinions which are relevant to the litigation. The appropriate universe should include a fair sampling of those purchasers most likely to partake of the alleged infringer's goods or services. Of the ten cities in which the Haley survey was conducted, eight had no "Domino's Pizza" outlets, and the outlets in the remaining two had been open for less than three months. Additionally, the persons interviewed consisted entirely of women found at home during six daylight hours who identified themselves as the member of the household primarily responsible for grocery buying. As plaintiff's sugar is sold primarily in grocery stores, participants in the Haley survey would have been repeatedly exposed to plaintiff's mark, but would have had little, if any, exposure to defendants' mark. Furthermore, the survey neglected completely defendants' primary customers—young, single, male college students. Thus, we do not believe that the proper universe was examined, and the result of the survey must therefore be discounted.

[T]he trial court discounted defendants' survey for largely the same reasons just discussed—it was conducted on the premises of "Domino's Pizza" outlets and therefore did not examine a proper survey universe, and the questioning procedures used were improper. Thus, defendants' survey is likewise not probative of the presence or absence of confusion.

Accordingly, we conclude that the trial court was clearly in error when it held defendants' use of the trademark "Domino's Pizza" was likely to cause confusion, mistake, or deception.

[S]ince defendants' use of the mark "Domino's Pizza" is not likely to confuse, mislead, or deceive the public, the district court's order and injunction to the contrary are set aside, and the judgment is REVERSED.

THE SQUIRT COMPANY v. THE SEVEN–UP COMPANY

United States District Court, Eastern District of Missouri, 1979.
207 U.S. Patent Quarterly 12.

■ HARPER, DISTRICT JUDGE.

[The Squirt Company, producers of a grapefruit-flavored soft drink named "Squirt," charged the Seven–Up Company with trademark infringement in naming their lemonade-flavored soft drink "Quirst." A survey performed by the Maritz Company was introduced as evidence of consumer confusion.]

We turn now to the methodology followed in the execution of the Maritz Survey. At three Low Cost Grocery Stores located in and around Phoenix, Arizona a store intercept study was conducted on July 20, 21 and 22, 1978. During the three-day period in which the study or survey was conducted all three of the Low Cost Stores had the soft drinks, SQUIRT and QUIRST, available for sale at the reduced price of ninety-nine cents for a six-pack of 12–ounce cans. Upon entering the grocery store all customers were given a coupon worth fifty cents off the regular price of one six-pack of 12–ounce cans of any flavor of non-alcoholic beverage, with the exception of cola flavor. The primary purpose of the fifty-cent coupon was to stimulate the purchase of non-cola soft drinks and thus increase the efficiency of the three-day survey by having a large sample.

After a customer had completed his shopping, gone through the checkout line, had his groceries bagged and was preparing to leave the store, he was intercepted by an interviewer and asked the following questions which were contained in a questionnaire: Question #1. "Did you get a coupon like this on your way into the grocery store?" (At the time of asking the question the interviewer displayed the fifty-cent off coupon described above.)

If the answer to Question #1 was "Yes," the interview continued and the respondent was then asked: Question #2: "Did you use your coupon?"

If the answer to Question #2 was "Yes," the interview continued and the following question was directed to the respondent: Question #3: "What brands of six-pack 12–ounce cans of non-alcoholic beverage other than cola flavor did you buy?"

The answers to Question #3 were recorded verbatim by the interviewer on the questionnaire. Following the recording of the responses to Question #3 the respondent was issued the following request: Question #4: "May I see the six-pack(s) of (each brand in the order mentioned in Question #3) you bought? I know it is an inconvenience to unpack your groceries so I will give you a $3.00 gift certificate good on any purchase of $3.00 or more at this store through July 30th if you will show me the six-pack(s) you bought."

The interviewers were instructed to record verbatim the exact brands of 12–ounce canned, non-alcoholic beverages which were shown to them by the respondent.

[F]ollowing the completion of the entire survey a tabulation was made of the number of respondents who correctly identified the brand purchased and of respondents who did not correctly identify the brands they had just previously purchased.

A compilation of the Maritz Survey results disclosed that a total of 1,016 persons were in fact interviewed. Of this total, some 884 persons answered "Yes" to Question #2 and thus used their fifty-cent coupon. Of the 884 persons who used their coupon, 839 responded to Question #3 by identifying the brands they purchased and then responded to Question #4 by displaying their beverage purchases to the interviewer. Of the total of 839, there were 70 persons who stated in answer to Question 3 the soft drink SQUIRT. Of the 70 persons who said they had SQUIRT, 65 in fact were able to display SQUIRT in response to Question #4. Three persons who said they had purchased SQUIRT, in fact had purchased QUIRST, while two persons of the total of 70 who said they purchased SQUIRT, in fact purchased the soft drink SPRITE. Thus, approximately 4.3% of the respondents, three out of the 70 who said they had purchased SQUIRT, when asked to display their purchases in fact had purchased QUIRST.

[A]s a starting point in this Court's evaluation of the Maritz Survey, we would point out that we know of no cases containing an actual market survey of the Maritz variety wherein an actual purchaser is asked to list the brands he has just purchased, and then asked to display the brands he has named, in order to determine the accuracy of his listed purchases. The cases which contain survey evidence that have been cited by the parties in their briefs are not of the Maritz type wherein consumer action or behavior is evaluated. Rather, the cases cited to this Court entail "opinion" type surveys, where typically a specific number of interviews are conducted either in a "purchasing" environment, such as a store or shopping center, or in a "non-purchasing" environment, such as the home or laboratory, and the respondent will be asked to express his or her opinion with respect to specific marks and whether they originate from the same source, or whether there is any relationship at all between two marks, etc.

[T]his Court does believe that the results of the Maritz survey are strong evidence of a likelihood of confusion between SQUIRT and QUIRST. First of all, the fact that the survey was conducted in a live market environment and measured actual consumer purchasing behavior as opposed to being conducted in the home and measuring consumer opinion, lends greater reliability to the survey results. As Judge Wyzanski pointed out in American Luggage Works v. United States Trunk Co., Inc., 158 F.Supp. 50, 116 USPQ 188 (Mass.1957); aff'd 259 F.2d 69, 118 USPQ 424 (1st Cir.1958), at page 53, 116 USPQ at page 190–191:

> "If the interviewee is not in a buying mood but is just in a friendly mood answering a pollster, his degree of attention is quite different from what it would be had he his wallet in his hand. Many men do not take the same trouble to avoid confusion when they are responding to sociological investigators as when they spend their cash."

[T]his Court cannot say that the 4.3% (three out of seventy) level of error between SQUIRT and QUIRST is de minimus or statistically insignificant, when it is considered in the context of the entire soft drink industry. [T]hese considerations lead us to the conclusion that the defendants are infringing the plaintiff's SQUIRT trademarks because the name QUIRST is likely to cause confusion, mistake or deception.

———

THE KROGER CO. v. JOHNSON & JOHNSON

United States District Court, Southern District of Ohio, 1983.
570 F.Supp. 1055.

■ CARL B. RUBIN, CHIEF JUDGE.

[Johnson & Johnson claimed that the Kroger Company and others had infringed its trademark in the analgesic "Tylenol" by naming their analgesics "Actenol," "Supernol," and "Hydenol" and packaging them in a manner likely to cause consumer confusion.]

A survey performed by Bruno and Ridgeway Research Associates, Inc., a marketing and advertising research firm, demonstrated the potential for consumer confusion between Tylenol and the three accused products. The survey indicated not only the likelihood of confusion among these brands, but also a belief by substantial numbers of those interviewed that the accused products were manufactured by Tylenol.[6] Although defendants attacked the methodology of the Bruno survey at trial, we are satisfied that it was conducted in a professional manner and may be considered as probative evidence on the issue of potential confusion.

[W]hile [Kroger] offered affidavits of 152 purchasers of Tylenol to the effect that they were not confused as to the nature of the product purchased or its origin, the Court does not find these affidavits controlling on the issue of potential confusion.[7]

[T]he preponderance of the evidence in this case establishes a likelihood of confusion between [Kroger's] products and that of [Johnson and Johnson], as well as confusion as to the source of [Kroger's] products.

LA VICTORIA FOODS v. CURTICE–BURNS

United States District Court, Western District of Washington, 1986.
No. C85–1557MTB (Unpublished).

■ ROBERT J. BRYAN.

FINDINGS OF FACT

[1] The plaintiff has continuously produced and marketed a unique Mexican-style salsa product under the SALSA SUPREMA trademark since

---

6. In the survey, consumers were asked to view a shelf of products containing [Kroger's] products as well as other national brand pain relievers for approximately five seconds. Afterwards, they were asked to identify those products which they had seen. Between 17 and 24% of the respondents claimed that they had seen Tylenol, when in fact it was not present on the shelf. The interviewees were then shown [Kroger's] products and asked who they believed made or manufactured that product. Twenty-three percent (23%) of the persons interviewed thought Actenol was manufactured by Tylenol. Forty percent (40%) of those persons interviewed with respect to Supernol and Hydenol likewise believed those products were manufactured by Tylenol.

7. Professor Dornoff noted the high probability of bias in the signing of these affidavits. The purchasers in question all mailed in and received a full rebate on the price paid for the product. They also received a double rebate if they consented to a personal interview. The affidavits were prepared by [Kroger's] counsel and the initial telephone interviews were conducted by counsel or members of his staff. Officials of [Kroger] obtained the affidavits during the personal interview. In view of the great probability of bias resulting from such techniques, as well as the unrepresentative nature of the sample, the Court attaches little weight to such evidence.

1968. The unique salsa which the plaintiff markets under the SALSA SUPREMA trademark is the leading seller in the plaintiff's product line.

[2] The SALSA SUPREMA trademark is duly registered on the Principal Register of the United States Patent and Trademark Office under the Lanham Act of 1946, as amended, 15 U.S.C.A. § 1051 *et seq.*, to La Victoria Foods, Inc. on April 26, 1977 for "Hot Sauce". The plaintiff is the owner of that registration and of the mark so registered. [P]laintiff is entitled to all of the benefits of its incontestable registration.

[3] The plaintiff has continuously sold, advertised and promoted its SALSA SUPREMA-marked product since 1968. The sales of this product have steadily increased. In 1980 the sales were in excess of $2,000,000. In 1984 they were in excess of $5,000,000 and the rate of sales in early 1986 indicated expected sales in excess of $7,000,000 per year. Since July 1984, the plaintiff has sold hundreds of thousands of jars of the SALSA–SUPREMA-marked product in the States of Washington, Oregon, Idaho, Montana and Alaska. From June 1979 through May 1986, the plaintiff spent in excess of $12,000,000 advertising and promoting its products, a substantial part of which has emphasized the SALSA SUPREMA product.

[4] Defendant began marketing both a Mexican-style salsa product and a tortilla chip product under the LA SUPREMA trademark in July 1984. The LA SUPREMA-marked products have been sold and marketed continuously in the States of Washington, Oregon, Idaho, Montana and Alaska since July 1984. Defendant has sold in excess of 1,700,000 jars of LA SUPREMA-marked salsa products with gross sales in excess of $1,700,000.

[5] The salsa products of plaintiff and defendant are sold in the same stores in the same geographic areas. The plaintiff's SALSA SUPREMA-marked salsa product is sold primarily as a general-purpose salsa in the Mexican food section of grocery stores and supermarkets. The SALSA SUPREMA product is also advertised and promoted as a dip. The defendant's LA SUPREMA-marked product is usually positioned in the chip and snack section of grocery stores and supermarkets and is primarily advertised and promoted as a dip.

[6] Plaintiff presented evidence of a survey designed by Dr. Elizabeth Loftus and conducted through Mr. John Burshek of Herbert Research, Inc. The survey was designed to determine the incidence of actual confusion between LA SUPREMA salsa and SALSA SUPREMA where the prospective purchaser hears information about one or the other of the products and then attempts to purchase that product in a store. Shoppers were intercepted on a random basis as they entered three different supermarkets in the Seattle–Tacoma area. Prospective purchasers of the products involved were screened from non-prospective purchasers by being asked the question "How many times have you eaten Mexican food in the past year?" If the interviewee responded in the affirmative, that person was then offered an incentive of $2 to purchase a salsa product which the interviewer named verbally. The interviewer asked the respondent to purchase one of "SALSA SUPREMA" or "LA SUPREMA Salsa." Those who accepted the offer were given a card reflecting the offer. The card also bore a code known only to

the interviewer that reflected which product the respondent had been asked to purchase. The respondent then proceeded into the store. The respondent was required to join the auditory stimuli given by the interviewer with a visual observation of the products in order to complete the test. When the respondent returned to the interviewer with a purchased product, the interviewer paid the promised $2 and recorded the name of the product purchased. The interviewer also recorded which product the interviewee had been asked to purchase. Three hundred and three people responded. One hundred and fifty three people were asked to purchase "SALSA SUPREMA" and one hundred and fifty were asked to purchase "LA SUPREMA salsa." The results were tabulated and a report was prepared.

[7]   The results of the plaintiff's auditory test indicated that there was an overall rate of actual confusion between the products in question of 11.9%. Both direct and reverse confusion were shown. Of those who were asked to purchase SALSA SUPREMA, 10.6% returned with LA SUPREMA Salsa, and 13.2% of those who were asked to purchase LA SUPREMA Salsa returned with SALSA SUPREMA. Dr. Loftus testified as to the design and results of the survey and Mr. Burshek testified as to the conducting of the survey. Both witnesses were credible, particularly as compared to the defendant's survey expert.

[8]   Dr. Loftus also approached ten grocery clerks at random in markets in the Seattle–Tacoma area and asked them where the "LA SUPREMA Salsa" was located. Seven of the ten directed her to the Mexican food section of the store when, in fact, the LA SUPREMA Salsa was located in the Chip and Snack section of the store. This is some evidence that those store personnel who are responsible for assisting the consuming public are themselves actually confused between these products and tends to confirm the results of the Loftus survey of prospective purchasers.

[9]   The defendant also conducted a survey. Consumers selected by a random procedure were telephoned and asked whether they had purchased "Mexican-style sauces or dips" within the last six months, along with several other preliminary questions. Those who qualified were offered an incentive to come to the offices of the entity that conducted the survey. Those who accepted the invitations were taken into a room with the interviewer and seated at a table where a box was positioned between the interviewer and the respondent. After the respondent was seated, the box was removed to reveal a jar of the defendant's LA SUPREMA Salsa standing on the table at a distance of less than an arm's length from the respondent. The box was left off the product for the remainder of the interview. The respondent was asked the question "What is the name of this product?" and was allowed to look at the jar of the defendant's product for as long as was required to answer the question. After that question was answered, the respondent was asked, "Do you know who makes this product?" If the respondent answered in the affirmative, the question "Who is it that makes this product?" was then asked. The answers were

recorded and the results were tabulated. Of the 201 people who were interviewed, 38.8% responded that the product was LA SUPREMA and another 20.5% responded with an answer which included LA SUPREMA or a close variant. Only 27 people said they knew who made the product. Of the 27 people, 21 said LA SUPREMA and one person said "Victoria."

[10]   The defendant's survey did not measure likelihood of confusion with the plaintiff's product. It was, if anything, merely a measure of the respondent's ability to read the defendant's label. There was no fair opportunity for the respondent to reveal any confusion which might have existed. The fact that one person, even while looking directly at the defendant's label from a distance of less than arm's length, said "Victoria" is of some slight probative value that confusion is likely.

[11]   The person who designed and conducted the defendant's survey testified with regard to that survey. His testimony was not credible. He appeared to be a partisan advocate. He was highly critical of the Loftus survey, but refused to acknowledge the very obvious substantial shortcomings in the design of his own survey and in the way in which it was conducted.

CONCLUSIONS OF LAW

[1]   There exists a likelihood of confusion to some appreciable degree between the plaintiff's trademark "SALSA SUPREMA" and defendant's trademark "LA SUPREMA" when defendant's trademark is used in connection with the word "salsa."

[2]   Defendant has infringed on plaintiff's "SALSA SUPREMA" trademark in violation of 15 U.S.C.A. § 1114 and 15 U.S.C.A. § 1125 in connection with the word "suprema." The appropriate remedy for such infringement is an injunction preventing the defendant from using the word "SUPREMA" or "SALSA SUPREMA" as a part of the brand name or trademark of any salsa product including their currently marketed product Bean Dip with salsa.

————

KIS v. FOTO FANTASY

United States District Court, Northern District of Texas, 2001.
204 F.Supp. 2d 968.

■ LYNN, DISTRICT JUDGE.

Before the Court is Defendants' Motion to Strike the Expert Report of Dr. Daniel J. Howard and to Exclude His Testimony from Trial.

[I]. Background

Plaintiffs [i.e., KIS] have filed suit against Defendants [i.e., Foto Fantasy] alleging, *inter alia,* that Defendants have violated the Lanham Act. Plaintiffs' Lanham Act claim stems from Defendants' use of drawings of Tom Cruise and Marilyn Monroe on the outside of their photo booths.

Defendants and Plaintiffs both own photo booths that are placed inside malls around the country. The booths operate by allowing the user to either have a picture taken inside of the booth, or to insert a photo brought into the booth by the user, so that the machine can transform the picture into a sketch. On the outside of Defendants' booths (a.k.a. "Portrait Studios") are sketches of Tom Cruise and Marilyn Monroe. On one corner of these celebrities' sketch images reads the phrase, "SCAN IN YOUR FAVORITE CELEBRITIES." Plaintiffs claim that the placement of these sketches on Defendants' photo booths violates the Lanham Act because it creates confusion as to the "affiliation, connection, or association" of Tom Cruise and Marilyn Monroe with Defendants' booths. [P]laintiffs argue that this confusion leads users to utilize Defendants' booths more than Plaintiffs' booths. To support this claim, Plaintiffs hired Dr. Howard to perform a survey to determine the amount of actual confusion engendered by the pictures of these celebrities on the outside of Defendants' machines.

[D]r. Howard [c]onducted his mall study, or "field experiment." He went to NorthPark Mall and selected 224 consumers for questioning. Dr. Howard picked these individuals "to match the demographics of the users of the Portrait Studio published by Foto[ ]Fantasy on its web site, as well as the demographics of users and potential users [he] observed at the Portrait Studio" in Grapevine Mills Mall. He divided the group in half, randomly assigning each participant to either the "experimental" or the "control" group.

After dividing the participants into the experimental and control groups, Dr. Howard gave every group member an envelope that contained the survey materials. In order to "avoid any possible contamination of the process," he then stood out of sight while the respondents looked through the materials and answered the questions. The only difference between the materials given to the control group and to the experimental group was the inclusion of the Tom Cruise sketch in the experimental group's packet. "Since that would be the only factor that differentiated the two groups, any reliable differences in the answers that the two groups gave to the same questions could only be attributable to their exposure to the Tom Cruise sketch."

Based on the survey results, Dr. Howard concluded that

the Tom Cruise sketch on the outside of the Portrait Studios results in the Portrait Studios being significantly more likely to capture consumers' attention[, and] significantly more likely to arouse the interest of consumers in the Portrait Studio, and [therefore consumers are] significantly more likely to purchase portraits from the Portrait Studio. I am also of the opinion that the sketch of Tom Cruise on the Portrait Studio results in approximately half of the consuming public believing that Tom Cruise endorses or approves of the Portrait Studio. I arrive at this conclusion by deducting the 7.1% of those in the control group who said they believed it likely or very likely that Tom Cruise endorsed or approved of the Portrait Studio from the 56.3% of those in the experimental group who responded the same way. By deducting the

7.1% from the 56.3%, I conclude that the "net" or "incremental" confusion rate is 49.2%.

Defendants complain that Dr. Howard's conclusions are unreliable and should be disregarded by the Court for three reasons. First, [D]r. Howard did not utilize a proper survey universe; *i.e.,* his [s]urvey participants did not mirror the actual consumers of Defendants' product. Second, the survey included leading questions that suggested the answer to the participants and resulted in a "demand effect" that skewed the survey data. Last, Dr. Howard's methodology did not reflect actual market conditions, as he only showed the survey participants pictures of the photo booth instead of an actual photo booth.

[II]. Proper Survey Universe

Defendants argue that the survey universe [w]as improper:

Dr. Howard did not . . . conduct the survey at a location that contains a photo booth, not to mention one owned or operated by any of the Defendants. Dr. Howard chose for his test location an upscale shopping mall in north Dallas that can hardly be said to reflect the consumer population to which his study should have been geared; that is, a population which is likely to encounter and utilize a Portrait Studio owned by Defendants. . . .

On the importance of a proper survey universe, Defendants rely primarily upon *Amstar Corp. v. Domino's Pizza, Inc.,* 615 F.2d 252 (5th Cir.1980), and *Jaret International, Inc. v. Promotion in Motion, Inc.,* 826 F.Supp. 69, 73–74 (E.D.N.Y.1993). These cases do not assist in proving Defendants' point, however.

Defendants quote *Amstar* for the proposition that "one of the most important factors in assessing the validity of an opinion poll is the adequacy of the 'survey universe,' that is, the persons interviewed must adequately represent the opinions which are relevant to the litigation." *Amstar,* 615 F.2d at 264. Indeed, the *Amstar* court did reject a survey proffered by the plaintiff in that case, who manufactured and sold Domino's Sugar. The plaintiff had introduced the survey to prove that consumers believed Domino's Sugar and Domino's Pizza were made by the same company or were related in some other way. The court rested its decision on the fact that the plaintiff's survey only polled "women found at home during six daylight hours who identified themselves as the member of the household primarily responsible for grocery buying." *Id.* The court found that, "[a]s plaintiff's sugar is sold primarily in grocery stores, participants in the . . . survey would have been repeatedly exposed to plaintiff's mark, but would have had little, if any, exposure to defendants' mark. Furthermore, the survey neglected completely defendants' primary customers[:] young, single, male college students." *Id.* In contrast, Dr. Howard attempted to replicate Defendants' consumer base. The claimed defects in Dr. Howard's survey universe are nothing like the flagrant methodological errors that inhered in the *Amstar* poll.

Thus, the cases cited by Defendants do not support the argument that the Court should disregard Dr. Howard's findings based on his survey universe. Although Dr. Howard could have improved the survey by conducting it at more than one mall, this is not a cause to throw out his findings. In fact, a similar report by Dr. Howard was held to survive a *Daubert* challenge for lack of geographic diversity. *See Harolds Stores, Inc. v. Dillard Dep't Stores, Inc.*, 82 F.3d 1533 (10th Cir.1996). In that case, Harold's Stores retained Dr. Howard to conduct a survey to " 'determine whether, and to what degree, Dillard's sale of Harold's copyrighted fabric designs inflicted damages to future sales of women's and men's clothing by Harold's.' " *Id.* at 1545. Dr. Howard's entire survey universe consisted of 1,231 female undergraduates at SMU. Dillard's objected to the universe of customers surveyed, arguing that it was too narrow. The court held, however, that Dr. Howard's testimony and report were admissible, finding that survey evidence should only be excluded "when the sample is clearly not representative of the universe it is intended to reflect." *See id.* at 1544 (internal quotation marks omitted). In contrast, "[t]echnical and methodological deficiencies in the survey, including the sufficiency of the universe sampled, bear on the weight of the evidence, not on the survey's admissibility." *Id.* The situation in *Harolds Stores* is much like the one at hand: In both, Dr. Howard attempted to assemble a survey participant group that conformed to the demographics supplied by Foto Fantasy. [A]lthough Dr. Howard could have conducted the survey with a larger respondent base, these defects go towards the weight, and not the admissibility, of the evidence.

III. *The Demand Effect*

Defendants argue that Dr. Howard's survey questions were leading and therefore tainted the participants' responses. The Court finds that the survey questions were not leading, however, as they did not suggest an answer to the respondents.[4] Defendants urge that even if the questions are not leading *per se,* they still suggest a possible association between Tom Cruise and the Portrait Studios that impermissibly influenced the participants' responses. In this argument, Defendants overlook the fact that Dr. Howard utilized a control group, one of the purposes of which was to monitor any possible demand effect the questions had on the respondents. As one district court found, "[t]he control cell is supposed to 'control' extraneous factors (known as 'noise')." *Novartis Consumer Health, Inc. v. Johnson & Johnson–Merck Consumer Pharm. Co.*, 129 F.Supp.2d 351, 365 n. 10 (D.N.J.2000). It further explained that " 'the control cell functions as a baseline and provides a measure of the degree to which respondents are likely to give an answer . . . because of other factors, such as the survey's questions, the survey's procedures, . . . or some other potential influence on a respondent's answer such as pre-existing beliefs.' " *Id.* (quoting the declaration of the expert who had conducted the survey). On this basis,

---

4. Dr. Howard asked, among other things, "How likely or unlikely is it that Tom Cruise has endorsed, or approves of, the Por- trait Studio?" The participants could choose from the following answers: very likely, like- ly, unsure, unlikely, and very unlikely.

Plaintiffs argue that, "[t]o the extent that something about the procedure or the questions in Dr. Howard's survey led consumers to see an endorsement where otherwise they might not have, that factor can be eliminated by subtracting the control group result from the test group result," which Dr. Howard purportedly did in determining the "net" confusion rate of 49.2%.

The Court finds that the use of the control group could have negated any real effect the form of the questions had on the participants. The fact that about 7% of the control group found it likely or very likely that Tom Cruise endorsed Defendants' Portrait Studios does suggest that something about the questions, the form of the survey, or something in the participants' background beliefs influenced them to find a relationship between the two even though they were not shown a picture of the Tom Cruise sketch that hangs outside Defendants' photo booths. Dr. Howard's subtracting of the 7.1% attributable to "noise" in arriving at his net estimation of confusion addresses this problem so that it does not present a reason for the Court to strike Dr. Howard's report and disregard his testimony.

IV.   Market Conditions

Defendants last argue that Dr. Howard's report fails to accurately reflect market conditions because [t]he survey participants were presented with an allegedly misleading picture of the Portrait Studio instead of with the actual Portrait Studio itself. [A]lthough it is clear from Dr. Howard's description of his experiment that it did not mirror actual market conditions in every possible way, Dr. Howard attempted, in his materials, to explain to the participants the mindset they should have in evaluating Defendants' photo booths. For example, the instructions to the questions told participants, "[w]hen answering these questions, assume that you were walking by a Portrait Studio." Dr. Howard also attempted to explain to the participants how the pictures of Tom Cruise and Marilyn Monroe fit into the overall design of the photo booths, stating that "[t]his 8 1/2 x 11 sketch is displayed on the outside of the Studio as an example of the Studio's work."

[I]n conclusion, the Court finds that Defendants' criticism of Dr. Howard's survey methodology, although it may be persuasive, goes only to the weight, and not the admissibility, of the evidence. Therefore, Defendants' Motion to Strike Dr. Howard's expert report and trial testimony is DENIED.

———

PHARMACIA CORP. v. ALCON LABORATORIES, INC.

United States District Court, District of New Jersey, 2002.
201 F.Supp. 2d 335.

■ Bassler, District Judge.

Pharmacia initiated this civil action on March 30, 2001 under the Lanham (Trademark) Act of 1946 and New Jersey statutory and common law.

On April 16, 2001, Pharmacia moved for a preliminary injunction to enjoin defendant Alcon from infringing [P]harmacia's federally registered Xalatan trademark in connection with Alcon's use of the name Travatan for the sale of a prostaglandin-based product used for the treatment of the eye disease glaucoma.

[T]he Diamond Survey

Alcon produced evidence in the form of a survey of the relevant population, that the marketplace is not confused. A well-designed survey of ophthalmologists and optometrists conducted by Prof. Shari Seidman Diamond shows a net confusion rate of 1.5%. (there is "no evidence that the name of Alcon's product Travatan is likely to cause confusion with the name of Pharmacia's product Xalatan in the relevant population," *i.e.,* ophthalmologists and optometrists). Dr. Diamond also testified at the evidentiary hearing. The Court found her to be a very credible witness.

Professor Diamond is a professor of law and psychology at Northwestern University School of Law and a senior research fellow at the American Bar Foundation. She is the author of the *Reference Guide to Survey Research* contained in the Federal Judicial Center's *Reference Guide on Scientific Evidence* (1994, 2000), as well as a similar chapter in West Publishing's four volume treatise, *Modern Scientific Evidence* (1997, 2000), and several other well-respected articles in the field.

Professor Diamond chose to survey a nationwide population of ophthalmologists and optometrists because they are the market gatekeepers with respect to the prescription glaucoma medications at issue in this case. Ophthalmologists and optometrists thus make the ultimate determination as to which medications pharmacists will dispense and end-users—patients—will receive.

[I]n order to ensure that the population surveyed was representative of glaucoma prescribers, Professor Diamond considered several lists of doctors from which to draw interviewees, including the membership list for the American Ophthalmology Association. Professor Diamond ultimately used a list assembled by the National Data Center because it is widely used for research purposes within the pharmaceutical industry and because it provided enough information about potential respondents' practice size and years of experience to allow for a stratified random sample.

Because doctors are a particularly busy population of potential respondents, Professor Diamond arranged for each one to receive an advance letter, as well as follow-up phone calls, to schedule interviews at a convenient time.

The Diamond Survey tested for product source confusion. [T]here were two cells in the survey: (1) a test cell of 200 prescribers that used a Travatan advertisement as the stimulus; and (2) a control cell, also of 200 prescribers, that used an identical Lumigan ® advertisement as the stimulus. The stimulus was designed to focus the respondent's attention primarily on the name of the product.

The questions that Professor Diamond selected for the survey ("What company do you believe puts out the product whose advertisement you just saw?;" "Please tell me whether or not you believe the company whose advertisement you just saw puts out any other medications for the eye;" and "Please tell me whether or not you believe that the company whose advertisement you just saw needs authorization, permission or approval from some other company in order to put out the product advertised."), are a standard type and format of questions used to gauge confusion in trademark cases. Pharmacia's survey expert, Walter McCullough, used virtually identical questions in a trademark confusion survey he designed in a prior infringement case.

Five percent of the test cell respondents confused the source of Xalatan ® and Travatan and 3.5% of control cell respondents confused the source of Xalatan ® and Lumigan ®, yielding net confusion of 1.5%.

Professor Diamond selected the survey firm D.S. Howard & Associates ("D.S. Howard") to conduct the survey because it specializes in medical surveys and medical marketing research, fields surveys for pharmaceutical companies for approximately 60% of its work and is staffed by surveyors with an academic background and a reputation for attention to detail.

Interviewers were instructed to record absolute and accurate verbatim responses and capture every word and sound uttered by respondents, including the "humms" and "ahhs," even if doing so meant simultaneously transcribing the responses in less than perfect penmanship.

[A] review of all the questionnaires, as well as monitoring reports and tapes of the interviews, confirms that the responses were recorded accurately and completely. [T]he raw data collected for this survey, in the form of the verbatim responses of doctors, was preserved and was made available to Pharmacia and the Court for review.

[T]he Court is aware that Pharmacia is not legally required to conduct a confusion survey. But under the circumstances of this case, Pharmacia's failure to conduct any confusion survey weighs against its request for a preliminary injunction. Such a failure, particularly when the trademark owner is financially able, justifies an inference "that the plaintiff believes the results of the survey will be unfavorable." *Charles Jacquin et Cie, Inc. v. Destileria Serralles, Inc.*, 921 F.2d 467, 475 (3d Cir.1990).

Pharmacia's attempt to explain away its decision not to conduct a confusion survey (economics) further supports the appropriateness of such an inference, in light of the fact that from July 2000 forward, Pharmacia conducted numerous surveys concerning the Travatan mark, but never attempted to assess whether Travatan was likely to cause confusion with Xalatan. Moreover, the results of that research show that over 95% of ophthalmologists were aware of Travatan and Xalatan as distinct products. The enormous sums Pharmacia invested in market research to prepare for the Travatan launch stand in stark contrast to its failure to conduct a confusion survey here, and fully warrant a negative inference regarding likelihood of confusion.

[P]rofessor Diamond's well-designed survey of ophthalmologists and optometrists, showing a net confusion rate of 1.5%, provides further evidence to support the Court's conclusion that no confusion is likely. *Henri's Food Prods. Co. v. Kraft, Inc.*, 717 F.2d 352, 358–59 (7th Cir.1983) (holding that 7.6% confusion finding is "a factor weighing against infringement"); *Pfizer Inc. v. Astra Pharm. Prods., Inc.*, 858 F.Supp. 1305, 1326 (S.D.N.Y. 1994) (adjusted confusion rate of 7.27% in a survey is "low" and insufficient evidence of likelihood of confusion); *see also* 5 McCarthy § 32:188, at 32–311 (4th ed. 2001) (generally, "figures below 20 percent become problematic because they can only be viewed against the background of other evidence . . .").

[P]harmacia's Opinions Regarding Likelihood of Confusion

Because Pharmacia has no marketplace evidence of likely or actual confusion, it emphasizes evidence in the form of expert opinion testimony. This evidence is insufficient to overcome the marketplace evidence that confusion is unlikely. Apart from consumer surveys, "[L]ay or even expert opinion about the likelihood of confusion is inadmissible or entitled to little weight." Richard L. Kirkpatrick, *Likelihood of Confusion in Trademark Law*, § 1.8.c, at 1–45 (PLI 1995); *Barnes Group*, 793 F.Supp. at 1293, 1301–02 (expert opinion that confusion was likely, offered without any supporting empirical data or marketplace observations, could not be relied on).

The opinions of Dr. Eisenberg and Mr. Di Domizio with regard to the likelihood of confusion between Travatan and Xalatan are based primarily on a subjective evaluation of the marks in light of their experience in the pharmaceutical industry (Di Domizio) or as an ophthalmologist (Eisenberg). There are no reported trademark cases in which a court has based its findings of a likelihood of confusion or dilution on the types of "opinions" on which Pharmacia relies. The bases for these opinions stand in stark contrast to the survey conducted by Professor Shari S. Diamond, J.D., Ph. D., which demonstrates persuasively a confusion rate of 1.5%.

[C]ONCLUSION

For the reasons discussed, the plaintiff's motion for a preliminary injunction is denied.

————

SMITH v. WAL–MART STORES, INC.

United States District Court, Northern District of Georgia, Atlanta Division, 2008.
537 F. Supp. 2d 1302.

■ TIMOTHY C. BATTEN, SR., DISTRICT JUDGE.

This action arises from the contention of Defendant Wal–Mart Stores, Inc. that its registered trademarks "WALMART"; "WAL–MART"; and "WAL★MART"; its registered word mark "ALWAYS LOW PRICES. AL-

WAYS"; and its "well-known smiley face mark" were infringed by Plaintiff Charles Smith's anti-Wal–Mart merchandise. Smith petitions the Court to declare his activities legal so that he may resume them without fear of incurring liability for damages; Wal–Mart counterclaims for an award of ownership of Smith's Wal–Mart-related domain names, an injunction precluding Smith from making commercial use of any designation beginning with the prefix "WAL," and an award of nominal damages.

[B]ackground

Smith is an avid and vocal critic of Wal–Mart. He believes that Wal–Mart has a destructive effect on communities, treats workers badly, and has a damaging influence on the United States as a whole—an influence so detrimental to the United States and its communities that Smith likens it to that of the Nazi regime. With the goals of stimulating discussions about Wal–Mart and getting others of like mind to join him in expressing strongly negative views about Wal–Mart, Smith created various designs and slogans that incorporated the word "Walocaust," a word Smith invented by combining the first three letters of Wal–Mart's name with the last six letters of the word "holocaust."

Smith created four basic Walocaust designs. One design depicted a blue stylized bird modeled to resemble a Nazi eagle grasping a yellow smiley face in the same manner that a Nazi eagle is typically depicted grasping a swastika. Above the bird image, the word "WAL★OCAUST" was printed in a blue font comparable to that commonly used by Wal–Mart. Two designs were text only: one design read, "I ♥ WAL★OCAUST[.] They have FAMILY VALUES and their ALCOHOL, TOBACCO and FIREARMS are 20% OFF"; and another design read, "WAL★OCAUST[.] Come for the LOW prices[,] stay for the KNIFE fights." The fourth was a graphical design that depicted the word WAL★OCAUST on a Wal–Mart-like storefront that also included the Nazi eagle image, a poster advertising family values and discounted alcohol, tobacco and firearms, and other images commenting negatively on Wal–Mart.

[S]mith arranged for some of his designs to be printed on t-shirts and other items like mugs, underwear, camisoles, teddy bears, bumper stickers and bibs that could be purchased through www.Cafe Press.com. He also placed text on his CafePress account home page that included harsh statements about Wal–Mart, such as "Walocaust: The World is Our Labor Camp. Walmart Sucks."

[W]al–Mart wrote to Smith and to CafePress, asserting that Smith's Walocaust CafePress webpage was violating Wal–Mart's trademark rights, and demanding that they cease selling all products imprinted with his various anti-Wal–Mart designs. Wal–Mart also objected to Smith's registration and use of the domain name www.walocaust.com, demanding that Smith cease using the domain name and transfer ownership of it to Wal–

Mart. In response, CafePress removed all of Smith's Wal–Mart-related merchandise from his online store so that only non-Wal–Mart-related merchandise remained available at www.cafepress.com/walocaust.

[W]al–Mart concedes that it has no marketplace evidence of actual consumer confusion. Instead, it presents [a] consumer research stud[y] conducted by Dr. Jacob Jacoby that purport[s] to prove that consumer confusion [is] likely.

The Jacoby Report

[D]eeming it impractical to test all of Smith's designs, Jacoby chose instead to test two products as representative of all of Smith's allegedly infringing products—the white t-shirt with the word "WAL★OCAUST" in blue font over the Nazi eagle clutching a yellow smiley face, and another white t-shirt that depicted the word "WAL–QAEDA" in a blue font as part of the phrase "SUPPORT OUR TROOPS. BOYCOTT WAL–QAEDA." [J]acoby engaged a market research firm to test each of the t-shirt designs in [a] "website" study intended to test for point-of-sale confusion.

The market research company conducted the stud[y] in a mall-inter-cept format. The company's researchers would approach people who appeared to be thirteen years old or older and ask a series of screening questions. [I]f the respondent met the qualifications, he or she was asked to go with the researcher to the mall's enclosed interviewing facility for a five-minute interview.[19]

[T]he respondents were exposed to a simulation of Smith's Walocaust CafePress homepage, [or] his Wal–Qaeda CafePress homepage.[20] [I]n each of the simulations, all of the hyperlinks were removed from the homepages except for the one hyperlink associated with the t-shirt that Jacoby had decided to test.

Jacoby directed the interviewers to begin each website interview by providing a URL to the respondent and asking the respondent to imagine that the URL was a search term the respondent had heard or seen somewhere and wanted to look up on the Internet. The interviewer would then have the respondent sit at a computer and type the URL into the browser. The URL would take the respondent to the simulated home page for testing.

The interviewer would then direct the respondent to look at the screen and scroll down the page "as [he or she] normally would" and click through to the first t-shirt on the screen. The respondent was then directed to click on the "view larger" box and look at the shirt as though he or she "found it interesting and [was] considering whether or not to order it...." The

19. The screening questionnaire provided to the Court indicates that the respondents who then participated in the surveys were given a monetary reward. Neither Jacoby's report nor any of the supporting survey documents disclosed the amount of the reward.

20. The simulations were reproduced on a compact disc; the respondents did not view Smith's actual web pages on the Internet.

interviewer would then ask the respondent [t]he consumer confusion questions.*

In order to be tallied as "confused," the respondent had to meet two tests. First, the respondent had to indicate either that the shirt came from Wal–Mart (first confusion series), came from a company that had some business connection or relationship with Wal–Mart (second confusion series), or came from a source that required or obtained permission from Wal–Mart (third confusion series). Second, the respondent had to indicate that his or her reason for that understanding was either because of the prefix "Wal," the name (or equivalent), the smiley face, or the star after the prefix "Wal." Thus, a respondent who believed that there was a connection between Wal–Mart and the t-shirt that he or she was shown but who did not mention the prefix "Wal," the name (or equivalent), the smiley face, or the star, would not be counted as "confused."

[There were] 287 reported responses to the [s]tudy. Jacoby reported that the survey reflected high levels of consumer confusion. [H]e claimed that the "website" study indicated a likelihood of confusion in almost forty-one percent of the respondents.[21]

[E]videntiary Objections

Whether a given survey constitutes acceptable evidence depends on the survey's ability to satisfy the demands of Federal Rule of Evidence 703, which requires consideration of the "validity of the techniques employed." 233–34 Fed. Jud. Ctr., Reference Manual on Sci. Evidence (2d ed.2002) (explaining that in the context of surveys for litigation purposes, "[t]he inquiry under Rule 703 [, which] focuses on whether facts or data are 'of a type reasonably relied upon by experts in the particular field in forming opinions or inferences upon the subject' . . . becomes, 'Was the . . . survey conducted in accordance with generally accepted survey principles, and were the results used in a statistically correct way?' ").

* [Ed Note: Elsewhere in the opinion, the Court described the consumer confusion questions:

> The first set of questions tested for confusion as to source. The interviewer would ask "which company or store" the respondent thought "put out" the shirt, and if the respondent named a company or store, the interviewer then asked what about the shirt made the respondent think the shirt was "put out" by that company or store. The second set of questions, which dealt with confusion as to connection or relationship, asked the respondent whether the company or store that "put out" the shirt had some "business connection or relationship with another company" and if so, with what company. The respondent was then asked why he or she believed the companies had a business connection or relationship. A third set of questions, aimed at testing for confusion as to authorization or sponsorship, asked whether the company that "put out" the shirt needed permission from another company to do so, and if so, which company. Finally, [h]e or she was then asked what the shirt made him or her "think of" and then "which company or store" the shirt brought to mind.]

21. Jacoby arrived at these numbers by averaging the net survey results for the Wal-ocaust and Wal–Qaeda t-shirts.

[S]mith cites several grounds for excluding the Jacoby survey. He argues that the survey is inadmissible because it (1) failed to identify the relevant consumer universe or used a consumer universe that was substantially overbroad; (2) failed to replicate shopping conditions as consumers would encounter them in the marketplace; [and] (3) was improperly leading. [S]mith further argues that even if the Court admits the survey, its consideration should be limited to only the two tested designs, despite Jacoby's claim that they are representative of all the designs Wal–Mart seeks to enjoin.

Web–Related Challenges

In undertaking to demonstrate likelihood of confusion in a trademark infringement case by use of survey evidence, the "appropriate universe should include a fair sampling of those purchasers most likely to partake of the alleged infringer's goods or services." Amstar Corp. v. Domino's Pizza, Inc., 615 F.2d 252, 264 (5th Cir.1980). Selection of the proper universe is one of the most important factors in assessing the validity of a survey and the weight that it should receive because "the persons interviewed must adequately represent the opinions which are relevant to the litigation." Id.

[S]mith hired Dr. Alan Jay Rosenblatt as a rebuttal witness to point out Internet-related deficiencies in Jacoby's survey methodology—particularly deficiencies in universe selection and replication of marketplace conditions—that he claims resulted from Jacoby's erroneous assumptions about how people reach and interact with websites. Smith uses Rosenblatt's expertise on Internet user experience and navigation to support his *Daubert* argument that because Jacoby surveyed an improperly broad universe and his survey design did not approximate the actual consumer marketplace experience, the Jacoby studies are legally insufficient to prove consumer confusion. [T]hus, Smith argues, the studies should be afforded little, if any, evidentiary value.

Survey Universe

The appropriate universe in this case is the consumers most likely to purchase Smith's Walocaust and Wal–Qaeda merchandise. *See Amstar Corp.,* 615 F.2d at 264. To qualify for [J]acoby's survey[], the respondent had to be over thirteen years of age and had to have in the past year bought, or would in the coming year consider buying, bumper stickers, t-shirts or coffee mugs with words, symbols or designs on them. [T]he respondent must also have (1) used the Internet in the past month to search for information about products or services and (2) either (a) in the past year used the Internet to buy or search for information about bumper stickers, t-shirts or coffee mugs with words, symbols or designs on them, or (b) in the coming year would consider buying over the Internet bumper stickers, t-shirts or coffee mugs with words, symbols or designs on them. Wal–Mart maintains that Jacoby's universe selection was proper. Smith counters that it was overly broad.

Although the universe Jacoby selected would include purchasers of Smith's Walocaust or Wal–Qaeda merchandise, the Court finds that it is significantly overbroad. Because Smith's merchandise was available only through his CafePress webstores and the links to his CafePress webstores from his Walocaust and Wal–Qaeda websites, it is likely that only a small percentage of the consumers in the universe selected by Jacoby would be potential purchasers of Smith's products. A survey respondent who purchases bumper stickers, t-shirts or coffee mugs with words, symbols or designs on them may buy such merchandise because the imprint represents his or her school, company, favorite sports team, cartoon character, social group, or any of hundreds of other interests or affiliations; he or she may have no interest at all in purchasing merchandise containing messages about Wal–Mart, pro or con. The respondent may buy from brick-and-mortar stores or well-known retailers with Internet storefronts without being aware of Smith's website or CafePress, or may have little interest in buying such merchandise over the Internet at all. Therefore, a respondent who clearly falls within Jacoby's survey universe may nevertheless have no potential to purchase Smith's imprinted products.

Shopping Experience

To be valid for the purposes of demonstrating actual confusion in a trademark infringement suit, it is necessary for a survey's protocol to take into account marketplace conditions and typical consumer behavior so that the survey may as accurately as possible measure the relevant "thought processes of consumers encountering the disputed mark ... as they would in the marketplace." Simon Prop. Group, 104 F.Supp.2d at 1038.

Smith contends that Jacoby's point-of-purchase study, which purported to measure consumer confusion over merchandise that Smith sold exclusively online, was improperly designed because it failed to take into account typical consumer Internet behavior.

[J]acoby's point-of-purchase survey called for interviewers to provide each respondent with specific "search terms" that would take the respondent to a simulation of one of Smith's websites. The respondent was asked to pretend that the resulting web page was of interest and to act accordingly (looking at the page and scrolling through it as the respondent would "normally" do), and then was directed to scroll down the page, below the first screen, and click on a specific t-shirt link. The respondent was not asked what message he or she took from the website or whether the website was in fact of interest. The survey protocol also gave the respondent no choice but to scroll down to the next screen and click on the t-shirt link, the only live link in the simulation.

In presenting Smith's website and directing the survey respondents to click on one specific t-shirt link, Jacoby's survey design presumed that all consumers who might be interested in a printed t-shirt, mug or bumper sticker would be equally likely to happen across Smith's designs, regardless of the respondent's level of interest in the messages on Smith's webpage.

Although, as Wal–Mart points out, it is possible that some consumers may view web pages randomly and may scroll through and clink on links on pages that are not of interest to them, the Court finds that the survey protocol did not sufficiently reflect actual marketplace conditions or typical consumer shopping behavior and therefore was unlikely to have elicited a shopping mindset that would have allowed Jacoby to accurately gauge actual consumer confusion.

Because Smith's merchandise was available only through his CafePress webstores and the links to his CafePress webstores from his Walocaust and Wal–Qaeda websites, it is unlikely that many consumers randomly happen across Smith's products. According to Rosenblatt's uncontroverted testimony, people do not come to websites randomly, and they do not move within websites randomly. A great majority of Internet users arrive at a particular website after searching specific terms via an Internet search engine or by following links from another website. The user makes a judgment based on contextual cues—what is shown about a prospective website from the text of a search result or what is said about a prospective website in the hyperlinked words and surrounding text of the website currently being viewed—in determining where to surf next. He moves from website to website, he moves within websites, and he performs actions such as signing a petition—or buying a product—by making choices based on what he sees and whether what he sees leads him to believe that going to the next page or following a link to another website will bring him to something he is interested in seeing, doing or buying.

In the marketplace, the visitor would be presented with a screen full of Smith's anti-Wal–Mart messages. Consumers who were interested in the messages on Smith's web pages would be motivated to choose the links that would eventually lead to his products, while those who were uninterested in Smith's messages would simply leave the page. Because the survey protocol directed the respondents to "pretend" to be interested in Smith's anti-Wal–Mart homepages and then directed them to click on a specific link, there is no assurance that the respondent actually read the homepage or would have been interested enough in it to be motivated to click on the t-shirt link. [A] reasonable person who was considering buying a t-shirt that references Al–Qaeda or the Holocaust would likely read the associated webpage at least well enough to see the harsh criticism of Wal–Mart.

[L]eading Questions

Smith [a]rgues that the wording of Jacoby's confusion questions was improperly leading. Although the challenged t-shirts were created and offered for sale by Charles Smith, an individual, via his CafePress webstore, the survey asked about sponsorship only in the context of companies or stores, such as in the survey's lead question, which asked, "[W]hich company or store do you think puts out this shirt?" Smith contends that this wording suggested to the respondent that the interviewer was looking for the name of a company or store, which would lead the respondent away from the answer that the shirt was put out by an individual who was criticizing a company. Wal–Mart counters that because Smith's merchandise was sold through his CafePress webstores, the questions were accurately worded and thus not misleading.

The Court agrees with Smith that the disputed questions improperly led respondents to limit their answers to companies or stores. Though Smith did offer his merchandise through his CafePress webstore, as Wal–Mart argues, the Court finds this characterization disingenuous; the party Wal–Mart sued for offering the Walocaust and Wal–Qaeda merchandise for sale is not a company or a store, but instead Charles Smith, an individual. Furthermore, Wal–Mart has failed to point to any authority supporting the use of the "company or store" language in a consumer "likelihood of confusion" apparel survey or any such surveys previously conducted by Jacoby. Thus, the Court must consider this weakness in determining the admissibility or evidentiary weight to be accorded the survey.

Testing Stimuli

Smith also argues that the Jacoby survey results should not be presumed to represent consumer reaction to any of the challenged merchandise that was not actually tested. Jacoby limited his surveys to testing two specific t-shirts (the Wal★ocaust smiley eagle shirt and the "SUPPORT OUR TROOPS" Wal–Qaeda shirt), and the conclusions stated in his report were narrowly drawn to refer to the tested t-shirts. At his deposition, however, he stated that because the tested shirts were "reasonably representative" of all the shirts that included the prefix "Wal" and the star, as in Wal★ocaust, or the prefix "Wal" and a hyphen, as in Wal–Qaeda, his results could be extrapolated from the tested t-shirts to all of the challenged t-shirts that shared those features.

[T]he Court finds that test results from one Walocaust or Wal–Qaeda t-shirt provide no data upon which to estimate consumer confusion regarding another Walocaust or Wal–Qaeda t-shirt. A consumer confused about the sponsorship of a shirt that says "SUPPORT OUR TROOPS [.] BOYCOTT WAL–QAEDA" may easily grasp the commentary in the more straightforwardly derogatory "WAL–QAEDA[.] Freedom Haters ALWAYS" concept. Similarly, a consumer confused over the sponsorship of a "Walocaust" shirt paired with an eagle and a smiley face might have a crystal clear understanding of the word's meaning when it is superimposed over a drawing of a Wal–Mart-like building paired with a sign that advertises family values and discounted alcohol, firearms, and tobacco or when it is presented along with the additional text "The World is Our Labor Camp. Walmart Sucks." As a result, this weakness will also impact the Court's assessment of the survey's evidentiary value.

Admissibility

Having identified numerous substantial flaws in Jacoby's survey, the Court must now determine whether the flaws limit the survey's evidentiary weight or are so substantial as to render the survey irrelevant or unreliable and therefore inadmissible under Federal Rule of Evidence 403, 702, or

703. Courts in the Eleventh Circuit typically decline to exclude likelihood of confusion surveys and instead consider a survey's technical flaws when determining the amount of evidentiary weight to accord the survey. Consequently, although this is a close case, the Court concludes that the better option is to admit the survey evidence and to consider the survey's flaws in determining the evidentiary weight to assign the survey in the likelihood of confusion analysis.

The Court finds, however, that because the survey tested only the "SUPPORT OUR TROOPS[.] BOYCOTT WAL–QAEDA" t-shirt and the Walocaust eagle t-shirt, it has no relevance to any of Smith's other Wal–Mart-related concepts. [T]he study is admissible only as to the two concepts that Jacoby actually tested. Even with regard to the tested concepts, the Court finds that the survey was so flawed that it does not create a genuine issue of material fact. Jacoby surveyed an overbroad universe, failed to adequately replicate the shopping experience, and asked leading questions.

[I]n sum, the Court is convinced that no fair-minded jury could find that a reasonable consumer is likely to be confused by the challenged marks. As a result, the Court GRANTS summary judgment to Smith on Wal–Mart's claims of trademark infringement [p]ractices. [S]mith may maintain his domain names and websites. He may also resume offering for sale via his Walocaust and Wal–Qaeda CafePress webstores his parodic WALOCAUST [and] WAL–QAEDA [n]ovelty merchandise.

———

MANUAL FOR COMPLEX LITIGATION (4TH ED. 2004)
Federal Judicial Center.

Parties who propose to offer sampling or survey evidence may want to consider whether to disclose details of the proposed sampling or survey methods to the opposing parties before the work is done (including the specific questions that will be asked, the introductory statements or instructions that will be given, and other controls to be used in the interrogation process). Objections can then be raised promptly and corrective measures taken before the survey is completed. A meeting of the parties' experts can expedite the resolution of problems affecting admissibility.

———

REFERENCE GUIDE ON SURVEY RESEARCH
Shari Seidman Diamond.
In Reference Manual on Scientific Evidence (2d ed. 2000).

The questions listed in this reference guide are intended to assist judges in identifying, narrowing, and addressing issues bearing on the adequacy of surveys either offered as evidence or proposed as a method for developing information. These questions can be (1) raised from the bench during a pretrial proceeding to determine the admissibility of the survey evidence; (2) presented to the contending experts before trial for their joint identification of disputed and undisputed issues; (3) presented to counsel with the expectation that the issues will be addressed during the examination of the experts at trial; or (4) raised in bench trials when a motion for a preliminary injunction is made to help the judge evaluate what weight, if any, the survey should be given. These questions are intended to improve the utility of cross-examination by counsel, where appropriate, not to replace it.

Purpose and Design of the Survey

A.   Was the Survey Designed to Address Relevant Questions?

B.   Was Participation in the Design, Administration, and Interpretation of the Survey Appropriately Controlled to Ensure the Objectivity of the Survey?

C.   Are the Experts Who Designed, Conducted, or Analyzed the Survey Appropriately Skilled and Experienced?

D.   Are the Experts Who Will Testify About Surveys Conducted by Others Appropriately Skilled and Experienced?

Population Definition and Sampling

A.   Was an Appropriate Universe or Population Identified?

B.   Did the Sampling Frame Approximate the Population?

C.   How Was the Sample Selected to Approximate the Relevant Characteristics of the Population?

D.   Was the Level of Nonresponse Sufficient to Raise Questions About the Representativeness of the Sample? If So, What Is the Evidence That Nonresponse Did Not Bias the Results of the Survey?

E.   What Procedures Were Used to Reduce the Likelihood of a Biased Sample?

F.   What Precautions Were Taken to Ensure That Only Qualified Respondents Were Included in the Survey?

Survey Questions and Structure

A.   Were Questions on the Survey Framed to Be Clear, Precise, and Unbiased?

B.   Were Filter Questions Provided to Reduce Guessing?

C.   Did the Survey Use Open–Ended or Closed–Ended Questions? How Was the Choice in Each Instance Justified?

D.   If Probes Were Used to Clarify Ambiguous or Incomplete Answers, What Steps Were Taken to Ensure That the Probes Were Not Leading and Were Administered in a Consistent Fashion?

E.   What Approach Was Used to Avoid or Measure Potential Order or Context Effects?

F.   If the Survey Was Designed to Test a Causal Proposition, Did the Survey Include an Appropriate Control Group or Question?

G.   What Limitations Are Associated with the Mode of Data Collection Used in the Survey?

    1.   In-person interviews

    2.   Telephone surveys

    3.   Mail surveys

    4.   Internet surveys

Surveys Involving Interviewers

A.   Were the Interviewers Appropriately Selected and Trained?

B.   What Did the Interviewers Know About the Survey and Its Sponsorship?

C.   What Procedures Were Used to Ensure and Determine That the Survey Was Administered to Minimize Error and Bias?

Data Entry and Grouping of Responses

A.   What Was Done to Ensure That the Data Were Recorded Accurately?

B.   What Was Done to Ensure That the Grouped Data Were Classified Consistently and Accurately?

Disclosure and Reporting

A.   When Was Information About the Survey Methodology and Results Disclosed?

B.   Does the Survey Report Include Complete and Detailed Information on All Relevant Characteristics?

C.   In Surveys of Individuals, What Measures Were Taken to Protect the Identities of Individual Respondents?

———

McCARTHY ON TRADEMARKS AND UNFAIR COMPETITION (4TH ED. 1996)

J. Thomas McCarthy.

It is notoriously easy for one survey expert to appear to tear apart the methodology of a survey taken by another. [O]ne must keep in mind that there is no such thing as a "perfect" survey. The nature of the beast is that it is a sample, albeit a scientifically constructed one. One must remain cognizant of the fact that, as Judge Anderson said of the survey evidence in the famous "Thermos" case, "any conclusion in this area cannot be reduced to a figure of unimpeachable accuracy but must, at best, be an approximation.''[8] Like any scientific method related to statistics in the social sciences, every survey, no matter how carefully constructed and conducted, has some potential flaws somewhere. The proper approach is to view such evidence with some understanding of the difficulty of devising and running a survey and to use any technical defects only to lessen evidentiary weight, not to reject the results out-of-hand.

[P]robably, a part of a lingering judicial skepticism about survey evidence can be laid at the feet of parties and their attorneys who, in a desperate search for *some kind* of evidence, offer, with a straight face, a haphazard, self-serving "survey." It may not be surprising that many judges view such purported "scientific evidence" with distaste. They know that the techniques of testing and sampling buyer reactions have been developed to a fairly high degree of accuracy. Thus, there is no real excuse for a biased survey which attempts to measure buyer reaction by means of leading or irrelevant questions asked in an environment far removed from the marketplace. The reason, of course, that accurate and scientifically precise surveys are not always offered is that they are costly. Perhaps the best that can be said is that no survey at all is better than a survey obtained "on the cheap." As weak arguments detract from even a strong case, a weak survey may detract from even the strongest case of trademark infringement.

––––––––

SOCIAL FACTS: SCIENTIFIC METHODOLOGY AS LEGAL PRECEDENT

Laurens Walker and John Monahan.
76 California Law Review 877 (1988).

Under the Federal Rules of Evidence, the analysis of the admissibility of social science research to prove a case-specific fact begins—and usually ends—with the question of "relevance." According to Rule 401:

"Relevant evidence" means evidence having any tendency to make the existence of any fact that is of consequence to the determination of the action more probable or less probable than it would be without the evidence.

There are two components to this definition: To be relevant, evidence must bear on a fact that is "of consequence" to the case, and must make that fact "more probable or less probable" than it would otherwise be.

[A.] Materiality

While it was once mired in the strictures of pleading, the question of whether evidence is "of consequence" or "material" to a fact in issue is now generally treated as a component of relevance. Materiality concerns

8. American Thermos Products Co. v.   134 U.S.P.Q. (BNA) 98 (D.Conn. 1962).]
Aladdin Industries, Inc. [207 F.Supp. 9, 21,

the relation between the proposition that the evidence is offered to demonstrate and the factual issues in the case. If the evidence is offered to prove a proposition that is not at issue, the evidence is immaterial and therefore irrelevant.

Whether proffered evidence is material depends upon the legal issue before the court: "[w]hat is 'in issue,' that is, within the range of the litigated controversy, is ... controlled by the substantive law."[32] In the context of social fact evidence, this means that even research flawlessly executed is inadmissible if the substantive law governing the case does not put in issue the fact that the research seeks to establish.

Questions of materiality are questions of substantive law, not questions of social science. Even without inquiring into the empirical merits of the evidence, it is proper for a court to exclude social science research that does not purport to demonstrate a fact with which the substantive law is concerned. Since judicial decisions based on the materiality prong of Rule 401 interpret the substantive law governing a case, they have the same precedential value as any other decisions of substantive law. Indeed, decisions on the materiality of social science evidence have uniformly been treated as precedent by subsequent courts.

[B.] Probative Value

To be relevant, evidence must make the existence of a fact "more probable or less probable" than it was before the evidence was offered. This component of relevance is usually referred to as "probative value" or "logical relevance." Evidence is logically relevant "only when the probability of finding that evidence given the truth of some hypothesis at issue in the case differs from the probability of finding the evidence given the falsity of the hypothesis at issue."[39] In the context of social science evidence, this means that even if the research directly addresses a fact of central concern to the substantive law, it will not be admitted unless the research data provides insight into the likelihood that the fact exists.

———

NOTES

1. Standard of Appellate Review. In Amstar Corporation v. Domino's Pizza, the Fifth Circuit applied the "clear error" standard for reviewing the trial court determination of consumer confusion. "Clear error" is the standard appellate courts normally use whenever they review a trial court determination of "adjudicative" fact. The reasons for this deference to trial courts have to do both with efficiency—so that appellate courts do not have to spend their time adjudicating factual issues already decided—and with accuracy—since the trial court actually observed the witnesses' testimony and the appellate court has only the "cold record" on which to rely, the

32. See C. McCormick, McCormick on Evidence 541 (3d ed. 1984).

39. Lempert, Modeling Relevance, 75 Mich.L.Rev. 1021, 1026 (1977).

trial court is generally in a better position to judge the facts. An appellate court makes its own findings of fact only to the extent that it determines what the facts are *not*—that the trial court was "clearly erroneous" in determining the facts based on the evidence in the record. In *Amstar*, for example, the appellate court held that the trial court was clearly in error when it held that the survey done by Amstar demonstrated consumer confusion between Domino's pizza and Domino's sugar.

2. Materiality and Probative Value. The "materiality" of social science evidence in trademark litigation is usually plain: the surveys address consumer confusion, which, given the language of the Lanham Act, is "of consequence" to the determination of trademark infringement. The dispute typically is whether the survey has probative value, that is, whether the survey makes it "more probable or less probable" that consumers are in fact confused. In La Victoria Foods v. Curtice–Burns, however, the court ruled that the defendant's survey—in which subjects were seated at a table on which there was a bottle of LA SUPREMA salsa and asked "What is the name of this product?"—was immaterial: "The defendant's survey did not measure likelihood of confusion with plaintiff's product. It was, if anything, a measure of the respondent's ability to read the defendant's label."

3. Admissibility versus Weight of the Evidence. The court in *Zippo* distinguished the "admissibility" of the survey evidence from the "weight" to be accorded it in determining consumer confusion. The court in *KIS* and the commentary by McCarthy also raise this distinction. According to Federal Rule of Evidence 401, evidence is relevant if it has "any tendency" to make a material fact "more probable or less probable than it would be without the evidence." According to Rule 402, "[a]ll relevant evidence is admissible" (unless its admission violates some other laws or rules; see Appendix A). Therefore, it is not necessary for social science evidence to be determinative of a fact at issue in the case, or even to make the existence of a fact such as consumer confusion "more likely than not," for the evidence to be admitted. As long as it has "any" tendency to demonstrate the existence of consumer confusion, the evidence is relevant and therefore presumptively admissible. While a particular survey may be admissible because it has at least some tendency to demonstrate a fact like consumer confusion, the methodology of the survey, or the way that the methodology was carried out, may be sufficiently flawed that the survey evidence should not be given much "weight" in determining whether consumers are likely to be confused.

4. Other Uses of Social Science Evidence in Trademark Law. The use of social science evidence in trademark law is by no means limited to the determination of consumer confusion. The Lanham Act also prohibits the granting of a trademark to a "generic" term, and allows for the cancellation of a valid trademark to a term that becomes generic. A generic term is the common name for a type of product made by many companies, "the name of a particular genus or class of which an individual article or service is but a member." Vision Center v. Opticks, Inc., 596 F.2d 111, 115 (5th Cir. 1979). Examples of terms that have been held to be generic are aspirin, cellophane, escalator, and thermos. Examples of terms that have been challenged as generic but have been held by courts to be valid trademarks are COKE, LEVI'S, POLAROID, and TEFLON. Social science evidence is often used to determine whether a term is the common designation for a type of product made by many companies, or whether it is associated by the public with a particular product or producer. For an account of this and other uses of social science evidence in trademark litigation—including the "secondary meaning" that can be acquired by "descriptive" terms—see K. Port, Trademark Law and Policy (2d ed. 2008).

5. Consumer Perceptions and Deceptive Advertising. Issues analogous to consumer confusion in Lanham Act trademark cases also arise in Lanham Act deceptive advertising cases under 15 U.S.C.A. § 1125(a). Inconsistencies found between the literal message of an advertisement and the listeners' or viewers' perceptions of the message have been found relevant to the issues of "miscomprehension," "deception," and "misleadingness." See Diamond and Dimitropoulos, Deception and Puffery in Advertising: Behavioral Science Implications for Regulation, in Advertising, Law and the Social Sciences (J. Lipton and B. Sales eds. 1993), and Preston and Richards, A Role for Consumer Belief in FTC and Lanham Act Deceptive Advertising Cases, 31 American Business Law Journal 1 (1993).

———

EMPIRICAL QUESTIONS WITHOUT EMPIRICAL ANSWERS

John Monahan and Laurens Walker.
1991 Wisconsin Law Review 569 (1991).

[W]hat should a court do in trademark or similar cases when the parties contest a "social fact" but do not bring forth [s]ocial science evidence in support of their assertions? Since social facts are explicitly within the purview of the Federal Rules of Evidence and similar state codes, the answer, it would seem, is to be found by identifying the party with the burden of proof and then asking whether that burden has been met.

The substantive law, of course, identifies the party with the burden of proof and also specifies the type of evidence that will be sufficient to meet that burden. In trademark infringement cases, to continue our example, the plaintiff—the owner of a registered mark—bears the burden of proving by a preponderance of the evidence that the latecomer's product will cause "consumer confusion."

[W]hile social science studies are not the only form of evidence for proving consumer confusion,[27] they are clearly the preferred form of

---

27. In Polaroid Corp. v. Polarad Elecs. Corp., 287 F.2d 492, 495 (2d Cir.1961), cert. denied, 368 U.S. 820 (1961), the Second Circuit specified a large number of factors of potential relevance in proving likely confusion, including the strength of the plaintiff's evidence for proving this "social fact." Failure of the plaintiff to introduce valid survey results may not be fatal to its claim of infringement, because other, less probative, forms of evidence bearing on consumer confusion may be available. But with courts beginning to draw adverse inferences from a lack of survey evidence, it will be a rare case where infringement is found in the absence of social science research.

More generally, failure to carry the burden of proof regarding an issue based on social fact will ordinarily result in victory for the opposing party, at least with respect to that issue in the case.

SELECTED BIBLIOGRAPHY

G. Dinwoodie and M. Janis, Trademarks and Unfair Competition: Law and Policy (2004).

P. Goldstein and E. Kitch, Unfair Competition, Trademark, Copyright, and Patent (2007).

E. Kitch and H. Perlman, Legal Regulation of the Competitive Process (5th ed. 1998).

Manta, In Search of Validity: A New Model for the Content and Procedural Treatment of Trademark Infringement Surveys, 24 Cardozo Arts and Entertainment Law Journal 1027 (2007).

SECTION II. OBSCENITY

In Interstate Circuit, Inc. v. Dallas, 390 U.S. 676, 88 S.Ct. 1298, 20 L.Ed.2d 225 (1968), Justice Harlan, dissenting, stated that "the subject of obscenity has produced a variety of views among members of the Court unmatched in any other course of constitutional adjudication. [In] 13 obscenity cases [i]n which signed opinions were written, [t]here has been a total of 55 separate opinions among the Justices." 390 U.S. at 704–705, 88 S.Ct. at 1314.

In Chapter Four, we deal with the controversial question of whether obscene materials are protected by the First Amendment. Here, we anticipate the Supreme Court's holding that "obscenity is not within the area of constitutionally protected speech or press," Roth v. United States, 354 U.S. 476, 485, 77 S.Ct. 1304, 1309, 1 L.Ed.2d 1498 (1957), and focus on the equally controversial question of how social science evidence can be used to determine whether a particular publication or film is obscene.

Before examining the ways that social science research has been used as evidence in obscenity litigation, we first consider whether social science evidence is admissible at all in such cases.

mark (for which advertising and sales figures are relevant evidence), defendant's bad faith adoption of the mark (for which instructions to a designer to imitate plaintiff's package are relevant evidence), and actual confusion (for which evidence of misdirected mail or phone calls is relevant). See S. Kane, Trademark Law: A Practitioner's Guide 117–37, 239–42 (1987).

A. THE ADMISSIBILITY OF SOCIAL SCIENCE EVIDENCE OF OBSCENITY

Until the 1970's, two issues regarding the use of social science evidence in obscenity litigation were extensively debated by the United States Supreme Court and by lower courts. The first was whether the Constitution *required* the prosecution to offer expert evidence of obscenity as part of proving its case beyond a reasonable doubt. The second was whether under the Constitution the defense must be *permitted* to offer expert evidence to rebut the prosecution's case.

PEOPLE v. MULLER

Court of Appeals of New York, 1884.
96 N.Y. 408.

■ ANDREWS, J.

The defendant on the trial called as witnesses an artist who had practiced painting for many years, and also a person who had been engaged in the study of art. They were asked by defendant's counsel whether there was a distinguishing line, as understood by artists, between pure art and obscene and indecent art. The question was objected to by the prosecutor and excluded by the court.

[I]ndeed there is but little scope for proof bearing upon the issue of decency or obscenity, beyond the evidence furnished by the picture itself. The question which was excluded, if intended to bring out the fact that pictures might be either decent or indecent, and that the canons of pure art would accept those of one class and reject those of the other, was properly overruled as an attempt to prove a self-evident proposition. If the question was intended to be followed by proof that, according to the standard of judgment adopted and recognized by artists, the photographs in question were not obscene or indecent, it was properly rejected for the reason that the issue was not whether in the opinion of witnesses, or of a class of people, the photographs were indecent or obscene, but whether they were so in fact, and upon this issue witnesses could neither be permitted to give their own opinions, or to state the aggregate opinion of a particular class or part of the community. To permit such evidence would put the witness in the place of the jury, and the latter would have no function to discharge. The testimony of experts is not admissible upon matters of judgment within the knowledge and experience of ordinary jurymen. The question whether a picture or writing is obscene is one of the plainest that can be presented to a jury, and under the guidance of a discreet judge there is little danger of their reaching a wrong conclusion. The opinions of witnesses would not aid the jury in reaching a conclusion, and their admission would contravene the general rule that facts and not opinions are to be given in evidence.

JACOBELLIS v. OHIO

Supreme Court of the United States, 1964.
378 U.S. 184, 84 S.Ct. 1676, 12 L.Ed.2d 793.

Oral Argument, April 1, 1964*

JUSTICE BLACK: How would you prove community standards?

MR. CORRIGAN [Representing the State of Ohio]: You prove community standards, Your Honor, by putting in evidence people who are [experts].

You are able to have these people testify as to whether or not this material is below or above the community standards and subject them to cross-examination as to the basis for their opinion.

[J]USTICE WHITE: What is wrong with the jury just deciding? Why is not the jury itself a representative of community standards without having any evidence or testimony as to what they are? [I]f it is a local standard, is not the jury, in theory at least, and perhaps in fact, the better judges than the experts brought in from outside?

MR. CORRIGAN: Your Honor, you have to make a record upon which to appeal. You have to have something.

[J]USTICE WHITE: Well, you do have the obscene publication.

MR. CORRIGAN: Yes, sir.

JUSTICE WHITE: Now, do you think you have to have expert testimony in addition to that?

[M]R. CORRIGAN: I think it is helpful in making a determination as to what the community standard is.

JUSTICE HARLAN: I suppose what you are really doing is saying that perhaps every juryman who sits on these cases has not read quite as widely as some others have, and I suppose what you are doing with this evidence is to expose a juryman to at least the views of other individuals in the community in the name of "community standard," to tell him, "consider this before you say this book is obscene," or "you are to consider that before you say it is not obscene."

Is not that what it really comes down to?

MR. CORRIGAN: That is exactly right, Your Honor.

———

JACOBELLIS v. OHIO

Supreme Court of the United States, 1964.
378 U.S. 184, 84 S.Ct. 1676, 12 L.Ed.2d 793.

■ MR. JUSTICE STEWART, concurring.

I have reached the conclusion [t]hat under the First and Fourteenth Amendments criminal laws in this area are constitutionally limited to hard-

* From Obscenity: The Complete Oral Arguments Before the Supreme Court in the Major Obscenity Cases (L. Friedman ed. 1970).

core pornography. I shall not today attempt further to define the kinds of material I understand to be embraced within that shorthand description; and perhaps I could never succeed in intelligibly doing so. But I know it when I see it, and the motion picture involved in this case is not that.

SMITH v. CALIFORNIA

Supreme Court of the United States, 1959.
361 U.S. 147, 80 S.Ct. 215, 4 L.Ed.2d 205.

■ Mr. Justice Frankfurter, concurring.

[There is a] right of one charged with obscenity—a right implicit in the very nature of the legal concept of obscenity—to enlighten the judgment of the tribunal, be it the jury or as in this case the judge, regarding the prevailing literary and moral community standards and to do so through qualified experts. It is immaterial whether the basis of the exclusion of such testimony is irrelevance, or the incompetence of experts to testify to such matters. The two reasons coalesce, for community standards or the psychological or physiological consequences of questioned literature can as a matter of fact hardly be established except through experts. Therefore, to exclude such expert testimony is in effect to exclude as irrelevant evidence that goes to the very essence of the defense and therefore to the constitutional safeguards of due process. The determination of obscenity no doubt rests with judge or jury. Of course the testimony of experts would not displace judge or jury in determining the ultimate question whether the particular book is obscene, any more than the testimony of experts relating to the state of the art in patent suits determines the patentability of a controverted device.

There is no external measuring rod for obscenity. Neither, on the other hand, is its ascertainment a merely subjective reflection of the taste or moral outlook of individual jurors or individual judges. Since the law through its functionaries is "applying contemporary community standards" in determining what constitutes obscenity, Roth v. United States, 354 U.S. 476, 489, 77 S.Ct. 1304, 1311, 1 L.Ed.2d 1498, it surely must be deemed rational, and therefore relevant to the issue of obscenity, to allow light to be shed on what those "contemporary community standards" are. Their interpretation ought not to depend solely on the necessarily limited, hit-or-miss, subjective view of what they are believed to be by the individual juror or judge. It bears repetition that the determination of obscenity is for juror or judge not on the basis of his personal upbringing or restricted reflection or particular experience of life, but on the basis of "contemporary community standards." Can it be doubted that there is a great difference in what is to be deemed obscene in 1959 compared with what was deemed obscene in 1859? The difference derives from a shift in community feeling regarding what is to be deemed prurient or not prurient by reason of the effects attributable to this or that particular writing. Changes in the intellectual and moral climate of society, in part doubtless due to the views and findings of specialists, afford shifting foundations for the attribution. What may well have been consonant "with mid-Victorian morals, does not seem to me to answer to the understanding and morality of the present time." United States v. Kennerley, 209 F. 119, 120. This was the view of Judge Learned Hand decades ago reflecting an atmosphere of propriety much closer to mid-Victorian days than is ours. Unless we disbelieve that the literary, psychological or moral standards of a community can be made fruitful and illuminating subjects of inquiry by those who give their life to such inquiries, it was violative of "due process" to exclude the constitutionally relevant evidence proffered in this case. [F]or the reasons I have indicated, I would make the right to introduce such evidence a requirement of due process in obscenity prosecutions.

MILLER v. CALIFORNIA

Supreme Court of the United States, 1973.
413 U.S. 15, 93 S.Ct. 2607, 37 L.Ed.2d 419.

■ MR. CHIEF JUSTICE BURGER delivered the opinion of the Court.

This is one of a group of "obscenity-pornography" cases being reviewed by the Court in a re-examination of standards enunciated in earlier cases involving what Mr. Justice Harlan called "the intractable obscenity problem." Interstate Circuit, Inc. v. Dallas, 390 U.S. 676, 704, 88 S.Ct. 1298, 1313, 20 L.Ed.2d 225 (1968) (concurring and dissenting).

Appellant conducted a mass mailing campaign to advertise the sale of illustrated books, euphemistically called "adult" material. After a jury trial, he was convicted of violating California Penal Code—311.2(a), a misdemeanor, by knowingly distributing obscene matter.

[T]he basic guidelines for the trier of fact must be: (a) whether "the average person, applying contemporary community standards" would find that the work, taken as a whole, appeals to the prurient interest, (b) whether the work depicts or describes, in a patently offensive way, sexual conduct specifically defined by the applicable state law; and (c) whether the work, taken as a whole, lacks serious literary, artistic, political, or scientific value.

[D]uring the trial, both the prosecution and the defense assumed that the relevant "community standards" in making the factual determination of obscenity were those of the State of California, not some hypothetical standard of the entire United States of America. Defense counsel at trial never objected to the testimony of the State's expert on community standards[12] or to the instructions of the trial judge on "statewide" standards.

---

12. The record simply does not support appellant's contention, belatedly raised on appeal, that the State's expert was unqualified to give evidence on California "communi-

[N]othing in the First Amendment requires that a jury must consider hypothetical and unascertainable "national standards" when attempting to determine whether certain materials are obscene as a matter of fact.

[I]t is neither realistic nor constitutionally sound to read the First Amendment as requiring that the people of Maine or Mississippi accept public depiction of conduct found tolerable in Las Vegas, or New York City.

————

PARIS ADULT THEATRE I v. SLATON

Supreme Court of the United States, 1973.
413 U.S. 49, 93 S.Ct. 2628, 37 L.Ed.2d 446.

■ MR. CHIEF JUSTICE BURGER delivered the opinion of the Court.

It should be clear from the outset that we do not undertake to tell the States what they must do, but rather to define the area in which they may chart their own course in dealing with obscene material.

[But it was not] error [for the trial court] to fail to require "expert" affirmative evidence that the materials were obscene when the materials themselves were actually placed in evidence. The films, obviously, are the best evidence of what they represent.[6]

————

KAPLAN v. CALIFORNIA

Supreme Court of the United States, 1973.
413 U.S. 115, 93 S.Ct. 2680, 37 L.Ed.2d 492.

■ MR. CHIEF JUSTICE BURGER delivered the opinion of the Court.

In Miller v. California, 413 U.S. 15, 93 S.Ct. 2607, 37 L.Ed.2d 419, the Court today holds that the " 'contemporary community standards of the State of California,' " as opposed to "national standards," are constitution-

ty standards." The expert, a police officer with many years of specialization in obscenity offenses, had conducted an extensive statewide survey and had given expert evidence on 26 occasions in the year prior to this trial. Allowing such expert testimony was certainly not constitutional error.

6. This is not a subject that lends itself to the traditional use of expert testimony. Such testimony is usually admitted for the purpose of explaining to lay jurors what they otherwise could not understand. Cf. 2 J. Wigmore, Evidence §§ 556, 559 (3d ed. 1940). No such assistance is needed by jurors in obscenity cases; indeed the "expert witness" prac-

tices employed in these cases have often made a mockery out of the otherwise sound concept of expert testimony. See *United States v. Groner,* 479 F.2d 577, 585–586 (C.A.5 1973); *id.,* at 587–588 (Ainsworth, J., concurring). "Simply stated, hard core pornography ... can and does speak for itself." *United States v. Wild,* 422 F.2d 34, 36 (C.A.2 1969), cert. denied, 402 U.S. 986, 91 S.Ct. 1644, 29 L.Ed.2d 152 (1971). We reserve judgment, however, on the extreme case, not presented here, where contested materials are directed at such a bizarre deviant group that the experience of the trier of fact would be plainly inadequate to judge whether the material appeals to the prurient interest.

ally adequate to establish whether a work is obscene. We also reject in Paris Adult Theatre I v. Slaton [413 U.S. 49, 93 S.Ct. 2628, 37 L.Ed.2d 446 (1973)] any constitutional need for "expert" testimony on behalf of the prosecution, or for any other ancillary evidence of obscenity, once the allegedly obscene material itself is placed in evidence. Paris Adult Theatre I, supra, 413 U.S., at 56, 93 S.Ct., at 2634–2635. The defense should be free to introduce appropriate expert testimony, see Smith v. California, 361 U.S. 147, 164–165, 80 S.Ct. 215, 224–225, 4 L.Ed.2d 205 (1959) (Frankfurter, J., concurring), but in "the cases in which this Court has decided obscenity questions since *Roth,* it has regarded the materials as sufficient in themselves for the determination of the question." *Ginzburg v. United States,* 383 U.S. 463, 465, 86 S.Ct. 942, 944, 16 L.Ed.2d 31 (1966).

HAMLING v. UNITED STATES

Supreme Court of the United States, 1974.
418 U.S. 87, 94 S.Ct. 2887, 41 L.Ed.2d 590.

■ Mr. Justice Rehnquist delivered the opinion of the Court.

Our holding in *Miller* that California could constitutionally proscribe obscenity in terms of a "statewide" standard did not mean that any such precise geographic area is required as a matter of constitutional law. [S]ince this case was tried in the Southern District of California, and presumably jurors from throughout that judicial district were available to serve on the panel which tried petitioners, it would be the standards of that "community" upon which the jurors would draw.

B.   Social Science Evidence of "Community Standards"

When *Miller, Paris Adult Theatre I,* and *Kaplan* were decided by the United States Supreme Court on the same day in 1973, the law regarding the admissibility of social science evidence in obscenity litigation was settled: the Constitution did not require the prosecution to offer expert evidence as part of proving its case, and the Constitution did require that the defense be permitted to offer expert evidence to rebut the prosecution's case.

In Pope v. Illinois, 481 U.S. 497, 107 S.Ct. 1918, 95 L.Ed.2d 439 (1987), the Supreme Court reaffirmed that "the first and second prongs of the *Miller* test—appeal to prurient interest and patent offensiveness—are issues of fact for the jury to determine applying contemporary community standards." 481 U.S. at 500, 107 S.Ct. at 1920. In the following cases, we examine the use of social science evidence to help determine these "community standards."

PEOPLE v. NELSON

Appellate Court of Illinois, Second District, 1980.
88 Ill.App.3d 196, 43 Ill.Dec. 476, 410 N.E.2d 476.

■ SEIDENFELD, PRESIDING JUSTICE.

Timothy D. Nelson was convicted after a jury trial of the offense of criminal obscenity. He was sentenced to a term of 45 days in jail and fined $1,000. Defendant appeals, contending that the trial court prejudicially erred in refusing to admit a public opinion poll on the issue of community standards and the proffered testimony of an expert witness analyzing the results of the poll.

[T]he witness is a Ph.D. and a social scientist who specializes in survey research methodology and the conducting of public opinion polls. His expertise as a social scientist and professional pollster were stipulated. [T]he target for the poll was the adult population of the State of Illinois. The sample was 770 persons. The State was divided into 77 areas of approximately equal population, and then using a random selection technique, representatives were sent out to conduct 770 interviews.

[T]he summary of the questions and results is included as an Appendix to this opinion. Dr. Bell described the concept of "consensus", stating that approximately 75% of the population would have to agree on a proposition before one could say there was a consensus. In analyzing the results of the 1978 Illinois community standard survey, he found that there was no consensus about whether it was acceptable or not acceptable to have depictions of sexually explicit materials provided under certain circumstances described in the questions. As the result of his expert analysis he concluded that there was no community standard regarding such depictions.

The prosecution objected to the expert analysis on the ground that there was no community standard shown by the survey and therefore that the testimony based on the inconclusive survey would invade the jury's province. The trial court ruled that both the survey evidence and the analysis invaded the province of the jury and that they were thus inadmissible.

[C]learly, a state-wide "community standard" based upon public acceptance of material claimed to be obscene is an essential element of proof of the charge.

Section 11–20(c)(4) of the Illinois Criminal Code provides, as relevant:

"In any prosecution for an offense under this Section evidence shall be admissible to show: * * * (4) The degree, if any, of public acceptance of the material in this State; * * * ". Ill.Rev.Stat.1977, ch. 38, par. 11–20(c)(4).

In view of the fact that no objections were made to the methodology or partiality of the survey the statutory provision makes the evidence admissible in our view since the results show "the degree if any, of the public acceptance of the [material]." It is apparent from the survey that the questions were framed with reference to Section 11–20(c)(4), since the members of the public are asked to state whether they feel it would be acceptable for the average adult in Illinois to see or buy sexually explicit materials. The questions and answers were relevant in that they showed that a majority of Illinois residents find depictions of "nudity and actual or pretended sexual activities" acceptable. This is relevant to the question of whether such depictions are "patently offensive" (for by definition acceptable materials are not offensive), and to the question whether such material appeals to "prurient interest."

[T]he survey results are strong evidence that the community standards would accept or at least would not reject the portrayal of sexually explicit material in movies when the access to the movies is limited to adult viewers. In fact, survey evidence may be the only way to prove degrees of acceptability of a product or material, as distinct from its availability. The State does not have the burden of introducing any evidence as to what the state-wide community standard is. But that cannot justify a court in denying the defendant the right to introduce the best evidence he can gather on this issue. Essentially the result of refusing the proffered evidence left the jurors with no way of knowing what the State standard might be. Particularly in this case, in which the jury *voir dire* showed that most of the jurors had lived all of their lives in the community of Rockford, did not read a paper from any other community within the State of Illinois and read few national magazines, it appears that the jurors would have little practical experience on which to base their opinion of what the state-wide community standard might be. This raises the great danger that the jurors may have applied a personal standard rather than a state-wide community standard. We conclude that the exclusion of the survey testimony was harmful and prejudicial error and requires that the case be remanded for a new trial.

The trial court, however, properly ruled that the commentary of the expert, exclusive of his foundation testimony, was inadmissible. The testimony of the expert that the survey results showed that there was no "consensus" in public opinion and therefore that there is no community standard by which to judge the obscenity of the material, is confusing for the jury. This comment is based on a social science concept which may be foreign to the jury. Further it focuses their attention on the nature and existence of the crime, perhaps thereby distracting them from a determination of guilt or innocence in the case at bar. Moreover, the survey results are clear and self-explanatory so that the jurors should have no difficulty in interpreting the results without expert aid.

[T]he judgment is therefore reversed and the cause remanded for a new trial in accordance with this opinion.

APPENDIX
SUMMARY—ILLINOIS COMMUNITY STANDARDS SURVEY

QUESTION: Is it your opinion that in recent years the standards in Illinois have changed so that depictions of nudity and sexual activities in movies and publications available only to adults are now more accept-able or less acceptable?

More acceptable 60.5%; less acceptable 25.7%; neither 7.8%; don't know 4.4%; no answer 1.3%; other .2%.

QUESTION: Do you think it is acceptable or not acceptable in Illinois for the average adult to see any depiction of actual or pretended sexual activities shown in movies and publications that he or she wants to?

Acceptable 58.1%; not acceptable 33.2%; neither 5.2%; no answer 3.5%.

GENERAL QUESTION

In your opinion, is it now all right or not all right in the State of Illinois for:

QUESTION: Adults who want to view them, to purchase magazines that depict nudity and actual or pretended sexual activities?

All right 63.1%; not all right 31.0%; neither 2.2%; no answer 3.6%.

QUESTION: Movie theaters, restricting attendance to adults only, to show films that depict nudity and actual or pretended sexual activities for adults who want to attend?

All right 59.2%; not all right 32.1%; neither 4.3%; no answer 4.4%.

QUESTION: Bookstores that restrict admittance to adults only to sell publications and movies depicting nudity and actual or pretended sexual activities for adults who want to go inside and purchase them?

All right 54.8%; not all right 37.3%; neither 4.0%; no answer 3.9%.

QUESTION: Arcades that restrict admittance to adults only to show films that depict nudity and actual or pretended sexual activities?

All right 48.7%; not all right 42.1%; neither 3.5%; no answer 5.7%.

QUESTION: Adults who want to, in the privacy of their homes, to see movies and publications that depict nudity and actual or pretended sexual activities?

All right 67.4%; not all right 25.7%; neither 2.9%; no answer 4.0%.

QUESTION: We have used the phrases "nudity" and "sexual activities" in the interview. What we mean by these terms is total male and/or female nudity, and sexual intercourse including all kinds of sexual variations. Is that what you understood we meant, or did you think we meant something else?

Understood 93.4%; something else 3.0%; neither 1.8%; no answer 1.8%.

———

SALIBA v. STATE

Court of Appeals of Indiana, Second District, 1985.
475 N.E.2d 1181.

■ SHIELDS, JUDGE.

Saliba was charged with exhibiting an obscene film in his adult book store in Indianapolis on November 12, 1981. The film which formed the basis for Saliba's conviction depicted three males involved in various homosexual activities. Prior to trial, Saliba employed Dr. Roderick Bell of California to conduct a public opinion poll to determine community standards in Marion County regarding the depiction of sexual activities in movies and publications. At trial and out of the jury's presence, Saliba offered into evidence the results of the poll designed by Dr. Bell. In support of the offer, Dr. Bell testified to his qualifications and explained the general nature of public opinion polls. Dr. Bell then extensively discussed the scientific methodology generally employed in conducting polls and detailed the specific techniques employed in conducting the poll at issue. Based on the design, execution, tabulation and verification of the instant poll, Dr. Bell opined that the poll was a valid measure of the degree of public acceptance of sexually explicit materials in Marion County.

The State objected to the poll's validity and [t]he trial judge ruled the poll inadmissible.

[S]urvey Evidence in Obscenity Prosecutions

As the State contends, the obscene character of materials may be determined by the jury based on a viewing of the allegedly offensive material. The State need not present an expert witness or other evidence of community standards.

However, expert evidence on this issue may be highly relevant. The jurors are not instructed to evaluate obscenity based on their personal opinions but are charged with applying contemporary community standards. In the absence of expert testimony, the jury's determination of contemporary community standards runs the risk of incorporating the individual juror's "necessarily limited, hit-or-miss subjective view" "on the basis of his personal upbringing or restricted reflection or particular experience of life." Smith v. California, 361 U.S. 147, 165, 80 S.Ct. 215, 225, 4 L.Ed.2d 205 (1959) (Frankfurter, J., concurring). Consequently, the defendant in an obscenity prosecution is entitled to introduce relevant and appropriate expert testimony on the issue of contemporary community standards. Kaplan v. California, 413 U.S. 115, 93 S.Ct. 2680, 37 L.Ed.2d 492.

Expert testimony based on a public opinion poll is uniquely suited to a determination of community standards. Perhaps no other form of evidence is more helpful or concise. [T]he alternative modes of introducing such evidence are less desirable. Zippo Manufacturing Co. v. Rogers Imports, Inc., 216 F.Supp. 670 (S.D.N.Y.1963) (leading case on survey evidence). For example, the presentation of in-court testimony from the entire target population or even a representative sample is patently impractical. And the use of an expert witness to testify regarding his or her opinion on community standards is not as direct or accurate as a public poll, even assuming an expert could qualify on the subject. The nature of public opinion polls renders them better suited to demonstrate contemporary community standards.

Admissibility of Survey Evidence

In the instant case, the State objected to the admission of the public opinion poll both on the grounds of relevancy and trustworthiness. Specifically, the State argued the poll's focus on overall community standards did not determine whether the film in question was obscene. Alternatively, the State argued the poll was improperly conducted and therefore unreliable. We will address each contention in turn.

A.   Relevancy

[O]ur probe into relevance is two-pronged. Were the questions in the poll relevant to a determination of 1) community standards in general and 2) the community's acceptance of viewing the particular film in question.

1.   General Community Standards

We first determine whether the questions in the poll were relevant to a determination of community standards. For example, question seven asked: "Do you personally think it is acceptable or not acceptable for the average adult to see any depiction of actual or pretended sexual activities shown in movies and publications that he or she wants to?" The balance of the questions in the poll merely changed the type and location of access to such materials to movies, books, or magazines and theaters, bookstores, or arcades. The poll therefore questioned the interviewees regarding their view of community acceptance of sexually explicit materials rather than their personal acceptance of such materials.

We must emphasize the majority of the community need not desire to view sexually explicit materials in order to establish community acceptance or tolerance of such materials. Rather, the issue concerns the population's perception of what is generally acceptable in the community considering the intended and probable recipients of the materials. The questions in the poll parallel the statutorily mandated standard; matter is "obscene" if "the average person, applying contemporary community standards" finds the material as a whole appeals to the prurient interest in sex. The poll's results were relevant evidence of the community standards which the jury was obligated to apply.

2.   Acceptance of Particular Film

We must also determine if the community acceptance of viewing "nudity and actual or pretended sexual activity", as phrased throughout the poll, is relevant to a determination of the acceptance of viewing the film in question. We also answer this inquiry in the affirmative. The poll defines "nudity and pretended or actual sexual activity" as "total male and/or female nudity, and sexual intercourse including all kinds of sexual variation." The sexual activity portrayed in the instant film fell within the definition of "nudity and actual or pretended sexual activity."

Although the poll did not present the interviewees with the ultimate question to be decided by the jury (i.e., whether the particular film was obscene), the poll was relevant to an application of community standards. [T]he failure to poll the population on the ultimate issue does not negate relevancy. The population's general opinion is probative, although not determinative, of community standards and, consequently, of the population's specific opinion of the film in question.

B.   Trustworthiness

Although the poll was relevant, we must also determine whether it was admissible. Relevant public opinion polls and other survey evidence are widely accepted as generally admissible if properly conducted. See generally Zippo, 216 F.Supp. at 682. Objections to admissibility usually arise because the contents of public opinion polls are generally not within the firsthand knowledge of the submitting witness; they may also constitute hearsay.

Several theories, however, have been advanced to justify the admission of public opinion polls. Some authorities classify polls as falling under the state of mind exception to the hearsay rule. Others characterize polls as hearsay but conclude the need for the evidence at trial and the circumstantial guarantees of trustworthiness justify admission. Still other authorities classify survey evidence as non-hearsay, and therefore directly rely on the rules governing admission of expert testimony generally. Id. In any event, it is now generally accepted neither the hearsay rule nor the requirement of firsthand knowledge bars the admission of properly conducted public opinion polls or surveys. As explained in the Advisory Committee's Note to Fed.R.Evid. 703: "Attention is directed to the validity of the techniques employed rather than the relatively fruitless inquiries whether hearsay is involved." 51 F.R.D. 404 (1971).

The admissibility of a public opinion poll depends primarily upon the presence of circumstantial guarantees of trustworthiness. 1 J. Moore, Moore's Federal Practice 2.712 (1982). Public opinion polls are surveys designed to elicit the state of mind of a targeted population ("universe") through an examination of a representative portion ("sample") of the universe. Through accepted statistical analysis, the sample data is used to project the opinion of the entire targeted population. In short, the circumstantial guarantees of trustworthiness are premised on 1) the use of generally accepted surveying techniques in conducting the poll and 2) adherence to statistically correct methods in conducting the poll and evaluating the results.

This twofold inquiry has led to the judicial development of [seven] foundational criteria which are generally accepted as scientifically necessary to insure a poll's reliability and, consequently, its admissibility. The proponent of a poll has the burden of establishing: 1) the poll was conducted by an expert in the field of surveying; 2) the relevant universe was examined; 3) a representative sample was drawn from the relevant universe; 4) the mode of questioning was "correct" (mail, telephone, personal interview, etc.); 5) the sample, questionnaire, and the interviews were designed in accordance with generally accepted standards; 6) the data gathered was accurately reported; and 7) the data was analyzed in a statistically correct manner. J. Moore, supra at 138. The adherence to this generally accepted methodology renders the poll's results admissible in the form of expert opinion.

Once these foundational requirements are established, subject to cross-examination, the poll is admissible. [G]iven an adequate foundation, questions regarding the technical adequacy of a poll affect the poll's weight only.

[D]r. Bell's foundation testimony explained the typical methodology used in conducting opinion polls and described the methodology employed in conducting the instant poll. Dr. Bell identified the "universe" as the adult population of Marion County. This "universe" was sampled by telephone using a random digit dialing technique, the currently preferred method of telephone interviewing. This technique used a list of telephone numbers randomly generated by computer in proportion to the number of lines for existing telephone prefixes. During the first two weeks of February, 1982, five hundred (500) adults from Marion County were questioned by interviewers from Herron Associates of Indianapolis, a field service. The interviewers were instructed and supervised by Dr. Bell. Dr. Bell prepared the questionnaire through the use of extensive "pretesting" techniques designed to insure the questions were understood by the interviewees. The interviewers were instructed to read the questionnaire to the interviewees and record the responses as designated by the accompanying "code sheet" or answer key. Once the interviews were complete, a subset of the sample was recontacted by the field supervisor to verify the interview took place and the responses were accurately coded. Dr. Bell then drew a subset of the subset to reverify. Dr. Bell testified this form of spot checking is the only accepted verification technique. The raw data was keyed into a computer for tabulation; Dr. Bell also supervised this data input. The results of the poll were 98% repeatable within a margin of error of 3% to 4%. Dr. Bell testified that the definitions, standards and methodologies described were used by "practically all" national polling organizations including Lou Harris. Dr. Bell's testimony alone provided a complete foundation for admission of the poll.

[T]he State's objections merely affected the poll's weight, not its admissibility. The survey was erroneously excluded.

Judgment reversed and cause remanded for a new trial.

COMMONWEALTH v. TRAINOR

Supreme Judicial Court of Massachusetts, Suffolk, 1978.
374 Mass. 796, 374 N.E.2d 1216.

■ WILKINS, JUSTICE.

The individual defendant and the corporate defendant were found guilty in February, 1976, after a jury waived trial, on all counts of indictments charging them with having possession of obscene matter in June, 1975, with intent to disseminate it.

[W]e come [t]o an issue with which this court has not dealt previously. The appellants argue that the judge improperly excluded a public opinion survey from evidence. Although, as will be seen, public opinion surveys are admissible in certain circumstances, we agree with the judge's decision to exclude the appellants' public opinion survey.

A properly conducted public opinion survey, offered through an expert in conducting such surveys, is admissible in an obscenity case if it tends to show relevant standards in the Commonwealth. We see no meaningful distinction between a properly conducted public opinion survey offered to show community norms and the testimony of an expert who states his views on the opinion of the public concerning the portrayal of certain allegedly obscene conduct. We have already recognized the admissibility of expert testimony of the latter type. We have said, citing Paris Adult Theatre I v. Slaton, 413 U.S. 49, 56, 93 S.Ct. 2628, 37 L.Ed.2d 446 (1973), that triers of fact "may consider expert testimony on the subject of Statewide standards, if any is offered in evidence, but also may disregard such evidence because the matter at issue may be per se sufficient evidence for a finding of prurience in most cases." Commonwealth v. 707 Main Corp., 357 N.E.2d 753, 761 (1976). Although expert testimony may be excluded, in the judge's discretion, if a subject is within the common knowledge of the average juror, the line between matters of common knowledge and matters beyond common knowledge often is not precise. If such expert testimony may give the jury appreciable assistance in resolving a fact question, it is admissible in the judge's discretion. Where the question is whether portrayals of sexual conduct are "obscene" under the statutory definition, it would be a rare case in which testimony from a qualified expert should be excluded on the ground that it would not be helpful to the trier of fact. Similarly, a properly conducted public opinion survey should be admitted. The question then is what is a properly conducted public opinion survey.

If the universe surveyed is relevant, if the sample questioned is representative of the relevant universe, if the questions are in a form appropriate to obtain unbiased answers within a reasonable margin of error, and if the pollster is qualified, the weight of authority supports the admission of a public opinion survey tending to prove a fact relevant to a material issue. See the leading, oft-cited case, Zippo Mfg. Co. v. Rogers Imports, Inc., 216 F.Supp. 670, 682 et seq. (S.D.N.Y.1963). However, where the methodology of the survey is deficient, the trial judge should exclude it.

We are not inclined to pause long to resolve whether a survey of people's opinions is hearsay and, if it is, whether it is admissible under the state of mind exception to the hearsay rule. Numerous authorities have admitted particular surveys under that hearsay exception. The focus should be on the techniques employed rather than on whether hearsay is involved.

See Fed.R.Evid. 703 and Note of the Advisory Committee, 56 F.R.D. 183, 283 (1972). A properly conducted public opinion survey itself adequately ensures a good measure of trustworthiness, and its admission may be necessary in the sense that no other evidence would be as good as the survey evidence or perhaps even obtainable as a practical matter. Of course, the judge will have to determine in his discretion whether the methodology of the survey was adequate to justify its admission. In certain instances, any weaknesses in the manner in which a poll was conducted might affect only the weight to be accorded the survey results rather than the admissibility of the survey in evidence.

In light of these principles, we consider the public opinion survey prepared for the defendants in this case. The defendants made an offer of proof of the testimony and exhibits relating to their survey. Two hundred adults, all residents of Boston, divided evenly by sex, were obtained from all sections of Boston by telephone solicitations conducted evenings, and each was interviewed. Each was offered $10 to come to an office in downtown Boston for an interview on an undisclosed subject relating to a pending court case. Trained personnel conducted the interviews shortly before trial. The defendants intended to introduce the results of the survey through an expert experienced in conducting public opinion surveys, who would have testified that the margin of error in the survey ranged from 6% to 10%.

The questions largely sought the personal views of each person interviewed: whether, in particular circumstances, he or she would be willing to have motion picture films shown or magazines sold depicting human sexual conduct. One question asked, for example, whether the individual would "personally be willing to have motion picture films or magazines showing human sexual intercourse between members of the opposite sex (*sic*) shown or sold" in (a) residential neighborhoods of Boston, (b) general commercial or business areas in Boston, (c) Boston adult entertainment districts, (d) under conditions where minors were excluded, or (e) in places clearly marked so that anyone not wanting to see them could avoid them. The interviewer suggested three answers: would be willing, would not be willing, or "[d]on't care one way or the other." If other answers such as no opinion or a qualified approval, were given, those answers also were tabulated. Similar questions were asked concerning each subject's willingness to allow the sale or showing of films or magazines depicting human masturbation, oral sex, or homosexual acts. Two other questions inquired into each subject's willingness to allow the sale of particular magazines which were shown to him or her. One of those magazines was the subject of one count in an indictment in this case.

As would be expected, the willingness of the subjects interviewed to have such films shown, or magazines sold, increased as the suggested place of the showing or sale moved from residential to adult entertainment areas, when minors were excluded from involvement, and when the nature of the material to be shown or sold was plainly indicated. In general, males were more willing to allow the showing or sale of such materials than females.

It is important to note certain facts not set forth in the offer of proof. There was no indication that the method of selection of the subjects to be interviewed assured a representative sample of the citizens of Boston. One might suspect that certain persons would decline to participate because of the method by which they were approached or because of their unwillingness or inability to take the time to participate in such interviews. The selection process was not shown to be free from producing a bias in the survey results.

The interrogation of residents of only Boston raises the question whether the survey results are competent to prove the standards of the Commonwealth as a whole. However, because the obscenity statute assumes the existence of a uniform, Statewide standard, we should not reject a representative and otherwise valid survey limited to a population as large as that of Boston.

Finally, and most significantly, we note the absence of any indication that the willingness, the lack of willingness, or the indifference of a group to the sale of sexually explicit magazines or the showing of sexually explicit films has any relevance to any issue material to this case. The survey results apparently were offered as bearing on the question whether the films and magazines involved in this case displayed sexual conduct in a patently offensive way. The offer of proof made no attempt to connect an acceptance of, or an indifference to, the showing or sale of that material with whether the particular sexual conduct involved in this case was depicted or described in a patently offensive way. Perhaps many people would not object to others' seeing such material, although they themselves regard that material as patently offensive. The offer of proof did not explain the relationship of the offered evidence to this fundamental factual question of patent offensiveness.

Because the offer of proof failed to demonstrate the representativeness of the persons interviewed and failed to show that the survey results were relevant to any material issue in the case, the judge was warranted in excluding the survey and expert testimony concerning it.

———

UNITED STATES v. PRYBA

United States District Court, Eastern District of Virginia, 1988.
678 F.Supp. 1225.

■ ELLIS, DISTRICT JUDGE.

Defendants sought to introduce the testimony of Dr. Joseph Scott, a sociologist with a background in statistical methodology. Dr. Scott conducted an "ethnographical" study which allegedly showed that the materials here in question are accepted by the adult community in the Alexandria division. According to Dr. Scott, an ethnographic study "looks at what is going on in the community." To get a look at "what is going on" in the

Alexandria Division of the Eastern District of Virginia, Dr. Scott did the following:

(1) He viewed the subject materials.

(2) He "probably went" to eighty or ninety bookstores, approximately sixty-nine of which sold what Dr. Scott described as "male sophisticate" magazines. He also visited about seventy-five video stores, of which forty-three sold adult videotapes.

(3) He talked to the operators and customers of the stores he visited about sexually explicit (male sophisticate) materials.

(4) He called newspaper editors and discussed with them the number and content of "letters to the editors" to ascertain the number and type of complaints relating to sexually explicit material.

As a result of this "ethnography," Dr. Scott was prepared to offer the jury his opinion that the "overwhelming majority" of adults in the community have at one time or another viewed sexually explicit material and that such materials, including the materials here in question, are readily acceptable by the average adult in the community. He prepared no report; he had only his notes. To reach his sweeping conclusion, Dr. Scott, who has never lived in Virginia, required only eight days.

The issue is whether such testimony is competent expert evidence of the prevailing community standards.[12] It is not.

[R]ule 104(a): Witness Must be Qualified

The Court holds that the bases of Dr. Scott's opinion are insufficient to qualify him as an expert either on contemporary community standards of obscenity in the Alexandria Division, or on the question whether the materials in issue are accepted by the community. Dr. Scott admits that ethnography is a "new approach" in the study of sexual mores. He described ethnography as a qualitative analysis of a community, a method used to "assess" community standards. "Ethnography is the work of describing a culture." J. Spradley, The Ethnographic Interview 3 (1979). The issue is whether Scott's ethnographic evidence properly reflects contemporary community standards. It does not. Stripped of its scientific disguise, Dr. Scott's so-called "ethnography" is shown to be nothing more than a series of interviews with dealers of sexually explicit materials and

12. Dr. Scott conceded that ethnography is a new approach to the study of community acceptance of sexually explicit material, but claimed that it is generally accepted in the social science field. Yet general acceptance of ethnography in the social sciences, even if true, does not mean that Dr. Scott's ethnography in this case qualifies him as an expert in the contemporary community standards of the Alexandria Division. Cf. Frye v. United States, 293 F. 1013 (D.C.Cir.1923). The problem here is that Dr. Scott's ethnography is not scientific in the sense understood in *Frye*. There is a difference between scientific studies and methodologies in the natural sciences and studies found acceptable in the social sciences. The former must typically meet more rigorous standards and be subject to reliable replication. Put more directly, Dr. Scott's interviews of adult video store clerks, store managers, and customers over an eight-day period is simply not science.

their customers. This is neither science, nor work requiring expertise. Moreover, Scott did not visit churches, community centers, garden clubs, Rotary Clubs or the like to develop a basis for his opinion. Also, Dr. Scott did not show the films or magazines here in issue to those whom he interviewed, but instead discussed only those sexually explicit materials sold in the stores that he visited. In sum, defendants have failed to establish how Scott's ethnography is related to the general community's acceptance of the specific materials in issue.

[A]lso, Scott's testimony must be excluded because it is predicated solely upon qualitative rather than quantitative analysis. Scott's analysis, i.e., talking to customers and vendors of sexually explicit material and reviewing letters to the editors of various publications, in no way demonstrates community acceptance of the materials here in issue. Scott's testimony, although perhaps reflecting availability of the materials surveyed, fails to evidence community acceptance. It is well-settled that mere availability does not equate with community acceptance. Scott offers no *quantitative* analysis for much of his male sophisticate material, such as sale or distribution figures, which might have been probative of community acceptance. Dr. Scott's ethnography, in essence, constitutes nothing more than a one-man, eight-day, unscientific poll of purveyors and purchasers of smut. To permit this so-called "study" to masquerade as expert testimony on Northern Virginia's contemporary community standards of obscenity is ludicrous. This "study" did not and could not make Dr. Scott a competent, reliable expert on the contemporary community standards on sexually explicit material in Northern Virginia. Accordingly, the Court excluded Dr. Scott's testimony as falling far short of even minimal standards under Rules 702 and 104 of the Federal Rules of Evidence.

THE LAW OF OBSCENITY (1976)

Fredrick Schauer.

One interpretation [of the term "patently offensive" in the *Miller* test of obscenity] asks whether the materials themselves would actually offend the average member of the community, or the majority of the community, or the community as a whole. [B]ut there is another possible interpretation, that asks not whether the materials offend the community or the average person, but whether the community or the average person is offended by the materials being available to those who wish to see them. In other words, are the community standards tolerant, even though most members of the community might themselves be offended by the materials. If so, it can be argued that the materials are not offensive to the community because they are restricted only to those who choose to see them. [T]hus, the survey may ask the respondents whether *they* are offended by the material, or whether they are offended by its availability in the community to those who want it.

ESTIMATING COMMUNITY STANDARDS: THE USE OF SOCIAL SCIENCE EVIDENCE IN AN OBSCENITY PROSECUTION

Daniel Linz, Edward Donnerstein, Kenneth C. Land, Patricia L. McCall, Joseph Scott, Bradley J. Shafer, Lee J. Klein, and Larry Lance.
55 Public Opinion Quarterly 80 (1991).*

The study reported here was proffered as evidence in the State of North Carolina v. Cinema Blue of Charlotte, Inc., 392 S.E.2d 136 (N.C.App. 1990). In this study, an attempt was made to gather social science data to inform the jury as to whether the average adult in Mecklenburg County, NC, applying contemporary community standards, would find that five movies and one magazine alleged to be obscene by the state, either appealed to a prurient interest in sex or were patently offensive.

[A] sample of Mecklenburg County residents were contacted by telephone. The sample was compiled through random digit dialing using a list of digits, not weighted by prefix, obtained from Survey Sampling Inc., Fairfield, Connecticut. Potential respondents who could not be reached were called back three times with next-day calling staggered by time. Once contacted, the respondents were administered an interview that involved four components: (1) selection of an adult respondent in the household 18 years old or over; (2) assessment of demographic characteristics including: age, education, race, and sex (the interviewers were instructed to recruit within quotas corresponding to the proportions within each of these demographic categories in the population); (3) subject recruitment "to possibly view a movie ... and fill out a questionnaire about it?" and (4) subject recruitment to possibly view "adult, X-rated sexually explicit films." Once respondents agreed to participate in the study, they were informed that they would receive $50.00 upon completion of the project, which, they were told, would last approximately two-and-a-half hours. Participants were then given the address of the study site.

[A] total of 614 adults completed the initial telephone interview. Of these, 380 respondents indicated that they would be willing to participate in a film-viewing project; 8 indicated they were "not sure," and 226 declined participation. From this group, a total of 284 respondents agreed to participate in the study once they were informed that they might be asked to watch an X-rated video. Of these respondents, 244 were scheduled for a film-viewing session. One hundred thirty-two subjects reported for a film-viewing session. One subject left once the video began, and two were dismissed with payment because all video viewing set-ups were being used simultaneously. A total of 129 subjects participated in the film [e]valuation study.

[S]ubjects reported to the viewing sessions not knowing if they would be asked to watch an X-rated film or a nonexplicit film. Subjects were randomly assigned to view either one of five sexually explicit films [o]r a nonexplicit control film.

Prefilm Questionnaire Administration

Subjects were [g]iven a questionnaire and instructed to take it to one of ten separate video viewing rooms and complete it. They were asked to indicate length of residence in Mecklenburg County, newspaper subscription, video movie consumption, cable subscription, political affiliation, political attitudes, religiosity, religious service attendance, attitudes about current events, education level, age, and religious affiliation. Most important, the following set of instructions were given and questions asked.

> The next few questions deal with X-rated videos and adult movies and magazines. The nudity and sex shown in these types of adult material include: nude bodies and close-up graphic depictions of a variety of sexual activities, such as sexual intercourse, ejaculation, bondage, oral sex, anal sex, group sex, and variations of these acts by adult performers.
>
> Do you think it *is* or *is not* tolerated in your community for the average adult to see adult movies, video cassettes, and magazines showing nudity and sex if they should want to?
>
> > Tolerated   1   2   3   4   5   6   7   8   Not Tolerated
>
> Do you believe you *should* be able to see any such showing of actual sex acts in adult movies, video cassettes, or magazines if you should want to?
>
> > Definitely No   1   2   3   4   5   6   7   8   Definitely Yes
>
> Some adult movies, video cassettes, and magazines show actual sex acts in great detail and with close-ups of sexual organs. Would viewing this type of material appeal to an unhealthy, shameful, or morbid interest in sex?
>
> > Definitely Yes   1   2   3   4   5   6   7   8   Definitely No

Film Viewing

Upon completing the prefilm questionnaire, subjects were instructed to return it to one of the staff members. The subject was then taken to the viewing room and shown how to turn off the video cassette recorder (VCR). Subjects were instructed at that time to turn off the VCR once they had viewed the videocassette and report to the staff person. The staff person then started the VCR and left the room. All subjects viewed the film alone, and their viewing was timed to ensure that they had viewed the film in its entirety.

Postfilm Questionnaire

When subjects returned from their movie viewing room, they were given a postfilm questionnaire and instructed to return to their room, alone, to complete it. This questionnaire assessed subject attitudes on a number of current issues, including gun control, censorship, and religious tolerance. Most important, they were given the following instructions and questions.

In the first questionnaire you filled out, we asked you about X-rated videos, adult movies, and adult magazines. We said that the nudity and sex shown in these adult materials include: nude bodies and close-up graphic depictions of a variety of sexual activities. This includes: sexual intercourse, ejaculation, bondage, oral sex, anal sex, group sex, and variations of these acts by adult performers.

Was the movie you saw today what you expected to see, given this definition of X-rated videos, adult movies, and magazines?

Definitely No   1 2 3 4 5 6 7 8   Definitely Yes

The next few questions deal *only* with the X-rated video that you saw today. The scenes you saw in this film may have included nude bodies and close-up graphic depictions of a variety of sexual activities, including: sexual intercourse, ejaculation, oral sex, anal sex, group sex, and variations of these acts by adult performers.

[T]his question was followed by questions on community tolerance and personal tolerance that were similar to those in the pretest. The appeal to prurient interest question was not preceded by the sentence concerning adult movies and videotapes in general, and reference was made, rather, to the particular film just viewed.

[C]ontrol Film Subjects

Control subjects [v]iewed a nonexplicit film (*Nothing in Common*). Their postfilm questionnaire did not include questions on whether the film they viewed met their definition of an "X-rated" film, and they were asked the prurient appeal question with the preface sentence in both the pre-and postfilm questionnaire. Otherwise, control subjects were treated in an identical manner to the sexually explicit film-viewing subjects.

Results

Subject Responses After Film Viewing and Comparisons Pre-and Postfilm Viewing

Table 4. Comparison of "[B]efore" and "After" Film Viewing (X-rated film viewing subjects only) on Beliefs About Community Tolerance, Viewing Materials, and Appeal to Shameful and Morbid Interest in Sex

	Before Film	After Film
"Do you think it *is* or *is not* tolerated in your community for the average adult to obtain and see adult movies, video cassettes, and magazines showing nudity and sex if they want to?"		
Tolerated	59.1%	52.7%
N	65	58
Not tolerated	40.9%	47.3%
N	45	52

	"Do you believe you *should* be able to see any such showing of actual sex acts in adult movies, video cassettes, or magazines if you want to?"	
Definitely yes	74.5%	75.19%
N	82	86
Definitely no	25.5%	24.81%
N	28	24

	"Some adult movies, videocassettes, and magazines show actual sex acts in great detail and with close-ups of sexual organs. Would viewing this type of material appeal to an unhealthy, shameful, or morbid interest in sex?"	
Definitely yes	43.6%	16.4%
N	48	18
Definitely no	56.4%	83.6%
N	62	92

Column [2] of table 4 shows the responses of subjects to the three critical questions after viewing the films. (It is important to remember that subjects were instructed to answer these questions *only* with reference to the film they had viewed that day.) For these analyses, responses were summed across all of the X-rated film-viewing conditions. As can be seen from the table, a majority of subjects believe that it is tolerated in their community for the average adult to obtain and see the adult video cassettes charged in the case. Seventy-five percent believe they personally should be able to see any such showing of actual sex acts in adult movies, video cassettes, or magazines, and 16% believe viewing the type of material charged in the case appealed to an unhealthy, shameful, or morbid interest in sex.

Changes pre-and postfilm viewing (again, summed across the five sexually explicit film conditions) were also examined for each of the three outcome variables by comparing the mean differences from pre-to postviewing. Comparisons of pre-and postfilm subject responses on the belief that these materials are tolerated in the community showed no significant change from pre-to postfilm viewing ($p > .15$). Likewise, there was no statistically significant change in subjects' opinions about whether they should be allowed to see such materials ($p > .50$). There was, however, a statistically significant change in subjects' perception that the materials appealed to a shameful, unhealthy, or morbid interest in sex before and after viewing. Subjects were less likely to find the materials appealed to such interests after viewing ($p < .0001$). Forty-four percent of the subjects believed that such material appealed to morbid, shameful, or unhealthy interest in sex before seeing a film. After they viewed a film, the percentage dropped to 16%.

Further Substantiation of the Findings

[I]t is necessary to rule out the possibility that answering the questions about tolerance/patent offensiveness and prurient appeal twice, once in the prefilm questionnaire and again in the postfilm questionnaire, might have caused subjects to think more carefully about these issues than they normally would, and lead them to change their opinion as a result of this reflection (a testing-effect bias). Specifically, it may be the case that the significant change from pre-to postfilm viewing on the questionnaire item about unhealthy, shameful, or morbid interest in sex that we observed was the result of subjects giving this question further consideration from the time of completing the prefilm questionnaire to the time they completed the postfilm questionnaire, and not the result of changing their opinions because they had seen the film. To test this possibility, we compared the responses of the neutral-film control group subjects before and after the film viewing on this questionnaire item. The results of this statistical test revealed a nonsignificant change between pre-and postfilm evaluations for the control group on the prurient appeal question ($p > .26$).

[D]iscussion

[A]t least two types of "tolerance" can be measured through a community survey—the opinions of a representative sample of persons about what they *think* the *community* tolerates, and the collective opinions of these same individuals about what they *personally* should be allowed to view. In this study, we asked subjects about both. The findings reported here (see table 4) indicate that a much lower percentage of people think the hypothetical "community" tolerates the films they just viewed than is the case when people are asked to report on what they personally tolerate (what they should be allowed to view). If we define community tolerance as the sum of individual responses about what people personally would tolerate, we would conclude that the community of Mecklenburg County is *overwhelmingly* tolerant of these materials, by a margin of 3 to 1.

[I]t might be informative to jurors for a social scientist to present evidence about *both* perceptions of the community and individual levels of tolerance. It should be acknowledged, however, that most policy decision making based on public opinion research relies on the summation of individual opinions rather than "guesses" by respondents about others' opinions and behaviors. As social scientists, we place far more confidence in a procedure whereby we ask people if they should personally be free to engage in a specific behavior (such as watching a movie) and summing these individual responses in order to obtain "the average" response, than we would be in asking people to report on what they *perceive* the "average" person would do in the same situation.

ST. JOHN v. STATE OF NORTH CAROLINA PAROLE COMMISSION

United States District Court, Western District of North Carolina, 1991.
764 F.Supp. 403.

■ ROBERT D. POTTER, DISTRICT JUDGE.

[Petitioners were convicted in a state court of selling obscene videotapes and sentenced to six years in prison. Having exhausted their appeals in state court, they filed a petition in federal court for a writ of habeas corpus. The Respondent—the Parole Commission that maintained custody of petitioners—moved for summary judgment dismissing the petition.]

[P]etitioners believe the following argument support[s] their contention that relief is available:

> The trial court excluded Petitioners' expert evidence in violation of Petitioners' right of confrontation and compulsory process pursuant to the Sixth Amendment and their due process rights pursuant to the Fourteenth Amendment.

[F]ilm Evaluation Study.

Petitioners attempted to introduce at trial a study involving focus groups that reviewed the films named in the indictment. According to Petitioners, the admission of such a study has never been attempted at an obscenity trial. Because the materials presented in the study were the films actually at issue, Petitioners argue that the trial court had no basis in law to exclude these studies.

Admittedly, the procedures utilized in the film evaluation study were designed to lead to the introduction of more relevant evidence than the other studies. Nonetheless, the Court does not believe that this fact alone requires the admission of the study. The proffered expert testimony revealed that only 20 to 24 people viewed each of the videotapes at issue.[11] Given the fact that the study was conducted in conditions exclusively in the control of Petitioners, the Court does not believe that Judge Gray was in error in finding that this evidence would be of no assistance to the 12 members of the community comprising the jury. Simply put, the Court believes that the record in this matter raises serious questions regarding whether those selected to participate in the study were "average" members of the community. The Court can envision large numbers of the community refusing to participate in a study that would expose them to the filth contained in the films at issue here. Even if it could be demonstrated that the focus groups were comprised of "average" citizens, the Court doubts whether the opinion of 20 to 24 persons would be of great assistance to the jury in deciding what in effect is a jury question—whether the films were obscene. Thus, the Court believes that the trial court did not deprive Petitioners of any constitutional right in excluding this study.

[R]espondents' motion for summary judgment is GRANTED.

———

11. Petitioners argue that the Court should not consider the small composition of the focus groups because the district attorney threatened to prosecute the experts for disseminating obscenity if the films were shown to the focus groups. [J]udge McMillan entered an order enjoining the district attorney from prosecuting the experts. However, the Fourth Circuit vacated that order as being unlawful. The Court does not believe that Petitioners can complain of the size of the focus groups in light of the Fourth Circuit's opinion.

NOTES

1. Focus Groups? The court referred to the conditions in the true experimental study later published by Linz et al as "focus groups." D. Stewart and P. Shamdasani, Focus Groups: Theory and Practice (1990), however, describe focus groups as follows: "The contemporary focus group interview generally involves 8 to 12 individuals who discuss a particular topic under the direction of a moderator who promotes interaction and assures that the discussion remains on the topic of interest." Id. at 10. Since the subjects in the Linz et al study watched a film in private and completed a written post-film questionnaire—never discussing their reactions to the film with another subject or with a "moderator"—"focus groups" would appear an inapt description of the methodology of the study the Petitioners had attempted to introduce at trial.

2. Obscenity Prosecutions. *Daubert v. Merrell Dow Pharmaceuticals* was decided in 1993. As of late 2009, there have been no reported opinions in which a court has subjected a survey of community standards of obscenity to a *Daubert* analysis. See Richards and Calvert, The 2008 Federal Obscenity Conviction of Paul Little and What It Reveals About Obscenity Law and Prosecutions, 11 Vanderbilt Journal of Entertainment and Technology Law 543 (2009).

SELECTED BIBLIOGRAPHY

Bedard and Gertz, Differences in Community Standards for the Viewing of Heterosexual and Homosexual Pornography, 12 International Journal of Public Opinion Research 324 (2000).

Boyce, Obscenity and Community Standards, 33 Yale Journal of International Law 299 (2008).

Obscenity and Pornography Decisions of the United States Supreme Court (M. Harrison and S. Gilbert eds. 2000).

Lindgren, Defining Pornography, 141 University of Pennsylvania Law Review 1153 (1993).

Richards and Calvert, The 2008 Federal Obscenity Conviction of Paul Little and What It Reveals About Obscenity Law and Prosecutions, 11 Vanderbilt Journal of Entertainment and Technology Law 543 (2009).

Section III.   Damages

The law of remedies is concerned with the kind of relief to be given to a plaintiff who has established that a defendant has violated a substantive right. An injunction, for example, can be issued by a court commanding a defendant to act or to avoid acting in a certain way (e.g., to cease using a given term as a trademark for a product), and disobeying the court's order can result in a fine or imprisonment for contempt. Another common remedy is damages. A person who suffers a legally recognized harm is often entitled to an award of damages. Damages are given to the plaintiff in the form of money, even if the plaintiff's injury was not pecuniary (e.g., pain and suffering). The primary purpose of damages is a compensatory one: to make up to the plaintiff for what he or she has lost. Separate from compensatory damages, a plaintiff may also be awarded punitive damages, whose common purpose is to punish the defendant in the case of particularly aggravated misconduct on the defendant's part. See D. Dobbs, Remedies (2nd ed. 1993).

Compensatory damages have traditionally been decided on an individual basis, with the jury or judge setting the amount of money to be awarded in rough proportion to the extent of the plaintiff's injury. See Robinson and Abraham, Collective Justice in Tort Law, 78 Virginia Law Review 1481, 1481–1490 (1992). In the case of "mass torts," however, in which large numbers of plaintiffs have been injured by a defendant or group of defendants, determining the amount of damages to be awarded to each individual plaintiff has threatened to overwhelm the legal system. Some courts have recently attempted to deal with this problem in a creative way: by employing sampling techniques derived from the social sciences.

HAROLDS STORES, INC. v. DILLARD DEPARTMENT STORES

United States Court of Appeals, Tenth Circuit, 1996.
82 F.3d 1533.

■ Baldock, Circuit Judge.

This appeal arises from a jury verdict entered in a copyright infringement action. Plaintiffs Harold's Stores, Inc. ("Harold's") and CMT Enterprises, Inc. ("CMT") filed suit against Defendant Dillard Department Stores, Inc. ("Dillard") alleging that Dillard infringed Harold's copyrighted fabric designs contained on women's garments, predominately skirts. [A] jury returned a verdict for Harold's. [D]illard appeals, arguing that [t]he district court erroneously admitted consumer survey evidence, and that it was entitled to judgment as a matter of law after trial.

[D]illard is a retail department store, operating 218 stores in 17 states. Harold's is a retail clothing store with 22 stores in 7 states, including 6 in Oklahoma and 7 in Texas. Women's clothing forms the majority of Harold's business. With the assistance of CMT, a garment manufacturer, Harold's designs and manufactures private label women's clothing, including skirts, that feature original print fabric designs. Harold's annually develops 70 to 80 print fabrics from original art that it purchases from art studios in Italy and New York. [H]arold's represents to its customers that the original print fabric garments are available solely from Harold's.

[O]n May 10, 1993, Rebecca Casey, C.E.O. of Harold's, received information that Dillard stores in Norman and Tulsa, Oklahoma were offering for sale skirts with print fabric patterns identical to print skirts that Harold's had sold during the previous 1991 to 1992 sales season. Ms. Casey dispatched two employees to a Dillard store to investigate. The employees returned with "sacks of garments" purchased at Dillard that upon first examination appeared identical to print skirts that Harold's had developed from original art and offered for sale at $78.00 to $80.00 apiece the year before. The Dillard skirts were priced at $28.00 to $30.00. Over the next few days, Harold's personnel discovered skirts substantially similar to Harold's own offered for sale in 26 different Dillard stores.

[P]rior to trial, Dillard stipulated that it had infringed 19 of Harold's copyrighted print fabrics. Dillard offered for sale a total of 22,000 garments manufactured using Harold's copyrighted print fabric designs, and placed advance orders for 15,000 more. Thus, Dillard offered for sale or had ordered a total of 37,000 garments which infringed Harold's copyrights.

The district court conducted a six-day jury trial on Harold's damages claims. To establish its damages, Harold's submitted opinion testimony from [D]r. Daniel Howard. [D]r. Howard, a marketing professor from Southern Methodist University ("SMU"), estimated Harold's damages. Based on the results of a survey of college-aged women who had visited a Harold's store or examined a Harold's catalog and visited a Dillard store during the relevant time, Dr. Howard calculated the damages Harold's suffered nationwide due to Dillard's infringement of Harold's copyrights. [O]ver Dillard's motion in limine and objections, the district court admitted Dr. Howard's survey, report, and testimony.

[D]illard contends the district erred in admitting Dr. Howard's survey. Dillard argues the district court abused its discretion in admitting the survey because: (1) Dr. Howard failed to survey a relevant universe of consumers, and (2) the survey was not material or probative to establish copyright damages.

We allow the admission of survey evidence "as an exception to the hearsay rule if the survey is material, more probative on the issue than other evidence and if it has guarantees of trustworthiness." Brunswick Corp. v. Spinit Reel Co., 832 F.2d 513, 522 (10th Cir.1987) (citing Fed. R.Evid. 803(24)); see also 5 Jack B. Weinstein & Margaret A. Berger, Weinstein's Evidence P 901(b)(9)[03] at 901–140 (1995) ("The admissibility of survey or sampling results depends upon two factors: necessity and trustworthiness."); Manual for Complex Litigation, Third, s 21.493 at 101 (1995) ("In some cases, sampling techniques may provide the only practicable means to collect and present relevant data."). "A survey is trustworthy if it is shown to have been conducted according to generally accepted survey principles." (Brunswick Corp., 832 F.2d at 522)

The survey should sample an adequate or proper universe of respondents. Exxon Corp. v. Texas Motor Exchange of Houston, Inc., 628 F.2d 500, 507 (5th Cir.1980). "[T]hat is, the persons interviewed must adequately represent the opinions which are relevant to the litigation." Amstar

Corp. v. Domino's Pizza, Inc., 615 F.2d 252, 264 (5th Cir.), cert. denied, 449 U.S. 899, 101 S.Ct. 268, 66 L.Ed.2d 129 (1980). The district court should exclude the survey "when the sample is clearly not representative of the universe it is intended to reflect." Bank of Utah v. Commercial Sec. Bank, 369 F.2d 19, 27 (10th Cir.1966), cert. denied, 386 U.S. 1018, 87 S.Ct. 1374, 18 L.Ed.2d 456 (1967). Technical and methodological deficiencies in the survey, including the sufficiency of the universe sampled, bear on the weight of the evidence, not the survey's admissibility. We review the district court's admission of a survey for an abuse of discretion.

At trial, Harold's claimed that Dillard's sale in 1993 of copyrighted skirts that Harold's sold in 1991 and 1992 injured Harold's reputation and goodwill, and damaged Harold's relations and future sales with present and prospective customers. Harold's retained Dr. Howard to offer opinion testimony in support of Harold's damages claims. As a basis for his testimony, Dr. Howard surveyed 1,231 female undergraduates at SMU in October 1993 using a single-page survey. The complete survey is set forth in the margin.[7] 578 of the 1,231 respondents reported that they had visited a Harold's store or looked at a Harold's catalog and visited a Dillard store during the relevant time periods. Dr. Howard used the universe of female undergraduates who were exposed to both Harold's and Dillard during the times at issue to "determine whether, and to what degree, Dillard's sale of Harold's copyrighted fabric designs inflicted damages to future sales of women's and men's clothing by Harold's." Aplee. Supp.App. at 2441, 2472.

Dillard maintains the district court abused its discretion in admitting the survey because the group surveyed was too narrow. Dillard argues that because Dr. Howard surveyed only female undergraduates at SMU, and from their responses extrapolated damages for all consumers that potentially would shop at a Harold's store, the survey was fatally flawed. According to Dillard, the proper universe encompasses "Harold's overall customers." Aplt. Reply Br. at 21.

7. Shopping Survey Instructions: Please respond to the following questions by placing a "x" in the space that most closely reflects your memories and your feelings about the issues addressed.

(1) Have you visited a Harold's store or looked at a Harold's catalog in the past two years (in 1991 or 1992)?

___yes ___no ___unsure

(2) Did you visit a Dillard's department store from May to August of this year(1993)?

___yes ___no ___unsure

CONTINUE THE SURVEY ONLY IF YOU ANSWERED "YES" TO #1 AND #2

(3) On any of your recent visits to Dillard's, have you seen any print skirts with patterns you thought of as being unique to Harold's?

___yes ___no ___unsure

(4) On any of your recent visits to Dillard's, have you seen any women's purses with designs you thought of as being unique to Harold's?

___yes ___no ___unsure

(5) How likely or unlikely is it that you will purchase clothes from Harold's within the next year?

very likely __:__:__:__:__ very unlikely

(6) Is this the first time you have answered these questions?

___yes ___no ___unsure

On this record, we cannot conclude the district court abused its discretion in admitting the survey. The district court conducted an extensive voir dire of Dr. Howard and satisfied itself that the survey was material, probative to the issue of copyright infringement damages, and conducted according to generally accepted survey principles. The record also reflects that Harold's laid an adequate foundation to admit the survey.

[W]e also conclude that Dr. Howard surveyed an adequate universe of respondents. Ms. Casey, CEO of Harold's, testified that college-aged women represent a critically important group to Harold's overall sales. Ms. Casey also testified that Harold's first store was located on a college campus and that Harold's intentionally locates its stores near college campuses to target the college market, primarily undergraduate women. Ms. Casey observed that in her view, the buying patterns of college-age women are "identical to our older customers." Aplt.App. at 1676. Testimony before the district court also established that purchasing patterns, consumer preferences, and the demand for Harold's products were similar for all Harold's stores, regardless of geographic location.

Because testimony before the district court established that college-age women comprise Harold's core customer base, this survey does not amount to an instance "when the sample is clearly not representative of the universe it is intended to reflect." Bank of Utah, 369 F.2d at 27. Instead, the record demonstrates that the universe of college-age women who had visited a Dillard store and either visited a Harold's store or looked at a Harold's catalog during the relevant time periods "represent the opinions which are relevant to the litigation." Amstar, 615 F.2d at 264. That is, the survey respondents' opinions are probative on the issue of whether and to what degree Dillard's infringement and sale of Harold's copyrighted fabric designs damaged Harold's future clothing sales. Thus, Dillard's contention that the survey was not probative or material to the issue of copyright infringement damages fails.

In sum, we hold the district court did not abuse its discretion in admitting the survey because Dr. Howard surveyed an adequate universe of respondents according to generally accepted survey principles. Consequently, any technical or methodological deficiencies in the manner in which Dr. Howard conducted the survey bear on the weight—not the admissibility—of the survey. We therefore reject Dillard's argument that the district court erred in admitting the survey because the survey respondents did not encompass "Harold's overall customers" and because the survey was, according to Dillard, not material or probative.

[D]illard [also] [m]aintains the district court erred in denying its Rule 50 (b) renewal motion for judgment as a matter of law because the evidence was insufficient to support the copyright damages award. Dillard contends that the survey evidence attested to by Dr. Howard did not provide reliable evidence of present or future reduced sales revenue as a result of reduced purchase intentions.

[H]arold's offered opinion testimony from Dr. Howard in support of its copyright infringement damages claims. Dr. Howard based his damages estimates on the survey. Of the universe of undergraduate women who had visited a Dillard store in 1993, (when Dillard offered the infringing skirts for sale), and visited a Harold's store or looked at a Harold's catalog in 1991 or 1992, Dr. Howard testified that the survey detected a reduced future purchase intention by respondents who saw print skirts at Dillard that they thought were unique to Harold's. Specifically, Dr. Howard testified that women who saw the infringing skirts at Dillard were some- what unlikely to purchase clothes from Harold's within the next year. In contrast, women who visited both stores but did not see skirts they thought of as unique to Harold's were, on the whole, fairly likely to shop at Harold's in the future. Dr. Howard reported that the women who saw the garments at issue at Dillard were 33.1% less likely to purchase garments at Harold's than women who visited both stores at the relevant time but did not view the infringing skirts.

Dr. Howard analyzed the survey data and estimated the damages Harold's suffered nationwide from Dillard's copyright infringement. Dr. Howard testified that Harold's suffered damages to goodwill, reputation, and sales to future and prospective customers in the range of $226,367.00 to $517,809.00.

Based on this evidence, the jury awarded Harold's and CMT actual damages of $312,000.00 on the copyright infringement claim. Viewing the evidence in the light most favorable to Harold's and drawing all reasonable inferences therefrom, SCFC ILC, Inc., 36 F.3d at 962, we conclude there was substantial evidence tending to support the jury's damages award on Harold's copyright infringement claim.

[I]n sum, we hold the district court did not err by [a]dmitting Dr. Howard's survey and [d]enying Dillard's renewal motion for judgment as a matter of law after trial.

[A]FFIRMED.

CIMINO v. RAYMARK INDUSTRIES, INC.

United States District Court, Eastern District of Texas, 1990.
751 F.Supp. 649.

■ ROBERT M. PARKER, CHIEF JUDGE.

The odyssey of asbestos litigation in the Eastern District of Texas has now entered its third decade. The trek started by Clarence Borel and Claude Tomplait has been marked by aimless wandering through the legal wilderness. The journey has taken its predicted toll. Raymark, Forty–Eight Insulations, Unarco, Standard Asbestos, Johns–Manville, Eagle–Picher, and now Celotex are bankrupt. Other defendants are clearly in the twilight of their participation. Four hundred and forty-eight members of the class have died waiting for their cases to be heard. The departed companies and plaintiffs have all been victims of a system that has seen a substantial majority of the compensation dollar go to witnesses and lawyers in the form of transaction costs. Transaction costs consumed $.61 of each asbestos-litigation dollar with $.37 going to defendants litigation costs; the plaintiffs receive only $.39 from each litigation dollar.

[T]he Court has now witnessed an evolution in defense strategy. [Defendants] have adopted a "fortress mentality" and are attempting to avoid liability by obstructing the Court's ability to provide a forum in these cases. It is a strategy that is not unique to East Texas, but is one that is being utilized all across the country. They assert a right to individual trials in each case and assert the right to repeatedly contest in each case every contestable issue involving the same products, the same warnings, and the same conduct. The strategy is a sound one; the defendants know that if the procedure in *Cimino* is not affirmed, these cases will never be tried.

If the Court could somehow close thirty cases a month, it would take six and one-half years to try these cases and there would be pending over 5,000 untouched cases at the present rate of filing. Transaction costs would be astronomical.

The great challenge presented to the Court by this litigation is to provide a fair and cost effective means of trying large numbers of asbestos cases.

[D]uring the course of the *Cimino* trial while the question of whether asbestos products were unreasonably dangerous was being litigated once again in Beaumont, the federal courtroom in Tyler was being used by the State Court of Appeals Judges because men in spacesuits were removing asbestos from their chambers.

THE PLAN

[O]n February 19, 1990, this Court certified a class under Fed.R.Civ.P. 23(b)(3) consisting of 3,031 plaintiffs with existing cases in the Eastern District of Texas, all claiming an asbestos-related injury or disease resulting from exposure to defendants' asbestos containing insulation products. Seven hundred thirty-three cases were removed as a result of being dismissed, severed or settled. The class consisting of 2,298 plaintiffs went to trial against Pittsburgh–Corning, Fibreboard, Celotex, Carey–Canada, and ACL.

PHASE I

[T]he issues were whether each asbestos containing insulation product manufactured by each defendant, settling and non-settling, was defective and unreasonably dangerous, the adequacy of warnings, the state of the art defense and the fiber type defense.

[P]HASE II

Phase II required a jury finding for each of nineteen worksites during certain time periods regarding which asbestos containing insulation products were used, which crafts were sufficiently exposed to asbestos fibers from those products for such exposure to be a producing cause of an asbestos-related injury or disease and an apportionment of causation among defendants, settling and non-settling.

In other words, the exposure questions to be submitted would be specific as to time, place, craft, and amounts of exposure.

PHASE III

Phase III is the damage issue. The 2,298 class members were divided into five disease categories based on the plaintiff's injury claims. The Court selected a random sample from each disease category as follows:

	SAMPLE SIZE	DISEASE CATEGORY POPULATION
Mesothelioma	15	32
Lung Cancer	25	186
Other Cancer	20	58
Asbestosis	50	1,050
Pleural Disease	50	972
TOTAL	160	2,298

The damage case of each trial sample class member randomly drawn was then submitted to a jury. Each plaintiff whose damage case was submitted to the jury is to be awarded his individual verdict and the average verdict for each disease category will constitute the damage award for each non-sample class member.

Plaintiffs have agreed to the procedure, thereby waiving their rights to individual damage determinations.

THE TRIAL

Phase I began with jury selection on February 6, 1990 and the verdict was returned March 29, 1990. The Court then granted the parties' request for additional preparation time between Phase I and Phases II and III. Two juries were selected on July 3, 1990. The juries sat together for the first five trial days which were devoted to general medical testimony. The juries were then divided and began hearing testimony on groups of plaintiffs and returning damage verdicts. The last verdict for the 160 individual damages cases was received October 5, 1990.

In all, the trial consumed 133 days of trial time and produced 25,348 pages of transcript prepared as daily copy. The docket sheet in the Clerk's office is 529 pages long. The Court has entered 373 signed Orders.

Prior to trial 1,885 sets of interrogatories were answered by the parties and 2,354 depositions were taken, with an additional 800 being taken during trial. Independent medical examinations were conducted of 1,400 plaintiffs.

During the course of the trial, 271 expert witnesses and 292 fact witnesses testified, 6,176 exhibits were received in evidence constituting 577,000 pages of documents. Fifty-eight individual lawyers participated in the in-court presentation of this case which was presided over in varying degrees by four district judges and three magistrates.

If all that is accomplished by this is the closing of 169 cases, then it was not worth the effort and will not be repeated.

PHASE II—STIPULATION

[P]rior to the Court drafting a verdict form for Phase II, the parties agreed to stipulate as to what the jury findings would have been had Phase II been tried to a jury. The parties stipulated that the jury would have apportioned causation among the defendants in the amounts of 10% causation for each of the non-settling defendants and 13% causation for the settling defendant Johns–Manville Corporation.

STATISTICS

Phase III of the plan utilizes the science of statistics, or more specifically, inferential statistics.

[A]cceptance of statistical evidence is now commonplace in the Courts. The following illustrations demonstrate the diverse legal contexts in which statistics, particularly random sampling, has been used. In trademark infringement suits, statistical sampling is useful in determining consumer product identification and confusion regarding trademarks. See Processed Plastic Co. v. Warner Communications, Inc., 675 F.2d 852, 854–58 (7th Cir.1982) (survey of children between the ages of 6 and 12 in order to determine if Plaintiff's toy car was confused with Defendant's "Dukes of Hazzard" toy car); Exxon Corp. v. Texas Motor Exchange, Inc., 628 F.2d 500 (5th Cir.1980) (survey of 515 licensed drivers indicated high possibility of confusion between "Texon" and "Exxon"); Zippo Manufacturing Co. v. Rogers Imports, Inc., 216 F.Supp. 670 (S.D.N.Y.1963).

[I]n the area of torts, statistics have been used to prove both liability and damages. The New Jersey Supreme Court has, in at least two cases, relied upon statistics showing the correlation between the theft of cars with keys left in the ignition and automobile accidents in the liability phase of a trial. See Hill v. Yaskin, 75 N.J. 139, 380 A.2d 1107 (1977); Zinck v. Whelan, 120 N.J.Super. 432, 294 A.2d 727 (1972). Courts frequently permit evidence of life-expectancy or mortality tables when determining damages. See Ageloff v. Delta Airlines, Inc., 860 F.2d 379 (11th Cir.1988); Espana v. United States, 616 F.2d 41 (2d Cir.1980); Larsen v. International Business Machines Corp., 87 F.R.D. 602 (E.D.Pa.1980) (use of work-life tables). Statistical evidence has proven to be particularly useful in the determination of lost or future revenues, profits or earnings. See In re Knickerbocker, 827 F.2d 281, 288–89 (8th Cir.1987) (court allowed expert to testify as to future revenues, based upon historical analysis and price predictions).

[T]he reasons the courts have come to rely on statistics are the same reasons that society embraces the science. It has been proved to provide information with an acceptable degree of accuracy and economy.

[A]gainst this backdrop, defendants assert that statistical methodology is somehow inappropriate for mass tort cases. This contention fails when examined under the same microscope used in other cases. The method incorporated into Phase III produces a level of economy in terms of both judicial resources and transaction cost that needs no elaboration. Moreover, defendants cannot possibly suggest that no form of statistical evidence is appropriate in this case. They frequently used statistics during this trial. At the outset, Owens–Illinois submitted a statistical analysis of a telephone survey conducted by Jury Analyst, Inc. on a sample of 500 people from each division in this district in support of its Motion to Transfer Venue. Defendants Fibreboard and Pittsburgh–Corning subsequently adopted that motion. The voluminous medical literature offered by both sides contains innumerable examples of statistical surveys and analysis.

Defendant Pittsburgh–Corning relied upon the testimony of Dr. Thomas Robert Savings to estimate the percentage of Pittsburgh–Corning products in the Golden Triangle area. Dr. Savings made an extensive statistical analysis to compute the estimated market share for Pittsburgh–Corning which was then extrapolated to the chemical plants in the area. The Court is of the opinion that defendants' extensive reliance upon statistical analysis and extrapolation considerably weakens their argument against the use of the same by the Court.

[D]UE PROCESS

Defendants object to the Court's plan and assert that due process, even in the asbestos context, entitles defendants to a traditional one-on-one trial in each of the 2,298 cases. In defendants' eyes there are no common issues, irrespective of the fact that the products in each trial would be identical, the warnings would be identical, and the exposure evidence for each worksite during the time periods inquired about for each craft would be identical.

[I]t is this Court's opinion that due process in the asbestos context should not be analyzed in the narrow, traditional, one-sided view of defendants, but should also encompass the impact on plaintiffs and even the obvious societal interest involved.

[D]amages must be determined in the aggregate. Whether it is by the mechanism of the Court's plan or by some other procedure approved or suggested by the Court of Appeals, without the ability to determine damages in the aggregate, the Court cannot try these cases.

IN RE ESTATE OF FERDINAND E. MARCOS HUMAN RIGHTS LITIGATION

United States District Court, District of Hawai'i, 1995.
910 F.Supp. 1460.

■ REAL, DISTRICT JUDGE.

Victims of torture, summary execution and disappearance filed suits for damages, in the form of a class action as well as individual direct actions, against the Estate of the former President of the Philippines, Ferdinand E. Marcos (MARCOS), for human rights violations.

[I]n 1986 MARCOS fled the Philippines and arrived in the State of Hawaii. MARCOS was a resident of Hawaii at the time he was served with the complaints that are the subject of this litigation but he died during the pendency of these actions. The Estate of Ferdinand E. Marcos (the ESTATE) has been substituted in MARCOS' place; his widow, Imelda Marcos, and his son, Ferdinand E. Marcos, Jr., have appeared before this Court as representatives of the ESTATE.

The action was tried in the three phases: (1) liability, (2) exemplary [i.e., punitive] damages, and (3) compensatory damages, over a nine year period—from 1986 to 1995. In the compensatory damages phase, Phase III, this Court allowed the jury to consider the damages to a random sample of plaintiffs as representative of the injuries suffered by those in the three subclasses; i.e. (1) plaintiffs who were tortured; (2) the families of those individuals who were the subjects of summary execution; and (3) the families of those who disappeared as the result of the actions of MARCOS.

[O]n September 22, 1992, in the liability phase of the trial, the jury found defendants liable to 10,059 plaintiffs, for the acts of torture, summary execution and disappearance. On February 23, 1994 the jury awarded plaintiffs $1.2 billion in exemplary damages.

In the compensatory damages phase, the class action plaintiffs presented their case to the jury by using damages sustained by a random sample of plaintiffs as representative of damages suffered by the entire class.

[A]t this time there are two issues before this Court. The primary question is whether the use by this Court of a random sample of plaintiffs, as representative of the injuries suffered by others in the class, violates defendant's due process rights. The second question is whether use of the random sample violates the defendant's Seventh Amendment right to a jury trial.

The ESTATE asserts random sampling is inappropriate for this case, and each claim should be individually tried. This Court holds otherwise. The use of aggregate procedures, with the help of an expert in the field of inferential statistics, for the purpose of determining class compensatory damages is proper.

James Dannemiller, an expert in the field of inferential statistics and survey sampling for twenty five years, assisted in this case. [M]r. Dannemiller testified that inferential statistics is a recognized science which uses mathematical equations to infer the probability of events occurring or not occurring. One branch of that science is the sampling theory, which deals with the selection of sample sizes sufficient to produce results that can be applied to a larger population from which the sample was selected with a specified probability of error. The formula Dannemiller used in this case is a well-known statistical tool that is found in Leslie Kish, Survey Sampling 53 (New York, John Wiley and Sons 1962) (KISH FORMULA).

Mr. Dannemiller testified under the KISH FORMULA, 137 randomly selected valid claims examined from a larger population of 9,541 validly submitted claims by class members would produce a 95% confidence level. The Court then considered the details of deposing 137 randomly selected claimants.

This Court appointed a Special Master, to facilitate the taking of depositions of 137 randomly selected plaintiffs. The Special Master's appointment had a three-fold purpose: first, he supervised the taking of the 137 depositions in the Philippines; second, he served as a court-appointed expert on damages, under Federal Rule of Evidence 706, to review the deposition transcripts along with the claim forms; finally, he made recommendations on compensatory damages for the 137 claimants as well as the remaining class members to the jury.

The depositions which the Special Master oversaw were noticed and taken in accordance with the Federal Rules of Civil Procedure. Although having notice of the depositions of the 137 class member sample and the names of the individual class members, the ESTATE chose not to participate and did not appear at any of the depositions, which were taken during October and November of 1994. Nor did the ESTATE choose to depose any of the 9,541 class members to test the procedure employed by the Court, or to acquire evidence to refute the fairness to the defendant of this random selection process using inferential statistical methodology.

The Special Master was directed by this Court to review the depositions for the following three elements: (1) whether the abuse claimed fell within one of the three definitions, with which the Court charged the jury at the liability phase of the trial; (2) whether the Philippine military or paramilitary was involved in such abuse; and (3) whether the abuse occurred during the period of September 1972 through February 1986.

[O]f the 137 randomly sampled claims, 67 were torture victims, 52 were execution victims and 18 were disappearance victims. Based upon the depositions of each of the 137 randomly selected class member's claims and review of all the claims of the remaining class members, the Special Master recommended damages under Philippine, International, and American law, for each of the three categories of claims. During the Special Master's testimony, the Court advised the jury that they, in determining damages, could accept, modify or reject the recommendations of the Special Master. The jury was also instructed that they could, independently, on the basis of the depositions of the 137 randomly chosen class members, make their own judgment as to the individual damages of the 137 claimants and the aggregate damages suffered by the class. [A]fter five days of deliberations, the jury returned a verdict of over $766 million, approximately $1 million less than the Special Master had recommended.

In his report and testimony, the Special Master made damage determinations for torture victims by ranking each claim from 1–5, with 5 representing the worst abuses and suffering. The torture claims were evaluated based upon Judge Real's decision in Trajano v. Imee Marcos–Manotoc, aff'd, In re: Estate of Ferdinand E. Marcos Litigation, 978 F.2d 493 (9th Cir.1992), cert. denied, 508 U.S. 972, 113 S.Ct. 2960, 125 L.Ed.2d 661 (1993), as part of this matter, and the following considerations: (1) physical torture, including what methods were used and/or abuses were suffered; (2) mental abuse, including fright and anguish; (3) amount of time torture lasted; (4) length of detention, if any; (5) physical and/or mental injuries; (6) victim's age; and (7) actual losses, including medical bills. Although each claim of torture could have been but were not totally unique, as the Court Appointed Expert on damages, the Special Master, was able to determine that there were sufficient similarities within a rating category to recommend a standard damage amount to each victim within that grouping.

[F]or computing the total amount of damages for summary execution and disappearance victims, depending on the individual facts, there were different variables which went into the equation: (1) torture prior to death or disappearance; (2) the actual killing or disappearance; (3) the victim's family's mental anguish; and (4) lost earnings.

[T]he utilization of random sampling was fully examined in Cimino v. Raymark Industries, Inc., 751 F.Supp. 649 (E.D.Tex.1990), an asbestos class action.

[D]ue Process

In a case such as this one, where there are 9,541 class members, most of whom live in other areas of the world, a balancing of interests must occur to obtain justice to the parties. A due process analysis must weigh defendant's claim to the right to trial in each individual case against judicial economy and manageability by use of a valid statistical procedure. [T]his Court was moved by the same concerns as Chief Judge Parker in Cimino. Here, individual trials for each of the 9,541 plaintiffs would take decades. Most of that time would be wasted since the nature of the injuries would be similar, if not identical, the testimony would be largely duplicative. Utilizing the procedure employed by the Court the injuries could be accurately categorized, and the source of the injuries would be identical. [I]nferential statistics with random sampling produces an acceptable due process solution to the troublesome area of mass tort litigation.

The issue remains whether this Court's use of inferential statistics in using aggregate procedures, denied defendant's their constitutional due process right to a one-on-one trial. This Court believes, "the aggregate trial is, in some vital respects, superior to the individual trial"[15] and does not violate the substantive or procedural due process rights of either the plaintiffs or the defendant.

15. Michael J. Saks and Peter David Blanck, "Justice Improved: The Unrecognized Benefits of Aggregation and Sampling in Mass Torts", 44 STAN.L.REV. 815, 827 (1992).

This Court finds persuasive the analysis of Professors Saks and Blank in their discussion that aggregate trials do not violate due process.

[S]eventh Amendment

The issue here is whether the use of random samples, in an aggregate trial, violates the Seventh Amendment right to a jury trial. [T]he Seventh Amendment provides no formula for the procedures to be used in a trial by jury. Rather, it is the rules of evidence and procedure that impact jury trials. Pragmatic application of these rules, consistent with justice, is all that is necessary for the presentation of the facts necessary for a jury determination. To claim otherwise certainly raises form over substance to a new level in today's jurisprudential world.

Here, the jury did determine the facts of the case, as the substance of the action was presented to the jury. There would be no benefit to either side in having the entire class testify given the repetition in the claims. Rule 23 of the Federal Rule of Civil Procedure does not mandate the presence of each member of the class. Therefore, by choosing a random sample of 137 claimants in an aggregate trial, neither side was deprived of even the form of their right to a jury trial. [D]efendant was given its day in court with the jury, by procedures facilitating the presentation of evidence by use of random sampling in an aggregate damage trial.

[C]ONCLUSION

The use of an aggregate procedure for determining compensatory damages, under the procedures followed in this litigation, was neither a violation of the parties' due process rights nor their right to a jury trial under the Seventh Amendment. The aggregation of compensatory damage claims vindicates important federal and international policies, permits justice to be done without unduly clogging the court system, and was shown to be fair to the defendant.

Judgment shall be entered for plaintiffs.

———

HILAO v. ESTATE OF MARCOS

United States Court of Appeals, Ninth Circuit, 1996.
103 F.3d 789.

■ FLETCHER, CIRCUIT JUDGE.

The Estate of Ferdinand E. Marcos appeals from a final judgment entered against it in a class-action suit after a trifurcated jury trial on the damage claims brought by a class of Philippine nationals (hereinafter collectively referred to as "Hilao") who were victims of torture, "disappearance", or summary execution under the regime of Ferdinand E. Marcos. [T]he district court allowed the use of a statistical sample of the class claims in determining compensatory damages.

[T]he Estate's challenge to the procedure used by the district court is very narrow. It challenges specifically only "the method by which [the district court] allowed the validity of the class claims to be determined": the master's use of a representative sample to determine what percentage of the total claims were invalid.

The grounds on which the Estate challenges this method are unclear. It states that to its knowledge this method "has not previously been employed in a class action". This alone, of course, would not be grounds for reversal, and in any case the method has been used before in an asbestos class-action case, the opinion in which apparently helped persuade the district court to use this method. See Cimino v. Raymark Indus., Inc., 751 F.Supp. 649, 659–667 (E.D.Tex.1990).

The Estate also argues that the method was "inappropriate" because the class consists of various members with numerous subsets of claims based on whether the plaintiff or his or her decedent was subjected to torture, "disappearance", or summary execution. The district court's methodology, however, took account of those differences by grouping the class members' claims into three subclasses.

Finally, the Estate appears to assert that the method violated its rights to due process because "individual questions apply to each subset of claims, i.e., whether the action was justified, the degree of injury, proximate cause, etc." It does not, however, provide any argument or case citation to explain how the methodology violated its due-process rights. Indeed, the "individual questions" it identifies—justification, degree of injury, proximate cause— are irrelevant to the challenge it makes: the method of determining the validity of the class members' claims. The jury had already determined that Philippine military or paramilitary forces on Marcos' orders—or with his conspiracy or assistance or with his knowledge and failure to act—had tortured, summarily executed, or "disappeared" untold numbers of victims and that the Estate was liable to them or their survivors. The only questions involved in determining the validity of the class members' claims were whether or not the human-rights abuses they claim to have suffered were proven by sufficient evidence.

Although poorly presented, the Estate's due-process claim does raise serious questions. Indeed, at least one circuit court has expressed "profound disquiet" in somewhat similar circumstances. In re Fibreboard Corp., 893 F.2d 706, 710 (5th Cir.1990). [O]n the other hand, the time and judicial resources required to try the nearly 10,000 claims in this case would alone make resolution of Hilao's claims impossible. See Cimino, 751 F.Supp. at 652–53 ("If the Court could somehow close thirty cases a month, it would take six and one-half years to try these [2,298] cases . . ."). The similarity in the injuries suffered by many of the class members would make such an effort, even if it could be undertaken, especially wasteful, as would the fact that the district court found early on that the damages suffered by the class members likely exceed the total known assets of the Estate.

While the district court's methodology in determining valid claims is unorthodox, it can be justified by the extraordinarily unusual nature of this case. " 'Due process,' unlike some legal rules, is not a technical conception with a fixed content unrelated to time, place and circumstances". Cafeteria and Restaurant Workers Union, Local 473 v. McElroy, 367 U.S. 886, 895, 81 S.Ct. 1743, 1748, 6 L.Ed.2d 1230 (1961). In Connecticut v. Doehr, 501 U.S. 1, 10, 111 S.Ct. 2105, 2112, 115 L.Ed.2d 1 (1991), a case involving prejudgment attachment, the Supreme Court set forth a test, based on the test of Mathews v. Eldridge, 424 U.S. 319, 96 S.Ct. 893, 47 L.Ed.2d 18 (1976), for determining whether a procedure by which a private party invokes state power to deprive another person of property satisfies due process: [F]irst, consideration of the private interest that will be affected by the [procedure]; second, an examination of the risk of erroneous deprivation through the procedures under attack and the probable value of additional or alternative safeguards; and third, ... principal attention to the interest of the party seeking the [procedure], with, nonetheless, due regard for any ancillary interest the government may have in providing the procedure or forgoing the added burden of providing greater protections. 501 U.S. at 11, 111 S.Ct. at 2112. The interest of the Estate that is affected is at best an interest in not paying damages for any invalid claims. If the Estate had a legitimate concern in the identities of those receiving damage awards, the district court's procedure could affect this interest. In fact, however, the Estate's interest is only in the total amount of damages for which it will be liable: if damages were awarded for invalid claims, the Estate would have to pay more. The statistical method used by the district court obviously presents a somewhat greater risk of error in comparison to an adversarial adjudication of each claim, since the former method requires a probabilistic prediction (albeit an extremely accurate one) of how many of the total claims are invalid. The risk in this case was reduced, though, by the fact that the proof-of-claim form that the district court required each class member to submit in order to opt into the class required the claimant to certify under penalty of perjury that the information provided was true and correct. Hilao's interest in the use of the statistical method, on the other hand, is enormous, since adversarial resolution of each class member's claim would pose insurmountable practical hurdles. The "ancillary" interest of the judiciary in the procedure is obviously also substantial, since 9,541 individual adversarial determinations of claim validity would clog the docket of the district court for years. Under the balancing test set forth in Mathews and Doehr, the procedure used by the district court did not violate due process. [T]he judgment of the district court is therefore

AFFIRMED.

■ RYMER, CIRCUIT JUDGE, concurring in part and dissenting in part.

Because I believe that determining causation as well as damages by inferential statistics instead of individualized proof raises more than "serious questions" of due process, I must dissent from [that Part] of the majority opinion.

[T]here is little question that Marcos caused tremendous harm to many people, but the question is which people, and how much. That, I think, is a question on which the defendant has a right to due process. If due process in the form of a real prove-up of causation and damages cannot be accomplished because the class is too big or to do so would take too long, then (as the Estate contends) the class is unmanageable and should not have been certified in the first place. As Judge Becker recently wrote for the Third Circuit in declining to certify a 250,000–member class in an asbestos action: "Every decade presents a few great cases that force the judicial system to choose between forging a solution to a major social problem on the one hand, and preserving its institutional values on the other. This is such a case." Georgine v. Amchem Prod., Inc., 83 F.3d 610, 617 (3d Cir.1996).

So is this. I think that due process dictates the choice: a real trial. I therefore dissent.

CIMINO v. RAYMARK INDUSTRIES, INC.

Unites States Court of Appeals, Fifth Circuit, 1998.
151 F.3d 297.

■ Garwood, Circuit Judge.

We begin by stating some very basic propositions. These personal injury tort actions for monetary damages are "a prototypical example of an action at law, to which the Seventh Amendment applies." Wooddell v. Intern. Broth. of Elec. Workers, 112 S.Ct. 494, 498 (1991). The Seventh Amendment applies notwithstanding that these are diversity cases. But because these are diversity cases, the Rules of Decision Act, 28 U.S.C. § 1652, and Erie R. Co. v. Tompkins, 58 S.Ct. 817, 822–23 (1938), with its seeming constitutional underpinning, mandate that the substantive law applied be that of the relevant state, here Texas. Substantive law includes not only the factual elements which must be found to impose liability and fix damages, but also the burdens of going forward with evidence and of persuasion thereon.

[T]hus, the question becomes: did the implemented trial plan include a litigated determination, consistent with the Seventh Amendment, of the Texas-law mandated issues of whether, as to each individual plaintiff, Pittsburgh Corning's product was a cause of his complained-of condition and, if so, the damages that plaintiff suffered as a result.

[W]ith one exception, noted below, we are aware of no appellate decision approving such a group, rather than individual, determination of cause in a damage suit for personal injuries to individuals at widely different times and places. [I]n Hilao v. Estate of Marcos, 103 F.3d 767 (9th Cir.1996), a divided panel of the Ninth Circuit in a rule 23(b)(3) class action permitted recoverable tort damages to be determined in a lump sum for the entire class. [H]ilao is distinguishable here; it did not operate under the constraints of the Rules of Decision Act or Erie; the present case, by contrast, does operate under those constraints. If Hilao is not thus distinguishable it is simply contrary to Fibreboard [893 F.2d 706 (5th Cir.1990)], which binds us and which in our opinion is in any event correct. Further, Hilao did not address—and there was apparently not presented to it any contention concerning—the Seventh Amendment. Finally, we find ourselves in agreement with the thrust of the dissenting opinion there. Id. at 788 ("Even in the context of a class action, individual causation and individual damages must still be proved individually").

In sum, as Fibreboard held, under Texas law causation must be determined as to "individuals, not groups." And, the Seventh Amendment gives the right to a jury trial to make that determination.

[W]e do not act in ignorance or disregard of the asbestos crises. In Amchem Products, Inc. v. Windsor, 117 S.Ct. 2231, 2237–38 (1997), the Supreme Court called attention to the report of the Judicial Conference's Ad Hoc Committee on Asbestos Litigation, stating that "Real reform, the report concluded, required federal legislation creating a national asbestos-dispute resolution scheme." Id. at 2238. The Court also observed, "The argument is sensibly made that a nationwide administrative claims processing regime would provide the most secure, fair, and efficient means of compensating victims of asbestos exposure. Congress, however, has not adopted such a solution." Id. at 2252 (footnote omitted). Nevertheless, the Court refused to stretch the law to fill the gap resulting from congressional inaction. As we said in Fibreboard, federal courts must remain faithful to Erie and must maintain "the separation of powers between the judicial and legislative branches." Id. at 711.(52) "The Judicial Branch can offer the trial of lawsuits. It has no power or competence to do more." Id. at 712.

We accordingly reverse the judgments before us.

———

SAMPLING DAMAGES*
Laurens Walker and John Monahan.
83 Iowa Law Review 545 (1998).

The astonishing number of claimants in mass tort litigation overwhelms traditional commitment to individual, case by case, adjudication of compensatory damage claims. Some cases have involved millions of claimants and many cases have involved thousands of injured persons seeking compensation. Numbers such as these rule out any serious consideration of individual trials and have prompted controversial experimentation by courts with various forms of aggregation. Among these experiments are three district courts which have endorsed a form of aggregation that centered on statistical sampling as a solution to what might be called the numbers problem. In Cimino v. Raymark Industries, Inc., the compensatory damage claims of 2298 persons were adjudicated by trying a random sample of 160 cases and applying the results to all of the remaining cases. A panel of the Fifth Circuit rejected the implemented plan. In re Estate of Marcos Human Rights Litigation involved the compensatory damage claims

* Laurens Walker and John Monahan,   (1998) (reprinted with permission). Sampling Damages, 83 Iowa L. Rev. 545

of 10,059 persons which were adjudicated by deposing a random sample of 137 claimants, aggregating the results, and presenting the depositions and the aggregated information to a jury at one trial. A panel of the Ninth Circuit upheld this implemented plan. In re Chevron, U.S.A. Inc. addressed three-thousand compensatory damage claims which were the subject of a plan to try a sample of thirty cases to provide a basis for disposing of the rest. The court of appeals rejected the plan because the proposed sample was not randomly drawn, but approved the use of random sampling.

Cimino, *Marcos* and *Chevron* involved important steps toward solution of the numbers problem in mass tort litigation, but they incorporate cautious, tentative measures that fail to realize the full potential of statistical sampling to solve many of the problems posed by throngs of claimants. The difficulty in all three cases is that the pretense of individual adjudication is maintained. In all three, time and money were wasted in an effort to provide a few claimants "individual" adjudication, while using a survey to resolve other claims. Our thesis is that a complete solution of the numbers problem in mass torts can only be achieved by abandoning any pretense of individual adjudication and randomly sampling damages without apology.

[T]he first step would be certification of a class of plaintiffs co-extensive with the population to be surveyed. This step would provide plaintiffs a class representative who could, with expert assistance, produce a survey and present it at a class trial. [A]fter certification, the class representative, charged with the burden of proof on damages, would employ an expert to conduct the damage survey. This choice would not need to be approved by the court or by the opposing party because the class representative would only be engaging in the traditional collection of evidence for use at trial.

[I]n our proposal, the trial judge would not take a role in planning or carrying out the survey. Instead, the class representative would ask the court to approve the admission at trial of the survey results. At that time, opposing parties would be invited to examine the survey and make any objections. Both the court and opposing parties would be presented a comprehensive report of the survey. The trial judge would apply the *Daubert* standards using the *Survey Research Guide* [see Diamond, above, p. 135] criteria, and either permit or refuse expert testimony describing the survey and results to the jury.

[T]he defendant would also have access to survey methodology to collect evidence regarding damages. In cases involving large stakes, the defendant might well choose to employ an expert and survey the opposing class members about their damages.

[F]inally, and in stark contrast to the *Cimino* and *Chevron* or *Marcos* models, under our proposal the results of the survey or surveys, if permitted by the court under *Daubert*, would be presented by expert testimony to the jury with the data aggregated to suggest a total amount of compensation to be divided among the class or among subclasses. No individual data would be presented to the jury and no individual damage verdicts would be required or permitted.

DUKES v. WAL–MART, INC.

United States Court of Appeals, Ninth Circuit, 2007.*
509 F.3d 1168.

■ PREGERSON, CIRCUIT JUDGE.

Plaintiffs filed a class action suit against Wal–Mart alleging sexual discrimination under Title VII of the 1964 Civil Rights Act. The district court certified the class with minor modifications to Plaintiffs' proposed class. [W]e affirm the district court, concluding that it did not abuse its discretion when it certified the class.

BACKGROUND

Plaintiffs' [C]omplaint, brought on behalf of six named plaintiffs and all others similarly situated, asserts claims against Wal–Mart for sex discrimination under Title VII of the 1964 Civil Rights Act. Plaintiffs allege that women employed in Wal–Mart stores: (1) are paid less than men in comparable positions, despite having higher performance ratings and greater seniority, and (2) receive fewer—and wait longer for—promotions to in-store management positions than men. Plaintiffs contend that Wal–Mart's strong, centralized structure fosters or facilitates gender stereotyping and discrimination, that the policies and practices underlying this discriminatory treatment are consistent throughout Wal–Mart stores, and that this discrimination is common to all women who work or have worked in Wal–Mart stores.

[C]LASS ACTION CAN PROCEED IN A WAY THAT IS BOTH MANAGEABLE AND IN ACCORDANCE WITH DUE PROCESS

The parties agree that this is the largest class certified in history. The district court was cognizant of this when it concluded that the class size, although large, was not unmanageable. [A]t this pre-merits stage, we [s]imply note that, because there are a range of possibilities [t]hat would allow this class action to proceed in a manner that is both manageable and in accordance with due process, manageability concerns present no bar to class certification here.

For example, in *Hilao v. Estate of Ferdinand Marcos*, 103 F.3d 767, 782–87 (9th Cir.1996), the district court employed [statistical sampling] to determine the amount of compensatory damages due the plaintiffs in a large class action. [O]n appeal, the *Hilao* court was presented with some of the same objections to its trial plan as Wal–Mart presents here. After a

---

* [Ed. Note: On February 13, 2009, the Ninth Circuit ordered that Dukes v. Wal–Mart be reheard en banc. "The three-judge panel opinion shall not be cited as precedent by or to any court of the Ninth Circuit." The case was reargued on March 24, 2009.]

lengthy discussion, however, the *Hilao* court rejected these challenges and approved of the trial plan. [B]ecause we see no reason why a similar procedure to that used in *Hilao* could not be employed in this case, we conclude that there exists at least one method of managing this large class action that, albeit somewhat imperfect, nonetheless protects the due process rights of all involved parties. Accordingly, we find no manageability-based reason to find this otherwise-certifiable class unsuited to class certification.

NOTE

1. Sampling Liability. Walker and Monahan, Sampling Liability, 85 Virginia Law Review 329 (1999), have suggested that sampling techniques used to determine damages might also be used to determine issues of liability:

> We propose as a model for determining liability in complex cases that the method of proof be determined by the cost of collecting information. Individualized information should be used where it is practical—i.e., cost effective—to obtain. If individual information is not practical to obtain, however, sampling should be used so that a judgment can be reached efficiently and expeditiously. The fundamental justification for this model is found in its capacity to avoid outcomes determined by the cost of gathering information. In a situation where critical information about liability is costly to obtain, one side can prevail simply because the relevant information costs too much for the other side to gather and not because of the merits as established by law. Id. at 343.

SELECTED BIBLIOGRAPHY

Robbennolt, Punitive Damage Decision Making: The Decisions of Citizens and Trial Court Judges, 26 Law and Human Behavior 315 (2002).

Saks and Blanck, Justice Improved: The Unrecognized Benefits of Aggregation and Sampling in the Trial of Mass Torts, 44 Stanford Law Review 815 (1992).

Saks, Hollinger, Wissler, Evans, and Hart, Reducing Variability in Civil Jury Awards, 21 Law and Human Behavior 243 (1997).

Sanders, Medical Criteria Acts: State Statutory Attempts to Control the Asbestos Litigation, 37 Southwestern University Law Review 671 (2008).

Walker and Monahan, Sampling Evidence at the Crossroads, 80 Southern California Law Review 969 (2007).

Willging, Beyond Maturity: Mass Tort Case Management in the Manual for Complex Litigation, 148 University of Pennsylvania Law Review 2225 (2000).

Wissler, Rector, and Saks, The Impact of Jury Instructions on the Fusion of Liability and Compensatory Damages, 25 Law and Human Behavior 125 (2001).

CHAPTER FOUR

SOCIAL SCIENCE USED TO MAKE LAW

In this chapter, we turn our attention to a second and much more controversial legal application of social science: its use to determine what Professor Kenneth Culp Davis called "legislative facts." Davis defined legislative facts as follows:

> When an agency [or court] wrestles with a question of law or policy, it is acting legislatively, [a]nd the facts which inform its legislative judgment may conveniently be denominated legislative facts.

Davis, An Approach to Problems of Evidence in the Administrative Process, 55 Harvard Law Review 364, 402 (1942).

Legislative facts, in other words, are facts that courts use when they make law (or "legislate"), rather than simply apply settled doctrine to resolve a dispute between particular parties to a case. While the determination of adjudicative facts affects only the litigants before the court, the determination of legislative facts influences the content of legal doctrine itself, and therefore affects many parties in addition to those who brought the case.

We begin our examination of the use of social science to make law by considering in more detail Professor Davis' concept of legislative fact. We then explore the law-making use of social science in both constitutional and common law. Finally, we present our own effort to reconceptualize legislative fact as "social authority."

SECTION I. LEGISLATIVE FACTS

In the sixty years since it was first articulated, the notion of legislative fact "has been widely accepted in the federal appellate courts." Broz v. Schweiker, 677 F.2d 1351, 1357 (11th Cir. 1982). The United States Supreme Court as well has invoked the term on numerous occasions, e.g., Concerned Citizens v. Pine Creek Conservancy Dist., 429 U.S. 651, 97 S.Ct. 828, 51 L.Ed.2d 116 (1977); Lockhart v. McCree, 476 U.S. 162, 106 S.Ct. 1758, 90 L.Ed.2d 137 (1986).

AN APPROACH TO PROBLEMS OF EVIDENCE IN THE ADMINISTRATIVE PROCESS

Kenneth Culp Davis.
55 Harvard Law Review 364 (1942).

The rules of evidence for finding facts which form the basis for creation of law and determination of policy should differ from the rules for finding facts which concern only the parties to a particular case.

[W]hen an agency finds facts concerning immediate parties—what the parties did, what the circumstances were, what the background conditions were—the agency is performing an adjudicative function, and the facts may conveniently be called adjudicative facts. When an agency wrestles with a question of law or policy, it is acting legislatively, just as judges have created the common law through judicial legislation, and the facts which inform its legislative judgment may conveniently be denominated legislative facts. The distinction is important; the traditional rules of evidence are designed for adjudicative facts, and unnecessary confusion results from attempting to apply the traditional rules to legislative facts.

The courts have generally treated legislative facts differently from adjudicative facts, even though the distinction has not been clearly articulated and explanations have been beclouded by an erroneous use of the concept of judicial notice. The distinction between legislative and adjudicative facts apparently has been clearly recognized only in constitutional cases, in which a category of "constitutional facts" has emerged. Often referred to as "social and economic data," constitutional facts are those which assist a court in forming a judgment on a question of constitutional law. [I]n *Muller v. Oregon,* for example, the Court considered factual information contained in a brief filed by Mr. Louis D. Brandeis, including "extracts from over ninety reports of committees, bureaus of statistics, commissioners of hygiene, inspectors of factories, both in this country and in Europe...." [208 U.S. 412, 420, 28 S.Ct. 324, 326, 52 L.Ed. 551 (1908)] After Brandeis became a justice he continued his extensive factual studies and wrote many opinions saturated with facts brought to light through his own researches.

[T]he Court's reliance on extra-record constitutional facts has become fairly familiar. But what has not been so generally recognized is that constitutional facts are only one manifestation of a larger category of facts which are utilized for informing a court's legislative judgment on questions of law and policy. In non-constitutional cases courts often use a similar type of legislative facts not developed through the evidence.

[N]ot only have Supreme Court justices frequently relied upon extra-record facts, but the facts relied upon in many instances do not come within the scope of judicial notice. Many of the facts used, for instance, clearly are not covered by the language of the American Law Institute's proposed *Code of Evidence:* "The judge may of his own motion take judicial notice of ... (b) specific facts so notorious as not to be the subject of reasonable dispute, and (c) specific facts and propositions of generalized knowledge which are capable of immediate and accurate demonstration by resort to easily accessible sources of indisputable accuracy...." [T]he boundaries of judicial notice prescribed by the proposed *Code* may, of course, be perfectly appropriate for adjudicative facts; they seem to me wholly inappropriate for legislative facts.

[T]he agency must be free to go outside the record and beyond the limits of judicial notice in informing itself of facts which enter into its judgment in molding law and formulating policy.

It is neither possible nor desirable to immunize adjudicators from acquiring new factual knowledge; they should have more of it, not less.

It is, after all, the facts which concern the parties to a particular proceeding, rather than generalized information, which best lend themselves to the usual processes of cross-examination and rebuttal. Briefs and oral arguments are often (though not always) better vehicles for presentation of legislative facts than testimony and documents. And when a court or administrative tribunal makes its own investigation, the safeguard usually lies in the petition for reargument (new briefs and oral arguments) rather than in the petition for a rehearing (new evidence).

NOTE

1. Judicial Notice. The Code of Evidence proposed by the American Law Institute was a precursor of the Federal Rules of Evidence enacted by Congress in 1975. Rule 201, "Judicial Notice of Adjudicative Facts", explicitly incorporates the distinction between legislative and adjudicative facts proposed by Davis in his 1942 article. The Advisory Committee appointed by the Supreme Court notes that Rule 201 "is the only evidence rule on the subject of judicial notice. It deals only with judicial notice of 'adjudicative' facts. No rule deals with judicial notice of 'legislative' facts." See Appendix A. Professors Saltzburg, Martin and Capra have stated that "[t]he most serious problem with Rule 201 may be its total failure to address legislative facts." S. Saltzburg, M. Martin, and D. Capra, Federal Rules of Evidence Manual 201.02[4] (9th ed. 2006).

FACTS IN LAWMAKING

Kenneth Culp Davis.
80 Columbia Law Review 931 (1980).

The ingredients of all lawmaking have to be policy ideas and facts, but the policy ideas are necessarily dependent, immediately or remotely, on facts. Two interrelated questions [a]re: (1) Should law require lawmakers to develop the facts that are relevant to their lawmaking? (2) Should law require lawmakers, before using facts in lawmaking, to allow interested parties to challenge the assumed facts?

[T]he judgment is an easy one that at least *sometimes* the law should require the relevant facts to be developed and should require them to be available to opposing persons for a pre-decision response. But when?

[W]hen facts used in lawmaking are (1) narrow and specific, (2) central or critical, (3) controversial, (4) unmixed with judgment or policy, (5) provable, and (6) in some degree about the parties or known mainly by them, the parties clearly should have a pre-decision chance to challenge them, and the requirement may even be imposed in the name of due process. But when the facts are (1) broad and general, (2) background or peripheral, (3) noncontroversial, (4) mixed with judgment or policy, (5) not easily provable, and (6) wholly unrelated to the parties, a court or agency may use them without even adverting to any possible problem of procedural fairness. When the six items are mixed—some at one end of the scale, some at the other, some toward the middle—the two questions of how much support the facts should have and of what procedural protection to give the parties may be difficult. Law cannot feasibly provide for all combinations and permutations, and in each instance a judgment must be made.

JUDICIAL, LEGISLATIVE, AND ADMINISTRATIVE LAWMAKING: A PROPOSED RESEARCH SERVICE FOR THE SUPREME COURT

Kenneth Culp Davis.
71 Minnesota Law Review 1 (1986).

The Supreme Court is often at its best on complex thinking problems, on philosophical or ethical or moral issues, on analysis or reasoning, and on issues of interpretation. The Court may often be at its worst on policy issues that are dependent upon understanding or instincts about legislative facts. Indeed, my impression is that, typically, the Court is basically baffled in trying to deal with legislative facts. The Court's treatment of legislative facts may be an especially weak area in its whole performance, and it seems to be fully aware of that weakness.

[W]hen the Supreme Court in deliberating about a case realizes that it needs legislative facts it does not have, what should it do? [A]nd what does it do?

What it does not do is easier to state. It *never* assigns the problem to a qualified staff for a study or investigation; it *never* gets the parties' response to such a study or investigation; and it *never* uses notice and comment procedure.

What the Supreme Court affirmatively does is quite various. It has no system. It tries one method after another, almost always with unsatisfactory results.

[W]hat sort of system might be established to supply the Court with needed studies of legislative facts? Brandeis briefs should be encouraged; the Court now welcomes them, but not many are filed. Perhaps law offices should more often engage appropriate scientific or professional specialists to contribute to the preparation of briefs. That would help but at best would be only a partial solution. The Supreme Court might employ specialists in sciences and social sciences to assist the Justices in somewhat the way law clerks do. But the Court is not geared to employing and managing such a staff, and a small staff would lack the needed diversification. Although having such a staff might be preferable to not having it, a much better idea is creation of a research organization outside the Court to make studies at the Court's request.

[I] propose that the Supreme Court after due deliberation should formally ask Congress to explore the potential for creating a research service to assist the Court. The sole purpose should be to increase the Court's freedom to obtain whatever research assistance it decides it needs. The Court should have the privilege of asking for research either on a problem about a pending case or about a narrow or broad area of law.

[T]he Court's use of the research service would rarely delay decisions. The service might be used in only about a half dozen decisions in each term, although it might be quite important in some of those cases.

SELECTED BIBLIOGRAPHY

D. Faigman, Constitutional Fictions: Unified Theory of Constitutional Facts (2008).

D. Faigman, Legal Alchemy: The Use and Misuse of Science in the Law (1999).

Handbook of Psychology in Legal Contexts 2d (R. Bull and D. Carson eds. 2003).

Levin, The Administrative Law Legacy of Kenneth Culp Davis, 42 San Diego Law Review 315 (2005).

J. Skeem, K. Douglas, and S. Lilienfeld (eds), Psychological Science in the Courtroom: Consensus and Controversy (2009).

A. Smith, Law, Social Science, and the Criminal Courts (2004).

SECTION II.   CONSTITUTIONAL LAW

A large portion of the lawmaking uses of social science have occurred in the context of constitutional law. In particular, decisions involving the First, Sixth, Eighth, and Fourteenth Amendments have often invoked social science to support a finding of "legislative fact." For historical reasons, we begin our analysis with the Fourteenth Amendment.

A. THE FOURTEENTH AMENDMENT: SCHOOL SEGREGATION

Section 1 of the Fourteenth Amendment to the Constitution, ratified in 1868, reads, in part:

No State shall make or enforce any law which shall abridge the privileges or immunities of citizens of the United States; nor shall any State deprive any person of life, liberty, or property, without due process of law; nor deny to any person within its jurisdiction the equal protection of the laws.

While many constitutional lawmaking uses of social science implicate the Fourteenth Amendment, none do so more directly than cases finding that the segregation of public schools by race or gender violates the Amendment's Equal Protection clause.

1. SEGREGATION BY RACE

The lawmaking uses of social science in litigation on the racial segregation of public schools fall into two categories. The first and earlier type of case dealt with the issue of whether the statutory segregation of schools by race violated the Fourteenth Amendment. The second and more recent type of case concerns the question of whether remedies for schools that have violated the Fourteenth Amendment can take into account affected parties' likely reactions to those remedies.

———

(a) "Separate but Equal"

Surely the best known use of social science in any area of law occurred when the United States Supreme Court in Brown v. Board of Education, 347 U.S. 483, 74 S.Ct. 686, 98 L.Ed. 873 (1954), cited several social science studies in overturning Plessy v. Ferguson, 163 U.S. 537, 16 S.Ct. 1138, 41 L.Ed. 256 (1896) to find that the racial segregation of public schools violates the equal protection clause of the Fourteenth Amendment. The court cited the studies in what has been called "the most controversial footnote in American constitutional law." Rosen, History and State of the Art of Applied Social Research in the Courts, in The Use/Nonuse/Misuse of Applied Social Research in the Courts 9 (M. Saks and C. Barron eds. 1980). *Brown* is generally regarded as the beginning of the modern era in the use of social science in law.

———

PLESSY v. FERGUSON

Supreme Court of the United States, 1896.
163 U.S. 537, 16 S.Ct. 1138, 41 L.Ed. 256.

■ MR. JUSTICE BROWN delivered the opinion of the court.

This case turns upon the constitutionality of an act of the General Assembly of the State of Louisiana, passed in 1890, providing for separate railway carriages for the white and colored races.

The first section of the statute enacts "that all railway companies carrying passengers in their coaches in this State, shall provide equal but separate accommodations for the white, and colored races, by providing two or more passenger coaches for each passenger train, or by dividing the passenger coaches by a partition so as to secure separate accommodations: Provided, That this section shall not be construed to apply to street railroads. No person or persons, shall be admitted to occupy seats in coaches, other than, the ones, assigned, to them on account of the race they belong to."

[T]he information filed in the criminal District Court charged in substance that Plessy, being a passenger between two stations within the State of Louisiana, was assigned by officers of the company to the coach used for the race to which he belonged, but he insisted upon going into a coach used by the race to which he did not belong. [Plessy] was ordered by the conductor to vacate said coach and take a seat in another assigned to persons of the colored race, and having refused to comply with such demand he was forcibly ejected with the aid of a police officer, and imprisoned in the parish jail to answer a charge of having violated the above act.

The constitutionality of this act is attacked upon the ground that it conflicts [w]ith the [F]ourteenth Amendment, which prohibits certain restrictive legislation on the part of the States.

[B]y the Fourteenth Amendment, all persons born or naturalized in the United States, and subject to the jurisdiction thereof, are made citizens of the United States and of the State wherein they reside; and the States are forbidden from making or enforcing any law which shall abridge the privileges or immunities of citizens of the United States, or shall deprive any person of life, liberty or property without due process of law, or deny to any person within their jurisdiction the equal protection of the laws.

[T]he object of the amendment was undoubtedly to enforce the absolute equality of the two races before the law, but in the nature of things it could not have been intended to abolish distinctions based upon color, or to enforce social, as distinguished from political equality, or a commingling of the two races upon terms unsatisfactory to either. Laws permitting, and even requiring, their separation in places where they are liable to be brought into contact do not necessarily imply the inferiority of either race to the other, and have been generally, if not universally, recognized as within the competency of the state legislatures in the exercise of their police power. The most common instance of this is connected with the establishment of separate schools for white and colored children, which has been held to be a valid exercise of the legislative power even by courts of

States where the political rights of the colored race have been longest and most earnestly enforced.

[W]e consider the underlying fallacy of the plaintiff's argument to consist in the assumption that the enforced separation of the two races stamps the colored race with a badge of inferiority. If this be so, it is not by reason of anything found in the act, but solely because the colored race chooses to put that construction upon it.

[L]egislation is powerless to eradicate racial instincts or to abolish distinctions based upon physical differences, and the attempt to do so can only result in accentuating the difficulties of the present situation. If the civil and political rights of both races be equal one cannot be inferior to the other civilly or politically. If one race be inferior to the other socially, the Constitution of the United States cannot put them upon the same plane.

———

THE PSYCHOLOGICAL EFFECTS OF ENFORCED SEGREGATION: A SURVEY OF SOCIAL SCIENCE OPINION

Max Deutscher and Isidor Chein.
26 The Journal of Psychology 259 (1948).

Final decision on the legality of enforced segregation, regardless of equal facilities, has not yet been rendered by the Supreme Court. Here too, social science evidence may be a significant if not crucial factor. For social scientists interested in "social engineering," this represents a concrete opportunity to apply the relevant findings of social science data.

The Problem

The present report is an attempt to gather the current opinions of social scientists about one aspect of the problem: namely, the psychological effects of enforced segregation, both on the group which enforces the segregation and on the group which is segregated. Since the purpose of the study was to gather material which would be relevant to a court decision, the focus was on aspects pertinent to the legal questions involved.

[S]ince anthropologists, psychologists, and sociologists have been most concerned with the development of individuals and their socialization, these were the social scientists whose views were sought.

[A] questionnaire and a covering letter were prepared for distribution to these 849 social scientists. Every effort was made to present the issue and to formulate the questions in as unbiased and unleading manner as possible.

[T]he questionnaire asked for opinions about the psychological effect of enforced segregation on both the segregated and segregating groups. About the effect on the segregated groups, respondents were asked to check one of the three following statements:

I believe that enforced segregation has detrimental psychological effects on members of racial and religious groups which are segregated, even if equal facilities are provided.

I believe that enforced segregation does not have detrimental psychological effects on members of racial and religious groups which are segregated, if equal facilities are provided.

I have not as yet formed an opinion on this issue.

In regard to the effect on the segregating groups, respondents were asked to check one of the three following statements:

I believe that enforced segregation has a detrimental psychological effect on the group which enforces the segregation, even if that group provides equal facilities for the members of the racial and religious groups which are segregated.

I believe that enforced segregation does not have a detrimental psychological effect on the group which enforces the segregation, if that group provides equal facilities for the members of the racial and religious groups which are segregated.

I have not as yet formed an opinion on this issue.

Results

[T]he results pertinent to Question 1 on the questionnaire are[:]

Ninety per cent of the total sample express the opinion that enforced segregation has detrimental psychological effects *on the segregated groups*. Two per cent believe that it has no harmful effects on the segregated group. Four per cent indicate that they have no opinion on this issue, while another 4 per cent did not answer this item even though they returned the questionnaire.

Opinions about the effects on the segregating groups (Question 2) show a similar distribution. Eighty-three per cent of the respondents believe that enforced segregation has detrimental psychological effects *on the group which enforces the segregation*. Four per cent express the opinion that it does not have harmful effects on the segregating group. Nine per cent say that they have not formed an opinion on this issue, and 5 per cent did not answer this item.

[I]t seems safe, therefore, to conclude from the above reported results that substantial majorities of social scientists who may be said to have some competence with regard to the matters under inquiry agree that enforced segregation is psychologically detrimental to both the segregated and enforcing groups even when equal facilities are provided.

———

RACIAL IDENTIFICATION AND PREFERENCE IN NEGRO CHILDREN*

Kenneth B. Clark and Mamie P. Clark.
In Readings in Social Psychology (1947).
(T. Newcomb and E. Hartley, eds.).

The specific problem of this study is an analysis of the genesis and development of racial identification as a function of ego development and self-awareness in Negro children.

[D]olls Test. The subjects were presented with four dolls, identical in every respect save skin color. Two of these dolls were brown with black hair and two were white with yellow hair. In the experimental situation these dolls were unclothed except for white diapers. The position of the head, hands, and legs on all the dolls was the same. For half of the subjects the dolls were presented in the order: white, colored, white, colored. For the other half the order of presentation was reversed. In the experimental situation the subjects were asked to respond to the following requests by choosing *one* of the dolls and giving it to the experimenter:

1. Give me the doll that you like to play with—(*a*) like best.

2. Give me the doll that is a nice doll.

3. Give me the doll that looks bad.

4. Give me the doll that is a nice color.

[S]ubjects

Two hundred fifty-three Negro children formed the subjects of this experiment. One hundred thirty-four of these subjects (southern group) were tested in segregated nursery schools and public schools in Hot Springs, Pine Bluff, and Little Rock, Arkansas. These children had had no experience in racially mixed school situations. One hundred nineteen subjects (northern group) were tested in the racially mixed nursery and public schools of Springfield, Massachusetts.

[N]orth-South Differences. From Table 8 it is clear that the southern children in segregated schools are less pronounced in their preference for the white doll, compared to the northern children's definite preference for this doll. Although still in a minority, a higher percentage of southern children, compared to northern, prefer to play with the colored doll or think that it is a "nice" doll.

* Excerpts adapted from READINGS IN SOCIAL PSYCHOLOGY, by Theodore M. Newcomb and Eugene L. Hartley, copyright 1947 by Holt, Rinehart and Winston, and renewed 1975 by Theodore M. Newcomb and Eugene L. Hartley, reprinted by permission of the publisher.

[Ed. Note: This is the original report of the data later included in K.B. Clark, Effect of Prejudice and Discrimination on Personality Development (Midcentury White House Conference on Children and Youth, 1950).]

TABLE 8

Choices of Subjects in Northern (Mixed Schools) and Southern (Segregated Schools) Groups (Requests 1 Through 4)*

Choice	North, percent	South, Percent
Request 1 (play with)		
colored doll	28	37
white doll	72	62
Request 2 (nice doll)		
colored doll	30	46
white doll	68	52
Request 3 (looks bad)		
colored doll	71	49
white doll	17	16
Request 4 (nice color)		
colored doll	37	40
white doll	63	57

A significantly higher percentage (71) of the northern children, compared to southern children (49) think that the brown doll looks bad. Also a slightly higher percent of the southern children think that the brown doll has a "nice color," while more northern children think that the white doll has a "nice color."

In general, it may be stated that northern and southern children in these age groups tend to be similar in the degree of their preference for the white doll—with the northern children tending to be somewhat more favorable to the white doll than are the southern children. The southern children, however, in spite of their equal favorableness toward the white doll, are significantly less likely to reject the brown doll (evaluate it negatively), as compared to the strong tendency for the majority of the northern children to do so.

———

NOTE

1. Interpretations of the Doll Data. The results of the Clark and Clark 1947 "doll study," to which Professor Kenneth Clark testified in one of the cases joined with *Brown*, were otherwise interpreted in van den Haag, Social Science Testimony in the Desegregation Cases—A Reply to Professor Kenneth Clark, 6 Villanova Law Review 69, 77 (1960):

> Whether it be granted that his tests show psychological damage to Negro children, the comparison between the responses of Negro children in segregated and in nonsegregated schools shows that "they do

* Individuals failing to make either choice not included, hence some percentages add to less than 100.

not differ" except that *Negro children in segregated schools "are less pronounced in their preference for the white doll" and more often think of the colored dolls as "nice" or identify with them.* In short, if Professor Clark's tests do demonstrate damage to Negro children, then they demonstrate that the damage is *less* with segregation and *greater* with congregation. Yet, Professor Clark told the Court that he was proving that "segregation inflicts injuries upon the Negro" by the very tests which, if they prove anything—which is doubtful—prove the opposite!

R. Kluger, Simple Justice (2004) at 356, described the interpretation Professor Clark placed on these data:

> The finding that Southern segregated black children showed much less inclination to reject the brown doll seemed a spot of special vulnerability, which Clark of course chose to avoid in his courtroom testimony. "Thurgood Marshall was very worried about that point," Clark comments. "But I believe, and I so argued at the time, that what the findings show is that the black children of the South were more adjusted to the feeling that they were not as good as whites and, because they felt defeated at an early age, did not bother using the device of denial. But that's not health. Adjusting to pathology is not health. The way the Northern kids were fighting it can be seen as a better sign. The little Southern children would point to the black doll and say, 'oh, yeah, that's me there—that's a nigger—I'm a nigger,' and they said it almost cheerfully. In the Northern cities, the question clearly threw the kids into a much more emotional state and often they'd point to the white doll."

> Marshall had weighed the risks of Clark's findings and decided that on balance they demonstrated injury to segregated Negro youngsters. "I wanted this kind of evidence on the record," he had said.

SIMPLE JUSTICE (REVISED AND EXPANDED ED. 2004)

Richard Kluger.

[A]fter sketching out his background and projective test methods with dolls [as an expert witness in Briggs v. Elliott, 98 F.Supp. 529 (E.D.S.C. 1951), later joined with Brown v. Board of Education, 347 U.S. 483, 74 S.Ct. 686, 98 L.Ed. 873 (1954)], Clark gave the essence of his findings as presented in his White House conference paper of the previous year: "I have reached the conclusion from the examination of my own results and from an examination of the literature in the entire field that discrimination, prejudice and segregation"—good to his word, he refused to single out school segregation—"have definitely detrimental effects on the personality development of the Negro child." He went on:

The essence of this detrimental effect is a confusion in the child's concept of his own self-esteem—basic feelings of inferiority, conflict, confusion in his self-image, resentment, hostility towards himself, hostility towards whites, intensification of ... a desire to resolve his basic conflict by sometimes escaping or withdrawing.

[C]lark then applied his general statements to the specific test results he obtained in Clarendon County: eleven of the sixteen black children thought the brown doll looked "bad"; ten of them considered the white doll the "nice" one [a]nd seven of the sixteen picked the white doll as the one like themselves.

The conclusion which I was forced to reach was that these children in Clarendon County, like other human beings who are subjected to an obviously inferior status in the society in which they live, have been definitely harmed in the development of their personalities; that the signs of instability in their personalities are clear, and I think that every psychologist would accept and interpret these signs as such.

It was a careful, low-key recitation, all the more stark for Clark's modulated manner. The psychologist hurriedly caught his breath and then braced himself for a relentless cross-examination. "I wasn't prepared for Mr. Figg's Southern gentility," he recalls.

Figg had sized up Clark's testimony and decided it would not adversely affect his case. He snipped away, trying to trivialize it rather than bludgeon it into inconsequence. No, Clark said, nobody else was present in the room while he tested each youngster. Yes, Clark said, he and his wife primarily had developed these particular tests, which had been given to about 400 children all together over the years. There was only a single sharp exchange between them as Figg tried to invoke the racist ideology of William Graham Sumner and other early sociologists that had prevailed half a century earlier but had been almost totally discredited by the academic world in the past two decades.

Q. Do you recognize the psychology that people, based upon the "universal consciousness of kind," social heritage and the degree of visibility of differences between the races and so forth—enters into the problem of dealing with the existence of two different races in great numbers in a particular area?

A. I do not recognize that at all, sir.

Q. You don't recognize that?

A. I do not recognize it as a principle which should govern democratic relations.

Q. Do you recognize that there is an emotional facet in the problem of two different races living in large numbers together in the same area?

A. I have just given you results which indicate the consequences of that kind of emotional tension.

Confronted with a determined and obviously quick-witted witness with expertise in an area that Figg knew relatively little about, the defense attorney did not force the issue. "You don't cross-examine in a probing way if you're not sure what the answers are going to be," notes Figg, who by then had had a dozen years' experience as a state prosecutor and knew the territory. "I was concerned about findings of fact, and once we determined that his testimony was based on very few children, that there were no witnesses to the tests, and that this was his own test method and not a well-established one, I didn't press the matter. His numbers were small and unimposing, so why should I have pushed it? In the courtroom, his manner was quiet and matter-of-fact. Nobody took it seriously."

The essence of Kenneth Clark's testimony, though, would be taken very seriously indeed before *Briggs* was finally resolved.

————

NOTE

1. **Doll Studies Reconsidered.** Gray–Little and Hafdahl, Factors Influencing Racial Comparisons of Self–Esteem: A Quantitative Review, 126 Psychological Bulletin 26 (2000) reviewed research on racial differences in self-esteem since the Clark and Clark studies. Their conclusions were as follows:

> Early research in this area, exemplified by the doll studies of racial preference, was viewed as demonstrating that Blacks have less self-regard than Whites. However, a meta-analytic synthesis of 261 comparisons, based largely on self-esteem scales and involving more than half a million respondents, revealed *higher* scores for Black than for White children, adolescents, and young adults. Id. at 26 (emphasis added).

————

THE EFFECTS OF SEGREGATION AND THE CONSEQUENCES OF DESEGREGATION: A SOCIAL SCIENCE STATEMENT*

Appendix to Appellants' Briefs

BROWN v. BOARD OF EDUCATION OF TOPEKA

Supreme Court of the United States, 1954.
347 U.S. 483, 74 S.Ct. 686, 98 L.Ed. 873.

The problem of the segregation of racial and ethnic groups constitutes one of the major problems facing the American people today. It seems desirable, therefore, to summarize the contributions which contemporary social science can make toward its resolutions. There are, of course, moral

* This statement was drafted and signed by the following sociologists, anthropologists, psychologists and psychiatrists, who have worked in the area of American race relations: [32 names are given].

and legal issues involved with respect to which the signers of the present statement cannot speak with any special authority and which must be taken into account in the solution of the problem. There are, however, also factual issues involved with respect to which certain conclusions seem to be justified on the basis of the available scientific evidence. It is with these issues only that this paper is concerned. Some of the issues have to do with the consequences of segregation, some with the problems of changing from segregated to unsegregated practices.

[I]

At the recent Mid-century White House Conference on Children and Youth, a fact-finding report on the effects of prejudice, discrimination and segregation on the personality development of children was prepared as a basis for some of the deliberations.[2] This report brought together the available social science and psychological studies which were related to the problem of how racial and religious prejudices influenced the development of a healthy personality. It highlighted the fact that segregation, prejudices and discriminations, and their social concomitants potentially damage the personality of all children—the children of the majority group in a some-what different way than the more obviously damaged children of the minority group.

The report indicates that as minority group children learn the inferior status to which they are assigned—as they observe the fact that they are almost always segregated and kept apart from others who are treated with more respect by the society as a whole—they often react with feelings of inferiority and a sense of personal humiliation.

[T]he report indicates that minority group children of all social and economic classes often react with a generally defeatist attitude and a lowering of personal ambitions. This, for example, is reflected in a lowering of pupil morale and a depression of the educational aspiration level among minority group children in segregated schools. In producing such effects, segregated schools impair the ability of the child to profit from the educational opportunities provided him.

[T]he preceding view is consistent with the opinion stated by a large majority (90%) of social scientists who replied to a questionnaire concerning the probable effects of enforced segregation under conditions of equal facilities. This opinion was that, regardless of the facilities which are provided, enforced segregation is psychologically detrimental to the members of the segregated group.[12]

2. Clark, K.B., Effect of Prejudice and Discrimination on Personality Development, Fact Finding Report Mid-century White House Conference on Children and Youth, Children's Bureau, Federal Security Agency, 1950 (mimeographed).

12. Deutscher, M. and Chein, I., The Psychological Effects of Enforced Segregation: A Survey of Social Science Opinion, J. Psychol., 1948, 26, 259–287.

[II]

Segregation is at present a social reality. Questions may be raised, therefore, as to what are the likely consequences of desegregation.

One such question asks whether the inclusion of an intellectually inferior group may jeopardize the education of the more intelligent group by lowering educational standards or damage the less intelligent group by placing it in a situation where it is at a marked competitive disadvantage. Behind this question is the assumption, which is examined below, that the presently segregated groups actually are inferior intellectually.

The available scientific evidence indicates that much, perhaps all, of the observable differences among various racial and national groups may be adequately explained in terms of environmental differences. It has been found, for instance, that the differences between the average intelligence test scores of Negro and white children decrease, and the overlap of the distribution increases, proportionately to the number of years that the Negro children have lived in the North. Related studies have shown that this change cannot be explained by the hypothesis of selective migration. It seems clear, therefore, that fears based on the assumption of innate racial differences in intelligence are not well founded.

[A] second problem that comes up in an evaluation of the possible consequences of desegregation involves the question of whether segregation prevents or stimulates interracial tension and conflict and the corollary question of whether desegregation has one or the other effect.

The most direct evidence available on this problem comes from observations and systematic study of instances in which desegregation has occurred. Comprehensive reviews of such instances clearly establish the fact that desegregation has been carried out successfully in a variety of situations although outbreaks of violence had been commonly predicted. Extensive desegregation has taken place without major incidents in the armed services in both Northern and Southern installations and involving officers and enlisted men from all parts of the country, including the South.

[U]nder certain circumstances desegregation not only proceeds without major difficulties, but has been observed to lead the emergence of more favorable attitudes and friendlier relations between races. Relevant studies may be cited with respect to housing, employment, the armed services and merchant marine, recreation agency, and general community life.

Much depends, however, on the circumstances under which members of previously segregated groups first come in contact with others in unsegregated situations. Available evidence suggests, first, that there is less likelihood of unfriendly relations when the change is simultaneously introduced into all units of a social institution to which it is applicable—e.g., all of the schools in a school system or all of the shops in a given factory. When factories introduced Negroes in only some shops but not in others the prejudiced workers tended to classify the desegregated shops as inferior, "Negro work." Such objections were not raised when complete integration was introduced.

The available evidence also suggests the importance of consistent and firm enforcement of the new policy by those in authority. It indicates also the importance of such factors as: the absence of competition for a limited number of facilities or benefits; the possibility of contacts which permit individuals to learn about one another as individuals; and the possibility of equivalence of positions and functions among all of the participants within the unsegregated situation. These conditions can generally be satisfied in a number of situations, as in the armed services, public housing developments, and public schools.

[III]

The problem with which we have here attempted to deal is admittedly on the frontiers of scientific knowledge. Inevitably, there must be some differences of opinion among us concerning the conclusiveness of certain items of evidence, and concerning the particular choice of words and placement of emphasis in the preceding statement. We are nonetheless in agreement that this statement is substantially correct and justified by the evidence, and the differences among us, if any, are of a relatively minor order and would not materially influence the preceding conclusions.

BROWN v. BOARD OF EDUCATION OF TOPEKA

Supreme Court of the United States, 1954.
347 U.S. 483, 74 S.Ct. 686, 98 L.Ed. 873.

■ MR. CHIEF JUSTICE WARREN delivered the opinion of the Court.

We come [t]o the question presented: Does segregation of children in public schools solely on the basis of race, even though the physical facilities and other "tangible" factors may be equal, deprive the children of the minority group of equal educational opportunities? We believe that it does.

[T]o separate them from others of similar age and qualifications solely because of their race generates a feeling of inferiority as to their status in the community that may affect their hearts and minds in a way unlikely ever to be undone. The effect of this separation on their educational opportunities was well stated by a finding in the Kansas case by a court which nevertheless felt compelled to rule against the Negro plaintiffs:

> "Segregation of white and colored children in public schools has a detrimental effect upon the colored children. The impact is greater when it has the sanction of the law; for the policy of separating the races is usually interpreted as denoting the inferiority of the negro group. A sense of inferiority affects the motivation of a child to learn. Segregation with the sanction of law, therefore, has a tendency to [retard] the educational and mental development of negro children and to deprive them of some of the benefits they would receive in a racial[ly] integrated school system."

Whatever may have been the extent of psychological knowledge at the time of Plessy v. Ferguson, this finding is amply supported by modern authority.[11] Any language in Plessy v. Ferguson contrary to this finding is rejected.

We conclude that in the field of public education the doctrine of "separate but equal" has no place. Separate educational facilities are inherently unequal. Therefore, we hold that the plaintiffs and others similarly situated for whom the actions have been brought are, by reason of the segregation complained of, deprived of the equal protection of the laws guaranteed by the Fourteenth Amendment.

JURISPRUDENCE*

Edmond Cahn.
30 New York University Law Review 150 (1955).

In the months since the utterance of the *Brown* [opinion], the impression has grown that the outcome, either entirely or in major part, was caused by the testimony and opinions of the scientists, and a genuine danger has arisen that even lawyers and judges may begin to entertain this belief. The word "danger" is used advisedly, because I would not have the constitutional rights of Negroes—or of other Americans—rest on any such flimsy foundation as some of the scientific demonstrations in these records.

[O]bviously, the *Brown* [opinion is] susceptible of more than one interpretation. My views do not agree with those of some very able commentators, who consider that the opinions show important marks of the psychologists' influence. Granting this variety of interpretations, does it really matter whether the Supreme Court relies or does not rely on the psychologists' findings? Does it make any practical difference?

I submit it does. In the first place, since the behavioral sciences are so very young, imprecise, and changeful, their findings have an uncertain expectancy of life. Today's sanguine asseveration may be cancelled by tomorrow's new revelation—or new technical fad. It is one thing to use the current scientific findings, however ephemeral they may be, in order to ascertain whether the legislature has acted reasonably in adopting some scheme of social or economic regulation; deference here is shown not so much to the findings as to the legislature. It would be quite another thing

11. K.B. Clark, Effect of Prejudice and Discrimination on Personality Development (Midcentury White House Conference on Children and Youth, 1950); Witmer and Kotinsky, Personality in the Making (1952), c. VI; Deutscher and Chein, The Psychological Effects of Enforced Segregation: A Survey of Social Science Opinion, 26 J. Psychol. 259 (1948); Chein, What are the Psychological Effects of Segregation Under Conditions of Equal Facilities?, 3 Int. J. Opinion and Attitude Res. 229 (1949); Brameld, Educational Costs, in Discrimination and National Welfare (MacIver, ed., 1949), 44–48; Frazier, The Negro in the United States (1949), 674–681. And see generally Myrdal, An American Dilemma (1944).

* Cahn, Jurisprudence, 30 New York University Law Review 150, 157–58, 167 (1955); reprinted with permission of the New York University Law Review.

to have our fundamental rights rise, fall, or change along with the latest fashions of psychological literature. Today the social psychologists—at least the leaders of the discipline—are liberal and egalitarian in basic approach. Suppose, a generation hence, some of their successors were to revert to the ethnic mysticism of the very recent past; suppose they were to present us with a collection of racist notions and label them "science." What then would be the state of our constitutional rights? Recognizing as we do how sagacious Mr. Justice Holmes was to insist that the Constitution be not tied to the wheels of any economic system whatsoever, we ought to keep it similarly uncommitted in relation to the other social sciences.

STELL v. SAVANNAH–CHATHAM COUNTY BOARD OF EDUCATION

United States District Court, Southern District of Georgia, 1963.
220 F.Supp. 667.

■ SCARLETT, DISTRICT JUDGE.

This is a class action in the right of the minor Negro plaintiffs as students in public schools of Savannah–Chatham County to enjoin defendant Board of Education from operating a bi-racial school system.

[T]he defendants [c]onceded the existence of a dual school system for white and Negro students in the City and County.

[A] motion to intervene on behalf of themselves and their class was made by minor white school children alleging that the separation of Negro and white children in the public schools was not determined solely by race or color but rather upon racial traits of educational significance as to which racial identity was only a convenient index.

Among these significant factors for consideration in devising a rational program best suited to the peculiar educational needs of Negro and white school children in separate schools were:

(a) differences in specific capabilities, learning progress rates, mental maturity, and capacity for education in general;

(b) differences in physical, psychical and behavioral traits.

The differences were alleged to be of such magnitude as to make it impossible for Negro and white children of the same chronological age to be effectively educated in the same classrooms.

It was alleged that to congregate children of such diverse traits in schools in the proportion and under the conditions existing in Savannah would seriously impair the educational opportunities of both white and Negro and cause them grave psychological harm.

[I]ntervenors [p]roduced Dr. Ernest van den Haag, a Professor of Social Philosophy at New York University and lecturer on sociology and social philosophy at the New School for Social Research. As with the other witnesses presented by the intervenors, plaintiffs conceded that Dr. van den Haag was an authority in his field. This witness reviewed for the Court a number of educational studies which investigated sources of group conflicts in the classroom and the patterns of association among students which affect their educational achievement. These studies, in whose conclusions Professor van den Haag concurred, show that inter-racial associational distinctions arise spontaneously in pre-school children without regard to whether they live in an area of segregated or integrated schooling. This is one aspect of group identification which every individual makes.

[A]ccording to this witness, any group having self-identification or associational preference closes its ranks in the presence of other groups. Prejudices, whether ethnic, religious or racial, increase rather than decrease in proportion to the degree of non-voluntary contact between separately identifiable groups. This is a psychological phenomenon which was noted in the time of Periclean Greece. Studies made of actual intermixing of groups in classrooms confirm the predicted result that an increase in cross-group contacts increases pre-existing racial hostility rather than ameliorates it. This group tension effect is greatest where obvious group identity criteria exist, such as physical appearance or variations in learning rate. Such groupings prevent a class having a natural homogeneity, multiply disciplinary problems in the classroom, and decrease attention to study.

Dr. van den Haag stated that acceptable group identifications are essential to the well-being of the individual. Any attempt to de-identify one's self with a natural grouping would be harmful.

[T]he proofs closed, plaintiffs renewed their objection of irrelevancy and moved to strike the evidence submitted by intervenors.

[I]n stating the basis for the objection to this evidence, counsel for plaintiffs said:

" * * * the law is settled by the Supreme Court in the Brown case that segregation itself injures negro children in the school system. That is what the Supreme Court's decision is all about, so we do not have to prove that."

A ruling on plaintiffs' objection therefore made it essential to consider the legal parameters of the Supreme Court's Brown decision.

[I]t is [a]pparent that the governance of the present issues by Brown is the question of whether the applicable portion of the determination in that case—the injury occurring through segregation as plaintiffs put it—is a finding of fact or a conclusion of law. For this let us look to the words and record in Brown.

[I]n Brown the Supreme Court stated for itself the nature of its inquiry:

"We come then to the question presented: Does segregation of children in public schools solely on the basis of race, even though the physical facilities and other 'tangible' factors may be equal, deprive the children of the minority group of equal educational opportunities?'' (347 U.S. p. 493, 74 S.Ct. p. 691)

Although it would appear sufficiently clear on its face that this calls for a conclusion of fact rather than law, we are confirmed when we find that Court looking to the testimonial and other evidence in the records before it and to a submission of scientific opinion rather than seeking the answer to this question in the law books.

From the Kansas record, the Court read:

"* * * the policy of separating the races is usually interpreted as denoting the inferiority of the negro group. A sense of inferiority affects the motivation of a child to learn. Segregation with the sanction of law, therefore, has a tendency to [retard] the educational and mental development of Negro children and to deprive them of some of the benefits they would receive in a racial[ly] integrated school system."

These are facts, not law. To make these findings the Kansas District Judge considered evidence—not cases. Whether Negroes in Kansas believed that separate schooling denoted inferiority, whether a sense of inferiority affected their motivation to learn and whether motivation to learn was increased or diminished by segregation was a question requiring evidence for decision. That was as much a subject for scientific inquiry as the braking distance required to stop a two-ton truck moving at ten miles an hour on dry concrete.

[T]he Supreme Court put at rest any residual question on the nature of its inquiry when it indicated its reliance on scientific information:

"Whatever may have been the extent of psychological knowledge at the time of Plessy v. Ferguson, [163 U.S. 537, 16 S.Ct. 1138, 41 L.Ed. 256,] this finding is amply supported by modern authority." 347 U.S. p. 494, 74 S.Ct. p. 692.

The teachings of psychology in 1896, in 1954, or in 1963 are inquiries requiring evidence in the same sense as repeated determinations of "seaworthiness." Actually, the non-legal authority to which the Court referred was neither testimonial nor documentary in character but came from a "Brandeis" type brief filed directly in the Supreme Court by the National Association for the Advancement of Colored People.

[T]he Supreme Court in Brown also had placed before it statements by scientists that separate schooling caused psychic injury to the Negro child. Here again the evidence in this case shows the contrary to be the fact. In this case, each witness testified that no such injury had been observed by him and in fact a dual school system is more favorable to the children involved in a psychological sense, avoids the injurious conflict arising from loss of racial identity, and results in a more successful educational program for the students of both races.

[T]he Court accordingly accepts the evidence given in the present case as having somewhat stronger indicia of truth than that on which the findings of potential injury were made in Brown.

[O]n the law these pupils of both races in Savannah–Chatham County are entitled to the best education available and on the unassailable facts that education is best given in separate schools adapted to their varying abilities. On the mandate of that law this Court gives judgment dismissing the complaint.

———

STELL v. SAVANNAH–CHATHAM COUNTY BOARD OF EDUCATION

United States Court of Appeals, Fifth Circuit, 1964.
333 F.2d 55.

■ GRIFFIN B. BELL, CIRCUIT JUDGE.

The District Court was bound by the decision of the Supreme Court in Brown. We reiterate that no inferior federal court may refrain from acting as required by that decision even if such a court should conclude that the Supreme Court erred either as to its facts or as to the law.

[W]e do not read the major premise of the decision of the Supreme Court in the first Brown case as being limited to the facts of the cases there presented. We read it as proscribing segregation in the public education process on the stated ground that separate but equal schools for the races were inherently unequal. This being our interpretation of the teaching of that decision, it follows that it would be entirely inappropriate for it to be rejected or obviated by this court.

[W]e hold that the District Court erred in failing to grant the preliminary injunction in the Savannah case.

———

NOTE

1. "Establishing" Social Science Findings: The Effect of Higher Courts on Lower Courts. In a study of seventeen school desegregation cases litigated during the 1970's, Sanders, Rankin–Widgeon, Kalmuss, and Chesler, The Relevance of "Irrelevant" Testimony: Why Lawyers Use Social Science Experts in School Desegregation Cases, 16 Law and Society Review 403 (1982), found that social scientists testifying for defendant school systems sometimes tried to reopen the legislative fact question addressed by the Supreme Court in footnote 11 of *Brown*. Perhaps because of the Fifth Circuit's decision in *Stell,* however, trial judges treated footnote 11 as dispositive. Sanders et al., id. at 414, quote one social scientist as follows:

> The legal doctrine is cast in concrete, and that's been one of my frustrations—it's as though the evidence is really immaterial. [I] remember in one case, I was talking with the judge from the witness box, and questioning some of the [social science] testimony in *Brown*. He

asked me, "are you questioning the facts of *Brown*?" And I said, "yes," and he said, "well, that's not admissible for you to be doing that."

Professors Perry and Melton, Precedential Value of Judicial Notice of Social Facts: Parham as an Example, 22 Journal of Family Law 633, 666–67 (1984), in this regard, make the following observation:

> It is well settled that findings of fact are not included in the *stare decisis* doctrine and have no precedential value beyond the original case. [H]owever, [w]hen a legal conclusion seems to rest on empirical assumptions (e.g., the psychological harm of school segregation), then those assumptions may become de facto conclusions of law which are not disputable.

FORCED JUSTICE: SCHOOL DESEGREGATION AND THE LAW (1995)*

David J. Armor.

The research on black self-esteem is of particular historical interest, given the original emphasis on this issue by the 1952 social science statement and the Supreme Court's decision in *Brown*. At that time low self-esteem was seen as the major psychological mechanism contributing to lower academic performance of black children (or any group of children, for that matter), and that view is still popular among many educators and some social scientists today.

The early versions of self-esteem theory, as applied to racial segregation, emerged from studies that used indirect or projective measures of self-esteem (the doll-playing techniques of Kenneth and Mamie Clark being the most prominent). During this period black children's preferences for white dolls were interpreted as rejection of their race and hence rejection of themselves. As the research on self-esteem became more extensive and more sophisticated during the 1960s, studies came to rely more on direct (self-report) measures of self-esteem, and earlier interpretations gave way to what came to be seen as a much more complex process. [T]he vast majority of these studies find that black self-esteem is either higher than or equal to white self-esteem.

[P]ossibly the results of the early doll studies were misinterpreted, and segregated black students did not in fact have lower personal self-esteem than white students at the time of *Brown*. Unfortunately, the theory that black self-esteem differed before *Brown* cannot be tested because no known studies using direct assessment of personal self-esteem were conducted during that period. What is known, with considerable certainty, is that from at least mid–1960s forward there is little evidence that black students have lower self-esteem than white students.

* Reprinted by permission of Oxford University Press.

If school segregation does not create low black self-esteem in the first place, then the question of whether desegregation raises black self-esteem may be somewhat academic. Nonetheless, numerous social science studies have compared the self-esteem of segregated and desegregated black students, and several reviews of these studies have been compiled. [O]f nearly fifty studies of desegregation and black self-esteem identified by these reviewers, only six had consistently positive effects. A much larger number—seventeen separate studies—found that school desegregation has adverse effects on black self-esteem.

[S]everal theories have been advanced to explain the adverse effects of desegregation on self-esteem. Most explanations rely on one of two possibilities: a social comparison phenomenon or racial prejudice. Desegregated black students may for the first time find themselves at a disadvantage academically or economically in comparison with white students, and these unfavorable comparisons lead to a lowered personal sense of worth. Desegregated black students may also experience racial prejudice or acts of discrimination for the first time, which may also have an impact on their personal self-esteem.

——————

SOCIAL SCIENCE AND SCHOOL DESEGREGATION: DID WE MISLEAD THE SUPREME COURT?

Stuart W. Cook.
5 Personality and Social Psychology Bulletin 420 (1979).

During the deliberations prior to its school desegregation decision in 1954 the Supreme Court had before it a Social Science Statement on the effects of segregation and desegregation. This article reassesses the quality of that Statement 25 years later. Key points in the Statement are compared to the results of subsequent research. Some points, e.g., no negative effect on the school achievement of white students, have been supported. Others, e.g., improvement in black self-esteem, are difficult to evaluate due to inconsistent and uninterpretable research findings. Still others, e.g., more favorable racial attitudes, cannot be compared to the research findings because desegregation was not carried out in accord with conditions that were specified as conducive to the outcomes predicted in the Statement.

[In sum,] there seems little reason to doubt the soundness of the information provided to the Supreme Court in the Social Science Statement of 1954. Regrettably, social scientists in the 1960's and 1970's misdirected their efforts, devoting countless hours to an unrewarding study of the confusing outcomes of desegregation carried out under conditions already known to minimize its effectiveness.

——————

SCHOOL DESEGREGATION: THE SOCIAL SCIENCE ROLE

Harold B. Gerard.
38 American Psychologist 869 (1983).

In his recent article [quoted above] Cook answers the question, Did we mislead the Court? His answer is No—principally, he goes on to say, because the conditions for real integration, which were outlined in the statement, are rarely met in the typical mixed classroom, although the framers argued that these conditions "can generally be satisfied in the public schools." Thirty-two prominent social scientists signed the statement. If I had been asked to do so, I probably would have signed it, too.

In retrospect, however, it was extraordinarily quixotic to assume that the following conditions specified in the statement [as conducive to successful desegregation] would or could be met in the typical school system: (a) firm and consistent endorsement by those in authority; (b) the absence of competition among the representatives of the different racial groups; (c) the equivalence of positions and functions among all participants in the desegregated setting; and (d) interracial contacts of the type that permit learning about one another as individuals. What could the framers have been thinking about while believing that the conjunction of these four conditions could be met in the typical American school? [F]or the four conditions to be met in the typical school, the teacher would have to be a social engineering whiz. How many of us with our supposed sophistication in group dynamics would undertake the task? The truly embarrassing question is, what do we actually know about intergroup contact that could really make a difference in the way a desegregation program is implemented?

[The authors of the statement] also argued that since President Eisenhower, as one of his first executive orders on entering the White House in 1953, desegregated the armed services, desegregation of the schools could also be successfully accomplished by government decree. This ignored marked differences between the military situation where men and women, black and white, were facing a common enemy in Korea and the complex nexus of circumstances represented by school desegregation, especially in the North. It also ignored the fact that in school desegregation the participants are children, and this engenders a good deal of emotion in their parents.

In his article, Cook attempted to evade the bad predictions [in the Social Science Statement] by blaming the system, but it was that self-same system about which the predictions were made, a system with which the framers were intimately acquainted. Excuse not accepted.

———

(b) "White Flight"

The constitutionality of "separate but equal" public schools having been resolved in the negative, much contemporary litigation concerns the remedies courts can order when they find a school system to be segregated. One issue that courts have had to confront repeatedly is whether, in fashioning a remedy, the Fourteenth Amendment permits them to take into account social science research on the likely behavioral reactions of the parties affected by the remedy. More plainly put, the question has been whether busing will result in "white flight," and, if so, whether this empirical conclusion should play any role in the decision to order busing.

MORGAN v. KERRIGAN

United States District Court, District of Massachusetts, 1975.
401 F.Supp. 216.

■ GARRITY, DISTRICT JUDGE.

[The district court had previously issued an opinion holding that Boston's public schools were unconstitutionally segregated according to race. The court then began extended consideration of a proposal to end this segregation. Among its requirements, this plan called for mandatory busing of approximately 21,000 students. During consideration of the proposed remedy, the Boston Home and School Association, an organization of parents, pointed out alleged defects in the plan, including its failure to allow for what the association claimed to be the predictable resegregative effects of white flight. The district court refused to consider the possibility of white flight.]

Inevitably, the court's primary concern in a desegregation case conflicts with other legitimate concerns. The remedy must accommodate these other interests. But the accommodation must reflect the primacy of the need to achieve equal opportunity in education. In its respect for a variety of interests, a desegregation plan resembles other equitable remedies. The Supreme Court has stated concisely a rough guideline for reconciling these interests.

> Having once found a violation, the district judge or school authorities should make every effort to achieve the greatest possible degree of actual desegregation, taking into account the practicalities of the situation. Davis v. Board of School Commissioners of Mobile County, 1971, 402 U.S. 33, 37, 91 S.Ct. 1289, 1292, 28 L.Ed.2d 577.

[S]ome of the parties have urged that the court limit the extent of actual desegregation lest children from middle class white families leave the public school system and to prevent racial turmoil and violence in Boston's schools and communities. The plaintiffs have argued, just as vigorously, that the court may not consider either "white flight" or the prospect of resistance to desegregation, in formulating the remedy. These prophecies of "white flight" and racial turmoil, like opposition itself, are not "practicalities" that can be weighed against the rights of the plaintiffs.[7]

---

7. Another ground for refusing to limit a remedy for fear of "white flight" is that a court would be presumptuous to try to predict the effect upon long-term trends in pop-

Opposition to a lawful desegregation remedy reflects no legitimate interest. Expression of that opposition constitutes a problem, of course, which the desegregation plan must confront in its implementation. But it does not constitute one of the "practicalities" to which the plan itself properly can make an accommodation. The court may not limit desegregation in deference to such opposition. To hold otherwise would be to trade away the constitutional rights of children to receive a desegregated education in order to appease parents and voters who prefer segregation to desegregation which involves forced busing, i.e., assignments to schools beyond walking distance. The impropriety of such an accommodation has long since been decided. The rule of law must prevail.

———

MORGAN v. KERRIGAN

United States Court of Appeals, First Circuit, 1976.
530 F.2d 401.

■ Coffin, Chief Judge.

[Judge Garrity's treatment of the white flight issue was one subject of appeal concerning the desegregation plan.]

These appeals present varied challenges to orders of the district court implementing a plan of desegregation for the public schools of Boston. The consolidated cases concern the remedy phase of litigation initiated by plaintiffs-appellees, representing a class of all black public school students and their parents, against, principally, the Boston School Committee and the Superintendent of Boston Public Schools. The liability phase came to an end in 1974 with a district court finding of substantial segregation in the entire school system intentionally brought about and maintained by official action over the years. Morgan v. Hennigan, 379 F.Supp. 410 (D.Mass.1974). We affirmed, Morgan v. Kerrigan, 509 F.2d 580 (1st Cir. 1974), and the Supreme Court denied certiorari, 421 U.S. 963, 95 S.Ct. 1950, 44 L.Ed.2d 449 (1975).

[T]he "White Flight" Controversy.

The district court ruled that "white flight," defined as the departure of white children from the Boston city schools to parochial, private, or suburban school systems, is not a practicality for which the plan must make an accommodation. Morgan v. Kerrigan, 401 F.Supp. at 233–34. The Mayor and the Association challenge this ruling as an abuse of discretion, claiming that "white flight" alters the effectiveness of a desegregation plan and leads to "resegregation" of the schools.

ulation movement of its adoption of a particular element, otherwise constitutionally required, in a desegregation plan. The masters received expert testimony on the subject of "white flight" from Boston's public schools during the current school year and concluded that the contention was a "misleading fiction."

White flight is an expression of opposition by individuals in the community to desegregation of the school system. From the inception of school desegregation litigation, accommodation of opposition to desegregation by failing to implement a constitutionally necessary plan has been impermissible.

Appellants contend, however, that white flight differs from other forms of opposition, because its effects, the withdrawal of white pupils from the school system, alter the effectiveness of the desegregation plan. The school system, they claim is "resegregated": the city school system largely black and other minority; the private and suburban systems, largely white.[29] To

29. Subsequent to the district court decision, we allowed to be filed, subject to a determination of relevance, voluminous affidavits and other materials by social scientists on the subject of white flight.

The admissibility of these submissions have been attacked as being outside the record, F.R.A.P. 10(a), and as hearsay. The materials have been defended as sociological data in the nature of "legislative facts" relevant to a determination of the law governing the district court in this matter.

For reasons we discuss in the text, we reject all these materials as irrelevant to the issues before us on this appeal. We include a brief synopsis of these materials to illustrate the difficulty in evaluating white flight if it were relevant.

The data submitted initially by the Association consists of an affidavit and report prepared by James S. Coleman, Professor of Sociology at the University of Chicago. Dr. Coleman states that his recent study shows that while there is decreasing segregation within school districts, segregation between school districts in the same metropolitan area is increasing; that rapid increase in loss of white children from central city schools follows immediately after school desegregation; and that as a consequence, desegregation has not significantly raised the levels of academic achievement of blacks.

Plaintiffs counter with the transcript of testimony given by Jane R. Mercer, Associate Professor of Sociology, University of California at Riverside, in a case involving Indianapolis. Her testimony shows that she studied desegregation in school districts throughout the state of California; that white exit to private schools is a short term phenomenon; and that declines in white population in the cities are part of a long term demographic trend independent of desegregation. The

plaintiffs also submit a paper written by Meyer Weinberg, Editor of *Integrated Education* magazine, which summarizes other studies showing white flight to be an avoidable phenomenon, not an inevitable consequence of mandatory desegregation. Weinberg's paper and another paper written by Professors Green of Michigan State University and Pettigrew of Harvard University, criticize Dr. Coleman's methodology, claiming that the source of his raw data is unknown; that failure to evaluate large cities which have been subject to massive desegregation orders separately from large cities which have not been subject to court orders undermines the study's relevancy; and that failure to control for other variables, which may be correlated with white flight, jeopardizes the validity of his conclusions.

Dr. Coleman replies in an affidavit filed with a copy of a working paper, "Trends in School Segregation, 1968–73". In his affidavit, Dr. Coleman states that the report previously filed with the court was prepared for oral delivery and was based on the attached working paper. He defends his methodology, states that his conclusions are consistent with the findings of the studies cited by Weinberg, and the studies conducted by Dr. Mercer. Dr. Coleman states that his study shows that massive white flight will occur when there is a significant decrease in segregation in a city where there is a high proportion of blacks in the central city and suburbs of a significantly different racial composition.

Plaintiffs, in rebuttal, file another study prepared by Christine H. Rossell, of Boston University. The Rossell study, prepared from data on 86 northern school districts subject to court ordered or legislatively enacted school desegregation, suggests that white flight is minimal and a temporary reaction to school desegregation. Plaintiffs claim that Dr.

prevent this result, appellants claim that the district court should consider white flight a "practicality", and limit the amount of desegregation to that level which would enjoy acceptance in the white community.[30]

There are two endemic flaws in this argument. First, in the trial on liability, evidence was presented that feeder patterns, district lines, and open transfer policies were established for the purpose of satisfying purported white community desires. This evidence resulted in a finding that the Boston schools were administered in violation of the Fourteenth Amendment. Appellants now ask that the district court, in devising a remedy for these violations, respond in the same way as the Boston School Committee did to the same perceived community attitudes: draw district lines, assign pupils to schools, and limit racial mixture to reduce "white flight". In other words, while appellants dwell upon the unpleasant prospect of an inner city black school system surrounded by suburban white school systems, the prospect contemplated by their approach is that of an

Rossell's study differs from Dr. Coleman's in that Dr. Rossell deals only with northern school districts subject to desegregation plans while Dr. Coleman does not distinguish between forms of desegregation.

In the final submission, Dr. Coleman defends his study against the Rossell findings, suggesting that her analysis is inadequate to examine the effects of desegregation on a core city school system. He further claims that his model has proved accurately predictive of the Boston experience.

Throughout this series of submissions this court has been burdened with reports written for sociologists by sociologists utilizing sophisticated statistical and mathematical techniques. We lack the expertise to evaluate these studies on their merits. We do come to one conclusion, however. The relationship between white flight and court ordered desegregation is a matter of heated debate among experts in sociology, and a firm professional consensus has not yet emerged.

Appellants have also filed with this court copies of the Boston School Department's current census of students according to race and minority group. The figures facially suggest loss of a significant number of white enrollees. We note, however, that the district court is currently studying the accuracy of past enrollment data. We decline to make any conclusions concerning the existence or non-existence of white flight on the sparse figures available to us.

30. Appellants suggested approach would necessarily involve the district court in something like the following analysis: (1)

take evidence concerning the prospects of white flight under the various plans proposed; (2) exclude the causes of such flight attributable to any historic trend, or such factors as overcrowding, transportation difficulties, deteriorated housing, taxes, crime, pollution, industrial migration, etc.; (3) make a judgment as to the effect which different levels of desegregation would have on white flight; and (4) select or devise that plan which will incorporate enough desegregation to bring about the maximum amount of inter-racial contact in the schools after taking account of the white flight such desegregation would be expected to induce.

The experts have difficulty in attempting to justify conclusions as to the effect of past desegregation plans on white flight, see note 29 supra; the task of making estimates of expected exodus of whites attributable to varying future desegregation plans would seem to be more difficult. Conceivably, public attitude sampling could be undertaken, using various hypotheses. This might involve questioning parents in a particular section or school district whether they would be likely to place their child elsewhere, or move, if the child were to attend a school which was x, y, or z percent black. The possibility is a real one that surveys would indicate that the prospect of any substantial amount of desegregation or busing would provoke sufficient expressions of intent to flee as to negate any desegregation plan. Alternatively, if expressed intentions were to be heavily discounted, their utility would accordingly diminish.

inner city segregated system, created unlawfully, but permitted to endure because the apprehension of massive white flight has made legal what had once been in violation of the constitution.

Second, appellants' claim that white flight destroys the effectiveness of the school desegregation plan, because of "resegregation" of the school system, founders on the constitutional definition of unlawful segregation. The Supreme Court has recently reemphasized that the constitutional right is to attend school in a unitary, non-discriminatory, public school system. It is not to attend school in a system which is comprised of students of a racial balance which exists in the general geographical area.

What the layman calls "resegregation" is not constitutionally recognized segregation. It is racial isolation imposed by historic school district boundaries or by individual choices to attend private institutions. This racial isolation becomes constitutionally significant only when the district boundaries are drawn with segregative intent, or when the state participates in the private institutions.

The constitution cannot solve all problems. On the contrary, to the extent that it demands that rights which have previously been overridden be enforced, it creates social problems. It inconveniences, sometimes substantially, law enforcement officers, prison wardens, university administrators, and government bureaucrats. And, when it allows tasteless books to be sold or movies shown, many are offended. But expectable individual, official or group reaction does not outweigh constitutional rights. We therefore must agree with another court which said, "concern over 'white flight' ... cannot become the higher value at the expense of rendering equal protection of the laws the lower value." Mapp v. Board of Education of Chattanooga, [525 F.2d 169], quoting 366 F.Supp. 1257, 1260 (E.D.Tenn. 1973).

The bright note in this otherwise somber picture is the care and imagination that the district court has displayed in structuring a diversified educational system offering superior opportunities for children, both white and black. The plan is not a mechanical device to ensure that the races share equally, but serves its constitutional goals within a framework offering educational hope for the children of the city. Nevertheless, federal courts have a limited jurisdiction and competence. To the extent that reorienting the Boston school system involves social expenses, it must be paid for in coin less dear than the constitutional rights of the city's citizens. Here as elsewhere, the Boston community must look to other institutions, city, state, federal and private, to contribute to an effort to vindicate the constitutional rights of its citizens at a minimum of social cost.

[W]e therefore affirm.

———

NOTE

1. Subsequent Research on White Flight in Boston. In R. Dentler and M. Scott, Schools on Trial: An Inside Account of the Boston Desegregation Case 224–226 (1981), the authors, who were appointed by Judge Garrity as experts to assist in designing the final desegregation plan in 1975, reflected upon the "white flight" issue in light of subsequent experience:

> White flight [in Boston] began in 1973 and reached a high velocity in 1975. Enrollments went from about 55 percent white in 1973 to 36 percent in 1980. Our efforts to account for this change lead us to think that roughly half of it was associated, however directly or indirectly, with desegregation.

> [T]here is no question as to whether white flight is occurring, although early in 1975 we were not able to foresee its scale and were tempted to downplay its importance in our public statements. [W]e did not anticipate the relocation of thousands of households to places far removed from the Greater Boston metropolitan area.

> Heavy white flight took place and it damaged not only school desegregation but also the income mix of students and the tax base of Boston.

In 2009, 13 percent of the students enrolled in Boston public schools were white. See http://www.bostonpublicschools.org/node/29.

D. Armor, Forced Justice: School Desegregation and the Law (1995),* summarized more recent research on white flight and white attitudes toward school desegregation as follows:

> The consensus at this point is that school desegregation contributes to white flight and that the flight can be quite large for some school systems, especially those systems that are larger, have higher minority concentrations, and have suburban or private school systems that can serve as alternatives for those who flee a desegregation plan or for new residents who want to avoid one. There is less consensus about whether some types of desegregation plans create more white flight than others and about the long-term consequences of white flight on effectiveness [of desegregation plans].

> The studies also show strong white parental support for various voluntary desegregation techniques such as magnet schools [a]nd no significant opposition to increasing the minority enrollment in their children's current schools. A significant fraction of white parents would object to sending their children to predominantly minority schools, however, and a large majority remain strongly opposed to the technique of mandatory busing—or to any method that would reassign their child to a distant school in a black neighborhood. Id. at 180, 203–204.

––––––

* From Forced Justice: School Desegregation and the Law by David J. Armor, copyright © 1995 by Oxford University Press, Inc. Used by permission of Oxford University Press, Inc.

PARENTS INVOLVED IN COMMUNITY SCHOOLS v. SEATTLE SCHOOL DISTRICT NO. 1

Supreme Court of the United States, 2007.
551 U.S. 701, 127 S.Ct. 2738, 168 L.Ed.2d 508.

■ CHIEF JUSTICE ROBERTS announced the judgment of the Court, and delivered the opinion of the Court with respect to Parts I, II, III–A, and III–C, and an opinion with respect to Parts III–B and IV, in which JUSTICES SCALIA, THOMAS, and ALITO join.

The school districts in these cases voluntarily adopted student assignment plans that rely upon race to determine which public schools certain children may attend. The Seattle school district classifies children as white or nonwhite; the Jefferson County school district as black or "other." In Seattle, this racial classification is used to allocate slots in oversubscribed high schools. In Jefferson County [Kentucky], it is used to make certain elementary school assignments and to rule on transfer requests. In each case, the school district relies upon an individual student's race in assigning that student to a particular school, so that the racial balance at the school falls within a predetermined range based on the racial composition of the school district as a whole. Parents of students denied assignment to particular schools under these plans solely because of their race brought suit, contending that allocating children to different public schools on the basis of race violated the Fourteenth Amendment guarantee of equal protection. The Courts of Appeals below upheld the plans. We granted certiorari, and now reverse.

III A

It is well established that when the government distributes burdens or benefits on the basis of individual racial classifications, that action is reviewed under strict scrutiny. As the Court recently reaffirmed, " 'racial classifications are simply too pernicious to permit any but the most exact connection between justification and classification.' " *Gratz v. Bollinger,* 539 U.S. 244, 270, 123 S.Ct. 2411, 156 L.Ed.2d 257 (2003) (quoting *Fullilove v. Klutznick,* 448 U.S. 448, 537, 100 S.Ct. 2758, 65 L.Ed.2d 902 (1980) (Stevens, J., dissenting); brackets omitted). In order to satisfy this searching standard of review, the school districts must demonstrate that the use of individual racial classifications in the assignment plans here under review is "narrowly tailored" to achieve a "compelling" government interest.

[A] government interest we have recognized as compelling for purposes of strict scrutiny is the interest in diversity in higher education upheld in *Grutter [v. Bollinger],* 539 U.S., at 328 [2003]. The specific interest found compelling in *Grutter* was student body diversity "in the context of higher education." *Ibid.* The diversity interest was not focused on race alone but encompassed "all factors that may contribute to student body diversity." *Id.,* at 337. We described the various types of diversity that the law school sought:

"[The law school's] policy makes clear there are many possible bases for diversity admissions, and provides examples of admittees who have lived or traveled widely abroad, are fluent in several languages, have overcome personal adversity and family hardship, have exceptional records of extensive community service, and have had successful careers in other fields." *Id.,* at 338 (brackets and internal quotation marks omitted).

[T]he entire gist of the analysis in *Grutter* was that the admissions program at issue there focused on each applicant as an individual, and not simply as a member of a particular racial group. The classification of applicants by race upheld in *Grutter* was only as part of a "highly individualized, holistic review," 539 U.S., at 337. As the Court explained, "[t]he importance of this individualized consideration in the context of a race-conscious admissions program is paramount." *Ibid.* The point of the narrow tailoring analysis in which the *Grutter* Court engaged was to ensure that the use of racial classifications was indeed part of a broader assessment of diversity, and not simply an effort to achieve racial balance, which the Court explained would be "patently unconstitutional." *Id.,* at 330.

In the present cases, by contrast, race is not considered as part of a broader effort to achieve "exposure to widely diverse people, cultures, ideas, and viewpoints," *ibid.*; race, for some students, is determinative standing alone. The districts argue that other factors, such as student preferences, affect assignment decisions under their plans, but under each plan when race comes into play, it is decisive by itself. It is not simply one factor weighed with others in reaching a decision, as in *Grutter*; it is *the* factor.

IV

[T]he parties and their *amici* debate which side is more faithful to the heritage of *Brown,* but the position of the plaintiffs in *Brown* was spelled out in their brief and could not have been clearer: "[T]he Fourteenth Amendment prevents states from according differential treatment to American children on the basis of their color or race." Brief for Appellants in Nos. 1, 2, and 4 and for Respondents in No. 10 on Reargument in *Brown I,* O.T.1953, p. 15 (Summary of Argument). What do the racial classifications at issue here do, if not accord differential treatment on the basis of race? As counsel who appeared before this Court for the plaintiffs in *Brown* put it: "We have one fundamental contention which we will seek to develop in the course of this argument, and that contention is that no State has any authority under the equal-protection clause of the Fourteenth Amendment to use race as a factor in affording educational opportunities among its citizens." Tr. of Oral Arg. in *Brown I,* p. 7 (Robert L. Carter, Dec. 9, 1952). There is no ambiguity in that statement. And it was that position that prevailed in this Court, which emphasized in its remedial opinion that what was "[a]t stake is the personal interest of the plaintiffs in admission to public schools as soon as practicable *on a nondiscriminatory basis,*" and what was required was "determining admission to the public schools *on a nonracial basis." Brown II, supra,* at 300–301 (emphasis added). What do the racial classifications do in these cases, if not determine admission to a public school on a racial basis?

Before *Brown,* schoolchildren were told where they could and could not go to school based on the color of their skin. The school districts in these cases have not carried the heavy burden of demonstrating that we should allow this once again—even for very different reasons. For schools that never segregated on the basis of race, such as Seattle, or that have removed the vestiges of past segregation, such as Jefferson County, the way "to achieve a system of determining admission to the public schools on a nonracial basis," *Brown II,* 349 U.S., at 300–301, is to stop assigning students on a racial basis. The way to stop discrimination on the basis of race is to stop discriminating on the basis of race.

■ JUSTICE THOMAS, concurring.

The dissent argues that the interest in integration has an educational element. The dissent asserts that racially balanced schools improve educational outcomes for black children. In support, the dissent unquestioningly cites certain social science research to support propositions that are hotly disputed among social scientists. In reality, it is far from apparent that coerced racial mixing has any educational benefits, much less that integration is necessary to black achievement.

Scholars have differing opinions as to whether educational benefits arise from racial balancing. Some have concluded that black students receive genuine educational benefits. See, *e.g.,* Crain & Mahard, Desegregation and Black Achievement: A Review of the Research, 42 L. & Contemp. Probs. 17, 48 (1978). Others have been more circumspect. See, *e.g.,* Henderson, Greenberg, Schneider, Uribe, & Verdugo, High Quality Schooling for African American Students, in Beyond Desegregation 166 (M. Shujaa ed. 1996) ("Perhaps desegregation does not have a single effect, positive or negative, on the academic achievement of African American students, but rather some strategies help, some hurt, and still others make no difference whatsoever. It is clear to us that focusing simply on demographic issues detracts from focusing on improving schools"). And some have concluded that there are no demonstrable educational benefits. See, *e.g.,* Armor & Rossell, Desegregation and Resegregation in the Public Schools, in Beyond the Color Line: New Perspectives on Race and Ethnicity in America 239, 251 (A. Thernstrom & S. Thernstrom eds.2002).

The *amicus* briefs in the cases before us mirror this divergence of opinion. Supporting the school boards, one *amicus* has assured us that "both early desegregation research and recent statistical and econometric analyses . . . indicate that there are positive effects on minority student achievement scores arising from diverse school settings." Brief for American Educational Research Association as *Amicus Curiae* 10. Another brief claims that "school desegregation has a modest positive impact on the achievement of African–American students." App. to Brief for 553 Social Scientists as *Amici Curiae* 13–14 (footnote omitted). Yet neither of those briefs contains specific details like the magnitude of the claimed positive effects or the precise demographic mix at which those positive effects begin to be realized. Indeed, the social scientists' brief rather cautiously claims the existence of any benefit at all, describing the "positive impact" as "modest," *id.,* at 13, acknowledging that "there appears to be little or no effect on math scores," *id.,* at 14, and admitting that the "underlying reasons for these gains in achievement are not entirely clear," *id.,* at 15.

Other *amici* dispute these findings. One *amicus* reports that "[i]n study after study, racial composition of a student body, when isolated, proves to be an insignificant determinant of student achievement." Brief for Dr. John Murphy et al. as *Amici Curiae* in No. 05–908, p. 8; see also *id.,* at 9 ("[T]here is no evidence that diversity in the K–12 classroom positively affects student achievement"). Another *amicus* surveys several social science studies and concludes that "a fair and comprehensive analysis of the research shows that there is no clear and consistent evidence of [educational] benefits." Brief for David J. Armor et al. as *Amici Curiae* 29.

[G]iven this tenuous relationship between forced racial mixing and improved educational results for black children, the dissent cannot plausibly maintain that an educational element supports the integration interest, let alone makes it compelling. See *[Missouri v.] Jenkins,* 515 U.S. [70 (1995)], at 121–122 (THOMAS, J., concurring) ("[T]here is no reason to think that black students cannot learn as well when surrounded by members of their own race as when they are in an integrated environment").

Perhaps recognizing as much, the dissent argues that the social science evidence is "strong enough to permit a democratically elected school board reasonably to determine that this interest is a compelling one." *Post,* at 38. This assertion is inexplicable. It is not up to the school board—the very government entities whose race-based practices we must strictly scrutinize—to determine what interests qualify as compelling under the Fourteenth Amendment to the United States Constitution. Rather, this Court must assess independently the nature of the interest asserted and the evidence to support it in order to determine whether it qualifies as compelling under our precedents. [Deferring to school boards] would leave our equal-protection jurisprudence at the mercy of elected government officials evaluating the evanescent views of a handful of social scientists. To adopt the dissent's deferential approach would be to abdicate our constitutional responsibilities.

[T]he dissent points to data that indicate that "black and white students in desegregated schools are less racially prejudiced than those in segregated schools." *Post,* at 40 (internal quotation marks omitted). [However], it is unclear whether increased interracial contact improves racial attitudes and relations. One researcher has stated that "the reviews of desegregation and intergroup relations were unable to come to any conclusion about what the probable effects of desegregation were ... [;] virtually all of the reviewers determined that few, if any, firm conclusions about the impact of desegregation on intergroup relations could be drawn." Schofield, School Desegregation and Intergroup Relations: A Review of the Literature, in 17 Review of Research in Education 356 (G. Grant ed.1991). Some studies have even found that a deterioration in racial attitudes seems to result from racial mixing in schools. See N. St. John, School Desegregation Outcomes for Children 67–68 (1975) ("A glance at [the data] shows that for either race positive findings are less common than negative findings"); Stephan, The Effects of School Desegregation: An Evaluation 30 Years After Brown, in Advances in Applied Social Psychology 183–186 (M. Saks & L. Saxe eds.1986). Therefore, it is not nearly as apparent as the dissent suggests that increased interracial exposure automatically leads to improved racial attitudes or race relations.

■ JUSTICE KENNEDY, concurring in part and concurring in the judgment.

This Nation has a moral and ethical obligation to fulfill its historic commitment to creating an integrated society that ensures equal opportunity for all of its children. A compelling interest exists in avoiding racial isolation, an interest that a school district, in its discretion and expertise, may choose to pursue. Likewise, a district may consider it a compelling interest to achieve a diverse student population. Race may be one component of that diversity, but other demographic factors, plus special talents and needs, should also be considered. What the government is not permitted to do, absent a showing of necessity not made here, is to classify every student on the basis of race and to assign each of them to schools based on that classification. Crude measures of this sort threaten to reduce children to racial chits valued and traded according to one school's supply and another's demand.

■ JUSTICE BREYER, with whom JUSTICE STEVENS, JUSTICE SOUTER, and JUSTICE GINSBURG join, dissenting.

The principal interest advanced in these cases to justify the use of race-based criteria goes by various names. Sometimes a court refers to it as an interest in achieving racial "diversity." Other times a court, like the plurality here, refers to it as an interest in racial "balancing." [R]egardless of its name, however, the interest at stake possesses three essential elements. First, there is a historical and remedial element: an interest in setting right the consequences of prior conditions of segregation. This refers back to a time when public schools were highly segregated, often as a result of legal or administrative policies that facilitated racial segregation in public schools.

[S]econd, there is an educational element: an interest in overcoming the adverse educational effects produced by and associated with highly segregated schools. Studies suggest that children taken from those schools and placed in integrated settings often show positive academic gains. See, e.g., Powell, Living and Learning: Linking Housing and Education, in Pursuit of a Dream Deferred: Linking Housing and Education Policy 15, 35 (J. Powell, G. Kearney, & V. Kay eds.2001) (hereinafter Powell); Hallinan, Diversity Effects on Student Outcomes: Social Science Evidence, 59 Ohio St. L.J. 733, 741–742 (1998) (hereinafter Hallinan).

Other studies reach different conclusions. See, *e.g.,* D. Armor, Forced Justice (1995). But the evidence supporting an educational interest in racially integrated schools is well established and strong enough to permit a democratically elected school board reasonably to determine that this interest is a compelling one.

Research suggests, for example, that black children from segregated educational environments significantly increase their achievement levels once they are placed in a more integrated setting. Indeed in Louisville itself the achievement gap between black and white elementary school students grew substantially smaller (by seven percentage points) after the integration plan was implemented in 1975. See Powell 35. Conversely, to take another example, evidence from a district in Norfolk, Virginia, shows that resegregated schools led to a decline in the achievement test scores of children of all races. *Ibid.*

One commentator, reviewing dozens of studies of the educational benefits of desegregated schooling, found that the studies have provided "remarkably consistent" results, showing that: (1) black students' educational achievement is improved in integrated schools as compared to racially isolated schools, (2) black students' educational achievement is improved in integrated classes, and (3) the earlier that black students are removed from racial isolation, the better their educational outcomes. See Hallinan 741–742. Multiple studies also indicate that black alumni of integrated schools are more likely to move into occupations traditionally closed to African–Americans, and to earn more money in those fields. See, *e.g.,* Schofield, Review of Research on School Desegregation's Impact on Elementary and Secondary School Students, in Handbook of Research on Multicultural Education 597, 606–607 (J. Banks & C. Banks eds.1995). Cf. W. Bowen & D. Bok, The Shape of the River 118 (1998) (hereinafter Bowen & Bok).

Third, there is a democratic element: an interest in producing an educational environment that reflects the "pluralistic society" in which our children will live. *Swann [v. Charlotte–Mecklenburg Bd. of Ed],* 402 U.S. [1 (1971)], at 16. It is an interest in helping our children learn to work and play together with children of different racial backgrounds. It is an interest in teaching children to engage in the kind of cooperation among Americans of all races that is necessary to make a land of three hundred million people one Nation.

Again, data support this insight. See, *e.g.,* Hallinan 745; Quillian & Campbell, Beyond Black and White: The Present and Future of Multiracial Friendship Segregation, 68 Am. Sociological Rev. 540, 541 (2003) (hereinafter Quillian & Campbell); Dawkins & Braddock, The Continuing Significance of Desegregation: School Racial Composition and African American Inclusion in American Society, 63 J. Negro Ed. 394, 401–403 (1994) (hereinafter Dawkins & Braddock); Wells & Crain, Perpetuation Theory and the Long–Term Effects of School Desegregation, 64 Rev. Educational Research 531, 550 (1994) (hereinafter Wells & Crain).

There are again studies that offer contrary conclusions. See, *e.g.,* Schofield, School Desegregation and Intergroup Relations, in 17 Review of Research in Education 356 (G. Grant ed.1991). Again, however, the evidence supporting a democratic interest in racially integrated schools is firmly established and sufficiently strong to permit a school board to determine, as this Court has itself often found, that this interest is compelling.

For example, one study documented that "black and white students in desegregated schools are less racially prejudiced than those in segregated schools," and that "interracial contact in desegregated schools leads to an increase in interracial sociability and friendship." Hallinan 745. See also Quillian & Campbell 541. Cf. Bowen & Bok 155. Other studies have found that both black and white students who attend integrated schools are more likely to work in desegregated companies after graduation than students who attended racially isolated schools. Dawkins & Braddock 401–403; Wells & Crain 550. Further research has shown that the desegregation of schools can help bring adult communities together by reducing segregated housing. Cities that have implemented successful school desegregation plans have witnessed increased interracial contact and neighborhoods that tend to become less racially segregated. Dawkins & Braddock 403. These effects not only reinforce the prior gains of integrated primary and secondary education; they also foresee a time when there is less need to use race-conscious criteria.

[F]or his part, Justice Thomas faults my citation of various studies supporting the view that school districts can find compelling educational and civic interests in integrating their public schools. He is entitled of course to his own opinion as to which studies he finds convincing— although it bears mention that even the author of some of Justice Thomas' preferred studies has found *some* evidence linking integrated learning environments to increased academic achievement. Cf. *ante,* at 15–17 (opinion of Thomas, J.) (citing Armor & Rossell, Desegregation and Resegregation in the Public Schools, in Beyond the Color Line 239 (A. Thernstrom & S. Thernstrom eds.2002)); Brief for Armor *et al.* as *Amici Curiae,* with Rosen, Perhaps Not All Affirmative Action is Created Equal, N.Y. Times, June 11, 2006 (quoting David Armor as commenting " '[w]e did find the [racial] achievement gap changing *significantly*' " and acknowledging that he " 'did find a modest association for math but not reading in terms of racial composition and achievement, but there's a big state variation' " (emphasis added)). If we are to insist upon unanimity in the social science literature before finding a compelling interest, we might never find one.

[B]rown held out a promise. It was a promise embodied in three Amendments designed to make citizens of slaves. It was the promise of true racial equality—not as a matter of fine words on paper, but as a matter of everyday life in the Nation's cities and schools. [T]he last half-century has witnessed great strides toward racial equality, but we have not yet realized

the promise of *Brown*. To invalidate the plans under review is to threaten the promise of *Brown*. The plurality's position, I fear, would break that promise. This is a decision that the Court and the Nation will come to regret.

———

2. SEGREGATION BY GENDER

Almost thirty years after *Brown* held that the segregation of public schools by race violated the Equal Protection clause of the Fourteenth Amendment, the Supreme Court addressed the question of whether the segregation of public schools by gender was also unconstitutional. The question arose in the context of a state-supported nursing school.

———

MISSISSIPPI UNIVERSITY FOR WOMEN v. HOGAN
Supreme Court of the United States, 1982.
458 U.S. 718, 102 S.Ct. 3331, 73 L.Ed.2d 1090.

■ Justice O'Connor delivered the opinion of the Court.

[Respondent Joe Hogan applied for admission to the Mississippi University for Women School of Nursing. Since by statute the University limited its enrollment to women applicants, Hogan was denied admission. The district court denied Hogan preliminary injunctive relief and the court of appeals reversed.]

This case presents the narrow issue of whether a state statute that excludes males from enrolling in a state-supported professional nursing school violates the Equal Protection Clause of the Fourteenth Amendment.

[T]he State's primary justification for maintaining the single-sex admissions policy of MUW's School of Nursing is that it compensates for discrimination against women and, therefore, constitutes educational affirmative action. As applied to the School of Nursing, we find the State's argument unpersuasive.

[M]ississippi has made no showing that women lacked opportunities to obtain training in the field of nursing or to attain positions of leadership in that field when the MUW School of Nursing opened its door or that women currently are deprived of such opportunities. In fact, in 1970, the year before the School of Nursing's first class enrolled, women earned 94 percent of the nursing baccalaureate degrees conferred in Mississippi and 98.6 percent of the degrees earned nationwide. United States Department of Health, Education, and Welfare, Earned Degrees Conferred: 1969–1970, 388 (1972). That year was not an aberration; one decade earlier, women had earned all the nursing degrees conferred in Mississippi and 98.9 percent of the degrees conferred nationwide. United States Department of Health, Education, and Welfare, Earned Degrees Conferred 1959–1960: Bachelor's and Higher Degrees 135 (1960). As one would expect, the labor force reflects the same predominance of women in nursing. When MUW's

School of Nursing began operation, nearly 98 percent of all employed registered nurses were female. United States Bureau of the Census, 1981 Statistical Abstract of the United States 402 (1981).

Rather than compensate for discriminatory barriers faced by women, MUW's policy of excluding males from admission to the School of Nursing tends to perpetuate the stereotyped view of nursing as an exclusively woman's job.[15] By assuring that Mississippi allots more openings in its state-supported nursing schools to women than it does to men, MUW's admissions policy lends credibility to the old view that women, not men, should become nurses, and makes the assumption that nursing is a field for women a self-fulfilling prophecy. Thus, we conclude that, although the State recited a "benign, compensatory purpose," it failed to establish that the alleged objective is the actual purpose underlying the discriminatory classification.

The policy is invalid also because it fails the second part of the equal protection test, for the State has made no showing that the gender-based classification is substantially and directly related to its proposed compensatory objective. To the contrary, MUW's policy of permitting men to attend classes as auditors fatally undermines its claim that women, at least those in the School of Nursing, are adversely affected by the presence of men.

MUW permits men who audit to participate fully in classes. Additionally, both men and women take part in continuing education courses offered by the School of Nursing, in which regular nursing students also can enroll. Deposition of Dr. James Strobel 56–60 and Deposition of Dean Annette K. Barrar 24–26. The uncontroverted record reveals that admitting men to nursing classes does not affect teaching style, Deposition of Nancy L. Herban 4, that the presence of men in the classroom would not affect the performance of the female nursing students, Tr. 61 and Deposition of Dean Annette K. Barrar 7–8, and that men in coeducational nursing schools do not dominate the classroom. Deposition of Nancy Herban 6. In sum, the record in this case is flatly inconsistent with the claim that excluding men from the School of Nursing is necessary to reach any of MUW's educational goals.

Thus, considering both the asserted interest and the relationship between the interest and the methods used by the State, we conclude that the State has fallen far short of establishing the "exceedingly persuasive justification" needed to sustain the gender-based classification. Accordingly, we hold that MUW's policy of denying males the right to enroll for credit in its School of Nursing violates the Equal Protection Clause of the Fourteenth Amendment.

---

15. Officials of the American Nurses Association have suggested that excluding men from the field has depressed nurses' wages. Hearings Before the United States Equal Employment Opportunity Commission on Job Segregation and Wage Discrimination 510–511, 517–518, 523 (April 1980). To the extent the exclusion of men has that effect, MUW's admissions policy actually penalizes the very class the State purports to benefit.

■ CHIEF JUSTICE BURGER, dissenting.

I agree generally with Justice Powell's dissenting opinion. I write separately, however, to emphasize that the Court's holding today is limited to the context of a professional nursing school. Since the Court's opinion relies heavily on its finding that women have traditionally dominated the nursing profession, it suggests that a State might well be justified in maintaining, for example, the option of an all-women's business school or liberal arts program.

■ JUSTICE BLACKMUN, dissenting.

While the Court purports to write narrowly, declaring that it does not decide the same issue with respect to "separate but equal" undergraduate institutions for females and males or with respect to units of MUW other than its School of Nursing, there is inevitable spillover from the Court's ruling today. That ruling, it seems to me, places in constitutional jeopardy any state-supported educational institution that confines its student body in any area to members of one sex, even though the State elsewhere provides an equivalent program to the complaining applicant. The Court's reasoning does not stop with the School of Nursing of the Mississippi University for Women.

■ JUSTICE POWELL, with whom JUSTICE REHNQUIST joins, dissenting.

[C]oeducation, historically, is a novel educational theory. From grade school through high school, college, and graduate and professional training, much of the nation's population during much of our history has been educated in sexually segregated classrooms.

[T]he sexual segregation of students has been a reflection of, rather than an imposition upon, the preference of those subject to the policy. It cannot be disputed, for example, that the highly qualified women attending the leading women's colleges could have earned admission to virtually any college of their choice. Women attending such colleges have chosen to be there, usually expressing a preference for the special benefits of single-sex institutions. Similar decisions were made by the colleges that elected to remain open to women only.[4]

The arguable benefits of single-sex colleges also continue to be recognized by students of higher education. The Carnegie Commission on Higher Education has reported that it "favor[s] the continuation of colleges for women. They provide an element of diversity ... and [an environment in which women] generally ... speak up more in their classes, ... hold more positions of leadership on campus, ... and have more role models and mentors among women teachers and administrators." Carnegie Report,

4. In announcing Wellesley's decision in 1973 to remain a women's college, President Barbara Newell said that "[t]he research we have clearly demonstrates that women's colleges produce a disproportionate number of women leaders and women in responsible positions in society; it does demonstrate that the higher proportion of women on the faculty the higher the motivation for women students." Carnegie Report, supra, in Babcock et al., Sex Discrimination and the Law, at 1014. Similarly rejecting coeducation in 1971, the Mount Holyoke Trustees Committee on Coeducation reported that "the conditions that historically justified the founding of women's colleges" continued to justify their remaining in that tradition. Ibid.

quoted in K. Davidson, R. Ginsburg, & H. Kay, Sex–Based Discrimination 814 (1975 ed.). A 10–year empirical study by the Cooperative Institutional Research Program of the American Counsel of Education and the University of California, Los Angeles also has affirmed the distinctive benefits of single-sex colleges and universities. As summarized in A. Astin, Four Critical Years 232 (1977), the data established that

> "[b]oth [male and female] single-sex colleges facilitate student involvement in several areas: academic, interaction with faculty, and verbal aggressiveness.... Men's and women's colleges also have a positive effect on intellectual self-esteem. Students at single-sex colleges are more satisfied than students at coeducational colleges with virtually all aspects of college life.... The only area where students are less satisfied is social life."[5]

[A] distinctive feature of America's tradition has been respect for diversity. [A]t stake in this case as I see it is the preservation of a small aspect of this diversity. But that aspect is by no means insignificant, given our heritage of available choice between single-sex and coeducational institutions of higher learning. The Court answers that there is discrimination. [B]ut, having found "discrimination," the Court finds it difficult to identify the victims. It hardly can claim that women are discriminated against. A constitutional case is held to exist solely because one man found it inconvenient to travel to any of the other institutions made available to him by the State of Mississippi. In essence he insists that he has a right to attend a college in his home community. This simply is not a sex discrimination case. The Equal Protection Clause was never intended to be applied to this kind of case.

ASSOCIATION AND ASSIMILATION

Deborah L. Rhode.
81 Northwestern University Law Review 106 (1986).

Contemporary justifications for sex-segregated schools generally take two forms. One rationale is remedial: gender segregation, like gender

---

5. In this Court the benefits of single-sex education have been asserted by the students and alumnae of MUW. One would expect the Court to regard their views as directly relevant to this case: "[I]n the aspect of life known as courtship or mate-pairing, the American female remains in the role of the pursued sex, expected to adorn and groom herself to attract the male. Without comment on the equities of this social arrangement, it remains a sociological fact.

"An institution of collegiate higher learning maintained exclusively for women is uniquely able to provide the education atmo-sphere in which some, but not all, women can best attain maximum learning potential. It can serve to overcome the historic repression of the past and can orient a woman to function and achieve in the still male dominated economy. It can free its students of the burden of playing the mating game while attending classes, thus giving academic rather than sexual emphasis. Consequently, many such institutions flourish and their graduates make significant contributions to the arts, professions and business." Brief for Mississippi University for Women Alumnae Assn. as Amicus Curiae 2–3.

preference in affirmative action programs, serves the short-term objective of overcoming women's historic disadvantages in educational and vocational pursuits. A second and broader rationale involves pluralism: single-sex education promotes values of cultural diversity and personal association analogous to those that traditionally have enjoyed first amendment protection.

The majority in *Hogan* chose to address only the first of these rationales. [P]articularly since this was the Court's first full opinion on single-sex schools, its analysis left much to be desired. As Justice Powell's dissent and Mississippi University for Women's brief noted, a substantial body of empirical research suggests that certain all-female learning environments serve remedial objectives. Compared with coeducational institutions, women's colleges reportedly have fostered greater verbal assertiveness, higher career aspirations, more intellectual self-esteem, expanded leadership opportunities, enhanced faculty-student contact, greater access to female role models, and more opportunities for women faculty or administrators. Presumably the state might have an interest in promoting some of these characteristics even for those in female-dominated professions. Why the Court declined even to mention this research, and instead relied on two witnesses' more speculative opinions, is not self-evident. It may be, as one amicus brief implied, that the university failed to make an adequate factual showing at trial. Alternatively, nursing schools have characteristics that cast doubt on the relevance of certain data regarding undergraduate programs; for example, their students are older, the percentage of male enrollees is unusually small, and opportunities for female faculty and access to female role models already are present. In either case, the majority's analysis begs for qualifications.

Equally problematic was the dissenting opinions' unqualified embrace of the university's remedial claim. Extolling the virtues of single-sex education, Justice Powell, joined by Chief Justice Burger and Justice Rehnquist, set forth a selective and superficial account of the available research. Moreover, as the Coalition of Women's Colleges has noted, much of the empirical data on which the dissent or its authorities relied is "outdated and generally insufficient to support a coherent argument." For example, it is unclear how attributes like greater verbal assertiveness and intellectual self-esteem in single-sex environments affect women's capacity to function in mixed environments.

[T]he pluralist defense of single-sex schools raises similar difficulties. It is true, as Justice Powell noted in *Hogan*, that generations of distinguished Americans have found "distinct advantages" in sexually segregated education. Yet comparable claims were made about racially segregated schools and clubs—claims that often rested on comparable stereotypes. Moreover, nothing in the standard pluralist argument serves to distinguish all-female from all-male schools as an antidote for "needless conformity."

[T]hus, the enhancement of some students' choices can come only at the cost of restricting others', and history leaves little doubt about which sex has paid the greater price for segregation. Even assuming that the pluralist defense somehow could be limited to women's schools, one cannot further suppose, as did the dissenters in *Hogan,* that perpetuating these institutions unequivocally "expands women's choices." To affirm the "honored traditions" of Mississippi University for Women, which focused on typing, teaching, nursing, and needlework, is to reinforce expectations that have constrained, not expanded, women's options. Lumping all women's schools into the same abstract category ignores the diversity in experience that such institutions have fostered.

[I]n the face of such competing concerns and conflicting data, the courts have steered a muddled course, and the prospects for improvement are not encouraging. Separate-but-equal as educational policy remains a perplexing misnomer. In some respects separate is better. In other respects it is worse. But never is it likely to be equal.

————

NOTES

1.   Standard of Review. Mississippi University for Women v. Hogan has been cited hundreds of times by lower courts, but not for its specific holding regarding the segregation by gender of nursing schools. Rather, the case has been cited as the definitive affirmation by the Supreme Court of an "intermediate" standard for reviewing the constitutionality of any state action involving gender. State action involving economic transactions—such as the maximum hour legislation at issue in Muller v. Oregon—is to be reviewed under a "rational basis" test: the legislation is to be upheld unless the means provided for achieving a legislative purpose bear no rational relationship to that purpose. Virtually all legislation passes this test. State action involving "fundamental" rights, such as freedom of speech, or "suspect" classifications, such as race, are subject to "strict scrutiny" by the courts: the legislation will be upheld only if there is a "compelling interest" at stake. Virtually all legislation fails this test. See Wilkinson, The Supreme Court, The Equal Protection Clause, and the Three Faces of Constitutionality, 61 Virginia Law Review 945 (1975). After *Hogan,* state action involving gender is reviewed according to a standard more demanding than rationality, but less demanding than strict scrutiny: the legislation will be upheld only if the State can show an "exceedingly persuasive justification" for a gender-based classification, which the State in *Hogan* failed to do.

2.   The Conclusions of Sociologists. In The Trial of a Mississippi Lawyer, The New York Times, May 15, 1983, § 6 (Magazine), at 62, 69, Wilbur Colom, Hogan's attorney at the oral argument before the Supreme Court, described one of the "ironic moments" of the case in which Colom, an African–American lawyer, invoked Edmond Cahn's criticism, above, of the *Brown* decision:

Thurgood Marshall, in 1954, arguing in *Brown,* had convinced the court to outlaw racial segregation in schools and base its decision on studies by social scientists that demonstrated segregated education adversely affected minorities. In the Hogan case, various studies were being used by those arguing for single-sex education to demonstrate that women learn better in an environment free from the disturbing influence of men. Turning to Justice Marshall, I contended that I did not want "my or anyone else's" constitutional rights to depend on the conclusions of sociologists.

3. Women's Colleges and Women Leaders. In footnote 4 of his dissent in Mississippi University for Women v. Hogan, Justice Powell cites approvingly the statement of Wellesley President Barbara Newell that "[t]he research we have clearly demonstrates that women's colleges produce a disproportionate number of women leaders and women in responsible positions in society." This research, however, is susceptible to other, less clear, interpretations. Tidball, Perspective on Academic Women and Affirmative Action, 54 Educational Record 130 (1973) is one of the most frequently cited studies asserting a causal relationship between attending a women's college and later achievement. She reported that all-female colleges produced a higher percentage of those listed in *Who's Who of American Women* between 1910 and 1950 than did coeducational institutions. As Rhode, Association and Assimilation, 81 Northwestern University Law Review 106, 139 (1986), notes:

> As a threshold matter, to view *Who's Who* listings as an adequate measure of achievement is to accept what many feminists have criticized as an impoverished understanding of individual worth, an understanding that historically has devalued women's contributions. But even assuming *arguendo* that an entry in *Who's Who* is an appropriate indication of success, one cannot infer a causal relationship from a correlation without controlling for a host of variables that Tidball's research failed to acknowledge. From her data, it is impossible to separate the effects of single-sex schools from the higher socioeconomic status and career orientation of their students. For example, had Ivy League institutions been open to women during the period of Tidball's study, the percentage of achievers from coeducational schools might have been substantially different.

UNITED STATES v. COMMONWEALTH OF VIRGINIA

United States District Court, Western District of Virginia, 1991.
766 F.Supp. 1407.

■ KISER, DISTRICT JUDGE.

It was in May of 1864 that the United States and the Virginia Military Institute (VMI) first confronted each other. That was a life-and-death engagement that occurred on the battlefield at New Market, Virginia. The combatants have again confronted each other, but this time the venue is in this court. Nonetheless, VMI claims the struggle is nothing short of a life-and-death confrontation—albeit figurative.

The conflict between the parties arises out of the United States' challenge to VMI's all-male admissions policy. The United States asserts that as a state-supported college, VMI's refusal to admit females to the Institute, regardless of their qualifications, violates the Equal Protection Clause of the Fourteenth Amendment. VMI counters by saying that although it discriminates against women, the discrimination is not invidious but rather to promote a legitimate state interest—diversity in education.

[Mississippi University for Women v.]Hogan involved admission of a single student into the nursing school, and the Court did not purport to extend its ruling to cover other programs at the school. 458 U.S. at 733, 102 S.Ct. at 3340 (Chief Justice Burger dissenting). These determinations require a fact-intensive examination of the practical considerations underlying the challenged policy. Many of the facts underlying the Supreme Court's rejection of the justification proffered in Hogan are not present here. In Hogan, Justice O'Connor's majority opinion emphasized that the

> uncontroverted record reveals that admitting men to nursing classes does not affect teaching style, ... that the presence of men in the classroom would not affect the performance of the female nursing students, ... and that men in coeducational nursing schools do not dominate the classroom.... In sum, the record in this case is flatly inconsistent with the claim that excluding men from the School of Nursing is necessary to reach any of MUW's educational goals.

Hogan, 458 U.S. at 731, 102 S.Ct. at 3339. The record in this case is directly to the contrary. The record is replete with testimony that single gender education at the undergraduate level is beneficial to both males and females. Moreover, the evidence establishes that key elements of the adversative VMI educational system, with its focus on barracks life, would be fundamentally altered, and the distinctive ends of the system would be thwarted, if VMI were forced to admit females and to make changes necessary to accommodate their needs and interests.

One of the most striking differences in the two cases is the reasons proffered to justify the discrimination. In Hogan, Mississippi maintained that a female-only admission policy at MUW was affirmative action which was justified to compensate women for past discrimination whereas, here, Virginia urges that a male-only admission policy at VMI promotes diversity within its statewide system of higher education. The Court found that Mississippi's proffered explanation failed both prongs of the intermediate scrutiny test, i.e., that it was not an important governmental objective and that the means of advancing the objective were not substantially related to the achievement of that objective. In contrast, diversity in education has been recognized both judicially and by education experts as being a legitimate objective. The sole way to attain single-gender diversity is to maintain a policy of admitting only one gender to an institution.

[O]ne empirical study in evidence, not questioned by any expert, demonstrates that single-sex colleges provide better educational experiences than coeducational institutions. Students of both sexes become more academically involved, interact with faculty frequently, show larger increases in intellectual self-esteem and are more satisfied with practically all aspects of college experience (the sole exception is social life) compared with their counterparts in coeducational institutions. Attendance at an all-male college substantially increases the likelihood that a student will carry out career plans in law, business and college teaching, and also has a substantial positive effect on starting salaries in business. Women's colleges increase the chances that those who attend will obtain positions of leadership, complete the baccalaureate degree, and aspire to higher degrees. Alexander Astin, Four Critical Years, (1977). This research was cited favorably by Justice Powell in his dissenting opinion in Hogan, 458 U.S. at 738–39, 102 S.Ct. at 3343–44. Viewed in the light of this very substantial authority favoring single-sex education, the VMI Board's decision to maintain an all-male institution is fully justified even without taking into consideration the other unique features of VMI's method of teaching and training. [W]hen one considers VMI's methods of education and the effect that admission of women into the institution will have, the Board's decision to remain an all-male institution is further reinforced. Expert testimony established that, even though some women are capable of all of the individual activities required of VMI cadets, a college where women are present would be significantly different from one where only men are present.

[P]hysical education requirements would have to be altered, at least for the women. The current program, where every student must pass precisely the same physical test before graduation, would prevent a disproportionate number of women from graduating, thus forcing VMI either to establish different requirements for women, or to eliminate or substantially reduce the requirements so that they could be applied to both sexes, which would remove one important part of the VMI system of education. The introduction of women into VMI would add a new set of stresses on the cadets, of a very different kind than the cadets now face. The belief that this would affect the educational program is well-founded in empirical evidence, and not based on an archaic stereotype.

[C]onclusion

Through its Board of Visitors at VMI, Virginia has set an objective of providing single-gender education for males. The evidence in the case, which is virtually uncontradicted, supports Virginia's view that substantial educational benefits flow from a single-gender environment, be it male or female, that cannot be replicated in a coeducational setting. This adds a measure of diversity to Virginia's overall system of education that would be missing if VMI were coeducational. The diversity is further enhanced by VMI's unique method of instruction which was applauded by all of the educational experts who testified. Thus, Virginia has sustained the requirement that gender discrimination serves an important state educational objective. Virginia also met the second prong of the Hogan test by proving that the objective of diversity of education is met by providing single-gender education. Obviously, the only means of attaining this goal is to exclude women from the all-male institution—VMI. But Virginia did not stop there. It enlarged on the single-gender diversity by maintaining an institution whose method of instruction is unique in all the world.

VMI is a different type of institution. It has set its eye on the goal of citizen-solider and never veered from the path it has chosen to meet that goal. VMI truly marches to the beat of a different drummer, and I will permit it to continue to do so.

APPENDIX: FINDINGS OF FACT

[D]ifferences Between Men and Women

A. Gender–Based Physiological Differences

[1]. High maximal lifting capacity refers to the ability to lift 50 kilograms to a height of 132 centimeters of distance, which corresponds to the tail board of a military truck. Approximately 7% of median college-age females possess high maximal lifting capacity, as compared with approximately 80% of males. Approximately 50% of median college-age females can engage in activities requiring a medium maximal lifting capacity, while 100% of median college-age males can engage in such activities.

[2]. On the average, college-age females perform a two-mile run approximately three minutes slower than the median for college-age males.

[3]. The median college-age female is not capable of performing push-ups equivalent to that of the median college-age male. Of the females tested, none was able to come close to meeting the push-up requirement of the VMI physical fitness test. The maximum number of push-ups by a female was 18, compared with a minimum requirement of 45 push-ups on the VMI fitness test.

[4]. Comparison of the United States Military Academy classes of 1989 and 1981 male and female cadets on the Army physical fitness tests, USMA indoor obstacle course test, and the USMA physical ability test, shows the following:

(a) Seven of eight physical tests show half (50th percentile) of the women performed below the bottom five percent of the men. The single exception is the Army physical fitness sit-up test, which was almost identical for the two groups.

(b) Three-quarters (75th percentile) of the women performed below the bottom five percent of the men in the indoor obstacle course and physical ability test push-up, standing long jump, modified basketball throw, and 300–yard shuttle run test.

(c) The 75th percentile of women for the class of 1989 Army physical fitness test push-up performance was equal to the 8th percentile performance for the men; and the 75th percentile women for the class of 1981 performance was equal to the 13th percentile performance for the men.

B. Gender–Based Developmental Differences

1. According to Dr. Richardson [an expert witness for VMI], the "nature of an experience that is growth-producing for a majority of women, according to the literature, is one that is supportive, is one that emphasizes positive motivation. I'm not saying that some women don't do well under adversative model, undoubtedly there are some who do, but you [do not] design educational experiences around the exception. You have to design them around the rule, and I think you would find that the doubting model ... the adversative model ... would have to be gradually adapt[ed] so that it incorporated more of the positive motivation, positive reenforcement."

2. A substantial body of contemporary scholarship and research supports the proposition that, although males and females have significant areas of developmental overlap, they also have differing developmental needs that are deep-seated.

[3]. Given these developmental differences females and males characteristically learn differently. Males tend to need an atmosphere of adversativeness or ritual combat in which the teacher is a disciplinarian and a worthy competitor. Females tend to thrive in a cooperative atmosphere in which the teacher is emotionally connected with the students.

[4]. Commenting on the scholarly literature and empirical evidence that single-sex education is desirable in light of gender-based developmental differences, the government's expert, Dr. Conrad [an expert witness for the United States], described the gender differences identified by researchers as "tendencies." He emphasized that the attributes of males and females in individual cases may diverge from these average tendencies. In other words, there are exceptions to the general rule.

UNITED STATES v. COMMONWEALTH OF VIRGINIA

United States Court of Appeals, Fourth Circuit, 1992.
976 F.2d 890.

■ NIEMEYER, CIRCUIT JUDGE.

The United States contends on appeal that enhancing diversity by offering a distinctive single-sex education to men only is not a legitimate state objective and that the Commonwealth and VMI have not established a sufficient justification for VMI's male-only admissions policy.

[T]he mission of VMI is to produce "citizen-soldiers, educated and honorable men who are suited for leadership in civilian life and who can provide military leadership when necessary." Focusing primarily on character development and leadership training through a unique and intense process, characterized as an "adversative" educational model drawn from earlier military training and English public schools, VMI's educational method emphasizes physical rigor, mental stress, absolute equality of treatment, absence of privacy, minute regulation of behavior, and indoctrination of values. The process is designed to foster in VMI cadets doubts about previous beliefs and experiences and to instill in cadets new values which VMI seeks to impart.

[T]he district court began its opinion by noting that in May 1864, during the Civil War, VMI cadets bravely fought Union troops at New Market, Virginia. The court continued, "the combatants have again confronted each other, but this time the venue is in this court." What was not said is that the outcome of each confrontation finds resolution in the Equal Protection Clause.

[T]o conduct the appropriate Fourteenth Amendment analysis in this case, we must determine whether the state policy of excluding women from admission to VMI is substantially related to an important policy or objective of Virginia. [W]e must first decide whether VMI's male-only admissions policy, maintained pursuant to state-delegated authority, is a classification justified by a fair and substantial relationship with the institution's mission of developing citizen soldiers, and this in turn leads to an examination of whether VMI's mission would be materially altered by the admission of women.

Much of the debate between the parties relates to the physiological differences between men and women and the question of a woman's ability to perform and endure the physical training included in VMI's program. While it is agreed by the parties that *some* women can meet the physical standards now imposed on men, it is also agreed that a smaller percentage of women can do so. Based on evidence about the experience of the service academies and the Marine Corps, the district court was justified in finding that if women were to be admitted, VMI would have to convert to a dual-track physical training program in order to subject women to a program equal in effect to that of men, and that, as found by a study conducted at West Point, cadets of both sexes would nevertheless perceive the treatment of them as unequal, leading to jealousy and resentment.

All the parties also agree that men and women would and should be entitled to some degree of privacy, at least to the extent that men and women not, in all respects, be exposed to each other. While again there was much debate among the parties as to the changes that might be required to accommodate this at VMI with the admission of women, all agreed that some accommodation would be necessary.

Finally, the parties have debated extensively the effect of cross-sexual confrontations that the adversative program would produce. Testimony was received that the deliberate harassment that upperclassmen give to "rats" [i.e., new cadets] would play out differently when the upperclassman is of one sex and the "rat" another. While the government attributed the predicted effect of this as stereotyping, the evidence supported the district court's finding that cross-sexual confrontation and interaction introduces additional elements of stress and distraction which are not accommodated by VMI's methodology. The court relied on testimony by experts and similar such observations made in the West Point study.

The sum of the changes that could be expected prompted the district court to conclude that if VMI became coeducational, it would offer "neither males nor females the VMI education that now exists." The court observed that "equal treatment would necessarily give way to fair treatment, thus undermining egalitarianism," which is a critical characteristic that now pervades several aspects of VMI's methodology. And the record supports the district court's findings that at least these three aspects of VMI's program—physical training, the absence of privacy, and the adversative approach—would be materially affected by coeducation, leading to a substantial change in the egalitarian ethos that is a critical aspect of VMI's training.

The district court's conclusions that VMI's mission can be accomplished only in a single-gender environment and that changes necessary to accommodate coeducation would tear at the fabric of VMI's unique methodology are adequately supported. And the district court was not clearly erroneous in concluding that if a court were to require the admission of women to VMI to give them access to this unique methodology, the decision would deny those women the very opportunity they sought because the unique characteristics of VMI's program would be destroyed by coeducation. The Catch–22 is that women are denied the opportunity when excluded from VMI and cannot be given the opportunity by admitting them, because the change caused by their admission would destroy the opportunity.

It is not the maleness, as distinguished from femaleness, that provides justification for the program. It is the homogeneity of gender in the process, regardless of which sex is considered, that has been shown to be related to the essence of the education and training at VMI.

The argument by the government that VMI's existing program is maintained as the result of impermissible stereotyping and overly broad generalizations, without a more detailed analysis, might lead, if accepted, to a finding that would impose a conformity that common experience rejects. Men and women are different, and our knowledge about the differences, physiological and psychological, is becoming increasingly more sophisticated. Indeed the evidence in this case amply demonstrated that single-genderedness in education can be pedagogically justifiable.

For instance, in a ten-year empirical study reported by Alexander W. Astin in *Four Critical Years: Effects of College on Beliefs, Attitudes, and Knowledge* (San Francisco: Jossey–Bass 1977), it was found that single-sex colleges have advantages over coeducational colleges in numerous areas. A summary of the report provided by the parties in this case states:

> Single-sex colleges show a pattern of effects on both sexes that is almost uniformly positive. Students of both sexes become more academically involved, interact with faculty frequently, show large increases in intellectual self-esteem, and are more satisfied with practically all aspects of college experience (the sole exception is social life) compared with their counterparts in coeducational institutions.

J.A.1830. In addition to providing substantial benefits to college students, single-sex education also has been found to have salutary consequences for sexual equality in the job market. In a study conducted by Marvin Bressler and Peter Wendell, *The Sex Composition of Selective Colleges and Gender Differences in Career Aspirations,* 51 J. Higher Educ. 650, 662 (1980), the authors observed that in single-sex colleges, the students were more likely to set aside initial, stereotypical job aspirations in favor of more sex-neutral aspirations. They concluded from their data,

> The available evidence thus fails to support the hypothesis that coeducation is a useful instrument for altering the imbalance in career aspirations of academically superior men and women undergraduates.

* * *

> [I]f all selective residential colleges reverted to single sex status, a notable fraction of all men and an even larger proportion of all women would probably renounce initial career commitments, a development which would have salutary consequences for sexual equality in the job market.

The experts for both sides in this case appear to agree with the conclusions reached in these studies.

Thus, while the data support a pedagogical justification for a single-sex education, they do not materially favor either sex. Both men *and* women appear to have benefited from single-sex education in a materially similar manner. The evidence about the VMI system suggests no differently. The problems that could be anticipated by coeducation at VMI, which are suggested by VMI generally to arise from physiological differences between men and women, needs for privacy, and cross-sexual confrontations, would not be anticipated in an all-female program with the same mission and methodology as that of VMI.

In summary, the record supports the conclusion that single-sex education is pedagogically justifiable, and VMI's system, which the district court found to include a holistic formula of training, even more so. It is not remarkable therefore that the government in its brief conceded, "[I]t is not our position that the Fourteenth Amendment embodies a per se bar to public single-sex education."

While this conclusion answers the question of whether VMI's male-only policy is justified by its institutional mission, the argument does not answer the larger question of whether the unique benefit offered by VMI's type of education can be denied to women by the state under a policy of diversity, which has been advanced as the justification and which was relied on by the district court.

The parties agree that VMI offers a unique combination of education and training that makes a positive contribution offered by no other institution. And the district court found, apparently without exception from any party, that "VMI's military program is absolutely unique. No other school in Virginia or in the United States, public or private, offers the same kind of rigorous military training as is available at VMI.'' The decisive question in this case therefore transforms to one of why the Commonwealth of Virginia offers the opportunity only to men. While VMI's institutional mission justifies a single-sex program, the Commonwealth of Virginia has not revealed a policy that explains why it offers the unique benefit of VMI's type of education and training to men and not to women. Although it is readily apparent from the evidence that the rigor of the physical training at VMI is tailored to males, in the context of a single-sex female institution, it could be adjusted without detrimental effect. No other aspect of the program has been shown to depend upon maleness rather than single-genderedness.

[I]f VMI's male-only admissions policy is in furtherance of a state policy of "diversity," the explanation of how the policy is furthered by affording a unique educational benefit only to males is lacking. A policy of diversity which aims to provide an array of educational opportunities, including single-gender institutions, must do more than favor one gender.

[I]n short, VMI has adequately defended a single-gender education and training program to produce "citizen soldiers," but it has not adequately explained how the maintenance of one single-gender institution gives effect to, or establishes the existence of, the governmental objective advanced to support VMI's admissions policy, a desire for educational diversity.

We are thus left with three conclusions: (1) single-gender education, and VMI's program in particular, is justified by a legitimate and relevant institutional mission which favors neither sex; (2) the introduction of women at VMI will materially alter the very program in which women seek to partake; and (3) the Commonwealth of Virginia, despite its announced policy of diversity, has failed to articulate an important policy that substantially supports offering the unique benefits of a VMI-type of education to men and not to women.

[I]n light of our conclusions and the generally recognized benefit that VMI provides, we do not order that women be admitted to VMI if alternatives are available. But VMI's continued status as a state institution is conditioned on the Commonwealth's satisfactorily addressing the findings we affirm and bringing the circumstances into conformity with the Equal Protection Clause of the Fourteenth Amendment. By commenting on the potential benefits of single-gender education while discussing the alleged governmental interest in support of VMI's admissions policies, we do not mean to suggest the specific remedial course that the Commonwealth should or must follow hereafter. Rather, we remand the case to the district court to give to the Commonwealth the responsibility to select a course it chooses, so long as the guarantees of the Fourteenth Amendment are satisfied. Consistent therewith, the Commonwealth might properly decide to admit women to VMI and adjust the program to implement that choice, or it might establish parallel institutions or parallel programs, or it might abandon state support of VMI, leaving VMI the option to pursue its own policies as a private institution. While it is not ours to determine, there might be other more creative options or combinations.

VACATED AND REMANDED FOR FURTHER PROCEEDINGS.

UNITED STATES v. VIRGINIA

Supreme Court of the United States, 1996.
518 U.S. 515, 116 S.Ct. 2264, 135 L.Ed.2d 735.

■ JUSTICE GINSBURG delivered the opinion of the Court.

In response to the Fourth Circuit's ruling, Virginia proposed a parallel program for women: Virginia Women's Institute for Leadership (VWIL). The 4–year, state-sponsored undergraduate program would be located at Mary Baldwin College, a private liberal arts school for women, and would be open, initially, to about 25 to 30 students. Although VWIL would share VMI's mission—to produce "citizen-soldiers"—the VWIL program would differ, as does Mary Baldwin College, from VMI in academic offerings, methods of education, and financial resources.

[V]irginia returned to the District Court seeking approval of its proposed remedial plan, and the court decided the plan met the requirements of the Equal Protection Clause. The District Court again acknowledged evidentiary support for these determinations: "[T]he VMI methodology could be used to educate women and, in fact, some women . . . may prefer the VMI methodology to the VWIL methodology." [852 F. Supp.], at 481. But the "controlling legal principles," the District Court decided, "do not require the Commonwealth to provide a mirror image VMI for women." Ibid. The court anticipated that the two schools would "achieve substantially similar outcomes." Ibid.

A divided Court of Appeals affirmed the District Court's judgment. 44 F.3d 1229 (C.A.4 1995). This time, the appellate court determined to give "greater scrutiny to the selection of means than to the [State's] proffered objective." Id., at 1236. The official objective or purpose, the court said, should be reviewed deferentially.

"[P]roviding the option of a single-gender college education may be considered a legitimate and important aspect of a public system of higher education," the appeals court observed, id., at 1238; that objective, the court added, is "not pernicious," id., at 1239.

[H]aving determined, deferentially, the legitimacy of Virginia's purpose, the court considered the question of means. Exclusion of "men at Mary Baldwin College and women at VMI," the court said, was essential to Virginia's purpose, for without such exclusion, the State could not "accomplish [its] objective of providing single-gender education." Ibid.

[T]he cross-petitions in this case present two ultimate issues. First, does Virginia's exclusion of women from the educational opportunities provided by VMI—extraordinary opportunities for military training and civilian leadership development—deny to women "capable of all of the individual activities required of VMI cadets," 766 F.Supp., at 1412, the equal protection of the laws guaranteed by the Fourteenth Amendment? Second, if VMI's "unique" situation, id., at 1413—as Virginia's sole single-sex public institution of higher education—offends the Constitution's equal protection principle, what is the remedial requirement?

[T]o summarize the Court's current directions for cases of official classification based on gender: Focusing on the differential treatment or denial of opportunity for which relief is sought, the reviewing court must determine whether the proffered justification is "exceedingly persuasive." The burden of justification is demanding and it rests entirely on the State. See Mississippi Univ. for Women, 458 U.S., at 724, 102 S.Ct., at 3336. The State must show "at least that the [challenged] classification serves 'important governmental objectives and that the discriminatory means employed' are 'substantially related to the achievement of those objectives.'" Ibid. (quoting Wengler v. Druggists Mutual Ins. Co., 446 U.S. 142, 150, 100 S.Ct. 1540, 1545, 64 L.Ed.2d 107 (1980)). The justification must be genuine, not hypothesized or invented post hoc in response to litigation. And it must not rely on overbroad generalizations about the different talents, capacities, or preferences of males and females.

[I]n support of its initial judgment for Virginia, a judgment rejecting all equal protection objections presented by the United States, the District Court made "findings" on "gender-based developmental differences." 766 F.Supp., at 1434–1435. These "findings" restate the opinions of Virginia's expert witnesses, opinions about typically male or typically female "tendencies." Id., at 1434. For example, "[m]ales tend to need an atmosphere of adversativeness," while "[f]emales tend to thrive in a cooperative atmosphere." Ibid. "I'm not saying that some women don't do well under [the] adversative model," VMI's expert on educational institutions testified, "undoubtedly there are some [women] who do"; but educational experiences must be designed "around the rule," this expert maintained, and not "around the exception." Ibid.

The United States does not challenge any expert witness estimation on average capacities or preferences of men and women. Instead, the United States emphasizes that time and again since this Court's turning point decision in Reed v. Reed, 404 U.S. 71, 92 S.Ct. 251, 30 L.Ed.2d 225 (1971), we have cautioned reviewing courts to take a "hard look" at generalizations or "tendencies" of the kind pressed by Virginia, and relied upon by the District Court. See O'Connor, Portia's Progress, 66 N.Y.U.L.Rev. 1546, 1551 (1991). State actors controlling gates to opportunity, we have instructed, may not exclude qualified individuals based on "fixed notions concerning the roles and abilities of males and females." Mississippi Univ. for Women, 458 U.S., at 725, 102 S.Ct., at 3336.

[V]irginia and VMI trained their argument on "means" rather than "end," and thus misperceived our precedent. Single-sex education at VMI serves an "important governmental objective," they maintained, and exclusion of women is not only "substantially related," it is essential to that objective. By this notably circular argument, the "straightforward" test

Mississippi Univ. for Women described, see 458 U.S., at 724–725, 102 S.Ct., at 3336–3337, was bent and bowed.

The State's misunderstanding and, in turn, the District Court's, is apparent from VMI's mission: to produce "citizen-soldiers," individuals

> " 'imbued with love of learning, confident in the functions and attitudes of leadership, possessing a high sense of public service, advocates of the American democracy and free enterprise system, and ready . . . to defend their country in time of national peril.' " 766 F.Supp., at 1425 (quoting Mission Study Committee of the VMI Board of Visitors, Report, May 16, 1986).

Surely that goal is great enough to accommodate women, who today count as citizens in our American democracy equal in stature to men. Just as surely, the State's great goal is not substantially advanced by women's categorical exclusion, in total disregard of their individual merit, from the State's premier "citizen-soldier" corps. Virginia, in sum, "has fallen far short of establishing the 'exceedingly persuasive justification,' " Mississippi Univ. for Women, 458 U.S., at 731, 102 S.Ct., at 3340, that must be the solid base for any gender-defined classification.

[I]n the second phase of the litigation, Virginia presented its remedial plan—maintain VMI as a male-only college and create VWIL as a separate program for women. [A] remedial decree, this Court has said, must closely fit the constitutional violation; it must be shaped to place persons unconstitutionally denied an opportunity or advantage in "the position they would have occupied in the absence of [discrimination]." See Milliken v. Bradley, 433 U.S. 267, 280, 97 S.Ct. 2749, 2757, 53 L.Ed.2d 745 (1977) (internal quotation marks omitted). The constitutional violation in this case is the categorical exclusion of women from an extraordinary educational opportunity afforded men. A proper remedy for an unconstitutional exclusion, we have explained, aims to "eliminate [so far as possible] the discriminatory effects of the past" and to "bar like discrimination in the future." Louisiana v. United States, 380 U.S. 145, 154, 85 S.Ct. 817, 822, 13 L.Ed.2d 709 (1965).

Virginia chose not to eliminate, but to leave untouched, VMI's exclusionary policy. For women only, however, Virginia proposed a separate program, different in kind from VMI and unequal in tangible and intangible facilities.

[V]WIL affords women no opportunity to experience the rigorous military training for which VMI is famed. [V]WIL students participate in ROTC and a "largely ceremonial" Virginia Corps of Cadets, see 44 F.3d, at 1234, but Virginia deliberately did not make VWIL a military institute. The VWIL House is not a military-style residence and VWIL students need not live together throughout the 4-year program, eat meals together, or wear uniforms during the school day. [V]WIL students receive their "leadership training" in seminars, externships, and speaker series, see 852 F.Supp., at 477, episodes and encounters lacking the "[p]hysical rigor, mental stress,

... minute regulation of behavior, and indoctrination in desirable values" made hallmarks of VMI's citizen-soldier training.

[V]irginia maintains that these methodological differences are "justified pedagogically," based on "important differences between men and women in learning and developmental needs," "psychological and sociological differences" Virginia describes as "real" and "not stereotypes." Brief for Respondents 28 (internal quotation marks omitted).

[I]n contrast to the generalizations about women on which Virginia rests, we note again these dispositive realities: VMI's "implementing methodology" is not "inherently unsuitable to women," 976 F.2d, at 899; "some women ... do well under [the] adversative model," 766 F.Supp., at 1434 (internal quotation marks omitted); "some women, at least, would want to attend [VMI] if they had the opportunity," id., at 1414; "some women are capable of all of the individual activities required of VMI cadets," id., at 1412, and "can meet the physical standards [VMI] now impose[s] on men," 976 F.2d, at 896. It is on behalf of these women that the United States has instituted this suit, and it is for them that a remedy must be crafted,[19] a remedy that will end their exclusion from a state-supplied educational opportunity for which they are fit, a decree that will "bar like discrimination in the future." Louisiana, 380 U.S., at 154, 85 S.Ct., at 822.

[V]irginia, in sum, while maintaining VMI for men only, has failed to provide any "comparable single-gender women's institution." Id., at 1241. Instead, the Commonwealth has created a VWIL program fairly appraised as a "pale shadow" of VMI in terms of the range of curricular choices and faculty stature, funding, prestige, alumni support and influence. [V]irginia's remedy does not match the constitutional violation; the State has shown no "exceedingly persuasive justification" for withholding from women qualified for the experience premier training of the kind VMI affords.

[F]or the reasons stated, the initial judgment of the Court of Appeals, 976 F.2d 890 (C.A.4 1992), is affirmed, the final judgment of the Court of Appeals, 44 F.3d 1229 (C.A.4 1995), is reversed, and the case is remanded for further proceedings consistent with this opinion.

It is so ordered.

■ Justice Scalia, dissenting.

The question to be answered [i]s whether the exclusion of women from VMI is "substantially related to an important governmental objective."

It is beyond question that Virginia has an important state interest in providing effective college education for its citizens. That single-sex instruction is an approach substantially related to that interest should be evident

---

19. Admitting women to VMI would undoubtedly require alterations necessary to afford members of each sex privacy from the other sex in living arrangements, and to adjust aspects of the physical training programs. See Brief for Petitioner 27–29; cf. note following 10 U.S.C.A. § 4342 (academic and other standards for women admitted to the Military, Naval, and Air Force Academies "shall be the same as those required for male individuals, except for those minimum essential adjustments in such standards required because of physiological differences between male and female individuals"). Experience shows such adjustments are manageable.

enough from the long and continuing history in this country of men's and women's colleges. But beyond that, as the Court of Appeals here stated: "That single-gender education at the college level is beneficial to both sexes is a *fact established in this case*." 44 F.3d 1229, 1238 (C.A.4 1995) (emphasis added).

The evidence establishing that fact was overwhelming—indeed, "virtually uncontradicted" in the words of the court that received the evidence, 766 F.Supp. 1407, 1415 (W.D.Va.1991). As an initial matter, Virginia demonstrated at trial that "[a] substantial body of contemporary scholarship and research supports the proposition that, although males and females have significant areas of developmental overlap, they also have differing developmental needs that are deep-seated." Id., at 1434. While no one questioned that for many students a coeducational environment was nonetheless not inappropriate, that could not obscure the demonstrated benefits of single-sex colleges. For example, the District Court stated as follows: "One empirical study in evidence, not questioned by any expert, demonstrates that single-sex colleges provide better educational experiences than coeducational institutions. Students of both sexes become more academically involved, interact with faculty frequently, show larger increases in intellectual self-esteem and are more satisfied with practically all aspects of college experience (the sole exception is social life) compared with their counterparts in coeducational institutions. Attendance at an all-male college substantially increases the likelihood that a student will carry out career plans in law, business and college teaching, and also has a substantial positive effect on starting salaries in business. Women's colleges increase the chances that those who attend will obtain positions of leadership, complete the baccalaureate degree, and aspire to higher degrees." Id., at 1412. See also id., at 1434–1435 (factual findings). "[I]n the light of this very substantial authority favoring single-sex education," the District Court concluded that "the VMI Board's decision to maintain an all-male institution is fully justified even without taking into consideration the other unique features of VMI's teaching and training." Id., at 1412. This finding alone, which even this Court cannot dispute, should be sufficient to demonstrate the constitutionality of VMI's all-male composition.

[T]he Court [d]ismisses the District Court's " 'findings' on 'gender-based developmental differences' " on the ground that "[t]hese 'findings' restate the opinions of Virginia's expert witnesses, opinions about typically male or typically female 'tendencies.' " (quoting 766 F.Supp., at 1434–1435). How remarkable to criticize the District Court on the ground that its findings rest on the evidence (i.e., the testimony of Virginia's witnesses)! That is what findings are supposed to do.

————

OFFICE OF THE ASSISTANT SECRETARY FOR CIVIL RIGHTS, U.S. DEPARTMENT OF EDUCATION (2007)

The U.S. Department of Education has amended the regulations implementing Title IX of the Education Amendments of 1972, applicable to nonvocational single-sex classes, extracurricular activities, and schools at the elementary and secondary education levels. These new regulations [t]ook effect on November 24, 2006. [T]itle IX prohibits discrimination on the basis of sex in education programs and activities receiving Federal financial assistance.

Summary of Title IX requirements for single-sex classes and extracurricular activities

The new regulations provide for a new exception to the general prohibition against single-sex classes and extracurricular activities. Under the former regulations, single-sex classes were generally prohibited in a coeducational school with specific limited exceptions, such as for sex education classes and contact sports in physical education classes. The new regulations retain the specific exceptions from the former regulations and add a new exception, which permits a recipient to provide single-sex nonvocational classes and extracurricular activities based on the recipient's "important objective." Each single-sex class or extracurricular activity must be based on the recipient's important objective.

The new regulations establish two important objectives upon which a recipient may base a single-sex class or extracurricular activity. The first important objective is to improve educational achievement of its students through a recipient's overall established policy to provide diverse educational opportunities. The second important objective is to meet the particular, identified educational needs of a recipient's students. Regardless of the recipient's important objective, the regulations require that the single-sex nature of the class or extracurricular activity be substantially related to achieving the recipient's important objective.

A recipient that chooses to provide single-sex classes or extracurricular activities is required to implement its important objective in an evenhanded manner with respect to male and female students. The regulations require that student enrollment in any single-sex class or extracurricular activity must be completely voluntary. The regulations also require that the recipient provide to all students, including the students excluded from the single-sex class or extracurricular activity based on sex, a substantially equal coeducational class or extracurricular activity in the same subject or activity. In addition to the required substantially equal coeducational class or extracurricular activity, a recipient, if necessary to comply with the requirement to implement its objective in an evenhanded manner, may also be required to provide a substantially equal single-sex class or extracurricular activity in the same subject or activity to students of the excluded sex.

After a recipient has established single-sex classes or extracurricular activities under this new regulatory exception, the regulations require recipients to conduct periodic self-evaluations of their single-sex classes or extracurricular activities at least every two years. Recipients are required to ensure through their self-evaluation that there is a substantial relationship between the single-sex nature of the class or activity and achievement of the important objective. Recipients also are required to ensure that their single-sex classes or extracurricular activities are based on genuine justifi-cations and do not rely on overly broad generalizations about the different talents, capacities, or preferences of either sex.

Summary of Title IX requirements for single-sex schools

With respect to requirements for offering single-sex public schools, the new regulations also provide more flexibility. The former regulations per-mitted a local educational agency (LEA) to offer a nonvocational single-sex school if it offered a corresponding school for students of the other sex. Under the Department's interpretation of the former requirements, the corresponding school must also have been a single-sex school. Under the new regulations, an LEA is permitted to offer a single-sex school to students of one sex if it provides a substantially equal school to students excluded from the single-sex school based on sex, but that school may be either single-sex or coeducational.

————

NOTES

1. Empirical Status. A report titled Early Implementation of Public Single–Sex Schools: Perceptions and Characteristics (2008) was published by the U.S. Department of Education and is available at http://www.ed.gov/about/offices/list/opepd/ppss/reports.html#singlesex. The report concluded at page xi:

> The results of the literature review were mixed, though the findings suggested some support for the premise that single-sex schooling can be helpful, especially for certain outcomes related to academic achieve-ment and more positive academic aspirations. The literature review did not, however, include any public single-sex schools in the United States; thus the findings should not be generalized to this population. In addition, the studies had some analytical weaknesses that may have inflated the statistical significance of their findings. Overall, there were more socio-emotional outcomes [e.g., increased self-confidence] favor-ing single-sex schools than academic outcomes favoring single-sex schools. In addition, more socio-emotional outcomes favored girls in single-sex schools (70 percent of 30 outcomes) than boys in single-sex schools (40 percent of 25 outcomes).

2. Constitutional Challenges. Many cases have been filed challenging the constitutionality of these amendments to Title IX, arguing that the amendments violate the Equal Protection Clause as interpreted in United States v. Virginia. On March 30, 2009, the first class action challenging the constitutionality of these amendments was certified in the U.S. District Court for the Western District of Kentucky, A.N.A. v. Breckinridge County Board of Education (Civil Action No. 3:08CV–4–S). For an update on the status of this and related litigation, see the ACLU Women's Right's Project,

Sex Segregated Schools: Separate and Unequal, available at http://www.
aclu.org/womensrights/edu/30129res20070614.html.

————

B.   THE FIRST AMENDMENT: OBSCENE OR VIOLENT ENTERTAINMENT

The First Amendment to the Constitution states that "Congress shall
make no law . . . abridging the freedom of speech, or of the press." Social
science research has been brought to bear on two First Amendment issues:
the state regulation of obscenity and of violent video games.

1.   OBSCENITY

In Chapter Three, we considered the use of social science evidence to
determine the factual question of whether a given film or publication
violated "community standards," and hence fulfilled one of the Supreme
Court's criteria for obscenity. Here, we examine the logically prior lawmaking question: can the State, consistent with the First Amendment, proscribe obscene material at all?

————

UNITED STATES v. ROTH

United States Court of Appeals, Second Circuit, 1956.
237 F.2d 796.

■ CLARK, CHIEF JUDGE.

[Samuel Roth was convicted by a district court jury of four counts of
mailing materials alleged to be "obscene, lewd, lascivious, filthy and of an
indecent character." He was sentenced to five years imprisonment. On
appeal, he attacked the statute as violating the First Amendment.]

We can understand all the difficulties of censorship of great literature,
and indeed the various foolish excesses involved in the banning of notable
books, without feeling justified in casting doubt upon all criminal prosecutions, both state and federal, of commercialized obscenity. A serious problem does arise when real literature is censored; but in this case no such
issues should arise, since the record shows only salable pornography. But
even if we had more freedom to follow an impulse to strike down such
legislation in the premises, we should need to pause because of our own
lack of knowledge of the social bearing of this problem, or consequences of
such an act;[4] and we are hardly justified in rejecting out of hand the

4. See Fuld, J., in Brown v. Kingsley
Books, Inc., 1 N.Y.2d 177 [(1956)], 151
N.Y.S.2d 639, 641, note 3, 134 N.E.2d 461,
463: "It is noteworthy that studies are for
the first time being made, through such scientific skills as exist, concerning the impact
of the obscene, in writings and other mass
media, on the mind and behavior of men,
women and children. (See, e.g., Jahoda and
Staff of Research Center for Human Rela-

strongly held views of those with competence in the premises as to the very direct connection of this traffic with the development of juvenile delinquency. We conclude, therefore, that the attack on constitutionality of this statute must here fail.

■ FRANK, CIRCUIT JUDGE (concurring).

[Appendix to concurring opinion.]

As a judge of an inferior court, I am constrained by opinions of the Supreme Court concerning the obscenity statute to hold that legislation valid. Since, however, I think [t]hat none of those opinions has carefully canvassed the problem in the light of the Supreme Court's interpretation of the First Amendment, especially as expressed by the Court in recent years, I deem it not improper to set forth, in the following, factors which I think deserve consideration in passing on the constitutionality of that statute.

[N]o adequate knowledge is available concerning the effects on the conduct of normal adults of reading or seeing the "obscene"

Suppose we assume, *arguendo*, that sexual thoughts or feelings, stirred by the "obscene," probably will often issue into overt conduct. Still it does not at all follow that that conduct will be anti-social. For no sane person can believe it socially harmful if sexual desires lead to normal, and not anti-social, sexual behavior since, without such behavior, the human race would soon disappear.

Doubtless, Congress could validly provide punishment for mailing any publications if there were some moderately substantial reliable data showing that reading or seeing those publications probably conduces to seriously harmful sexual conduct on the part of normal adult human beings. But we have no such data.

Suppose it argued that whatever excites sexual longings might *possibly* produce sexual misconduct. That cannot suffice: Notoriously, perfumes sometimes act as aphrodisiacs, yet no one will suggest that therefore Congress may constitutionally legislate punishment for mailing perfumes.

[E]ffect of "obscenity" on adult conduct

To date there exist, I think, no thorough-going studies by competent persons which justify the conclusion that normal adults' reading or seeing of the "obscene" probably induces anti-social conduct. Such competent studies as have been made do conclude that so complex and numerous are the causes of sexual vice that it is impossible to assert with any assurance that "obscenity" represents a ponderable causal factor in sexually deviant adult behavior. [W]hat little competent research has been done, points definitely in a direction precisely opposite to that assumption.

tions, New York University [1954]. The Impact of Literature: A Psychological Discussion of Some Assumptions in the Censorship Debate.)"

[T]he following is a recent summary of studies of [the relationship of obscenity to juvenile delinquency][33] "(1) Scientific studies of juvenile delinquency demonstrate that those who get into trouble, and are the greatest concern of the advocates of censorship, are far less inclined to read than those who do not become delinquent. [(2)] Sheldon and Eleanor Glueck, who are among the country's leading authorities on the treatment and causes of juvenile delinquency, have recently published the results of a ten-year study of its causes. They exhaustively studied approximately 90 factors and influences that might lead to or explain juvenile delinquency; but the Gluecks gave no consideration to the type of reading material, if any were read by the delinquents. This is, of course, consistent with their finding that delinquents read very little. When those who know so much about the problem of delinquency among youth—the very group about whom the advocates of censorship are most concerned—conclude that what delinquents read has so little effect upon their conduct that it is not worth investigating in an exhaustive study of causes, there is good reason for serious doubts concerning the basic hypothesis on which obscenity censorship is dependent. (3) The many other influences in society that stimulate sexual desire are so much more frequent in their influence and so much more potent in their effect that the influence of reading is likely, at most, to be relatively insignificant in the composite of forces that lead an individual into conduct deviating from the community sex standards.... And the studies demonstrating that sex knowledge seldom results from reading indicates the relative unimportance of literature in sexual thoughts and behavior as compared with other factors in society."

Judge Clark, however, speaks of "the strongly held views of those with competence in the premises as to the very direct connection" of obscenity "with the development of juvenile delinquency." He cites and quotes from a recent opinion of the New York Court of Appeals and an article by Judge Vanderbilt, which in turn, cite the writings of persons thus described by Judge Clark as "those with competence in the premises." One of the cited writings is a report, by Dr. Jahoda and associates, entitled The Impact of Literature: A Psychological Discussion of Some Assumptions in the Censorship Debate (1954). I have read this report (which is a careful survey of all available studies and psychological theories). I think it expresses an attitude quite contrary to that indicated by Judge Clark. In order to avoid any possible bias in my interpretation of that report, I thought it well to ask Dr. Jahoda to write her own summary of it, which, with her permission, I shall quote. (In doing so, I am following the example of Mr. Justice Jackson who, in Federal Trade Commission v. Ruberoid Co., 343 U.S. 470, 485, 72 S.Ct. 800, 809, 96 L.Ed. 1081, acknowledged that he relied on "an unpublished treatise", i.e., one not available to the parties. If that practice is proper, I think it similarly proper to quote an author's unpublished interpretation of a published treatise.) Dr. Jahoda's summary reads as follows:

33. Lockhart & McClure, Literature.   38 Minn.L.Rev. (1954), 295, 385–386.
The Law of Obscenity and the Constitution,

"Persons who argue for increased censorship of printed matter often operate on the assumption that reading about sexual matters or about violence and brutality leads to anti-social actions, particularly to juvenile delinquency. An examination of the pertinent psychological literature has led to the following conclusions:

"1.   There exists no research evidence either to prove or to disprove this assumption definitively.

"2.   In the absence of scientific proof two lines of psychological approach to the examination of the assumption are possible: (a) a review of what is known on the causes of juvenile delinquency; and (b) review of what is known about the effect of literature on the mind of the reader.

"3.   In the vast research literature on the causes of juvenile delinquency there is no evidence to justify the assumption that reading about sexual matters or about violence leads to delinquent acts. Experts on juvenile delinquency agree that it has no single cause. Most of them regard early childhood events, which precede the reading age, as a necessary condition for later delinquency. At a later age, the nature of personal relations is assumed to have much greater power in determining a delinquent career than the vicarious experiences provided by reading matter. Juvenile delinquents as a group read less, and less easily, than non-delinquents. Individual instances are reported in which so-called 'good' books allegedly influenced a delinquent in the manner in which 'bad' books are assumed to influence him.

"Where childhood experiences and subsequent events have combined to make delinquency psychologically likely, reading could have one of two effects: it could serve a trigger function releasing the criminal act or it could provide for a substitute outlet of aggression in fantasy, dispensing with the need for criminal action. There is no empirical evidence in either direction.

"4.   With regard to the impact of literature on the mind of the reader, it must be pointed out that there is a vast overlap in content between all media of mass communication. The daily press, television, radio, movies, books and comics all present their share of so-called 'bad' material, some with great realism as reports of actual events, some in clearly fictionalized form. It is virtually impossible to isolate the impact of one of these media on a population exposed to all of them. Some evidence suggests that the particular communications which arrest the attention of an individual are in good part a matter of choice. As a rule, people do not expose themselves to everything that is offered, but only to what agrees with their inclinations."

[M]aybe some day we will have enough reliable data to show that obscene books and pictures do tend to influence children's sexual conduct adversely. Then a federal statute could be enacted which would avoid constitutional defects by authorizing punishment for using the mails or interstate shipments in the sale of such books and pictures to children.

———

NOTES

1. Judicial Notice. In his concurring opinion in United States v. Roth, Judge Frank "thought it well to ask Dr. Jahoda to write her own summary" of the research on the relationship between obscenity and crime. See Federal Rule of Evidence 201 and the Advisory Committee Note in Appendix A and the American Bar Association's Code of Judicial Conduct (1999), which provides in Canon 3:

> A judge shall not initiate, permit, or consider ex parte communications, or consider other communications made to the judge outside the presence of the parties concerning a pending or impending proceeding.

In Commentary, the Code states "An appropriate and often desirable procedure for a court to obtain the advice of a disinterested expert on legal issues is to invite the expert to file a brief amicus curiae."

In this regard, T. Marvell, in a major study of appellate courts, Appellate Courts and Lawyers (1978), reported numerous instances of judges seeking informal expert assistance. For example, one judge said that he talked to his doctor during an annual physical examination about the practical effect a proposed ruling would have on surgeons' dealings with their patients. Marvell noted, id. at 98, 99:

> Some judges send their clerks to professors rather than go themselves, and clerks are not likely to get advice without being directed to do so. [T]his advice is ordinarily obtained over the telephone or in informal meetings; written communication about the cases outside regular channels is uncommon.

> [M]uch, if not most of the information sought [i]s information about [legislative] facts, such as the practical consequences of a proposed ruling. [T]heoretically, outsiders are not supposed to know anything about the court's deliberations. But by asking for advice a judge would imply that he is writing on the case, and he may disclose how he is leaning. For this reason questions are generally posed in the abstract without giving the name or specific facts of the case.

2. Burden of Proof. The Supreme Court ultimately upheld the Second Circuit's Roth decision, 354 U.S. 476, 77 S.Ct. 1304, 1 L.Ed.2d 1498 (1957), with Justice Brennan writing for the court and concluding that "obscenity is not within the area of constitutionally protected speech or press." Justice Douglas (joined by Justice Black) dissented, however, citing at 510–511, 77 S.Ct. at 1322–1323, the same data as Judge Frank in his concurrence:

> If we were certain that impurity of sexual thoughts impelled to action, we would be on less dangerous ground in punishing the distributors of this sex literature. But it is by no means clear that

obscene literature, as so defined, is a significant factor in influencing substantial deviations from the community standards. [T]he absence of dependable information on the effect of obscene literature on human conduct should make us wary. It should put us on the side of protecting society's interest in literature, except and unless it can be said that the particular publication has an impact on action that the government can control.

REPORT OF THE COMMISSION ON OBSCENITY AND PORNOGRAPHY (1970)

A number of empirical studies conducted recently by psychiatrists, psychologists, and sociologists attempted to assess the effects of exposure to explicit sexual materials. [T]he findings of available research are summarized below.

[C]riminal and Delinquent Behavior

Delinquent and nondelinquent youth report generally similar experiences with explicit sexual materials. Exposure to sexual materials is widespread among both groups. The age of first exposure, the kinds of materials to which they are exposed, the amount of their exposure, the circumstances of exposure, and their reactions to erotic stimuli are essentially the same, particularly when family and neighborhood backgrounds are held constant. There is some evidence that peer group pressure accounts for both sexual experience and exposure to erotic materials among youth. A study of a heterogeneous group of young people found that exposure to erotica had no impact upon moral character over and above that of a generally deviant background.

Statistical studies of the relationship between availability of erotic materials and the rates of sex crimes in Denmark indicate that the increased availability of explicit sexual materials has been accompanied by a decrease in the incidence of sexual crime. Analysis of police records of the same types of sex crimes in Copenhagen during the past 12 years revealed that a dramatic decrease in reported sex crimes occurred during this period and that the decrease coincided with changes in Danish law which permitted wider availability of explicit sexual materials. Other research showed that the decrease in reported sexual offenses cannot be attributed to concurrent changes in the social and legal definitions of sex crimes or in public attitudes toward reporting such crimes to the police, or in police reporting procedures.

Statistical studies of the relationship between the availability of erotic material and the rates of sex crimes in the United States presents a more complex picture. During the period in which there has been a marked increase in the availability of erotic materials, some specific rates of arrest for sex crimes have increased (e.g., forcible rape) and others have declined (e.g., overall juvenile rates). For juveniles, the overall rate of arrests for sex crimes decreased even though arrests for nonsexual crimes increased by more than 100%. For adults, arrests for sex offenses increased slightly more than did arrests for nonsex offenses. The conclusion is that, for America, the relationship between the availability of erotica and changes in sex crime rates neither proves nor disproves the possibility that availability of erotica leads to crime, but the massive overall increases in sex crimes that have been alleged do not seem to have occurred.

Available research indicates that sex offenders have had less adolescent experience with erotica than other adults. They do not differ significantly from other adults in relation to adult experience with erotica, in relation to reported arousal or in relation to the likelihood of engaging in sexual behavior during or following exposure. Available evidence suggests that sex offenders' early inexperience with erotic material is a reflection of their more generally deprived sexual environment. The relative absence of experience appears to constitute another indicator of atypical and inadequate sexual socialization.

In sum, empirical research designed to clarify the question has found no evidence to date that exposure to explicit sexual materials plays a significant role in the causation of delinquent or criminal behavior among youth or adults. The Commission cannot conclude that exposure to erotic materials is a factor in the causation of sex crime or sex delinquency.

Dissent by Commissioners Morton A. Hill, S.J., and Winfrey C. Link, Concurred in by Charles H. Keating, Jr.

We feel impelled to issue this report in vigorous dissent.

The conclusions and recommendations in the majority report will be found deeply offensive to Congress and to tens of millions of Americans. And what the American people do not know is that the scanty and manipulated evidence contained within this report is wholly inadequate to support the conclusions and sustain the recommendations. Thus, both conclusions and recommendations are, in our view, fraudulent.

What the American people have here for the two million dollars voted by Congress, and paid by the taxpayer, is a shoddy piece of scholarship that will be quoted ad nauseam by cultural polluters and their attorneys within society.

The fundamental "finding" on which the entire report is based is: that "empirical research" has come up with "no reliable evidence to indicate that exposure to explicitly sexual materials plays a significant role in the causation of delinquent or criminal behavior among youth or adults."

The inference from this statement, i.e., pornography is harmless, is not only insupportable on the slanted evidence presented; it is preposterous. How isolate one factor and say it causes or does not cause criminal behavior? How determine that one book or one film caused one man to commit rape or murder? A man's entire life goes into one criminal act. No one factor can be said to have caused that act.

The Commission has deliberately and carefully avoided coming to grips with the basic underlying issue. The government interest in regulating pornography has always related primarily to the prevention of moral corruption and *not* to prevention of overt criminal acts and conduct, or the protection of persons from being shocked and/or offended.

The basic question is whether and to what extent society may establish and maintain certain moral standards. If it is conceded that society has a legitimate concern in maintaining moral standards, it follows logically that government has a legitimate interest in at least attempting to protect such standards against any source which threatens them.

[W]e believe it is impossible, and totally unnecessary, to attempt to prove or disprove a cause-effect relationship between pornography and criminal behavior.

———

PARIS ADULT THEATRE I v. SLATON

Supreme Court of the United States, 1973.
413 U.S. 49, 93 S.Ct. 2628, 37 L.Ed.2d 446.

■ MR. CHIEF JUSTICE BURGER delivered the opinion of the Court.

[In two cases decided on the same day, Miller v. California, 413 U.S. 15, 93 S.Ct. 2607, 37 L.Ed.2d 419 (1973), and Paris Adult Theatre I v. Slaton, the Supreme Court established the obscenity "test" currently in use. Chief Justice Burger, writing in *Miller* for five members of the court, stated, "The basic guidelines for the trier of fact must be: (a) whether 'the average person, applying contemporary community standards' would find that the work, taken as a whole, appeals to the prurient interest, (b) whether the work depicts or describes, in a patently offensive way, sexual conduct specifically defined by the applicable state law; and (c) whether the work, taken as a whole, lacks serious literary, artistic, political, or scientific value." 413 U.S. at 24, 93 S.Ct. at 2614. The Supreme Court considered the empirical issues raised by obscenity statutes in *Paris,* which concerned a Georgia civil proceeding to enjoin the showing of allegedly obscene films at two "adult" theaters in Atlanta. The trial judge had dismissed the complaint, and the Georgia Supreme Court had reversed the dismissal.]

We hold that there are legitimate state interests at stake in stemming the tide of commercialized obscenity, even assuming it is feasible to enforce effective safeguards against exposure to juveniles and to passersby. Rights and interests "other than those of the advocates are involved." Breard v. Alexandria, 341 U.S. 622, 642 (1951). These include the interest of the public in the quality of life and the total community environment, the tone of commerce in the great city centers, and, possibly, the public safety itself.

The Hill–Link Minority Report of the Commission on Obscenity and Pornography indicates that there is at least an arguable correlation between obscene material and crime.[8]

[B]ut, it is argued, there are no scientific data which conclusively demonstrate that exposure to obscene material adversely affects men and women or their society. It is urged on behalf of the petitioners that, absent such a demonstration, any kind of state regulation is "impermissible." We reject this argument. It is not for us to resolve empirical uncertainties underlying state legislation, save in the exceptional case where that legislation plainly impinges upon rights protected by the Constitution itself. Mr. Justice Brennan, speaking for the Court in Ginsberg v. New York, 390 U.S. 629, 642–643, 88 S.Ct. 1274, 1282, 20 L.Ed.2d 195 (1968), said: "We do not demand of legislatures 'scientifically certain criteria of legislation.' Noble State Bank v. Haskell, 219 U.S. 104, 110 (31 S.Ct. 186, 187) 55 L.Ed. 112." Although there is no conclusive proof of a connection between antisocial behavior and obscene material, the legislature of Georgia could quite reasonably determine that such a connection does or might exist. In deciding *Roth*, this Court implicitly accepted that a legislature could legitimately act on such a conclusion to protect *"the social interest in order and morality."* Roth v. United States, 354 U.S., at 485, 77 S.Ct. at 1309, quoting Chaplinsky v. New Hampshire, 315 U.S. 568, 572, 62 S.Ct. 766, 769, 86 L.Ed. 1031 (1942) (emphasis added in *Roth*).

From the beginning of civilized societies, legislators and judges have acted on various unprovable assumptions. Such assumptions underlie much lawful state regulation of commercial and business affairs. [O]n the basis of these assumptions both Congress and state legislatures have, for example, drastically restricted associational rights by adopting antitrust laws, and have strictly regulated public expression by issuers of and dealers in securities. [U]nderstandably those who entertain an absolutist view of the First Amendment find it uncomfortable to explain why rights of association, speech, and press should be severely restrained in the marketplace of goods and money, but not in the marketplace of pornography.

8. The Report of the Commission on Obscenity and Pornography 390–412 (1970). For a discussion of earlier studies indicating "a division of thought [among behavioral scientists] on the correlation between obscenity and socially deleterious behavior," Memoirs v. Massachusetts, [383 U.S. 413, 86 S.Ct. 975, 16 L.Ed.2d 1 (1966)] at 451, and references to expert opinions that obscene material may induce crime and antisocial conduct, see id., at 451–453 (Clark, J., dissenting). Mr. Justice Clark emphasized:

"While erotic stimulation caused by pornography may be legally insignificant in itself, there are medical experts who believe that such stimulation frequently manifests itself in criminal sexual behavior or other antisocial conduct. For example, Dr. George W. Henry of Cornell University has expressed the opinion that obscenity, with its exaggerated and morbid emphasis on sex, particularly abnormal and perverted practices, and its unrealistic presentation of sexual behavior and attitudes, may induce antisocial conduct by the average person. A number of sociologists think that this material may have adverse effects upon individual mental health, with potentially disruptive consequences for the community.

"Congress and the legislatures of every State have enacted measures to restrict the distribution of erotic and pornographic material, justifying these controls by reference to evidence that antisocial behavior may result in part from reading obscenity." Id., at 452–453, 86 S.Ct., at 994–995 (footnotes omitted).

Likewise, when legislatures and administrators act to protect the physical environment from pollution and to preserve our resources of forests, streams, and parks, they must act on such imponderables as the impact of a new highway near or through an existing park or wilderness area. [T]he fact that a congressional directive reflects unprovable assumptions about what is good for the people, including imponderable aesthetic assumptions, is not a sufficient reason to find that statute unconstitutional.

If we accept the unprovable assumption that a complete education requires the reading of certain books, and the well nigh universal belief that good books, plays, and art lift the spirit, improve the mind, enrich the human personality, and develop character, can we then say that a state legislature may not act on the corollary assumption that commerce in obscene books, or public exhibitions focused on obscene conduct, have a tendency to exert a corrupting and debasing impact leading to antisocial behavior?

[T]he sum of experience, including that of the past two decades, affords an ample basis for legislatures to conclude that a sensitive, key relationship of human existence, central to family life, community welfare, and the development of human personality, can be debased and distorted by crass commercial exploitation of sex. Nothing in the Constitution prohibits a State from reaching such a conclusion and acting on it legislatively simply because there is no conclusive evidence or empirical data.

FACTS IN LAWMAKING

Kenneth Culp Davis.
80 Columbia Law Review 931 (1980).

The Court in *Paris* relied on a 1970 minority report of two of the nineteen members of the Commission on Obscenity and Pornography, and said that the question of legislative fact was "arguable" on one side, without saying whether it was "arguable" on the other side.

[T]he Court's inaccurate factfinding in the *Paris* case is obviously deplorable, but the deficiencies run much deeper: (1) The Court should recognize its affirmative responsibility to assure that reasonably available legislative facts that may affect its lawmaking are adequately developed. (2) When facts presented by the parties are inadequate, it should, unless it does its own research, either request factual briefs on designated questions or remand for factual development on those questions. (3) When extra record facts are crucial in its lawmaking, it should address the question whether procedural fairness requires that parties be given a pre-decision chance to challenge the facts it uses.

NEW YORK v. FERBER

Supreme Court of the United States, 1982.
458 U.S. 747, 102 S.Ct. 3348, 73 L.Ed.2d 1113.

■ Justice White delivered the opinion of the Court.

[Paul Ferber, the proprietor of a Manhattan bookstore, sold an undercover police officer two films of young boys masturbating. He was convicted under a state statute prohibiting promotion of a sexual performance by a child under sixteen years old. The New York Court of Appeals reversed, holding that the statute—which did not require proof that the performance be obscene—violated the First Amendment. The Supreme Court granted certiorari "presenting the single question: 'To prevent the abuse of children who are made to engage in sexual conduct for commercial purposes, could the New York State Legislature, consistent with the First Amendment, prohibit the dissemination of material which shows children engaged in sexual conduct, regardless of whether such material is obscene?' "]

Like obscenity statutes, laws directed at the dissemination of child pornography run the risk of suppressing protected expression by allowing the hand of the censor to become unduly heavy. For the following reasons, however, we are persuaded that the States are entitled to greater leeway in the regulation of pornographic depictions of children.

First. It is evident beyond the need for elaboration that a state's interest in "safeguarding the physical and psychological well being of a minor" is "compelling." [T]he prevention of sexual exploitation and abuse of children constitutes a government objective of surpassing importance. [S]uffice it to say that virtually all of the States and the United States have passed legislation proscribing the production of or otherwise combatting "child pornography." The legislative judgment, as well as the judgment found in the relevant literature, is that the use of children as subjects of pornographic materials is harmful to the physiological, emotional, and mental health of the child.[9] That judgment, we think, easily passes muster under the First Amendment.

---

9. "[T]he use of children as ... subjects of pornographic materials is very harmful to both the children and the society as a whole." S.Rep. No. 95–438, p. 5 (1978). It has been found that sexually exploited children are unable to develop healthy affectionate relationships in later life, have sexual dysfunctions, and have a tendency to become sexual abusers as adults. Schoettle, Child Exploitation: A Study of Child Pornography, 19 J.Am.Acad. Child Psych. 289, 296 (1980) (hereafter cited as Child Exploitation); Schoettle, Treatment of the Child Pornography Patient, 137 Am.J.Psych. 1109, 1110 (1980); Densen–Gerner, Child Prostitution and Child Pornography: Medical, Legal and Societal Aspects of the Commercial Exploita-

tion of Children, reprinted in U.S. Dept. of Health and Human Services, Sexual Abuse of Children: Selected Readings 77, 80 (1980) (hereafter cited as Commercial Exploitation) (sexually exploited children predisposed to self-destructive behavior such as drug and alcohol abuse or prostitution). See generally A. Burgess & L. Holmstrom, Accessory-to-Sex: Pressure, Sex and Secrecy, in A. Burgess, A. Groth, L. Holmstrom, and S. Sgroi, Sexual Assault of Children and Adolescents 85, 94 (1978); V. DeFrancis, Protecting the Child Victim of Sex Crimes Committed by Adults, 169 (1969); Ellerstein & Canavan, Sexual Abuse of Boys, 134 Am.J.Diseases of Children 255, 256–257 (1980); Finch, Adult Seduction of the Child: Effects on the Child,

Second. The distribution of photographs and films depicting sexual activity by juveniles is intrinsically related to the sexual abuse of children in at least two ways. First, the materials produced are a permanent record of the children's participation and the harm to the child is exacerbated by their circulation.[10] Second, the distribution network for child pornography must be closed if the production of material which requires the sexual exploitation of children is to be effectively controlled. Indeed, there is no serious contention that the legislature was unjustified in believing that it is difficult, if not impossible, to halt the exploitation of children by pursuing only those who produce the photographs and movies.

[T]hird. The advertising and selling of child pornography provides an economic motive for and is thus an integral part of the production of such materials, an activity illegal throughout the Nation. "It rarely has been suggested that the constitutional freedom for speech and press extends its immunity to speech or writing used as an integral part of conduct in violation of a valid criminal statute." Giboney v. Empire Storage & Ice Co., 336 U.S. 490, 498, 69 S.Ct. 684, 688, 93 L.Ed. 834 (1949).

[F]ourth. The value of permitting live performances and photographic reproductions of children engaged in lewd sexual conduct is exceedingly modest, if not *de minimis*. We consider it unlikely that visual depictions of children performing sexual acts or lewdly exhibiting their genitals would often constitute an important and necessary part of a literary performance or scientific or educational work.

[F]ifth. Recognizing and classifying child pornography as a category of material outside the protection of the First Amendment is not incompatible with our earlier decisions. "The question whether speech is, or is not, protected by the First Amendment often depends on the content of the speech." Young v. American Mini Theatres, 427 U.S. 50, 66, 96 S.Ct. 2440, 2450, 49 L.Ed.2d 310 (Opinion of JUSTICE STEVENS, joined by THE CHIEF JUSTICE, JUSTICE WHITE, and JUSTICE REHNQUIST). [T]hus it is not rare that a

Med. Aspects of Human Sexuality 170, 185 (Mar.1973); Groth, Sexual Trauma in the Life Histories of Rapists and Child Molesters, 4 Victimology 10 (1979). Sexual molestation by adults is often involved in the production of child sexual performances. Sexual Exploitation of Children, A Report to Illinois General Assembly by the Illinois Legislative Investigatory Comm'n at 30–31 (1980) (hereafter cited as Ill.Comm'n). When such performances are recorded and distributed, the child's privacy interests are also invaded.

10. As one authority has explained:

"[P]ornography poses an even greater threat to the child victim than does sexual abuse or prostitution. Because the child's actions are reduced to a recording, the pornography may haunt him in future years, long after the original misdeed took place. A child who has posed for the camera must go through life knowing that the recording is circulating within the mass distribution system for child pornography." Shouvlin, Preventing the Sexual Exploitation of Children: A Model Act, 17 Wake Forest L.Rev. 535, 545 (1981).

See also Schoettle, Child Exploitation, at 292 ("[I]t is the fear of exposure and the tension of keeping the act secret that seem to have the most profound emotional repercussions"); Note, Protection of Children from Use in Pornography: Toward Constitutional and Enforceable Legislation, 12 U.Mich.J. Law Reform 295, 301 (1979) (interview with child psychiatrist) ("The victims knowledge of publication of the visual material increases the emotional and psychic harm suffered by the child.").

content-based classification of speech has been accepted because it may be appropriately generalized that within the confines of the given classification, the evil to be restricted so overwhelmingly outweighs the expressive interests, if any, at stake, that no process of case-by-case adjudication is required. When a definable class of material such as that covered by § 263.15, bears so heavily and pervasively on the welfare of children engaged in its production we think the balance of competing interests is clearly struck and that it is permissible to consider these materials as without the protection of the First Amendment.

———

NOTE

1. Case Studies and Retrospective Surveys. Among the authorities Justice White cited in support of his statement that "it has been found that sexually exploited children are unable to develop healthy affectionate relationships in later life, have sexual dysfunctions, and have a tendency to become sexual abusers as adults," is Schoettle, Treatment of the Child Pornography Patient, 137 American Journal of Psychiatry 1109 (1980). That article is a brief case study of "Kathy," a 12–year old girl who, along with her siblings, engaged in photographed sexual acts with adults and with each other. The principal findings of this report are as follows, id. at 1109–1110:

> After police investigation of the child pornography ring, Kathy and her family were referred to our sex abuse clinic for psychiatric evaluation and weekly therapy. At the first session Kathy's complaints related to feeling guilty about being accused of involving her younger siblings in the sexual exploration schemes. [K]athy's history and presentation were consistent with a diagnosis of sexual deviation with associate depression.

Another study Justice White cited is Groth, Sexual Trauma in the Life Histories of Rapists and Child Molesters, 4 Victimology 10, 11 (1979), where the author stated:

> The subjects for this study consisted of 348 men convicted of sexual assault and referred to a security treatment center for diagnostic observation. Most of these offenders were recidivists. [D]ata pertaining to sexual trauma in the life histories of these men were retrieved through interviews with these subjects and/or a study of their clinical records. Sexual trauma was operationally defined as any sexual activity witnessed or experienced which was emotionally upsetting or disturbing to the subject. As a comparison group, sixty-two male law enforcement officers were administered an anonymous questionnaire in regard to sexual trauma experienced during their development. This police sample was roughly comparable to the offender sample in regard to age and socio-economic background.

[E]vidence of some form of sexual trauma during their developmental years (ages one-fifteen) was found in the life histories of 106
(31 percent) of the subjects. No evidence of any sexual trauma was
found for 203 (58 percent) of the subjects, and no data were available
for thirty-nine (11 percent) of the subjects in this study. In comparison,
only two (3 percent) of the sample of law enforcement officers reported
any history of sexual trauma during their formative years.

REPORT OF THE ATTORNEY GENERAL'S COMMISSION ON PORNOGRAPHY (1986)

Summary for Violent and Nonviolent Sexually Explicit Materials.

In evaluating the results for sexually violent material, it appears that
exposure to such materials (1) leads to a greater acceptance of rape myths
and violence against women; (2) have more pronounced effects when the
victim is shown enjoying the use of force or violence; (3) is arousing for
rapists and for some males in the general population; and (4) has resulted
in sexual aggression against women in the laboratory.

[R]esearch has further demonstrated that such attitudes as rape myth
acceptance and acceptance of violence against women are correlated with
arousal to such materials and with "real-world" sexual aggression and that
subjects who have demonstrated sexual aggression in the laboratory are
also more likely to report using coercion and force in their actual sexual
interactions. The validation of the measures used in his studies, the use of
physiological measures of arousal, and the attempt to systematically examine patterns among different populations with a variety of measures,
arousal, attitudinal and behavioral, all tend to provide the type of conver-
gent validation we feel is required of social science evidence.

We are less confident about the findings for nonviolent sexually explicit
materials and we hasten to add that this is not necessarily because this
class of materials has no effects but because the wide variety of effects
obtained needs to be more systematically examined and explained.

[I]t is clear that the conclusion of "no negative effects" advanced by
the 1970 Commission is no longer tenable. It is also clear that catharsis, as
an explanatory model for the impact of pornography, is simply unwarrant-
ed by evidence in this area, nor has catharsis fared well in the general area
of mass media effects and anti-social behavior.

This is not to say, however, that the evidence as a whole is comprehensive enough or definitive enough. While we have learned much more since
1970, even more areas remain to be explored.

What do we know at this point?

—It is clear that many sexually explicit materials, particularly of the
commercial variety, that are obviously designed to be arousing, *are,* in fact,
arousing, both to offenders and nonoffenders.

—Rapists appear to be aroused by both forced as well as consenting sex depictions while nonoffenders (our college males) are less aroused by depictions of sexual aggression. On the other hand, when these portrayals show the victim as "enjoying" the rape, these portrayals similarly elicit high arousal levels.

—Arousal to rape depictions appears to correlate with attitudes of acceptance of rape myths and sexual violence and both these measures likewise correlate with laboratory-observed aggressive behaviors.

—Depictions of sexual violence also increase the likelihood that rape myths are accepted and sexual violence toward women condoned. Such attitudes have further been found to be correlated with laboratory aggression toward women. Finally, there is also some evidence that laboratory aggression toward women correlates with self-reported sexually aggressive behaviors.

What we know about the effects of nonviolent sexually explicit material is less clear. There are tentative indications that negative effects in the areas of attitudes might also occur, particularly from massive exposure. The mechanics of such effects need to be elaborated more fully, however, particularly in light of more recent findings that suggest that degrading themes might have effects that differ from non violent, non-degrading sexually explicit materials. This is clearly an area that deserves further investigation.

—There are suggestions that pornography availability may be one of a nexus of socio-cultural factors that has some bearing on rape rates in this country. Other cross-cultural data, however, offer mixed results as well so these findings have to be viewed as tentative at best.

—We still know very little about the causes of deviancy and it is important to examine the developmental patterns of offenders, particularly patterns of early exposure. We do have some convergence on the data from some rapists and males in the general population in the areas of arousal and attitudes but again, this remains to be examined more closely.

Clearly, the need for more research remains as compelling as ever.

STATEMENT OF DR. JUDITH BECKER AND ELLEN LEVINE

The Commission sought to break down pornography into the various types of sexually explicit material available in our society. Unfortunately, social science research to date has not uniformly followed any such categorization (although we certainly suggest that future researchers consider this option), and the attempt to force the available social science data to fit the Commission's categories is fruitless. That is why in this statement the conclusions and interpretations of what the social science data *says* and *does not say* follow the research, not the Commission, categories.

First, it is essential to state that the social science research has not been designed to evaluate the relationship between exposure to pornography and the commission of sexual crimes; therefore efforts to tease the current data into proof of a causal link between these acts simply cannot be accepted. Furthermore, social science does not speak to harm, on which this Commission report focuses. Social science research speaks of a relationship among variables or effects that can be positive or negative.

Research has evaluated adults rather than children, and it is the latter who are most likely to be influenced by pornography. Studies have relied almost exclusively on male college student volunteers, which means that the "generalizability" of this data is extremely limited. The only other category studied in depth is sex offenders. Information from the sex-offender population must be interpreted with care because it may be self-serving. The research conducted to date has been correlational and experimental. Despite these limitations, the research data can be interpreted to indicate the following:

A.   In a laboratory setting, exposure to sexually violent stimuli has a negative effect on research subjects as measured by acceptance of rape myth and aggression and callousness toward women. We do not know, however, how long this attitudinal change is sustained without further stimulation; more importantly, we do not know whether and why such an attitudinal change might transfer into a behavioral change. There is reason for concern about these findings because we do know that experience with sex offenders indicates they harbor belief systems and attitudes consistent with deviant sexual practices (e.g. "women enjoy being raped" or "sexual acts with a child are a way of showing love and affection to that child"). We know further that such attitudes appear to be a precursor and maintainer of actual deviant behavior in an offender population. Although we believe the potential exists for attitudinal changes to translate into behavioral changes in some circumstances, this possibility needs considerable additional investigation.

B.   Very little social-science research has been conducted evaluating the impact of non-violent degrading material on the average adult. Furthermore, there is a problem of definition about what constitutes "degrading material." We strongly encourage further research to define and evaluate the impact of such material.

C.   Although research findings are far from conclusive, the preponderance of existing data indicates that non-violent and non-degrading sexually explicit materials do not have a negative effect on adults.

D.   In documents attached to the main report mention has been made of a possible relationship between circulation rates of pornographic magazines and sex crime rates. One of the authors of the study on which the Commission has based its conclusion, Murray Straus, has written to explain his own research, which he suggested was being misinterpreted. "I do not believe that this research demonstrates that pornography causes rape.... In general the scientific evidence clearly indicates that if one is concerned with the effects of media on rape, the problem lies in the prevalence of violence in the media, not on sex in the media."

E.   To date there is no single comprehensive theory that is agreed upon to explain the development of paraphilic behavior. Human behavior is complex and multi-causal. To say that exposure to pornography in and of itself causes an individual to commit a sexual crime is simplistic, not supported by the social science data, and overlooks many of the other variables that may be contributing causes. Research must be conducted on the development of sexual interest patterns if we are to understand and control paraphilic behavior.

F.   Unfortunately, little is known about the impact of sexually explicit material on children. Ethically and morally one could not and would not conduct experiments to examine such a relationship. We do know that adolescents and young adults are large consumers of these materials, and little is yet known about its impact on this population. We underscore the statement made in the main body of the Commission's report regarding social science research: "In many respects, research is still at a fairly rudimentary stage, and with few attempts to standardize categories of analysis, self-reporting questionnaires, types of stimulus materials, description of stimulus materials, measurement of effects and related problems. We recommend that moneys be made available to fund further research on this topic."

THE ATTORNEY GENERAL'S COMMISSION ON PORNOGRAPHY: THE GAPS BETWEEN "FINDINGS" AND FACTS

Daniel Linz, Steven D. Penrod, and Edward Donnerstein.
1987 American Bar Foundation Research Journal 713 (1987).

The Commission maintains that there is a "causal relationship" between exposure to sexually violent pornography and negative changes in certain attitudes toward and perceptions of women, as well as increased aggression toward women. This statement is accurate as long as it refers to the results of laboratory studies examining sexually violent images. In the typical study, men are first exposed to depictions that show the female victim "enjoying" or reacting in a positive fashion to her mistreatment, and they are then asked to report on their attitudes and beliefs about rape victims and/or administer electric shocks or other forms of "punishment" to a female victim. The results of these studies have generally indicated that male subjects exposed to sexual violence of this sort show (1) changes in the perception of a rape victim (e.g., seeing her as less injured and more responsible for her assault); (2) changes in the perception of a rapist (e.g., seeing him as less responsible for his actions and as deserving less punishment); (3) greater acceptance of certain "rape myths"; and (4) more aggressive behavior toward a female target than control subjects. Depictions involving victims who abhor their experience *produce similar outcomes* depending on the population exposed to these materials.

However, there are at least two important considerations that should be kept in mind when applying the results of these social psychological experiments to legal decision making about pornography and obscenity. The first consideration is whether the changes in attitudes and behaviors following exposure to sexually violent material are due primarily to the sexually explicit context in which the violence is depicted, or to the violence itself, regardless of sexual explicitness. The second consideration is a methodological qualification that involves a familiar criticism of laboratory investigations of aggressive behavior.

Is Sexual Explicitness Necessary for Harmful Effects to Occur?

Depictions of women "enjoying" the application of force and of women as the deserving victims of sexual and nonsexual violence are pervasive in the mass media.

In a [r]ecent pair of studies, two of the authors of this essay systematically examined the relative contributions of the aggressive and sexual components of violent pornography. In the first study, male college students were angered by either a male or a female confederate and were then shown one of four different films. The first film [contained] aggressive pornography. The second was X-rated but contained no aggression or sexual coercion. Subjects rated the second film just as sexually and physiologically arousing as the first film. The third film contained scenes of aggression against women but without any sexual content. Subjects rated it as less sexually and physiologically arousing than the previous two films. The final film was of neutral content.

After viewing the films, the men were given the opportunity to aggress against male or female confederates of the experiment. The results showed that the men who viewed the film that was both aggressive and pornographic displayed the highest level of aggression against the woman, but the aggression-only film produced more aggression against the woman than did the sexually explicit film that contained no violence or coercion. In fact, there were no differences in aggression against the female target for subjects in the sex-only film condition and in the neutral film condition. In the second study, subjects who viewed the combination of sex and violence displayed higher levels of aggressive behavior than subjects in the sex-only group, and subjects exposed to the violence-only depiction also exhibited higher levels of aggression than the sex-only group.

[G]eneralizations From Laboratory Experiments

In addition to the fact that many of the experimental studies upon which the Commission bases its findings did not employ obscene or pornographic stimuli, the Commission also fails to exercise proper caution about generalizing the results of these studies to violent behavior outside the laboratory. Despite the higher level of causal certainty accorded the laboratory experiment relative to other forms of investigation, laboratory assessments of the effects of violent mass media on behavior are susceptible to many criticisms concerning external validity—for example, the extent to which findings obtained under laboratory conditions can be applied to persons, situations, and times outside the laboratory.

[T]he Commission should have acknowledged at least a few of the most important of those criticisms. Among them would be: (1) laboratory subjects may not perceive themselves as inflicting harm when experimenters ask them to perform very artificial forms of aggression in their interactions with a confederate; (2) outside the laboratory violence is not sanctioned, but inside the laboratory aggression is condoned, even encouraged, after the subject has viewed violent material; (3) all the studies examine subjects from a very narrow segment of the general population; (4) laboratory experiments may be generally susceptible to what has been termed an "experimenter demand effect," wherein subjects attempt to guess and then confirm the experimenter's hypothesis; (5) usually only studies that obtain positive results are published; and (6) no one yet has been able to come up with either an acceptable operational definition of aggressive behavior on the part of the subject who is supposedly reacting to the film or other media event, or an acceptable definition of what actually constitutes violence in the media depiction itself.

NOTES

1. External Validity of Research on Violent Pornography. One of the dependent measures in the research on violent pornography has been a question asking subjects the likelihood they would commit a rape "if they could not get caught." One study found that 51 percent of undergraduate males responded that their likelihood of committing a rape under these conditions was greater than zero. "It would seem highly inappropriate to argue that those subjects who indicated a possibility of engaging in rape, particularly under the hypothetical circumstances of being assured of not being caught, are actually likely to rape. This self-report, however, may be an indication of a tendency that in combination with other factors and in an exaggerated form may indeed be predictive of such assaults." Malamuth, Haber, and Feshbach, Testing Hypotheses Regarding Rape: Exposure to Sexual Violence, Sex Differences, and the "Normality" of Rapists, 14 Journal of Research in Personality 121, 134 (1980).

2. Ethics of Research on Violent Pornography. Clearly, the researchers conducting the studies described above could not terminate the research at the point that the subjects reported an increase in the likelihood of committing a rape, even under the hypothetical condition of not being caught. Rather, at the conclusion of the research, the "experimenter then brought the subject a debriefing sheet, which, for subjects who were exposed to rape depictions, stressed the violent nature of rape and presented several points designed to dispel rape myths. [A]ssessments of the effectiveness of such debriefings [c]onducted as long as 4 months following research participation [c]onsistently show that the overall impact of research participation that includes exposure to rape portrayals followed by debriefings is a reduction in subjects' acceptance of rape myths." Malamuth and Check, Sexual Arousal to Rape Depictions: Individual Differences, 92 Journal of Abnormal Psychology 55, 59 (1983).

3. Moral Decay and Social Harm. Linz, Donnerstein, Shafer, Land, McCall, and Graesser, Discrepancies between the Legal Code and Community Standards for Sex and Violence: An Empirical Challenge to Traditional Assumptions in Obscenity Law, 29 Law and Society Review 127 (1995), report a study in which residents of western Tennessee were randomly assigned to view sexually explicit films at issue in an obscenity case, violent films, or control films (neither sexually explicit nor violent). The researchers report finding tolerance for depictions of consensual sexual behavior, but substantial disapproval of violent sexual behavior such as rape or bondage. "Obscenity law with its emphasis on 'moral decay' appears to lie outside the community's scope of concern. Instead, the possible harms of exposure to violence appear most troubling." Id. at 160–161. Linz et al conclude that these and other research results now "suggest that prosecutions most closely aligned with both community standards and harmful effects as identified by empirical research would involve materials that feature rape or other forms of sexual violence rather than consenting sexual depictions." Id. at 162.

----

2. VIOLENT VIDEO GAMES

In recent years, First Amendment freedom of expression litigation has focused not on obscenity but on attempts by many states to civilly regulate or to criminally proscribe the exposure of minors to interactive video games that depict physical—but not sexual—violence. The key empirical question in this ongoing litigation is whether playing violent video games either harms minors or causes minors to harm others.

AMERICAN AMUSEMENT MACHINE ASSOCIATION v. KENDRICK

United States Court of Appeals, Seventh Circuit, 2001.
244 F.3d 572.

■ POSNER, CIRCUIT JUDGE.

The manufacturers of video games and their trade association seek to enjoin, as a violation of freedom of expression, the enforcement of an Indianapolis ordinance that seeks to limit the access of minors to video games that depict violence. Denial of a preliminary injunction has precipitated this appeal.

The ordinance defines the term "harmful to minors" to mean "an amusement machine that predominantly appeals to minors' morbid interest in violence or minors' prurient interest in sex, is patently offensive to prevailing standards in the adult community as a whole with respect to what is suitable material for persons under the age of eighteen (18) years, lacks serious literary, artistic, political or scientific value as a whole for persons under" that age, and contains either "graphic violence" or "strong sexual content." "Graphic violence," which is all that is involved in this case (so far as appears, the plaintiffs do not manufacture [v]ideo games that have "strong sexual content"), is defined to mean "an amusement machine's visual depiction or representation of realistic serious injury to a human or human-like being where such serious injury includes amputation, decapitation, dismemberment, bloodshed, mutilation, maiming or disfiguration."

[T]he ordinance brackets violence with sex, and the City asks us to squeeze the provision on violence into a familiar legal pigeonhole, that of obscenity, which is normally concerned with sex and is not protected by the First Amendment. [I]n general [however], the concerns [about obscenity and violence] are different. The main worry about obscenity, the main reason for its proscription, is not that it is harmful, which is the worry behind the Indianapolis ordinance, but that it is offensive. A work is classified as obscene not upon proof that it is likely to affect anyone's conduct, but upon proof that it violates community norms regarding the permissible scope of depictions of sexual or sex-related activity. *Miller v. California,* 413 U.S. 15, 24 [(1973)]. [N]o proof that obscenity is harmful is required either to defend an obscenity statute against being invalidated on constitutional grounds or to uphold a prosecution for obscenity. Offensiveness is the offense.

[B]ut offensiveness is not the basis on which Indianapolis seeks to regulate violent video games. [T]he basis of the ordinance, rather, is a belief that violent video games cause temporal harm by engendering aggressive attitudes and behavior, which might lead to violence.

[T]he City rightly does not rest on "what everyone knows" about the harm inflicted by violent video games. [T]he City instead appeals to social science to establish that games such as "The House of the Dead" and "Ultimate Mortal Kombat 3," games culturally isomorphic with (and often derivative from) movies aimed at the same under 18 crowd, are dangerous to public safety. The social science evidence on which the City relies consists primarily of the pair of psychological studies [w]hich are reported in Craig A. Anderson & Karen E. Dill, "Personality Processes and Individual Differences–Video Games and Aggressive Thoughts, Feelings, and Behavior in the Laboratory and in Life," 78 *J. Personality & Soc. Psych.* 772 (2000). Those studies do not support the ordinance. There is no indication that the games used in the studies are similar to those in the record of this case or to other games likely to be marketed in game arcades in Indianapolis. The studies do not find that video games have ever caused anyone to commit a violent act, as opposed to feeling aggressive, or have caused the average level of violence to increase anywhere. And they do not suggest that it is the *interactive* character of the games, as opposed to the violence of the images in them, that is the cause of the aggressive feelings. The studies thus are not evidence that violent video games are any more harmful to the consumer or to the public safety than violent movies or other violent, but passive, entertainments. It is highly unlikely that they are more harmful, because "passive" entertainment aspires to be interactive too and often succeeds. When Dirty Harry or some other avenging hero kills off a string of villains, the audience is expected to identify with him, to revel in his success, to feel their own finger on the trigger. It is conceivable that pushing a button or manipulating a toggle stick engenders an even deeper surge of aggressive joy, but of that there is no evidence at all.

[C]ommon sense says that the City's claim of harm to its citizens from these games is implausible, at best wildly speculative. Common sense is sometimes another word for prejudice, and the common sense reaction to the Indianapolis ordinance could be overcome by social scientific evidence, but has not been.

[T]he plaintiffs are entitled to a preliminary injunction. [T]he judgment is therefore reversed, and the case remanded with instructions to enter a preliminary injunction.

ENTERTAINMENT SOFTWARE ASS'N v. BLAGOJEVICH

United States District Court, Northern District of Illinois, Eastern Division, 2005.
404 F.Supp.2d 1051.

■ KENNELLY, DISTRICT JUDGE.

Plaintiffs Entertainment Software Association [et al.] sued several state and local officials seeking to enjoin the enforcement of Illinois's Violent Video Games Law [VVGL]. Plaintiffs moved for a preliminary injunction, and the Court ordered a hearing. All parties consented to combine the preliminary injunction hearing with trial on the merits.

[T]he VVGL establishes criminal penalties for selling or renting violent video games to minors. [T]he statute defines "violent video games" as those that include:

depictions of or simulations of human-on-human violence in which the player kills or otherwise causes serious physical harm to another human. "Serious physical harm" includes depictions of death, dismemberment, amputation, decapitation, maiming, disfigurement, mutilation of body parts, or rape.

[P]laintiffs sought declaratory and injunctive relief against enforcement of the VVGL [o]n the ground that the statutes violate their constitutional right to free expression.

[T]his Court held an evidentiary hearing on the effect of violent video games on youth. [D]r. Craig Anderson, a psychologist and professor at Iowa State University, testified on behalf of the defendants. Dr. Anderson summarized research, including his own, regarding the relationship between minors' exposure to violent video games and aggressive thoughts and behavior. Based on this research, Dr. Anderson testified that "it seems clear that exposure to violent video games increases aggressive behavior, aggressive thinking, physiological arousal, aggressive feelings, and is also associated with a decrease in prosocial behavior." [H]e stated:

> In violent video games, you rehearse really the whole sequence [of aggression]. You rehearse, you practice being vigilant, that is, looking for the source of the threat. You practice identifying sources of threat. You practice making decisions about how to respond to that threat. And eventually, you actually carry out some form of action, typically a violent action to deal with that threat, clicking a mouse or something on the keyboard or a pretend sort of gun of some kind.

[O]ne of the articles Dr. Anderson published involved two studies of the effects of violent video games on measures of aggression of college students. This study provided the basis for the Indianapolis ordinance regulating violent video games that was struck down in *Kendrick. Kendrick,* 244 F.3d at 578. In the first study, Dr. Anderson and Dr. Karen Dill of Lenoir–Rhyne College conducted a survey of college students regarding exposure to violent video games and aggressive behavior. [D]r. Anderson found "a strong positive correlation between video game exposure and aggressive behavior." He conceded, however, that once the results were adjusted to exclude non-serious behavior, such as throwing snowballs, less than ten percent of the participants reported engaging in aggressive behavior. Dr. Anderson also indicated that exposure to violent video games only incrementally affected the amount of aggressive behavior they engaged in.

In a second study, Dr. Anderson conducted an experiment in which participants played a violent video game, *Wolfenstein 3D,* or a non-violent video game, *Myst.* The participants were then asked to participate in a task in which they were supposed to "compete" with someone outside the room and administer a noise blast to the "loser" whenever they won. Based on this experiment, Dr. Anderson concluded that violent video games caused an increase in aggressive behavior, because participants who played *Myst* administered a longer noise blast than the participants who played *Wolfenstein 3D.*[1] In his testimony, however, Dr. Anderson stated that the difference between the two groups was a matter of milliseconds.

Dr. Anderson also discussed [a]dditional studies he conducted using college students. In [one] experiment, half the students played violent video games and half played non-violent video games. They were then given a list of partially completed words—many of which could have been completed to form an aggressive word—and asked the participants to finish the words. The students who played the violent video game were more likely to fill in the blank to form an aggressive word, leading Dr. Anderson and his

---

1. [Ed. Note: There appears to be a typographical error in this sentence. In fact, participants who played *Wolfenstein 3D* administered a longer noise blast than the participants who played *Myst.* See Anderson and Dill, Video Games and Aggressive Thoughts, Feelings, and Behavior in the Laboratory and in Life, 78 Journal of Personality and Social Psychology 772 (2000)].

colleagues to conclude that exposure to the violent video game had increased their aggressive thoughts.

[D]r. Anderson stated that there has only been one reliable longitudinal study into the impact of violent video games on aggression in minors. Such studies, which examine the effects of a particular variable at two or more points in time, are important because they can measure longer term effects, rule out alternative explanations for particular behavior, and help identify the cause of a particular behavior. In this study, which is still undergoing peer review, Dr. Douglas Gentile, a colleague of Dr. Anderson's at Iowa State University, interviewed third-, fourth-, and fifth-graders about the level of violence in the video games they played during the six month period of the study. Then, using reports from parents and teachers, he determined the child's level of aggressive behavior at the beginning and end of the study to assess whether such behavior had increased.

According to Dr. Anderson, Dr. Gentile's longitudinal study showed that those children with a higher exposure to violent video games were more likely to have been in a fight by the end of the study, even after controlling for whether the child had been in a fight—and likely had a proclivity for aggression—before the study began. From this longitudinal study, Dr. Anderson concluded that "[w]hat is clear is that regardless of the *initial cause,* playing violent video games still makes children *more* aggressive." Douglas A. Gentile and Craig A. Anderson, *Violent Video Games: The Effects on Youth, and Public Policy Implications, in Children, Culture, and Violence,* at 232 (N. Dowd et. al. eds.) (forthcoming) (emphasis in original). The total increase in aggressive behavior between the beginning and end of the study, however, was not very large; there was a high (0.4 to 0.5) correlation between aggression at the beginning and end of the study; and at most, only four percent of the increase in aggression was associated with exposure to video game violence.

[D]r. Jeffrey Goldstein, a social psychologist at the University of Utrecht in the Netherlands, and Dr. Dmitri Williams, an assistant professor of communications at the University of Illinois at Urbana–Champaign, testified for the plaintiffs. [T]hey agreed that there is a correlation between exposure to video game violence and increases in aggressive cognition and behavior, but disagreed with Dr. Anderson's conclusion that the research establishes that exposure to violent video games causes increases in aggressive thinking and behavior.

Dr. Goldstein and Dr. Williams shared a number of the same concerns with the methodology and conclusions of research regarding violent video games cited by Dr. Anderson. With regard to methodology, they were concerned that these studies defined aggressive thoughts and behavior vaguely (e.g., equating aggressive play with aggressive behavior), [and] administered problematic tests for measuring aggression (e.g., [n]oise blasts). [W]ith regard to their conclusions, Dr. Goldstein and Dr. Williams noted that Dr. Anderson not only had failed to cite any peer-reviewed studies that had shown a definitive causal link between violent video game play and aggression, but had also ignored research that reached conflicting conclusions.

[E]ven if one were to accept the proposition that playing violent video games increases aggressive thoughts or behavior, there is no evidence that this effect is at all significant. Dr. Anderson provided no evidence supporting the view that playing violent video games has a lasting effect on aggressive thoughts and behavior—in other words, an effect that lingers more than a short time after the player stops playing the game.

[A]ll parties agree that the VVGL is a content-based regulation subject to the strictest scrutiny under the First Amendment. [T]he plaintiffs's challenge to the VVGL is, contrary to defendants' claims, governed by the Seventh Circuit's decision in *Am. Amusement Machine Assoc. v. Kendrick,* 244 F.3d 572 (7th Cir.2001).

[D]efendants have come nowhere near making the necessary showing in this case. [A]t most, researchers have been able to show a correlation between playing violent video games and a slightly increased level of aggressive thoughts and behavior. With these limited findings, it is impossible to know which way the causal relationship runs: it may be that aggressive children may also be attracted to violent video games. One unpublished article by Dr. Anderson's colleague Dr. Gentile [c]oncludes there is a causal relationship between violent video game play and aggression in children. The evidence is not, however, sufficient to establish a compelling interest in regulating the games at hand.

[P]laintiffs are unquestionably entitled to a permanent injunction barring enforcement of [t]he VVGL.

C. The Sixth Amendment: Juries and Witnesses

The Sixth Amendment to the Constitution reads in part as follows:

In all criminal prosecutions, the accused shall enjoy the right to a speedy and public trial, by an impartial jury of the State and district wherein the crime shall have been committed, [and] to be confronted with the witnesses against him.

Social science research has been heavily implicated in Sixth Amendment issues in recent years. One issue that has received much attention concerns the minimum size of the group needed to constitute a "jury." Another concerns whether juries that decide capital cases are "impartial."

1. JURY SIZE

The number of decision-makers varies dramatically in different procedural systems. In some cultures, it is traditional to assemble an entire community to render a verdict; in other cultures, a single judge hears cases. The number of persons necessary to constitute a jury for purposes of the Sixth Amendment has been the focus of a number of Supreme Court cases since 1970.

WILLIAMS v. FLORIDA

Supreme Court of the United States, 1970.
399 U.S. 78, 90 S.Ct. 1893, 26 L.Ed.2d 446.

■ MR. JUSTICE WHITE delivered the opinion of the Court.

[After trial to a six-member jury, petitioner was convicted in a Florida court of robbery, and sentenced to life imprisonment. Petitioner challenged the Florida law which required that a six-member jury try all non-capital criminal cases as contrary to the Sixth and Fourteenth Amendments of the U.S. Constitution.]

In Duncan v. Louisiana, 391 U.S. 145, 88 S.Ct. 1444, 20 L.Ed.2d 491 (1968), we held that the Fourteenth Amendment guarantees a right to trial by jury in all criminal cases that—were they to be tried in a federal court—would come within the Sixth Amendment's guarantee. Petitioner's trial for robbery on July 3, 1968, clearly falls within the scope of that holding. The question in this case then is whether the constitutional guarantee of a trial by "jury" necessarily requires trial by exactly 12 persons, rather than some lesser number—in this case six. We hold that the 12–man panel is not a necessary ingredient of "trial by jury," and that respondent's refusal to impanel more than the six members provided for by Florida law did not violate petitioner's Sixth Amendment rights as applied to the States through the Fourteenth.

We had occasion in Duncan v. Louisiana, supra, to review briefly the oft-told history of the development of trial by jury in criminal cases. That history revealed a long tradition attaching great importance to the concept of relying on a body of one's peers to determine guilt or innocence as a safeguard against arbitrary law enforcement. That same history, however, affords little insight into the considerations that gradually led the size of that body to be generally fixed at 12. Some have suggested that the number 12 was fixed upon simply because that was the number of the presentment jury from the hundred, from which the petit jury developed. Other, less circular but more fanciful reasons for the number 12 have been given, "but they were all brought forward after the number was fixed," and rest on little more than mystical or superstitious insights into the significance of "12." Lord Coke's explanation that the *"number of twelve* is much respected *in holy writ,* as 12 *apostles,* 12 *stones,* 12 *tribes, etc.,"* is typical. In short, while sometime in the 14th century the size of the jury at common law came to be fixed generally at 12, that particular feature of the jury system appears to have been a historical accident, unrelated to the great purposes which gave rise to the jury in the first place. The question before us is whether this accidental feature of the jury has been immutably codified into our Constitution.

[T]here is absolutely no indication in "the intent of the framers" [of the Constitution] of an explicit decision to equate the constitutional and common-law characteristics of the jury.

Nothing in this history suggests, then, that we do violence to the letter of the Constitution by turning to other than purely historical considerations to determine which features of the jury system, as it existed at common law, were preserved in the Constitution. The relevant inquiry, as we see it, must be the function that the particular feature performs and its relation to the purposes of the jury trial. Measured by this standard, the 12–man requirement cannot be regarded as an indispensable component of the Sixth Amendment.

The purpose of the jury trial, as we noted in *Duncan,* is to prevent oppression by the Government. "Providing an accused with the right to be tried by a jury of his peers gave him an inestimable safeguard against the corrupt or overzealous prosecutor and against the complaint, biased, or eccentric judge." Duncan v. Louisiana, supra, at 156. Given this purpose, the essential feature of a jury obviously lies in the interposition between the accused and his accuser of the commonsense judgment of a group of laymen, and in the community participation and shared responsibility that results from that group's determination of guilt or innocence. The performance of this role is not a function of the particular number of the body that makes up the jury. To be sure, the number should probably be large enough to promote group deliberation, free from outside attempts at intimidation, and to provide a fair possibility for obtaining a representative cross-section of the community. But we find little reason to think that these goals are in any meaningful sense less likely to be achieved when the jury numbers six, than when it numbers 12—particularly if the requirement of unanimity is retained. And, certainly the reliability of the jury as a factfinder hardly seems likely to be a function of its size.

It might be suggested that the 12–man jury gives a defendant a greater advantage since he has more "chances" of finding a juror who will insist on acquittal and thus prevent conviction. But the advantage might just as easily belong to the State, which also needs only one juror out of twelve insisting on guilt to prevent acquittal. What few experiments have occurred—usually in the civil area—indicate that there is no discernible difference between the results reached by the two different-sized juries.[48] In short, neither currently available evidence nor theory[49] suggests that the

---

48. See Wiehl, [The Six Man Jury, 4 Gonzaga Law Review 35, 40–41 (1968)]; Tamm, [The Five–Man Civil Jury, 51 Geo. L.J. 120, 134–136 (1962)]; Cronin, Six–Member Juries Tried in Massachusetts District Court, 42 J.Am.Jud.Soc., 136 (1958). See also New Jersey Experiments with Six–Man Jury, 9 Bull. of the Section of Jud.Admin. of the ABA (May 1966); Phillips, A Jury of Six in All Cases, 30 Conn.B.J. 354 (1956).

49. Studies of the operative factors contributing to small group deliberation and decisionmaking suggest that jurors in the minority on the first ballot are likely to be influenced by the proportional size of the majority aligned against them. See H. Kalven & H. Zeisel, The American Jury 462–463, 488–489 (1966); C. Hawkins, Interaction and Coalition Realignments in Consensus–Seeking Groups: A Study of Experimental Jury

12–man jury is necessarily more advantageous to the defendant than a jury composed of fewer members.

[W]e conclude, in short, as we began: the fact that the jury at common law was composed of precisely 12 is a historical accident, unnecessary to effect the purposes of the jury system and wholly without significance "except to mystics." Duncan v. Louisiana, supra, 391 U.S., at 182, 88 S.Ct. at 1466 (Harlan, J., dissenting). To read the Sixth Amendment as forever codifying a feature so incidental to the real purpose of the Amendment is to ascribe a blind formalism to the Framers which would require considerably more evidence than we have been able to discover in the history and language of the Constitution or in the reasoning of our past decisions. [C]onsistent with this holding, we conclude that petitioner's Sixth Amendment rights, as applied to the States through the Fourteenth Amendment, were not violated by Florida's decision to provide a six-man rather than a 12–man jury.

———

COLGROVE v. BATTIN

Supreme Court of the United States, 1973.
413 U.S. 149, 93 S.Ct. 2448, 37 L.Ed.2d 522.

■ Mr. Justice Brennan delivered the opinion of the Court.

In Williams v. Florida, 399 U.S. 78, 90 S.Ct. 1893, 26 L.Ed.2d 446 (1970), the Court sustained the constitutionality of a Florida statute providing for six-member juries in certain criminal cases. The constitutional challenge rejected in that case relied on the guarantees of jury trial secured the accused by Art. III, § 2, cl. 3, of the Constitution and by the Sixth Amendment. We expressly reserved, however, the question whether "additional references to the 'common law' that occur in the Seventh Amendment might support a different interpretation" with respect to jury trial in civil cases. Id., at 92 n. 30, 90 S.Ct., at 1901. We conclude that they do not.

The pertinent words of the Seventh Amendment are: "In Suits at common law ... the right of trial by jury shall be preserved...." On its face, this language is not directed to jury characteristics, such as size, but

Deliberations 13, 146, 156, Aug. 17, 1960 (unpublished thesis on file at Library of Congress); cf. Asch, Effects of Group Pressure Upon the Modification and Distortion of Judgments in Readings in Social Psychology 2 (G. Swanson, T. Newcomb & E. Hartley et al., eds., 1952). See generally Note, On Instructing Dead-locked Juries, 78 Yale L.J. 100, 108 and n. 30 (and authorities cited), 110–111 (1968). Thus if a defendant needs initially to persuade four jurors that the State has not met its burden of proof in order to escape ultimate conviction by a 12–man jury, he arguably escapes by initially persuading half that number in a six-man jury: random reduction, within limits, of the absolute number of the jury would not affect the outcome. See also C. Joiner, Civil Justice and the Jury 31, 83 (1962) (concluding that the deliberative process should be the same in either the six-or 12–man jury).

rather defines the kind of cases for which jury trial is preserved, namely, "suits at common law."

[C]onsistently with the historical objective of the Seventh Amendment, our decisions have defined the jury right preserved in cases covered by the Amendment, as "the substance of the common-law right of trial by jury, as distinguished from mere matters of form or procedure...." Baltimore & Carolina Line, Inc. v. Redman, 295 U.S. 654, 657, 55 S.Ct. 890, 891, 79 L.Ed. 1636 (1935). The Amendment, therefore, does not "bind the federal courts to the exact procedural incidents or details of jury trial according to the common law in 1791," Galloway v. United States, 319 U.S. 372, 390, 63 S.Ct. 1077, 1087, 87 L.Ed. 1458 (1943).

[O]ur inquiry turns, then, to whether a jury of 12 is of the substance of the common-law right of trial by jury. Keeping in mind the purpose of the jury trial in criminal cases to prevent government oppression, *Williams,* 399 U.S., at 100, 90 S.Ct., at 1905, and, in criminal and civil cases, to assure a fair and equitable resolution of factual issues, Gasoline Products Co. v. Champlin Co., 283 U.S. 494, 498, 51 S.Ct. 513, 514, 75 L.Ed. 1188 (1931), the question comes down to whether jury performance is a function of jury size. In *Williams,* we rejected the notion that "the reliability of the jury as a factfinder ... [is] a function of its size," 399 U.S., at 100–101, 90 S.Ct., at 1906, and nothing has been suggested to lead us to alter that conclusion. Accordingly, we think it cannot be said that 12 members is a substantive aspect of the right of trial by jury.

[T]here remains, however, the question whether a jury of six satisfies the Seventh Amendment guarantee of "trial by jury." We had no difficulty reaching the conclusion in *Williams* that a jury of six would guarantee an accused the trial by jury secured by Art. III and the Sixth Amendment. Significantly, our determination that there was "no discernible difference between the results reached by the two different-sized juries," 399 U.S., at 101, 90 S.Ct., at 1906, drew largely upon the results of studies of the operations of juries of six in civil cases. Since then, much has been written about the six-member jury, but nothing that persuades us to depart from the conclusion reached in *Williams.*[15] Thus, while we express no view as to

---

15. Arguments, pro and con, on the effectiveness of a jury of six compared to a jury of 12 will be found in Devitt, [The Six Man Jury in the Federal Court, 53 F.R.D. 273 (1971)]; Augelli, [Six–Member Juries in Civil Actions in the Federal Judicial System, 3 Seton Hall L.Rev. 281 (1972)]; Croake, [Memorandum on the Advisability and Constitutionality of Six Man Juries and ⅚ Verdicts in Civil Cases, 44 N.Y.State B.J. 385 (1972)]; Fisher, [The Seventh Amendment and the Common Law: No Magic in Numbers, 56 F.R.D. 507 (1973)]; Bogue & Fritz, The Six–Man Jury, 17 S.D.L.Rev. 285 (1972); Moss, The Twelve Member Jury in Massachusetts— Can it be Reduced?, 56 Mass.L.Q. 65 (1971); Zeisel, ... And Then There Were None: The Diminution of the Federal Jury, 38 U.Chi. L.Rev. 710 (1971); Zeisel, The Waning of the American Jury, 58 A.B.A.J. 367 (1972); Gibbons, The New Minijuries: Panacea or Pandora's Box?, 58 A.B.A.J. 594 (1972); Kaufman, The Harbingers of Jury Reform, 58 A.B.A.J. 695 (1972); Whalen, Remarks on Resolution of 7th Amendment Jury Trial Requirement, 54 F.R.D. 148 (1972); Note, Right to Twelve–Man Jury, 84 Harv.L.Rev. 165 (1970); Note, Reducing the Size of Juries, 5 U.Mich.J.L.Reform 87 (1971); Note, The Effect of Jury Size on the Probability of Conviction: An Evaluation of Williams v. Florida, 22 whether any number less than six would suffice,[16] we conclude that a jury of six satisfies the Seventh Amendment's guarantee of trial by jury in civil cases.

IGNORANCE OF SCIENCE IS NO EXCUSE*

Michael Saks.
10 Trial 18 (1974).

The briefs presented by opposing counsel [in Williams v. Florida and Colgrove v. Battin] were oblivious to well established social science findings and/or methodological principles which would have supported the appellant. In short, the law's confrontation with some relatively simple empirical questions was simply an embarrassment. Let us look with some care at the treatment of the jury size issue.

Defendant Williams was convicted of a crime which, under Florida law, was tried to a jury of six rather than 12. Williams appealed on grounds that included the fact that his conviction was by what he argued was an unconstitutionally small jury. When the case reached the US Supreme Court, the Court asserted that an answer to the question lay not in law nor in history, but in a functional analysis of the jury purpose. That is, do the characteristics or behavior of a six-person jury differ in such a way or to

Case W.Res.L.Rev. 529 (1971); Comment, Defendant's Right to a Jury Trial—Is Six Enough?, 59 Ky.L.J. 997 (1971).

Professor Zeisel has suggested that the six-member jury is more limited than the 12-member jury in representing the full spectrum of the community, and this in turn may result in differences between the verdicts reached by the two panels. Zeisel, supra, 38 U.Chi.L.Rev., at 716–719.

On the other hand, one study suggests that the decrease in the size of the jury from 12 to six is conducive to a more open discussion among the jurors, thereby improving the quality of the deliberative process. Note, supra, 5 U.Mich.J.L.Reform, at 99–106. See also C. Joiner, Civil Justice and the Jury 31, 83 (1962) (concluding prior to *Williams* that the deliberative process should be the same in either six-or 12–member juries).

In addition, four very recent studies have provided convincing empirical evidence of the correctness of the *Williams* conclusion that "there is no discernible difference between the results reached by the two different-sized juries." Note, Six–Member and Twelve–Member Juries: An Empirical Study of Trial Results, 6 U.Mich.J.L.Reform 671

(1973); Institute of Judicial Administration, A Comparison of Six-and Twelve–Member Civil Juries in New Jersey Superior and County Courts (1972); Note, An Empirical Study of Six-and Twelve–Member Jury Decision–Making Processes, 6 U.Mich.J.L.Reform 712 (1973); Bermant & Coppock, Outcomes of Six-and Twelve–Member Jury Trials: An Analysis of 128 Civil Cases in the State of Washington, 48 Wash.L.Rev. 593 (1973).

16. What is required for a "jury" is a number large enough to facilitate group deliberation combined with a likelihood of obtaining a representative cross section of the community. Williams v. Florida, 399 U.S., at 100, 90 S.Ct., at 1905. It is undoubtedly true that at some point the number becomes too small to accomplish these goals, but, on the basis of presently available data, that cannot be concluded as to the number six. See Tamm, A Proposal for Five–Member Civil Juries in the Federal Courts, 50 A.B.A.J. 162 (1964); Tamm, The Five–Man Civil Jury: A Proposed Constitutional Amendment, 51 Geo.L.J. 120 (1962).

such a degree from that of a 12–person jury that the former will not fulfill the jury's purpose as well as the latter. Although the opinion stated that the case entirely turned on this set of empirical questions, it dealt with them in only three paragraphs. The Court concluded that there were no differences—that either size would do as well in providing a representative cross-section of the community, in being reliable and accurate, in providing for the jury minority's ability to resist majority pressure, that there would be equal amounts of deliberation, and that the likelihood of conviction would remain the same.

How did the Court know the answers to these questions? It knew because "experiments" on the effects of reduced jury size in the civil area all showed "no discernible difference." Footnote 48 of the Court's opinion cites six such "experiments." One reference consisted of an unsupported assertion that there would be no differences; three were reports of haphazard observations by officials in courts using six-member juries, who said they saw no differences; another was a report that a jurisdiction was trying out six-member juries; and the sixth was an article on the economic advantages to be expected from reduced jury size. As Professor Hans Zeisel commented in a critique of this use by the Court of non-studies, "this is scant evidence by any standards."[8] Not one of the references even began to address competently the empirical questions the Court posed for itself.

Footnote 49 is perhaps more incredible. A number of genuine empirical studies were cited to support the contention that "... jurors in the minority ... are likely to be influenced by the proportional size of the majority aligned against them." That is to say, a jury split 10–2 is equivalent to one split 5–1 in terms of the minority's ability to defend its view, because both represent 83%–17% splits. Each of the studies cited, however, found exactly the opposite to be true. They found that it is the absolute rather than the relative size of the opposition that determined factional influence, and that having an ally (10–2) as compared to having no ally (5–1) makes an enormous difference. This is a classic and widely known finding in social psychology research on conformity. The presence of an ally is one of the most powerful known facilitators of minority resistance to conformity pressure.

In asserting that there would be a negligible difference in the ability of 12–member and six-member juries to provide a representative cross-section of the community, the court ignored what is obvious to every social scientist: that when sampling from heterogeneous populations, sample size (12 versus 6) determines how well minority groups in the population will be represented. In sampling from a population stratified 90%/10%, for example, we can predict from our knowledge of sampling theory that 72% of 12–member juries will include one or more members of the minority, but that only 47% of the 6–member samples will. Still, this is only a statistical prediction, and a sincere empiricist would want to see empirical evidence.

8. Zeisel, ... And Then There Were None: Diminution of the Federal Jury, 38 Chicago L.Rev. 710 (1974).

In my own experiments on 12–member versus six-member juries I compared the number of large and the number of small juries that had one or more blacks present. Blacks composed 10% of the population from which these jurors were drawn. Instead of the 72% to 47% contrast predicted, I found an 82% to 32% difference.[10] Not many people would term this difference "negligible."

After the decision in Williams v. Florida, the first empirical studies aimed directly at the effects of group size on jury behavior were conducted. By the time Colgrove v. Battin was heard, four such studies had been published and were considered by the Court. This might be viewed as progress. The Court did look at empirical studies and did understand the stated findings.

What the Court did not realize was that not all empirical studies are equal. As Zeisel and Shari Diamond make clear in a recent paper[12], the validity of empirical studies differs, and the intelligent use of empirical evidence requires a critical evaluation of the research. An empirical finding is only as good as the methods used to find it. Thus, the methods used in an empirical study must be scrutinized. The importance of method cannot be overstressed. Method is the overlooked, but more important term, in the phrase "scientific method." Studies using poor methods tell one nothing; but they can seriously mislead because their findings still may properly be called "empirical."

The four empirical studies cited in Colgrove v. Battin, because of their faulty methods, said much less than the Court thought they were saying.

Two of the studies[13] compared the behavior of six-member and 12–member civil juries in two jurisdictions where litigants were able to choose which jury size the case would be tried to. The studies found no difference in outcomes that exceeded chance levels.

One of the studies examined more than just the verdicts reached. It found that the 12–member jury, compared to the six-member, deliberated longer, awarded three times as much damages, and, most curiously, required about twice as much trial time. The researchers correctly discounted these differences by noting that attorneys did not choose their jury size carelessly. Attorneys tended to select 12–member juries for cases involving large amounts of damages sought and/or more complex issues. That accounts for the difference in trial times and awards. And the notion is fully supported by the additional findings that in cases scheduled for trial before 12–member juries, there were significantly more settlements, and those settlements were for triple the amount of settlements in six-member juries.

10. [Reported in M. Saks, Jury Verdicts (1977).]

12. Zeisel & Diamond, "Convincing Empirical Evidence" on the Six-member Jury, 41 Chicago L.Rev. 281 (1974).

13. Bermant, G. & Coppock, R. Outcomes of Six-and Twelve-member Jury Trials: An Analysis of 128 Civil Cases in the State of Washington, 48 Washington Law Review 593 (1973); Institute of Judicial Administration, A Comparison of Six-and Twelve-member Juries in New Jersey Superior and County Courts (1972).

What is operating here is known in social science jargon as a "confound." A confound exists when several potential causes vary simultaneously. Under such conditions it is difficult and usually impossible to know which potential cause is responsible for changes in performance. Thus, in comparing large juries hearing more complex and more costly cases to small juries hearing less complex and less costly cases, one cannot know whether it is jury size, complexity, or damages sought which is responsible for the various observed differences.

The researchers are probably correct in suggesting that it is complexity and not jury size that created all of those undesirable differences. What they ignore, however, is that while the confound (differential complexity and damages sought) can create differences that are not due to the variable of major interest (jury size), it can mask a difference that is in fact caused by the major variable. When the researchers saw a difference they didn't like, they explained it away by pointing to the confound. When they saw a non-difference they did like, they made believe the confound wasn't there. Given the procedures by which the data were collected and analyzed, one is simply unable to know what effect, if any, jury size did have.

A third study compared a sample of 12–member jury decisions made prior to a statutory reduction in jury size to a sample of six-person jury decisions made after the change.[14] Here, attorney choice of jury size could not be a factor since attorneys had no choice. But there were other potential confounds. The most serious was that not only did the jury size change, but a mediation board was created to try to settle auto negligence cases. The vital data are not provided by the study, but a plausible possibility is that lawyers, in keeping with their behavior in the study discussed above, tended to use the mediation board to settle the expensive and/or complex cases, rather than trust them to a jury. Thus, after the statutory changes, expensive or complex cases would be siphoned off, and the cases tried to six-member juries would therefore tend to be less complex. And we are back where we were in the previous two studies. The study's findings that no difference occurred in the direction of verdicts is still unreliable. We cannot *know* that there was a difference due to jury size, but, given the available data, we cannot be assured that a change in the kinds of cases that went to trial did not mask an actual difference due to jury size.

A fundamental strategy for avoiding the problem of confounds is to do a "true experiment." This was what the fourth study did.[15] In a true experiment the research procedures assure that only the variables of interest are permitted to vary systematically. In the study under discussion, the same case was presented to all juries by videotape and jurors were randomly assigned to sit as a six-member jury or a twelve-member jury. This assured that the only difference between the six-member and 12–member juries was their size.

14. Mills, Six-member and Twelve-member Juries: An Empirical Study of Trial Results, 6 University of Michigan Journal of Law Reform 671 (1973).

15. Kessler, An Empirical Study of Six-member and Twelve-member Jury Decision-making Processes, 6 University of Michigan Journal of Law Reform 712 (1973).

But the achieving of such non-ambiguity is often at a cost. An obvious cost in this experiment is the fact that the study is now of mock juries and not real juries making decisions about real defendants. That is less of a problem than it seems at first blush; such "laboratory" studies are virtually never contradicted by "real-world" studies of the same phenomena. But there are other costs that a controlled experiment can—but need not—fall victim to.

The study in question did not avoid these heavy losses. College undergraduates were used rather than adult jurors. The number of juries used was only 16—8 large and 8 small. All competent social scientists know that the ability of a study to detect effects is determined in part by the sample size. A good way to guarantee that a study will find "no differences" is to use a very small sample size. If there is in reality a 1% difference between large and small juries in the number of verdicts favoring the defendant, it would require about 10,000 juries to insure statistically reliable detection of that difference. A sample size of 16 can be sure of detecting differences between proportions of verdicts only if the difference is 25% or greater. Also, the videotaped trial that was used happened to be so heavily weighted to the defendant that not a single verdict favored the plaintiff. If there is no variability in a dependent variable (verdicts), there is no possible way to see how jury size affects the variability. These are only the major flaws in this experiment, but it should be clear that they alone are adequate to insure that the only finding that could have come from this study was "no difference between the different-sized juries."

Interestingly enough, these empirical studies note that in Williams v. Florida the Court made its conclusions on the question of jury size effects without the benefit of empirical evidence. That's why the studies were conducted—to provide such empirical evidence. But because of glaring shortcomings, these studies contribute nothing to establishing the answer. The final irony is that in Colgrove v. Battin the Court referred to these studies as "convincing empirical evidence." As Zeisel and Diamond point out in their analysis of that "convincing empirical evidence," the expertise required to spot the major flaws in that empirical research is modest. And the expertise required to know when one is dealing with empirical evidence and when one is dealing with bald assertions is even easier to come by. Yet the Court and the respective advocates have consistently failed to exercise the modest expertise that could have prevented this remarkable incompetence. The Court currently believes the matter of equality of performance for different-size juries is now well established, when in truth there is still no evidence to support such a conclusion.

BALLEW v. GEORGIA

Supreme Court of the United States, 1978.
435 U.S. 223, 98 S.Ct. 1029, 55 L.Ed.2d 234.

■ MR. JUSTICE BLACKMUN announced the judgment of the Court and delivered an opinion in which MR. JUSTICE STEVENS joined.

[Ballew was the manager of the Paris Adult Theatre in Atlanta, Georgia. He was charged in a two-count misdemeanor accusation with "distributing obscene materials in violation of Georgia Code Section 26–2101 in that the said accused did, knowing the obscene nature thereof, exhibit a motion picture film entitled 'Behind the Green Door' that contained obscene and indecent scenes." Ballew was brought to trial in the Criminal Court of Fulton County; the practice of this court was to try misdemeanor cases before juries of five persons, pursuant to Georgia law. Ballew's motion that the court impanel a twelve-person jury was denied, and the trial proceeded with the smaller jury panel, which returned guilty verdicts on both counts. Ballew's state appeals, on several grounds, including a Sixth Amendment challenge of the five-person jury, were unsuccessful. The United States Supreme Court granted certiorari.]

This case presents the issue whether a state criminal trial to a jury of only five persons deprives the accused of the right to trial by jury guaranteed to him by the Sixth and Fourteenth Amendments. Our resolution of the issue requires an application of principles enunciated in Williams v. Florida, 399 U.S. 78, 90 S.Ct. 1893, 26 L.Ed.2d 446 (1970), where the use of a six-person jury in a state criminal trial was upheld against constitutional attack.

[W]hen the Court in *Williams* permitted the reduction in jury size—or, to put it another way, when it held that a jury of six was not unconstitutional—it expressly reserved ruling on the issue whether a number smaller than six passed constitutional scrutiny. Id., at 91 n. 28, 90 S.Ct., at 1901. The Court refused to speculate when this so-called "slippery slope" would become too steep. We face now, however, the two-fold question whether a further reduction in the size of the state criminal trial jury does make the grade too dangerous, that is, whether it inhibits the functioning of the jury as an institution to a significant degree, and, if so, whether any state interest counterbalances and justifies the disruption so as to preserve its constitutionality.

Williams v. Florida and Colgrove v. Battin, 413 U.S. 149, 93 S.Ct. 2448, 37 L.Ed.2d 522 (1973) (where the Court held that a jury of six members did not violate the Seventh Amendment right to a jury trial in a civil case), generated a quantity of scholarly work on jury size.[10] These writings do not

10. E.g., M. Saks, Jury Verdicts (1977) (hereinafter cited as Saks); Bogue & Fritz, The Six-Man Jury, 17 S.D.L.Rev. 285 (1972); Davis, Kerr, Atkin, Holt, & Mech, The Decision Processes of 6–and 12–Person Mock Juries Assigned Unanimous and Two–Thirds Majority Rules, 32 J. of Personality & Soc. Psych. 1 (1975); Diamond, A Jury Experiment Reanalyzed, 7 U.Mich.J.L. Reform 520 (1974); Friedman, Trial by Jury: Criteria for Convictions, Jury Size and Type I and Type II Errors, 26–2 Am.Stat. 21 (Apr.1972) (hereinafter cited as Friedman); Institute of Judicial Administration, A Comparison of Six-and Twelve–Member Civil Juries in New Jersey Superior and County Courts (1972). Lempert, Uncovering "Nondiscernible" Differences: Empirical Research and the Jury–Size Cases, 73 Mich.L.Rev. 643 (1975) (hereinafter cited as Lempert); Nagel & Neef, Deductive Modeling to Determine an Optimum Jury Size and Fraction Required to Convict, 1975 Wash. U.L.Q. 933 (hereinafter cited as Nagel & Neef); New Jersey Criminal Law Revision Commission, Six–Member Juries (1971); Pabst, Statistical Studies of the Costs of Six-

draw or identify a bright line below which the number of jurors would not be able to function as required by the standards enunciated in *Williams*. On the other hand, they raise significant questions about the wisdom and constitutionality of a reduction below six. We examine these concerns:

First, recent empirical data suggest that progressively smaller juries are less likely to foster effective group deliberation. At some point, this decline leads to inaccurate fact-finding and incorrect application of the common sense of the community to the facts. Generally, a positive correlation exists between group size and the quality of both group performance and group productivity.[11] A variety of explanations have been offered for this conclusion. Several are particularly applicable in the jury setting. The smaller the group, the less likely are members to make critical contributions necessary for the solution of a given problem.[12] Because most juries are not permitted to take notes, see Forston, Sense and Non–Sense: Jury Trial Communication, 1975 B.Y.U.L.Rev. 601, 631–633, memory is important for accurate jury deliberations. As juries decrease in size, then, they are less likely to have members who remember each of the important pieces of evidence or argument.[13] Furthermore, the smaller the group, the less likely it is to overcome the biases of its members to obtain an accurate

Man versus Twelve–Man Juries, 14 Wm. & Mary L.Rev. 326 (1972) (hereinafter cited as Pabst); Saks, Ignorance of Science Is No Excuse, 10 Trial 18 (Nov.–Dec.1974); Zeisel, Twelve is Just, 10 Trial 13 (Nov.–Dec.1974); Zeisel, . . . And Then There Were None: The Diminution of the Federal Jury, 38 U.Chi. L.Rev. 710 (1971) (hereinafter cited as Zeisel); Zeisel, The Waning of the American Jury, 58 A.B.A.J. 367 (1972); Zeisel & Diamond, "Convincing Empirical Evidence" on the Six Member Jury, 41 U.Chi.L.Rev. 281 (1974) (hereinafter cited as Zeisel & Diamond); Note, The Effect of Jury Size on the Probability of Conviction: An Evaluation of Williams v. Florida, 22 Case W.Res.L.Rev. 529 (1971) (hereinafter cited as Note, Case W.Res.); Note, Six–Member and Twelve–Member Juries: An Empirical Study of Trial Results, 6 U.Mich.J.L. Reform 671 (1973); Note, An Empirical Study of Six-and Twelve–Member Jury Decision–Making Processes, 6 U.Mich.J.L. Reform 712 (1973).

Some of these studies have been pressed upon us by the parties. Brief for Petitioner 7–9; Tr. of Oral Arg. 26–27.

We have considered them carefully because they provide the only basis, besides judicial hunch, for a decision about whether smaller and smaller juries will be able to fulfill the purpose and functions of the Sixth Amendment. Without an examination about how juries and small groups actually work, we would not understand the basis for the conclusion of Mr. Justice Powell that "a line has to be drawn somewhere." We also note that The Chief Justice did not shrink from the use of empirical data in Williams v. Florida, 399 U.S. 78, 100–102, 105, 90 S.Ct. 1893, 1905–1907, 1908, 26 L.Ed.2d 446 (1970), when the data were used to support the constitutionality of the six-person criminal jury, or in Colgrove v. Battin, 413 U.S. 149, 158–160, 93 S.Ct. 2448, 2453–2454, 37 L.Ed.2d 522 (1973), a decision also joined by Mr. Justice Rehnquist.

11. Two researchers have summarized the findings of 31 studies in which the size of groups from 2 to 20 members was an important variable. They concluded that there were no conditions under which smaller groups were superior in the quality of group performance and group productivity. Thomas & Fink, Effects of Group Size, 60 Psych.Bull. 371, 373 (1963), cited in Lempert 685. See Saks 77 et seq., 107.

12. See Faust, Group versus Individual Problem–Solving, 59 J.Ab. & Soc.Psych. 68, 71 (1959), cited in Lempert 685 and 686.

13. Saks 77 et seq.; see Kelley & Thibaut, Group Problem Solving, 4 Handbook of Soc.Psych. 68–69 (2d ed., G. Lindzey & E. Anderson 1969) (hereinafter cited as Kelley & Thibaut).

result.[14] When individual and group decisionmaking were compared, it was seen that groups performed better because prejudices of individuals were frequently counterbalanced, and objectivity resulted. Groups also exhibited increased motivation and self-criticism. All these advantages, except, perhaps, self-motivation, tend to diminish as the size of the group diminishes.[15] Because juries frequently face complex problems laden with value choices, the benefits are important and should be retained. In particular, the counterbalancing of various biases is critical to the accurate application of the common sense of the community to the facts of any given case.

Second, the data now raise doubts about the accuracy of the results achieved by smaller and smaller panels. Statistical studies suggest that the risk of convicting an innocent person (Type I error) rises as the size of the jury diminishes.[16] Because the risk of not convicting a guilty person (Type II error) increases with the size of the panel,[17] an optimal jury size can be selected as a function of the interaction between the two risks. Nagel and Neef concluded that the optimal size, for the purpose of minimizing errors, should vary with the importance attached to the two types of mistakes. After weighting Type I error as 10 times more significant than Type II, perhaps not an unreasonable assumption, they concluded that the optimal jury size was between six and eight. As the size diminished to five and below, the weighted sum of errors increased because of the enlarging risk of the conviction of innocent defendants.[18]

Another doubt about progressively smaller juries arises from the increasing inconsistency that results from the decreases. Saks argued that the "more a jury type fosters consistency, the greater will be the proportion of juries which select the correct (i.e., the same) verdict and the fewer 'errors' will be made." Saks 86–87. From his mock trials held before undergraduates and former jurors, he computed the percentage of "correct" decisions rendered by 12–person and 6–person panels. In the student experiment, 12–person groups reached correct verdicts 83% of the time; 6–person panels reached correct verdicts 69% of the time. The results for the former-juror study were 71% for the 12–person groups and 57% for the 6–person groups. Ibid. Working with statistics described in H. Kalven & H. Zeisel, The American Jury 460 (1966), Nagel and Neef tested the average conviction propensity of juries, that is, the likelihood that any given jury of a set would convict the defendant.[19] They found that half of all 12–person

14. Lempert 687–688, citing Barlund, A Comparative Study of Individual, Majority, and Group Judgment, 58 J.Ab. & Soc.Psych. 55, 59 (1959); see Kelley & Thibaut 67.

15. Lempert 687–688, citing Barlund, supra n. 14, pp. 58–59.

16. Friedman; Nagel & Neef.

17. Nagel & Neef 945.

18. Id., at 946–948, 956, 975. Friedman reached a similar conclusion. He varied the appearance of guilt in his statistical study.

The more guilty the person appeared, the greater the chance that a 6–member panel would convict when a 12–member panel would not. As jury size was reduced, the risk of Type I error would increase, Friedman said, without a significant corresponding advantage in reducing Type II error. Friedman 23.

19. Nagel & Neef 952, 971, concluded that the average juror had a propensity to convict more frequently than to acquit, a tendency designated by the figure .677. In juries would have average conviction propensities that varied by no more than 20 points. Half of all six-person juries, on the other hand, had average conviction propensities varying by 30 points, a difference they found significant in both real and percentage terms.[20] Lempert reached similar results when he considered the likelihood of juries to compromise over the various views of their members, an important phenomenon for the fulfillment of the commonsense function. In civil trials averaging occurs with respect to damages amounts. In criminal trials it relates to numbers of counts and lesser included offenses.[21] And he predicted that compromises would be more consistent when larger juries were employed. For example, 12–person juries could be expected to reach extreme compromises in 4% of the cases, while 6–person panels would reach extreme results in 16%.[22] All three of these *post*-Williams studies, therefore, raise significant doubts about the consistency and reliability of the decisions of smaller juries.

Third, the data suggest that the verdicts of jury deliberation in criminal cases will vary as juries become smaller, and that the variance amounts to an imbalance to the detriment of one side, the defense. Both Lempert and Zeisel found that the number of hung juries would diminish as the panels decreased in size. Zeisel said that the number would be cut in half—from 5% to 2.4% with a decrease from 12 to 6 members.[23] Both studies emphasized that juries in criminal cases generally hang with only one, or more likely two, jurors remaining unconvinced of guilt.[24] Also, group theory suggests that a person in the minority will adhere to his position more frequently when he has at least one other person supporting his argument.[25] In the jury setting the significance of this tendency is demonstrated by the following figures: If a minority viewpoint is shared by 10% of the community, 28.2% of 12–member juries may be expected to have no minority representation, but 53.1% of 6–member juries would have none. Thirty-four percent of 12–member panels could be expected to have two minority members, while only 11% of 6–member panels would have two.[26] As the numbers diminish below six, even fewer panels would have one member with the minority viewpoint and still fewer would have two. The chance for hung juries would decline accordingly.

Fourth, what has just been said about the presence of minority viewpoint as juries decrease in size foretells problems not only for jury decisionmaking, but also for the representation of minority groups in the

other words, if the average jury considered the average case 67.7% of the jurors would vote to convict.

20. With the average juror having a conviction propensity of .677, the average 12–member jury propensities ranged from .579 to .775. The average six-member jury propensities ranged from .530 to .830. Id., at 971–972.

21. Lempert 680.

22. Accord, Zeisel 718; Note, Case W.Res. 547.

23. Zeisel 720; accord Lempert 676. But see Saks 89–90.

24. Lempert 674–677; Zeisel 719.

25. Asch, Effects of Group Pressure upon the Modification and Distortion of Judgments in Group Dynamics Research and Theory, 189, 195–197 (2d ed., 1960), cited in Lempert 673.

26. Id., at 669, 677.

community. The Court repeatedly has held that meaningful community participation cannot be attained with the exclusion of minorities or other identifiable groups from jury service.

[A]lthough the Court in *Williams* concluded that the six-person jury did not fail to represent adequately a cross-section of the community, the opportunity for meaningful and appropriate representation does decrease with the size of the panels. Thus, if a minority group constitutes 10% of the community, 53.1% of randomly selected six-member juries could be expected to have no minority representative among their members, and 89% not to have two.[27] Further reduction in size will erect additional barriers to representation.

Fifth, several authors have identified in jury research methodological problems tending to mask differences in the operation of smaller and larger juries.[28] For example, because the judicial system handles so many clear cases, decisionmakers will reach similar results through similar analyses most of the time. One study concluded that smaller and larger juries could disagree in their verdicts in no more than 14% of the cases.[29] Disparities, therefore, appear in only small percentages. Nationwide, however, these small percentages will represent a large number of cases. And it is with respect to those cases that the jury trial right has its greatest value. When the case is close, and the guilt or innocence of the defendant is not readily apparent, a properly functioning jury system will insure evaluation by the sense of the community and will also tend to insure accurate factfinding.[30]

Studies that aggregate data also risk masking case-by-case differences in jury deliberations. The authors, H. Kalven and H. Zeisel, of The American Jury (1966), examined the judge-jury disagreement. They found that judges held for plaintiffs 57% of the time and that juries held for plaintiffs 59%, an insignificant difference. Yet case-by-case comparison revealed judge-jury disagreement in 22% of the cases. Id., at 63, cited in Lempert 656. This casts doubt on the conclusion of another study that compared the aggregate results of civil cases tried before 6–member juries

---

27. Ibid.; Saks 90.

28. Lempert 648–653; Nagel & Neef 934–937; Saks, Ignorance of Science Is No Excuse, supra n. 10, at 19; Zeisel & Diamond 283–291; Note, Case W.Res. 535.

29. Lempert 648–653.

30. Zeisel and Diamond have criticized one of the more important studies supporting smaller juries. See n. 34, infra. In Note, An Empirical Study of Six-and Twelve–Member Jury Decision–Making Processes, 6 U.Mich. J.L. Reform 712 (1973), the author tested the deliberations of larger and smaller panels by showing to sets of both sizes the video tape of a single mock civil trial. The case concerned an automobile accident and turned on whether the plaintiff had been speeding. If so, Michigan law precluded recovery because of contributory negligence. Of the 16 juries tested, not one found for the plaintiff. This led Zeisel and Diamond to conclude: "The evidence in the case overwhelmingly favored the defendant.... This overpowering bias makes the experiment irrelevant. On the facts of this case, any jury under any rules would probably have arrived at the same verdict. Hence, to conclude from this experiment that jury size generally has no effect on the verdict is impermissible." Zeisel & Diamond 287. See also Diamond, A Jury Experiment Reanalyzed, 7 U.Mich.J.L. Reform 520 (1974). The criticized study was cited and relied upon by the Court in Colgrove v. Battin, 413 U.S. 149, 159, n. 15, 93 S.Ct. 2448, 2454, 37 L.Ed.2d 522 (1973).

with those of 12–member jury trials.[31] The investigator in that study had claimed support for his hypothesis that damages awards did not vary with the reduction in jury size. Although some might say that figures in the aggregate may have supported this conclusion, a closer view of the cases reveals greater variation in the results of the smaller panels, i.e., a standard deviation of $58,335 for the 6–member juries, and of $24,834 for the 12–member juries.[32] Again, the averages masked significant case-by-case differences that must be considered when evaluating jury function and performance.

While we adhere to, and reaffirm our holding in *Williams v. Florida,* these studies, most of which have been made since *Williams* was decided in 1970, lead us to conclude that the purpose and functioning of the jury in a criminal trial is seriously impaired, and to a constitutional degree, by a reduction in size to below six members. We readily admit that we do not pretend to discern a clear line between six members and five. But the assembled data raise substantial doubt about the reliability and appropriate representation of panels smaller than six. Because of the fundamental importance of the jury trial to the American system of criminal justice, any further reduction that promotes inaccurate and possibly biased decision-making, that causes untoward differences in verdicts, and that prevents juries from truly representing their communities, attains constitutional significance.

[T]he empirical data cited by Georgia do not relieve our doubts. The State relies on the Saks study for the proposition that a decline in the number of jurors will not affect the aggregate number of convictions or hung juries. Tr. of Oral Arg. 27. This conclusion, however, is only one of several in the Saks study; that study eventually concludes:

> "Larger juries (size twelve) are preferable to smaller juries (six). They produce longer deliberations, more communication, far better community representation, and, possibly, greater verdict reliability (consistency)." Saks 107.

Far from relieving our concerns, then, the Saks study supports the conclusion that further reduction in jury size threatens Sixth and Fourteen Amendment interests.

Methodological problems prevent reliance on the three studies that do purport to bolster Georgia's position. The reliability of the two Michigan studies cited by the State has been criticized elsewhere.[34] The critical

---

31. See Note, Six–Member and Twelve–Member Juries: An Empirical Study of Trial Results, 6 U.Mich.J.L. Reform 671 (1973). This also was cited and relied upon in Colgrove v. Battin, 413 U.S., at 159 n. 15, 93 S.Ct. 2448, n. 15.

32. Zeisel & Diamond 289–290. These authors also criticized the Michigan study because it ignored two other important changes that had occurred when the size of

civil juries was decreased from 12 to 6 members: A mediation board, which encouraged settlements, had been introduced, and rules that permitted discovery of insurance policy limits had taken effect. See Saks 43.

34. Note, Six–Member and Twelve–Member Juries: An Empirical Study of Trial Results, 6 U.Mich.J.L. Reform 671 (1973) (a statistical study of actual jury results), and Note, An Empirical Study of Six-and Twelve-problem with the Michigan laboratory experiment, which used a mock civil trial, was the apparent clarity of the case. Not one of the juries found for the plaintiff in the tort suit; this masked any potential difference in the decisionmaking of larger and smaller panels. The results also have been doubted because in the experiment only students composed the juries, only 16 juries were tested, and only a video tape of the mock trial was presented.[35] The statistical review of the results of actual jury trials in Michigan erroneously aggregated outcomes. It is also said that it failed to take account of important changes of court procedure initiated at the time of the reduction in size from 12 to 6 members.[36] The Davis study, which employed a mock criminal trial for rape, also presented an extreme set of facts so that none of the panels rendered a guilty verdict.[37] None of these three reports, therefore, convinces us that a reduction in the number of jurors below six will not affect to a constitutional degree the functioning of juries in criminal trials.

With the reduction in the number of jurors below six creating a substantial threat to Sixth and Fourteenth Amendment guarantees, we must consider whether any interest of the State justifies the reduction. We find no significant state advantage in reducing the number of jurors from six to five.

The States utilize juries of less than 12 primarily for administrative reasons. Savings in court time and in financial costs are claimed to justify the reductions.[38] The financial benefits of the reduction from 12 to 6 are substantial; this is mainly because fewer jurors draw daily allowances as they hear cases.[39] On the other hand, the asserted saving in judicial time is not so clear. Pabst in his study found little reduction in the time for voir dire with the six-person jury because many questions were directed at the veniremen as a group.[40] Total trial time did not diminish, and court delays and backlogs improved very little. The point that is to be made, of course, is that a reduction in size from six to five or four or even three would save the

Member Jury Decision–Making Processes, 6 U.Mich.J.L. Reform 712 (1973) (a laboratory experiment using a mock trial), were both criticized in Saks 43–46, and in Zeisel & Diamond 286–290. The second study was criticized in Diamond, A Jury Experiment Reanalyzed, 7 U.Mich.J.L. Reform 520 (1974). The Michigan studies were advanced by the State at oral argument. Tr. of Oral Arg. 27.

35.   Saks 45.

36.   Id., at 43–44; Zeisel & Diamond 288–290.

37.   Davis, et al., supra n. 10, at 7, criticized in Saks 49–51.

38.   See New Jersey Criminal Law Revision Commission, Six–Member Juries (1971); Bogue & Fritz, The Six–Man Jury, 17 S.D.L.Rev. 285 (1972).

39.   It has been said that a reduction from 12 jurors to 6 throughout the federal system could save at least $4 million annually. Zeisel, Twelve is Just, 10 Trial 13 (Nov.–Dec. 1974). Another study calculated a saving in jury man-hours of 41.9% with the reduction to six members. Pabst, Statistical Studies of the Costs of Six–Man versus Twelve–Man Juries, 14 Wm. & Mary L.Rev. 326, 328 (1972).

40.   Id., at 327; Zeisel, Twelve is Just, supra. But see Institute of Judicial Administration, A Comparison of Six-and Twelve–Member Civil Juries in New Jersey Superior and County Courts 27–28 (1972); New Jersey Criminal Law Revision Commission, Six–Member Juries 3–4 (1971); Thompson, Six Will Do, 10 Trial 12, 14 (Nov.–Dec. 1974).

States little. They could reduce slightly the daily allowances, but with a reduction from six to five the saving would be minimal. If little time is gained by the reduction from 12 to 6, less will be gained with a reduction from 6 to 5. Perhaps this explains why only two States, Georgia and Virginia, have reduced the size of juries in certain nonpetty criminal cases to five. Other States appear content with six members or more. In short, the State has offered little or no justification for its reduction to five members.

Petitioner, therefore, has established that his trial on criminal charges before a five-member jury deprived him of the right to trial by jury guaranteed by the Sixth and Fourteenth Amendments.

■ Mr. Justice Powell, with whom The Chief Justice and Mr. Justice Rehnquist join, concurring in the judgment.

I concur in the judgment, as I agree that use of a jury as small as five members, with authority to convict for serious offenses, involves grave questions of fairness. As the opinion of Mr. Justice Blackmun indicates, the line between five-and six-member juries is difficult to justify, but a line has to be drawn somewhere if the substance of jury trial is to be preserved. [I] have reservations as to the wisdom—as well as the necessity—of Mr. Justice Blackmun's heavy reliance on numerology derived from statistical studies. Moreover, neither the validity nor the methodology employed by the studies cited was subjected to the traditional testing mechanisms of the adversary process. The studies relied on merely represent unexamined findings of persons interested in the jury system.

For these reasons I concur only in the judgment.

PEOPLE v. DISTRICT COURT

Supreme Court of Colorado, 1981.
634 P.2d 44.

Larry J. Dirgo was charged by information in the District Court of Boulder County with the offense of criminal mischief. [T]he case was set for a jury trial on May 14, 1981. On the day before the trial the defendant Dirgo moved the court for a trial to a jury of one person. His motion was based upon section 18–1–406(4), C.R.S. 1973 (1978 Repl. Vol. 8), which provides:

"(4) Except as to class 1 felonies, the defendant in any felony or misdemeanor case may, with the approval of the court, elect, at any time before verdict, to be tried by a number of jurors less than the number to which he would otherwise be entitled."

The statutorily prescribed jury to which one accused of a felony is entitled is a jury of twelve persons. Section 18–1–406(1), C.R.S.1973 (1978 Repl. Vol. 8). The district court, although expressing doubts about the wisdom of the procedure, concluded that the statute permitted a jury of one person and therefore the court granted Dirgo's motion. The district attorney sought relief from this order and we issued our rule to show cause.

It is fundamental that one accused of a felony is constitutionally entitled to a jury trial. It is also clear that the accused may waive his constitutional right to a jury.

The preliminary question for determination is whether under section 18–1–406(4) above set forth, one accused of a felony, other than a class 1 felony, may, with the approval of the court, elect to be tried by a number of jurors less than the number to which he would otherwise be entitled.

In Williams v. Florida, 399 U.S. 78, 90 S.Ct. 1893, 26 L.Ed.2d 446 (1970), the validity of a Florida statute was challenged, which provided for a jury of six in all criminal cases except capital cases where a jury of twelve was constitutionally mandated. The Supreme Court held as follows:

> "... then is whether the constitutional guarantee of a trial by 'jury' necessarily requires trial by exactly 12 persons, rather than some lesser number—in this case six. We hold that the 12–man panel is not a necessary ingredient of 'trial by jury,' and that respondent's refusal to impanel more than the six members provided for by Florida law did not violate petitioner's Sixth Amendment rights as applied to the States through the Fourteenth."

It is thus not constitutionally impermissible under the United States Constitution to impanel a jury of six rather than twelve to try a felony case other than a capital case.

We find no language in the Colorado Constitution which mandates that one accused of a felony may not elect to be tried by a jury numbering less than twelve persons. The enactment of the statute under consideration, section 18–1–406(4), is a recognition that public policy does not demand a jury of twelve in non-capital felony cases. Reinforced by the rationale of *Williams, supra,* we hold that one accused of a felony, other than a capital offense, may at his election, subject to the statutorily required approval of the court, be tried to a jury of less than twelve persons.

We next consider the validity of the trial court's determination that the defendant could be tried by a jury of one. We hold that the court's ruling was erroneous.

Initially, we observe that section 18–1–406(4) does not speak in terms of a single juror, but rather of a "number of *jurors* less than the number to which he would otherwise be entitled." (Emphasis added.) More importantly, the term "jury" connotes a deliberative body of persons. The word "jury" has been defined as:

> "A body of men sworn to give a verdict upon some matter submitted to them; ... a body of men selected according to law, impaneled and sworn to inquire into and try any matter of fact, and to give their verdict according to the evidence legally produced." Webster's Third New International Dictionary, 1966.

In *Williams,* supra, the Supreme Court speaking to the size of a jury stated:

> "... the essential feature of a jury obviously lies in the interposition between the accused and his accuser of the commonsense judgment of a *group of laymen,* and in the community participation and shared responsibility that results from that group's determination of guilt or innocence. The performance of this role is not a function of the particular number of the body that makes up the jury. To be sure, the number should probably be large enough to promote group deliberation, free from outside attempts at intimidation, and to provide a fair possibility for obtaining a representative cross-section of the community...." (Emphasis added.)

It is thus obvious that a jury may not be composed of a single person. If the accused desires a one person determination of his guilt or innocence, he may waive the jury and be tried by the court.

We are thus left with the question of what minimum number of persons may compose a constitutional jury in a non-capital felony case if a defendant elects under the statute to be tried by a jury of less than the number to which he is entitled. We are guided in our determination by the decision in Ballew v. Georgia, 435 U.S. 223, 98 S.Ct. 1029, 55 L.Ed.2d 234 (1978). In that case the petitioner was accused of a misdemeanor which under the Georgia statute was triable by a jury of five persons. He contended he was entitled to a jury of twelve. The Supreme Court held that a jury of less than six persons substantially threatens Sixth and Fourteenth Amendment guarantees and held that the Georgia statute was unconstitutional.

The essence of the Court's reasoning, as previously expounded in *Williams v. Florida,* supra, was that since the purpose of a jury trial is to prevent oppression by the government and to safeguard against corrupt and overzealous prosecution, that purpose could be attained by participation of the community in the determination of guilt and by the application of the common sense of laymen who as jurors consider the case. This function could only be served by a jury of sufficient size to promote group deliberation, to insulate the members of the jury from outside intimidation, and to provide a representative cross section of the community. The Supreme Court held in *Williams* that a jury of six could adequately perform that function and satisfy the underlying purposes of a jury.

In *Ballew,* supra, the Court had before it numerous empirical studies concerning the minimum size below which the number of jurors would not be able to function as required by the standards enunciated in *Williams,* *supra.* The Court in *Ballew* concluded as follows:

> "While we adhere to, and reaffirm our holding in *Williams v. Florida,* these studies, most of which have been made since *Williams* was decided in 1970, lead us to conclude that the purpose and functioning of the jury in a criminal trial is seriously impaired, and to a constitutional degree, by a reduction in size to below six members. We readily admit that we do not pretend to discern a clear line between six members and five. But the assembled data raise substantial doubt about the reliability and appropriate representation of panels smaller

than six. Because of the fundamental importance of the jury trial to the American system of criminal justice, any further reduction that promotes inaccurate and possibly biased decisionmaking, that causes untoward differences in verdicts, and that prevents juries from truly representing their communities, attains constitutional significance."

The defendant Dirgo in the present case is not asserting a denial of a constitutional jury. However, in our view, to allow Dirgo to elect to be tried by a jury of less than six persons would submit the issue of his guilt or innocence to a body of persons insufficient in number to function in accordance with the standards set forth in *Williams,* supra, and thus not qualify as a valid jury.

For the foregoing reasons we draw the line at six persons and hold that one accused of a non-capital felony who elects, pursuant to section 18–1–406(4), to be tried by a jury of less than twelve persons may not be tried by a jury of less than six persons. It follows that a jury of one as requested and ordered in this case is no jury at all.

OPINION OF THE JUSTICES

Supreme Court of New Hampshire, 1981.
121 N.H. 480, 431 A.2d 135.

The following request of the Senate for an opinion of the justices was adopted on May 27, 1981, and filed with the supreme court on June 3, 1981:

"Whereas, the Senate has under consideration HB 698 which reduces the number of persons serving on juries in civil cases from 12 to 6; and

"Whereas, some members of the Senate question the constitutionality of certain aspects of the proposed legislation;

"Now, therefore, be it

"Resolved by the Senate;

"That the Justices of the Supreme Court are respectfully requested to give their opinion and answer the following question:

"Do any provisions of HB 698 in the form as passed by the House of Representatives violate any provision of the United States Constitution or of the New Hampshire Constitution?"; and

"That the clerk of the Senate transmit copies of this resolution and HB 698 as passed by the House of Representatives, to the Justices of the Supreme Court."

The following answer was returned.

To the Honorable Senate:

The undersigned justices of the supreme court reply as follows to your request filed in this court on June 3, 1981.

We need not devote considerable discussion to your inquiry regarding the constitutionality of House bill 698 under the federal constitution. In passing, however, we note that the Justices of the Supreme Court of the United States have expressed divergent views in their individual opinions on the subject matter.

In Williams v. Florida, 399 U.S. 78, 90 S.Ct. 1893, 26 L.Ed.2d 446 (1970), the Supreme Court of the United States in considering a Sixth Amendment question sustained a Florida statute providing for the use of unanimous six-member juries in all but capital cases, holding that the twelve-member jury is not a necessary ingredient of a "trial by jury." In Colgrove v. Battin, 413 U.S. 149, 159–60, 93 S.Ct. 2448, 2454, 37 L.Ed.2d 522 (1973), the Supreme Court of the United States held that a *federal district court* procedural rule providing for six-member juries in civil cases did not violate the Seventh Amendment's guarantee of trial by jury in civil cases.

Since the *Williams,* supra and *Colgrove,* supra decisions, writings of legal scholars with empirical studies, leading to considerable debate regarding the impact of six-member juries, have been legion. For a listing of several of these articles, see Ballew v. Georgia, 435 U.S. 223, 231 n. 10, 98 S.Ct. 1029, 1034 n. 10, 55 L.Ed.2d 234 (1978). In *Ballew,* supra, the Supreme Court held that a jury of less than six in a criminal trial violated the Sixth and Fourteenth Amendments to the Constitution. When Justice Blackmun wrote the majority opinion in *Ballew,* he had the benefit of the post-*Williams* data, and he discussed several studies that suggested: "that progressively smaller juries are less likely to foster effective group deliberation," and that "[a]t some point, this decline leads to inaccurate fact-finding and incorrect application of the common sense of the community to the facts," 435 U.S. at 232, 98 S.Ct. at 1035; "that the risk of convicting an innocent person . . . rises as the size of the jury diminishes," id. at 234, 98 S.Ct. at 1036; that "[t]he chance for hung-juries would decline," id. at 236, 98 S.Ct. at 1037; and that "[f]urther reduction in size will erect additional barriers to [minority] representation," id. at 237, 98 S.Ct. at 1037. *See generally* Note, The Jury Size Question in Pennsylvania: Six of One and a Dozen of the Other, 53 Temple L.Q. 89, 90 n. 5–7 (1980) (discussing studies regarding these problems).

Although Justice Blackmun's majority opinion in *Ballew* expressed these concerns in the context of a decision regarding a further reduction of criminal trial juries from six to five, we note that these problems may also arise in the context of reducing the size of juries in civil cases from twelve to six.

Justice Marshall, in a footnote to his dissent in *Colgrove,* supra, noted that "the Seventh Amendment is one of the few remaining provisions in the Bill of Rights which has not been held to be applicable to the states" through the Fourteenth Amendment. 413 U.S. at 169 n. 4, 93 S.Ct. at 2459 n. 4. Accordingly, although House Bill 698 might pass muster under the federal constitution, the determination of its propriety falls squarely within this State's power to apply its own constitutional provisions regarding trial by jury. See First Nat'l Bank of Olathe v. Clark, 226 Kan. 619, 622, 602 P.2d 1299, 1302 (1979).

In 1859, the New Hampshire House of Representatives asked the justices of this court whether the legislature had the power to change the law to provide for petit juries numbering less than twelve. In responding to the House of Representatives this court stated:

> "We regard it as a well settled and unquestioned rule of construction that the language used by the legislature, in the statutes enacted by them, and that used by the people in the great paramount law which controls the legislature as well as the people, is to be always understood and explained *in that sense in which it was used at the time when the constitution and the laws were adopted.*"

Opinion of the Justices, 41 N.H. 550, 551 (1860). (Emphasis added.) The court examined the meaning of the terms "jury" and "trial by jury" at the time of the adoption of our constitution, concluding that:

> "[W]e are of opinion that no body of less than twelve men, though they should be by law denominated a jury, would be a jury within the meaning of the constitution; nor would a trial by such a body, though called a trial by jury, be such, within the meaning of that instrument. *We think, therefore, that the legislature have no power so to change the law in relation to juries, as to provide that petit juries may be composed of a less number than twelve,* nor to provide that a number of the petit jury, less than the whole number, can render a verdict...."

Id. at 552 (emphasis added); see Copp v. Henniker, 55 N.H. 179, 193 (1875). We reaffirm this decision, believing that the vitality of its conclusion remains today, especially in light of the number of empirical studies that have questioned the impact of the six-member jury on our court system. We therefore answer your question as it pertains to the New Hampshire Constitution, N.H. Const., Pt. I, Art. 20, in the affirmative.

GONZALEZ v. FLORIDA

Supreme Court of the United States, 2008.
129 S.Ct. 647.

Brief On Petition For Writ of Certiorari*

Amici Curiae are university professors whose teaching and scholarship have addressed historical, behavioral, and constitutional questions about jury size and jury performance. We urge the Court to grant certiorari in *Gonzalez v. Florida* on the question of whether the Sixth Amendment permits criminal juries smaller than twelve.

* Brief of Steven G. Calabresi, Shari S. Diamond, Phoebe C. Ellsworth, Samuel R. Gross, Valerie Hans, Saul Kassin, Stephan Landsman, Richard O. Lempert, Steven D. Penrod, Mary R. Rose, Michael J. Saks, and Neil Vidmar.

[T]he Functional Equivalence Test and its Application

When the *Williams* Court [399 U.S. 78 (1970)] concluded that twelve jurors were not required, it devised a test of the constitutionality of juries of varying sizes: To be constitutional a jury must perform as well as the twelve-person unanimous jury performed. [We refer to this test as *"functional equivalence."*]

[I]n the nearly unanimous view of scholars from various disciplines, the application of the functional equivalence test in *Williams* was deeply flawed. In 1970, the Court had little empirical research from which to draw in conducting its inherently empirical analysis. What little it had it misread or misinterpreted. [T]he most constitutionally significant error in *Williams* was the failure to realize that juries of six are substantially less likely than juries of twelve to contain even a single member of a minority group. For example, based on statistical sampling theory, a group which constitutes 10% of a population would, all else equal, be represented on 72% of twelve-person juries but on only 47% of six-person juries. The findings of many empirical studies have been in line with the statistical models. The most recent such study found that at least one member of a minority group (which constituted 25.8% of jurors remaining after challenges were completed) was seated on all but 2% of twelve-person juries, while 28% of six-person juries contained none of them at all.

[C]urrent Jurisprudence of Jury Size

Current jurisprudence governing the constitutionality of jury size is largely a void. Eight years after inventing the functional equivalence test, the Court tacitly abandoned it in *Ballew v. George*, 435 U.S. 223 (1978). In *Ballew* the court unanimously declared Georgia's five-person criminal juries to be below the constitutional minimum, but none of the four opinions in the case employed the functional equivalence test to reach that conclusion.

Justice Blackmum announced the judgment of the Court in an opinion joined only by Justice Stevens. That opinion reviewed at length numerous studies and commentaries which together showed that the factual conclusions in *Williams* were empirically and theoretically mistaken. Bafflingly, however, the opinion relied on those studies–comparing the performance of *six-person* juries to *twelve-person* juries–to conclude that *five-person* juries are unconstitutional.

[A]fter *Ballew*, there is no longer any coherent framework for analyzing constitutional jury-size questions. Not surprisingly, a split has developed among state courts. [S]ome state courts have found the dicta of the Court's jury-size opinions more illuminating than the holdings. Other states might adopt various jury sizes and, with no rational guidance from this Court on how to assess the federal constitutionality of those juries, confusions will multiply.

Conclusion

The jury-size cases weave together erroneous empirical factfinding with mistaken history, producing an incoherent statement of the law which should be troubling to legal theorists of various perspectives–originalists, empiricists, and doctrinalists alike. The amici urge the court to grant certiorari.

————

NOTE

1. Denial. The Supreme Court denied the above petition in Gonzalez v. Florida, ___ U.S. ___, 129 S.Ct. 647, 172 L.Ed.2d 627 (2008).

————

2.   DEATH–QUALIFIED JURIES

In many states, in cases in which the death penalty is a statutory option, juries render two verdicts in a "bifurcated" or split trial. The first verdict, after the "guilt phase" of the trial, is whether the defendant is guilty or not guilty (or not guilty by reason of insanity) of the crime charged or of a lesser crime. If the defendant is found guilty of the capital offense charged, the second verdict, after the "sentencing phase" of the trial, is whether the defendant should receive the death penalty or a prison sentence. The same jury renders both verdicts.

In all criminal cases, potential jurors are screened by the prosecutor, defense counsel, and the judge during a proceeding known as voir dire. Potential jurors can be eliminated "for cause" if the judge finds reason to believe that they may not be able to render a fair verdict, for example, if they are related to, or friends of, the defendant or the victim. (Each side also has a limited number of "peremptory" challenges by which it can strike a juror without giving any reason.)

In capital cases, an additional form of screening is employed in many states in which potential jurors are eliminated from both the guilt phase and the penalty phase—that is, from the entire trial—if they state during voir dire that they are so opposed to the death penalty that they will not consider voting for execution if the defendant is found guilty. This form of screening is known as "death-qualification."

————

WITHERSPOON v. ILLINOIS

Supreme Court of the United States, 1968.
391 U.S. 510, 88 S.Ct. 1770, 20 L.Ed.2d 776.

■ MR. JUSTICE STEWART delivered the opinion of the Court.

The petitioner was brought to trial in 1960 in Cook County, Illinois, upon a charge of murder. The jury found him guilty and fixed his penalty at death. At the time of his trial an Illinois statute provided:

"In trials for murder it shall be a cause for challenge of any juror who shall, on being examined, state that he has conscientious scruples against capital punishment, or that he is opposed to the same."

[T]he issue before us is a narrow one. It does not involve the right of the prosecution to challenge for cause those prospective jurors who state that their reservations about capital punishment would prevent them from making an impartial decision as to the defendant's guilt. Nor does it involve the State's assertion of a right to exclude from the jury in a capital case those who say that they could never vote to impose the death penalty or that they would refuse even to consider its imposition in the case before them. For the State of Illinois did not stop there, but authorized the prosecution to exclude as well all who said that they were opposed to capital punishment and all who indicated that they had conscientious scruples against inflicting it.

[T]he petitioner contends that a State cannot confer upon a jury selected in this manner the power to determine guilt. He maintains that such a jury, unlike one chosen at random from a cross-section of the community, must necessarily be biased in favor of conviction, for the kind of juror who would be unperturbed by the prospect of sending a man to his death, he contends, is the kind of juror who would too readily ignore the presumption of the defendant's innocence, accept the prosecution's version of the facts, and return a verdict of guilt. To support this view, the petitioner refers to what he describes as "competent scientific evidence that death-qualified jurors are partial to the prosecution on the issue of guilt or innocence."[10]

The data adduced by the petitioner, however, are too tentative and fragmentary to establish that jurors not opposed to the death penalty tend to favor the prosecution in the determination of guilt.[11] We simply cannot

---

10. In his brief, the petitioner cites two surveys, one involving 187 college students, W.C. Wilson, Belief in Capital Punishment and Jury Performance (Unpublished Manuscript, University of Texas, 1964), and the other involving 200 college students, F.J. Goldberg, Attitude Toward Capital Punishment and Behavior as a Juror in Simulated Capital Cases (Unpublished Manuscript, Morehouse College, undated). In his petition for certiorari, he cited a study based upon interviews with 1,248 jurors in New York and Chicago. A preliminary, unpublished summary of the results of that study stated that "a jury consisting only of jurors who have no scruples against the death penalty is likely to be more prosecution prone than a jury on which objectors to the death penalty sit," and that "the defendant's chances of acquittal are somewhat reduced if the objectors are excluded from the jury." H. Zeisel, Some Insights Into the Operation of Criminal Juries 42

(Confidential First Draft, University of Chicago, November 1957).

11. During the post-conviction proceedings here under review, the petitioner's counsel argued that the prosecution-prone character of "death-qualified" juries presented "purely a legal question," the resolution of which required "no additional proof" beyond "the facts ... disclosed by the transcript of the voir dire examination...." Counsel sought an "opportunity to submit evidence" in support of several contentions unrelated to the issue involved here. On this issue, however, no similar request was made, and the studies relied upon by the petitioner in this Court were not mentioned. We can only speculate, therefore, as to the precise meaning of the terms used in those studies, the accuracy of the techniques employed, and the validity of the generalizations made. Under these circumstances, it is not surprising that the *ami-*

conclude, either on the basis of the record now before us or as a matter of judicial notice, that the exclusion of jurors opposed to capital punishment results in an unrepresentative jury on the issue of guilt or substantially increases the risk of conviction. In light of the presently available information, we are not prepared to announce a *per se* constitutional rule requiring the reversal of every conviction returned by a jury selected as this one was.

It does not follow, however, that the petitioner is entitled to no relief. For in this case the jury was entrusted with two distinct responsibilities: first, to determine whether the petitioner was innocent or guilty; and second, if guilty, to determine whether his sentence should be imprisonment or death. It has not been shown that this jury was biased with respect to the petitioner's guilt. But it is self-evident that, in its role as arbiter of the punishment to be imposed, this jury fell woefully short of that impartiality to which the petitioner was entitled under the Sixth and Fourteenth Amendments.

If the State had excluded only those prospective jurors who stated in advance of trial that they would not even consider returning a verdict of death, it could argue that the resulting jury was simply "neutral" with respect to penalty. But when it swept from the jury all who expressed conscientious or religious scruples against capital punishment and all who opposed it in principle, the State crossed the line of neutrality. In its quest for a jury capable of imposing the death penalty, the State produced a jury uncommonly willing to condemn a man to die.

[S]pecifically, we hold that a sentence of death cannot be carried out if the jury that imposed or recommended it was chosen by excluding veniremen for cause simply because they voiced general objections to the death penalty or expressed conscientious or religious scruples against its infliction. No defendant can constitutionally be put to death at the hands of a tribunal so selected.

Whatever else might be said of capital punishment, it is at least clear that its imposition by a hanging jury cannot be squared with the Constitution. The State of Illinois has stacked the deck against the petitioner. To execute this death sentence would deprive him of his life without due process of law.

GRIGSBY v. MABRY

United States District Court, Eastern District of Arkansas, 1983.
569 F.Supp. 1273.

■ EISELE, CHIEF JUDGE.

Pending before the Court are the habeas corpus petitions of James T. Grigsby [a]nd Ardia McCree, who have been in the custody of the Arkansas

cus curiae brief filed by the NAACP Legal Defense and Educational Fund finds it necessary to observe that, with respect to bias in favor of the prosecution on the issue of guilt, the record in this case is "almost totally lacking in the sort of factual information that would assist the Court."

Department of Correction since their convictions for capital murder. Each petitioner contends that his conviction must be set aside due to the exclusion for cause at the guilt determination phase of his trial of certain venirepersons who during *voir dire* professed adamant scruples against the death penalty.

[A]s a result of *Witherspoon* both those who are able to make an impartial decision on the defendant's guilt and those who are not are excluded from participating in that decision if they, on *voir dire,* express adamant opposition to the death penalty, i.e., if they would, at any later sentencing phase, "automatically" vote against the death penalty without regard to the evidence in the case. Jurors possessing such strong scruples against the death penalty are referred to as "*Witherspoon* Excludables" or "WEs." [T]he petitioner in *Witherspoon* attempted to persuade the Supreme Court on the basis of logic and intuition that those persons who expressed attitudes in favor of the death penalty would, as jurors, "favor the prosecution in the determination of guilt." [T]he petitioner in *Witherspoon* expressly declined the "opportunity to submit evidence" on the guilt-proneness issue. It is true that at the appellate level the petitioner asked the Supreme Court to judicially notice summaries of some early social scientific research. [T]he Supreme Court found this data "too tentative and fragmentary to establish that jurors not opposed to the death penalty tend to favor the prosecution in the determination of guilt." Indeed, those data were very "tentative and fragmentary."

[T]he Supreme Court noted in *Witherspoon* that the items which it was asked to judicially notice had not been introduced into evidence or subjected to the fact-finding process. Therefore, the Court was left to: "... speculate ... as to the precise meaning of the terms used in the studies, the accuracy of the techniques employed and the validity of the generalizations made." Id. at 517 n. 11, 88 S.Ct. at 1774 n. 11. The Court ultimately refused to find, based upon the record or judicial notice, "that the exclusion of jurors opposed to capital punishment results in an unrepresentative jury on the issue of guilt...." Id. at 517–18, 88 S.Ct. at 1774–75. By this determination the Supreme Court refused to adopt a *per se* guilt phase rule. Instead, it invited further study, leaving it open for future defendants to attempt to prove that juries death-qualified by *Witherspoon* standards were "less than neutral with respect to guilt." See id. at 518, 88 S.Ct. at 1775.

The petitioners in the case at bar have responded to the Supreme Court's invitation with a plethora of well-documented scientific research that does not suffer from the numerous deficiencies attributed to the research in *Witherspoon*.

[After Witherspoon, these] questions remained: (1) Are there among those in the group adamantly opposed to the death penalty (the WEs) persons who could fairly and impartially try the guilt/innocence issue if they did not have to participate in the sentencing phase, and (2), if so, does the exclusion of such persons deprive the defendant at the guilt phase of a representative jury, or result in a jury that is more prone to convict than would be a jury from which such persons were not excluded?

The term "nullifier" is used to describe a prospective juror who states that he would be unable to try the issue of the defendant's guilt/innocence upon the basis of the evidence and the law. In the death-penalty context this is the person who would say, "I cannot vote a defendant guilty regardless of the evidence if I know that, should he be convicted, someone else [the court or some other jury] might impose the death penalty." These nullifiers are described in *Witherspoon* as those persons who make it unmistakably clear that their attitude toward the death penalty "would prevent them from making an impartial decision as to the defendant's guilt." See 391 U.S. at 513, 88 S.Ct. at 1772. It is, of course, agreed by all that "nullifiers" are properly excluded from both the guilt/innocence phase and the sentencing phase of a capital case. But it is urged that no proper reason exists for the exclusion of the impartial WEs at the guilt/innocence phase. For this reason they are sometimes referred to as "Guilt–Phase Includables."

Using this terminology all *"Witherspoon* Excludables" (WEs) may be divided into "Nullifiers" and "Guilt Phase Includables."

This court must decide on the basis of the evidence presented if there are differences, material to jury performance, between those qualified to serve under *Witherspoon* standards and those who are excluded by such standards.

[Research on this topic has been] undertaken by Dr. Phoebe Ellsworth and her colleagues Dr. Joan C. Harrington, Dr. William Thompson, Dr. Claudia Cowan and Raymond M. Bukaty in 1979. The studies were designed to replicate the results of earlier studies using more sophisticated experimental and control techniques and to attempt to gain some insight into the reasons that death-qualified jurors might be more conviction prone than non-death qualified jurors who could fairly try the issue of guilt-innocence in capital trials.

The transcript of Dr. Ellsworth's testimony in the *Hovey* case [Hovey v. Superior Court, 28 Cal.3d 1, 168 Cal.Rptr. 128, 616 P.2d 1301 (1980)] was received in evidence here. Dr. Haney relied upon that transcript together with the studies themselves for the purpose of explaining the full thrust and effect of those studies. It will be recalled that the California Supreme Court found Dr. Ellsworth's work very persuasive.

The subjects of the five *Ellsworth* studies were all drawn from the same panel of 288 adult, jury-eligible citizens in Santa Clara and San Mateo counties in California. They were recruited by using a jury list from the local court and by advertising for volunteers. Forty-five percent had prior jury service. Each subject was read an introductory statement and was asked to assume that he or she was a prospective juror in a criminal case being questioned by a judge. The statement explained the bifurcated process by which capital trials are presently conducted in this country. Each was then asked the following question:

Which of the following expresses what you would do if you were a juror for the first (guilt/innocence) part of the trial?

a. I would follow the judge's instructions and decide the question of guilt or innocence in a fair and impartial manner based on the evidence and the law or

b. I would not be fair and impartial in deciding the question of guilt or innocence, knowing that if the person was convicted he or she might get the death penalty.

Those who chose (b) were then excluded from participation in any of the studies. This eliminated the "nullifiers," leaving only those who could sit as impartial jurors at the guilt-innocence phase of capital trials.

The subjects were also inquired of as follows:

The judge will ask you this question:

Is your attitude toward the death penalty such that as a juror you would never be willing to impose it in any case, no matter what the evidence was or would you consider voting to impose it in at least some cases?

a. I would be unwilling to impose it in any case.

b. I would consider voting to impose it in some cases.

The answers identified the *Witherspoon* Excludables, or, more precisely, the "Guilt Phase Includables" (since the nullifiers had already been removed) on the one hand and identified those who were death-qualified on the other hand. With this information Dr. Ellsworth and her colleagues were able to compare the voting behavior of the subjects in all five studies. The final sample was composed of 258 death-qualified subjects and 30 WEs.

The *Ellsworth* studies did not use random sampling techniques. In fact they often restricted the number of WEs so that, in the deliberation studies, simulated juries could be composed of differing percentages of WEs, i.e., so that such 12–person juries could have 0, 1, 2, 3 or 4, but not more than 4 WEs.

Since random techniques were not employed no claim is made that it is possible to generalize from the numbers of WEs and death-qualified in the subject pool to the population at large.

In the *Ellsworth Conviction Proneness Study 1979*, [t]he stimulus used was a 2–hour videotape re-enactment of an actual murder trial in Massachusetts. It was prepared by Dr. Hastie for use in his own work and was loaned to Dr. Ellsworth for her study. She revised it somewhat and substituted California jury instructions. The tape included opening statements, the direct and cross-examination of seven witnesses, closing arguments and one-half hour of jury instructions. It was filmed in a Massachusetts courtroom using a judge, a prosecutor and a defense attorney to portray those same roles in the film. Probably no simulation, even of an actual trial, will be completely satisfactory to an experienced judge or lawyer. But the Court finds this videotape to be a high quality and realistic stimulus. The tape is in evidence in its entirety.

After viewing the videotape each subject was asked to vote for one of four verdicts: (1) guilty of first degree murder, (2) guilty of second degree murder, (3) guilty of voluntary manslaughter, or (4) not guilty by reason of self-defense or excusable homicide. The results were as follows:

ELLSWORTH CONVICTION-PRONENESS STUDY

DISTRIBUTION OF INITIAL VERDICTS
(BY DEATH-QUALIFIED/EXCLUDABLE)

It will be seen that most voted for manslaughter or acquittal. Few voted for first or second degree murder. Among these there were no significant differences but when the manslaughter and not guilty votes are considered the typical pattern emerges. About half of the death-qualified jurors voted to convict of manslaughter while only approximately one-fourth of the *Witherspoon* excludables so voted. Put another way 46.7% of WEs voted to acquit as compared with 22.1% of the death-qualified.

Considering only guilty and not guilty votes this study shows a 25% greater guilty vote by death-qualified subjects compared to WEs (77.9% versus 53.3%). Note the following graph:

ELLSWORTH CONVICTION-PRONENESS STUDY
PERCENT VOTING GUILTY
(BY DEATH-QUALIFIED/EXCLUDABLE)

Dr. Ellsworth then proceeded to determine the effect that systematic exclusion of WEs would have on the number of not guilty votes in a case such as that portrayed. She assumed that 17.2% of the jury eligible population would be made up of WEs. The Court finds this to have been a valid assumption based upon the attitudinal surveys. She then determined that such systematic exclusion would result in 31% fewer initial votes to acquit. Using the accepted and familiar method of multiple regression (so frequently used in racial discrimination cases), Dr. Ellsworth excluded other possibly relevant factors that might arguably account for such differences, e.g., age, gender, area of residence, or prior jury experience. This study provides strong evidence for the opinion, so often expressed by petitioners' experts, that death penalty attitudes are a far better predictor of juror voting behavior than any other single characteristic.

The results of this study are significant and demonstrate that persons who are death-qualified by *Witherspoon* standards are substantially more likely to vote to acquit than are persons excluded by those standards.* This study marks the culmination of some fifteen years of research demonstrating the divergent juror voting propensities of death-qualified versus excludable jurors.

* [Ed. Note: There appears to be a typographical error in this sentence. Either "death-qualified" should be "disqualified," or "acquit" should be "convict."]

Can the behavior of *juries* be predicted from the results of studies revealing the attitudes and voting behavior of individual *jurors*? Dr. Hastie answers this in the affirmative, basing his opinion in part upon the findings of Hans Zeisel and Harry Kalven in *The American Jury* [(1966)]. One of those findings, based upon extensive empirical investigation, is that the first ballot preferences of a majority of jurors in a given case is the single most accurately predictive factor in determining the final verdict outcome by that jury. Since first ballots are frequently taken prior to any extensive jury deliberations, the attitudes which each juror brings to the jury room turn out to be very important in explaining the differences that surface upon the initial ballot. The evidence shows that there is a strong propensity for *initial majority* verdicts to be the same as the *final unanimous* verdict. Therefore, studies of individual juror attitudes provide reliable information about final jury verdicts.

Dr. Hastie's own studies also support his opinion. His research shows that "initial faction size" constitutes the best predictive factor in determining final verdict outcomes, i.e., the verdict initially selected by the largest faction will most likely become the jury's final verdict. So the extent of initial agreement, prior to jury deliberation, is most often decisive of the final outcome.

The Court finds that the systematic exclusion of WEs from capital juries will reduce the number of cases with an initial majority, or largest faction, in favor of acquittal or in favor of a lesser included offense and will thereby substantially lessen the likelihood of acquittal and the likelihood of a vote of guilty to a lesser-included offense when the final unanimous jury verdict comes in.

[T]he phrase "fireside induction" has been used to refer to "those common sense empirical generalizations about human behavior which derive from introspection, anecdotal evidence, and culturally transmitted beliefs."[14]

[H]ere the fireside inductions clearly support the contentions of petitioners. If asked, "Does the removal of all prospective jurors with adamant objections to the death penalty result in a jury more prone to convict?" Trial lawyers and judges will answer, "yes, of course." If asked, "Does the usual process of death qualification itself, as observed time and again, prejudice the defendant?" The answer, "yes, clearly."

Yet it is always possible that our dearly held "fireside induction" may be proved to have been in error, to be nothing more than professional superstition. And the U.S. Supreme Court in *Witherspoon* itself counsels against embracing *per se* rules based upon judicial notice or intuition without the benefit of empirical studies.

The research has been done. The studies have been introduced into evidence and explained. What do they show? They prove that what we

---

14. Meehl, Law and Fireside Inductions: Some Reflections of a Clinical Psychol-ogist, in Law Justice and the Individual in Society (J. Tapp & F. Levine Eds.1977).

"knew" all along is in fact true. The trial lawyers and judges could have been wrong but in this case at least they were right.

[M]r. Grigsby is now deceased. The Court will therefore set aside the conviction of Mr. McCree only and direct the respondent, within 90 days, to retry him or to set him free.

LOCKHART v. McCREE

Supreme Court of the United States, 1986.
476 U.S. 162, 106 S.Ct. 1758, 90 L.Ed.2d 137.

■ JUSTICE REHNQUIST delivered the opinion of the Court.

In this case we address the question left open by our decision nearly 18 years ago in Witherspoon v. Illinois, 391 U.S. 510, 88 S.Ct. 1770, 20 L.Ed.2d 776 (1968): Does the Constitution prohibit the removal for cause, prior to the guilt phase of a bifurcated capital trial, of prospective jurors whose opposition to the death penalty is so strong that it would prevent or substantially impair the performance of their duties as jurors at the sentencing phase of the trial? We hold that it does not.

[T]he District Court held a hearing on the "death qualification" issue in July 1981, receiving in evidence numerous social science studies concerning the attitudes and beliefs of "*Witherspoon*-excludables," along with the potential effects of excluding them from the jury prior to the guilt phase of a bifurcated capital trial. In August 1983, the court concluded, based on the social science evidence, that "death qualification" produced juries that "were more prone to convict" capital defendants than "non-death-qualified" juries. Grigsby v. Mabry, 569 F.Supp., at 1323. The court ruled that "death qualification" thus violated both the fair cross-section and impartiality requirements of the Sixth and Fourteenth Amendments, and granted McCree habeas relief.

The Eighth Circuit found "substantial evidentiary support" for the District Court's conclusion that the removal for cause of "*Witherspoon*-excludables" resulted in "conviction-prone" juries, and affirmed the grant of habeas relief on the ground that such removal for cause violated McCree's constitutional right to a jury selected from a fair cross-section of the community. Grigsby v. Mabry, 758 F.2d, at 229.

[B]efore turning to the legal issues in the case, we are constrained to point out what we believe to be several serious flaws in the evidence upon which the courts below reached the conclusion that "death qualification" produces "conviction-prone" juries.[3] McCree introduced into evidence some

---

3. McCree argues that the "factual" findings of the District Court and the Eighth Circuit on the effects of "death qualification" may be reviewed by this Court only under the "clearly erroneous" standard of Federal Rule of Civil Procedure 52(a). Because we do not ultimately base our decision today on the invalidity of the lower courts' "factual" findings, we need not decide the "standard of review" issue. We are far from persuaded, fifteen social science studies in support of his constitutional claims, but only six of the studies even purported to measure the potential effects on the guilt-innocence determination of the removal from the jury of *"Witherspoon*-excludables."[4] Eight of the remaining nine studies dealt solely with generalized attitudes and beliefs about the death penalty and other aspects of the criminal justice system, and were thus, at best, only marginally relevant to the constitutionality of McCree's conviction.[5] The fifteenth and final study dealt with the effects on prospective jurors of *voir dire* questioning about their attitudes toward the death penalty,[6] an issue McCree raised in his brief to this Court but that counsel for McCree admitted at oral argument would not, standing alone, give rise to a constitutional violation.[7]

however, that the "clearly erroneous" standard of Rule 52(a) applies to the kind of "legislative" facts at issue here. See generally Dunagin v. City of Oxford, Mississippi, 718 F.2d 738, 748, n. 8 (C.A.5 1983) (en banc) (plurality opinion of Reavley, J.). The difficulty with applying such a standard to "legislative" facts is evidenced here by the fact that at least one other Court of Appeals, reviewing the same social science studies as introduced by McCree, has reached a conclusion contrary to that of the Eighth Circuit. See Keeten v. Garrison, 742 F.2d 129, 133, n. 7 (C.A.4 1984) (disagreeing that studies show relationship between generalized attitudes and behavior as jurors), cert. pending, No. 84—187.

4. The Court of Appeals described the following studies as "conviction-proneness surveys": H. Zeisel, Some Data on Juror Attitudes Toward Capital Punishment (University of Chicago Monograph 1968) (Zeisel); W. Wilson, Belief in Capital Punishment and Jury Performance (unpublished manuscript, University of Texas, 1964) (Wilson); Goldberg, Toward Expansion of *Witherspoon*: Capital Scruples, Jury Bias, and Use of Psychological Data to Raise Presumptions in the Law, 5 Harv.Civ.Rights–Civ.Lib.L.Rev. 53 (1970) (Goldberg); Jurow, New Data on the Effect of a "Death Qualified" Jury on the Guilt Determination Process, 84 Harv.L.Rev. 567 (1971) (Jurow); and Cowan, Thompson, & Ellsworth, The Effects of Death Qualification on Jurors' Predisposition to Convict and on the Quality of Deliberation, 8 Law & Hum.Behav. 53 (1984) (Cowan–Deliberation). In addition, McCree introduced evidence on this issue from a Harris Survey conducted in 1971. Louis Harris & Associates, Inc., Study No. 2016 (1971) (Harris–1971).

5. The Court of Appeals described the following studies as "attitudinal and demographic surveys": Bronson, On the Conviction Proneness and Representativeness of the Death–Qualified Jury: An Empirical Study of Colorado Veniremen, 42 U.Colo.L.Rev. 1 (1970); Bronson, Does the Exclusion of Scrupled Jurors in Capital Cases Make the Jury More Likely to Convict? Some Evidence from California, 3 Woodrow Wilson L.J. 11 (1980); Fitzgerald & Ellsworth, Due Process vs. Crime Control: Death Qualification and Jury Attitudes, 8 Law & Hum.Behav. 31 (1984); and Precision Research, Inc., Survey No. 1286 (1981). In addition, McCree introduced evidence on these issues from Thompson, Cowan, Ellsworth, & Harrington, Death Penalty Attitudes and Conviction Proneness, 8 Law & Hum.Behav. 95 (1984); Ellsworth, Bukaty, Cowan, & Thompson, The Death–Qualified Jury and the Defense of Insanity, 8 Law & Hum.Behav. 81 (1984); A. Young, Arkansas Archival Study (unpublished, 1981); and various Harris, Gallup, and National Opinion Research Center polls conducted between 1953 and 1981.

6. McCree introduced evidence on this issue from Haney, On the Selection of Capital Juries: The Biasing Effects of the Death–Qualification Process, 8 Law & Hum.Behav. 121 (1984).

7. We would in any event reject the argument that the very process of questioning prospective jurors at *voir dire* about their views of the death penalty violates the Constitution. McCree concedes that the State may challenge for cause prospective jurors whose opposition to the death penalty is so strong that it would prevent them from impartially determining a capital defendant's guilt or innocence. *Ipso facto,* the State must be given the opportunity to identify such prospective jurors by questioning them at *voir dire* about their views of the death penalty.

Of the six studies introduced by McCree that at least purported to deal with the central issue in this case, namely, the potential effects on the determination of guilt or innocence of excluding *"Witherspoon*-excludables" from the jury, three were also before this Court when it decided *Witherspoon, supra.*[8] There, this Court reviewed the studies and concluded:

"The data adduced by the petitioner . . . are too tentative and fragmentary to establish that jurors not opposed to the death penalty tend to favor the prosecution in the determination of guilt. We simply cannot conclude, either on the basis of the record now before us or as a matter of judicial notice, that the exclusion of jurors opposed to capital punishment results in an unrepresentative jury on the issue of guilt or substantially increases the risk of conviction. In light of the presently available information, we are not prepared to announce a *per se* constitutional rule requiring the reversal of every conviction returned by a jury selected as this one was." Id., at 517–518, 88 S.Ct., at 1774–75 (footnote omitted).

It goes almost without saying that if these studies were "too tentative and fragmentary" to make out a claim of constitutional error in 1968, the same studies, unchanged but for having aged some eighteen years, are still insufficient to make out such a claim in this case.

Nor do the three post-*Witherspoon* studies introduced by McCree on the "death qualification" issue provide substantial support for the *"per se* constitutional rule"* McCree asks this Court to adopt. All three of the "new" studies were based on the responses of individuals randomly selected from some segment of the population, but who were not actual jurors sworn under oath to apply the law to the facts of an actual case involving the fate of an actual capital defendant.[9] We have serious doubts about the value of these studies in predicting the behavior of actual jurors. In addition, two of the three "new" studies did not even attempt to simulate the process of jury deliberation,[10] and none of the "new" studies was able to predict to what extent, if any, the presence of one or more *"Witherspoon*-excludables" on a guilt-phase jury would have altered the outcome of the guilt determination.[11]

---

8. The petitioner in *Witherspoon* cited the Wilson and Goldberg studies, and a prepublication draft of the Zeisel study.

9. The Harris–1971 study polled 2,068 adults from throughout the United States, the Cowan–Deliberation study involved 288 jury-eligible residents of San Mateo and Santa Clara Counties in California, and the Jurow study was based on the responses of 211 employees of the Sperry Rand Corporation in New York.

10. The Harris–1971 and Jurow studies did not allow for group deliberation, but rather measured only individual responses.

11. Justice Marshall's dissent refers to an "essential unanimity" of support among social-science researchers and other academics for McCree's assertion that "death qualification" has a significant effect on the outcome of jury deliberations at the guilt phase of capital trials. See post, at 6. At least one of the articles relied upon by the dissent candidly acknowledges, however, that its conclusions ultimately must rest on "[a] certain amount of . . . conjecture" and a willingness "to transform behavioral suspicions into doctrine." Finch & Ferraro, The Empirical Challenge to Death Qualified Juries: On Further

Finally, and most importantly, only one of the six "death qualification" studies introduced by McCree even attempted to identify and account for the presence of so-called "nullifiers," or individuals who, because of their deep-seated opposition to the death penalty, would be unable to decide a capital defendant's guilt or innocence fairly and impartially.[12] McCree concedes, as he must, that "nullifiers" may properly be excluded from the guilt-phase jury, and studies that fail to take into account the presence of such "nullifiers" thus are fatally flawed.[13] Surely a *"per se* constitutional rule" as far-reaching as the one McCree proposes should not be based on the results of the lone study that avoids this fundamental flaw.

Having identified some of the more serious problems with McCree's studies, however, we will assume for purposes of this opinion that the studies are both methodologically valid and adequate to establish that "death qualification" in fact produces juries somewhat more "conviction-prone" than "non-death-qualified" juries. We hold, nonetheless, that the Constitution does not prohibit the States from "death qualifying" juries in capital cases.

The Eighth Circuit ruled that "death qualification" violated McCree's right under the Sixth Amendment, as applied to the States via incorporation through the Fourteenth Amendment, to a jury selected from a representative cross-section of the community. But we do not believe that the fair cross-section requirement can, or should, be applied as broadly as that court attempted to apply it. We have never invoked the fair cross-section principle to invalidate the use of either for-cause or peremptory challenges to prospective jurors, or to require petit juries, as opposed to jury panels or venires, to reflect the composition of the community at large.

[B]ut even if we were willing to extend the fair cross-section requirement to petit juries, we would still reject the Eighth Circuit's conclusion that "death qualification" violates that requirement. The essence of a "fair cross-section" claim is the systematic exclusion of "a 'distinctive' group in the community." [Duren v. Missouri] 439 U.S., at 364, 99 S.Ct., at 668. In our view, groups defined solely in terms of shared attitudes that would prevent or substantially impair members of the group from performing one

Examination, 65 Neb.L.Rev. 21, 67 (1986). As the authors of the article explain:

"[U]ncertainty inheres in every aspect of the capital jury's operation, whether one focuses on the method of identifying excludables or the deliberative process through which verdicts are reached. So it is that, some seventeen years after *Witherspoon,* no definitive conclusions can be stated as to the frequency or the magnitude of the effects of death qualification.

* * *

"Nor is it likely that further empirical research can add significantly to the current understanding of death qualification. The true magnitude of the phenomenon of conviction proneness is probably unmeasurable, given the complexity of capital cases and capital adjudication." Id., at 66–67.

12. Only the Cowan–Deliberation study attempted to take into account the presence of "nullifiers."

13. The effect of this flaw on the outcome of a particular study is likely to be significant. The Cowan–Deliberation study revealed that approximately 37% of the *"Witherspoon*-excludables" identified in the study were also "nullifiers."

of their duties as jurors, such as the "*Witherspoon*-excludables" at issue here, are not "distinctive groups" for fair cross-section purposes.

[T]he group of "*Witherspoon*-excludables" involved in the case at bar differs significantly from the groups we have previously recognized as "distinctive." "Death qualification," unlike the wholesale exclusion of blacks, women, or Mexican–Americans from jury service, is carefully designed to serve the State's concededly legitimate interest in obtaining a single jury that can properly and impartially apply the law to the facts of the case at both the guilt and sentencing phases of a capital trial. There is very little danger, therefore, and McCree does not even argue, that "death qualification" was instituted as a means for the State to arbitrarily skew the composition of capital-case juries.

Furthermore, unlike blacks, women, and Mexican–Americans, "*Witherspoon*-excludables" are singled out for exclusion in capital cases on the basis of an attribute that is within the individual's control. It is important to remember that not all who oppose the death penalty are subject to removal for cause in capital cases; those who firmly believe that the death penalty is unjust may nevertheless serve as jurors in capital cases so long as they state clearly that they are willing to temporarily set aside their own beliefs in deference to the rule of law. Because the group of "*Witherspoon*-excludables" includes only those who cannot and will not conscientiously obey the law with respect to one of the issues in a capital case, "death qualification" hardly can be said to create an "appearance of unfairness."

Finally, the removal for cause of "*Witherspoon*-excludables" in capital cases does not prevent them from serving as jurors in other criminal cases, and thus leads to no substantial deprivation of their basic rights of citizenship. They are treated no differently than any juror who expresses the view that he would be unable to follow the law in a particular case.

In sum, "*Witherspoon*-excludables," or for that matter any other group defined solely in terms of shared attitudes that render members of the group unable to serve as jurors in a particular case, may be excluded from jury service without contravening any of the basic objectives of the fair cross-section requirement. It is for this reason that we conclude that "*Witherspoon*-excludables" do not constitute a "distinctive group" for fair cross-section purposes, and hold that "death qualification" does not violate the fair cross-section requirement.

McCree argues that, even if we reject the Eighth Circuit's fair cross-section holding, we should affirm the judgment below on the alternative ground, adopted by the District Court, that "death qualification" violated his constitutional right to an impartial jury. McCree concedes that the individual jurors who served at his trial were impartial, as that term was defined by this Court in cases such as Irvin v. Dowd, 366 U.S. 717, 723, 81 S.Ct. 1639, 1643, 6 L.Ed.2d 751 (1961) ("It is sufficient if the juror can lay aside his impression or opinion and render a verdict based on the evidence presented in court"), [I]nstead, McCree argues that his jury lacked impartiality because the absence of "*Witherspoon*-excludables" "slanted" the jury in favor of conviction.

We do not agree. McCree's "impartiality" argument apparently is based on the theory that, because all individual jurors are to some extent predisposed towards one result or another, a constitutionally impartial *jury* can be constructed only by "balancing" the various predispositions of the individual *jurors*. Thus, according to McCree, when the State "tips the scales" by excluding prospective jurors with a particular viewpoint, an impermissibly partial jury results. We have consistently rejected this view of jury impartiality, including as recently as last Term when we squarely held that an impartial *jury* consists of nothing more than "*jurors* who will conscientiously apply the law and find the facts." Wainwright v. Witt, 469 U.S. 412, 423, 105 S.Ct. 844, 852, 83 L.Ed.2d 841 (1985) (emphasis added).

The view of jury impartiality urged upon us by McCree is both illogical and hopelessly impractical. McCree characterizes the jury that convicted him as "slanted" by the process of "death qualification." But McCree admits that exactly the same twelve individuals could have ended up on his jury through the "luck of the draw," without in any way violating the constitutional guarantee of impartiality. Even accepting McCree's position that we should focus on the *jury* rather than the individual *jurors,* it is hard for us to understand the logic of the argument that a given jury is unconstitutionally partial when it results from a State-ordained process, yet impartial when exactly the same jury results from mere chance. On a more practical level, if it were true that the Constitution required a certain mix of individual viewpoints on the jury, then trial judges would be required to undertake the Sisyphean task of "balancing" juries, making sure that each contains the proper number of Democrats and Republicans, young persons and old persons, white-collar executives and blue-collar laborers, and so on. Adopting McCree's concept of jury impartiality would also likely require the elimination of peremptory challenges, which are commonly used by both the State and the defendant to attempt to produce a jury favorable to the challenger.

[I]n our view, it is simply not possible to define jury impartiality, for constitutional purposes, by reference to some hypothetical mix of individual viewpoints. Prospective jurors come from many different backgrounds, and have many different attitudes and predispositions. But the Constitution presupposes that a jury selected from a fair cross-section of the community is impartial, regardless of the mix of individual viewpoints actually represented on the jury, so long as the jurors can conscientiously and properly carry out their sworn duty to apply the law to the facts of the particular case. We hold that McCree's jury satisfied both aspects of this constitutional standard. The judgment of the Court of Appeals is therefore

Reversed.

■ Justice Marshall, with whom Justice Brennan and Justice Stevens join, dissenting.

With a glib nonchalance ill-suited to the gravity of the issue presented and the power of respondent's claims, the Court upholds a practice that allows the State a special advantage in those prosecutions where the charges are the most serious and the possible punishments, the most severe. The State's mere announcement that it intends to seek the death penalty if the defendant is found guilty of a capital offense will, under today's decision, give the prosecution license to empanel a jury especially likely to return that very verdict. Because I believe that such a blatant disregard for the rights of a capital defendant offends logic, fairness, and the Constitution, I dissent.

[I]n the wake of *Witherspoon,* a number of researchers set out to supplement the data that the Court had found inadequate in that case. The results of these studies were exhaustively analyzed by the District Court in this case, see Grigsby v. Mabry (*Grigsby II*), 569 F.Supp. 1273, 1291–1308 (E.D.Ark.1983), and can be only briefly summarized here.[2] The data strongly suggest that death qualification excludes a significantly large subset—at least 11% to 17%—of potential jurors who could be impartial during the guilt phase of trial.[3] Among the members of this excludable class are a disproportionate number of blacks and women.

The perspectives on the criminal justice system of jurors who survive death qualification are systematically different from those of the excluded jurors. Death-qualified jurors are, for example, more likely to believe that a defendant's failure to testify is indicative of his guilt, more hostile to the insanity defense, more mistrustful of defense attorneys, and less concerned about the danger of erroneous convictions. This pro-prosecution bias is reflected in the greater readiness of death-qualified jurors to convict or to convict on more serious charges. And, finally, the very process of death qualification—which focuses attention on the death penalty before the trial has even begun—has been found to predispose the jurors that survive it to believe that the defendant is guilty.

2. Most of the studies presented here were also comprehensively summarized in Hovey v. Superior Court [28 Cal.3d 1, 168 Cal.Rptr. 128, 616 P.2d 1301 (1980)]. Because the California Supreme Court found the studies had not accounted for jurors who could be excluded because they would automatically vote for the death penalty where possible, that court ultimately rejected a defendant's constitutional challenge to death qualification. But see Kadane, After *Hovey:* A Note on Taking Account of the Automatic Death Penalty Jurors, 8 Law & Hum.Behav. 115 (1984).

3. Bronson, On the Conviction Proneness and Representativeness of the Death-Qualified Jury: An Empirical Study of Colorado Veniremen, 12 U.Colo.L.Rev. 1 (1970) (using classification only approximating *Witherspoon* standard, and finding 11% of subjects *Witherspoon*-excludable); Bronson, Does the Exclusion of Scrupled Jurors in Capital Cases Make the Jury More Likely to Convict? Some Evidence from California, 3

Woodrow Wilson L.J. 11 (1980) (using more appropriate *Witherspoon* question and finding 93% overlap of "strongly opposed" group in prior Bronson study with *Witherspoon*-excludables); Jurow, New Data on the Effect of a "Death Qualified Jury" on the Guilt Determination Process, 84 Harv.L.Rev. 567 (1971) (finding only 10% of sample excludable, but likely to have underestimated size of class in general population because sample 99% white and 80% male); Fitzgerald & Ellsworth, Due Process vs. Crime Control: Death Qualification and Jury Attitudes, 8 Law & Hum.Behav. 31 (1984) (random sample with nullifiers screened out finding 17% still excludable under *Witherspoon*); A. Young, Arkansas Archival Study (unpublished, 1981) (14% of jurors questioned in *voir dire* transcripts excludable); Precision Research, Inc., Survey No. 1286 (1981) (11% excludable, not counting nullifiers).

The evidence thus confirms, and is itself corroborated by, the more intuitive judgments of scholars and of so many of the participants in capital trials—judges, defense attorneys, and prosecutors.

[R]espondent's case would of course be even stronger were he able to produce data showing the prejudicial effects of death qualification upon actual trials. Yet until a State permits two separate juries to deliberate on the same capital case and return simultaneous verdicts, defendants claiming prejudice from death qualification should not be denied recourse to the only available means of proving their case, recreations of the *voir dire* and trial processes. See Grigsby v. Mabry, 758 F.2d, at 237 ("[I]t is the courts who have often stood in the way of surveys involving real jurors and we should not now reject a study because of this deficiency").

The chief strength of respondent's evidence lies in the essential unanimity of the results obtained by researchers using diverse subjects and varied methodologies. Even the Court's haphazard jabs cannot obscure the power of the array. Where studies have identified and corrected apparent flaws in prior investigations, the results of the subsequent work have only corroborated the conclusions drawn in the earlier efforts. Thus, for example, some studies might be faulted for failing to distinguish within the class of *Witherspoon*-excludables, between nullifiers (whom respondent concedes may be excluded from the guilt phase) and those who could assess guilt impartially. Yet their results are entirely consistent with those obtained after nullifiers had indeed been excluded. See, *e.g.*, Cowan, Thompson, & Ellsworth, The Effects of Death Qualification on Jurors Predisposition to Convict and on the Quality of Deliberation, 8 Law & Hum.Behav. 53 (1984). And despite the failure of certain studies to "allow for group deliberations," the value of their results is underscored by the discovery that initial verdict preferences, made prior to group deliberations, are a fair predictor of how a juror will vote when faced with opposition in the jury room. See Cowan, Thompson, & Ellsworth, supra, at 68–69; see also R. Hastie, S. Penrod, & N. Pennington, Inside the Jury 66 (1983); H. Kalven & H. Zeisel, The American Jury 488 (1966).

The evidence adduced by respondent is quite different from the "tentative and fragmentary" presentation that failed to move this Court in *Witherspoon.* 391 U.S., at 517, 88 S.Ct., at 1774. Moreover, in contrast to *Witherspoon,* the record in this case shows respondent's case to have been "subjected to the traditional testing mechanisms of the adversary process," Ballew v. Georgia, 435 U.S. 223, 246, 98 S.Ct. 1029, 1042, 55 L.Ed.2d 234 (1978) (Powell, J., concurring in judgment). At trial, respondent presented three expert witnesses and one lay witness in his case in chief, and two additional lay witnesses in his rebuttal. Testimony by these witnesses permitted the District Court, and allows this Court, better to understand the methodologies used here and their limitations. Further testing of respondent's empirical case came at the hands of the State's own expert witnesses. Yet even after considering the evidence adduced by the State, the Court of Appeals properly noted: "there are no studies which contradict the studies submitted [by respondent]; in other words, all of the document-ed studies support the district court's findings." 758 F.2d, at 238.

[F]aced with the near unanimity of authority supporting respondent's claim that death qualification gives the prosecution a particular advantage in the guilt phase of capital trials, the majority here makes but a weak effort to contest that proposition. Instead, it merely assumes for the purposes of this opinion "that 'death-qualification' in fact produces juries somewhat more 'conviction-prone' than 'non-death-qualified' juries," and then holds that this result does not offend the Constitution. This disregard for the clear import of the evidence tragically misconstrues the settled constitutional principles that guarantee a defendant the right to a fair trial and an impartial jury whose composition is not biased toward the prosecu-tion.

OVERRULED: JURY NEUTRALITY IN CAPITAL CASES

Samuel R. Gross.
21 Stanford Lawyer 11 (1986).

At the outset, I should make my point of view clear. I argued the *Lockhart* case in the Supreme Court on behalf of the respondent, Mr. Ardia McCree, and I lost. Needless to say, I am not a detached observer.

[I]n the Supreme Court, the American Psychological Association filed a brief amicus curiae evaluating the social scientific evidence, and concluded that "without credible exception, the research studies show that death-qualified juries are prosecution prone [and] unrepresentative," and that "the research clearly satisfies the criteria for evaluating the methodological soundness, reliability and utility of empirical research." But the Supreme Court finds fault.

The Court begins its discussion of the empirical record by observing that "McCree introduced into evidence some fifteen social science stud-ies. . . ."; five paragraphs later the Court concludes that it should not base its holding on the one "lone study" that it found worthy of consideration. I will mention only a few of the steps in the remarkable winnowing process that happens in between:

Several of the studies show that jurors who are excluded by death qualification differ greatly from those who remain, in their attitudes toward the criminal justice system—on questions such as whether a defen-dant who does not testify in his own defense is probably guilty. The Court immediately dismisses these studies as "at best, only marginally relevant" because they "dealt solely with generalized attitudes," and never considers them again.

Three of the remaining studies—which show directly that death-qualified jurors are more likely to vote to convict than those who are excluded—had been presented to the Supreme Court in *Witherspoon*.

Therefore, the Court says, "[I]t goes almost without saying that if these studies were 'too tentative and fragmentary' . . . in 1968, the same studies, unchanged but having aged some eighteen years, are still insufficient." [B]ut [t]he fact that these studies were *insufficient* to prove a claim *by themselves* hardly means that they can be written off and ignored entirely when they are presented together with other evidence—which is exactly what the Supreme Court does.

One of McCree's studies shows that the *process* of questioning jurors about their death penalty attitudes predisposes them to believe that the defendant is guilty. The Court disposes of this study by pointing out that "counsel for McCree admitted at oral argument" that this problem "would not, standing alone, give rise to a constitutional violation." Needless to say, the effects of this type of questioning do not occur (and were not litigated) "standing alone"—they are an inseparable aspect of the process of identifying and excluding death penalty opponents—but the Supreme Court, having made this apparently irrelevant observation, acts as if it has one less study to think about.

The most striking thing about the Supreme Court's method of treating the social scientific studies on death qualification is what the Court does *not* do. The Court never even attempts to weigh all the evidence collectively, and reach a decision on the underlying facts. On this claim, that would have been easy: the evidence in support is uncommonly strong—and it is supported by anecdotal wisdom and common sense—while the evidence in opposition is non-existent. Instead, the Supreme Court shops around to find some objection to each study, and having found one, however tenuous, it rules that study out of bounds.

[M]cCree argued that because death qualification increases the likelihood of conviction, it undermines the impartiality of the jury. The Court finds this argument "both illogical and hopelessly impractical" because "McCree admits that exactly the same twelve individuals [who convicted him] could have ended up on his jury through the 'luck of the draw,' without in any way violating the constitutional guarantee of impartiality. . . . [I]t is hard for us to understand the logic of the argument that a given jury is unconstitutionally partial when it results in a State-ordained process, yet impartial when exactly the same jury results from mere chance." I have difficulty believing that the Court really means this. All-white juries can occur by chance; does that make them constitutional if they "result from a State-ordained process"? And what is the reach of this test? Residential segregation could occur by chance; so could an all-male work force. Does that make the arguments against them illogical and impractical when it is proven that chance had nothing to do with it?

[T]he Court could have held, as a matter of law, that the biasing effects of death qualification are immaterial, without taking on the task of contradicting a body of proof that no one seriously doubts. But that would have made their legal argument sound callous: "You may have proven that your jury was biased toward conviction, but it doesn't matter, not even if you are executed as a result." On the other hand, the Court could have held that the evidence is still insufficient without adding a tortuous legal holding—but that would have posed even greater difficulties. Such a decision would have rested on a single shaky leg: on an empirical question where the scientific community is uncommonly single minded, the Supreme Court has little credibility to assert the opposite. Worse, a holding based solely on the insufficiency of the evidence would have been an invitation for future litigation based on additional studies and even fuller records, and the last thing the Court wanted was to face this claim again.

———

NOTE

1. External Validity. The amicus brief filed by the American Psychological Association in the *Lockhart* case addressed the issue of the generalization of the research findings to actual juries:

> [One] criticism concerns the fact that the studies compared death-qualified and excludable jurors, rather than death-qualified and typical criminal juries. Inevitably, juries composed of a mixture of death-qualified and GPI [Guilt Phase Includable] jurors will fall somewhere between a jury composed solely of GPIs or DQs [Death–Qualifieds]. Death-qualified jurors are more conviction prone than such mixed juries would be. Thus, the size of the difference between the pure WE [Witherspoon–Excludable] and pure DQ groups in the research studies cannot be taken as an accurate estimate of the size of the difference between jury verdicts, although the existence and direction of the effect is clear from the studies. The precise magnitude of difference in a given case will change as a result of many variables, e.g., quality of lawyering, first ballot verdict, number of WEs on mixed juries, strength of the evidence.
>
> The research demonstrates that the composition of juries in terms of death penalty attitudes is an important variable and that over the long run eliminating GPIs will increase the number of guilty verdicts.

———

D. THE EIGHTH AMENDMENT: THE DEATH PENALTY

The Eighth Amendment to the Constitution reads as follows:

Excessive bail shall not be required, nor excessive fines imposed, nor cruel and unusual punishments inflicted.

Social science research has been used in recent years to address the "cruel" and the "unusual" prongs of the Eighth Amendment. The "cruelty" issue arises in cases that consider whether the death penalty deters crime. The "unusual" issue is the focus of cases contending that the death penalty is applied in a discriminatory manner. In addition, most recently, courts have used social science to address the issue of whether the execution of certain kinds of offenders constitutes an "excessive" sanction.

1. DETERRENCE

The "cruelty" prong of the Eighth Amendment has been invoked in arguments that the death penalty results in the gratuitous infliction of suffering since execution lacks the penological justification of deterring crime. Social science research has been heavily emphasized by both sides in this debate.

FURMAN v. GEORGIA

Supreme Court of the United States, 1972.
408 U.S. 238, 92 S.Ct. 2726, 33 L.Ed.2d 346.

■ Per Curiam.

Certiorari was granted limited to the following question: "Does the imposition and carrying out of the death penalty in [these cases] constitute cruel and unusual punishment in violation of the Eighth and Fourteenth Amendments?" 403 U.S. 952, 91 S.Ct. 2287, 29 L.Ed.2d 863 (1971). The Court holds that the imposition and carrying out of the death penalty in these cases constitute cruel and unusual punishment in violation of the Eighth and Fourteenth Amendments. The judgment in each case is therefore reversed insofar as it leaves undisturbed the death sentence imposed, and the cases are remanded for further proceedings.

■ Justice Marshall, concurring.

The most hotly contested issue regarding capital punishment is whether it is better than life imprisonment as a deterrent to crime.

[T]horsten Sellin, one of the leading authorities on capital punishment, has urged that [t]he death penalty [does not deter murderers. Sellin's] evidence has its problems, however. One is that there are no accurate figures for capital murders; there are only figures on homicides and they, of course, include noncapital killings. A second problem is that certain murders undoubtedly are misinterpreted as accidental deaths or suicides, and there is no way of estimating the number of such undetected crimes. A third problem is that not all homicides are reported. Despite these difficulties, most authorities have assumed that the proportion of capital murders in a State's or nation's homicide statistics remains reasonably constant, and that the homicide statistics are therefore useful.

Sellin's statistics demonstrate that there is no correlation between the murder rate and the presence or absence of the capital sanction. He compares States that have similar characteristics and finds that irrespective of their position on capital punishment, they have similar murder rates. In the New England States, for example, there is no correlation between executions and homicide rates. The same is true for Midwestern States, and for all others studied. Both the United Nations and Great Britain have acknowledged the validity of Sellin's statistics.

Sellin also concludes that abolition and/or reintroduction of the death penalty had no effect on the homicide rates of the various States involved. This conclusion is borne out by others who have made similar inquiries and by the experience of other countries. Despite problems with the statistics, Sellin's evidence has been relied upon in international studies of capital punishment.

[D]espite the fact that abolitionists have not proved non-deterrence beyond a reasonable doubt, they have succeeded in showing by clear and convincing evidence that capital punishment is not necessary as a deterrent to crime in our society. This is all that they must do. We would shirk our judicial responsibilities if we failed to accept the presently existing statistics and demanded more proof. It may be that we now possess all the proof that anyone could ever hope to assemble on the subject. But, even if further proof were to be forthcoming, I believe there is more than enough evidence presently available for a decision in this case.

[I]n light of the massive amount of evidence before us, I see no alternative but to conclude that capital punishment cannot be justified on the basis of its deterrent effect.

■ MR. CHIEF JUSTICE BURGER, with whom MR. JUSTICE BLACKMUN, MR. JUSTICE POWELL and MR. JUSTICE REHNQUIST join, dissenting.

[A] controversial question is whether the death penalty acts as a superior deterrent. Those favoring abolition find no evidence that it does.[21] Those favoring retention start from the intuitive notion that capital punishment should act as the most effective deterrent and note that there is no convincing evidence that it does not. Escape from this empirical stalemate is sought by placing the burden of proof on the States and concluding that they have failed to demonstrate that capital punishment is a more effective deterrent than life imprisonment. Numerous justifications have been advanced for shifting the burden, and they are not without their rhetorical appeal. However, these arguments are not descended from established constitutional principles, but are born of the urge to bypass an unresolved factual question. Comparative deterrence is not a matter that lends itself to precise measurement; to shift the burden to the States is to provide an illusory solution to an enormously complex problem. If it were proper to put the States to the test of demonstrating the deterrent value of capital punishment, we could just as well ask them to prove the need for life imprisonment or any other punishment. Yet I know of no convincing evidence that life imprisonment is a more effective deterrent than 20 years' imprisonment, or even that a $10 parking ticket is a more effective deterrent than a $5 parking ticket. In fact, there are some who go so far as to challenge the notion that any punishments deter crime. If the States are unable to adduce convincing proof rebutting such assertions, does it then follow that all punishments are suspect as being "cruel and unusual"

21. See, e.g., Sellin, Homicides in Retentionist and Abolitionist States, in Capital Punishment 135 et seq. (T. Sellin ed. 1967); Schuessler, The Deterrent Influence of the Death Penalty, 284 Annals 54 (1952).

within the meaning of the Constitution? On the contrary, I submit that the questions raised by the necessity approach are beyond the pale of judicial inquiry under the Eighth Amendment.

[I]f today's opinions demonstrate nothing else, they starkly show that this is an area where legislatures can act far more effectively than courts.

[T]he preference for legislative action is justified by the inability of the courts to participate in the debate at the level where the controversy is focused. The case against capital punishment is not the product of legal dialectic, but rests primarily on factual claims, the truth of which cannot be tested by conventional judicial processes. The five opinions in support of the judgments differ in many respects, but they share a willingness to make sweeping factual assertions, unsupported by empirical data, concerning the manner of imposition and effectiveness of capital punishment in this country. Legislatures will have the opportunity to make a more penetrating study of these claims with the familiar and effective tools available to them as they are not to us.

The highest judicial duty is to recognize the limits on judicial power and to permit the democratic processes to deal with matters falling outside of those limits.

GREGG v. GEORGIA

Supreme Court of the United States, 1976.
428 U.S. 153, 96 S.Ct. 2909, 49 L.Ed.2d 859.

■ Justice Stewart announced the judgment of the Court.

[This case presented the question of whether the imposition of the death sentence under a Georgia statute would be "cruel and unusual" punishment under the Eighth and Fourteenth Amendments of the Constitution. The case was, to some extent, a successor to Furman v. Georgia, 408 U.S. 238, 92 S.Ct. 2726, 33 L.Ed.2d 346 (1972), where the court held that a prior version of the statute was unconstitutional because of the broad discretion it accorded juries to impose or withhold the death penalty. In *Gregg,* one consideration was whether the death sentence resulted in the gratuitous infliction of suffering because it lacked the penological justification of deterring crime. The presence of this issue led members of the court to consider the deterrent effect, if any, of the death sentence.]

Statistical attempts to evaluate the worth of the death penalty as a deterrent to crimes by potential offenders have occasioned a great deal of debate.[31] The results simply have been inconclusive. As one opponent of capital punishment has said:

31. See, e.g., Peck, The Deterrent Effect of Capital Punishment: Ehrlich and His Critics, 85 Yale L.J. 359 (1976); Baldus & Cole, A Comparison of the Work of Thorsten Sellin and Isaac Ehrlich on the Deterrent Effect of Capital Punishment, 85 Yale L.J. 170 (1975); Bowers & Pierce, The Illusion of Deterrence in Isaac Ehrlich's Research on

"[A]fter all possible inquiry, including the probing of all possible methods of inquiry, we do not know, and for systematic and easily visible reasons cannot know, what the truth about this 'deterrent' effect may be. . . .

"The inescapable flaw is . . . that social conditions in any state are not constant through time, and that social conditions are not the same in any two states. If an effect were observed (and the observed effects, one way or another, are not large) then one could not at all tell whether any of this effect is attributable to the presence or absence of capital punishment. A 'scientific'—that is to say, a soundly based— conclusion is simply impossible, and no methodological path out of this tangle suggests itself." C. Black, Capital Punishment: The Inevitability of Caprice and Mistake 25–26 (1974).

Although some of the studies suggest that the death penalty may not function as a significantly greater deterrent than lesser penalties,[32] there is no convincing empirical evidence either supporting or refuting this view. We may nevertheless assume safely that there are murderers, such as those who act in passion, for whom the threat of death has little or no deterrent effect. But for many others, the death penalty undoubtedly is a significant deterrent. There are carefully contemplated murders, such as murder for hire, where the possible penalty of death may well enter into the cold calculus that preceded the decision to act. And there are some categories of murder, such as murder by a life prisoner, where other sanctions may not be adequate.[34]

The value of capital punishment as a deterrent of crime is a complex factual issue the resolution of which properly rests with the legislatures, which can evaluate the results of statistical studies in terms of their own local conditions and with a flexibility of approach that is not available to the courts. Furman v. Georgia, [408 U.S.] at 403–405, 92 S.Ct., at 2810– 2812 (Burger, C.J., Dissenting). Indeed, many of the post-*Furman* statutes reflect just such a responsible effort to define those crimes and those criminals for which capital punishment is most probably an effective deterrent.

Capital Punishment, 85 Yale L.J. 187 (1975); Ehrlich, The Deterrent Effect of Capital Punishment: A Question of Life and Death, 65 Am.Econ.Rev. 397 (June 1975); Hook, The Death Sentence, in The Death Penalty in America 146 (H. Bedau ed. 1967); T. Sellin, The Death Penalty, A Report for the Model Penal Code Project of the American Law Institute (1959).

32. See, e.g., The Death Penalty in America, supra, at 258–332; Report of the Royal Commission on Capital Punishment, 1949–1953, Cmd. 8932.

34. We have been shown no statistics breaking down the total number of murders into the categories described above. The over-

all trend in the number of murders committed in the nation, however, has been upward for some time. In 1964, reported murders totaled an estimated 9,250. During the ensuing decade, the number reported increased 123%, until it totaled approximately 20,600 in 1974. In 1972 the year *Furman* was announced, the total estimated was 18,520. Despite a fractional decrease in 1975 as compared with 1974, the number of murders increased in the three years immediately following *Furman* to approximately 20,400, an increase of almost 10%. See FBI, Uniform Crime Reports, for 1964, 1972, 1974, and 1975, Preliminary Annual Release.

■ JUSTICE MARSHALL, dissenting.

[I]n *Furman,* I canvassed the relevant data on the deterrent effect of capital punishment. 408 U.S. at 347–354, 92 S.Ct. at 2781–2785.[2] The state of knowledge at that point, after literally centuries of debate, was summarized as follows by a United Nations Committee:

> "It is generally agreed between the retentionists and abolitionists, whatever their opinions about the validity of comparative studies of deterrence, that the data which now exist show no correlation between the existence of capital punishment and lower rates of capital crime."[3]

The available evidence, I concluded in *Furman,* was convincing that "capital punishment is not necessary as a deterrent to crime in our society." Id. at 353.

The Solicitor General in his *amicus* brief in these cases relies heavily on a study by Isaac Ehrlich,[4] reported a year after *Furman,* to support the contention that the death penalty does deter murder. Since the Ehrlich study was not available at the time of *Furman* and since it is the first scientific study to suggest that the death penalty may have a deterrent effect, I will briefly consider its import.

The Ehrlich study focused on the relationship in the Nation as a whole between the homicide rate and "execution risk"—the fraction of persons convicted of murder who were actually executed. Comparing the differences in homicide rate and execution risk for the years 1933 to 1969, Ehrlich found that increases in execution risk were associated with increases in the homicide rate.[5] But when he employed the statistical technique of multiple regression analysis to control for the influence of other variables posited to have an impact on the homicide rate,[6] Ehrlich found a negative correlation between changes in the homicide rate and changes in execution risk. His tentative conclusion was that for the period from 1933 to 1967 each additional execution in the United States might have saved eight lives.[7]

The methods and conclusions of the Ehrlich study have been severely criticized on a number of grounds.[8] It has been suggested, for example, that

---

2. See e.g., T. Sellin, The Death Penalty, A Report for the Model Penal Code Project of the American Law Institute (1959).

3. United Nations, Department of Economic and Social Affairs, Capital Punishment, pt. II, & 159, p. 123 (1968).

4. I. Ehrlich, The Deterrent Effect of Capital Punishment: A Question of Life and Death (Working Paper No. 18, National Bureau of Economic Research, Nov. 1973); Ehrlich, The Deterrent Effect of Capital Punishment: A Question of Life and Death, 65 Am. Econ.Rev. 397 (June 1975).

5. Id. at 409.

6. The variables other than execution risk included probability of arrest, probability

of conviction given arrest, national aggregate measures of the percentage of the population between age 14 and 24, the unemployment rate, the labor force participation rate, and estimated per capita income.

7. Id. at 398, 414.

8. See Passell & Taylor, The Deterrent Effect of Capital Punishment: Another View (unpublished Columbia University Discussion Paper 74–7509, Mar.1975), reproduced in Brief for Petitioner App. E in Jurek v. Texas, O.T.1975, No. 75–5844; Passell, The Deterrent Effect of the Death Penalty: A Statistical Test, 28 Stan.L.Rev. 61 (1975); Baldus & Cole, A Comparison of the Work of Thorsten Sellin & Isaac Ehrlich on the Deterrent Efthe study is defective because it compares execution and homicide rates on a nationwide, rather than a state-by-state, basis. The aggregation of data from all States—including those that have abolished the death penalty—obscures the relationship between murder and execution rates. Under Ehrlich's methodology, a decrease in the execution risk in one State combined with an increase in the murder rate in another State would, all other things being equal, suggest a deterrent effect that quite obviously would not exist. Indeed, a deterrent effect would be suggested if, once again all other things being equal, one State abolished the death penalty and experienced no change in the murder rate, while another State experienced an increase in the murder rate.

The most compelling criticism of the Ehrlich study is that its conclusions are extremely sensitive to the choice of the time period included in the regression analysis. Analysis of Ehrlich's data reveals that all empirical support for the deterrent effect of capital punishment disappears when the five most recent years are removed from his time series—that is to say, whether a decrease in the execution risk corresponds to an increase or a decrease in the murder rate depends on the ending point of the sample period. This finding has cast severe doubts on the reliability of Ehrlich's tentative conclusions. Indeed, a recent [s]tudy, based on Ehrlich's theoretical model but using cross-section state data for the years 1950 and 1960, found no support for the conclusion that executions act as a deterrent.

The Ehrlich study, in short, is of little, if any, assistance in assessing the deterrent impact of the death penalty. The evidence I reviewed in *Furman* remains convincing, in my view, that "capital punishment is not necessary as a deterrent to crime in our society." 408 U.S., at 353, 92 S.Ct., at 2784. The justification for the death penalty must be found elsewhere.

———

DETERRENCE AND INCAPACITATION: ESTIMATING THE EFFECTS OF CRIMINAL SANCTIONS ON CRIME RATES

Panel on Research on Deterrent and Incapacitative Effects, National Academy of Sciences (1978).

The question of whether capital punishment has any additional deterrent effect beyond that associated with imprisonment has been a subject of intense debate for generations. Periodically, this debate emerges as a

fect of Capital Punishment, 85 Yale L.J. 170 (1975); Bowers & Pierce, The Illusion of Deterrence in Isaac Ehrlich's Research on Capital Punishment, 85 Yale L.J. 187 (1975); Peck, The Deterrent Effect of Capital Punishment: Ehrlich and His Critics, 85 Yale L.J. 359 (1976). See also Ehrlich, Deterrence: Evidence and Inference, 85 Yale L.J. 209 (1975); Ehrlich, Rejoinder, 85 Yale L.J. 368 (1976).

In addition to the items discussed in text, criticism has been directed at the quality of Ehrlich's data, his choice of explanatory variables, his failure to account for the interdependence of those variables, and his assumptions as to the mathematical form of the relationship between the homicide rate and the explanatory variables.

matter of major public concern. This has happened most recently in the series of U.S. Supreme Court decisions[54] regarding the constitutionality of capital punishment. In the most recent of the Supreme Court decisions, complex technical evidence on the deterrent effect of capital punishment was brought into the debate by the Solicitor General, who introduced an analysis by Ehrlich in his *amicus curiae* brief.

The Ehrlich analysis showed a negative association over time between United States national homicide rates and the number of executions per homicide conviction, a proxy for the probability of execution. This association has been interpreted as demonstrating that capital punishment deters homicide and has been carried to the point of estimating the number of homicides averted per execution. Ehrlich's analysis contradicted earlier analyses that found no evidence that capital punishment deters homicide.

[W]hile all the earlier studies failed to find evidence of a deterrent effect, they suffer from a number of methodological weaknesses. The most serious flaw was the general failure to control adequately for the variety of demographic, cultural, and socioeconomic factors, other than the death penalty, that influence murder rates. Examining "similar" contiguous states or the same jurisdiction over short time periods represents some effort to hold these factors constant, but, when dealing with rare events like homicides and executions where the numbers are quite small, the crudeness of these controls could easily mask any effects that may exist. In addition, there were no controls for differences in noncapital sanctions, which could also influence homicide rates.

In some studies, different jurisdictions were compared on the basis of their statutes regarding capital punishment rather than by their practice, when the latter may be the more relevant factor affecting deterrence. Additionally, these analyses usually failed to separate the number of capital homicides (those homicides for which capital punishment was a legal sanction) from total homicides as the dependent variable, and variations in the larger number of noncapital homicides in the total could have masked a deterrent effect.

[E]hrlich, using time-series data for 1933–1969 in which homicides and executions were aggregated for the entire United States, reports a deterrent effect for executions. There have been a number of reanalyses of data equivalent to that used by Ehrlich. All of these reanalyses have shown that Ehrlich's findings are sensitive to minor technical variations in the analysis. These variations include changes in the mathematical form of the relationship of homicide rates to their determinants (e.g., a multiplicative form compared to a linear one) and the variables included as determinants of homicide (e.g., including the aggregate crime index as a determinant). These reanalyses either reversed the direction of the presumed effect or greatly reduced its magnitude.

54. Furman v. Georgia, 408 U.S. 238 (1972); Fowler v. North Carolina, 95 Sup.Ct. 223; Jurek v. Texas, 96 Sup.Ct. 2950; Woodson v. North Carolina, 96 Sup.Ct. 2978; Proffitt v. Florida; 96 Sup.Ct. 2976; and Gregg v. Georgia, 96 Sup.Ct. 2909.

The most striking sensitivity of Ehrlich's findings is to the time period over which the analysis is conducted. No negative association is found for 1933–1961, so that the results are determined by the effect in 1962–1969. But during those eight years, *all* crime rates rose dramatically, and the frequency of executions declined (and had ceased by 1968). Thus, to conclude that a deterrent effect exists, one must assume that the steady rise in homicides over this eight-year period was caused at least in part by the decline in executions and that the trends in executions and in homicides were not generated either independently or by some common third cause, which might also account for the rise in other crimes. If one makes these assumptions, statistical analyses contribute no further information to the test of the deterrence hypothesis. Moreover, the failure to discern any deterrent effect in the earlier 1933–1961 period, when there was more fluctuation in both homicide and execution rates, still remains unexplained.

In summary, the flaws in the null-effect results and the sensitivity of the Ehrlich results to minor variations in model specification and their serious temporal instability lead the Panel to conclude that the results of the analyses on capital punishment provide no useful evidence on the deterrent effect of capital punishment.

Our conclusion should not be interpreted as meaning that capital punishment does not have a deterrent effect, but rather that there is currently no evidence for determining whether it does have a deterrent effect. Furthermore, we are skeptical that the death penalty, so long as it is used relatively rarely, can ever be subjected to the kind of statistical analysis that would validly establish the presence or absence of a deterrent effect.

Our conclusion on the current evidence does not imply that capital punishment should or should not be imposed. The deterrent effect of capital punishment and its magnitude reflect only one aspect of the many considerations involved in the choice of the use of the death penalty. Those considerations include issues related to the value of human life, the moral justification of killing by government, and the appropriate form of public outrage at heinous crimes—all of which are likely to dominate policy decisions in comparison to inevitably crude estimates of the deterrent effects.

---

2. DISCRIMINATION

The "unusual" prong of the Eighth Amendment has been the focus of arguments that the death penalty is invoked with disproportionate frequency on defendants whose victims have been white. The issue here has revolved around one major social science study of the application of the death penalty.

McCLESKEY v. KEMP

Supreme Court of the United States, 1987.
481 U.S. 279, 107 S.Ct. 1756, 95 L.Ed.2d 262.

■ Justice Powell delivered the opinion of the Court.

McCleskey, a black man, was convicted of two counts of armed robbery and one count of murder in the Superior Court of Fulton County, Georgia, on October 12, 1978. McCleskey's convictions arose out of the robbery of a furniture store and the killing of a white police officer during the course of the robbery.

[T]he jury recommended that he be sentenced to death on the murder charge and to consecutive life sentences on the armed robbery charges. The court followed the jury's recommendation and sentenced McCleskey to death.

On appeal, the Supreme Court of Georgia affirmed the convictions and the sentences.

McCleskey [f]iled a petition for a writ of habeas corpus in the federal District Court for the Northern District of Georgia. His petition raised 18 claims, one of which was that the Georgia capital sentencing process is administered in a racially discriminatory manner in violation of the Eighth and Fourteenth Amendments to the United States Constitution. In support of his claim, McCleskey proffered a statistical study performed by Professors David C. Baldus, George Woodworth, and Charles Pulaski (the Baldus study) that purports to show a disparity in the imposition of the death sentence in Georgia based on the race of the murder victim and, to a lesser extent, the race of the defendant. The Baldus study is actually two sophisticated statistical studies that examine over 2,000 murder cases that occurred in Georgia during the 1970s. The raw numbers collected by Professor Baldus indicate that defendants charged with killing white persons received the death penalty in 11% of the cases, but defendants charged with killing blacks received the death penalty in only 1% of the cases. The raw numbers also indicate a reverse racial disparity according to the race of the defendant: 4% of the black defendants received the death penalty, as opposed to 7% of the white defendants.

Baldus also divided the cases according to the combination of the race of the defendant and the race of the victim. He found that the death penalty was assessed in 22% of the cases involving black defendants and white victims; 8% of the cases involving white defendants and white victims; 1% of the cases involving black defendants and black victims; and 3% of the cases involving white defendants and black victims. Similarly, Baldus found that prosecutors sought the death penalty in 70% of the cases involving black defendants and white victims; 32% of the cases involving white defendants and white victims; 15% of the cases involving black defendants and black victims; and 19% of the cases involving white defendants and black victims.

Baldus subjected his data to an extensive analysis, taking account of 230 variables that could have explained the disparities on nonracial grounds. One of his models concludes that, even after taking account of 39 nonracial variables, defendants charged with killing white victims were 4.3 times as likely to receive a death sentence as defendants charged with killing blacks. According to this model, black defendants were 1.1 times as likely to receive a death sentence as other defendants. Thus, the Baldus study indicates that black defendants, such as McCleskey, who kill white victims have the greatest likelihood of receiving the death penalty.

The District Court held an extensive evidentiary hearing on McCleskey's petition. Although it believed that McCleskey's Eighth Amendment claim was foreclosed by the Fifth Circuit's decision in Spinkellink v. Wainwright, 578 F.2d 582, 612–616 (1978), cert. denied, 440 U.S. 976, 99 S.Ct. 1548, 59 L.Ed.2d 796 (1979), it nevertheless considered the Baldus study with care. It concluded that McCleskey's "statistics do not demonstrate a prima facie case in support of the contention that the death penalty was imposed upon him because of his race, because of the race of the victim, or because of any Eighth Amendment concern." McCleskey v. Zant, 580 F.Supp. 338, 379 (N.D.Ga.1984). As to McCleskey's Fourteenth Amendment claim, the court found that the methodology of the Baldus study was flawed in several respects. Because of these defects, the Court held that the Baldus study "fail[ed] to contribute anything of value" to McCleskey's claim. Id., at 372 (emphasis omitted). Accordingly, the Court dismissed the petition. [T]he Court of Appeals affirmed the dismissal by the District Court of McCleskey's petition for a writ of habeas corpus, with three judges dissenting as to McCleskey's claims based on the Baldus study. We granted certiorari, and now affirm.

McCleskey's first claim is that the Georgia capital punishment statute violates the Equal Protection Clause of the Fourteenth Amendment.[7]

[O]ur analysis begins with the basic principle that a defendant who alleges an equal protection violation has the burden of proving "the existence of purposeful discrimination." Whitus v. Georgia, 385 U.S. 545, 550, 87 S.Ct. 643, 646, 17 L.Ed.2d 599 (1967). A corollary to this principle is that a criminal defendant must prove that the purposeful discrimination "had a discriminatory effect" on him. Wayte v. United States, 470 U.S. 598, 608, 105 S.Ct. 1524, 1531, 84 L.Ed.2d 547 (1985). Thus, to prevail under the Equal Protection Clause, McCleskey must prove that the decisionmakers in his case acted with discriminatory purpose. He offers no evidence specific to his own case that would support an inference that racial considerations played a part in his sentence. Instead, he relies solely on the

7. Although the District Court rejected the findings of the Baldus study as flawed, the Court of Appeals assumed that the study is valid and reached the constitutional issues. Accordingly, those issues are before us. As did the Court of Appeals, we assume the study is valid statistically without reviewing the factual findings of the District Court. Our assumption that the Baldus study is statistically valid does not include the assumption that the study shows that racial considerations actually enter into any sentencing decisions in Georgia. Even a sophisticated multiple regression analysis such as the Baldus study can only demonstrate a *risk* that the factor of race entered into some capital sentencing decisions and a necessarily lesser risk that race entered into any particular sentencing decision.

Baldus study.[11] McCleskey argues that the Baldus study compels an inference that his sentence rests on purposeful discrimination. McCleskey's claim that these statistics are sufficient proof of discrimination, without regard to the facts of a particular case, would extend to all capital cases in Georgia, at least where the victim was white and the defendant is black.

The Court has accepted statistics as proof of intent to discriminate in certain limited contexts. First, this Court has accepted statistical disparities as proof of an equal protection violation in the selection of the jury venire in a particular district. [S]econd, this Court has accepted statistics in the form of multiple regression analysis to prove statutory violations under Title VII.

But the nature of the capital sentencing decision, and the relationship of the statistics to that decision, are fundamentally different from the corresponding elements in the venire-selection or Title VII cases. Most importantly, each particular decision to impose the death penalty is made by a petit jury selected from a properly constituted venire. Each jury is unique in its composition, and the Constitution requires that its decision rest on consideration of innumerable factors that vary according to the characteristics of the individual defendant and the facts of the particular capital offense. Thus, the application of an inference drawn from the general statistics to a specific decision in a trial and sentencing simply is not comparable to the application of an inference drawn from general statistics to a specific venire-selection or Title VII case. In those cases, the statistics relate to fewer entities, and fewer variables are relevant to the challenged decisions. [A]ccordingly, we reject McCleskey's equal protection claims.

McCleskey also argues that the Baldus study demonstrates that the Georgia capital sentencing system violates the Eighth Amendment.

[I]n light of our precedents under the Eighth Amendment, McCleskey cannot argue successfully that his sentence is "disproportionate to the crime in the traditional sense." See Pulley v. Harris, 465 U.S. 37, 43, 104 S.Ct. 871, 875, 79 L.Ed.2d 29 (1984). He does not deny that he committed a murder in the course of a planned robbery, a crime for which this Court has determined that the death penalty constitutionally may be imposed. Gregg v. Georgia, 428 U.S., at 187, 96 S.Ct., at 2931. His disproportionality claim "is of a different sort." Pulley v. Harris, supra, 465 U.S., at 43, 104 S.Ct., at 875. McCleskey argues that the sentence in his case is disproportionate to the sentences in other murder cases.

[T]o evaluate McCleskey's challenge, we must examine exactly what the Baldus study may show. Even Professor Baldus does not contend that

---

11. McCleskey's expert testified:

"Models that are developed talk about the effect on the average. They do not depict the experience of a single individual. What they say, for example, [is] that on the average, the race of the victim, if it is white, increases on the average the probability ... (that) the death sentence would be given.

"Whether in a given case that is the answer, it cannot be determined from statistics." 580 F.Supp., at 372.

his statistics prove that race enters into any capital sentencing decisions or that race was a factor in McCleskey's particular case. Statistics at most may show only a likelihood that a particular factor entered into some decisions. There is, of course, some risk of racial prejudice influencing a jury's decision in a criminal case. There are similar risks that other kinds of prejudice will influence other criminal trials. The question "is at what point that risk becomes constitutionally unacceptable," Turner v. Murray, 476 U.S. 28, 36, n. 8, 106 S.Ct. 1683, 1688, n. 8, 90 L.Ed.2d 27 (1986). McCleskey asks us to accept the likelihood allegedly shown by the Baldus study as the constitutional measure of an unacceptable risk of racial prejudice influencing capital sentencing decisions. This we decline to do.

[A]t most, the Baldus study indicates a discrepancy that appears to correlate with race. Apparent disparities in sentencing are an inevitable part of our criminal justice system. The discrepancy indicated by the Baldus study is "a far cry from the major systemic defects identified in *Furman*," Pulley v. Harris, 465 U.S., at 54, 104 S.Ct., at 881. As this Court has recognized, any mode for determining guilt or punishment "has its weaknesses and the potential for misuse." Singer v. United States, 380 U.S. 24, 35, 85 S.Ct. 783, 790, 13 L.Ed.2d 630 (1965). Specifically, "there can be 'no perfect procedure for deciding in which cases governmental authority should be used to impose death.'" Zant v. Stephens, 462 U.S. 862, 884, 103 S.Ct. 2733, 2746, 77 L.Ed.2d 235 (1983) (quoting Lockett v. Ohio, 438 U.S., at 605, 98 S.Ct., at 2965 (plurality opinion of Burger, C.J.)). Despite these imperfections, our consistent rule has been that constitutional guarantees are met when "the mode [for determining guilt or punishment] itself has been surrounded with safeguards to make it as fair as possible." Singer v. United States, supra, 380 U.S., at 35, 85 S.Ct., at 790. Where the discretion that is fundamental to our criminal process is involved, we decline to assume that what is unexplained is invidious. In light of the safeguards designed to minimize racial bias in the process, the fundamental value of jury trial in our criminal justice system, and the benefits that discretion provides to criminal defendants, we hold that the Baldus study does not demonstrate a constitutionally significant risk of racial bias affecting the Georgia capital-sentencing process.

Two additional concerns inform our decision in this case. First, McCleskey's claim, taken to its logical conclusion, throws into serious question the principles that underlie our entire criminal justice system. The Eighth Amendment is not limited in application to capital punishment, but applies to all penalties. Thus, if we accepted McCleskey's claim that racial bias has impermissibly tainted the capital sentencing decision, we could soon be faced with similar claims as to other types of penalty.[38] Moreover, the claim that his sentence rests on the irrelevant factor of race

---

38. Studies already exist that allegedly demonstrate a racial disparity in the length of prison sentences. See, e.g., Spohn, Gruhl, & Welch, The Effect of Race on Sentencing: A Reexamination of an Unsettled Question, 16 Law & Soc.Rev. 71 (1981–1982); Unnever, Frazier & Henretta, Race Differences in Criminal Sentencing, 21 Sociological Q. 197 (1980).

easily could be extended to apply to claims based on unexplained discrepancies that correlate to membership in other minority groups, and even to gender.[40] Similarly, since McCleskey's claim relates to the race of his victim, other claims could apply with equally logical force to statistical disparities that correlate with the race or sex of other actors in the criminal justice system, such as defense attorneys[41], or judges. Also, there is no logical reason that such a claim need be limited to racial or sexual bias. If arbitrary and capricious punishment is the touchstone under the Eighth Amendment, such a claim could—at least in theory—be based upon any arbitrary variable, such as the defendant's facial characteristics,[43] or the physical attractiveness of the defendant or the victim,[44] that some statistical study indicates may be influential in jury decisionmaking. As these examples illustrate, there is no limiting principle to the type of challenge brought by McCleskey. The Constitution does not require that a State eliminate any demonstrable disparity that correlates with a potentially irrelevant factor in order to operate a criminal justice system that includes capital punishment. As we have stated specifically in the context of capital punishment, the Constitution does not "plac[e] totally unrealistic conditions on its use." Gregg v. Georgia, 428 U.S., at 199, n. 50, 96 S.Ct., at 2937, n. 50.

Second, McCleskey's arguments are best presented to the legislative bodies. It is not the responsibility—or indeed even the right—of this Court to determine the appropriate punishment for particular crimes. It is the legislatures, the elected representatives of the people, that are "constituted to respond to the will and consequently the moral values of the people." Furman v. Georgia, 408 U.S., at 383, 92 S.Ct., at 2800 (Burger, C.J.,

---

40. See Chamblin, The Effect of Sex on the Imposition of the Death Penalty (paper presented at a symposium of the Amer. Psych. Assn., entitled "Extra-legal Attributes Affecting Death Penalty Sentencing," New York City, Sept., 1979); Steffensmeier, Effects of Judge's and Defendant's Sex on the Sentencing of Offenders, 14 Psychology 3 (1977).

41. See Johnson, Black Innocence and the White Jury, 83 Mich.L.Rev. 1611, 1625–1640, and n. 115 (1985) (citing Cohen & Peterson, Bias in the Courtroom: Race and Sex Effects of Attorneys on Juror Verdicts, 9 Social Behavior & Personality 81 (1981)); Hodgson & Pryor, Sex Discrimination in the Courtroom: Attorney's Gender and Credibility, 55 Psychological Rep. 483 (1984).

43. See Kerr, Bull, MacCoun, & Rathborn, Effects of victim attractiveness, care and disfigurement on the judgments of American and British mock jurors, 24 Brit. J. Social Psych. 47 (1985); Johnson, supra, 1638, n. 128 (citing Shoemaker, South, & Lowe, Facial Stereotypes of Deviants and

Judgments of Guilt or Innocence, 51 Social Forces 427 (1973)).

44. Some studies indicate that physically attractive defendants receive greater leniency in sentencing than unattractive defendants, and that offenders whose victims are physically attractive receive harsher sentences than defendants with less attractive victims. Smith & Hed, Effects of Offenders' Age and Attractiveness on Sentencing by Mock Juries, 44 Psychological R. 691 (1979); Kerr, Beautiful and Blameless: Effects of Victim Attractiveness and Responsibility on Mock Jurors' Verdicts, 4 Personality and Social Psych. Bull. 479 (1978). But see Baumeister & Darley, Reducing the Biasing Effect of Perpetrator Attractiveness in Jury Simulation, 8 Personality and Social Psych. Bull. 286 (1982); Schwibbe & Schwibbe, Judgment and Treatment of People of Varied Attractiveness, 48 Psychological R. 11 (1981); Weiten, The Attraction–Leniency Effect in Jury Research: An Examination of External Validity, 10 J. Applied Social Psych. 340 (1980).

dissenting). Legislatures also are better qualified to weigh and "evaluate the results of statistical studies in terms of their own local conditions and with a flexibility of approach that is not available to the courts," Gregg v. Georgia, supra, 428 U.S., at 186, 96 S.Ct., at 2931. Capital punishment is now the law in more than two thirds of our States. It is the ultimate duty of courts to determine on a case-by-case basis whether these laws are applied consistently with the Constitution. Despite McCleskey's wide ranging arguments that basically challenge the validity of capital punishment in our multi-racial society, the only question before us is whether in his case, the law of Georgia was properly applied. We agree with the District Court and the Court of Appeals for the Eleventh Circuit that this was carefully and correctly done in this case.

■ JUSTICE BRENNAN, dissenting.

It is important to emphasize at the outset that the Court's observation that McCleskey cannot prove the influence of race on any particular sentencing decision is irrelevant in evaluating his Eighth Amendment claim. Since Furman v. Georgia, 408 U.S. 238, 92 S.Ct. 2726, 33 L.Ed.2d 346 (1972), the Court has been concerned with the *risk* of the imposition of an arbitrary sentence, rather than the proven fact of one. *Furman* held that the death penalty "may not be imposed under sentencing procedures that create a substantial risk that the punishment will be inflicted in an arbitrary and capricious manner." Godfrey v. Georgia, 446 U.S., at 427, 100 S.Ct., at 1764.

[T]he Court assumes the statistical validity of the Baldus study, and acknowledges that McCleskey has demonstrated a risk that racial prejudice plays a role in capital sentencing in Georgia. Nonetheless, it finds the probability of prejudice insufficient to create constitutional concern. Close analysis of the Baldus study, however, in light of both statistical principles and human experience, reveals that the risk that race influenced McCleskey's sentence is intolerable by any imaginable standard.

The Baldus study indicates that, after taking into account some 230 nonracial factors that might legitimately influence a sentencer, the jury *more likely than not* would have spared McCleskey's life had his victim been black. The study distinguishes between those cases in which (1) the jury exercises virtually no discretion because the strength or weakness of aggravating factors usually suggests that only one outcome is appropriate; and (2) cases reflecting an "intermediate" level of aggravation, in which the jury has considerable discretion in choosing a sentence. McCleskey's case falls into the intermediate range. In such cases, death is imposed in 34% of white-victim crimes and 14% of black-victim crimes, a difference of 139% in the rate of imposition of the death penalty.

In other words, just under 59%—almost 6 in 10—[of the] defendants comparable to McCleskey would not have received the death penalty if their victims had been black.

Furthermore, even examination of the sentencing system as a whole, factoring in those cases in which the jury exercises little discretion, indicates the influence of race on capital sentencing. For the Georgia system as a whole, race accounts for a six percentage point difference in the rate at which capital punishment is imposed. Since death is imposed in 11% of all white-victim cases, the rate in comparably aggravated black-victim cases is 5%. The rate of capital sentencing in a white-victim case is thus 120% greater than the rate in a black-victim case. Put another way, over half—55%—of defendants in white-victim crimes in Georgia would not have been sentenced to die if their victims had been black. Of the more than 200 variables potentially relevant to a sentencing decision, race of the victim is a powerful explanation for variation in death sentence rates—as powerful as nonracial aggravating factors such as a prior murder conviction or acting as the principal planner of the homicide.

These adjusted figures are only the most conservative indication of the risk that race will influence the death sentences of defendants in Georgia. Data unadjusted for the mitigating or aggravating effect of other factors show an even more pronounced disparity by race. The capital sentencing rate for all white-victim cases was almost *11 times* greater than the rate for black-victim cases. Furthermore, blacks who kill whites are sentenced to death at nearly *22 times* the rate of blacks who kill blacks, and more than *7 times* the rate of whites who kill blacks.

In addition, prosecutors seek the death penalty for 70% of black defendants with white victims, but for only 15% of black defendants with black victims, and only 19% of white defendants with black victims. Since our decision upholding the Georgia capital-sentencing system in *Gregg,* the State has executed 7 persons. All of the 7 were convicted of killing whites, and 6 of the 7 executed were black. Such execution figures are especially striking in light of the fact that, during the period encompassed by the Baldus study, only 9.2% of Georgia homicides involved black defendants and white victims, while 60.7% involved black victims.

McCleskey's statistics have particular force because most of them are the product of sophisticated multiple-regression analysis. Such analysis is designed precisely to identify patterns in the aggregate, even though we may not be able to reconstitute with certainty any individual decision that goes to make up that pattern. Multiple-regression analysis is particularly well-suited to identify the influence of impermissible considerations in sentencing, since it is able to control for permissible factors that may explain an apparent arbitrary pattern. While the decision-making process of a body such as a jury may be complex, the Baldus study provides a massive compilation of the details that are most relevant to that decision. As we held in the Title VII context last term in Bazemore v. Friday, 478 U.S. 385, 106 S.Ct. 3000, 92 L.Ed.2d 315 (1986), a multiple-regression analysis need not include every conceivable variable to establish a party's case, as long as it includes those variables that account for the major factors that are likely to influence decisions. In this case, Professor Baldus in fact conducted additional regression analyses in response to criticisms and suggestions by the District Court, all of which confirmed, and some of which even strengthened, the study's original conclusions.

The statistical evidence in this case thus relentlessly documents the risk that McCleskey's sentence was influenced by racial considerations. This evidence shows that there is a better than even chance in Georgia that race will influence the decision to impose the death penalty; a majority of defendants in white-victim crimes would not have been sentenced to die if their victims had been black. In determining whether this risk is acceptable, our judgment must be shaped by the awareness that "[t]he risk of racial prejudice infecting a capital sentencing proceeding is especially serious in light of the complete finality of the death sentence." Turner v. Murray, 476 U.S. 28, 35, 106 S.Ct. 1683, 1688, 90 L.Ed.2d 27 (1986), and that "[i]t is of vital importance to the defendant and to the community that any decision to impose the death sentence be, and appear to be, based on reason rather than caprice or emotion." Gardner v. Florida, 430 U.S. 349, 358, 97 S.Ct. 1197, 1204, 51 L.Ed.2d 393 (1977). In determining the guilt of a defendant, a state must prove its case beyond a reasonable doubt. That is, we refuse to convict if the chance of error is simply less likely than not. Surely, we should not be willing to take a person's life if the chance that his death sentence was irrationally imposed is *more* likely than not. In light of the gravity of the interest at stake, petitioner's statistics on their face are a powerful demonstration of the type of risk that our Eighth Amendment jurisprudence has consistently condemned.

LAW AND STATISTICS IN CONFLICT: REFLECTIONS ON McCLESKEY v. KEMP*

David C. Baldus, George Woodworth, and Charles A. Pulaski, Jr.
In Handbook of Psychology and Law (D.K. Kagehiro and W.S. Laufer eds. 1992).

We believe that the Court's refusal in *McCleskey* to accept the normal rules of statistical inference reflects considerations going well beyond the methodological justifications by Justice Powell. One factor working against McCleskey's equal protection arguments may have been that the principle of racial equality underlying the equal protection clause of the Fourteenth Amendment was not as heavily implicated in his case as it is in more typical civil rights cases. As a convicted murderer, McCleskey did not enjoy the same status of an "oppressed minority" as claimants in housing, employment, and school discrimination cases.

In addition, the principal basis of *McCleskey's* discrimination claims was not evidence of discrimination against black defendants, but rather against defendants whose victims were white. This difference constitutes another deviation from the typical civil rights model in which the claimants suffered adverse treatment or denial of benefits on the basis of their gender or race, factors over which they had no control. It may appear inappropri-

* Baldus, Woodworth, and Pulaski, Law and Statistics in Conflict: Reflections on McCleskey v. Kemp, in Handbook of Psychol- ogy and Law, 265–69 (Kagehiro and Laufer eds. 1992), reprinted with kind permission of Springer Science and Business Media.

ate to allow a defendant who "chose" his victim to invoke that person's race as a basis for obtaining relief under the Constitution.

To be sure, to the extent that capital punishment produces benefits for either the white or black community, race-of-victim discrimination does adversely affect the black community as a whole. Specifically, discrimination on the basis of the race of the victim means that any beneficial effects produced by capital punishment are disproportionately allocated to the white community. Also, race-of-victim discrimination represents a distinct insult to the black community in that it conveys the message that black lives are worth less than white lives, regardless of the motivation for the differential in treatment. Nevertheless, as a class, black murder defendants are not adversely affected by race-of-victim discrimination. In fact, because most killers of black victims are blacks themselves, the suppressed rate of death sentencing in black-victim cases means that fewer black defendants receive the death sentence than would otherwise be the case.

We do not intend to suggest, however, that the Court cares little about race-of-victim discrimination. Indeed, Justice Powell's opinion in Booth v. Maryland [482 U.S. 496, 107 S.Ct. 2529, 96 L.Ed.2d 440 (1987)], decided two months after McCleskey, reflects the Court's continuing concerns. *Booth* held that Maryland's use of detailed Victim Information Statements (VIS) in penalty trials violated the Eighth Amendment.

> The VIS in this case provided the jury with two types of information. First, it described the personal characteristics of the victims and the emotional impact of the crimes on the family. Second, it set forth the family members' opinions and characterizations of the crimes and the defendant. For the reasons stated below, we find that this information is irrelevant to a capital-sentencing decision, and that its admission creates a constitutionally unacceptable risk that the jury may impose the death penalty in an arbitrary and capricious manner. [Id. at 503, 107 S.Ct. at 2533].

Moreover, Justice Powell explained his concern about the Victim Information Statements' description of the personal characteristics of the decedent in the following footnote:

> We are troubled by the implication that defendants whose victims were assets to their community are more deserving of punishment than those whose victims are perceived to be less worthy. Of course, our system of justice does not tolerate such distinctions. [Id. at 506, n. 8, 107 S.Ct. at 2534, n. 8].

This language clearly demonstrates a continuing commitment to a principled nondiscriminatory death-sentencing system, especially as it applies to the characteristics of the victim. Certainly, if the Court condemned jury consideration of the victim's character, it clearly would condemn the consideration of the victim's race by either prosecutors or jurors.

Of course, the *Booth* decision does raise an obvious question: How can one reconcile the Court's decision in *Booth* which, on the basis of a completely undocumented risk, invalidated the use of Victim Impact Statements, with the Court's ruling two months earlier in *McCleskey* that empirical evidence was incapable of proving a "constitutionally significant risk of racial bias"? It may also be relevant that, in cases like *Booth,* the Court can comfortably assess the risk of arbitrariness and capriciousness in individual cases based solely on unproven hunches about the effects of certain rules and procedures without recourse to empirical evidence about those effects. This preference for hunches or intuition may very well reflect an insecurity about the Justices' own abilities to assess properly quantitative evidence of the type presented in *McCleskey.* The Court may fear that subsequent analysis will demonstrate that it incorrectly interpreted the empirical data on which its findings were based. Furthermore, one can understand why relatively untrained judges, confronted with massive quantities of data and conflicting expert opinions about the validity and probative force of statistically derived inferences, might have greater confidence in intuitively derived conclusions than the pronouncements of statisticians. If the Court felt more confident about its ability to distinguish good from bad empirical studies, it might be more willing to accept such studies as a basis for its decisions. Certainly, without such confidence, one can understand a reluctance to rely upon an empirical study, no matter how well-regarded by the experts.

Uncertainty about the validity of empirical research does not, however, appear to offer a plausible explanation for the Court's rejection of McCleskey's claim and its seemingly contrary ruling in *Booth*. The likely explanation, we think, is that cases like *Booth,* which vacate death sentences on ad hoc grounds, will at most affect only a few defendants and lack any potential for producing a large-scale disruptive effect on state death-sentencing systems generally. A ruling for McCleskey, in contrast, carried the potential for a serious disruption of current death-sentencing practices both in Georgia and in other death-sentencing jurisdictions.

[A] ruling in McCleskey's favor could have seriously disrupted the U.S. death-sentencing system. The United States Supreme Court has labored for 15 years to develop a body of doctrine which would allow the states to resume routine executions under standards which would satisfy the requirements of the Constitution. In the eyes of many proponents of the death penalty, however, the Court's efforts have been woefully ineffective and have merely frustrated the desires of the people to get on with the executions. At the time of the *McCleskey* decision, more than 3,000 death sentences had been imposed, but fewer than 100 had been actually carried out through the execution. A finding in favor of McCleskey, whether based upon the jury discrimination model or an employment discrimination model, which would have led to the scrutiny of each individual death sentence, would likely have led to the wholesale staying of executions until each jurisdiction's death-sentencing could be legitimated through an empirical study. A delay of 5 years in executions as a consequence would not have seemed unlikely. The outcry against the Court from such a policy would have been predictable.

[Justice Powell] suggested a final possible explanation for the Court's decision. In it, he indicated that because the Eighth Amendment applies to the entire criminal justice system, a holding that evidence of race or sex discrimination in a criminal justice system could expose it to a successful Eighth Amendment challenge would potentially jeopardize the entire criminal justice system. He envisioned a virtual invasion of statisticians and social scientists who could potentially bring the entire criminal justice system to its knees.

To be sure, as noted above, a ruling favorable to McCleskey would have disrupted the death-sentencing systems of some states, at least for the short term; but Justice Powell's apprehension of a parade of social scientists and statisticians disrupting the courts appears to be greatly exaggerated. In the first place, the only social science research relevant to judicial proceedings would be field research conducted in actual courts. Most of the social science studies cited by Justice Powell were not field studies but experiments that used students as mock jurors. In the second place, field research of the type Justice Powell fears is expensive, extremely time-consuming, and, because of its applied nature, generally not favored by funding sources. The relatively small amount of judicial field research done to date is suggestive of the few incentives that the system offers to produce it. Third, most of the field research conducted to date tends to undercut the farfetched claims Justice Powell thinks social scientists would be inclined to support. That research does not suggest that the criminal justice system is systematically biased or invidious, or that it characteristically functions arbitrarily or irrationally. To be sure, there is substantial evidence of sentencing disparities among similarly situated offenders, but most of the available evidence does not suggest that these disparities are correlated with sex, physical appearance, or any of the other factors hypothesized by the Court. In fact, with respect to the issue of discrimination against minority defendants, the literature suggests that further empirical inquiry may increase public confidence in the basic fairness of the system.

Finally, we find it distressing that a majority of the Supreme Court would choose to reject a claim based upon invidious racial discrimination because of the work load that a ruling in the claimant's favor might entail in later cases. Former Chief Justice Burger frequently urged Congress to conduct a "judicial impact study" before enacting new legislation. Justice Powell's avowed concerns in *McCleskey* have the same flavor, but, given the constitutional character of the rights asserted, seem much less appropriate.

JUSTICE LEWIS F. POWELL, JR. (1994)*
John C. Jeffries, Jr.

Powell stated his position most succinctly in an early memorandum urging his colleagues not to hear McCleskey's case. First, it was hard to

* Reprinted with the permission of Scribner, a Division of Simon and Schuster, from LOUIS F. POWELL, JR.: A BIOGRAPHY by John C. Jeffries, Jr. Copyright © 1994 by John C. Jeffries, Jr., and with the permission of the author.

know what to make of statistics. "[S]entencing judges and juries are constitutionally *required* to consider a host of individual-specific circumstances in deciding whether to impose capital punishment. No study can take all of these individual circumstances into account, precisely because they are fact-specific as to each defendant." Of course, taking all factors into account was precisely what Baldus and his colleagues had tried to do, but Powell was uneasy with this kind of evidence. As he said elsewhere, "[m]y understanding of statistical analysis ... ranges from limited to zero."

He also did not know what constitutional weight to give to the statistical effect of the *victim's* race. "[O]ne would expect that if there were race-based sentencing, the Baldus study would show a bias based on the *defendant's* race," but the "study suggests *no* such effect...." Differential treatment of defendants based on the race of their victims was hard to understand as racial bias against defendants.

Finally, Powell thought the overall picture revealed by the figures was decidedly positive. The "study tends to show that the system operates rationally as a general matter: The death penalty was most likely in those cases with the most severe aggravating factors and the least mitigating factors, and least likely in the opposite cases. The pattern suggests precisely the kind of careful balancing of individual factors that the Court required in *Gregg*,"

[P]owell did not see the case as condoning racism but simply as recognizing the inevitable variations in any nonmandatory death penalty.

[I]n conversation with the author in the summer of 1991, Powell was asked whether he would change his vote in any case:

"Yes, *McCleskey v. Kemp*."

"Do you mean you would now accept the argument from statistics?"

"No, I would vote the other way in any capital case."

"In *any* capital case?"

"Yes."

"Even in *Furman v. Georgia*?"

"Yes. I have come to think that capital punishment should be abolished."

———

NOTES

1. Court–Ordered Research. The defendant in People v. Jackson, 28 Cal.3d 264, 168 Cal.Rptr. 603, 618 P.2d 149 (1980), an African–American male, was convicted of murdering two white women and sentenced to death. The California Supreme Court affirmed the conviction but appointed a retired state appellate justice as a referee and ordered him "to take evidence and make findings of fact with respect to defendant's contentions that death sentences in California have been discriminatorily imposed on the basis of (1) the race of the victim, (2) the race of the defendant, and/or (3) the gender of the defendant." In re Jackson, Crim. 22165, Minutes of the California Supreme Court, May 3, 1984. After the referee had spent three years and one million dollars commissioning this research, a new majority of the California Supreme Court quashed the study. "Our order, dated May 3, 1984, expanding the reference to include claims of discriminatory application of the death penalty in California on the basis of race and sex, is vacated without prejudice to a renewed application for an expanded or separate reference which alleges a prima facie case not inconsistent with McCleskey v. Kemp (1987), 481 U.S. 279, 95 L.Ed.2d 262." In re Jackson, Crim. 22165, Minutes of the California Supreme Court, October 27, 1987.

2.   Certificates of Non–Discrimination. The Omnibus Drug Initiative of 1988, Pub.L. No. 100–690, codified at 21 U.S.C. § 848(*o*)(1), "Death Penalty for Drug–Related Killings," states as follows:

> In any hearing held before a jury under this section, the court shall instruct the jury that in its consideration of whether the sentence of death is justified it shall not consider the race, color, religious beliefs, national origin, or sex of the defendant or the victim, and that the jury is not to recommend a sentence of death unless it has concluded that it would recommend a sentence of death for the crime in question no matter what the race, color, religious beliefs, national origin, or sex of the defendant, or the victim, may be. The jury shall return to the court a certificate signed by each juror that consideration of the race, color, religious beliefs, national origin, or sex of the defendant or the victim was not involved in reaching his or her individual decision, and that the individual juror would have made the same recommendation regarding a sentence for the crime in question no matter what the race, color, religious beliefs, national origin, or sex of the defendant, or the victim, may be.

———

BAZE v. REES

Supreme Court of the United States, 2008.
___ U.S. ___, 128 S.Ct. 1520, 170 L.Ed.2d 420.

■ CHIEF JUSTICE ROBERTS announced the judgment of the Court and delivered an opinion, in which JUSTICE KENNEDY and JUSTICE ALITO join.

Like 35 other States and the Federal Government, Kentucky has chosen to impose capital punishment for certain crimes. As is true with respect to each of these States and the Federal Government, Kentucky has altered its method of execution over time to more humane means of carrying out the sentence. That progress has led to the use of lethal injection by every jurisdiction that imposes the death penalty.

Petitioners in this case—each convicted of double homicide—acknowledge that the lethal injection procedure, if applied as intended, will result in a humane death. They nevertheless contend that the lethal injection protocol is unconstitutional under the Eighth Amendment's ban on "cruel and unusual punishments," because of the risk that the protocol's terms might not be properly followed, resulting in significant pain.

The trial court [r]ecognized that "[t]here are no methods of legal execution that are satisfactory to those who oppose the death penalty on moral, religious, or societal grounds," but concluded that Kentucky's procedure "complies with the constitutional requirements against cruel and unusual punishment."

[T]hroughout our history, whenever a method of execution has been challenged in this Court as cruel and unusual, the Court has rejected the challenge. Our society has nonetheless steadily moved to more humane methods of carrying out capital punishment. The firing squad, hanging, the electric chair, and the gas chamber have each in turn given way to more humane methods, culminating in today's consensus on lethal injection. The broad framework of the Eighth Amendment has accommodated this progress toward more humane methods of execution, and our approval of a particular method in the past has not precluded legislatures from taking the steps they deem appropriate, in light of new developments, to ensure humane capital punishment. There is no reason to suppose that today's decision will be any different.[7]

The judgment below concluding that Kentucky's procedure is consistent with the Eighth Amendment is, accordingly, affirmed.

■ JUSTICE STEVENS, concurring in the judgment.

In *Gregg v. Georgia,* 428 U.S. 153 (1976), we explained that unless a criminal sanction serves a legitimate penological function, it constitutes "gratuitous infliction of suffering" in violation of the Eighth Amendment. We then identified three societal purposes for death as a sanction: incapacitation, deterrence, and retribution. In the past three decades, however, each of these rationales has been called into question.

While incapacitation may have been a legitimate rationale in 1976, the recent rise in statutes providing for life imprisonment without the possibility of parole demonstrates that incapacitation is neither a necessary nor a sufficient justification for the death penalty.[10] Moreover, a recent poll

7. We do not agree with Justice STEVENS that anything in our opinion undermines or remotely addresses the validity of capital punishment. The fact that society has moved to progressively more humane methods of execution does not suggest that capital punishment itself no longer serves valid purposes; we would not have supposed that the case for capital punishment was stronger when it was imposed predominantly by hanging or electrocution.

10. Forty-eight States now have some form of life imprisonment without parole, with the majority of statutes enacted within the last two decades. See Note, A Matter of Life and Death: The Effect of Life–Without–

indicates that support for the death penalty drops significantly when life without the possibility of parole is presented as an alternative option.[11] And the available sociological evidence suggests that juries are less likely to impose the death penalty when life without parole is available as a sentence.[12]

The legitimacy of deterrence as an acceptable justification for the death penalty is also questionable, at best. Despite 30 years of empirical research in the area, there remains no reliable statistical evidence that capital punishment in fact deters potential offenders.[13] In the absence of such evidence, deterrence cannot serve as a sufficient penological justification for this uniquely severe and irrevocable punishment.

We are left, then, with retribution as the primary rationale for imposing the death penalty. And indeed, it is the retribution rationale that animates much of the remaining enthusiasm for the death penalty[14]. As Lord Justice Denning argued in 1950, " 'some crimes are so outrageous that society insists on adequate punishment, because the wrong-doer deserves it, irrespective of whether it is a deterrent or not.' " 428 U.S., at 184, n. 30. Our Eighth Amendment jurisprudence has narrowed the class of offenders eligible for the death penalty to include only those who have committed outrageous crimes defined by specific aggravating factors. It is the cruel treatment of victims that provides the most persuasive arguments

Parole Statutes on Capital Punishment, 119 Harv. L.Rev. 1838, 1839, 1841–1844 (2006).

11. See R. Dieter, Sentencing For Life: Americans Embrace Alternatives to the Death Penalty (Apr.1993), http://www. death penalty info.org/article.php?scid=45 & did=481.

12. In one study, potential capital jurors in Virginia stated that knowing about the existence of statutes providing for life without the possibility of parole would significantly influence their sentencing decision. In another study, a significant majority of potential capital jurors in Georgia said they would be more likely to select a life sentence over a death sentence if they knew that the defendant would be ineligible for parole for at least 25 years. See Note, 119 Harv. L.Rev., at 1845. Indeed, this insight drove our decision in *Simmons v. South Carolina,* 512 U.S. 154 (1994), that capital defendants have a due process right to require that their sentencing juries be informed of their ineligibility for parole.

13. Admittedly, there has been a recent surge in scholarship asserting the deterrent effect of the death penalty, see, *e.g.,* Mocan & Gittings, Getting Off Death Row: Commuted Sentences and the Deterrent Effect of Capital Punishment, 46 J. Law & Econ. 453 (2003); Adler & Summers, Capital Punishment Works, Wall Street Journal, Nov. 2, 2007, p. A13, but there has been an equal, if not greater, amount of scholarship criticizing the methodologies of those studies and questioning the results, see, *e.g.,* Fagan, Death and Deterrence Redux: Science, Law and Causal Reasoning on Capital Punishment, 4 Ohio St. J.Crim. L. 255 (2006); Donohue & Wolfers, Uses and Abuses of Empirical Evidence in the Death Penalty Debate, 58 Stan. L.Rev. 791 (2005).

14. Retribution is the most common basis of support for the death penalty. A recent study found that 37% of death penalty supporters cited "an eye for an eye/they took a life/fits the crime" as their reason for supporting capital punishment. Another 13% cited "They deserve it." The next most common reasons-"sav[ing] taxpayers money/cost associated with prison" and deterrence-were each cited by 11% of supporters. See Dept. of Justice, Bureau of Justice Statistics, Sourcebook of Criminal Justice Statistics 147 (2003) (Table 2.55), online at http:// www. albany.edu/sourcebook/pdf/t255.pdf.

for prosecutors seeking the death penalty. A natural response to such heinous crimes is a thirst for vengeance.

At the same time, [o]ur society has moved away from public and painful retribution towards ever more humane forms of punishment. State-sanctioned killing is therefore becoming more and more anachronistic. In an attempt to bring executions in line with our evolving standards of decency, we have adopted increasingly less painful methods of execution, and then declared previous methods barbaric and archaic. But by requiring that an execution be relatively painless, we necessarily protect the inmate from enduring any punishment that is comparable to the suffering inflicted on his victim. This trend, while appropriate and required by the Eighth Amendment's prohibition on cruel and unusual punishment, actually undermines the very premise on which public approval of the retribution rationale is based. See, *e.g.,* Kaufman–Osborn, Regulating Death: Capital Punishment and the Late Liberal State, 111 Yale L.J. 681, 704 (2001) (explaining that there is "a tension between our desire to realize the claims of retribution by killing those who kill, and ... a method [of execution] that, because it seems to do no harm other than killing, cannot satisfy the intuitive sense of equivalence that informs this conception of justice"); A. Sarat, When the State Kills: Capital Punishment and the American Condition 60–84 (2001).

Full recognition of the diminishing force of the principal rationales for retaining the death penalty should lead this Court and legislatures to reexamine the question recently posed by Professor Salinas, a former Texas prosecutor and judge: "Is it time to Kill the Death Penalty?" See Salinas, 34 Am. J.Crim. L. 39 (2006). The time for a dispassionate, impartial comparison of the enormous costs that death penalty litigation imposes on society with the benefits that it produces has surely arrived.

[J]ustice White was exercising his own judgment in 1972 when he provided the decisive vote in *Furman,* the case that led to a nationwide reexamination of the death penalty. His conclusion that death amounted to "cruel and unusual punishment in the constitutional sense" as well as the "dictionary sense," rested on both an uncontroversial legal premise and on a factual premise that he admittedly could not "prove" on the basis of objective criteria. [Furman v. Georgia,] 408 U.S. [238 (1972)], at 312, 313 (concurring opinion). As a matter of law, he correctly stated that the "needless extinction of life with only marginal contributions to any discernible social or public purposes ... would be patently excessive" and violative of the Eighth Amendment. *Id.,* at 312. As a matter of fact, he stated, "like my Brethren, I must arrive at judgment; and I can do no more than state a conclusion based on 10 years of almost daily exposure to the facts and circumstances of hundreds and hundreds of federal and state criminal cases involving crimes for which death is the authorized penalty." *Id.,* at 313. I agree with Justice White that there are occasions when a Member of this Court has a duty to make judgments on the basis of data that falls short of absolute proof.

[O]f special concern to me are rules that deprive the defendant of a trial by jurors representing a fair cross section of the community. Litigation involving both challenges for cause and peremptory challenges has persuaded me that the process of obtaining a "death qualified jury" is really a procedure that has the purpose and effect of obtaining a jury that is biased in favor of conviction.

[Another] significant concern is the risk of discriminatory application of the death penalty. While that risk has been dramatically reduced, the Court has allowed it to continue to play an unacceptable role in capital cases. Thus, in *McCleskey v. Kemp,* 481 U.S. 279 (1987), the Court upheld a death sentence despite the "strong probability that [the defendant's] sentencing jury ... was influenced by the fact that [he was] black and his victim was white." *Id.,* at 366 (STEVENS, J., dissenting).

[I]n sum, just as Justice White ultimately based his conclusion in *Furman* on his extensive exposure to countless cases for which death is the authorized penalty, I have relied on my own experience in reaching the conclusion that the imposition of the death penalty represents "the pointless and needless extinction of life with only marginal contributions to any discernible social or public purposes. A penalty with such negligible returns to the State [is] patently excessive and cruel and unusual punishment violative of the Eighth Amendment." *Furman,* 408 U.S., at 312 (White, J., concurring).

The conclusion that I have reached with regard to the constitutionality of the death penalty itself makes my decision in this case particularly difficult. It does not, however, justify a refusal to respect precedents that remain a part of our law. This Court has held that the death penalty is constitutional, and has established a framework for evaluating the constitutionality of particular methods of execution. Under those precedents, [I] am persuaded that the evidence adduced by petitioners fails to prove that Kentucky's lethal injection protocol violates the Eighth Amendment. Accordingly, I join the Court's judgment.

■ JUSTICE SCALIA, with whom JUSTICE THOMAS joins, concurring in the judgment.

I write separately to provide what I think is needed response to Justice STEVENS' separate opinion. [A]ccording to Justice STEVENS, the death penalty promotes none of the purposes of criminal punishment because it neither prevents more crimes than alternative measures nor serves a retributive purpose. He argues that "the recent rise in statutes providing for life imprisonment without the possibility of parole" means that States have a ready alternative to the death penalty. Moreover, "[d]espite 30 years of empirical research in the area, there remains no reliable statistical evidence that capital punishment in fact deters potential offenders." Taking the points together, Justice STEVENS concludes that the availability of alternatives, and what he describes as the unavailability of "reliable statistical evidence," renders capital punishment unconstitutional. In his view, the benefits of capital punishment—as compared to other forms of punishment such as life imprisonment—are outweighed by the costs.

These conclusions are not supported by the available data. Justice STEVENS' analysis barely acknowledges the "significant body of recent evidence that capital punishment may well have a deterrent effect, possibly a quite powerful one." Sunstein & Vermeule, Is Capital Punishment Morally Required? Acts, Omissions, and Life–Life Tradeoffs, 58 Stan. L.Rev. 703, 706 (2006); see also *id.,* at 706, n. 9 (listing the approximately half a dozen studies supporting this conclusion). According to a "leading national study," "each execution prevents some eighteen murders, on average." *Id.,* at 706. "If the current evidence is even roughly correct . . . then a refusal to impose capital punishment will effectively condemn numerous innocent people to death." *Ibid.*

Of course, it may well be that the empirical studies establishing that the death penalty has a powerful deterrent effect are incorrect, and some scholars have disputed its deterrent value. But that is not the point. It is simply not our place to choose one set of responsible empirical studies over another in interpreting the Constitution. Nor is it our place to demand that state legislatures support their criminal sanctions with foolproof empirical studies, rather than commonsense predictions about human behavior. "The value of capital punishment as a deterrent of crime is a complex factual issue the resolution of which properly rests with the legislatures, which can evaluate the results of statistical studies in terms of their own local conditions and with a flexibility of approach that is not available to the courts." *Gregg, supra,* at 186 (joint opinion of Stewart, Powell, and STEVENS, JJ.). Were Justice STEVENS' current view the constitutional test, even his own preferred criminal sanction—life imprisonment without the possibility of parole—may fail constitutional scrutiny, because it is entirely unclear that enough empirical evidence supports that sanction as compared to alternatives such as life with the possibility of parole.

But even if Justice STEVENS' assertion about the deterrent value of the death penalty were correct, the death penalty would yet be constitutional (as he concedes) if it served the appropriate purpose of retribution. I would think it difficult indeed to prove that a criminal sanction fails to serve a retributive purpose—a judgment that strikes me as inherently subjective and insusceptible of judicial review.

---

3. EXCESSIVE SANCTION

In Atkins v. Virginia, 536 U.S. 304, 122 S.Ct. 2242, 153 L.Ed.2d 335 (2002), the Supreme Court held that executing people with mental retardation constituted an "excessive" sanction in violation of the Eighth and Fourteenth Amendments to the Unites States Constitution. Three years later, the court applied a similar analysis, informed by social science, to hold that the execution of offenders who were under the age of 18 when they committed their crimes was also unconstitutional. Three years after that, the court found that the execution of offenders for the rape of children that did not result in the childrens' deaths was unconstitutional.

—————

ROPER v. SIMMONS

Supreme Court of the United States, 2005.
543 U.S. 551, 125 S.Ct. 1183, 161 L.Ed.2d 1.

■ JUSTICE KENNEDY delivered the opinion of the Court.

This case requires us to address ... whether it is permissible under the Eighth and Fourteenth Amendments to the Constitution of the United States to execute a juvenile offender who was older than 15 but younger than 18 when he committed a capital crime. [A]t the age of 17, when he was still a junior in high school, Christopher Simmons, the respondent here, committed murder. About nine months later, after he had turned 18, he was tried and sentenced to death.

[B]ecause the death penalty is the most severe punishment, the Eighth Amendment applies to it with special force. *Thompson*, 487 U.S., at 856 (O'CONNOR, J., concurring in judgment). Capital punishment must be limited to those offenders who commit "a narrow category of the most serious crimes" and whose extreme culpability makes them "the most deserving of execution." *Atkins [536 U.S. 304 (2002)]* at 319.

[T]hree general differences between juveniles under 18 and adults demonstrate that juvenile offenders cannot with reliability be classified among the worst offenders. First, as any parent knows and as the scientific and sociological studies respondent and his *amici* cite tend to confirm, "[a] lack of maturity and an underdeveloped sense of responsibility are found in youth more often than in adults and are more understandable among the young. These qualities often result in impetuous and ill-considered actions and decisions." *Johnson [509 U.S. 350 (1993)]*, at 367; see also *Eddings*, *[455 U.S. 104 (1982)]*, at 115–116 ("Even the normal 16–year–old customarily lacks the maturity of an adult"). It has been noted that "adolescents are overrepresented statistically in virtually every category of reckless behavior." Arnett, Reckless Behavior in Adolescence: A Developmental Perspective, 12 Developmental Review 339 (1992). In recognition of the comparative immaturity and irresponsibility of juveniles, almost every State prohibits those under 18 years of age from voting, serving on juries, or marrying without parental consent.

The second area of difference is that juveniles are more vulnerable or susceptible to negative influences and outside pressures, including peer pressure. *Eddings, supra*, at 115 ("Youth is more than a chronological fact. It is a time and condition of life when a person may be most susceptible to influence and to psychological damage"). This is explained in part by the prevailing circumstance that juveniles have less control, or less experience with control, over their own environment. See Steinberg & Scott, Less Guilty by Reason of Adolescence: Developmental Immaturity, Diminished

Responsibility, and the Juvenile Death Penalty, 58 Am. Psychologist 1009, 1014 (2003) (hereinafter Steinberg & Scott) ("As legal minors, [juveniles] lack the freedom that adults have to extricate themselves from a criminogenic setting").

The third broad difference is that the character of a juvenile is not as well formed as that of an adult. The personality traits of juveniles are more transitory, less fixed. See generally E. Erikson, Identity: Youth and Crisis (1968).

These differences render suspect any conclusion that a juvenile falls among the worst offenders. The susceptibility of juveniles to immature and irresponsible behavior means "their irresponsible conduct is not as morally reprehensible as that of an adult." *Thompson, supra,* at 835 (plurality opinion). Their own vulnerability and comparative lack of control over their immediate surroundings mean juveniles have a greater claim than adults to be forgiven for failing to escape negative influences in their whole environment. The reality that juveniles still struggle to define their identity means it is less supportable to conclude that even a heinous crime committed by a juvenile is evidence of irretrievably depraved character. From a moral standpoint it would be misguided to equate the failings of a minor with those of an adult, for a greater possibility exists that a minor's character deficiencies will be reformed. Indeed, "the relevance of youth as a mitigating factor derives from the fact that the signature qualities of youth are transient; as individuals mature, the impetuousness and recklessness that may dominate in younger years can subside." *Johnson, supra,* at 368; see also Steinberg & Scott 1014 ("For most teens, [risky or antisocial] behaviors are fleeting; they cease with maturity as individual identity becomes settled. Only a relatively small proportion of adolescents who experiment in risky or illegal activities develop entrenched patterns of problem behavior that persist into adulthood").

In *Thompson,* a plurality of the Court recognized the import of these characteristics with respect to juveniles under 16, and relied on them to hold that the Eighth Amendment prohibited the imposition of the death penalty on juveniles below that age. 487 U.S., at 833–838. We conclude the same reasoning applies to all juvenile offenders under 18.

Once the diminished culpability of juveniles is recognized, it is evident that the penological justifications for the death penalty apply to them with lesser force than to adults. We have held there are two distinct social purposes served by the death penalty: " 'retribution and deterrence of capital crimes by prospective offenders.' " *Atkins,* 536 U.S., at 319 (quoting *Gregg* v. *Georgia,* 428 U.S. 153, 183 (1976) (joint opinion of Stewart, Powell, and STEVENS, JJ.)). As for retribution, we remarked in *Atkins* that "if the culpability of the average murderer is insufficient to justify the most extreme sanction available to the State, the lesser culpability of the mentally retarded offender surely does not merit that form of retribution." 536 U.S., at 319. The same conclusions follow from the lesser culpability of the juvenile offender. Whether viewed as an attempt to express the community's moral outrage or as an attempt to right the balance for the wrong to the victim, the case for retribution is not as strong with a minor as with an adult. Retribution is not proportional if the law's most severe penalty is imposed on one whose culpability or blameworthiness is diminished, to a substantial degree, by reason of youth and immaturity.

As for deterrence, it is unclear whether the death penalty has a significant or even measurable deterrent effect on juveniles, as counsel for the petitioner acknowledged at oral argument. In general we leave to legislatures the assessment of the efficacy of various criminal penalty schemes. Here, however, the absence of evidence of deterrent effect is of special concern because the same characteristics that render juveniles less culpable than adults suggest as well that juveniles will be less susceptible to deterrence. In particular, as the plurality observed in *Thompson*, "the likelihood that the teenage offender has made the kind of cost-benefit analysis that attaches any weight to the possibility of execution is so remote as to be virtually nonexistent." 487 U.S., at 837. To the extent the juvenile death penalty might have residual deterrent effect, it is worth noting that the punishment of life imprisonment without the possibility of parole is itself a severe sanction, in particular for a young person.

In concluding that neither retribution nor deterrence provides adequate justification for imposing the death penalty on juvenile offenders, we cannot deny or overlook the brutal crimes too many juvenile offenders have committed. Certainly it can be argued, although we by no means concede the point, that a rare case might arise in which a juvenile offender has sufficient psychological maturity, and at the same time demonstrates sufficient depravity, to merit a sentence of death. Indeed, this possibility is the linchpin of one contention pressed by petitioner and his *amici*. They assert that even assuming the truth of the observations we have made about juveniles' diminished culpability in general, jurors nonetheless should be allowed to consider mitigating arguments related to youth on a case-by-case basis, and in some cases to impose the death penalty if justified.

[W]e disagree. The differences between juvenile and adult offenders are too marked and well understood to risk allowing a youthful person to receive the death penalty despite insufficient culpability. [I]t is difficult even for expert psychologists to differentiate between the juvenile offender whose crime reflects unfortunate yet transient immaturity, and the rare juvenile offender whose crime reflects irreparable corruption. See Steinberg & Scott 1014–1016. As we understand it, this difficulty underlies the rule forbidding psychiatrists from diagnosing any patient under 18 as having antisocial personality disorder, a disorder also referred to as psychopathy or sociopathy, and which is characterized by callousness, cynicism, and contempt for the feelings, rights, and suffering of others. American Psychiatric Association, Diagnostic and Statistical Manual of Mental Disorders 701–706 (4th ed. text rev. 2000); see also Steinberg & Scott 1015. If trained psychiatrists with the advantage of clinical testing and observation refrain, despite diagnostic expertise, from assessing any juvenile under 18 as having antisocial personality disorder, we conclude that States should refrain from asking jurors to issue a far graver condemnation—that a juvenile offender merits the death penalty. When a juvenile offender commits a heinous crime, the State can exact forfeiture of some of the most basic liberties, but the State cannot extinguish his life and his potential to attain a mature understanding of his own humanity.

[T]he Eighth and Fourteenth Amendments forbid imposition of the death penalty on offenders who were under the age of 18 when their crimes were committed. The judgment of the Missouri Supreme Court setting aside the sentence of death imposed upon Christopher Simmons is affirmed.

■ JUSTICE SCALIA, with whom THE CHIEF JUSTICE and JUSTICE THOMAS join, dissenting.

[T]oday's opinion provides a perfect example of why judges are ill equipped to make the type of legislative judgments the Court insists on making here. To support its opinion that States should be prohibited from imposing the death penalty on anyone who committed murder before age 18, the Court looks to scientific and sociological studies, picking and choosing those that support its position. It never explains why those particular studies are methodologically sound; none was ever entered into evidence or tested in an adversarial proceeding. As THE CHIEF JUSTICE has explained:

> "Methodological and other errors can affect the reliability and validity of estimates about the opinions and attitudes of a population derived from various sampling techniques. Everything from variations in the survey methodology, such as the choice of the target population, the sampling design used, the questions asked, and the statistical analyses used to interpret the data can skew the results." *Atkins, supra,* at 326–327 (dissenting opinion) (citing R. Groves, Survey Errors and Survey Costs (1989); 1 C. Turner & E. Martin, Surveying Subjective Phenomena (1984)).

In other words, all the Court has done today, to borrow from another context, is to look over the heads of the crowd and pick out its friends.

We need not look far to find studies contradicting the Court's conclusions. As petitioner points out, the American Psychological Association (APA), which claims in this case that scientific evidence shows persons under 18 lack the ability to take moral responsibility for their decisions, has previously taken precisely the opposite position before this very Court. In its brief in *Hodgson* v. *Minnesota,* 497 U.S. 417 (1990), the APA found a "rich body of research" showing that juveniles are mature enough to decide whether to obtain an abortion without parental involvement. Brief for APA as *Amicus Curiae,* O. T. 1989, No. 88–805 etc., p. 18. The APA brief, citing psychology treatises and studies too numerous to list here, asserted: "By middle adolescence (age 14–15) young people develop abilities similar to adults in reasoning about moral dilemmas, understanding social rules and laws, [and] reasoning about interpersonal relationships and interpersonal problems." *Id.,* at 19–20 (citations omitted). Given the nuances of scientific methodology and conflicting views, courts—which can only consider the limited evidence on the record before them—are ill equipped to determine which view of science is the right one. Legislatures "are better qualified to weigh and 'evaluate the results of statistical studies in terms of their own local conditions and with a flexibility of approach that is not available to the courts.'" *McCleskey* v. *Kemp,* 481 U.S. 279, 319 (1987) (quoting *Gregg, supra,* at 186).

Even putting aside questions of methodology, the studies cited by the Court offer scant support for a categorical prohibition of the death penalty for murderers under 18. At most, these studies conclude that, *on average,* or *in most cases,* persons under 18 are unable to take moral responsibility for their actions. Not one of the cited studies opines that all individuals under 18 are unable to appreciate the nature of their crimes.

Moreover, the cited studies describe only adolescents who engage in risky or antisocial behavior, as many young people do. Murder, however, is more than just risky or antisocial behavior. It is entirely consistent to believe that young people often act impetuously and lack judgment, but, at the same time, to believe that those who commit premeditated murder are—at least sometimes—just as culpable as adults. Christopher Simmons, who was only seven months shy of his 18th birthday when he murdered Shirley Crook, described to his friends *beforehand*—"in chilling, callous terms," as the Court puts it, *ante,* at 1—the murder he planned to commit. He then broke into the home of an innocent woman, bound her with duct tape and electrical wire, and threw her off a bridge alive and conscious.

[N]or does the Court suggest a stopping point for its reasoning. If juries cannot make appropriate determinations in cases involving murderers under 18, in what other kinds of cases will the Court find jurors deficient? We have already held that no jury may consider whether a mentally deficient defendant can receive the death penalty, irrespective of his crime. See *Atkins,* 536 U.S., at 321. Why not take other mitigating factors, such as considerations of childhood abuse or poverty, away from juries as well? Surely jurors "overpowered" by "the brutality or cold-blooded nature" of a crime, *ante,* at 19, could not adequately weigh these mitigating factors either.

———

KENNEDY v. LOUISIANA

Supreme Court of the United States, 2008.
___ U.S. ___, 128 S.Ct. 2641, 171 L.Ed.2d 525.

■ JUSTICE KENNEDY delivered the opinion of the Court.

Patrick Kennedy, the petitioner here, seeks to set aside his death sentence under the Eighth Amendment. He was charged by the respondent, the State of Louisiana, with the aggravated rape of his then–8–year–old stepdaughter. After a jury trial petitioner was convicted and sentenced to death under a state statute authorizing capital punishment for the rape of a child under 12 years of age. This case presents the question whether the Constitution bars respondent from imposing the death penalty for the rape of a child where the crime did not result, and was not intended to result, in death of the victim. We hold the Eighth Amendment prohibits the death penalty for this offense. The Louisiana statute is unconstitutional.

[I]t must be acknowledged that there are moral grounds to question a rule barring capital punishment for a crime against an individual that did not result in death. These facts illustrate the point. Here the victim's fright, the sense of betrayal, and the nature of her injuries caused more prolonged physical and mental suffering than, say, a sudden killing by an unseen assassin. The attack was not just on her but on her childhood. For this reason, we should be most reluctant to rely upon the language of the plurality in *Coker [v. Georgia*, 433 U.S. 584 (1977)], which posited that, for the victim of rape, "life may not be nearly so happy as it was" but it is not beyond repair. 433 U. S., at 598. Rape has a permanent psychological, emotional, and sometimes physical impact on the child. See C. Bagley & K. King, Child Sexual Abuse: The Search for Healing 2–24, 111–112 (1990); Finkelhor & Browne, Assessing the Long–Term Impact of Child Sexual Abuse: A Review and Conceptualization in Handbook on Sexual Abuse of Children 55–60 (L. Walker ed. 1988). We cannot dismiss the years of long anguish that must be endured by the victim of child rape.

It does not follow, though, that capital punishment is a proportionate penalty for the crime. The constitutional prohibition against excessive or cruel and unusual punishments mandates that the State's power to punish "be exercised within the limits of civilized standards." *Trop [v. Dulles]*, 356 U. S. [86], at 99, 100 [(1958)] (plurality opinion). Evolving standards of decency that mark the progress of a maturing society counsel us to be most hesitant before interpreting the Eighth Amendment to allow the extension of the death penalty, a hesitation that has special force where no life was taken in the commission of the crime.

[C]onsistent with evolving standards of decency and the teachings of our precedents, we conclude that, in determining whether the death penalty is excessive, there is a distinction between intentional first-degree murder on the one hand and nonhomicide crimes against individual persons, even including child rape, on the other.

[I]n reaching our conclusion we find significant the number of executions that would be allowed under respondent's approach. The crime of child rape, considering its reported incidents, occurs more often than first-degree murder. Approximately 5,702 incidents of vaginal, anal, or oral rape of a child under the age of 12 were reported nationwide in 2005; this is almost twice the total incidents of intentional murder for victims of all ages (3,405) reported during the same period. See Inter–University Consortium for Political and Social Research, National Incident–Based Reporting System, 2005, Study No. 4720, http://www.icpsr.umich.edu (as visited June 12, 2008, and available in Clerk of Court's case file). Although we have no reliable statistics on convictions for child rape, we can surmise that, each year, there are hundreds, or more, of these convictions just in jurisdictions that permit capital punishment. Cf. Brief for Louisiana Association of Criminal Defense Lawyers et al. as *Amici Curiae* 1–2, and n. 2 (noting that there are now at least 70 capital rape indictments pending in Louisiana and estimating the actual number to be over 100). As a result of existing rules, only 2.2% of convicted first-degree murderers are sentenced to death, see Blume, Eisenberg, & Wells, Explaining Death Row's Population and Racial Composition, 1 J. of Empirical Legal Studies 165, 171 (2004). But under respondent's approach, the 36 States that permit the death penalty could sentence to death all persons convicted of raping a child less than 12 years of age. This could not be reconciled with our evolving standards of decency and the necessity to constrain the use of the death penalty.

[O]ur decision is consistent with the justifications offered for the death penalty. *Gregg [v. Georgia,* 428 U.S. 153 (1976)] instructs that capital punishment is excessive when it is grossly out of proportion to the crime or it does not fulfill the two distinct social purposes served by the death penalty: retribution and deterrence of capital crimes.

As in *Coker,* here it cannot be said with any certainty that the death penalty for child rape serves no deterrent or retributive function. Cf. *Gregg, supra,* at 185–186 (joint opinion of Stewart, Powell, and STEVENS, JJ.) ("[T]here is no convincing empirical evidence either supporting or refuting th[e] view [that the death penalty serves as a significantly greater deterrent than lesser penalties]. We may nevertheless assume safely that there are murderers . . . for whom . . . the death penalty undoubtedly is a significant deterrent").

[I]n considering whether retribution is served, among other factors we have looked to whether capital punishment "has the potential . . . to allow the community as a whole, including the surviving family and friends of the victim, to affirm its own judgment that the culpability of the prisoner is so serious that the ultimate penalty must be sought and imposed." *Panetti* v. *Quarterman,* 551 U. S. 930 (2007). In considering the death penalty for nonhomicide offenses this inquiry necessarily also must include the question whether the death penalty balances the wrong to the victim.

It is not at all evident that the child rape victim's hurt is lessened when the law permits the death of the perpetrator. Capital cases require a long-term commitment by those who testify for the prosecution, especially when guilt and sentencing determinations are in multiple proceedings. In cases like this the key testimony is not just from the family but from the victim herself. During formative years of her adolescence, made all the more daunting for having to come to terms with the brutality of her experience, L. H. [the victim] was required to discuss the case at length with law enforcement personnel. In a public trial she was required to recount once more all the details of the crime to a jury as the State pursued the death of her stepfather. Cf. G. Goodman et al., Testifying in Criminal Court: Emotional Effects on Child Sexual Assault Victims 50, 62, 72 (1992). And in the end the State made L. H. a central figure in its decision to seek the death penalty, telling the jury in closing statements: "[L. H.] is asking you, asking you to set up a time and place when he dies."

Society's desire to inflict the death penalty for child rape by enlisting the child victim to assist it over the course of years in asking for capital punishment forces a moral choice on the child, who is not of mature age to make that choice. The way the death penalty here involves the child victim in its enforcement can compromise a decent legal system; and this is but a subset of fundamental difficulties capital punishment can cause in the administration and enforcement of laws proscribing child rape.

There are, moreover, serious systemic concerns in prosecuting the crime of child rape that are relevant to the constitutionality of making it a capital offense. The problem of unreliable, induced, and even imagined child testimony means there is a "special risk of wrongful execution" in some child rape cases. This undermines, at least to some degree, the meaningful contribution of the death penalty to legitimate goals of punishment. Studies conclude that children are highly susceptible to suggestive questioning techniques like repetition, guided imagery, and selective reinforcement. See Ceci & Friedman, The Suggestibility of Children: Scientific Research and Legal Implications, 86 Cornell L. Rev. 33, 47 (2000) (there is "strong evidence that children, especially young children, are suggestible to a significant degree-even on abuse-related questions"); Gross, Jacoby, Matheson, Montgomery, & Patil, Exonerations in the United States 1989 Through 2003, 95 J. Crim. L. & C. 523, 539 (2005) (discussing allegations of abuse at the Little Rascals Day Care Center); see also Quas, Davis, Goodman, & Myers, Repeated Questions, Deception, and Children's True and False Reports of Body Touch, 12 Child Maltreatment 60, 61–66 (2007) (finding that 4–to 7–year–olds "were able to maintain [a] lie about body touch fairly effectively when asked repeated, direct questions during a mock forensic interview").

Similar criticisms pertain to other cases involving child witnesses; but child rape cases present heightened concerns because the central narrative and account of the crime often comes from the child herself. She and the accused are, in most instances, the only ones present when the crime was committed. And the question in a capital case is not just the fact of the crime, including, say, proof of rape as distinct from abuse short of rape, but details bearing upon brutality in its commission. These matters are subject to fabrication or exaggeration, or both. See Ceci and Friedman, *supra;* Quas, *supra.* Although capital punishment does bring retribution, and the legislature here has chosen to use it for this end, its judgment must be weighed, in deciding the constitutional question, against the special risks of unreliable testimony with respect to this crime.

With respect to deterrence, if the death penalty adds to the risk of non-reporting, that, too, diminishes the penalty's objectives. Underreporting is a common problem with respect to child sexual abuse. See Hanson, Resnick, Saunders, Kilpatrick, & Best, Factors Related to the Reporting of Childhood Rape, 23 Child Abuse & Neglect 559, 564 (1999) (finding that about 88% of female rape victims under the age of 18 did not disclose their abuse to authorities); Smith et al., Delay in Disclosure of Childhood Rape: Results From A National Survey, 24 Child Abuse & Neglect 273, 278–279

(2000) (finding that 72% of women raped as children disclosed their abuse to someone, but that only 12% of the victims reported the rape to authorities). Although we know little about what differentiates those who report from those who do not report, one of the most commonly cited reasons for nondisclosure is fear of negative consequences for the perpetrator, a concern that has special force where the abuser is a family member, see Goodman–Brown, Edelstein, Goodman, Jones, & Gordon, Why Children Tell: A Model of Children's Disclosure of Sexual Abuse, 27 Child Abuse & Neglect 525, 527–528 (2003); Smith, *supra,* at 283–284 (finding that, where there was a relationship between perpetrator and victim, the victim was likely to keep the abuse a secret for a longer period of time, perhaps because of a "greater sense of loyalty or emotional bond"); Hanson, *supra,* at 565–566, and Table 3 (finding that a "significantly greater proportion of reported than nonreported cases involved a stranger"). The experience of the *amici* who work with child victims indicates that, when the punishment is death, both the victim and the victim's family members may be more likely to shield the perpetrator from discovery, thus increasing underreporting. As a result, punishment by death may not result in more deterrence or more effective enforcement.

In addition, by in effect making the punishment for child rape and murder equivalent, a State that punishes child rape by death may remove a strong incentive for the rapist not to kill the victim. Assuming the offender behaves in a rational way, as one must to justify the penalty on grounds of deterrence, the penalty in some respects gives less protection, not more, to the victim, who is often the sole witness to the crime. See Rayburn, Better Dead Than R(ap)ed?: The Patriarchal Rhetoric Driving Capital Rape Statutes, 78 St. John's L. Rev. 1119, 1159–1160 (2004). It might be argued that, even if the death penalty results in a marginal increase in the incentive to kill, this is counterbalanced by a marginally increased deterrent to commit the crime at all. Whatever balance the legislature strikes, however, uncertainty on the point makes the argument for the penalty less compelling than for homicide crimes.

Each of these propositions, standing alone, might not establish the unconstitutionality of the death penalty for the crime of child rape. Taken in sum, however, they demonstrate the serious negative consequences of making child rape a capital offense. These considerations lead us to conclude, in our independent judgment, that the death penalty is not a proportional punishment for the rape of a child.

[T]he judgment of the Supreme Court of Louisiana upholding the capital sentence is reversed. This case is remanded for further proceedings not inconsistent with this opinion.

■ Justice Alito, with whom The Chief Justice, Justice Scalia, and Justice Thomas join, dissenting.

With respect to the question of the harm caused by the rape of child in relation to the harm caused by murder, it is certainly true that the loss of human life represents a unique harm, but that does not explain why other grievous harms are insufficient to permit a death sentence. [T]he rape of any victim inflicts great injury, and "[s]ome victims are so grievously injured physically or psychologically that life *is* beyond repair." *Coker*, 433 U. S., at 603 (opinion of Powell, J.). Long-term studies show that sexual abuse is "grossly intrusive in the lives of children and is harmful to their normal psychological, emotional and sexual development in ways which no just or humane society can tolerate." C. Bagley & K. King, Child Sexual Abuse: The Search for Healing 2 (1990). It has been estimated that as many as 40% of 7–to 13–year–old sexual assault victims are considered "seriously disturbed." A. Lurigio, M. Jones, & B. Smith, Child Sexual Abuse: Its Causes, Consequences, and Implications for Probation Practice, 59 Sep Fed. Probation 69, 70 (1995). Psychological problems include sudden school failure, unprovoked crying, dissociation, depression, insomnia, sleep disturbances, nightmares, feelings of guilt and inferiority, and self-destructive behavior, including an increased incidence of suicide.

The deep problems that afflict child-rape victims often become society's problems as well. Commentators have noted correlations between childhood sexual abuse and later problems such as substance abuse, dangerous sexual behaviors or dysfunction, inability to relate to others on an interpersonal level, and psychiatric illness. Handbook on Sexual Abuse of Children 7 (L. Walker ed. 1988). Victims of child rape are nearly 5 times more likely than nonvictims to be arrested for sex crimes and nearly 30 times more likely to be arrested for prostitution. *Ibid.*

The harm that is caused to the victims and to society at large by the worst child rapists is grave. It is the judgment of the Louisiana lawmakers and those in an increasing number of other States that these harms justify the death penalty. The Court provides no cogent explanation why this legislative judgment should be overridden.

SELECTED BIBLIOGRAPHY

A. The Fourteenth Amendment: School Desegregation

J. Jackson, Social Scientists for Social Justice: Making the Case Against Segregation (2001).

Jackson, The Scientific Attack on *Brown v. Board of Education*, 1954–1964, 59 American Psychologist 530 (2004).

Lucas and Paret, Law, Race, and Education in the United States, 1 Annual Review of Law and Science 203 (2005).

M. Robinson and R. Bonnie, Law Touched Our Hearts: A Generation Remembers Brown v. Board of Education (2009).

Ryan, The Limited Influence of Social Science Evidence in Modern Desegregation Cases, 81 North Carolina Law Review 1161 (2003).

Sanders, *Brown v. Board of Education*: An Empirical Reexamination of Its Effects on Federal District Courts, 29 Law and Society Review 731 (1995).

Schofield and Hausmann, School Desegregation and Social Science Research, 59 American Psychologist 538 (2004).

Simson, Separate But Equal and Single–Sex Schools, 90 Cornell Law Review 443 (2005).

P. Strum, Women in the Barracks: The VMI Case and Equal Rights (2002).

B. The First Amendment: Obscene and Violent Entertainment

C. Anderson, D. Gentile, and K. Buckley, Violent Video Game Effects on Children and Adolescents: Theory, Research, and Public Policy (2007).

Anderson and Gentile, Media Violence, Aggression, and Public Policy, in Beyond Common Sense: Psychological Science in the Courtroom (E. Borgida and S. Fiske eds. 2008).

Chananie, Violent Videogames, Crime, and the Law: Looking for Proof of a Causal Connection, 26 Developments in Mental Health Law 27 (2007).

Dean, Returning the Pig to Its Pen: A Pragmatic Approach to Regulating Minors' Access to Violent Video Games, 75 George Washington Law Review 136 (2006).

Dionne, Pornography, Morality, and Harm: Why *Miller* Should Survive *Lawrence*, 15 George Mason Law Review 611 (2008).

Ferguson, Rueda, Cruz, Ferguson, Fritz, and Smith, Violent Video Games and Aggression: Causal Relationship or Byproduct of Family Violence and Intrinsic Violence Motivation? 35 Criminal Justice and Behavior 311 (2008).

Koppelman, Does Obscenity Cause Moral Harm?, 105 Columbia Law Review 1635 (2005).

Malamuth and Huppin, Drawing the Line on Virtual Child Pornography: Bringing the Law in Line with the Research Evidence, 31 New York University Review of Law and Social Change 773 (2007).

C. Nowlin, Judging Obscenity: A Critical History of Expert Evidence (2003).

Saunders, Shielding Children from Violent Video Games Through Ratings Offender Lists, 41 Indiana Law Review 55 (2008).

Seto, Maric, and Barbaree, The Role of Pornography in the Etiology of Sexual Aggression, 6 Aggression and Violent Behavior 35 (2001).

C. The Sixth Amendment: Juries

Butler, The Impact of Death Qualification, Belief in a Just World, Legal Authoritarianism, and Locus of Control on Venirepersons' Evaluations of Aggravating and Mitigating Circumstances in Capital Trials, 25 Behavioral Sciences and the Law 57 (2007).

Butler, The Role of Death Qualification in Venirepersons' Susceptibility to Victim Impact Statements, 14 Psychology, Crime and Law, 133 (2008).

Cohen and Smith, The Death of Death–Qualification, 59 Case Western Reserve Law Review 87 (2008).

Diamond, Beyond Fantasy and Nightmare: A Portrait of the Jury, 54 Buffalo Law Review 717 (2006).

Diamond, How Jurors Deal With Expert Testimony and How Judges Can Help, 16 Journal of Law and Policy 47 (2007).

Diamond, Truth, Justice, and the Jury, 26 Harv. J. of Law & Public Policy 143 (2003).

Diamond and Rose, Real Juries, 1 Annual Review of Law and Social Science 255 (2005).

Diamond, Rose, and Murphy, Revisiting the Unanimity Requirement: The Behavior of the Non–Unanimous Civil Jury, 100 Northwestern Law Review 201 (2006).

Diamond, Rose, Murphy, and Smith, Juror Questions During Trial: A Window Into Juror Thinking, 59 Vanderbilt Law Review 1927 (2006).

Diamond, Vidmar, Rose, Ellis, and Murphy, Jury Discussions During Civil Trials: Studying an Arizona Innovation, 45 University of Arizona Law Review 1 (2003).

V. Hans, Business on Trial: The Civil Jury and Corporate Responsibility (2000).

Hans, Jury Systems Around the World, 4 Annual Review of Law and Social Science 275 (2008).

Heuer and Penrod, Juror Notetaking and Question Asking During Trials: A National Field Experiment, 18 Law and Human Behavior 121 (1994).

Kaye, And Then There Were Twelve: Statistical Reasoning, the Supreme Court, and the Size of the Jury, 68 California Law Review 1004 (1980).

Kaye and Koehler, Can Jurors Understand Probabilistic Evidence?, 154 Journal of the Royal Statistical Association 75 (1991).

Koehler, Train Our Jurors, in Heuristics and the Law (G. Gigerenzer and C. Engel eds. 2006).

Mott, Hans, and Simpson, What's Half a Lung Worth? Civil Jurors' Accounts of Their Award Decision Making, 24 Law and Human Behavior 401 (2000).

Reifman, Gusick, and Ellsworth, Real Jurors' Understanding of the Law in Real Cases, 16 Law and Human Behavior 539 (1992).

Rose and Seidman, Judging Bias: Juror Confidence and Judicial Rulings on Challenges for Cause, 42 Law & Society Review 513 (2008).

Rose, Ellison, and Diamond, Preferences for Juries over Judges across Racial and Ethnic Groups, 89 Social Science Quarterly 372 (2008).

Saks and Marti, A Meta–Analysis of the Effects of Jury Size, 21 Law and Human Behavior 451 (1997).

Smith and Saks, The Case For Overturning *Williams v. Florida* and The Six–Person Jury: History, Law, and Empirical Evidence, 60 Florida Law Review 441 (2008).

Sommers, On Racial Diversity and Group Decision–Making: Identifying Multiple Effects of Racial Composition on Jury Deliberations, 90 Journal of Personality and Social Psychology 597 (2006).

Sommers and Ellsworth, How Much do We Really Know About Race and Juries? A Review of Social Science Theory and Research, 78 Chicago–Kent Law Review 997 (2003).

Sommers and Ellsworth, White Juror Bias: An Investigation of Prejudice Against Black Defendants in American Courtrooms, 7 Psychology, Public Policy, and Law 201 (2001).

Steblay Hosch, Culhane, and McWethy, The Impact on Juror Verdicts of Judicial Instruction to Disregard Inadmissible Evidence: A Meta–Analysis, 30 Law and Human Behavior 469 (2006).

Vidmar, Expert Evidence, the Adversary System, and the Jury, 95 American Journal of Public Health S137 (2005).

N. Vidmar and V. Hans, American Juries: The Verdict (2007).

D.   The Eighth Amendment: The Death Penalty

Baldus, Woodworth, and Grosso, Race and Proportionality Since *McCleskey v. Kemp*: Different Actors with Mixed Strategies of Denial and Avoidance, 39 Columbia Human Rights Law Review 139 (2007).

Conley, Turnier, and Rose, The Racial Ecology of the Courtroom: An Experimental Study of Juror Response to the Race of Criminal Defendants, 2000 Wisconsin Law Review 1185 (2000).

Donohue and Wolfers, Uses and Abuses of Empirical Evidence in the Death Penalty Debate, 58 Stanford Law Review 791 (2005).

Eberhardt, Davies, Purdie–Vaughns, and Johnson, Looking Deathworthy: Perceived Stereotypicality of Black Defendants Predicts Capital–Sentencing Outcomes, 17 Psychological Science 383 (2006).

Eisenberg, Death Sentence Rates and County Demographics: An Empirical Study, 90 Cornell Law Review 347 (2005).

Eisenberg, Garvey, and Wells, The Deadly Paradox of Capital Jurors, 74 Southern California Law Review 371 (2001).

Ellsworth, Unpleasant Facts: The Supreme Court's Response to Empirical Research on Capital Punishment, in Challenging Capital Punishment: Legal and Social Science Approaches (K. Haas and J. Inciardi eds. 1988).

Ellsworth and Gross, Social Science and the Evolving Standards of Death Penalty Law, in Beyond Common Sense: Psychological Science in the Courtroom (E. Borgida and S. Fiske eds. 2008).

Fagan, Death and Deterrence Redux: Science, Law and Causal Reasoning on Capital Punishment, 4 Ohio State Journal of Criminal Law 255 (2006).

Fagan and Bakhshi, McClesky at 20: New Frameworks for Racial Equality in the Criminal Law, 39 Columbia Human Rights Law Review 1 (2007).

Fagan and Meares, Punishment, Deterrence and Social Control: The Paradox of Punishment in Minority Communities, 6 Ohio State Journal of Criminal Law 173 (2008).

Fagan, Zimring, and Geller, Capital Punishment and Capital Murder: Market Share and the Deterrent Effects of the Death Penalty, 84 Texas Law Review 1803 (2006).

Gross and Ellsworth, Second Thoughts: Americans' Views on the Death Penalty at the Turn of the Century, in Capital Punishment and the American Future (S. Garvey ed. 2001).

C. Haney, Death by Design: Capital Punishment as a Social Psychological System (2005).

Hood and Hoyle, The Death Penalty in Global Perspective, in 38 Crime and Justice (M. Tonry ed. 2009).

Katt, *Roper* and the Scientific Amicus, 49 Jurimetrics 253 (2009).

Nadler, Flouting the Law, 83 Texas Law Review 1399 (2005).

Steinberg, Adolescent Development and Juvenile Justice, 5 Annual Review of Clinical Psychology 47 (2009).

Steinberg, Cauffman, Woolard, Graham, and Banich, Are Adolescents Less Mature Than Adults? Minors' Access to Abortion, the Juvenile Death Penalty, and the Alleged APA "Flip–Flop," American Psychologist (in press).

Tonry, Learning from the Limitations of Deterrence Research in 37 Crime and Justice: A Review of Research (M. Tonry ed, 2008).

Weisberg, The Death Penalty Meets Social Science: Deterrence and Jury Behavior Under New Scrutiny, 1 Annual Review of Law and Social Science 151 (2005).

Zimring, Criminology and Its Discontents, 46 Criminology 255 (2008).

SECTION III. COMMON LAW

While the bulk of the lawmaking uses of social science clearly have occurred in the area of constitutional law, common law has also seen the application of empirical research. We consider here two topics where social science studies have been relied upon to change the course of the common law. The first concerns rules of evidence and trial management. The second deals with tort liability.

A. RULES OF EVIDENCE AND TRIAL MANAGEMENT

1. THE EXCLUSIONARY RULE

The Fourth Amendment to the Constitution reads as follows:

The right of the people to be secure in their persons, houses, papers, and effects, against unreasonable searches and seizures, shall not be violated, and no Warrants shall issue, but upon probable cause, supported by Oath or affirmation, and particularly describing the place to be searched, and the persons or things to be seized.

Weeks v. United States, 232 U.S. 383, 34 S.Ct. 341, 58 L.Ed. 652 (1914), held that evidence seized in violation of the Fourth Amendment could not be used against the defendant in federal criminal prosecutions. Since the time of *Weeks,* this has been known as the "exclusionary rule."

———

WOLF v. COLORADO

Supreme Court of the United States, 1949.
338 U.S. 25, 69 S.Ct. 1359, 93 L.Ed. 1782.

■ Mr. Justice Frankfurter delivered the opinion of the Court.

The precise question for consideration is this: Does a conviction by a State court for a State offense deny the "due process of law" required by the Fourteenth Amendment, solely because evidence that was admitted at the trial was obtained under circumstances which would have rendered it inadmissible in a prosecution for violation of a federal law in a court of the United States because there deemed to be an infraction of the Fourth Amendment as applied in Weeks v. United States, 232 U.S. 383, 34 S.Ct. 341, 58 L.Ed. 652?

[T]he security of one's privacy against arbitrary intrusion by the police—which is at the core of the Fourth Amendment—is basic to a free society. It is therefore implicit in "the concept of ordered liberty" and as such enforceable against the States through the Due Process Clause. The knock at the door, whether by day or by night, as a prelude to a search, without authority of law but solely on the authority of the police, did not need the commentary of recent history to be condemned as inconsistent with the conception of human rights enshrined in the history and the basic constitutional documents of English-speaking peoples.

Accordingly, we have no hesitation in saying that were a State affirmatively to sanction such police incursion into privacy it would run counter to the guaranty of the Fourteenth Amendment. But the ways of enforcing such a basic right raise questions of a different order. How such arbitrary conduct should be checked, what remedies against it should be afforded, the means by which the right should be made effective, are all questions that are not to be so dogmatically answered as to preclude the varying solutions which spring from an allowable range of judgment on issues not susceptible of quantitative solution.

In Weeks v. United States, supra, this Court held that in a federal prosecution the Fourth Amendment barred the use of evidence secured through an illegal search and seizure. [T]he immediate question is whether the basic right to protection against arbitrary intrusion by the police demands the exclusion of logically relevant evidence obtained by an unreasonable search and seizure because, in a federal prosecution for a federal crime, it would be excluded. As a matter of inherent reason, one would suppose this to be an issue as to which men with complete devotion to the protection of the right of privacy might give different answers. When we find that in fact most of the English-speaking world does not regard as vital to such protection the exclusion of evidence thus obtained, we must hesitate to treat this remedy as an essential ingredient of the right. The contrariety of views of the States is particularly impressive in view of the careful reconsideration which they have given the problem in the light of the *Weeks* decision. [T]he [state] jurisdictions which have rejected the *Weeks* doctrine have not left the right to privacy without other means of protection. Indeed, the exclusion of evidence is a remedy which directly serves only to protect those upon whose person or premises something incriminating has been found. We cannot, therefore, regard it as a departure from basic standards to remand such persons, together with those who emerge scatheless from a search, to the remedies of private action and such protection as the internal discipline of the police, under the eyes of an alert public opinion, may afford. Granting that in practice the exclusion of evidence may be an effective way of deterring unreasonable searches, it is not for this Court to condemn as falling below the minimal standards assured by the Due Process Clause a State's reliance upon other methods which, if consistently enforced, would be equally effective.

[W]e hold, therefore, that in a prosecution in a State court for a State crime the Fourteenth Amendment does not forbid the admission of evidence obtained by an unreasonable search and seizure.

■ Mr. Justice Murphy, dissenting.

The conclusion is inescapable that but one remedy exists to deter violations of the search and seizure clause. That is the rule which excludes illegally obtained evidence. Only by exclusion can we impress upon the zealous prosecutor that violation of the Constitution will do him no good. And only when that point is driven home can the prosecutor be expected to emphasize the importance of observing constitutional demands in his instructions to the police.

If proof of the efficacy of the federal rule were needed, there is testimony in abundance in the recruit training programs and in-service courses provided the police in states which follow the federal rules.[5] St. Louis, for example, demands extensive training in the rules of search and seizure, with emphasis upon the ease with which a case may collapse if it

---

5. The material which follows is gleaned from letters and other material from Commissioners of Police and Chiefs of Police in twenty-six cities. Thirty-eight large cities in the United States were selected at random, and inquiries directed concerning the instructions provided police on the rules of search and seizure. Twenty-six replies have been received to date. Those of any significance are mentioned in the text of this opinion. The sample is believed to be representative, but it cannot, of course, substitute for a thorough-going comparison of present-day police procedures by a completely objective observer. A study of this kind would be of inestimable value.

depends upon evidence obtained unlawfully. Current court decisions are digested and read at roll calls. The same general pattern prevails in Washington, D.C. In Dallas, officers are thoroughly briefed and instructed that "the courts will follow the rules very closely and will detect any frauds." In Milwaukee, a stout volume on the law of arrest and search and seizure is made the basis of extended instruction. Officer preparation in the applicable rules in Jackson, Mississippi, has included the lectures of an Associate Justice of the Mississippi Supreme Court. The instructions on evidence and search and seizure given to trainees in San Antonio carefully note the rule of exclusion in Texas, and close with this statement: "Every police officer should know the laws and the rules of evidence. Upon knowledge of these facts determines whether the ... defendant will be convicted or acquitted.... When you investigate a case ... remember throughout your investigation that only admissible evidence can be used."

But in New York City, we are informed simply that "copies of the State Penal Law and Code of Criminal Procedure" are given to officers, and that they are "kept advised" that illegally obtained evidence may be admitted in New York courts. In Baltimore, a "Digest of Laws" is distributed, and it is made clear that the statutory section excluding evidence "is limited in its application to the trial of misdemeanors.... It would appear ... that ... evidence illegally obtained may still be admissible in the trial of felonies." In Cleveland, recruits and other officers are told of the rules of search and seizure, but "instructed that it is admissible in the courts of Ohio. The Ohio Supreme Court has indicated very definitely and clearly that Ohio belongs to the 'admissionist' group of states when evidence obtained by an illegal search is presented to the court." A similar pattern emerges in Birmingham, Alabama.

The contrast between states with the federal rule and those without it is thus a positive demonstration of its efficacy. There are apparent exceptions to the contrast—Denver, for example, appears to provide as comprehensive a series of instructions as that in Chicago, although Colorado permits introduction of the evidence and Illinois does not. And, so far as we can determine from letters, a fairly uniform standard of officer instruction appears in other cities, irrespective of the local rule of evidence. But the examples cited above serve to ground an assumption that has motivated this Court since the *Weeks* case: that this is an area in which judicial action has positive effect upon the breach of law; and that, without judicial action, there are simply no effective sanctions presently available.

MAPP v. OHIO

Supreme Court of the United States, 1961.
367 U.S. 643, 81 S.Ct. 1684, 6 L.Ed.2d 1081.

■ Mr. Justice Clark delivered the opinion of the court.

[A]fter declaring that the "security of one's privacy against arbitrary intrusion by the police" is "implicit in 'the concept of ordered liberty' and

as such enforceable against the States through the Due Process Clause,"
and announcing that it "stoutly adhere[d]" to the *Weeks* decision, the
Court decided [in Wolf v. Colorado] that the *Weeks* exclusionary rule would
not then be imposed upon the States as "an essential ingredient of the
right." 338 U.S., at 27–29, 69 S.Ct., at 1362. The Court's
reasons for not
considering essential to the right to privacy, as a curb imposed upon the
States by the Due Process Clause, that which decades before had been
posited as part and parcel of the Fourth Amendment's limitation upon
federal encroachment of individual privacy, were bottomed on factual
considerations.

While they are not basically relevant to a decision that the exclusionary
rule is an essential ingredient of the Fourth Amendment as the right it
embodies is vouch-safed against the States by the Due Process Clause, we
will consider the current validity of the factual grounds upon which *Wolf*
was based.

The Court in *Wolf* first stated that "[t]he contrariety of views of the
States" on the adoption of the exclusionary rule of *Weeks* was "particularly
impressive" (338 U.S. at page 29, 69 S.Ct. at page 1362); and, in this
connection, that it could not "brush aside the experience of States which
deem the incidence of such conduct by the police too slight to call for a
deterrent remedy ... by overriding the [States'] relevant rules of evidence." At pages 31–32 of U.S., at page 1363 of 69 S.Ct. While in 1949,
prior to the *Wolf* case, almost two-thirds of the States were opposed to the
use of the exclusionary rule, now, despite the *Wolf* case, more than half of
those since passing upon it, by their own legislative or judicial decision,
have wholly or partly adopted or adhered to the *Weeks* rule.

Significantly, among those now following the rule is California, which,
according to its highest court, was "compelled to reach that conclusion
because other remedies have completely failed to secure compliance with
the constitutional provisions...." People v. Cahan, 44 Cal.2d 434, 445, 282
P.2d 905, 911 (1955). In connection with this California case, we note that
the second basis elaborated in *Wolf* in support of its failure to enforce the
exclusionary doctrine against the States was that "other means of protection" have been afforded "the right to privacy." 338 U.S., at page 30, 69
S.Ct., at page 1362. The experience of California that such other remedies
have been worthless and futile is buttressed by the experience of other
States.

[I]t, therefore, plainly appears that the factual considerations supporting the failure of the *Wolf* Court to include the *Weeks* exclusionary rule
when it recognized the enforceability of the right to privacy against the
States in 1949, while not basically relevant to the constitutional consideration, could not, in any analysis, now be deemed controlling.

[T]oday we once again examine *Wolf's* constitutional documentation of
the right to privacy free from unreasonable state intrusion, and, after its
dozen years on our books, are led by it to close the only courtroom door

remaining open to evidence secured by official lawlessness in flagrant abuse of that basic right, reserved to all persons as a specific guarantee against that very same unlawful conduct. We hold that all evidence obtained by searches and seizures in violation of the Constitution is, by that same authority, inadmissible in a state court.

———

UNITED STATES v. LEON

Supreme Court of the United States, 1984.
468 U.S. 897, 104 S.Ct. 3405, 82 L.Ed.2d 677.

■ JUSTICE WHITE delivered the opinion of the Court.

[Acting on the basis of information from a confidential informant who claimed to have witnessed a drug sale take place at a given address approximately five months previously, officers of the Burbank, California, Police Department began a surveillance of the address. During this surveillance, a number of persons with previous drug convictions were observed entering a home and leaving with small packages. A police officer applied for a warrant to search the homes and automobiles of the individuals observed. The application, which had been reviewed by several Deputy District Attorneys, was granted by a state superior court judge. The ensuing searches produced large quantities of cocaine, and Antonio Leon and several others were indicted on drug-related charges. The defendants filed motions to suppress the evidence seized pursuant to the warrant. The District Court found that, while the police had acted reasonably and in good faith, the warrant upon which their search was based was insufficient to establish probable cause for a search, because it failed to establish the credibility of the confidential informant and because the information provided by the informant was "stale." The District Court, therefore, suppressed much of the evidence as having been obtained in violation of the Fourth Amendment. The government appealed to the Court of Appeals for the Ninth Circuit, which affirmed the District Court. The government's petition for certiorari to the Supreme Court presented the question "[w]hether the Fourth Amendment exclusionary rule should be modified so as not to bar the admission of evidence seized in reasonable, good faith reliance on a search warrant that is subsequently held to be defective."]

The Fourth Amendment contains no provision expressly precluding the use of evidence obtained in violation of its commands, and an examination of its origin and purposes makes clear that the use of fruits of a past unlawful search or seizure "work[s] no new Fourth Amendment wrong." United States v. Calandra, 414 U.S. 338, 354, 94 S.Ct. 613, 623, 38 L.Ed.2d 561 (1974). The wrong condemned by the Amendment is "fully accomplished" by the unlawful search or seizure itself, ibid., and the exclusionary rule is neither intended nor able to "cure the invasion of the defendant's rights which he has already suffered." Stone v. Powell, [428 U.S. 465, 96 S.Ct. 3037, 49 L.Ed.2d 1067 (1976)] at 540 (White, J., dissenting). The rule thus operates as "a judicially created remedy designed to safeguard Fourth

Amendment rights generally through its deterrent effect, rather than a personal constitutional right of the person aggrieved." United States v. Calandra, supra, 414 U.S. at 348, 94 S.Ct. at 620.

Whether the exclusionary sanction is appropriately imposed in a particular case, our decisions make clear, is "an issue separate from the question whether the Fourth Amendment rights of the party seeking to invoke the rule were violated by police conduct." Illinois v. Gates, [462 U.S. 213, 103 S.Ct. 2317, 76 L.Ed.2d 527 (1983)]. Only the former question is currently before us, and it must be resolved by weighing the costs and benefits of preventing the use in the prosecution's case-in-chief of inherently trustworthy tangible evidence obtained in reliance on a search warrant issued by a detached and neutral magistrate that ultimately is found to be defective.

The substantial social costs exacted by the exclusionary rule for the vindication of Fourth Amendment rights have long been a source of concern. "Our cases have consistently recognized that unbending application of the exclusionary sanction to enforce ideals of governmental rectitude would impede unacceptably the truth-finding functions of judge and jury." United States v. Payner, 447 U.S. 727, 734, 100 S.Ct. 2439, 2445, 65 L.Ed.2d 468 (1980). An objectionable collateral consequence of this interference with the criminal justice system's truth-finding function is that some guilty defendants may go free or receive reduced sentences as a result of favorable plea bargains.[6] Particularly when law enforcement officers have

---

6. Researchers have only recently begun to study extensively the effects of the exclusionary rule on the disposition of felony arrests. One study suggests that the rule results in the nonprosecution or nonconviction of between 0.6% and 2.35% of individuals arrested for felonies. Davies, A Hard Look at What We Know (and Still Need to Learn) About the "Costs" of the Exclusionary Rule: The NIJ Study and Other Studies of "Lost" Arrests, 1983 A.B.F.Res.J. 611, 621. The estimates are higher for particular crimes the prosecution of which depends heavily on physical evidence. Thus, the cumulative loss due to nonprosecution or nonconviction of individuals arrested on felony drug charges is probably in the range of 2.8% to 7.1%. Id. at 680. Davies' analysis of California data suggests that screening by police and prosecutors results in the release because of illegal searches or seizures of as many as 1.4% of all felony arrestees, Id. at 650, that 0.9% of felony arrestees are released because of illegal searches or seizures at the preliminary hearing or after trial, id. at 653, and that roughly 0.5% of all felony arrestees benefit from reversals on appeal because of illegal searches. Id. at 654. See also K. Brosi, A Cross–City Comparison of Felony Case Pro-

cessing 16, 18–19 (1979); Report of the Comptroller General of the United States, Impact of the Exclusionary Rule on Federal Criminal Prosecutions 10–11, 14 (1979); F. Feeney, F. Dill & A. Weir, Arrests Without Convictions: How Often They Occur and Why 203–206 (1983); National Institute of Justice, The Effects of the Exclusionary Rule: A Study in California 1–2 (1982); Nardulli, The Societal Cost of the Exclusionary Rule: An Empirical Assessment, 1983 A.B.F.Res.J. 585, 600. The exclusionary rule also has been found to affect the plea-bargaining process. S. Schlesinger, Exclusionary Injustice: The Problem of Illegally Obtained Evidence 63 (1977). But see Davies, supra, at 668–669; Nardulli, supra, at 604–606.

Many of these researchers have concluded that the impact of the exclusionary rule is insubstantial, but the small percentages with which they deal mask a large absolute number of felons who are released because the cases against them were based in part on illegal searches or seizures. "[A]ny rule of evidence that denies the jury access to clearly probative and reliable evidence must bear a heavy burden of justification, and must be carefully limited to the circumstances in which it will pay its way by deterring official acted in objective good faith or their transgressions have been minor, the magnitude of the benefit conferred on such guilty defendants offends basic concepts of the criminal justice system. Stone v. Powell, supra, at 490, 96 S.Ct. at 3050. Indiscriminate application of the exclusionary rule, therefore, may well "generat[e] disrespect for the law and the administration of justice." Id. at 491. Accordingly, "[a]s with any remedial device, the application of the rule has been restricted to those areas where its remedial objectives are thought most efficaciously served." United States v. Calandra, supra, 414 U.S. at 348, 94 S.Ct. at 670.

[W]e have frequently questioned whether the exclusionary rule can have any deterrent effect when the offending officers acted in the objectively reasonable belief that their conduct did not violate the Fourth Amendment. "No empirical researcher, proponent or opponent of the rule, has yet been able to establish with any assurance whether the rule has a deterrent effect. . . ." United States v. Janis, 428 U.S. at 452, n. 22, 96 S.Ct. at 3031, n. 22. But even assuming that the rule effectively deters some police misconduct and provides incentives for the law enforcement profession as a whole to conduct itself in accord with the Fourth Amendment, it cannot be expected, and should not be applied, to deter objectively reasonable law enforcement activity.

[T]his is particularly true, we believe, when an officer acting with objective good faith has obtained a search warrant from a judge or magistrate and acted within its scope. In most such cases, there is no police illegality and thus nothing to deter. It is the magistrate's responsibility to determine whether the officer's allegations establish probable cause and, if so, to issue a warrant comporting in form with the requirements of the Fourth Amendment. In the ordinary case, an officer cannot be expected to question the magistrate's probable-cause determination or his judgment that the form of the warrant is technically sufficient. "[O]nce the warrant issues, there is literally nothing more the policeman can do in seeking to comply with the law." Id. at 498, 96 S.Ct. at 3054 (Burger, C.J., concurring). Penalizing the officer for the magistrate's error, rather than his own, cannot logically contribute to the deterrence of Fourth Amendment violations.

We conclude that the marginal or nonexistent benefits produced by suppressing evidence obtained in objectively reasonable reliance on a subsequently invalidated search warrant cannot justify the substantial costs of exclusion.

[A]ccordingly, the judgment of the Court of Appeals is Reversed.

■ Justice Blackmun, concurring.

I write separately, [t]o underscore what I regard as the unavoidably provisional nature of today's decisions.

unlawlessness." Illinois v. Gates, 462 U.S., at 257–258, 103 S.Ct., at 2342 (White, J., concurring in the judgment). Because we find that the rule can have no substantial deterrent effect in the sorts of situations under consideration in this case, we conclude that it cannot pay its way in those situations.

As the Court's opinion in this case makes clear, the Court has narrowed the scope of the exclusionary rule because of an empirical judgment that the rule has little appreciable effect in cases where officers act in objectively reasonable reliance on search warrants. Because I share the view that the exclusionary rule is not a constitutionally compelled corollary of the Fourth Amendment itself, I see no way to avoid making an empirical judgment of this sort, and I am satisfied that the Court has made the correct one on the information before it. Like all courts, we face institutional limitations on our ability to gather information about "legislative facts," and the exclusionary rule itself has exacerbated the shortage of hard data concerning the behavior of police officers in the absence of such a rule. See United States v. Janis, 428 U.S. 433, 448–453, 96 S.Ct. 3021, 3029–3031, 49 L.Ed.2d 1046 (1976). Nonetheless, we cannot escape the responsibility to decide the question before us, however imperfect our information may be, and I am prepared to join the Court on the information now at hand.

What must be stressed, however, is that any empirical judgment about the effect of the exclusionary rule in a particular class of cases necessarily is a provisional one. By their very nature, the assumptions on which we proceed today cannot be cast in stone. To the contrary, they now will be tested in the real world of state and federal law enforcement, and this Court will attend to the results. If it should emerge from experience that, contrary to our expectations, the good faith exception to the exclusionary rule results in a material change in police compliance with the Fourth Amendment, we shall have to reconsider what we have undertaken here. The logic of a decision that rests on untested predictions about police conduct demands no less.

If a single principle may be drawn from this Court's exclusionary rule decisions, from *Weeks* through Mapp v. Ohio, 367 U.S. 643, 81 S.Ct. 1684, 6 L.Ed.2d 1081 (1961), to the decisions handed down today, it is that the scope of the exclusionary rule is subject to change in light of changing judicial understanding about the effects of the rule outside the confines of the courtroom.

■ JUSTICE BRENNAN, with whom JUSTICE MARSHALL joins, dissenting.

[T]he Court seeks to justify this result on the ground that the "costs" of adhering to the exclusionary rule in cases like those before us exceed the "benefits." But the language of deterrence and of cost/benefit analysis, if used indiscriminately, can have a narcotic effect. It creates an illusion of technical precision and ineluctability. It suggests that not only constitutional principle but also empirical data supports the majority's result. When the Court's analysis is examined carefully, however, it is clear that we have not been treated to an honest assessment of the merits of the exclusionary rule, but have instead been drawn into a curious world where the "costs" of excluding illegally obtained evidence loom to exaggerated heights and where the "benefits" of such exclusion are made to disappear with a mere wave of the hand.

[T]he Court's decisions over the past decade have made plain that the entire enterprise of attempting to assess the benefits and costs of the exclusionary rule in various contexts is a virtually impossible task for the judiciary to perform honestly or accurately. Although the Court's language in those cases suggests that some specific empirical basis may support its analyses, the reality is that the Court's opinions represent inherently unstable compounds of intuition, hunches, and occasional pieces of partial and often inconclusive data. In *Calandra,* for example, the Court, in considering whether the exclusionary rule should apply in grand jury proceedings, had before it no concrete evidence whatever concerning the impact that application of the rule in such proceedings would have either in terms of the long-term costs or the expected benefits. To the extent empirical data is available regarding the general costs and benefits of the exclusionary rule, it has shown, on the one hand, as the Court acknowledges today, that the costs are not as substantial as critics have asserted in the past, and, on the other hand, that while the exclusionary rule may well have certain deterrent effects, it is extremely difficult to determine with any degree of precision whether the incidence of unlawful conduct by police is now lower than it was prior to *Mapp.* See United States v. Janis, 428 U.S., at 449–453 and n. 22, 96 S.Ct., at 3029–3031 and n. 22; Stone v. Powell, 428 U.S., at 492, n. 32, 96 S.Ct., at 3051, n. 32.[9] The Court has sought to turn this uncertainty to its advantage by casting the burden of proof upon proponents of the rule, see e.g., United States v. Janis, 428 U.S., at 453–454, 96 S.Ct., at 3031–3032. "Obviously," however, "the assignment of the burden of proof on an issue where evidence does not exist and cannot be obtained is outcome determinative. [The] assignment of the burden is merely a way of announcing a predetermined conclusion."[10]

By remaining within its redoubt of empiricism and by basing the rule solely on the deterrence rationale, the Court has robbed the rule of legitimacy. A doctrine that is explained as if it were an empirical proposition but for which there is only limited empirical support is both inherently unstable and an easy mark for critics. The extent of this Court's fidelity to Fourth Amendment requirements, however, should not turn on such statistical uncertainties. I share the view, expressed by Justice Stewart for the Court in Faretta v. California, 422 U.S. 806, 95 S.Ct. 2525, 45 L.Ed.2d 562 (1975), that "[p]ersonal liberties are not based on the law of averages." Id. at 834, 95 S.Ct. at 2540. Rather than seeking to give effect to the liberties secured by the Fourth Amendment through guesswork about deterrence, the Court should restore to its proper place the principal framed 70 years ago in *Weeks* that an individual whose privacy has been invaded in violation of the Fourth Amendment has a right grounded in that Amendment to

9. See generally on this point, Davies, A Hard Look at What We Know (and Still Need to Learn) About the "Costs" of the Exclusionary Rule: The NIJ Study and Other Studies of "Lost" Arrests, 1983 Am.Bar Found. Res.J. 611, 627–629; Canon, Ideology and Reality in the Debate over the Exclusionary Rule: A Conservative Argument for its Retention, 23 S.Tex.L.J. 559, 561–563 (1982); Critique, On the Limitation of the Empirical Evaluation of the Exclusionary Rule: A Critique of the Spiotto Research and United States v. Calandra, 69 N.W.U.L.Rev. 740 (1974).

10. Dworkin, Fact Style Adjudication and the Fourth Amendment: The Limits of Lawyering, 48 Ind.L.J. 329, 332–333 (1973).

prevent the government from subsequently making use of any evidence so obtained.

[E]ven if I were to accept the Court's general approach to the exclusionary rule, I could not agree with today's result.

[A]t the outset, the Court suggests that society has been asked to pay a high price—in terms either of setting guilty persons free or of impeding the proper functioning of trials—as a result of excluding relevant physical evidence in cases where the police, in conducting searches and seizing evidence, have made only an "objectively reasonable" mistake concerning the constitutionality of their actions. But what evidence is there to support such a claim?

Significantly, the Court points to none, and, indeed, as the Court acknowledges, recent studies have demonstrated that the "costs" of the exclusionary rule—calculated in terms of dropped prosecutions and lost convictions—are quite low. Contrary to the claims of the rule's critics that exclusion leads to "the release of countless guilty criminals," Bivens v. Six Unknown Federal Narcotics Officers, 403 U.S. 388, 416, 91 S.Ct. 1999, 2014, 29 L.Ed.2d 619 (Burger, C.J., dissenting), these studies have demonstrated that federal and state prosecutors very rarely drop cases because of potential search and seizure problems. For example, a 1979 study prepared at the request of Congress by the General Accounting Office reported that only 0.4% of all cases actually declined for prosecution by federal prosecutors were declined primarily because of illegal search problems. Report of the Comptroller General of the United States, Impact of the Exclusionary Rule on Federal Criminal Prosecutions 14 (1979). If the GAO data are restated as a percentage of *all* arrests, the study shows that only 0.2% of all felony arrests are declined for prosecution because of potential exclusionary rule problems. See Davies, A Hard Look at What We Know (and Still Need to Learn) About the "Costs" of the Exclusionary Rule: The NIJ Study and Other Studies of "Lost" Arrests, 1983 Am.Bar Found.Res.J. 611, 635.[11] Of

---

11. In a series of recent studies, researchers have attempted to quantify the actual costs of the rule. A recent National Institute of Justice study based on data for the four year period 1976–1979 gathered by the California Bureau of Criminal Statistics showed that 4.8% of all cases that were declined for prosecution by California prosecutors were rejected because of illegally seized evidence. National Institute of Justice, Criminal Justice Research Report—The Effects of the Exclusionary Rule: A Study in California 1 (1982). However, if these data are calculated as a percentage of all arrests that were declined for prosecution, they show that only 0.8% of all arrests were rejected for prosecution because of illegally seized evidence. See Davies, supra, at 619.

In another measure of the rule's impact—the number of prosecutions that are dismissed or result in acquittals in cases where evidence has been excluded—the available data again show that the Court's past assessment of the rule's costs has generally been exaggerated. For example, a study based on data from 9 mid-sized counties in Illinois, Michigan and Pennsylvania reveals that motions to suppress physical evidence were filed in approximately 5% of the 7,500 cases studied, but that such motions were successful in only 0.7% of all these cases. Nardulli, The Societal Cost of the Exclusionary Rule: An Empirical Assessment, 1983 Am.Bar Found. Res.J. 585, 596. The study also shows that only 0.6% of all cases resulted in acquittals because evidence had been excluded. Id. at 600. In the GAO study, suppression motions course, these data describe only the costs attributable to the exclusion of evidence in all cases; the costs due to the exclusion of evidence in the narrower category of cases where police have made objectively reasonable mistakes must necessarily be even smaller. The Court, however, ignores this distinction and mistakenly weighs the aggregated costs of exclusion in *all* cases, irrespective of the circumstances that led to exclusion, against the potential benefits associated with only those cases in which evidence is excluded because police reasonably but mistakenly believe that their conduct does not violate the Fourth Amendment. When such faulty scales are used, it is little wonder that the balance tips in favor of restricting the application of the rule.

What then supports the Court's insistence that this evidence be admitted? Apparently, the Court's only answer is that even though the costs of exclusion are not very substantial, the potential deterrent effect in these circumstances is so marginal that exclusion cannot be justified. The key to the Court's conclusion in this respect is its belief that the prospective deterrent effect of the exclusionary rule operates only in those situations in which police officers, when deciding whether to go forward with some particular search, have reason to know that their planned conduct will violate the requirements of the Fourth Amendment. If these officers in fact understand (or reasonably should understand because the law is well-settled) that their proposed conduct will offend the Fourth Amendment and that, consequently, any evidence they seize will be suppressed in court, they will refrain from conducting the planned search. In those circumstances, the incentive system created by the exclusionary rule will have the hoped-for deterrent effect. But in situations where police officers reasonably (but mistakenly) believe that their planned conduct satisfies Fourth Amendment requirements—presumably either (a) because they are acting on the basis of an apparently valid warrant, or (b) because their conduct is only later determined to be invalid as a result of a subsequent change in the law or the resolution of an unsettled question of law—then such officers will have no reason to refrain from conducting the search and the exclusionary rule will have no effect.

[T]he flaw in the Court's argument, however, is that its logic captures only one comparatively minor element of the generally acknowledged deterrent purposes of the exclusionary rule. To be sure, the rule operates to some extent to deter future misconduct by individual officers who have had evidence suppressed in their own cases. But what the Court overlooks is that the deterrence rationale for the rule is not designed to be, nor should it be thought of as, a form of "punishment" of individual police officers for

were filed in 10.5% of all federal criminal cases surveyed, but of the motions filed, approximately 80–90% were denied. GAO Report, supra, at 8, 10. Evidence was actually excluded in only 1.3% of the cases studied, and only 0.7% of all cases resulted in acquittals or dismissals after evidence was excluded. Id. at 9–11. See Davies, supra, at 660. And in another study based on data from cases during 1978 and 1979 in San Diego and Jacksonville, it was shown that only 1% of all cases resulting in nonconviction were caused by illegal searches. Feeney, Dill & Weir, Arrests Without Conviction: How Often They Occur and Why (1983). See generally Davies, supra, at 663.

their failures to obey the restraints imposed by the Fourth Amendment. Instead, the chief deterrent function of the rule is its tendency to promote institutional compliance with Fourth Amendment requirements on the part of law enforcement agencies generally. Thus, as the Court has previously recognized, "over the long term, [the] demonstration [provided by the exclusionary rule] that our society attaches serious consequences to violation of constitutional rights is thought to encourage those who formulate law enforcement policies, and the officers who implement them, to incorporate Fourth Amendment ideals into their value system." Stone v. Powell, 428 U.S. at 492, 96 S.Ct. at 3051. It is only through such an institution-wide mechanism that information concerning Fourth Amendment standards can be effectively communicated to rank and file officers.[13]

If the overall educational effect of the exclusionary rule is considered, application of the rule to even those situations in which individual police officers have acted on the basis of a reasonable but mistaken belief that their conduct was authorized can still be expected to have a considerable long-term deterrent effect. If evidence is consistently excluded in these circumstances, police departments will surely be prompted to instruct their officers to devote greater care and attention to providing sufficient information to establish probable cause when applying for a warrant, and to review with some attention the form of the warrant that they have been issued, rather than automatically assuming that whatever document the magistrate has signed will necessarily comport with Fourth Amendment requirements.

After today's decision, however, that institutional incentive will be lost. Indeed, the Court's "reasonable mistake" exception to the exclusionary rule will tend to put a premium on police ignorance of the law.

---

13. Although specific empirical data on the systemic deterrent effect of the rule is not conclusive, the testimony of those actually involved in law enforcement suggests that, at the very least, the *Mapp* decision had the effect of increasing police awareness of Fourth Amendment requirements and of prompting prosecutors and police commanders to work towards educating rank and file officers. For example, as former New York Police Commissioner Murphy explained the impact of the *Mapp* decision: "I can think of no decision in recent times in the field of law enforcement which had such a dramatic and traumatic effect.... I was immediately caught up in the entire program of reevaluating our procedures, which had followed the *Defore* rule, and modifying, amending, and creating new policies and new instructions for implementing *Mapp*.... Retraining sessions had to be held from the very top administrators down to each of the thousands of foot patrolmen." Murphy, Judicial Review of Police Methods in Law Enforcement: The Problem of Compliance by Police Departments, 44 Tex.L.Rev. 939, 941 (1966).

Further testimony about the impact of the *Mapp* decision can be found in the statement of Deputy Commissioner Reisman: "The *Mapp* case was a shock to us. We had to reorganize our thinking, frankly. Before this, nobody bothered to take out search warrants. Although the U.S. Constitution requires warrants in most cases, the U.S. Supreme Court had ruled that evidence obtained without a warrant—illegally, if you will—was admissible in state courts. So the feeling was, why bother? Well, once that rule was changed we knew we had better start teaching our men about it." N.Y. Times, April 28, 1965, at 50, col. 1.

STATE v. NOVEMBRINO

Supreme Court of New Jersey, 1987.
105 N.J. 95, 519 A.2d 820.

■ Stein, J.

Defendant, Ottavio Novembrino, was indicted for possession of controlled dangerous substances [a]nd possession of controlled dangerous substances with intent to distribute. [A] motion to suppress evidence was filed.

[T]he Appellate Division concluded that the affidavit failed to establish probable cause:

> The affidavit here involved simply revealed that a police informant concluded for unknown reasons that defendant was a drug dealer, that a person previously arrested for possession of cocaine was seen at defendant's gas station engaged in some unspecified activities which caused a detective, whose education, training and experiences are unknown, to conclude that criminal activities in the form of violations of Title 24 were taking place at the gas station. The totality of the circumstances spelled out in the affidavit failed to contain a single objective fact tending to engender a "well grounded suspicion" that a crime was being committed. * * * We conclude, therefore, that probable cause was not established. [State v. Novembrino, 200 N.J.Super. 229, 236, 491 A.2d 37 (1985) (citation omitted).]

The State also argued that if probable cause was not established, the evidence should nevertheless be admissible on the basis of the good-faith exception recognized by the United States Supreme Court in *Leon*. The Appellate Division acknowledged that if *Leon* were followed in New Jersey, it would apply retroactively and thereby determine the admissibility of the evidence obtained at defendant's station. A majority of the Appellate Division was also satisfied that Detective Higgins had objectively and reasonably relied upon the warrant, which had been issued by a detached and neutral judge. Accordingly, the Appellate Division majority found that the record adequately raised the issue whether the good-faith exception should be applied under our State Constitution.

A majority of the Appellate Division panel determined that New Jersey should not recognize the good-faith exception because it would undermine the constitutional requirement of probable cause. [W]e granted the State's motion for leave to appeal.

[I]t is an established principle of our federalist system that state constitutions may be a source of "individual liberties more expansive than those conferred by the Federal Constitution." PruneYard Shopping Center v. Robins, 447 U.S. 74, 81, 100 S.Ct. 2035, 2040, 64 L.Ed.2d 741, 752 (1980).

[T]his Court has frequently resorted to our own State Constitution in order to afford our citizens broader protection of certain personal rights than that afforded by analogous or identical provisions of the federal

Constitution. Although the language of article I, paragraph 7 of the New Jersey Constitution is virtually identical with that of the fourth amendment, we have held in other contexts that it affords our citizens greater protection against unreasonable searches and seizures than does the fourth amendment.

In this case, defendant urges that we construe our state-constitutional protection against unreasonable searches and seizures to preclude recognition of the good-faith exception to the exclusionary rule established in *Leon*. The Attorney General and the Hudson County Prosecutor argue that we should follow the Supreme Court's modification of the exclusionary rule and construe article I, paragraph 7 of our Constitution in a manner consistent with the good-faith exception. Our conclusion as to which of these courses to follow is strongly influenced by what we perceive to be the likely impact of our decision on the privacy rights of our citizens and the enforcement of our criminal laws, matters of "particular state interest" that afford an appropriate basis for resolving this issue on independent state grounds.

[T]he Attorney General and the County Prosecutors Association adopted in February 1985 a joint policy statement intended to achieve the "institutionalization of a systematic search warrant review procedure in New Jersey." The policy statement, which applies to all State, County, and municipal officers, requires that "[a]ll applications for search warrants shall be reviewed by the Attorney General or his designees, or the appropriate County Prosecutor, or his designees, prior to their submission to the Courts for authorization." The Court has been informed, in response to its direct inquiry, that this policy statement has been implemented without exception in every county in the State. We are also cognizant of the significant and recurring search warrant training programs offered regularly to municipal court judges throughout the state. We assume that the likely effect of such a statewide policy requiring competent legal review of search warrant applications, combined with the training programs for municipal judges, would be to enhance the extent of compliance with the probable-cause standard and minimize the incidents of suppression of evidence because of defectively-issued warrants.[33]

---

33. In his dissenting opinion in *Leon*, Justice Brennan emphasized that statistical studies on a national basis also suggest that the "costs" of the exclusionary rule are minimal:

[I]ndeed, as the Court acknowledges, recent studies have demonstrated that the "costs" of the exclusionary rule—calculated in terms of dropped prosecutions and lost convictions—are quite low. Contrary to the claims of the rule's critics that exclusion leads to "the release of countless guilty criminals," Bivens v. Six Unknown Federal Narcotics Agents, 403 U.S. 388, 416, 29 L.Ed.2d 619, 91 S.Ct. 1999 [2014] (Burger, C.J., dissenting), these studies have demonstrated that federal and state prosecutors very rarely drop cases because of potential search and seizure problems. For example, a 1979 study prepared at the request of Congress by the General Accounting Office reported that only 0.4% of all cases actually declined for prosecution by federal prosecutors were declined primarily because of illegal search problems. Report of the Comptroller General of the United States, Impact of the Exclusionary Rule on Federal Criminal Prosecutions 14 (1979). If the GAO data are restated as a percentage of *all* arrests, the study shows

In this connection, a survey performed by the Administrative Office of the Courts with respect to suppression motions in ten counties during the six-month period of December 1, 1985, to May 31, 1986, reveals that of the 1082 motions filed, 540 motions have been resolved. Of these, 38 were granted and all of the granted motions involved warrantless searches. In addition, the study examined all of the granted suppression motions in three of the ten counties for an additional six-month period and in two additional counties during a twelve-month period. Out of 44 granted motions, only one suppression order involved a search warrant defective for lack of probable cause. Administrative Office of the Courts, Report on Suppression Motions, July 30, 1986. This survey was not statewide and examined a limited sample of suppression motions. Nevertheless, its results suggest that currently in New Jersey the grant of motions to suppress evidence obtained pursuant to defective search warrants is relatively uncommon and apparently poses no significant obstacle to law-enforcement efforts.

[O]ne obvious consequence of the application of the exclusionary rule in New Jersey has been the encouragement of law-enforcement officials to comply with the constitutionally-mandated probable-cause standard in order to avoid the suppression of evidence. The *Leon* rule avoids suppression of evidence even if the constitutional standard is violated, requiring only that the officer executing the defective warrant have an objectively reasonable basis for relying on it. Whatever else may be said for or against the *Leon* rule, the good-faith exception will inevitably and inexorably diminish the quality of evidence presented in search-warrant applications. By eliminating any cost for noncompliance with the constitutional requirement of probable cause, the good-faith exception assures us that the constitutional standard will be diluted.

[U]ltimately, we focus on the inevitable tension between the proposed good-faith exception and the guarantee contained in our State Constitution that search warrants "shall not issue except upon probable cause." In the twenty-five years during which we have applied the exclusionary rule in New Jersey, we have perceived no dilution of our probable-cause standard; rather, efforts to comply with the constitutional mandate have been enhanced. Nor do we perceive that application of the exclusionary rule has in

that only 0.2% of all felony arrests are declined for prosecution because of potential exclusionary rule problems. See Davies, A Hard Look at What We Know (and Still Need to Learn) About the "Costs" of the Exclusionary Rule: The NIJ Study and Other Studies of "Lost" Arrests, 1983 Am.Bar Found. Res.J. 611, 635. Of course, these data describe only the costs attributable to the exclusion of evidence in all cases; the costs due to the exclusion of evidence in the narrower category of cases where police have made objectively reasonable mistakes must necessarily be even smaller. The Court, however, ignores this distinction and mistakenly weighs the aggregated costs of exclusion in *all* cases, irrespective of the circumstances that led to exclusion against the potential benefits associated with only those cases in which evidence is excluded because police reasonably but mistakenly believe that their conduct does not violate the Fourth Amendment. When such faulty scales are used, it is little wonder that the balance tips in favor of restricting the application of the rule. [United States v. Leon, 468 U.S. at 950–51, 104 S.Ct. at 3441–42, 82 L.Ed.2d at 716–17 (Brennan, J., dissenting).]

any significant way impaired the ability of law-enforcement officials to enforce the criminal laws. The statistical evidence is to the contrary.

[J]ustice Blackmun, concurring in Leon, cautioned us as to the "unavoidably provisional nature" of the decision, 468 U.S. at 927, 104 S.Ct. at 3424, 82 L.Ed.2d at 701, and warned that if "the good faith exception to the exclusionary rule results in a material change in police compliance with the Fourth Amendment, we shall have to reconsider what we have undertaken here," id. at 928, 104 S.Ct. at 3424, 82 L.Ed.2d at 702. We suspect that Justice Blackmun's forebodings may be prophetic indeed. In our view, erosion of the probable-cause guarantee will be a corollary to the good-faith exception. We think it quite possible that the damage to the constitutional guarantee may reach such a level as to cause the Court to reconsider its experiment with the fourth amendment.

We see no need in New Jersey to experiment with the fundamental rights protected by the fourth-amendment counterpart of our State Constitution. We will not subject the procedures that vindicate the fundamental rights guaranteed by article 1, paragraph 7 of our State Constitution— procedures that have not diluted the effectiveness of our criminal justice system—to the uncertain effects that we believe will inevitably accompany the good-faith exception to the federal exclusionary rule.

The judgment of the Appellate Division is affirmed.

NOTES

1. Special Masters. In an article cited by both the majority and the dissent in *Leon,* Davies, A Hard Look at What We Know (and Still Need to Learn) About the "Costs" of the Exclusionary Rule: The NIJ Study and Other Studies of "Lost" Arrests, 1983 American Bar Foundation Research Journal 611, 688 n. 447 (1983), made the following suggestion:

> If an empirical question appears to be central to an appellate decision, perhaps it would be appropriate for an appellate court to appoint a master to take expert testimony to provide the court with a more fully developed record on the empirical data and the quality and completeness of the research relied on.

2. Tort Remedies. When the United States Supreme Court in Wolf v. Colorado declined to apply the federal exclusionary rule to state prosecutions, it noted that states could choose instead to rely on "the remedies of private action," i.e., to allow tort suits against police officers who violate a citizen's Fourth Amendment rights. When it overturned the *Wolf* decision in Mapp v. Ohio, however, the Court noted the "obvious futility" of remedies such as tort action to secure the Fourth Amendment.

Opponents of the exclusionary rule continue to promote tort suits against police officers alleged to have engaged in illegal searches as an alternative to excluding evidence from criminal proceedings. Casper, Benedict, and Perry, The Tort Remedy in Search and Seizure Cases: A Case

Study in Juror Decision Making, 13 Law and Social Inquiry 279 (1988), reviewed the empirical literature on such suits and conclude that defendant police officers prevail about three-quarters of the time and that, when plaintiffs win, the damages awarded are relatively minor (e.g., about a third of the plaintiffs who won received less than $1,000, and 85% received less than $10,000). In a simulation study with persons called for jury service in Cook County, Illinois, Casper and his colleagues found that substituting the municipality (i.e., the city that employed the police officer) as the defendant, or substituting the federal government as the plaintiff, did not affect the incidence or size of damage awards. Denying jurors information about the outcome of the search, however—that is, not telling jurors whether the allegedly illegal search uncovered evidence of crime—increased both the incidence and the size of damages awarded.

----

2.   IMPEACHMENT OF A WITNESS

When a witness testifies at trial, his or her credibility is often contested. One way that an attorney cross-examining a witness may try to impeach the witness' testimony—to raise doubts in jurors' minds about the witness' credibility—is to introduce evidence that the witness has been convicted of a crime in the past. The rationale for this form of impeachment is the proposition that a person who has been convicted of crime is less worthy of belief than a person who has not been convicted. In a criminal case, when the witness is also the defendant, the risk of allowing the admission of such evidence is that the jury may use it for purposes other than the assessment of credibility, such as to support an inference that the witness must be guilty of the crime charged, since he or she has been found guilty before.

PEOPLE v. ALLEN

Supreme Court of Michigan, 1988.
429 Mich. 558, 420 N.W.2d 499.

■ BRICKLEY, JUSTICE.

[Five criminal cases in which the defendants were convicted by a jury were appealed. In each case, the defendant had testified in his own behalf, and the state had impeached the testimony by telling the jury of the defendant's prior criminal convictions.]

These cases were consolidated in order to resolve differing interpretations of the application of MRE [Michigan Rule of Evidence] 609(a) to the practice of impeaching criminal defendants by prior conviction.[1] [W]e also

----

1. MRE 609 reads in pertinent part:

"(a) General rule. For the purpose of attacking the credibility of a witness, evidence that he has been convicted of a crime shall be admitted if elicited from him or established by public record during cross-examination but only if take this opportunity to promulgate an amendment to MRE 609(a) which will apply to all cases tried after March 1, 1988. (See appendix A.) It provides for bright-line rules that recognize and exclude certain prior convictions which are inherently more prejudicial than probative and allows admission of those convictions which are inherently more probative than prejudicial.

[A] jury should not be allowed to consider the defendant's guilt of the crime before it on the basis of evidence of his propensity for crime. Finding a person guilty of a crime is not a pleasant or easy assignment for a representative group of twelve people. It is much easier to conclude that a person is bad than that he did something bad. Hence the appetite for more knowledge of the defendant's background and the slippery slope toward general "bad man" evidence.

This appetite presents three types of impropriety. First, that jurors may determine that although defendant's guilt in the case before them is in doubt, he is a bad man and should therefore be punished. Second, the character evidence may lead the jury to lower the burden of proof against the defendant, since, even if the guilty verdict is incorrect, no "innocent" man will be forced to endure punishment. Third, the jury may determine that on the basis of his prior actions, the defendant has a propensity to commit crimes, and therefore he probably is guilty of the crime with which he is charged. All three of these dimensions suggest a likelihood that innocent persons may be convicted.

The danger then is that a jury will misuse prior conviction evidence by focusing on the defendant's general bad character, rather than solely on his character for truthtelling.

[I]n spite of the likelihood of prejudice, it can be argued, and indeed the dissent does so eloquently, that a limiting instruction will suffice.

[T]he notion that a limiting instruction can prevent misuse of prior conviction evidence is simply mistaken, as it asks the jury to do what it cannot. This view is supported by a number of empirical studies. A Canadian study concluded that

> "present research leaves little doubt that knowledge of a previous conviction biases a case against the defendant. The likelihood that a jury will convict the defendant is significantly higher if the defendant's record is made known to the jury. *The fact that the defendant has a*

"(1) the crime was punishable by death or imprisonment in excess of one year under the law under which he was convicted, or the crime involved theft, dishonesty or false statement, regardless of the punishment, and

"(2) the court determines that the probative value of admitting this evidence on the issue of credibility outweighs its prejudicial effect and articulates on the record the factors considered in making the determination."

record permeates the entire discussion of the case, and appears to affect the juror's perception and interpretation of the evidence in the case.

"*. . . These effects are present in spite of the fact that jurors were given specific instructions to ignore the fact of record while assessing the defendant's guilt.*" Hans & Doob, *Section 12 of the Canada Evidence Act and the deliberations of simulated juries,* 18 Crim.L.Q. 235, 251 (1976) (emphasis added).

Perhaps most disturbing was the study's conclusion that

"jurors used [prior conviction evidence] only minimally in considering the issue of credibility." *Id.* at 247.

Thus, the intended use of the evidence was of little actual importance.

Another study observed that the notion of a successful limiting instruction, with respect to character evidence, runs counter to the basic evaluative mechanisms discussed above.

"The assumption that people can differentiate the use of information goes directly against what is known as the 'halo' effect: the phenomenon by which a person will infer positive characteristics about a person where favourable information has been received and will infer negative characteristics about someone where unfavourable information has been received. As Rosenberg and Olshan (1970) [citing Rosenberg & Olshan, *Evaluative and descriptive aspects in personality perception,* J of Personality and Soc Psyc, 16, 619–626 (1970)] have pointed out, 'Studies using [the technique by which a subject is asked to infer characteristics about an individual on the basis of information about other characteristics] . . . have consistently shown that subjects infer favourable traits from one or more favourable stimulus traits and infer unfavourable traits from unfavourable stimulus traits' (p. 619). Thus, if a person is told one negative thing about another person, he is going to assume other negative things. With respect to s. 12 of the Canada Evidence Act, it follows that we would expect that if a juror hears that an accused has one unfavourable characteristic (e.g., that he has a criminal record) he will then think of that accused as a generally bad person. If this same juror is then asked to judge the guilt of the accused, he will be likely to infer that the accused is guilty of the crime in question." Doob & Kirshenbaum, *Some empirical evidence on the effect of s. 12 of the Canada Evidence Act upon an accused,* 15 Crim.L.Q. 88, 89–90 (1972–1973).

One of the researchers in the University of Chicago report leading to publication of *The American Jury* stated that the jury examinations revealed

" 'almost universal inability and/or unwillingness either to understand or follow the court's instruction on the use of defendant's prior criminal record for impeachment purposes. The jurors almost universally used defendant's record to conclude that he was a bad man and hence was more likely than not guilty of the crime for which he was then standing trial.' "

"Letter from Dale W. Broeder, Associate Professor, the University of Nebraska College of Law, who conducted intensive jury interviews, to Yale Law Journal, dated March 14, 1960, on file in Yale Law Library." Note, *Other crimes evidence at trial: Of balancing and other matters,* 70 Yale L J 763, 777, n 89 (1961).

In a far less scientific study, the Columbia Journal of Law and Social Problems conducted a random national survey of trial judges and criminal defense attorneys. When asked whether they believed jurors were able to follow limiting instructions concerning the use of prior conviction evidence, ninety-eight percent of the responding attorneys answered negatively, and, even more disturbingly, forty-three percent of the responding judges agreed. Note, *To take the stand or not to take the stand: The dilemma of the defendant with a criminal record,* 4 Colum J of Law & Social Problems 215, 218 (1968).

The most recent study of this problem concluded that mock jurors used prior conviction evidence to "help them judge the likelihood that the defendant committed the crime charged" in spite of limiting instructions. Wissler & Saks, *On the inefficacy of limiting instructions: When jurors use prior conviction evidence to decide on guilt,* 9 Law & Human Behavior 37, 44 (1985). Most telling was the fact that a higher conviction rate was found where, all else being the same, the impeaching crime was murder than where the impeaching crime was perjury. Id. at 43. The only explanation for this last result is that the prior conviction evidence was not used exclusively to evaluate credibility. This is emphasized by the fact that the researchers found that there was no significant difference between the mock jurors' ratings of defendant's credibility when a prior conviction was introduced and when one was not. Id. at 41. They concluded that "[t]he credibility ratings of defendant did not vary as a function of prior conviction," while "[c]onviction rates [did vary] as a function of prior conviction. . . ." Id.

[I]n light of the overwhelming tendency for jurors, and even trial and appellate judges to misuse prior conviction evidence, it is our view that there is an "overwhelming probability" that most prior conviction evidence introduced for the purpose of impeachment will be considered as if it had been introduced to show that the defendant acted in conformity with his criminal past. See *Richardson v. Marsh,* 481 U.S. 200, 107 S.Ct. 1702, 95 L.Ed.2d 176 (1987).

The dissenters criticize us for making behavioral judgments and relying on studies in reaching this determination. They critique at length the conclusions and methodologies of the studies we have cited. We do not agree with their conclusions, but welcome their critique of these materials as social science experiments cannot serve as the primary basis for judicial decision. Many fundamental principles of our jurisprudence are based on assumptions of human behavior that have never been, and in most cases cannot be, scientifically tested. We also note that the rule we modify today, and that the dissent urges us to leave as is, was the result of assumptions about jury behavior and the effectiveness of limiting instructions that were accompanied by relatively little analysis or study.

The studies cited are nevertheless relevant, support our view, and deserve consideration. In citing them, however, we do not suggest that the amendment of MRE 609 is based solely upon them. The rule change is instead based upon the underlying principles of our legal system and our perception that these principles are not served by the scope of prior-conviction impeachment which is presently permitted.

Some of the most cherished and well-accepted of these principles have been defined by jurists who were willing to state the obvious. The obvious in this area is that criminal defendants are prejudiced by prior conviction evidence as presently allowed and that leaving the question to trial judges has not been successful.

[W]e, therefore, in the words of the dissent, act not on the basis of studies, but on the "common-sense premise" that some prior convictions are more probative than others, that some are inherently more prejudicial, and that it is absurd to suggest that jurors will be able to avoid improper consideration of a defendant's criminal character once it has become known to them.

APPENDIX A
REVISED MRE 609
IMPEACHMENT BY EVIDENCE OF CONVICTION OF CRIME

(a) General rule. For the purpose of attacking the credibility of a witness, evidence that the witness has been convicted of a crime shall not be admitted unless the evidence has been elicited from the witness or established by public record during cross-examination, and

(1) the crime contained an element of dishonesty or false statement, or

(2) the crime contained an element of theft, and

(A) the crime was punishable by imprisonment in excess of one year or death under the law under which the witness was convicted, and

(B) the court determines that the evidence has significant probative value on the issue of credibility and, if the witness is the defendant in a criminal trial, the court further determines that the probative value of the evidence outweighs its prejudicial effect.

(b) Determining probative value and prejudicial effect. For purposes of the probative value determination required by subrule (a)(2)(B), the court shall consider only the age of the conviction and the degree to which a conviction of the crime is indicative of veracity. If a determination of prejudicial effect is required, the court shall consider only the conviction's similarity to the charged offense and the possible effects on the decisional process if admitting the evidence causes the defendant to elect not to testify. The court must articulate, on the record, the analysis of each factor.

■ BOYLE, JUSTICE (dissenting).

The majority has today replaced the trial judge's discretionary authority to advance the truth-seeking process with its own view of the proper use of impeachment evidence.

[T]he majority has looked to empirical studies of mock jurors by behavioral psychologists to design these new rules. The very use of the concept that jurors "mediate" their conclusions through other perceptions bespeaks the majority's application of behavioral decision theory to the jury system. The majority fails to acknowledge, however, that simulations of the jury process are conceded even by proponents of "psycholegal" research to be "imperfect tools for answering empirical questions," Kerr & Bray, *The Psychology of the Courtroom* (New York: Academic Press, 1982), p 318. Notwithstanding such reservations and ignoring the fact that the prosecution must introduce sufficient evidence in the case in chief to support guilt beyond a reasonable doubt, the majority states that it is much easier for a jury to conclude that "a person is bad than that he did something bad," and then flatly asserts that the limiting instructions do not accomplish their purpose.

One study the majority believes deserves consideration involves forty-eight mock jurors being advised of seven prior similar convictions, Doob & Kirshenbaum, *Some empirical evidence on the effect of § 12 of the Canada Evidence Act upon an accused,* 15 Crim.L.Q. 88, 93 (1972–73). It is this study which provides the "halo effect" explanation in the majority opinion.[18]

The most recent study cited by the majority is based on observations of 160 persons approached in Laundromats, supermarkets, bus terminals, and private homes who were asked to determine guilt or innocence of a

---

18.   The majority quotes at length from this study. Forty-eight persons were individually approached in and around various public buildings. Each was read a four-hundred-word description of a case of breaking and entering. Each was asked, "How likely do you think it is that he is guilty?" Each was asked to respond on a scale that ran from one (definitely guilty) to seven (definitely not guilty). Points three and five were labeled as "probably guilty" and "probably not guilty," respectively.

Twelve persons read the case and rated (Group 1); twelve persons read, in addition, that the defense attorney decided not to put his client on the stand because there was no purpose (Group 2); twelve persons were told that the defendant testified "but did not give any important evidence" and that the defendant was impeached with five prior felonies for breaking and entering an occupied dwelling and twice for possession of stolen property (Group 3); and twelve persons were told,

in addition to the convictions, the limiting instruction of the judge (Group 4). The results were:

Average Ratings of Guilt

Group 1	4.00
Group 2	4.33
Group 3	3.25
Group 4	3.00

The study concludes on the basis of the data that the presence of a record has a dramatic effect. I would expect that random disagreement in so small a sample could account for all of the difference, but, regardless, this study can hardly be urged as support for the majority's result.

There is simply no real basis for comparison between the methodology of this study and that of the courtroom. These are forty-eight individual ratings without a trial, evidence, voir dire, argument, witnesses, instructions, or deliberation, and the prior conviction evidence is overwhelming and unrepresentative.

hypothetical defendant from a two-page case summation. This study concludes that mock jurors are more likely to convict a defendant when advised of conviction of a prior *similar* crime, not, as the majority implies, of any prior conviction—a result that supports the current approach of our jurisprudence to this category of case. Similarly, the study's observation that the participants' rating of the hypothetical defendant's credibility did not vary as a function of prior conviction is used by the majority to support its conclusion that a limiting instruction has no effect on how jurors use prior conviction evidence. It is obvious even to the untutored, however, that the fact that there was no significant variation in the mock jurors' evaluation of the "defendant's" credibility is equally explained by the fact that there was no real defendant to evaluate. As the authors of this study themselves note:

> "One should be cautious in generalizing from the results of this study to jurors in a real trial. First, the ratio of trial evidence to prior conviction information is much lower in simulations than in actual trials. In an actual trial, the greater richness of evidence and actors probably provides jurors with more bases for forming credibility judgments than the subjects in our simulation had." Wissler & Saks, *On the inefficacy of limiting instructions: When jurors use prior conviction evidence to decide on guilt,* 9 Law & Human Behavior 37, 46 (1985).

Finally, not only was there no real defendant, no actual deliberation or explanation of the limiting instruction, the most telling indication of the absence of persuasive weight in this study is the fact that the observation the majority finds most important, that is, that all else being the same, the "conviction" rate was higher where the impeaching crime was murder, is a conclusion drawn from a survey of *twenty* people, fourteen of whom opined that the defendant was guilty.

[T]he fact is that there is no demonstrable evidence that juries resolve doubtful cases on the basis that the defendant is a "bad man" and should be punished, that juries lower the burden of proof even if a guilty verdict would be incorrect, that juries convict because of a belief that the defendant's convictions indicate that he is probably guilty of the crime charged, or that juries incorrectly convict where a defendant does not take the stand because of fear of impeachment. Thus, there is no basis other than the majority's preference for its own rules for the statements that there is an "overwhelming tendency for jurors . . . to misuse prior conviction evidence," or that MRE 609 presents a "likelihood that innocent persons may be convicted."

———

3.   PERMITTING JURORS TO ASK QUESTIONS OF A WITNESS

A final illustration of the use of social science research to construct rules of evidence and rules of trial management addresses the issue of whether judges should allow jurors to ask questions of a witness at trial.

———

SECURITIES AND EXCHANGE COMMISSION v. KOENIG

United States Court of Appeals, Seventh Circuit, 2009.
557 F.3d 736.

■ EASTERBROOK, CHIEF JUDGE.

Waste Management, Inc., grew at an average annual rate of 26% from 1979 through 1991. When growth fell off, James Koenig, its Chief Financial Officer, decided to improve appearances. He devised several accounting strategies that a jury found to be fraudulent. The district judge imposed a civil penalty of about $2.1 million and ordered Koenig to disgorge the bonuses he received ($831,500, plus more than $1.2 million in prejudgment interest). [S]everal of Koenig's arguments [on appeal] concern trial management.

[P]rinciple 13(C) of the ABA's American Jury Project recommends that judges permit jurors to ask questions of witnesses. The Final Report of the Seventh Circuit's American Jury Project 15–24 (Sept. 2008) concurs, with the proviso that jurors should submit their questions to the judge, who will edit them and pose appropriate, non-argumentative queries. District judges throughout the Seventh Circuit participated in that project. The judges, the lawyers for the winning side, and, tellingly, the lawyers for the losing side, all concluded (by substantial margins) that when jurors were allowed to ask questions, their attention improved, with benefits for the overall quality of adjudication. Keeping the jurors' minds on their work is an especially vital objective during a long trial about a technical subject, such as accounting. The district judge in this case permitted jurors to submit questions to him. Some were asked; others were reformulated and asked; some were not asked, when the judge thought them inappropriate or repetitive.

Koenig contends that permitting the jurors to participate in this fashion is a reversible error. That can't be because any statute or rule of procedure bans the process. There is no such statute or rule. Nor has any court of appeals forbidden the judge to ask questions submitted by the jurors. The ABA and Seventh Circuit jury projects found benefits; so have scholars. See, e.g., Shari Seidman Diamond, Mary R. Rose, Beth Murphy & Sven Smith, *Juror Questions During Trial: A Window into Juror Thinking,* 59 Vand. L.Rev.1927 (2006); Nicole L. Mott, *The Current Debate on Juror Questions,* 78 Chi.-Kent L.Rev. 1099 (2003).

In opposition to these studies, Koenig has only occasional judicial skepticism. For example, we said more than a decade ago that questions from jurors are "fraught with risks". *United States v. Feinberg,* 89 F.3d 333, 336 (7th Cir.1996). Similar statements are easy to find. E.g., *DeBenedetto v. Goodyear Tire & Rubber Co.,* 754 F.2d 512, 516 (4th Cir.1985); *United States v. Ajmal,* 67 F.3d 12, 14 (2d Cir.1995). These expressions reflect concern that allowing jurors to ask questions will lead them to take positions too early in the trial, emulating the advocates by choosing sides and becoming argumentative rather than reflective. The jury projects and other studies were designed to find out whether these risks are realized so frequently that they overcome the benefits, such as keeping jurors alert and focused. Now that several studies have concluded that the benefits exceed the costs, there is no reason to disfavor the practice. Like other issues of trial management—may jurors take notes? should written jury instructions and copies of exhibits be sent to the jury room during deliberations?—whether to allow the jurors to pose questions is a topic committed to the sound discretion of the judge. That discretion was not abused in this case; to the contrary, the judge's decision, like his supervision of the questioning process, was well considered and sensible.

Koenig contends that the judge should have limited the jurors to "clarifying" questions, but jurors' perspectives are so different from those of lawyers that it is difficult to see how such a limit could be enforced (or why it would be appropriate). Testimony that seems clear to a specialist in accounting or securities law may be confusing to a juror encountering these subjects for the first time, so a juror may see as "clarifying" a question that the lawyer sees as unnecessary or obtuse. A judge should serve as a filter for questions and eliminate or rephrase those that are irrelevant or disguised argument (as the judge at this trial did); more than that a court of appeals cannot sensibly demand.

[K]oenig sees in some of the proposed questions (principally those filtered out by the judge) signs that a few jurors had made up their minds or taken an adversarial position in mid-trial. It is dangerous to draw such inferences from questions; judges often ask pointed questions of both sides, and it would be a mistake to infer from these questions that the judge was leaning against *both* litigants. No matter. Koenig's position seems to be that ignorance is bliss: if some jurors have reached a tentative conclusion in mid-trial, it is best not to know it. Why? Jurors must be impartial, but like everyone else they respond to evidence and may think that they know enough even when lawyers want to feed them more. [L]awyers should want to *know* when some jurors are tending the other side's way, so that they can make adjustments to their presentations in an effort to supply whatever proof the jurors think vital, but missing. Just as questions from the bench can supply insight that helps lawyers make a stronger case, so questions from jurors can help lawyers tailor their presentations. Keeping jurors silent won't prevent them from reacting to the evidence; it will just make it harder for lawyers to know how things are going. It is a lot easier (and more reliable) to read jurors' questions than to read the expressions on their faces.

The judgment is affirmed.

B.   TORT LIABILITY

Another example of social science research being used to shape the common law can be found in the area of tort liability. The principal issue in the development of tort law on which social science has been brought to bear has been "foreseeability," that is, the degree to which a defendant should have known that his or her behavior could result in harm to another.

ZINCK v. WHELAN

Superior Court of New Jersey, Appellate Division, 1972.
120 N.J.Super. 432, 294 A.2d 727.

■ CONFORD, P.J.A.D.

[Patrick Schoudt, the defendant, parked his father's car on a residential street in front of their house on the evening of June 24, 1970. The car was unlocked and the key left in the ignition. During the night, a group of teenagers stole the car and later crashed into a car driven by the plaintiffs, who were severely injured. The plaintiffs sued Schoudt for negligently leaving his key in the ignition of the unlocked car, but the trial judge granted summary judgment in favor of Schoudt.]

Basically the key to duty, negligence and proximate cause in the fact-pattern under review is the foreseeability *vel non* to a reasonable man of an unreasonably *enhanced hazard,* when a motor vehicle is left unlocked in a public place with key in the ignition, of both the theft or misappropriation of the vehicle and an ensuing mishandling of it by the taker with death, injury or destruction of property of others lawfully using the highways as the result.

[C]ommon-law courts having evolved the law of negligence, they are obviously free to and should mold its application as developing experience and sound judgment counsel in the broad public interest and in the interests of justice. The fact that New Jersey has no pertinent legislation in the field under consideration is no bar against our courts performing their traditional common-law function in this regard. In undertaking to do so, however, courts should inform themselves on the basis of such reliable empirical data as are available. Such data were not available in 1951 when we decided Saracco v. Lyttle [78 A.2d 288 (App.Div.1951)]. However, the data now at hand, taken in conjunction with social trends which are commonly known, indicate that the hazard of car theft is rapidly growing and that both its relationship to keys being left in the ignitions of unlocked vehicles and the extraordinary correlation between thefts and disastrous incidental accidents are far clearer now than in the days when the doctrine of no-proximate-cause in this area was getting its foothold in judicial thought.

Some of the data is mentioned in [t]he recent District of Columbia Circuit Court of Appeals opinion in Gaither v. Myers, 404 F.2d at 222, particularly the allusion therein to the estimated accident rate for stolen cars being 200 times the normal accident rate. But there is much other concordant, convincing data from sources supplied us by appellants which we deem reliable.

In 1950 the national rate of stolen vehicles per 100,000 population was about 100. President's Commission on Law Enforcement and Administration of Justice, Task Force Report: Crime and its Impact—An Assessment, at 27 (1967). In 1970 the rate was 453.5, an increase of over 350%. United Crime Reports: Crime in the United States (1970) (promulgated by F.B.I.) ("Uniform Crime Reports"). The 1964 rate was 242. Since 1960 the rate increased 149.7%. That increase has been four times greater than both the percentage increase in automobile registrations generally and that of persons aged 15–24 years. 1970 Uniform Crime Reports, at 28.

As of 1964 50% of the thefts involved minors under 18. Uniform Crime Reports, at 19. 42% of the cars stolen had the keys left in the ignition or the ignition unlocked. Id. at 20. "Most auto thefts, two-thirds, occur at night, and over one-half of the thefts are from private residences, apartments and/or from streets in residential areas." Id. at 20.

In 1966 the Department of Justice conducted a survey of this subject. See Hearings on H.R. 15215 before Subcommittee No. 5 of the House Committee on the Judiciary, 90th Congress, 2d Session, at 31–39 (1968) ("Justice Department Survey"). This was based upon questionnaires returned by 1,659 convicted car thieves involved in 4,077 offenses. The survey showed that 59% of the cars stolen had the keys left in the ignition or the switch unlocked. Justice Department Survey, at 32. 18.2% of the cars taken were subsequently involved in accidents. Id. at 33.

Since 1967 the Attorney General of New Jersey has promulgated an annual statistical crime summary. Uniform Crime Reports of New Jersey. The 1969 report (at 57) indicates a rise in auto theft of 25% from 1967 to 1969. 48% of the thefts were by persons under 18. Ibid. Over 45% of the thefts were from the streets of residential areas and more than 70% occurred at night. Id. at 59. Inquiries of owners of cars stolen indicated that 34% professed to be unable to inform the police as to whether the key was in the ignition or whether the car was locked; but of those who purported to remember, the key was left in the ignition or elsewhere in the vehicle in 17% of the cases. Id. at 59. In any event, the same report (at 59) observes:

> The degree of negligence of motor vehicle operator in most cases dictates whether or not the theft will occur. The portion of thefts attributed to the professional car thief is relatively small when compared to that portion perpetrated by the non-professional whose actions depend chiefly on the opportunities afforded by careless operators who fail to take normal safeguards when leaving a motor vehicle unattended.

We think the reasonably prudent motor car operator can today justly be held to an awareness of the gravamen of the foregoing data, if not of the specific figures, which may vary from time to time, locality to locality or from one study to another. As noted above, on March 1, 1967 the United States Attorney General publicly announced the start of the Justice Department's National Auto Theft Prevention Campaign, a drive against the very problem here of concern. The campaign has continued since, abetted by wide media and other publicity. Automobile owners are continuously warned to remove the key and lock the vehicle when parking. [A]s to the question of Patrick's negligence in leaving the key in the ignition, a fact issue for the jury was clearly presented. The cover of darkness and absence of surveillance was an inviting setting for the taking. The car was inferably left in the street for the night. And the statistical data cited above indicate that thefts from residential streets, or after nightfall, are of relatively high incidence.

Judgment reversed.

————

HILL v. YASKIN

Supreme Court of New Jersey, 1977.
75 N.J. 139, 380 A.2d 1107.

■ CLIFFORD, J.

Plaintiff William E. Hill, a Camden police officer, was injured on October 8, 1971 when his police car collided with a vehicle which he was pursuing. The vehicle, owned by defendant Judith A. Yaskin, had been stolen the previous day from a parking lot operated by defendant Camden Parking Services, Inc. (Camden Parking). Suit was commenced against Yaskin and Camden Parking bottomed on the admitted fact that the ignition key had been left in the vehicle while it was parked in the lot. Specifically, the Complaint charged that defendant Yaskin "so negligently and carelessly allowed her motor vehicle to be * * * unattended, so as to allow the unknown driver to take and use the same." As to defendant Camden Parking the charge was that the Yaskin vehicle had been left unattended, with the keys placed in the ignition, on the specific instructions of the lot owner, and that this conduct on the part of Camden Parking constituted negligence.

The trial court granted summary judgment in favor of both defendants and the Appellate Division affirmed.

[W]hat the issue before us comes down to is whether there was a duty owed to plaintiff by either defendant or both of them.

[T]his "duty" aspect of foreseeability was concisely set forth by Judge Conford, in the stolen vehicle context, in Zinck v. Whelan, [294 A.2d 727 at 734 (1972)] wherein he noted:

[B]asically the key to duty, negligence and proximate cause in the fact-pattern under review is the foreseeability *vel non* to a reasonable man of an unreasonably *enhanced hazard,* when a motor vehicle is left unlocked in a public place with key in the ignition, of both the theft or misappropriation of the vehicle and an ensuing mishandling of it by the taker with death, injury or destruction of property of others lawfully using the highways as the result.

The *Zinck* court fortified its "enhanced hazard" approach by reference to empirical data indicating the danger involved in leaving ignition keys in unattended vehicles. 120 N.J.Super. at 446–49, 294 A.2d 727. The continuing validity of such data may be recognized by reference to a recent study conducted by the Law Enforcement Assistance Administration [L.E.A.A.]. A report entitled Preliminary Study of the Effectiveness of Auto Anti–Theft Devices (Nat'l Inst. of Law Enforcement and Crim. Justice, L.E.A.A., U.S. Dept. of Justice 1975) [hereinafter *LEAA Study*] indicates that in at least 24% of the cases considered, the means used by a thief to mobilize a stolen car was a key. *LEAA Study* at 4–5. The study's conclusion on this point was that

> a significant number of the stolen and recovered cars involved keys left in the ignition lock or concealed in the car (under a mat or above the sun visor, for example). It would thus appear that owner/operator action may have directly contributed to a very large proportion of these thefts. [Id. at 4.]

This same study further concluded that the accident rate for stolen cars is 47 times greater than the rate for the general public. Id. at 29.

With this impressive array of statistical information as a backdrop, we have no hesitancy in concluding that summary judgment should not have been entered in favor of either defendant.

[I]t should be acknowledged that our search here is essentially one for desirable policy. In this area, the issue being whether the plaintiff William Hill's injured interest is one which falls within the protection of the rule he invokes, our function is "altogether an excursion into the domain of policy." Or, as put more succinctly by Chief Justice Weintraub, "[w]hether a duty exists is ultimately a question of fairness." Goldberg v. Housing Auth. of Newark, 186 A.2d at 293. As we view the matter, there is nothing unfair in requiring defendants to go to trial on the question of whether they should have foreseen that the leaving of Yaskin's automobile unattended under the circumstances recited above unreasonably increased the hazard of its theft and subsequent mishandling—particularly where that hazard could have so easily been substantially reduced.

[J]udgment reversed. The cause is remanded to the Law Division for trial as to both defendants.

———

McCLENAHAN v. COOLEY

Supreme Court of Tennessee, 1991.
806 S.W.2d 767.

■ DROWOTA, JUSTICE.

In this action for the wrongful death of his wife and two children and personal injuries to another child, William McClenahan, Plaintiff–Appellant, appeals the dismissal of his lawsuit against Glenn Cooley, Defendant–Appellee, by the Circuit Court of Bradley County. The central issue presented in this litigation is whether a jury should be permitted to determine the issue of proximate causation in cases where the keys are left in the ignition of a parked automobile that is subsequently stolen and thereafter involved in an accident.

[T]he facts to be taken as true in this case reveal that on May 20, 1988, at approximately 11 a.m., the Defendant, Glenn Cooley, drove his 1981 Pontiac Bonneville automobile to a bank located in the public parking lot of a shopping center in Athens. The Defendant left the keys in the ignition to his parked automobile while he went inside of the bank to transact business. While the Defendant was in the bank, a thief spotted the keys in the ignition of the vehicle, started the engine, and began driving down the interstate where he was spotted by a state trooper. When the thief exited the interstate a short time later, a high speed chase ensued on the busiest stretch of highway in Cleveland at the lunchtime hour. The thief was pursued by police officers approximately 80 miles per hour approaching the most dangerous intersection in the city. When the vehicles reached the intersection, the thief ran a red light traveling in excess of 80 miles per hour and slammed into another vehicle broadside.

[T]he Plaintiff brought an action predicated upon negligence per se and common law negligence for the wrongful death of his wife and the two children, and for injuries to the child who survived. The complaint alleges that the Defendant knew or should have known that it was unlawful to leave the keys in the ignition of an unattended vehicle; that he knew or should have known that it was unsafe to do so; and that he knew or should have known that the place where he had parked the vehicle, complete with keys in the ignition, created a foreseeable likelihood that the vehicle would be stolen. The claim is made by the Plaintiff that the actions of the thief are a foreseeable and/or expected result of the Defendant's purported negligence.

[G]iving foremost consideration to the established principles of common law negligence, we conclude, as many other jurisdictions have, that leaving a key in the ignition of an unattended automobile in an area where the public has access, be it public or private property, could be found by a reasonable jury to be negligent, whether or not a prohibitory statute is involved. The mere fact that an automobile is parked on private property and no statute is violated should not in all cases dictate a determination of absolute non-liability. The basic issue is foreseeability, both as to proximate causation and superseding intervening cause, and that is a question of fact rather than of law upon which reasonable minds can and do differ, at least where the accident has occurred during the flight of the thief relatively close thereto in time and distance.[8] [W]e thus expressly reject the contention that an intervening criminal act under the circumstances presented here automatically breaks the chain of causation as a matter of law, concluding instead that reasonable minds can differ as to whether a person

---

8. A study conducted by the United States Department of Justice reveals that 42.3 percent of all automobiles stolen during the period covered by the study were left unattended with the keys in the ignition and that the rate of accidents involving such stolen vehicles was 200 times the normal accident rate. See 45 A.L.R.3d at 797.

of ordinary prudence and intelligence through the exercise of reasonable diligence could foresee, or should have foreseen, the theft of an unattended automobile with the keys in the ignition left in an area where the public has access, and could likewise foresee the increased risk to the public should a theft occur.

[F]or the foregoing reasons, the judgment of the trial court is reversed and the case remanded for proceedings consistent with this opinion.

NOTE

1. "Dramshop" and Convenience Store Liability. The extension of tort liability to liquor stores—"dramshops"—when minors or intoxicated persons who purchase alcohol are later involved in car crashes has also invoked empirical research findings. For example, in McClellan v. Tottenhoff, 666 P.2d 408 (Wyo. 1983), the Supreme Court of Wyoming overturned a precedent to hold that a liquor store could be sued for selling alcohol to a minor who later became intoxicated and caused a fatal collision. The court stated that "[t]he fact that the risk to the traveling public may readily be recognized and foreseen is supported by disturbing statistics," id. at 415, and recited data that over half of all fatal crashes in Wyoming involved alcohol, and in nearly one-fourth of these, the driver was a minor. In a further extension of tort liability to convenience stores, the court in West v. East Tennessee Pioneer Oil Co., 172 S.W.3d 545, 551 (Tenn. 2005) held:

> It is common knowledge that drunk driving directly results in accidents, injuries, and deaths. [T]he severity of the risk posed by drunken driving in this state is clearly indicated in Tennessee Department of Safety statistics which reveal that alcohol related automobile accidents led to 2,498 deaths in Tennessee between 1998 and 2003. *Dep't of Safety Internet–DUI Statistics: Known Alcohol Related Crashes* (2005). [B]ased upon the foregoing analysis, we conclude that a convenience store employee owes a duty of reasonable care to persons on the roadways, including the plaintiffs, not to sell gasoline to a person whom the employee knows (or reasonably ought to know) to be intoxicated and to be the driver of the motor vehicle.

SELECTED BIBLIOGRAPHY

A. Common Law

Alschuler, "Close Enough for Government Work": The Exclusionary Rule After *Leon,* 1984 Supreme Court Review 309 (1984).

Demaine, In Search of an Anti–Elephant: Confronting the Human Inability to Forget Inadmissible Evidence, 16 George Mason Law Review 99 (2008).

Dripps, Living with *Leon,* 95 Yale Law Journal 906 (1986).

LaFave, The Smell of *Herring*: A Critique of the Supreme Court's Latest Assault on the Exclusionary Rule, 99 Journal of Criminal Law and Criminology ___ (2009).

Perrin, Caldwell, Chase, and Fagan, If It's Broken, Fix It: Moving Beyond the Exclusionary Rule, 83 Iowa Law Review 669 (1998).

Sklansky, Is the Exclusionary Rule Obsolete?, 5 Ohio State Journal of Criminal Law 567 (2008).

Taslitz, The Expressive Fourth Amendment: Rethinking the Good Faith Exception to the Exclusionary Rule, 76 Mississippi Law Journal 483 (2006).

Uchida and Bynum, Search Warrants, Motions to Suppress and "Lost Cases:" The Effects of the Exclusionary Rule in Seven Jurisdictions, 81 Journal of Criminal Law and Criminology 1034 (1991).

B. Tort Liability

Conaway, The Continuing Search for Solutions to the Drinking Driver Tragedy and the Problem of Social Host Liability, 82 Northwestern Law Review 403 (1988).

Malkin and Voon, Social Hosts' Responsibility for Their Intoxicated Guests: Where Courts Fear to Tread, 15 Torts Law Journal 62 (2007).

Stout, Sloan, Liang, and Davies, Reducing Harmful Alcohol–Related Behaviors: Effective Regulatory Methods, 61 Journal of Studies on Alcohol 402 (2000).

Section **IV.** Social Authority

In both constitutional and common law, courts have relied heavily upon Davis's concept of "legislative fact" for theoretical guidance in dealing with social science research. In our own work on the lawmaking uses of social science, however, we have become increasingly disenchanted with "legislative fact" and increasingly frustrated with the lack of direction—illustrated in the cases presented above—that it provides courts confronted with empirical questions. We have developed an alternative theoretical concept that we believe brings more coherence to the task of incorporating social science research in the judicial lawmaking process. We call our perspective "social authority."

———

SOCIAL AUTHORITY: OBTAINING, EVALUATING, AND ESTABLISHING SOCIAL SCIENCE IN LAW

John Monahan and Laurens Walker.
134 University of Pennsylvania Law Review 477 (1986).

It is difficult to gainsay the recent conclusion that "a viable formulation of rules ... with regard to legislative facts has not proven feasible."[37]

---

37. E. Cleary, K. Broun, G. Dix, E. Gelhorn, D. Kaye, R. Meisenholder, E. Roberts & J. Strong, McCormick on Evidence 937 (3d ed. 1984).

[R]ather, improvement in the use of social science information in the courts may be possible only "within the perimeters of a new concept,"[39] a concept that would fundamentally alter the way in which courts view social science materials.

We propose *social authority* as such a concept. We argue that courts should treat social science research relevant to creating a rule of law as a source of authority rather than as a source of facts. More specifically we propose that courts treat social science research as they would legal precedent under the common law.

[O]ur initial case for the jurisprudential plausibility of viewing social science as a form of authority takes this observation as its point of departure: while empirical research has some of the characteristics of fact, it has some of the characteristics of law as well. Until now, courts and commentators have attended to the similarity between social science and fact, and have largely ignored the similarity between social science and law.

[I]   A. *Similarity Between Social Science and Fact*

The principal similarity between social science research and fact is that both are *positive*—both concern the way the world *is*, with no necessary implications for the way the world *ought* to be. Both refer to the empirical reality that we infer from our senses, rather than to the value we impute to that reality. Law, in contrast, is *normative*. It does not describe how people *do* behave, but rather prescribes how they *should* behave.

B. *Similarity Between Social Science and Law*

The principal similarity between social science research and law is that both are *general*—both produce principles applicable beyond particular instances. Facts, in contrast, are specific to particular instances. Social science research, though derived from specific empirical data, typically addresses persons, situations, and time periods beyond those present in a particular investigation. Indeed, the purpose of most scientific research is to obtain knowledge that, while surely not immutable, holds true for many people over considerable time and in a variety of places. Because of this generality, the conclusions of empirical research are sometimes metaphorically described as scientific laws.

Like social science, law, particularly court decisions in a commonlaw system, derives from specific empirical events (the facts of a case), but speaks more broadly. It is this attribute of generality that is described as the "precedential effect" or authoritative nature of a court decision. A decision takes on the mantle of legal authority in subsequent litigation precisely to the extent that the decision transcends the people, situation, and time present in the original case. Indeed, the way to deny legal

---

39. Id. at 938.

authority to a court decision is to deny its generality by claiming that the decision is limited to its own facts.

[C.] *The Criterion for Classification*

[I]f we have made our threshold case that it is jurisprudentially possible for social science research to be classified as either law or fact, the next question concerns the nature of the argument that is to decide which classification should be used. Of two plausible classification schemes, how does one choose between them? How, in other words, does one decide which similarities—the similarities to law or the similarities to fact—are the most important? The question is taxonomic, and the extensive literature in the field of classification yields a clear answer: the better classification is the one that is most useful.

[T]he adequacy of our proposal—that social science research be treated by the courts as courts treat legal precedent rather than as fact—depends, therefore, upon the quality of the judicial management procedures that flow from this social authority classification, as compared with the existing procedures that result from the fact classification.

[W]hat implications flow from conceiving of social science as more akin to law than to fact? We offer a series of proposals addressed to the three questions that have proved most vexing to American courts when empirical studies appear relevant to rendering a decision: (1) how should courts obtain information from the social sciences?; (2) how should they evaluate it?; and (3) how should they treat the empirical conclusions established by other courts?

The heuristic presumption with which we approach each question is that courts should treat social science data the same way they treat legal precedent.

[II] A. *Obtaining Social Authority*

From a theory that posits social science as a source of authority in the law flow two corollary propositions regarding how a court should obtain empirical research: the parties should present empirical research to the court in briefs rather than by testimony; and the court may locate social science studies through its own research.

1. WRITTEN BRIEFS FROM THE PARTIES

[I]f the research is more analogous to law than to fact, the parties should present the research to the court in the same manner that they would offer legal precedents, that is, in written briefs rather than by oral testimony. Parties wishing to argue that a prior legal decision should be taken as precedent for the present case do not do so by introducing as a witness the judge who wrote the prior opinion. Similarly, the oral testimony of the authors of social science research should not be the vehicle by which the research is introduced in court.

[2.]   Independent Judicial Investigation

[T]reating empirical research as a source of authority rather than as a type of fact can provide the principled direction now lacking on the issue of whether judges should locate research independently. The analogy is plain: as courts are free to find legal precedents that the parties have not presented, they should also have the power to locate social science research through independent investigation. Courts are not limited to the case precedents contained in the parties' briefs and are not required to remand for further hearings to develop a record in which case precedents can be introduced. Likewise, they should not be limited to the briefs or required to remand to obtain scientific research.

[B.]   *Evaluating Social Authority*

[C]ourts assign precedential value to prior judicial decisions by a process that is neither clear nor simple. One need not unpack the whole jurisprudence of precedent, however, to arrive at an appreciation of the factors on which courts rely in evaluating prior cases. At least four indices of precedential persuasiveness can be easily abstracted from the jurisprudential literature: (1) cases decided by courts higher in the appellate structure have more weight than lower court decisions; (2) better reasoned cases have more weight than poorly reasoned cases; (3) cases involving facts closely analogous to those in the case at issue have more weight than cases involving easily distinguished facts; and (4) cases followed by other courts have more weight than isolated cases.

We realize that these indicia of precedential value cannot be applied literally to the evaluation of social science research. Scientific studies themselves, for example, are not "decided" by or "appealed" to varying levels of the judiciary. Yet, as we hope to demonstrate, the principles courts use to distinguish cases in terms of their precedential worth bear a striking similarity to the principles used by social scientists to distinguish research studies in terms of their scientific worth. We propose, therefore, that courts evaluate scientific research studies along four dimensions analogous to the four dimensions used to evaluate case precedent. Courts should place confidence in a piece of scientific research to the extent that the research (1) has survived the critical review of the scientific community; (2) has employed valid research methods; (3) is generalizable to the case at issue; and (4) is supported by a body of other research.

[C.]   *Establishing Social Authority*

Finally, we must consider a special issue in evaluating social science research: How should a court evaluate a study that another court has already evaluated? Studies of first impression may be evaluated as we propose, but additional considerations arise when another court previously has relied upon, or rejected, a particular piece of research. If the research has been evaluated by a court in another jurisdiction, the evaluation of the former court may be treated much as its conclusions of law are treated. That is, its value as precedent could be determined according to the guidelines we have developed. Yet, what of research that has been evaluated by a court in the same jurisdiction as the court presently reviewing it? The issue arises often, and in two legally distinct situations.

1. THE EFFECT OF LOWER COURT EVALUATION OF SOCIAL SCIENCE RESEARCH UPON APPELLATE COURTS

If empirical studies are considered to be matters of fact, appellate courts would appear to be bound by lower court evaluations of the studies, at least if the lower court evaluations were not "clearly erroneous." [A]ppellate courts commonly resort to the distinction between legislative facts and adjudicative facts to avoid the untenable result of being bound by two inconsistent lower court evaluations of the same research, neither of which is "clearly erroneous." Lower court findings of adjudicative facts, according to this view, are not reviewable on appeal (unless clearly erroneous), but lower court findings of legislative facts are reviewable.

We reach the same result, but by a more parsimonious route. Since appellate courts are not bound by lower courts' conclusions of law, they should not be bound by lower courts' conclusions regarding empirical research. A reviewing court is completely free to evaluate *de novo* any precedent used in a lower court decision. Similarly, the court should be unconstrained in its ability to reevaluate any social science research upon which a lower court relied in creating a rule of law.

[2.] THE EFFECT OF APPELLATE COURT EVALUATION OF SOCIAL SCIENCE RESEARCH UPON LOWER COURTS

[C]onsistent with our position on social authority, we suggest that appellate courts' evaluation of social science research should affect lower courts to the same extent that their evaluation of case precedent affects lower courts.

To say that lower courts should be influenced by the conclusions that appellate courts have derived from social science research in the same way that they are influenced by the rules that the courts abstract from prior cases, however, does not mean that lower courts need be merely passive recipients of the empirical judgments issued above. Just as new legal cases and commentary can develop and recast a given rule of law, so too new research and analysis—not previously considered by an appellate court—can change the empirical conclusions upon which a rule of law rests.

[W]e believe that if courts treat social science research as social authority, fewer judicial opinions will rely upon social science material, but the material that is used will be of much higher quality. Poor studies will be screened out, and exemplary research will become more apparent. In this way, the development of fair and efficient rules of law that rely in part upon empirical propositions will be facilitated.

———

EMPIRICAL QUESTIONS WITHOUT EMPIRICAL ANSWERS

John Monahan and Laurens Walker.
1991 Wisconsin Law Review 569 (1991).

The issue here is how courts are to proceed when they acknowledge that an empirical proposition is a predicate for a rule of law, but lack "social authority" bearing on that proposition. Since the course of action courts take might differ depending upon whether the empirical assumption arises in the context of the common law or in the context of judicial review of state action, we consider each situation separately.

A.   Empirical Assumptions in the Common Law

[C]onceiving of social science research, when used to create a legal rule, as more analogous to law itself than to fact (i.e., as a form of "social authority"), suggests the following heuristic: how do courts decide legal issues in the absence of precedent? That is, how do courts proceed in cases of "first impression"?

The predominant answer is that courts, faced with the necessity of deciding a novel case, often proceed by articulating the competing interests at stake and then formulating a rule that balances those interests to promote a desirable public policy. Empirical questions about the nature of those competing interests, and about the consequences of a policy giving priority to one of them may weigh heavily in the balancing process. When empirical assumptions are supported by "social authority" in the form of social science research, that research is often cited and relied upon in balancing interests and formulating a legal rule. When no research, or inadequate research, exists to support empirical assumptions, however, the courts fulfill their obligation to render a decision by relying upon those empirical assumptions that seem most *plausible*. Based on their experience and intuition, along with whatever information may be available, judges will *speculate* on what would be the likely impact of valid social science research on the empirical assumptions at issue.

[T]he great advantage of judicial candor about the role of empirical assumptions and the speculative nature of their resolution, then, is that the common law is left open to change as new social authority bearing on those assumptions becomes available. A corollary of this candor is that it clearly signals to the social science research community, and the government agencies that fund their research, the importance of empirical assumptions in the law (the judiciary's "working hypotheses"), and the receptiveness of courts to obtaining social authority bearing on them.

In the making of common law, therefore, courts often cannot avoid basing legal rules on empirical assumptions. Frequently, those assumptions will lack support in the form of social authority provided by the parties, or otherwise found by the court through its own independent research. In such cases, courts should rely upon the most plausible assumptions available at the time of the decision and allow future developments in experience or in research to modify these assumptions. This, of course, is how the common law always evolves.

B. *Empirical Assumptions in Judicial Review of State Action*

Judicial review of the decisions of other branches of government is a vast topic. We shall simplify our analysis by focusing on judicial review under the Equal Protection Clause of the fourteenth amendment and, specifically, on two sharply divergent tests for reviewing legislation.

[1]. THE RATIONALITY STANDARD

[T]wo concepts have been articulated as being central to judicial review under the standard of rationality: the "presumption" that the legislature acted rationally to pursue legitimate ends in enacting the statute, and the "burden of proof" to the contrary being placed on those challenging the statute. We believe, however, that both "presumption" and "burden of proof" are inapposite extrapolations; they are concepts developed in the arena of social facts and cannot properly be applied to the realm occupied by social authority.

[R]ather than employing the evidentiary concepts of case-specific social facts in judicial decisionmaking, we believe that concepts more appropriate to the "legislative" or "authoritative" nature of the inquiry should be adopted. Instead of stating that there is a "presumption of constitutionality" under the rationality standard, it would be more helpful to state that there was an "assumption of constitutionality." That is, under the "rationality" standard, *courts normally will accept as plausible the empirical assumptions made by the legislature in enacting a statute.* The challenger's burden is to demonstrate that these empirical assumptions are implausible. This is not a burden of "proof," however, since "proof" can be provided only by "evidence." Rather, the responsibility is one of "argument:" under the rationality standard, *it is the challenger's responsibility to convince the court to reject as implausible the empirical assumptions made by the legislature in enacting a statute.* This responsibility is met by providing the court with empirical research—"social authority"—the results of which so contradict the assumptions made by the legislature that it would be implausible ("irrational") to maintain them.

[W]hen courts consider a statute under the rationality standard and determine that the statute is based on empirical assumptions for which no adequate empirical support exists, the statute will normally be upheld. Only when the challenger presents—or the court finds through its own efforts—social authority sufficient to convince the court that the assumptions made by the legislature are implausible should the statute fail rationality review. Just as the common law judge is permitted to proceed by plausible speculation in a case of first impression, courts initially accept as plausible the empirical assumptions of the legislature. By such deference, courts acknowledge the legislature's primacy as a lawmaking institution. An empirical challenge to this deference, we believe, should be treated much as a legal argument challenging legislation is treated. It should be evaluated by criteria designed to test law-like social authority—rather than by criteria for reviewing factual evidence.

2.   THE STRICT SCRUTINY STANDARD

[T]he same two concepts traditionally employed for judicial review under the rationality standard, "presumption" and "burden of proof," appear central to judicial review under the strict scrutiny standard as well. Under the strict scrutiny standard, however, the presumption and burden are shifted. The presumption here is of unconstitutionality and the burden is on the state to prove otherwise. In addition, the strict scrutiny standard changes the nature of what is to be proven. The state must prove not merely that the ends it sought were "legitimate" and the means it chose were "rationally related" to achieving those ends—that is, that the legislature had a "plausible" justification for the statute. Rather, the state must prove that the ends it sought were "compelling" and the means it chose were "necessary" to their achievement—that is, that the legislature had a "valid" justification for the statute.

[W]e believe that both "presumption" and "burden of proof" are inappropriate extrapolations of social facts to the realm properly occupied by social authority. As with the rationality basis test, clarity would be brought to the strict scrutiny standard by adopting concepts more appropriate to the "legislative" or "authoritative" nature of the inquiry. Instead of stating that there is a "presumption of unconstitutionality" under the strict scrutiny standard, it would be more helpful to state that there is an "assumption of unconstitutionality." That is, under the "strict scrutiny" standard, *courts normally will reject as invalid the empirical assumptions made by the legislature in enacting a statute.* The "burden" is on the state to demonstrate that these assumptions are valid. As in the rationality standard, this is not a burden of "proof," since "proof" can be provided only by "evidence." Rather, the responsibility is again one of "argument": *it is the state's responsibility to convince the court to accept as valid the empirical assumptions made by the legislature in enacting a statute.* This responsibility is met by providing the court with empirical research— "social authority"—the results of which support the assumptions made by the legislature. Thus, strict scrutiny of a statute based on empirical assumptions for which no adequate empirical support exists should result in invalidation of the statute. Only when the state presents—or the court finds through its own research—sufficient social authority to convince the court that the assumptions made by the legislature are valid should a statute pass the strict scrutiny test. For statutes that impinge on fundamental interests or that classify on suspect bases, the respect ordinarily accorded by courts to the empirical assumptions of the legislature is much less. These special cases constitute an exception to the typical judicial deference to the legislature's primacy as a lawmaking institution. As with rationality review, however, casting the issue in terms of law-like "social authority" rather than in terms of factual evidence clarifies for courts the process of obtaining and evaluating research, and therefore, assists substantially in determining whether the state's responsibility has been met.

SELECTED BIBLIOGRAPHY

Acker, Social Science in Supreme Court Criminal Cases and Briefs: The Actual and Potential Contribution of Social Scientists as Amici Curiae, 14 Law and Human Behavior 25 (1990).

Faigman, To Have and Have Not: Assessing the Value of Social Science to the Law as Science and Policy, 38 Emory Law Journal 1005 (1989).

Faigman, "Normative Constitutional Fact Finding": Exploring the Empirical Component of Constitutional Interpretation, 139 University of Pennsylvania Law Review 541 (1991).

D. Faigman, Laboratory of Justice: The Supreme Court's 200–Year Struggle to Integrate Science and the Law (2005).

Hafemeister and Melton, The Impact of Social Science Research on the Judiciary, in Reforming the Law: Impact of Child Development Research (G. Melton ed. 1987).

Keeton, Legislative Facts and Similar Things: Deciding Disputed Premise Facts, 73 Minnesota Law Review 1 (1988).

Meares and Harcourt, Transparent Adjudication and Social Science Research in Constitutional Criminal Procedure, 90 Journal of Criminal Law and Criminology 733 (2000).

Monahan and Walker, A Judges' Guide to Using Social Science, 43 Court Review 156 (2007).

Roesch, Golding, Hans, and Reppucci, Social Science and the Courts: The Role of Amicus Curiae Briefs, 15 Law and Human Behavior 1 (1991).

Saks, Judicial Attention to the Way the World Works, 75 Iowa Law Review 1011 (1990).

CHAPTER FIVE

SOCIAL SCIENCE USED TO PROVIDE CONTEXT

It is commonplace to distinguish two fundamental uses of social science research in deciding legal cases. The first is to determine facts—what Kenneth Culp Davis called "adjudicative facts" and what we called "social facts" in Chapter 3. The second is to assist in making law—what Davis called "legislative facts" and what we called "social authority" in Chapter 4. Yet a reading of recent cases reveals a great number that seem anomalous by this method of classification. In these cases, social science is used neither as case-specific fact nor as authority for lawmaking. Instead, a third use of social science in deciding cases has emerged in recent years, one that combines elements of each of the two conventional applications to provide judges and juries with a general context for determining factual issues in particular cases.

In this chapter, we first identify and define this third use of social science research, which we call "social framework." We then examine a variety of ways in which social science is employed to provide decision makers with frameworks for determining future, present, and past facts.

SECTION I.   SOCIAL SCIENCE AS CONTEXT

In the typical case in which social science research is used to determine facts, such as the trademark and obscenity cases described in Chapter 3, the research is done by one or both parties to the lawsuit and involves the actual items whose attributes—e.g., "likelihood of confusion" or "patent offensiveness"—are in dispute. In the typical case in which social science is used to make law, such as the constitutional or common law cases described in Chapter 4, the research is broadly-based and involves the parties only as exemplars of more general findings—e.g., the effects of segregated education on the self-esteem of all African–American children, or the deterrent value of the exclusionary rule on police officers as a class. In this third, hybrid, use of social science, however, research that appears to have the general, broadly-based characteristics usually associated with lawmaking is used to determine case-specific issues, a function usually conceived as fact-finding.

SOCIAL FRAMEWORKS: A NEW USE OF SOCIAL SCIENCE IN LAW

Laurens Walker and John Monahan.
73 Virginia Law Review 559 (1987).

Most of the uses of social science in court fall into either the "legislative fact" or "adjudicative fact" categories. Within the past several years, however, courts have increasingly begun to use research in ways that do not correspond to either of the traditional classifications. There are strong indications that a new, third use of social science in law is emerging. Notable examples can be found in cases concerning eyewitness identification, assessments of dangerousness, battered women, and sexual victimization.

Social Framework as an Organizing Concept

[In these cases] social science was not being used to provide "legislative facts." [N]either party contemplated a change in any rule of law. Rather, accepting the rules of law governing his or her respective case, the party introducing the research was attempting to demonstrate that the findings would assist the jury to decide the specific factual issues being litigated.

At the same time, [s]ocial science was not being used [in these cases] to provide "adjudicative facts" either. [In] none of the [cases] were the parties to the case involved in the research at all. The expert witnesses relied heavily—and in some of the cases, exclusively—on "off the rack" research studies published before the events that gave rise to the litigation took place, studies performed by researchers and using subjects with no knowledge of the case at bar.

Yet the way social science was used in these cases—while neither legislative nor adjudicative fact—does have some of the hallmarks of each. In each case, the research being introduced shared the critical characteristic of legislative fact—generality. The studies bore on issues at trial only as those issues were particular instances of larger empirical relationships that had been uncovered.

[H]owever, as in cases involving the use of social research to determine adjudicative facts, the studies here were introduced solely to help resolve specific factual issues disputed by the immediate parties to the case, issues whose resolution had no substantive significance beyond the case at hand.

[T]he research used in these [cases], then, is not pure legislative or adjudicative fact but rather incorporates the essential aspects of both of the established categories. We therefore propose a new category, which we term social framework, to refer to the use of general[31] conclusions from social science research in determining factual issues in a specific case.

[M]easuring social frameworks according to broad evidentiary policy reveals no general bar to this third use of social science in law. Social frameworks can make the existence of a fact at issue in a legal proceeding

---

31. The conclusions of social science research are "general" to the extent that they are informed by a theory of some aspect of human behavior.

more probable or less probable than it would otherwise appear. Frameworks run little risk of inflaming a juror's emotions or taking advantage of a juror's credulity. They can, with careful presentation, clarify rather than confuse the issues to be decided at trial. Frameworks often tell jurors something they do not already know, or disabuse them of common but erroneous perceptions. And while the use of frameworks should be constrained by the concerns expressed in the rule against character evidence, numerous exceptions to that rule suggest ample opportunity for the application of frameworks.

SELECTED BIBLIOGRAPHY

Fraher, Adjudicative Facts, Non–Evidence Facts, and Permissible Jury Background Information, 62 Indiana Law Journal 333 (1987).

Meadow and Sunstein, Statistics, Not Experts, 51 Duke Law Journal 629 (2001).

Mosteller, Syndromes and Politics in Criminal Trials and Evidence Law, 46 Duke Law Journal 461 (1996).

Tanford, Thinking About Elephants: Admonitions, Empirical Research and Legal Policy, 60 University of Missouri–Kansas City Law Review 645 (1992).

SECTION II.   CONTEXTS FOR DETERMINING FUTURE FACTS

At many junctures, the law calls for an estimation of what will happen in the future. The likelihood of future criminality, for example, is frequently treated as an issue of fact in bail, parole, sexually violent predator, and death penalty statutes. Increasingly, the foreseeable likelihood of harm is a central fact in determining tort liability when the harm is realized. The following cases examine the use of social science to provide decision makers with empirical contexts for determining each of these "facts."

A.   BAIL

The prediction of one type of behavior, failure to appear at trial, has long played a central role in determining the pretrial release of criminal defendants. More recently, the prediction of another type of behavior, crime while awaiting trial, has been included among the factors to be considered in making pretrial release decisions.

––––––

REPORT OF THE COMMITTEE ON THE JUDICIARY UNITED STATES SENATE, 1983

Senate Report Number 98–225.

Comprehensive Crime Control Act of 1983: Title I–Bail Reform

The concept of permitting an assessment of defendant dangerousness in the pretrial release decision has been widely supported, and has been specifically endorsed by such diverse groups as the American Bar Association, the National Conference of Commissioners on Uniform State Laws, the National District Attorneys Association, and the National Association of Pretrial Service Agencies. In addition, the laws of several States recognize the validity of weighing the issue of the risk a released defendant may pose to community safety, and the release provisions of District of Columbia Code, passed by the Congress in 1970, specifically recognize that defendant dangerousness is an appropriate consideration in setting conditions of pretrial release and may also serve as a basis for pretrial detention.

This broad base of support for giving judges the authority to weigh risks to community safety in pretrial release decisions is a reflection of the deep public concern, which the Committee shares, about the growing problem of crimes committed by persons on release. In a recent study of release practices in eight jurisdictions, approximately one out of every six defendants in the sample studied were rearrested during the pretrial period—one-third of these defendants were rearrested more than once, and some were rearrested as many as four times.[14] Similar levels of pretrial criminality were reported in a study of release practices in the District of Columbia, where thirteen percent of all felony defendants released were rearrested. Among defendants released on surety bond, which under the District of Columbia Code, like the Bail Reform Act, is the form of release reserved for those defendants who are the most serious bail risks, pretrial rearrest occurred at the alarming rate of twenty-five percent.[15] The disturbing rate of recidivism among released defendants requires the law to recognize that the danger a defendant may pose to others should receive at least as much consideration in the pretrial release determination as the likelihood that he will not appear for trial.

In facing the problem of how to change current bail laws to provide appropriate authority to deal with dangerous defendants seeking release, the Committee concluded that while such measures as permitting consideration of community safety in setting release conditions and providing for revocation of release upon the commission of a crime during the pretrial period may serve to reduce the rate of pretrial recidivism, and that these measures therefore should be incorporated in this chapter, there is a small but identifiable group of particularly dangerous defendants as to whom neither the imposition of stringent release conditions nor the prospect of revocation of release can reasonably assure the safety of the community or other persons. It is with respect to this limited group of offenders that the courts must be given the power to deny release pending trial.

---

14. Lazar Institute, Pretrial Release: An Evaluation of Defendant Outcomes and Program Impact 48 (Washington, D.C., August 1981).

15. Institute for Law and Social Research, Pretrial Release and Misconduct in the District of Columbia 41 (April 1980).

BAIL REFORM ACT OF 1984

18 U.S.C. § 3142.

(f) Detention hearing

The judicial officer shall hold a hearing to determine whether any condition or combination of conditions [w]ill reasonably assure the appearance of [a criminal defendant at trial] as required and the safety of any other person and the community—

(1) upon motion of the attorney for the Government, in a case that involves—

(A) a crime of violence;

(B) an offense for which the maximum sentence is life imprisonment or death;

(C) an offense for which a maximum term of imprisonment of ten years or more is prescribed in the Controlled Substances Act (21 U.S.C.A. 801 et seq.), the Controlled Substances Import and Export Act (21 U.S.C.A. 951 et seq.), or section 1 of the Act of September 15, 1980 (21 U.S.C.A. 955a); or

(D) any felony if such person has been convicted of two or more offenses described in subparagraphs (A) through (C) of this paragraph, or two or more State or local offenses that would have been offenses described in subparagraphs (A) through (C) of this paragraph if a circumstance giving rise to Federal jurisdiction had existed, or a combination of such offenses; or

(2) upon motion of the attorney for the Government or upon the judicial officer's own motion in a case, that involves—

(A) a serious risk that such person will flee; or

(B) a serious risk that such person will obstruct or attempt to obstruct justice, or threaten, injure, or intimidate, or attempt to threaten, injure, or intimidate, a prospective witness or juror.

[(g)] Factors to be considered

The judicial officer shall, in determining whether there are conditions of release that will reasonably assure the appearance of the person as required and the safety of any other person and the community, take into account the available information concerning:

(1) the nature and circumstances of the offense charged, including whether the offense is a crime of violence or involves a narcotic drug;

(2) the weight of the evidence against the person;

(3) the history and characteristics of the person, including:

(A) the person's character, physical and mental condition, family ties, employment, financial resources, length of residence in the community, community ties, past conduct, history relating to drug or alcohol abuse, criminal history, and record concerning appearance at court proceedings; and

(B) whether, at the time of the current offense or arrest, the person was on probation, on parole, or on other release pending trial, sentencing, appeal, or completion of sentence for an offense under Federal, State, or local law; and

(4) the nature and seriousness of the danger to any person or the community that would be posed by the person's release.

UNITED STATES v. SALERNO

Supreme Court of the United States, 1987.
481 U.S. 739, 107 S.Ct. 2095, 95 L.Ed.2d 697.

■ CHIEF JUSTICE REHNQUIST delivered the opinion of the Court.

The Bail Reform Act of 1984 allows a federal court to detain an arrestee pending trial if the government demonstrates by clear and convincing evidence after an adversary hearing that no release conditions "will reasonably assure ... the safety of any other person and the community." The United States Court of Appeals for the Second Circuit struck down this provision of the Act as facially unconstitutional, because, in that court's words, this type of pretrial detention violates "substantive due process."

[T]he Court of Appeals concluded that "the Due Process Clause prohibits pretrial detention on the ground of danger to the community as a regulatory measure, without regard to the duration of the detention." 794 F.2d, at 71. Respondents characterize the Due Process Clause as erecting an impenetrable "wall" in this area that "no governmental interest—rational, important, compelling or otherwise—may surmount." Brief for Respondents 16.

We do not think the Clause lays down any such categorical imperative. We have repeatedly held that the government's regulatory interest in community safety can, in appropriate circumstances, outweigh an individual's liberty interest. For example, in times of war or insurrection, when society's interest is at its peak, the government may detain individuals whom the government believes to be dangerous. See Ludecke v. Watkins, 335 U.S. 160, 68 S.Ct. 1429, 92 L.Ed. 1881 (1948) (approving unreviewable Executive power to detain enemy aliens in time of war); Moyer v. Peabody, 212 U.S. 78, 84–85, 29 S.Ct. 235, 236–237, 53 L.Ed. 410 (1909) (rejecting due process claim of individual jailed without probable cause by Governor in time of insurrection). Even outside the exigencies of war, we have found that sufficiently compelling governmental interests can justify detention of dangerous persons. Thus, we have found no absolute constitutional barrier to detention of potentially dangerous resident aliens pending deportation proceedings. Carlson v. Landon, 342 U.S. 524, 537–542, 72 S.Ct. 525, 532–535, 96 L.Ed. 547 (1952); Wong Wing v. United States, 163 U.S. 228, 16 S.Ct. 977, 41 L.Ed. 140 (1896). We have also held that the government may detain mentally unstable individuals who present a danger to the public, Addington v. Texas, 441 U.S. 418, 99 S.Ct. 1804, 60 L.Ed.2d 323 (1979), and dangerous defendants who become incompetent to stand trial, Jackson v. Indiana, 406 U.S. 715, 731–739, 92 S.Ct. 1845, 1854–1858, 32 L.Ed.2d 435 (1972); Greenwood v. United States, 350 U.S. 366, 76 S.Ct. 410, 100 L.Ed. 412 (1956). We have approved of postarrest regulatory detention of juveniles when they present a continuing danger to the community. Schall v. Martin [467 U.S. 253 (1984)]. Even competent adults may face substantial liberty restrictions as a result of the operation of our criminal justice system. If the police suspect an individual of a crime, they may arrest and hold him until a neutral magistrate determines whether probable cause exists. Gerstein v. Pugh, 420 U.S. 103, 95 S.Ct. 854, 43 L.Ed.2d 54 (1975). Finally, respondents concede and the Court of Appeals noted that an arrestee may be incarcerated until trial if he presents a risk of flight, see Bell v. Wolfish, 441 U.S., at 534, 99 S.Ct., at 1871, or a danger to witnesses.

Respondents characterize all of these cases as exceptions to the "general rule" of substantive due process that the government may not detain a person prior to a judgment of guilt in a criminal trial. Such a "general rule" may freely be conceded, but we think that these cases show a sufficient number of exceptions to the rule that the congressional action challenged here can hardly be characterized as totally novel. Given the well-established authority of the government, in special circumstances, to restrain individuals' liberty prior to or even without criminal trial and conviction, we think that the present statute providing for pretrial detention on the basis of dangerousness must be evaluated in precisely the same manner that we evaluated the laws in the cases discussed above.

The government's interest in preventing crime by arrestees is both legitimate and compelling. De Veau v. Braisted, 363 U.S. 144, 155, 80 S.Ct. 1146, 1152, 4 L.Ed.2d 1109 (1960). In *Schall*, supra, we recognized the strength of the State's interest in preventing juvenile crime. This general concern with crime prevention is no less compelling when the suspects are adults. Indeed, "[t]he harm suffered by the victim of a crime is not dependent upon the age of the perpetrator." Schall v. Martin, 467 U.S., at 264–265, 104 S.Ct., at 2410. The Bail Reform Act of 1984 responds to an even more particularized governmental interest than the interest we sustained in *Schall*. The statute we upheld in *Schall* permitted pretrial detention of any juvenile arrested on any charge after a showing that the individual might commit some undefined further crimes. The Bail Reform Act, in contrast, narrowly focuses on a particularly acute problem in which the government interests are overwhelming. The Act operates only on individuals who have been arrested for a specific category of extremely serious offenses. 18 U.S.C.A. § 3142(f). Congress specifically found that these individuals are far more likely to be responsible for dangerous acts in the community after arrest. See S.Rep. No. 98–225, pp. 6–7. Nor is the Act by any means a scattershot attempt to incapacitate those who are merely suspected of these serious crimes. The government must first of all demonstrate probable cause to believe that the charged crime has been committed by the arrestee, but that is not enough. In a full-blown adversary hearing, the government must convince a neutral decisionmaker by clear and convincing evidence that no conditions of release can reasonably assure the safety of the community or any person. 18 U.S.C.A. § 3142(f). While the government's general interest in preventing crime is compelling, even this interest is heightened when the government musters convincing proof that the arrestee, already indicted or held to answer for a serious crime, presents a demonstrable danger to the community. Under these narrow circumstances, society's interest in crime prevention is at its greatest.

[A]s we stated in *Schall*, "there is nothing inherently unattainable about a prediction of future criminal conduct." Id., (at 278, 104 S.Ct., at 2417).

[T]he judgment of the Court of Appeals is therefore *reversed*.

NOTE

1. Bail Guidelines in Operation. J. Goldkamp, M. Gottfredson, P. Jones, and D. Weiland, Personal Liberty and Community Safety: Pretrial Release in the Criminal Court (1995), describe the development and implementation of bail guidelines in several cities. In Maricopa County (Phoenix), Arizona, for example, the researchers gathered data on a large number of variables from 2,200 felony cases. Defendants were followed for 90 days following pretrial release to determine the extent of failure to appear at trial or rearrest for a new crime. Statistical analyses identified eight factors that were predictive of failure to appear (FTA) or recidivism. These factors were combined in a "Classification Worksheet" that is completed by the local Pretrial Services Agency on all defendants in jail. The worksheet is reproduced below.

Risk Group Calculations			
Check the Applicable Categories Below		Enter Below	
Beginning Score of....		1	1
☐ Prior FTAs	☐ One	36	
	☐ Two or more	40	
☐ Police: Flight Risk Facts	☐ Police note facts defendant might flee	67	
☐ Property Offense	☐ Charges involve Property	34	
☐ Defendant Lives Alone	☐ Lives alone	37	
☐ Robbery Offense	☐ Charges involve robbery	45	

	Police Risk with FTAs	☐ With one prior FTA............. 8 ☐ With two or more............... 17
☐	Police Risk and Lives Alone	☐ Police: flight risk and lives alone 28
	TOTAL COLUMN IN SPACE AT RIGHT	

Points	Risk Group
1 to 34	Group 1 [ ]
35 to 67	Group 2 [ ]
68 to 107	Group 3 [ ]
108 or more	Group 4 [ ]

"Police" refers to a notation on the police arrest report that the arresting officer believes that the defendant poses a risk of flight.

The follow-up revealed the following rates of "failure" (FTA or rearrest) while on pretrial release:

Risk Group	Percent Failure
1	7
2	15
3	20
4	53

The total failure rate was 17 percent. Approximately two-thirds of the failures were rearrests and one-third were FTA.

Based on this research, courts in Maricopa County rely on the risk group classification, along with a ranking of the severity of the pending charges, as "guidelines" in making bail decisions. Courts accept the guideline suggestions in 78 percent of the cases (interview with the Maricopa County Pretrial Services Agency, April 2009). For example, a low score on the seriousness of the charges (e.g., assault, drug possession) and placement in Risk Group 1 or 2 results in a presumptive guideline decision of release on the defendant's own recognizance. A high score on the seriousness of the charges (e.g., murder, sexual assault) and a placement in Risk Group 4 results in a guideline suggestion for bail being set for $10,000 to $20,000, which often results in pretrial detention. Evaluation of the use of guidelines in Maricopa County showed that when courts deviate from the guidelines, they almost always impose higher bail than the guidelines recommend.

B. PAROLE

In many states, the role of the judge in criminal sentencing is simply to set the upper bound of time that a convicted offender can spend in prison, within the constraints of the applicable sentencing statute. The actual time spent incarcerated—up to the court-imposed maximum—is determined by an administrative agency, often called a parole board. These agencies are created by statute or, in a few states, are incorporated in the state constitution. Some parole boards, in setting the length of time an offender spends in prison, make explicit reference to social science estimates of the likelihood that he or she will offend again.

————

GEORGIA STATE BOARD OF PARDONS AND PAROLES
Parole Consideration and Eligibility (2008).

The Parole Board [d]etermined that it was in the public's best interest to adopt [P]arole Decision Guidelines that incorporate a scientifically based, data-driven risk instrument with new time to serve guidelines. [T]he Board's new Parole Decision Guidelines represent its best effort to protect the public from harm by maximizing the utility of the state's prison system by ensuring that the most dangerous offenders are incarcerated for the longest period of time possible, given the State's available resources.

The Hearing Examiner cross-references the offender's Crime Severity Level and Risk to Re–Offend Score on the Guidelines Grid component of the Parole Decision Guidelines System.

The Guidelines Grid provides a months-to-serve or a percentage of the prison sentence recommendation for the Board's consideration. The Board adopted various percentages of the sentence for Level VIII offenses, rather than an across-the-board percentage (*e.g.*, 90%), because the law governing parole guidelines requires that the guidelines take into consideration not just the severity of the crime, but "the inmate's conduct, and the social factors which the board has found to have value predicting the probability of further criminal behavior."

The Board may accept or reject the recommendation from the Guidelines. The Board specifically reserves the right to exercise its discretion under Georgia Law to disagree with the recommendation resulting from application of the Parole Decision Guidelines and to make an independent decision to deny parole or to establish a Tentative Parole Month at any time prior to sentence expiration.

————

GEORGIA STATE BOARD OF PARDONS AND PAROLES
Crime Severity Levels (2008).

The Crime Severity Level is selected from the table of offenses listed below. [I]f the inmate is serving a sentence for multiple offenses, the most serious offense will determine the Crime Severity Level.

LEVEL I

Bad checks—Under $2,000

Credit card theft

Theft of vehicle—not to sell; 1st offense

LEVEL II

Bad checks—$2,000 or more

Theft—$1,000 to $4,999

Theft of vehicle—not to sell; 2nd offense

LEVEL III

Terroristic threats

Theft—$5,000 to $10,000

Theft of vehicle to sell

LEVEL IV

Arson—over $2,000

Burglary, non-dwelling—over $5,000

Theft—over $10,000

LEVEL V

Aggravated assault, no injury or weapon

Arson

Identity fraud

LEVEL VI

Burglary, unoccupied dwelling

Cocaine or methamphetamine possession, 200–399 grams

Marijuana possession, 10 to 1,999 pounds

LEVEL VII

Attempted armed robbery

Attempted kidnapping

Attempted aggravated sexual battery

LEVEL VIII

Aggravated assault, with injury or weapon

Burglary, occupied residence

Child molestation

————

GEORGIA STATE BOARD OF PARDONS AND PAROLES
Risk to Re–Offend Score Chart (2008).

The Parole Board will use the following factors to compute a Risk to Re–Offend Score for each inmate it considers for parole using its Parole Guidelines System.

A.   Number of Felony Convictions
       None = 0
       1–2 = 1
       3 = 2
       4–5 = 3
       6–7 = 4
       8 = 5
       9 or more = 6

B.   Number of Prior Prison Incarcerations:
       None = 0
       1 = 1
       2 = 3
       3 = 4
       4 or more = 6

C.   Current Prison Sentenced Offenses (score is cumulative) includes:

       Offense(s) not listed = 0
       Burglary = 1
       Drug possession = 1
       Forgery = 2
       Felony obstruction of an officer = 3
       Theft = 5

D.   Age at Current Prison Admission:
       20 or less = 0
       More than 20 to 40 = minus 1
       More than 40 = minus 2

E.   History of drug or alcohol abuse:
       No = 0
       Yes = 2

F.   Employed at time of current arrest:
       No = 0
       Yes = minus 3

Total Risk to Re–Offend Score:

———

GEORGIA STATE BOARD OF PARDONS AND PAROLES
Parole Decision Guidelines, Time to Serve Grid (2008).

Risk to Re–Offend Score	Low (–5 to +2)	Medium (3–6)	High (7+)
Crime Severity Level			
1	17 months	20 months	22 months
2	20 months	22 months	26 months

Risk to Re–Offend Score	Low (–5 to +2)	Medium (3–6)	High (7+)
3	22 months	24 months	28 months
4	24 months	28 months	32 months
5	34 months	42 months	50 months
6	40 months	50 months	65 months
7	44 months	60 months	76 months
8	65% of sentence	75% of sentence	90% of sentence

———

NOTES

1. **Range of Months-to-Serve.** The number of recommended months-to-serve given in the above Grid are mid-points on a somewhat broader distribution of months-to-serve. For example, for Crime Severity Level 1, with a Low Risk to Re–Offend Score, the mid-point of recommended months-to-serve is 17 months, with a lower limit of 15 months and a higher limit of 19 months. Seventy-five percent of all cases in a given cell receive the mid-point of the recommended months-to-serve, with 25 percent receiving either the lower or the higher end of the recommended months-to-serve range (interview with the Research, Evaluation and Technology Division, Georgia State Board of Pardons and Paroles, May 2009).

2. **Validation Research.** The Risk to Re–Offend Score was developed by studying the criminal behavior of 33,465 inmates released from Georgia prisons between 2002 and 2003 and followed in the community for three years (interview with Applied Research Services, Inc., May, 2009). "Failure" was defined as any new felony conviction during this three-year period. Failure rates were as follows:

> Low Risk to Re–Offend Score   18%
> Medium Risk to Re–Offend Score   27%
> High Risk to Re–Offend Score   39%

3. **Constitutionality.** The constitutionality of Georgia's use of the actuarial risk assessment in setting recommended months-to-serve was upheld against an inmate's Fourteenth Amendment challenge in Sultenfuss v. Snow, 35 F.3d 1494 (11th Cir.1994).

4. **Other States.** The Michigan Department of Corrections developed an Assaultive Risk Screening Sheet to aid in parole decision making. Information on 350 variables was collected on each of 1200 male inmates released on parole. The dependent measure was arrest and return to prison for the commission of a new *violent* crime during the first 14 months on parole. Statistical analyses were then performed to ascertain which combination of the 350 variables was associated with recidivism. The flow chart below emerged.

This flow chart was then applied to a new group of male prisoners released on parole. The following results were obtained:

Assaultive Risk Screening Scores

	Very Low	Low	Middle	High	Very High
Percent Failure	3	7	12	21	40

A male prisoner's score on the Assaultive Risk Screening Sheet figures heavily in the Parole Board's determination of the length of time he will spend in prison. For example, 71 percent of those who score Very Low, but only 17 percent of those who score Very High, are paroled at their earliest release date. (Research Division, Michigan Department of Corrections, March 2009).

An attempt to generalize the Assaultive Risk Screening Sheet to female parolees was not successful. Both because of the small number of female prisoners (approximately 4 percent of the prison population) and because of the low rate of violent recidivism among these women (less than one-third of the male rate), it was not possible to obtain reliable data. For example, between 1974 and 1978, a total of only 10 female prisoners in the state scored in the Very High range of the Assaultive Risk Screening Sheet, and only one of these ("10 percent") committed a new violent crime on parole. Murphy, Final Report: Michigan Female Risk Prediction Study (1988). In light of this research, the Michigan Department of Corrections issued Policy Directive Number 05.01.135 in 1998. Section II (B) of this Directive reads: "All newly committed female prisoners shall be automatically designated very low risk without being screened."

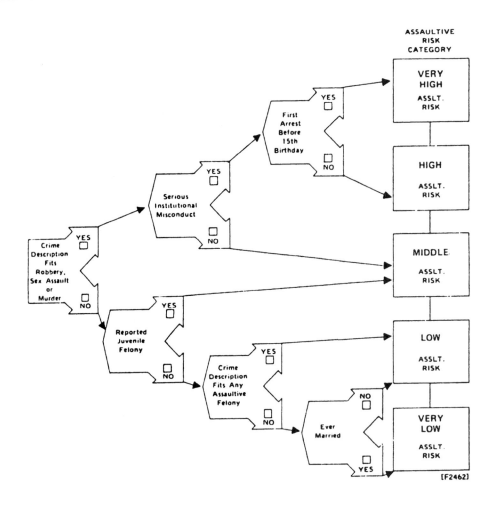

C. CIVIL COMMITMENT OF SEXUALLY VIOLENT PREDATORS

Civil commitment—the involuntary hospitalization of a person with a serious mental illness, such as schizophrenia, who is also "dangerous to self or others"—has long been accepted in all American jurisdictions. See O'Connor v. Donaldson, 422 U.S. 563, 95 S.Ct. 2486, 45 L.Ed.2d 396 (1975). In recent years, however, some states have enacted a new form of civil commitment whereby a person convicted of and imprisoned for a sexual offense, if found at the end of his or her criminal sentence to possess a "mental abnormality" or a "personality disorder"—rather than a serious mental illness—and to be likely to commit a new sexual offense in the future, can be transferred from prison to a mental hospital for an indefinite period.

KANSAS v. HENDRICKS

Supreme Court of the United States, 1997.
521 U.S. 346, 117 S.Ct. 2072, 138 L.Ed.2d 501.

■ JUSTICE THOMAS delivered the opinion of the Court.

In 1994, Kansas enacted the Sexually Violent Predator Act, which establishes procedures for the civil commitment of persons who, due to a "mental abnormality" or a "personality disorder," are likely to engage in "predatory acts of sexual violence." Kan. Stat. Ann. § 59–29a01 et seq. (1994). The State invoked the Act for the first time to commit Leroy Hendricks, an inmate who had a long history of sexually molesting children, and who was scheduled for release from prison shortly after the Act became law. Hendricks challenged his commitment on, inter alia, "substantive" due process, double jeopardy, and ex post facto grounds. The Kansas Supreme Court invalidated the Act, holding that its precommitment condition of a "mental abnormality" did not satisfy what the court perceived to be the "substantive" due process requirement that involuntary civil commitment must be predicated on a finding of "mental illness." In re Hendricks, 259 Kan. 246, 261, 912 P.2d 129, 138 (1996).

[T]he Act defined a "sexually violent predator" as:

"any person who has been convicted of or charged with a sexually violent offense and who suffers from a mental abnormality or personality disorder which makes the person likely to engage in the predatory acts of sexual violence." § 59–29a02(a).

A "mental abnormality" was defined, in turn, as a "congenital or acquired condition affecting the emotional or volitional capacity which predisposes the person to commit sexually violent offenses in a degree constituting such person a menace to the health and safety of others." § 59–29a02(b).

[T]he statute thus requires proof of more than a mere predisposition to violence; rather, it requires evidence of past sexually violent behavior and a present mental condition that creates a likelihood of such conduct in the future if the person is not incapacitated. As we have recognized, "[p]revious instances of violent behavior are an important indicator of future violent tendencies." Heller v. Doe, 509 U.S. 312, 323 (1993); see also Schall v. Martin, 467 U.S. 253, 278 (1984) (explaining that "from a legal point of view there is nothing inherently unattainable about a prediction of future criminal conduct").

A finding of dangerousness, standing alone, is ordinarily not a sufficient ground upon which to justify indefinite involuntary commitment. We have sustained civil commitment statutes when they have coupled proof of dangerousness with the proof of some additional factor, such as a "mental illness" or "mental abnormality." See, e.g., Heller, supra, at 314–315 (Kentucky statute permitting commitment of "mentally retarded" or "mentally ill" and dangerous individual). These added statutory requirements serve to limit involuntary civil confinement to those who suffer from a volitional impairment rendering them dangerous beyond their control.

The Kansas Act is plainly of a kind with these other civil commitment statutes: It requires a finding of future dangerousness, and then links that finding to the existence of a "mental abnormality" or "personality disorder" that makes it difficult, if not impossible, for the person to control his dangerous behavior. The precommitment requirement of a "mental abnormality" or "personality disorder" is consistent with the requirements of these other statutes that we have upheld in that it narrows the class of persons eligible for confinement to those who are unable to control their dangerousness.

Hendricks nonetheless argues that our earlier cases dictate a finding of "mental illness" as a prerequisite for civil commitment. He then asserts that a "mental abnormality" is not equivalent to a "mental illness" because it is a term coined by the Kansas Legislature, rather than by the psychiatric community. Contrary to Hendricks' assertion, the term "mental illness" is devoid of any talismanic significance. [W]e have never required state legislatures to adopt any particular nomenclature in drafting civil commitment statutes. [T]o the extent that the civil commitment statutes we have considered set forth criteria relating to an individual's inability to control his dangerousness, the Kansas Act sets forth comparable criteria and Hendricks' condition doubtless satisfies those criteria. The mental health professionals who evaluated Hendricks diagnosed him as suffering from pedophilia, a condition the psychiatric profession itself classifies as a serious mental disorder. See, e.g., [American Psychiatric Association, Diagnostic and Statistical Manual of Mental Disorders (4th ed. 1994)], at 524–525, 527–528. Hendricks even conceded that, when he becomes "stressed out," he cannot "control the urge" to molest children. This admitted lack of volitional control, coupled with a prediction of future dangerousness, adequately distinguishes Hendricks from other dangerous persons who are perhaps more properly dealt with exclusively through criminal proceedings. Hendricks' diagnosis as a pedophile, which qualifies as a "mental abnormality" under the Act, thus plainly suffices for due process purposes.

We granted Hendricks' cross-petition to determine whether the Act violates the Constitution's double jeopardy prohibition or its ban on ex post facto lawmaking. The thrust of Hendricks' argument is that the Act establishes criminal proceedings; hence confinement under it necessarily constitutes punishment. He contends that where, as here, newly enacted "punishment" is predicated upon past conduct for which he has already been convicted and forced to serve a prison sentence, the Constitution's Double Jeopardy and Ex Post Facto Clauses are violated.

[A]s a threshold matter, commitment under the Act does not implicate either of the two primary objectives of criminal punishment: retribution or deterrence. The Act's purpose is not retributive because it does not affix culpability for prior criminal conduct. Instead, such conduct is used solely for evidentiary purposes, either to demonstrate that a "mental abnormality" exists or to support a finding of future dangerousness. [N]or can it be said that the legislature intended the Act to function as a deterrent. Those persons committed under the Act are, by definition, suffering from a "mental abnormality" or a "personality disorder" that prevents them from exercising adequate control over their behavior. Such persons are therefore unlikely to be deterred by the threat of confinement.

[W]here the State has "disavowed any punitive intent"; limited confinement to a small segment of particularly dangerous individuals; provided strict procedural safeguards; directed that confined persons be segregated from the general prison population and afforded the same status as others who have been civilly committed; recommended treatment if such is possible; and permitted immediate release upon a showing that the individual is no longer dangerous or mentally impaired, we cannot say that it acted with punitive intent. We therefore hold that the Act does not establish criminal proceedings and that involuntary confinement pursuant to the Act is not punitive. Our conclusion that the Act is nonpunitive thus removes an essential prerequisite for both Hendricks' double jeopardy and ex post facto claims.

[W]e hold that the Kansas Sexually Violent Predator Act comports with due process requirements and neither runs afoul of double jeopardy principles nor constitutes an exercise in impermissible ex post facto lawmaking. Accordingly, the judgment of the Kansas Supreme Court is reversed.

———

NOTES

1. Personality Disorder. The American Psychiatric Association's Diagnostic and Statistical Manual of Mental Disorders (4th Edition–Text Revision, 2000) (DSM–IV–TR) of defines personality disorder as "an enduring pattern of inner experience and behavior that deviates markedly from the expectations of the individual's culture, is pervasive and inflexible, has an onset in adolescence or early adulthood, is stable over time, and leads to distress or impairment." The Manual lists ten types of personality disorder: *Paranoid Personality Disorder* ("a pattern of distrust and suspiciousness such that others' motives are interpreted as malevolent"); *Schizoid Personality Disorder* ("a pattern of detachment from social relationships and a restricted range of emotional expression"); *Schizotypal Personality Disorder* ("a pattern of acute discomfort in close relationships, cognitive or perceptual distortions, and eccentricities of behavior"); *Antisocial Personality Disorder* ("a pattern of disregard for, and violation of, the rights of others"); *Borderline Personality Disorder* ("a pattern of instability in interpersonal relationships, self-image, and affects, and marked impulsivity"); *Histrionic Personality Disorder* ("a pattern of excessive emotionality and attention seeking"); *Narcissistic Personality Disorder* ("a pattern of grandiosity, need for admiration, and lack of empathy"); *Avoidant Personality Disorder* ("a pattern of social inhibition, feelings of inadequacy, and hypersensitivity to negative evaluation"); *Dependent Personality Disorder* ("a pattern of submissive and clinging behavior related to an excessive need to be taken care of"); and *Obsessive–Compulsive Personality Disorder* ("a pattern of preoccupation with orderliness, perfectionism, and control"). Id. at 685.

2. Sexually Violent Predator Statutes. Since Kansas v. Hendricks, 19 states in addition to Kansas have adopted Sexually Violent Predator statutes. The most recent estimate is that 4,534 persons—virtually all male—are currently civilly committed under these statutes. K. Gookin, Comparison of State Laws Authorizing Involuntary Commitment of Sexually Violent Predators (2007).

———

SEXUALLY VIOLENT PREDATORS ACT

Virginia Code Ann. § 37.1–70 et seq. (2006).

"Sexually violent predator" means any person who (i) has been convicted of a sexually violent offense or has been charged with a sexually violent offense and is unrestorably incompetent to stand trial [a]nd (ii) because of a mental abnormality or personality disorder, finds it difficult to control his predatory behavior which makes him likely to engage in sexually violent acts.

[T]he CRC [Commitment Review Committee] shall consist of seven members to be appointed as follows: (i) three full-time employees of the Department of Corrections, appointed by the Director; (ii) three full-time employees of the Department [of Mental Health, Mental Retardation and Substance Abuse Services], appointed by the Commissioner, at least one of whom shall be a psychiatrist or psychologist licensed to practice in the Commonwealth of Virginia who is skilled in the diagnosis of mental abnormalities and personality disorders associated with violent sex offenders; and (iii) one assistant or deputy attorney general, appointed by the Attorney General.

[E]ach month, the Director [of the Department of Corrections] shall review the database [of prisoners incarcerated for sexually violent offenses] and identify all [p]risoners who are scheduled for release from prison within 10 months from the date of such review who receive a score of five or more on the Static–99 or a similar score on a comparable, scientifically validated instrument as designated by the Commissioner [of the Department of Mental Health, Mental Retardation and Substance Abuse Services], or a score of four on the Static–99 or a like score instrument on a comparable, scientifically validated instrument if the sexually violent offense [was one in which] the victim was under the age of 13 and suffered physical bodily injury. [U]pon the identification of such prisoners, the Director shall forward their names [t]o the CRC for assessment.

[C]RC assessments [s]hall include a mental health examination, including a personal interview, of the prisoner or defendant by a licensed psychiatrist or a licensed clinical psychologist who is designated by the Commissioner who [is] not a member of the CRC [and who] shall determine whether the prisoner is a sexually violent predator.

[F]ollowing the examination and review of a prisoner, [t]he CRC shall recommend that such prisoner (i) be committed as a sexually violent predator pursuant to this chapter; (ii) not be committed, but be placed in a conditional release program as a less restrictive alternative; or (iii) not be committed because he does not meet the definition of a sexually violent predator.

[T]he Attorney General or the respondent shall have the right to a trial by jury. [I]f a jury determines that the respondent is a sexually violent predator, a unanimous verdict shall be required. [T]he court or jury shall determine whether, by clear and convincing evidence, the respondent is a sexually violent predator. [A]ll proceedings conducted hereunder are civil proceedings.

[A]ny person committed pursuant to this chapter shall be placed in the custody of the Department [of Mental Health, Mental Retardation and Substance Abuse Services] for control, care, and treatment until such time as the person's mental abnormality or personality disorder has so changed that the person will not present an undue risk to public safety.

[T]he committing court shall conduct a hearing 12 months after the date of commitment to assess each respondent's need for secure inpatient treatment. A hearing for assessment shall be conducted at yearly intervals for five years and at biennial intervals thereafter. [T]he burden of proof at the hearing shall be on the Commonwealth to prove to the Court by clear and convincing evidence that the respondent remains a sexually violent predator.

NOTES

1. **The Static–99.** The Static–99 is an actuarial risk assessment instrument consisting of ten empirically-derived risk factors. A. Harris, A. Phenix, R. Hanson, and D. Thornton, Static–99 Coding Rules Revised (2003). The risk factors and their scoring are as follows:

Risk factor	Score
1. Young	
Aged 25 or older	0
Aged 18–24.99	1
2. Ever lived with a lover for at least 2 years?	
Yes	0
No	1
3. Index non-sexual violence (any convictions)	
No	0
Yes	1

Risk factor	Score
4. Prior non-sexual violence (any convictions)	
No	0
Yes	1
5. Prior Sex Offenses	
None	0
1 conviction or 1–2 charges	1
2–3 convictions or 3–5 charges	2
4+ convictions or 6+ charges	3
6. Prior Sentencing Dates (excluding index offense)	
3 or less	0
4 or more	1
7. Any convictions for non-contact sex offense	
No	0
Yes	1
8. Any unrelated victims	
No	0
Yes	1
9. Any stranger victims	
No	0
Yes	1
10. Any male victims	
No	0
Yes	1

The total score on the Static–99 consists of the sum of the scores on the 10 individual items. The authors note:

> This instrument is not recommended for females, young offenders (those having an age of less than 18 years at time of release) or for offenders who have only been convicted of prostitution related offences, pimping, public toileting (sex in public locations with consenting adults) or possession of pornography/indecent materials. The STATIC–99 is not recommended for use with those who have never committed a sexual offence, nor is it recommended for making recommendations regarding the determination of guilt or innocence in those accused of a sexual offence. Id. at 5.

2. Recidivism Estimates. The most recent five and ten-year recidivism estimates for the Static–99 are based on 64 studies. Helmus, Hanson, and Thornton, Reporting Static–99 in Light of New Research on Recidivism Norms, 21 Newsletter of the Association for the Treatment of Sexual Abusers 38 (Winter, 2009). In the estimates reported below, violent recidivism includes sexually violent recidivism. The first number in each column refers to the lower-bound of the empirical recidivism estimate, and the second number to the upper-bound of the empirical recidivism estimate.

For example, based on existing research, an offender who scored 5 on the Static–99 would have a likelihood of sexually violent recidivism of 10 to 23% over the next five years and 12 to 32% over the next ten years; he would also have a likelihood of generally violent recidivism of 25 to 39% over the next five years, and 32 to 48% over the next ten years,

	Sexual Recidivism (%)		Violent Recidivism (%)	
Static–99 Score	5 years	10 years	5 years	10 years
0	2–8	2–13	9–17	9–26
1	3–10	3–16	11–20	11–30
2	4–13	4–19	14–24	15–34
3	6–16	6–23	17–29	20–38
4	8–19	8–27	21–34	25–43
5	10–23	12–32	25–39	32–48
6	14–28	17–37	31–45	39–53
7	17–33	23–43	37–51	47–58
8	22–38	31–49	43–57	55–63
9	28–44	40–54	50–62	63–67
10+	35–50	50–60	57–68	70–72

The authors' recommendation is for the evaluator to report recidivism estimates in two stages.

> The first stage involves reporting an empirically-derived range of recidivism risk. [T]he second stage involves making a professional judgment as to where a particular offender is likely to fall within that range. This judgment represents a separate task from reporting the empirical recidivism rates; currently, there is no research to assess how well evaluators are able to make this judgment. Until further research is conducted, however, this professional judgment is unavoidable. Id. at 41.

See http://www.static99.org for periodic updates of these recidivism estimates.

———

D. CAPITAL PUNISHMENT

The death penalty statutes of several states specify that execution of first-degree murderers is contingent upon the jury making the factual finding that the defendant is likely to repeat his or her violent acts. Some social scientists have served as expert witnesses for the prosecution and some for the defense in capital sentencing hearings to provide estimates of the risk that defendants pose. Other social scientists have participated in writing briefs and as expert witnesses at hearings, challenging the empirical basis of the estimates of risk that their colleagues offer.

———

BAREFOOT v. ESTELLE

Supreme Court of the United States, 1983.
463 U.S. 880, 103 S.Ct. 3383, 77 L.Ed.2d 1090.

■ Justice White delivered the opinion of the Court.

[Thomas Barefoot was convicted of the capital murder of a police officer. At a separate sentencing hearing, the same jury considered the two questions put to it under the Texas death penalty statute: whether the conduct causing the death was "committed deliberately and with reasonable expectation that the death of the deceased or another would result," and whether "there is a probability that the defendant would commit criminal acts of violence that would constitute a continuing threat to society." The jury's affirmative answer to both questions required the imposition of the death penalty.]

Petitioner's merits submission is that his death sentence must be set aside because the Constitution of the United States barred the testimony of the two psychiatrists who testified against him at the punishment hearing. [I]t is urged that psychiatrists, individually and as a group, are incompetent to predict with an acceptable degree of reliability that a particular criminal will commit other crimes in the future and so represent a danger to the community.

[T]he suggestion that no psychiatrist's testimony may be presented with respect to a defendant's future dangerousness is somewhat like asking us to disinvent the wheel. In the first place, it is contrary to our cases. If the likelihood of a defendant committing further crimes is a constitutionally acceptable criterion for imposing the death penalty, which it is, Jurek v. Texas, 428 U.S. 262, 96 S.Ct. 2950, 49 L.Ed.2d 929 (1976), and if it is not impossible for even a lay person sensibly to arrive at that conclusion, it makes little sense, if any, to submit that psychiatrists, out of the entire universe of persons who might have an opinion on the issue, would know so little about the subject that they should not be permitted to testify. In *Jurek*, seven Justices rejected the claim that it was impossible to predict future behavior and that dangerousness was therefore an invalid consideration in imposing the death penalty.

[A]cceptance of petitioner's position that expert testimony about future dangerousness is far too unreliable to be admissible would immediately call into question those other contexts in which predictions of future behavior are constantly made [such as the civil commitment of the mentally ill.]

[I]n the second place, the rules of evidence generally extant at the federal and state levels anticipate that relevant, unprivileged evidence should be admitted and its weight left to the factfinder, who would have the benefit of cross examination and contrary evidence by the opposing party. Psychiatric testimony predicting dangerousness may be countered not only as erroneous in a particular case but as generally so unreliable that it should be ignored. If the jury may make up its mind about future dangerousness unaided by psychiatric testimony, jurors should not be barred from hearing the views of the State's psychiatrists along with opposing views of the defendant's doctors.

Third, petitioner's view mirrors the position expressed in the *amicus* brief of the American Psychiatric Association (APA). [H]owever, the same view was presented and rejected in Estelle v. Smith, [451 U.S. 454, 101 S.Ct. 1866, 68 L.Ed.2d 359 (1981).] We are no more convinced now that the view of the APA should be converted into a constitutional rule barring an entire category of expert testimony. We are not persuaded that such testimony is almost entirely unreliable and that the factfinder and the adversary system will not be competent to uncover, recognize, and take due account of its shortcomings.

The *amicus* does not suggest that there are not other views held by members of the Association or of the profession generally. Indeed, as this case and others indicate, there are those doctors who are quite willing to testify at the sentencing hearing, who think, and will say, that they know what they are talking about, and who expressly disagree with the Association's point of view.[7] Furthermore, their qualifications as experts are regularly accepted by the courts. If they are so obviously wrong and should be discredited, there should be no insuperable problem in doing so by calling members of the Association who are of that view and who confidently assert that opinion in their *amicus* brief. Neither petitioner nor the Association suggests that psychiatrists are always wrong with respect to future dangerousness, only most of the time. Yet the submission is that this category of testimony should be excised entirely from all trials. We are unconvinced, however, at least as of now, that the adversary process cannot be trusted to sort out the reliable from the unreliable evidence and opinion about future dangerousness, particularly when the convicted felon has the opportunity to present his own side of the case.

[T]he judgment of the District Court is affirmed.

■ JUSTICE BLACKMUN, with whom JUSTICE BRENNAN and JUSTICE MARSHALL join, [d]issenting.

[T]he Court holds that psychiatric testimony about a defendant's future dangerousness is admissible, despite the fact that such testimony is wrong two times out of three. The Court reaches this result—even in a capital case—because, it is said, the testimony is subject to cross-examination and impeachment. In the present state of psychiatric knowledge, this is too much for me.

[At the sentencing hearing, Dr. Grigson, a prosecution psychiatrist, testified on the basis of a hypothetical question, without having examined

7. [W]e are aware that many mental health professionals have questioned the usefulness of psychiatric predictions of future dangerousness in light of studies indicating that such predictions are often inaccurate.

[A]ll of these professional doubts about the usefulness of psychiatric predictions can be called to the attention of the jury. Petitioner's entire argument, as well as that of Justice Blackmun's dissent, is founded on the premise that a jury will not be able to separate the wheat from the chaff. We do not share in this low evaluation of the adversary process.

Barefoot, that] he could diagnose Barefoot "within reasonable psychiatric certainty" as an individual with "a fairly classical, typical, sociopathic personality disorder." He placed Barefoot in the "most severe category" of sociopaths (on a scale of one to ten, Barefoot was "above ten"), and stated that there was no known cure for the condition. Finally, Doctor Grigson testified that whether Barefoot was in society at large or in a prison society there was a *"one hundred percent and absolute"* chance that Barefoot would commit future acts of criminal violence that would constitute a continuing threat to society.

[T]he American Psychiatric Association (APA), participating in this case as *amicus curiae,* informs us that "[t]he unreliability of psychiatric predictions of long-term future dangerousness is by now an established fact within the profession." The APA's best estimate is that *two out of three* predictions of long-term future violence made by psychiatrists are wrong. The Court does not dispute this proposition, and indeed it could not do so; the evidence is overwhelming. For example, [J]ohn Monahan, recognized as "the leading thinker on this issue" even by the State's expert witness at Barefoot's federal habeas corpus hearing, concludes that "the 'best' clinical research currently in existence indicates that psychiatrists and psychologists are accurate in no more than one out of three predictions of violent behavior," even among populations of individuals who are mentally ill and have committed violence in the past. J. Monahan, The Clinical Prediction of Violent Behavior 47–49 (1981). [N]either the Court nor the State of Texas has cited a single reputable scientific source contradicting the unanimous conclusion of professionals in this field that psychiatric predictions of long-term future violence are wrong more often than they are right.[2]

[T]hus, the Court's remarkable observation that "[n]either petitioner nor the [APA] suggests that psychiatrists are *always wrong* with respect to future dangerousness, *only most of the time,*" misses the point completely, and its claim that this testimony was no more problematic than "other

2. Among the many other studies reaching this conclusion are APA Task Force Report. Clinical Aspects of the Violent Individual 28 (1974) (90% error rate "[u]nfortunately . . . is the state of the art") (APA, Clinical Aspects); Steadman & Morrissey, The Statistical Prediction of Violent Behavior, 5 Law & Human Behavior 263, 271–273 (1981); Dix, Expert Prediction Testimony in Capital Sentencing; Evidentiary and Constitutional Considerations, 19 Am.Crim.L.Rev. 1, 16 (1981); Schwitzgebel, Prediction of Dangerousness and Its Implications for Treatment, in W. Curran, A. McGarry & C. Petty, Modern Legal Medicine, Psychiatry, and Forensic Science 783, 784–786 (1980); Cocozza & Steadman, Prediction in Psychiatry: An Example of Misplaced Confidence in Experts, 25 Soc.Probs. 265, 272–273 (1978); Report of the [American Psychological Association's] Task Force on the Role of Psychology in the Criminal Justice System, 33 Am.Psychologist 1099, 1110 (1978); Steadman & Cocozza, Psychiatry, Dangerousness and the Repetitively Violent Offender, 69 J. Crim.L. & Criminology 226, 227, 230 (1978); Cocozza & Steadman, The Failure of Psychiatric Predictions of Dangerousness: Clear and Convincing Evidence, 29 Rutgers L.Rev. 1084, 1101 (1976); Diamond, The Psychiatric Prediction of Dangerousness, 123 U.Pa.L.Rev. 439, 451–452 (1974); Ennis & Litwak, Psychiatry and the Presumption of Expertise: Flipping Coins in the Courtroom, 62 Calif.L.Rev. 693, 711–716 (1974). A relatively early study making this point is Rome, Identification of the Dangerous Offender, 42 F.R.D. 185 (1968).

relevant evidence against any defendant in a criminal case," is simply incredible. Surely, this Court's commitment to ensuring that death sentences are imposed reliably and reasonably requires that nonprobative and highly prejudicial testimony on the ultimate question of life or death be excluded from a capital sentencing hearing.

Despite its recognition that the testimony at issue was probably wrong and certainly prejudicial, the Court holds this testimony admissible because the Court is "unconvinced . . . that the adversary process cannot be trusted to sort out the reliable from the unreliable evidence and opinion about future dangerousness." One can only wonder how juries are to separate valid from invalid expert opinions when the "experts" themselves are so obviously unable to do so. Indeed, the evidence suggests that juries are not effective at assessing the validity of scientific evidence. Giannelli, Scientific Evidence, 80 Colum.L.Rev., at 1239–1240, and n. 319.

[U]ltimately, when the Court knows full well that psychiatrists' predictions of dangerousness are specious, there can be no excuse for imposing on the defendant, on pain of his life, the heavy burden of convincing a jury of laymen of the fraud.

———

NOTE

1. Further Developments. The dissent in *Barefoot* quoted one researcher as concluding that "psychiatrists and psychologists are accurate in no more than one out of three predictions of violent behavior." While that was a valid summary of the empirical evidence in the mid–1980's, subsequent research has reported accuracy rates for violence risk assessment higher than previously obtained. J. Monahan, H. Steadman, E. Silver, P. Appelbaum, P. Robbins, E. Mulvey, L. Roth, T. Grisso, and S. Banks, Rethinking Risk Assessment: The MacArthur Study of Mental Disorder and Violence (2001), assessed over 1,000 people in psychiatric facilities on over 100 risk factors for future violence to others. Patients were followed in the community for several months after discharge from the hospital. The researchers were able to combine the risk factors statistically—rather than clinically—in such a way as to place all subjects into one of five groups, with rates of serious violence in the next several months of 1, 8, 26, 56, and 76 percent, respectively. That is, in the highest group, three-out-of-four people predicted to be violent were later found to commit a violent act in the community, rather than the one-out-of-three accuracy rate for clinical prediction quoted in *Barefoot*. Among the risk factors that predicted violence in different groups of patients were prior arrests, substance abuse, having been abused as a child, one's father having abused drugs, having fantasies about being violent, male gender, and young age. Violence risk assessment software based on these data has been developed. J. Monahan, H. Steadman, P. Appelbaum, T. Grisso, E. Mulvey, L. Roth, P. Robbins, S. Banks, and E. Silver, The Classification of Violence Risk (2005).

———

STATE v. DAVIS

Supreme Court of New Jersey, 1984.
96 N.J. 611, 477 A.2d 308.

■ Per Curiam.

On April 12, 1983, defendant, Steven Raymond Davis, was indicted for murder. Defendant subsequently pled guilty, and, pursuant to the provisions of N.J.S.A. 2C:11–3c, a penalty trial was scheduled.

[O]n February 8, 1984, defense counsel advised the State that he intended to proffer, in mitigation of a death penalty verdict pursuant to N.J.S.A. 2C:11–3c(5)(h), the expert testimony of Professor Marvin E. Wolfgang, Ph.D. Dr. Wolfgang would testify as to the contents of a report prepared by him on February 7, 1984, that asserted that defendant was a likely candidate "for a thirty year sentence instead of a death sentence" because empirical studies demonstrate that a defendant sharing Mr. Davis' statistical profile "would never again commit another serious crime of any kind" after serving the mandatory minimum thirty year term. The statute provides that if the jury does not determine to impose the death penalty, the defendant shall be sentenced to a term of life imprisonment in which he shall not be eligible for release on parole until he has served a minimum term of thirty years.

Dr. Wolfgang holds a doctorate in sociology and is a member of the faculty of the department of sociology at the University of Pennsylvania. A review of his *curriculum vitae* and published works reveals that for more than twenty-five years a principal focus of Dr. Wolfgang's research has been the study of criminal violence, with specific emphasis upon the psychological and sociological determinants of violent crime. Dr. Wolfgang is described by defendant and *amicus* as an "eminent criminologist" who is an "expert in statistics." He holds no degrees in psychology or psychiatry, and has had no formal training in those fields.

Dr. Wolfgang's report on behalf of Mr. Davis was not based on any personal evaluation of defendant. (In fact, Dr. Wolfgang has never met Mr. Davis.) Rather, the professor relied upon demographic "features" that defendant possessed, and then selectively drew upon statistical research that demonstrates a low rate of recidivism among offenders sharing these demographic features.

His four-page report notes Mr. Davis' present age and that "he will be 57 years old were he sentenced to 30 years without parole as a minimum sentence." Dr. Wolfgang then cites his own research findings and "national statistics" to demonstrate that males aged 55–59 are highly unlikely to commit homicide. Moreover, "after age 29, as age increases crime rates decrease." Next, Dr. Wolfgang notes that according to statistics presented in a 1980 report of the U.S. Department of Justice and in a 1969 study by the New York Division of Parole, murderers are the least likely to commit subsequent offenses of any sort upon release from prison. Thus, according to Dr. Wolfgang, "the best available research shows that persons convicted of first degree murder * * * have the lowest rates of future offending among all types of offenders." The report proceeds to assert that

> [t]aking these factors into account, and recognizing that Mr. Davis has no previous crime record, that he would have served a minimum of 30 years in prison, and were he given this sentence, that he would minimally be 57 years old at the time of release, our conclusion is that Mr. Davis would never again commit another serious crime of any kind.

The State moved to exclude Dr. Wolfgang's testimony on the ground that it is irrelevant to any mitigating factor properly before the jury. The trial court ruled that the proffered testimony would be excluded during the penalty phase since the statement in no way pertained to Mr. Davis' individual character. The court concluded that while "the question of potential for rehabilitation" may be testified to as part of the indicia of a defendant's character, "the statistical approach doesn't tell us anything at all about a given defendant."

[N]J.S.A. 2C:11–3c(5) provides, in pertinent part:

> The mitigating factors which may be found by the jury or the court are:

* * *

> (h) Any other factor which is relevant to the defendant's character or record or to the circumstances of the offense.

The parties to this action do not dispute that a defendant's potential for rehabilitation is an aspect of his character, and therefore may be considered as a factor militating in favor of a sentence less than death in the penalty phase of a capital proceeding. It is the means by which this defendant seeks to make the showing—through the introduction of statistical evidence of the rehabilitative potential of similarly situated defendants—that has prompted this appeal.

We determine that evidence consisting of statistical data based upon empirical studies can assist the jury in the penalty phase of a capital proceeding in evaluating an individual defendant's potential for rehabilitation as an aspect of his character presented as a mitigating factor under N.J.S.A. 2C:11–3c(5)(h). Accordingly, we hold that, subject to appropriate standards concerning its competency (such as its scientific reliability and the qualifications of the expert witness), evidence of this nature is relevant and admissible.

Evidence of empirical studies and findings, including the statistical presentation and analysis of data, may under appropriate circumstances be sufficiently related to a defendant's rehabilitative potential to satisfy the statutory threshold of relevancy. Such evidence may, in effect, encapsulate ordinary human experience and provide an appropriate frame of reference for a jury's consideration of a defendant's character. For example, insofar as the proffered report in this case focuses primarily on defendant's present age and his age at the time of his earliest possible release, it can be noted that age, as a demographic variable, has consistently been found to be strongly related to subsequent criminal activity. See, e.g., Cocozza & Steadman, "Some Refinements in the Prediction of Dangerous Behavior," 131 Am.J. of Psychiatry 1012 (1974) (examination of possible importance of variables other than those having to do with prior criminal activity, including variety of social and demographic factors, reveals that only one, age, is highly related to predictions of future violence).

Moreover, this kind of information, when presented by experts, can supplement or explain ordinary human experience and can assist laypersons in the deliberative process to reach sound determinations concerning an individual's character. Indeed, it has been observed that a layperson with access to relevant statistics can assess a defendant's rehabilitative potential at least as well as, and possibly better than, those with psychiatric training in this area. Barefoot v. Estelle, 463 U.S. 880, 103 S.Ct. 3383, 77 L.Ed.2d 1090, 1122 (1983) (Blackmun, J., dissenting) (citing American Psychiatric Association Task Force Report, Clinical Aspects of the Violent Individual 28 (1974)); see also J. Monahan, The Clinical Prediction of Violent Behavior, 47–49 (1981) ("the 'best' clinical research currently in existence indicates that psychiatrists and psychologists are accurate in no more than one out of three predictions of violent behavior"); Steadman & Morrissey, "The Statistical Prediction of Violent Behavior," 5 Law & Human Behavior 263, 271–73 (1981); Cocozza & Steadman, "The Failure of Psychiatric Predictions of Dangerousness: Clear and Convincing Evidence," 29 Rutgers L.Rev. 1084, 1101 (1976).

[A]ccordingly, it is our ruling that the proposed testimony of the defendant's expert, reflected in the report proffered in this case, generally satisfies broad standards of relevancy and is therefore admissible as a mitigating factor in the penalty phase of a capital proceeding, pursuant to N.J.S.A. 2C:11–3c(5)(h).

We do not, and, indeed, on this record cannot, determine that the report, in the form presented, is admissible in respects other than relevancy. We consider the report merely as a proffer, sufficient to pose the legal question as to whether the type of evidence it represents satisfies standards of relevancy under N.J.S.A. 2C:11–3c(5)(h). We nonetheless deem it appropriate to comment generally on other aspects of admissibility that will undoubtedly arise in the penalty phase of the trial upon defendant's attempt to introduce this evidence.

The evidence as proffered relates to a subject matter that is appropriately within the competence of experts or specialists. Consequently, the testifying expert witness, Dr. Wolfgang, must be qualified. Further, the subject matter of his testimony must be established as scientifically reliable. We stress, however, that the conventional standards of competency, relating to both the expert's qualifications and the scientific reliability of the subject matter, are not to be strictly applied in this context—the penalty phase of a capital proceeding—in which the choice before the jury is between life and death.

[T]o the extent that evidence of the type sought to be proffered in the case at bar arguably may suffer shortcomings when measured by strict rules of evidential relevance and competence, such deficits will go to the weight of the testimony, properly relegating to the adversarial process the task of "separating the wheat from the chaff." Barefoot v. Estelle, supra, 463 U.S. at ___, 103 S.Ct. at 3398, 77 L.Ed.2d at 1109 (psychiatric testimony concerning defendant's future dangerousness offered pursuant to specific provision in Texas death penalty statute held admissible despite fact that such testimony is not based on personal examination of defendant).

However, relaxed standards for admissibility are not to be equated with automatic admissibility. Judicial tolerance is not judicial license. For example, in this case the court may, upon a persuasive showing, consider the report, or any of its component parts, incomplete and therefore unhelpful. Arguably, the report could, upon countervailing proofs presented by the prosecutor through cross-examination or rebuttal evidence, be considered untrustworthy because of its failure to consider the educational background, employment history, familial status, criminal record, or some other important demographic factor relating to the potential for rehabilitation. It might also be considered flawed because of its use of, or its undifferentiated emphasis upon, statistical data based upon race, gender, or some other suspect characteristic.[2] The court must retain discretion to exclude the evidence, in whole or in part, if its probative value is substantially outweighed by its unfounded or speculative character and the risk of confusion of the essential issues.

————

NOTE

1. Group Statistics and Individual Cases. Dawes, Faust, and Meehl, Clinical Versus Actuarial Judgment, 243 Science 1668 (1989), reviewed the social science literature on the relative accuracy of clinical and statistical prediction. They located nearly 100 comparative studies. "In virtually every one of these studies, the actuarial method has equalled or surpassed the clinical method, sometimes slightly and sometimes substantially." Id. at 1669.

A common anti-actuarial argument, or misconception, is that group statistics do not apply to single individuals or events. The argument abuses basic principles of probability. Although individuals

---

2. In this regard we note that Dr. Wolfgang's proffered report refers to race—i.e., that defendant is a "white male"—as a demographic factor. The use of such a variable may have unacceptably invidious implications, bearing upon the ultimate admissibility of the expert's testimony. We mention this circumstance, but do not further consider the issue because it has not been raised or addressed in the present appeal and, further, it has not been shown to what extent Dr. Wolfgang's proposed testimony will coincide with his report in all of its present detail. We assume that the parties and trial court will be alert to this issue in the sentencing proceeding.

and events may exhibit unique features, they typically share common features with other persons or events that permit tallied observations or generalizations to achieve predictive power. An advocate of this anti-actuarial position would have to maintain, for the sake of logical consistency, that if one is forced to play Russian roulette a single time and is allowed to select a gun with one or five bullets in the chamber, the uniqueness of the event makes the choice arbitrary. Id. at 1672.

A more recent review disaggregated studies in terms of the type of behavior being predicted and concluded that "one area in which the statistical method is most clearly superior to the clinical approach is the prediction of violence." Aegisdottir et al., The Meta–Analysis of Clinical Judgment Project: Fifty-six Years of Accumulated Research on Clinical Versus Statistical Prediction, 34 Counseling Psychologist 341, 368 (2006).

SALDANO v. TEXAS

Supreme Court of the United States, 2000.
530 U.S. 1212, 120 S.Ct. 2214, 147 L.Ed.2d 246.

Brief in Opposition to Petition for Writ of Certiorari

Saldano's Crime

In 1996, the Petitioner, Victor Hugo Saldano, was convicted of capital murder in Collin County, Texas, for the murder of Paul King. [N]either Saldano nor his accomplice knew Mr. King, and the crime appears to have been random. [P]rior to his trial, Saldano told the jailer that he had shot Mr. King four times, and then once in the head just to make sure he was dead. Saldano said he felt nothing when he shot Mr. King.

The Admittance of Race as a Factor in Determining Future Dangerousness

In the penalty phase of Saldano's trial, the jury [w]as charged with finding beyond a reasonable doubt the probability that Saldano would commit criminal acts of violence that would constitute a continuing threat to society. The jury was instructed that the burden of proving this "future dangerousness" lay solely on the prosecution.

The jury was presented with more than enough evidence to warrant its finding of "future dangerousness." [T]his evidence includes the facts that: (1) the circumstances of Saldano's capital offense demonstrate that it was particularly random, callous, cruel, and bold; (2) Saldano expressed no remorse for the slaying of his victim and has even stated that he felt nothing at the time of the killing; (3) Saldano was engaged in an escalating series of criminal activities prior to the killing of his victim; and (4) Saldano's relatively young age.

During the sentencing phase of Saldano's trial, the prosecution presented testimony on the issue of Saldano's future dangerousness, including evidence that there were twenty-four factors to be weighed in determining future dangerousness, one of which was Saldano's race. The witness testified that African–Americans and Hispanics are over-represented in prison compared to their percentage of the general population. He explained that "race itself may not explain the over-representation, so there are other subrealities that may have to be considered." Further, the witness testified that because Saldano was from Argentina, he would be considered Hispanic. As the Texas Court of Criminal Appeals recognized, the prosecution's witness "testified that because [Saldano] is Hispanic, this was a factor weighing in the favor of future dangerousness." At the conclusion of the witness's direct testimony, the State admitted into evidence a series of exhibits consisting of flip-charts that listed each of the factors the jury was to weigh in determining future dangerousness. The charts had marks next to each factor that was said to apply to Saldano, including race.

Counsel for Saldano did not object to the introduction of testimony regarding race. Instead, defense counsel cross-examined regarding the reliability of the data and whether Saldano, as a Argentinian, fit within the category of Hispanic.

[W]hile not mentioning race specifically, in closing argument the prosecution told the jury to rely on the twenty-four factors provided by its witness. The jury was told to take the formula of twenty-four factors and "plug it in." The jury found that Saldano was a future danger to society and that there were not sufficient mitigating factors to warrant life imprisonment. Accordingly, the trial court sentenced Saldano to the death penalty.

ARGUMENT

[T]he sole issue raised by Saldano is whether the Texas Court of Criminal Appeals erred in upholding his death sentence, despite the improper introduction of testimony inviting the use of race as a factor in determining future dangerousness, due to his counsel's failure to object. Because the use of race in Saldano's sentencing seriously undermined the fairness, integrity, or public reputation of the judicial process, Texas confesses error and agrees that Saldano is entitled to a new sentencing hearing.

[D]espite the fact that sufficient proper evidence was submitted to the jury to justify the finding of Saldano's future dangerousness, the infusion of race as a factor for the jury to weigh in making its determination violated his constitutional right to be sentenced without regard to the color of his skin.

Conclusion

For the reasons stated, Texas respectfully requests that the Court grant the petition, vacate the trial court's imposition of sentence on Saldano, and remand the case to the trial court with instructions that Saldano receive a new sentencing hearing in which race is not considered.

———

SALDANO v. TEXAS

Supreme Court of the United States, 2000.
530 U.S. 1212, 120 S.Ct. 2214, 147 L.Ed.2d 246.

The motion of petitioner for leave to proceed in forma pauperis and the petition for a writ of certiorari are granted. The judgment is vacated and the case is remanded to the Court of Criminal Appeals of Texas for further consideration in light of the confession of error by the Solicitor General of Texas.

———

TEXAS CODE OF CRIMINAL PROCEDURE, 2001

Article 37.07(3)(a)(2): Admissibility in a Criminal Trial of Race or Ethnicity As a Predictor of Future Criminal Behavior

Evidence may not be offered by the state to establish that the race or ethnicity of the defendant makes it likely that the defendant will engage in future criminal conduct.

———

E.   Tort Liability

The determination of bail and prison sentences, the initiation of civil commitment, and the imposition of capital punishment are often premised on assessments of risk that are provided by social scientists. Among the goals of these interventions is the prevention of the forecasted behavior. Social scientists have also been involved in cases assigning tort liability when "foreseeable" harmful conduct has not been prevented. By the way it assigns tort liability, many believe that the law induces greater care in assessing risk on the part of those charged with the duty to do so.

———

TARASOFF v. REGENTS OF THE UNIVERSITY OF CALIFORNIA

Supreme Court of California, 1976.
17 Cal.3d 425, 131 Cal.Rptr. 14, 551 P.2d 334.

■ Tobriner, Justice.

On October 27, 1969, Prosenjit Poddar killed Tatiana Tarasoff. Plaintiffs, Tatiana's parents, allege that two months earlier Poddar confided his intention to kill Tatiana to Dr. Lawrence Moore, a psychologist employed by the Cowell Memorial Hospital at the University of California at Berkeley. They allege that on Moore's request, the campus police briefly detained Poddar, but released him when he appeared rational. They further claim that Dr. Harvey Powelson, Moore's superior, then directed that no further action be taken to detain Poddar. No one warned plaintiffs of Tatiana's peril.

[P]laintiffs' complaints predicate liability on two grounds: defendants' failure to warn plaintiffs of the impending danger and their failure to bring about Poddar's confinement pursuant to the Lanterman–Petris–Short Act (Welf. & Inst.Code, § 5000ff.) Defendants, in turn, assert that they owed no duty of reasonable care to Tatiana and that they are immune from suit under the California Tort Claims Act of 1963 (Gov.Code, § 810ff.).

We shall explain that defendant therapists cannot escape liability merely because Tatiana herself was not their patient. When a therapist determines, or pursuant to the standards of his profession should determine, that his patient presents a serious danger of violence to another, he incurs an obligation to use reasonable care to protect the intended victim against such danger. The discharge of this duty may require the therapist to take one or more of various steps, depending upon the nature of the case. Thus it may call for him to warn the intended victim or others likely to apprise the victim of the danger, to notify the police, or to take whatever other steps are reasonably necessary under the circumstances.

[T]he second cause of action can be amended to allege that Tatiana's death proximately resulted from defendants' negligent failure to warn Tatiana or others likely to apprise her of her danger. Plaintiffs contend that as amended, such allegations of negligence and proximate causation, with resulting damages, establish a cause of action. Defendants, however, contend that in the circumstances of the present case they owed no duty of care to Tatiana or her parents and that, in the absence of such duty, they were free to act in careless disregard of Tatiana's life and safety.

In analyzing this issue, we bear in mind that legal duties are not discoverable facts of nature, but merely conclusory expressions that, in cases of a particular type, liability should be imposed for damage done.

[T]he most important of these considerations in establishing duty is foreseeability. [W]hen the avoidance of foreseeable harm requires a defendant to control the conduct of another person, or to warn of such conduct, the common law has traditionally imposed liability only if the defendant bears some special relationship to the dangerous person or to the potential victim. Since the relationship between a therapist and his patient satisfies this requirement, we need not here decide whether foreseeability alone is sufficient to create a duty to exercise reasonable care to protect a potential victim of another's conduct.

[A]lthough plaintiffs' pleadings assert no special relation between Tatiana and defendant therapists, they establish as between Poddar and defendant therapists the special relation that arises between a patient and his doctor or psychotherapist. Such a relationship may support affirmative duties for the benefit of third persons. Thus, for example, a hospital must exercise reasonable care to control the behavior of a patient which may endanger other persons. A doctor must also warn a patient if the patient's condition or medication renders certain conduct, such as driving a car, dangerous to others.

[D]efendants contend, however, that imposition of a duty to exercise reasonable care to protect third persons is unworkable because therapists cannot accurately predict whether or not a patient will resort to violence. In support of this argument amicus representing the American Psychiatric Association and other professional societies cites numerous articles which indicate that therapists, in the present state of the art, are unable reliably to predict violent acts; their forecasts, amicus claims, tend consistently to overpredict violence, and indeed are more often wrong than right.[10] Since predictions of violence are often erroneous, amicus concludes, the courts should not render rulings that predicate the liability of therapists upon the validity of such predictions.

The role of the psychiatrist, who is indeed a practitioner of medicine, and that of the psychologist who performs an allied function, are like that of the physician who must conform to the standards of the profession and who must often make diagnoses and predictions based upon such evaluations. Thus the judgment of the therapist in diagnosing emotional disorders and in predicting whether a patient presents a serious danger of violence is comparable to the judgment which doctors and professionals must regularly render under accepted rules of responsibility.

We recognize the difficulty that a therapist encounters in attempting to forecast whether a patient presents a serious danger of violence. Obviously we do not require that the therapist, in making that determination, render a perfect performance; the therapist need only exercise "that reasonable degree of skill, knowledge, and care ordinarily possessed and exercised by members of [that professional specialty] under similar circumstances." Bardessono v. Michels (1970) 3 Cal.3d 780, 788, 91 Cal.Rptr. 760, 764, 478 P.2d 480, 484. Within the broad range of reasonable practice and treatment in which professional opinion and judgment may differ, the therapist is free to exercise his or her own best judgment without liability; proof, aided by hindsight, that he or she judged wrongly is insufficient to establish negligence.

In the instant case, however, the pleadings do not raise any question as to failure of defendant therapists to predict that Poddar presented a serious danger of violence. On the contrary, the present complaints allege that defendant therapists did in fact predict that Poddar would kill, but were negligent in failing to warn. Amicus contends, however, that even when a therapist does in fact predict that a patient poses a serious danger of violence to others, the therapist should be absolved of any responsibility for failing to act to protect the potential victim. In our view, however once a therapist does in fact determine, or under applicable professional standards

---

10. See, e.g., People v. Burnick (1975) 14 Cal.3d 306, 325–328, 121 Cal.Rptr. 488, 535 P.2d 352; Monahan, The Prevention of Violence, in Community Mental Health in the Criminal Justice System (Monahan ed. 1975); Diamond, The Psychiatric Prediction of Dangerousness (1975) 123 U.Pa.L.Rev. 439; Ennis & Litwack, Psychiatry and the Presumption of Expertise: Flipping Coins in the Courtroom (1974) 62 Cal.L.Rev. 693.

reasonably should have determined, that a patient poses a serious danger of violence to others, he bears a duty to exercise reasonable care to protect the foreseeable victim of that danger. While the discharge of this duty of due care will necessarily vary with the facts of each case, in each instance the adequacy of the therapist's conduct must be measured against the traditional negligence standard of the rendition of reasonable care under the circumstances.

[T]he risk that unnecessary warnings may be given is a reasonable price to pay for the lives of possible victims that may be saved. We would hesitate to hold that the therapist who is aware that his patient expects to attempt to assassinate the President of the United States would not be obligated to warn the authorities because the therapist cannot predict with accuracy that his patient will commit the crime.

Defendants further argue that free and open communication is essential to psychotherapy. [T]he giving of a warning, defendants contend, constitutes a breach of trust which entails the revelation of confidential communications. We recognize the public interest in supporting effective treatment of mental illness and in protecting the rights of patients to privacy, and the consequent public importance of safeguarding the confidential character of psychotherapeutic communication. Against this interest, however, we must weigh the public interest in safety from violent assault.

[W]e conclude that the public policy favoring protection of the confidential character of patient-psychotherapist communications must yield to the extent to which disclosure is essential to avert danger to others. The protective privilege ends where the public peril begins.

Our current crowded and computerized society compels the interdependence of its members. In this risk-infested society we can hardly tolerate the further exposure to danger that would result from a concealed knowledge of the therapist that his patient was lethal. If the exercise of reasonable care to protect the threatened victim requires the therapist to warn the endangered party or those who can reasonably be expected to notify him, we see no sufficient societal interest that would protect and justify concealment.

––––––––

NOTES

1. **The Impact of *Tarasoff* on Psychotherapists.** To evaluate the effects of the *Tarasoff* decision on the practice of psychotherapy, the Stanford Law Review surveyed 1,200 California psychologists and psychiatrists. The respondents indicated that they saw an average of more than one case per month that they believed to be "potentially dangerous."

One-quarter of those responding to the survey said that they now gave more attention in their therapy sessions to the possibility of their patients' violent behavior. One-third of the psychiatrists and psychologists surveyed had increased the frequency with which they consulted colleagues concerning cases in which violence was an issue. Over half reported an increase in their own anxiety concerning the entire topic of "dangerousness" as a result of the *Tarasoff* decision. The survey also revealed that, as a result of *Tarasoff*, almost one-fifth of the respondents had decided to avoid asking questions that could yield information bearing on the likelihood of violent behavior by their patients. Even more reported that they had changed their recordkeeping procedures in an effort to avoid legal liability they might otherwise incur as a result of *Tarasoff*. "Some therapists ceased keeping detailed records; others began keeping *more* detailed records, including information that might justify any decisions they made and thereby trying to create a favorable evidentiary record for future litigation." Note, Where the Peril Begins: A Survey of Psychotherapists to Determine the Effects of *Tarasoff*, 31 Stanford Law Review 165, 182, n. 88 (1978).

Givelber, Bowers, and Blitch, *Tarasoff*: Myth and Reality: An Empirical Study of Private Law In Action, 1984 Wisconsin Law Review 443 (1984), surveyed the effects of the *Tarasoff* decision on a representative sample of psychiatrists, psychologists, and social workers in the eight largest standard metropolitan statistical areas in the United States. Virtually all therapists in California, and the great majority outside California, had heard of *Tarasoff* or "a case like it." The researchers stated that "it is a fair guess that there is no other legal decision, with the possible exception of controversial cases such as *Brown v. Board of Education,* which could command this level of recognition among a subgroup of lay persons." Id. at 457–458.

Further, the survey found that more than half of the therapists *outside* California believed that they were "legally bound" by the California Supreme Court's decision in *Tarasoff* because they mistakenly thought that the decision "applied to their professions." As the authors noted, "[t]he proponents of the *Tarasoff* duty, having won an initial battle in California, have, in essence, won the entire war without firing another shot." Id. at 485.

More recently, Pabian, Welfel, and Beebe, Psychologists' Knowledge of Their States' Laws Pertaining to *Tarasoff*–Type Situations, 40 Professional Psychology: Research and Practice 8 (2009), surveyed psychologists in four states and concluded:

> Most psychologists (76.4%) were misinformed about their state laws, believing that they had a legal duty to warn when they did not, or assuming that warning was their only legal option when other protective actions less harmful to client privacy were allowed. Moreover, in spite of the inaccuracy of their knowledge, many respondents were confident that they understood the duty to protect in their own state. Id. at 8.

2. The Impact of Tarasoff on Patients. Buckner and Firestone, "Where the Peril Begins": 25 Years After *Tarasoff*, 21 Journal of Legal Medicine 187 (2000), reviewed the literature on the effects of the *Tarasoff* decision on persons undergoing psychotherapy. They concluded:

Based upon the case law and surveys over the past 25 years, even if confidentiality must be breached, the earlier anticipated negative effects have not materialized. There is just no evidence thus far that patients have been discouraged from coming to therapy, or discouraged from speaking freely once there, for fear that their confidentiality will be breached. Id. at 221.

THOMPSON v. COUNTY OF ALAMEDA

Supreme Court of California, 1980.
27 Cal.3d 741, 167 Cal.Rptr. 70, 614 P.2d 728.

■ RICHARDSON, JUSTICE.

We recite the gravamen of plaintiffs' causes of action as contained in their amended complaint. Plaintiffs, husband and wife, and their minor son lived in the City of Piedmont, a few doors from the residence of the mother of James F. (James), a juvenile offender. Prior to the incident in question, James had been in the custody and under the control of County and had been confined in a county institution under court order. County knew that James had "latent, extremely dangerous and violent propensities regarding young children and that sexual assaults upon young children and violence connected therewith were a likely result of releasing [him] into the community." County also knew that James had "indicated that he would, if released, take the life of a young child residing in the neighborhood." (James gave no indication of which, if any, young child he intended as his victim.) County released James on temporary leave into his mother's custody at her home, and "[a]t no time did [County] advise and/or warn [James' mother], the local police and/or parents of young children within the immediate vicinity of [James' mother's] house of the known facts. . . ." Within 24 hours of his release on temporary leave, James murdered plaintiffs' son in the garage of James' mother's home.

[D]UTY TO WARN THE LOCAL POLICE, THE NEIGHBORHOOD PARENTS, OR THE JUVENILE'S CUSTODIAN

We now examine the principal and most troublesome contentions of plaintiffs, namely, that County is liable for its failure to warn the local police and the parents of neighborhood children that James was being released or, alternatively, to warn James' mother of his expressed threat.

[B]y their very nature parole and probation decisions are inherently imprecise. According to a recent study by the California Probation Parole and Correction Association, during 1977 in California a total of 315,143 persons (225,331 adults and 89,912 juveniles) were supervised on probation. (The Future of Probation, A Report of the CPPCA Committee on the Future of Probation (Jul. 1979) p. 15.) During the same year, cases removed from probation because of violations totaled 13.4 percent in the superior courts, 14.8 percent in the lower courts, and 11.5 percent in the juvenile courts. (*Id.,* at pp. 27–28.) Additionally, a large number of parole violations occur. National parole violation rates reflect that 18–20 percent of parolees fail on one-year follow-up, 25 percent on two-year follow-up, and 26 percent on three-year follow-up. (*Id.,* at p. 35.) Although we fully recognize that not all violations involve new or violent offenses, a significant proportion do.

[B]earing in mind the ever present danger of parole violations, we nonetheless conclude that public entities and employees have no affirmative duty to warn of the release of an inmate with a violent history who has made *nonspecific threats of harm directed at nonspecific victims.* Obviously aware of the risk of failure of probation and parole programs the Legislature has nonetheless as a matter of public policy elected to continue those programs even though such risks must be borne by the public.

Similar general public policy considerations were described in a recent analysis of the *Tarasoff* issue. The author reasoned: "Assume that one person out of a thousand will kill. Assume also that an exceptionally accurate test is created which differentiates with 95% effectiveness those who will kill from those who will not. If 100,000 people were tested, out of the 100 who would kill 95 would be isolated. Unfortunately, out of the 99,900 who would not kill, 4,995 people would also be isolated as potential killers. In these circumstances, it is clear that we could not justify incarcerating all 5,090 people. If, in the criminal law, it is better that ten guilty men go free than that one innocent man suffer, how can we say in the civil commitment area that it is better that fifty-four harmless people be incarcerated lest one dangerous man be free? [Citation.]" (Comment, *Tarasoff* and the Psychotherapist's Duty to Warn (1975) 12 San Diego L.Rev. 932, 942–943, fn. 75.)

Furthermore, we foresee significant practical obstacles in the imposition of a duty in the form that plaintiffs seek, concluding that it would be unwieldy and of little practical value. As previously indicated a large number of persons are released and supervised on probation and parole each year in this state. Notification to the public at large of the release of each offender who has a history of violence and who has made a generalized threat at some time during incarceration or while under supervision would, in our view, produce a cacophony of warnings that by reason of their sheer volume would add little to the effective protection of the public.

[I]n summary, whenever a potentially dangerous offender is released and thereafter commits a crime, the possibility of the commission of that crime is statistically foreseeable. Yet the Legislature has concluded that the benefits to society from rehabilitative release programs mandate their continuance. Within this context and for policy reasons the duty to warn depends upon and arises from the existence of a prior threat to a specific identifiable victim. In those instances in which the released offender poses a predictable threat of harm to a named or readily identifiable victim or group of victims who can be effectively warned of the danger, a releasing agent may well be liable for failure to warn such persons. Despite the tragic events underlying the present complaint, plaintiffs' decedent was not a known, identifiable victim, but rather a member of large amorphous public group of potential targets. Under these circumstances we hold that County had no affirmative duty to warn plaintiffs, the police, the mother of the juvenile offender, or other local parents.

————

BRADY v. HOPPER

United States District Court, District of Colorado, 1983.
570 F.Supp. 1333.

■ JOHN P. MOORE, DISTRICT JUDGE.

This matter comes before the Court on defendant's motion to dismiss. Consequently, the well-pleaded allegations of fact must be accepted as true, and the facts must be construed in a light most favorable to the pleader.

[P]laintiffs James Scott Brady, Timothy John McCarthy, and Thomas K. Delahanty were all shot and seriously injured by John W. Hinckley, Jr. ("Hinckley") in his attempt to assassinate President Reagan on March 30, 1981, in Washington, D.C. The defendant, Dr. John J. Hopper, Jr., is the psychiatrist who had been treating Hinckley from late October, 1980, until March, 1981.

Plaintiffs' complaint alleges that Dr. Hopper was negligent in examining, diagnosing, and treating Hinckley in conformity with reasonable standards of psychiatric care.

[T]he complaint alleges that Dr. Hopper knew or should have known that Hinckley was a danger to himself or others, and that Dr. Hopper either possessed or had access to, information which would have indicated that Hinckley identified with the assassin in the movie "Taxi Driver"; that he was collecting books and articles on political assassination; and that Hinckley possessed guns and ammunition. (Complaint ¶ 28). According to the complaint, Hinckley's parents were aware of and concerned about their son's worsening condition, and contacted Dr. Hopper and recommended that their son be hospitalized. (Complaint ¶¶ 13–17). Despite the possibility Hinckley might have been amenable to that idea, Dr. Hopper recommended that Hinckley not be hospitalized, and that treatment continue on an outpatient basis. (Complaint ¶ 18).

The rest of Hinckley's strange story is well known. In March, 1981, Hinckley left Denver and traveled across the country to Washington, D.C. On March 30, 1981, he attempted to assassinate President Reagan, and, in the process, shot and injured plaintiffs. Hinckley was subsequently tried for these crimes and found not guilty by reason of insanity. He is currently confined to St. Elizabeth's Hospital where he is receiving medical and psychiatric care.

The gravamen of plaintiffs' complaint is that if Dr. Hopper had properly performed his professional duties, he would have controlled Hinckley's behavior; therefore, Hinckley would not have made the presidential assassination attempt.

[S]ummary of the Arguments

The primary issue raised by defendant's motion is whether the relationship between therapist and patient gives rise to a legal duty such that Dr. Hopper can be held liable for the injuries caused to plaintiffs by Hinckley. The Restatement (Second) of Torts ¶ 315 states as follows:

> There is no duty so to control the conduct of a third person as to prevent him from causing physical harm to another unless
>
> (a) a special relation exists between the actor and the third person which imposes a duty upon the actor to control the third person's conduct, or
>
> (b) a special relation exists between the actor and the other which gives to the other a right to protection.

The thrust of defendant's argument is that the relationship between Dr. Hopper and Hinckley, that of a therapist and outpatient, is not a "special relationship" which gives rise to a duty on the part of the therapist to control the actions of the patient. In other words, defendant asserts that the therapist-outpatient relationship lacks sufficient elements of control required to bring the therapist within the language of ¶ 315.

[D]efendant next argues that the duty to control the violent acts of another does not arise absent specific threats directed to a reasonably identifiable victim. The leading case on a therapist's liability for the violent actions of a patient is Tarasoff v. Regents of University of California, 17 Cal.3d 425, 131 Cal.Rptr. 14, 551 P.2d 334 (1976). In Tarasoff, the patient communicated to the therapist specific threats and his intention to kill an unnamed—although readily identifiable—girl. The therapist informed law enforcement authorities of these threats, but failed to warn the girl or her parents. The California Supreme Court held that when a therapist determines (or pursuant to the standards of his profession should determine) that his patient presents a serious danger of violence to another, he is then obligated to take reasonable care to protect the intended victim against such danger. The court further held in such cases reasonable care may include the duty to warn the intended victim.

In Thompson v. County of Alameda, 27 Cal.3d 741, 167 Cal.Rptr. 70, 614 P.2d 728 (1980), the California Supreme Court again faced the question of the extent of liability to a third party for the dangerous acts of another. In *Thompson,* a juvenile offender known to have dangerous propensities was confined in a county institution. This patient had made generalized threats regarding his intention to kill, but had made no specific threats regarding any identifiable person. The county institution released the patient on temporary leave, and, within a day, the patient killed a young boy in his neighborhood. The court refused to extend *Tarasoff* to a setting where there was no identifiable victim. Instead, it took a more limited approach to the duty to warn, and concluded that even in the case of a person with a history of violence, no duty existed when the person had made only nonspecific threats of harm directed at nonspecific victims. Id. at 614 P.2d 735.

In essence, defendant argues that the instant case presents an even clearer basis than *Thompson* for a finding of no duty. It is argued that even according to the allegations in the complaint, Hinckley had no history of violence directed to persons other than himself; he had no history of arrests; no previous hospitalizations arising from any violent episodes; and in fact, he did not appear to be a danger to others. Thus, defendant asserts, this case involves, and plaintiffs have pled, none of the "warning signs" by which Hinckley's conduct or mental state would give rise to a duty on the part of Dr. Hopper.

[P]laintiffs have responded to each of the arguments. First plaintiffs assert that the therapist-outpatient relationship between Dr. Hopper and Hinckley was a "special relationship" within the meaning of Restatement (Second) of Torts ¶ 315. Plaintiffs argue that the duty to warn imposed in Tarasoff was premised on the assumption that such a special relationship exists between psychotherapist and patient.

[P]laintiffs further argue the duty to control is not limited to those situations where the patient makes specific threats to specific persons. According to plaintiffs, a duty on the part of the therapist arises whenever violence by the patient is foreseeable. In other words, depending on the nature of the patient's behavior, the therapist's duty is multifaceted: it may be to warn the potential victim or law enforcement authorities; it may be to take steps to have the patient confined; it may be to warn the patient's family or guardian of the potential danger; or it may be to take whatever action seems appropriate under the circumstances.

[D]iscussion

In my opinion, the main issue raised by the pleadings and briefs is not simply whether the therapist-outpatient relationship is a "special relationship" which gives rise to a legal duty on the part of the therapist; rather the key issue is to what extent was Dr. Hopper obligated to protect these particular plaintiffs from this particular harm? It is implicit in the majority of cases in this area that the therapist-patient relationship is one which under certain circumstances will give rise to a duty on the part of the therapist to protect third persons from harm. Tarasoff v. Regents of University of California, supra. However, the existence of a special relationship does not necessarily mean that the duties created by that relationship are owed to the world at large. It is fundamental that the duty owed be measured by the foreseeability of the risk and whether the danger created is sufficiently large to embrace the specific harm. Palsgraf v. Long Island R. Co., 248 N.Y. 339, 162 N.E. 99 (1928).

[A]ccepting as true the facts alleged in the complaint and viewing them in a light most favorable to plaintiffs, it is my conclusion that plaintiffs' injuries were not foreseeable; therefore, the plaintiffs fall outside of the scope of defendant's duty. Nowhere in the complaint are there allegations that Hinckley made any threats regarding President Reagan, or indeed that he ever threatened anyone. At most, the complaint states that if Dr. Hopper had interviewed Hinckley more carefully, he would have discovered that Hinckley was obsessed with Jody Foster and the movie "Taxi Driver", that he collected books on Ronald Reagan and political assassination, and that he practiced with guns. According to plaintiffs, if Dr. Hopper had properly performed his professional duties, he would have learned that Hinckley suffered from delusions and severe mental illness, as opposed to being merely maladjusted. Even assuming all of these facts and many of plaintiffs' conclusions to be true, the allegations are still insufficient to create a legal duty on the part of Dr. Hopper to protect these plaintiffs from the specific harm.

The parties have for the most part cast their arguments in terms of whether the relationship between Dr. Hopper and *Hinckley* gave rise to a particular duty on the part of Dr. Hopper. However, the legal obstacle to the maintenance of this suit is that there is no relationship between Dr. Hopper and *plaintiffs* which creates any legal obligation from Dr. Hopper to these plaintiffs. As explained by Justice Cardozo, negligence is a matter of relation between the parties, and must be founded upon the foreseeability of harm to the person in fact injured. Palsgraf v. Long Island R. Co., 162 N.E. at 101.

The question of whether a legal duty should be imposed necessarily involves social policy considerations. See Prosser, Law of Torts § 43, 257 (4th Ed.1971). In the present case, there are cogent policy reasons for limiting the scope of the therapist's liability. To impose upon those in the counseling professions an ill-defined "duty to control" would require therapists to be ultimately responsible for the actions of their patients. Such a rule would closely approximate a strict liability standard of care, and therapists would be potentially liable for all harm inflicted by persons presently or formerly under psychiatric treatment. Human behavior is simply too unpredictable, and the field of psychotherapy presently too inexact, to so greatly expand the scope of therapists' liability. In my opinion, the "specific threats to specific victims" rule states a workable, reasonable, and fair boundary upon the sphere of a therapist's liability to third persons for the acts of their patients.

The present case is one which makes application of the previously stated rules and policy considerations particularly difficult. Plaintiffs' injuries are severe and their damages extensive. Their plight as innocent bystanders to a bizarre and sensational assassination attempt is tragic and evokes great sympathy. Nevertheless, the question before the Court is whether Dr. Hopper can be subjected to liability as a matter of law for the injuries inflicted upon plaintiffs by Hinckley. I conclude that under the facts pleaded in the complaint, the question must be answered in the negative.

Accordingly, it is ordered that defendant's motion to dismiss is granted.

NOTE

1. Negligent Warning. In Hopewell v. Adebimpe, Court of Common Pleas of Allegheny County, Pennsylvania, Civil Case No. G.D. 78–28756, 130 Pittsburgh Legal Journal 107 (1982), a patient sued her psychiatrist for breaching the confidentiality provisions of the state Mental Health Procedures Act. The psychiatrist had sent the following letter to the patient's employer, without the patient's consent, Id. at 108:

RE: Rebecca Hopewell

Dear Sir:

In the course of a psychiatric interview which took place in my office on October 2, the above-named reported feelings of being so enraged about her work situation that she "will blow up and hurt somebody very seriously if the harassment does not stop".

This information is being relayed to you because there is a legal precedent requiring it and is not to be taken as an estimate of the probability that the threat will actually be carried out. It is, however, important that the person or persons at risk be notified. In this case I believe that her immediate supervisor should know of this letter.

Yours sincerely,

/s/VICTOR R. ADEBIMPE, M.D.

The court granted summary judgment for the plaintiff, commenting, Id. at 108–109, as follows:

In [cases such as this], the psychologist, psychiatrist or psychotherapist is generally confronted with the dilemma of having to choose between the patient or his potential victim. On the one hand the professional must seek to protect the confidentiality of the privileged psychotherapist-patient communication while on the other hand he is faced with the possible imposition of tort liability for failure to disclose and warn third persons of the threatened harm.

While certain jurisdictions such as the State of California in the landmark decision of Tarasoff v. Regents of the University of California have specifically recognized the duty of the psychotherapist to warn the person potentially harmed of the pending danger where the therapist either in fact had determined that the patient presented a serious danger of violence to the third person, or pursuant to the standard of the profession should have so determined, the Commonwealth of Pennsylvania has effectively eliminated the psychotherapist enigma by striking the balance in favor of confidentiality through the passage of appropriate statutory law.

Section 111 of the "Mental Health Procedures Act", Act of July 9, 1976, P.L. 817, No. 143, 50 P.S. Section 7111, entitled "Confidentiality of records" provides in pertinent part:

> *"In no event [s]hall privileged communication, whether written or oral, be disclosed to anyone without [w]ritten consent."* (Emphasis added)

When, as in the case at hand, the words of a statute are clear and free from all ambiguity, the letter of it is not to be disregarded under the pretext of pursuing its spirit. The Court does not have the slightest doubt that the disclosure by Dr. Adebimpe of the confidential and privileged communication as set forth in this letter of October 3, 1978, without the prior written consent of the Plaintiff, Rebecca Hopewell, violated Section 111 of the Act.

In light of the great publicity the *Tarasoff* decision received in national mental health publications, Dr. Adebimpe evidently believed that it was a "legal precedent" in Pennsylvania as well as in California. In 1998—16 years after *Hopewell v. Adebimpe*—the Pennsylvania Supreme Court adopted a version of *"Tarasoff* liability." See Emerich v. Philadelphia Center for Human Development, Inc., 554 Pa. 209, 720 A.2d 1032 (1998).

CIVIL CODE OF CALIFORNIA, 1985

§ 43.92. Psychotherapists; duty to warn of threatened violent behavior of patient; immunity from monetary liability

(a) There shall be no monetary liability on the part of, and no cause of action shall arise against, any person who is a psychotherapist as defined in Section 1010 of the Evidence Code in failing to warn of and protect from a patient's threatened violent behavior or failing to predict and warn of and protect from a patient's violent behavior except where the patient has communicated to the psychotherapist a serious threat of physical violence against a reasonably identifiable victim or victims.

(b) If there is a duty to warn and protect under the limited circumstances specified above, the duty shall be discharged by the psychotherapist making reasonable efforts to communicate the threat to the victim or victims and to a law enforcement agency.

SELECTED BIBLIOGRAPHY

A. Bail

Goldkamp, Prediction in Criminal Justice Policy Development, in Prediction and Classification: Criminal Justice Decision Making (D. Gottfredson and M. Tonry eds. 1987).

Goldkamp and Vilcica, Judicial Discretion and the Unfinished Agenda of American Bail Reform: Lessons from Philadelphia's Evidence–Based Judicial Strategy, 47 Studies in Law, Politics, and Society 115 (2009).

Note, The Trial of Pretrial Dangerousness: Preventive Detention After *United States v. Salerno,* 75 Virginia Law Review 639 (1989).

B. Parole

Carson, A Risk Management Approach to Legal Decision–Making About "Dangerous" People, in Law and Uncertainty (R. Baldwin ed. 1997).

B. Harcourt, Against Prediction: Profiling, Policing, and Punishing in an Actuarial Age (2007).

Harcourt, Criminal Profiling and Prediction, 5 Annual Review of Law and Social Science (2009).

Rice, Violent Offender Research and Implications for the Criminal Justice System, 52 American Psychologist 414 (1997).

Zimring and Hawkins, Dangerousness and Criminal Justice, 85 Michigan Law Review 481 (1986).

C. Civil Commitment of Sexually Violent Predators

Carlsmith, Monahan, and Evans, The Function of Punishment in the "Civil" Commitment of Sexually Violent Predators, 25 Behavioral Sciences and the Law 437 (2007).

Hanson, The Psychological Assessment of Risk for Crime and Violence, Canadian Psychology (in press).

Hanson and Morton–Bourgon, The Accuracy of Recidivism Risk Assessments for Sexual Offenders: A Meta–Analysis of 118 Prediction Studies, 21 Psychological Assessment 1 (2009).

Janus and Prentky, Sexual Predator Laws: A Two–Decade Retrospective, 21 Federal Sentencing Reporter 90 (2008).

Monahan, A Jurisprudence of Risk Assessment: Forecasting Harm Among Prisoners, Predators, and Patients, 92 Virginia Law Review 391 (2006).

Prentky, Janus, Barbaree, Schwartz, and Kafka, Sexually Violent Predators in the Courtroom: Science on Trial, 12 Psychology, Public Policy, and Law 357 (2006).

Rice and Harris, Sexual Aggressors, in Modern Scientific Evidence: The Law and Science of Expert Testimony, 2008–2009 ed. (D. Faigman, M. Saks, J. Sanders, and E. Cheng eds. 2008).

D. Capital Punishment

Cunningham, Reidy, and Sorensen, Assertions of "Future Dangerousness" at Federal Capital Sentencing: Rates and Correlates of Subsequent Prison Misconduct and Violence, 32 Law and Human Behavior 46 (2008).

Cunningham and Sorensen, Capital Offenders in Texas Prisons: Rates, Correlates, and an Actuarial Analysis of Violent Misconduct, 31 Law and Human Behavior 553 (2007).

Edens, Buffington–Vollum, Keilen, Roskamp, and Anthony, Predictions of Future Dangerousness in Capital Murder Trials: Is it Time to "Disinvent the Wheel?", 29 Law and Human Behavior 55 (2005).

C. Slobogin, Proving the Unprovable: The Role of Law, Science, and Speculation in Adjudicating Culpability and Dangerousness (2006).

Sorensen and Pilgrim, An Actuarial Risk Assessment of Violence Posed By Capital Murder Defendants, 90 Journal of Criminal Law and Criminology 1251 (2000).

E. Tort Liability

Appelbaum, Zonana, Bonnie, and Roth, Statutory Approaches to Limiting Psychiatrists' Liability for Their Patients' Violent Acts, 146 American Journal of Psychiatry 821 (1989).

Backstrom, Unveiling the Truth When It Matters Most: Implementing the *Tarasoff* Duty for California's Attorneys, 73 Southern California Law Review 139 (1999).

The Duty to Protect: Ethical, Legal, and Professional Considerations for Mental Health Professionals (J. Werth, E. Welfel, and G. Benjamin eds 2008).

Dvoskin and Heilbrun, Risk Assessment and Release Decision–Making: Toward Resolving the Great Debate, 29 Journal of the American Academy of Psychiatry and the Law 6 (2001).

Kachigian and Felthous, Court Responses to *Tarasoff* Statutes, 32 Journal of the American Academy of Psychiatry and Law 263 (2004).

McNiel, Binder, and Fulton, Management of Threats of Violence Under California's Duty-to-Protect Statute, 155 American Journal of Psychiatry 1097 (1998).

Monahan, Limiting Therapist Exposure to *Tarasoff* Liability: Guidelines for Risk Containment, 48 American Psychologist 242 (1993).

Monahan, Steadman, Robbins, Appelbaum, Banks, Grisso, Heilbrun, Mulvey, Roth, and Silver, An Actuarial Model of Violence Risk Assessment for Persons with Mental Disorders, 56 Psychiatric Services 810 (2005).

Monahan, Structured Risk Assessment of Violence, in Textbook of Violence Assessment and Management (R. Simon and K. Tardiff, eds.) (2008).

Monahan, *Tarasoff* at Thirty: How developments in science and policy shape the common law. 75 University of Cincinnati Law Review 497 (2006).

SECTION III. CONTEXTS FOR DETERMINING PRESENT FACTS

Unlike the use of social science to provide contexts for determining facts that will occur in the future—a use that educates the decisions of judges or jurors—the use of social science to supply contexts for determining facts that are in the process of occurring informs the decisions of law enforcement officers. Many law enforcement situations are characterized by (a) the clear knowledge that violations of the law are occurring; (b) the presence of large numbers of persons ("suspects") who could be the ones violating the law; and (c) a lack of resources to investigate each of these persons. In some of these situations, the police have found it useful to rely upon social science characterizations of potential violators to assist in giving priority to their investigations.

The typical case in this area concerns a person who exhibited the behavioral characteristics of known groups of persons who have engaged in given criminal acts, and who therefore was stopped and questioned. The ensuing investigation uncovered contraband, and the person was arrested. At trial, the defendant attempts to have the evidence suppressed, arguing that the initial investigation violated the Fourth Amendment, since social science data do not give rise to probable cause needed for a search or even to the reasonable suspicion needed for a brief investigatory "stop" according to Terry v. Ohio, 392 U.S. 1, 88 S.Ct. 1868, 20 L.Ed.2d 889 (1968).

We consider here the use of social science to provide contexts for determining "present" facts relating to illegal weapons, illegal aliens, and illegal drugs.

A. ILLEGAL WEAPONS

Metal detectors and "skyjacker profiles" are forms of screening airline passengers for the presence of illegal weapons. The "skyjacker profile" is the one use of social science to provide a context for determining an ongoing fact—whether a given passenger is carrying a weapon—that occasions little controversy.

UNITED STATES v. LOPEZ

United States District Court, Eastern District of New York, 1971.
328 F.Supp. 1077.

■ WEINSTEIN, DISTRICT JUDGE.

[Two Deputy United States Marshals questioned Lopez and a companion at Kennedy Airport after an employee of Pan American Airlines "pointed out the two passengers as 'selectees'—persons whose 'profile' suggested a substantial likelihood that they were potential hijackers; who had activated a magnetometer, a metal detection device; and who, upon request, had failed to produce identification." When the marshals frisked Lopez for a weapon, they found heroin, arrested him, and charged him with concealing and facilitating the transportation of heroin. He moved to suppress the evidence taken from his person.]

[I]n October 1968 a Task Force was appointed to consider methods of combating the increasing number of airline hijackings. A number of interested agencies including the Federal Aeronautics Administration, the Department of Justice and the Department of Commerce were represented. This Task Force included individuals trained in several disciplines including psychology, law, engineering and administration. Dr. John T. Dailey, a well-trained psychologist with a broad practical background in education and government personnel, took a leading role in developing and testing the Task Force ideas. At the hearing he testified at length and impressed the Court with his skill and honesty.

One of the serious problems faced by the Task Force was that many millions of passengers use air transportation. Any practical procedure would have to permit maximum access to aircraft with minimal inconvenience and embarrassment to passengers and almost no delay in the operations of the airlines.

Among the investigations undertaken by this group were a detailed study of the characteristics of all the then known hijackers and of the air traveling public. Background investigations of hijackers as well as visual and photographic studies of boarding air passengers were relied upon. Among the findings were (1) hijackers were generally not highly motivated and resourceful and (2) they shared certain characteristics markedly distinguishing them from the general traveling public.

[O]ne sample consisting of 500,000 screened passengers showed that only 1,406 satisfied the profile—.28%. Approximately one-half of those were nevertheless permitted to board immediately after failing to activate the magnetometer, leaving 712, or .14% to be interviewed. Of those interviewed, 283, approximately one-third, were actually searched. Therefore, only .05% of the sample were ultimately subjected to a preventive weapons frisk. Twenty persons were denied boarding—approximately ⅟₁₅ of those searched and of these, 16 were arrested. In sum, almost everyone (99.86%) of the one-half million persons passed swiftly through the boarding process without even being asked a question and 99.95% boarded without being searched.

In another sample of 226,000 screened passengers .57% were selected as meeting the profile; .28% were interviewed; and .13% were searched. It was reported that none were searched "involuntarily" and only 24 were denied boarding.

[T]hat the risk of hijacking is greatly increased when a passenger possesses weapons can hardly be doubted. In the 80 hijacking incidents involving planes of United States registry up to June of 1970, there were 55 firearms, 20 knives, 14 alleged bombs, 3 razors or razor blades, 1 BB gun, 1 tear gas pen, and 1 broken bottle.

In camera testimony was persuasive that the characteristics of the potential hijackers chosen for the profile were well calculated to eliminate safe persons while isolating those likely to be dangerous. No one can be certain, of course, that anyone failing all the tests of the system will be a hijacker. In fact, approximately 14 out of every 15 people who were searched proved to have no weapons and were then permitted to proceed. Moreover, as the facts detailed below indicate, there is always the risk that a soundly designed process will be abused by ignorant, careless or malevolent personnel. As one commentator pointed out "permitting *any* use of certain mathematical methods entails a sufficiently high risk of misuse, or a risk of misuse sufficiently costly to avoid, that it would be irrational not to take such misuse into account when deciding whether to permit the methods to be employed at all." Tribe, Trial by Mathematics: Precision and Ritual in the Legal Process, 84 Harv.L.Rev. 1329, 1331 (1971) (emphasis in original).

Measured against the air traveling population as a whole, the method is highly effective in narrowing the group which needs particular attention. Where the risks of hijacking to passengers and crew and to the viability of the entire industry are so great we cannot say on balance that use of the system is imprudent. Whether it meets the reasonableness test of the Constitution is an issue dealt with below.

[T]he testimony revealed that studies underlying the profile were thorough. Procedures followed in developing it were adequate. Appropriate statistical, sociological and psychological data and techniques were utilized. The profile is a highly effective procedure for isolating potential hijackers.

After studying known hijackers, the task force compiled twenty-five to thirty characteristics in which hijackers differed significantly from the air-traveling public. By putting only a few of them together they could obtain a reliable combination sharply differentiating potential hijackers from non-hijackers.

During the testing period and shortly thereafter in 1969 the task force studied an additional sample of 30 new hijackers and found that over 90% of that group would have met the profile. There has been a continuous process of reevaluation in light of new hijackings and changes in trends of hijacking. Thus far the original profile has retained validity.

[T]he anti-hijacking system is unusual in that it provides statistics showing the precise probabilities involved. Based upon the surveys available, out of every approximately 15 persons who are frisked one person is found with a weapon. Thus the probability that any person who is selected to be frisked has a weapon is approximately 6%. We know that the frisk is conducted in private with as much courtesy as the circumstances permit and that those who are frisked and allowed to go on their way generally welcome the protective measures taken in their behalf rather than resent them. The substantial interest in preserving the integrity and safety of air travel by preventing hijacking is obvious. In light of the circumstances, a 6% danger of arms suffices to justify a frisk.

The statistics discussed earlier indicate that only somewhere on the order of ¹⁄₁₀ of 1% of all passengers screened are actually frisked and that included in that .1% are practically all of the potential hijackers. The procedure, as designed, operates on purely objective criteria independent of race, color, or creed. It is well calculated to winnow out potential hijackers while occasioning a bare minimum of inconvenience to a very small percentage of the flying public—an inconvenience which most subjects seem, in fact, to accept. A United States Marshal would be imprudent were he to refuse to heed the warning given to him by the system. A narrowly circumscribed protective weapons "pat-down" or "frisk" is constitutionally permissible under these circumstances.

[W]e reach this conclusion recognizing that the system used is disquieting. Employing a combination of psychological, sociological, and physical sciences to screen, inspect and categorize unsuspecting citizens raises visions of abuse in our increasingly technological society. Proposals based upon statistical research designed to predict who might commit crimes and giving them the special attention of law enforcement agencies is particularly disturbing. There is a basis for

> ". . . what anti-utopians like Huxley and Orwell have forecast—though . . . these dismal despotisms will be far more stable and effective than their prophets have foreseen. For they will be equipped with techniques of inner-manipulation as unobtrusively fine as gossamer." T. Roszak, The Making of a Counter Culture xiii (1969).

Undoubtedly there are persons with objectively observable characteristics who provide a higher statistical probability of danger than the population as a whole. But our criminal law is based on the theory that we do not condemn people because they are potentially dangerous. We only prosecute illegal acts. Putting a group of potential violators in custody on the ground that this group contained all or nearly all of the people who would commit crimes in the future would raise the most serious constitutional issues. The procedure before us accomplishes no such result and raising such specters does not assist in a rational evaluation of the anti-hijacking program. This system does not constitute a first step along the road to preventive detention of potentially dangerous classes of persons.

[W]hile candidly recognizing the disquieting possibilities suggested by the techniques of the anti-hijacking campaign, we are unpersuaded that the rights of air travellers generally have been or will be violated by the proper application of this system. We ought not be frightened out of taking sensible protective steps by the possibilities of misuse so long as our courts are in a position to prevent abuse should it arise.

SUPPRESSION IN THIS CASE

While evidence discovered during a frisk pursuant to this anti-hijacking procedure would normally be admissible, the special circumstances of the instant case require suppression. The Pan American Passenger Service Manager issued a memorandum on July 22, 1970 purporting to "update" the "profile" to be applied in the anti-hijacking screening procedure. This action was not authorized by Pan American Security Services, the United States Marshal Service, or the Federal Aeronautics Administration. It eliminated one criterion included in the official profile established by the F.A.A. and added two additional categories.

Both the government and Pan American disowned the memorandum and indicated that it had been withdrawn. Neither were able, however, to assure the Court that the boarding area personnel responsible for applying the profile to passengers on November 14, 1970 had not read the memorandum and were not following it. Under the circumstances, the Court must assume that the "updated" profile was, in fact, employed in selecting the defendant.

The one characteristic eliminated by this supplemental memorandum effectively excised from the screening procedure one of the fundamental characteristics of hijackers as described by Dr. Dailey during *in camera* testimony. One of the characteristics added introduced an ethnic element for which there is no experimental basis, thus raising serious equal protection problems. The second added criterion called for an act of individual judgment on the part of airline employees. The effect of these changes was to destroy the essential neutrality and objectivity of the approved profile.

In evaluating the constitutionality of the system that was actually in operation on the day in question we cannot now rely on the statistics presented to the Court since the properly conducted samplings utilized the official Task Force profile. These statistics were critical in our determination that this system was an appropriate method of protecting air travellers.

The procedure instituted to detect hijackers becomes unacceptable when abused in the manner described in this case. The approved system survives constitutional scrutiny only by its careful adherence to absolute objectivity and neutrality. When elements of discretion and prejudice are interjected it becomes constitutionally impermissible.

[T]he anti-hijacking system can be a valuable and effective method of protecting millions of air travellers from the threat of violence and sudden death in the air. Properly supervised it is also constitutional. Abuses such as the one which occurred in this case must, however, be eliminated if evidence obtained in its operation is to be used in our Courts.

CONCLUSION

Defendant's motion to suppress evidence must be granted. Since without this evidence the government has no case, the indictment is dismissed.

NOTE

1. Use of the "Profile." Lopez was sent through a magnetometer only after he was noticed to exhibit the characteristics of a potential hijacker. It was FAA policy in 1971 to use the magnetometer only on those persons who "fit the profile." In 1973, the policy changed to the currently existing one, whereby all airline passengers, not just specially selected ones, pass through a magnetometer. There was then no need for a behavioral "profile" to identify persons likely to be in the possession of weapons, since the magnetometer accomplished this task by screening everyone. The FAA therefore discontinued the use of the hijacker profile in 1973.

In 1980, however, there was a series of plane hijackings in which the hijacker had boarded the plane in the possession of a plastic flask filled with gasoline, and a cigarette lighter. The plastic flask had not activated the magnetometer. As of 1980, the FAA began to deploy the hijacker profile again in order to identify persons who would hijack a plane with the use of a nonmetallic weapon.

FINAL REPORT TO PRESIDENT CLINTON

White House Commission on Aviation Safety and Security, 1997.
Vice President Al Gore, Chairman.

[Recommendation:] Complement technology with automated passenger profiling.

Profiling can leverage an investment in technology and trained people. Based on information that is already in computer databases, passengers could be separated into a very large majority who present little or no risk, and a small minority who merit additional attention. Such systems are employed successfully by other agencies, including the Customs Service. By utilizing this process Customs is better able to focus its resources and attention. As a result, many legitimate travelers never see a customs agent anymore—and drug busts are way up. The FAA and Northwest Airlines are developing an automated profiling system tailored to aviation security, and the Commission supports the continued development and implementation of such a system.

To improve and promote passenger profiling, the Commission recommends three steps. First, FBI, CIA, and ATF should evaluate and expand the research into known terrorists, hijackers, and bombers needed to develop the best possible profiling system. They should keep in mind that such a profile would be most useful to the airlines if it could be matched against automated passenger information which the airlines maintain.

Second, the FBI and CIA should develop a system that would allow important intelligence information on known or suspected terrorists to be used in passenger profiling without compromising the integrity of the intelligence or its sources. Similar systems have been developed to give environmental scientists access to sensitive data collected by satellites.

Third, the Commission will establish an advisory board on civil liberties questions that arise from the development and use of profiling systems.

[A]ugmenting Recommendation

[T]he Commission supports the development and implementation of manual and automated profiling systems, such as the one under development by the FAA and Northwest Airlines. The Commission strongly believes the civil liberties that are so fundamentally American should not, and need not, be compromised by a profiling system. Consistent with this viewpoint, the Commission sought the counsel of leading experts in the civil liberties field. The Commission recommends the following safeguards:

66666666 666666666666

1. No profile should contain or be based on material of a constitutionally suspect nature—e.g., race, religion, national origin of U.S. citizens. The Commission recommends that the elements of a profiling system be developed in consultation with the Department of Justice and other appropriate experts to ensure that selection is not impermissibly based on national origin, racial, ethnic, religious or gender characteristics.

2. Factors to be considered for elements of the profile should be based on measurable, verifiable data indicating that the factors chosen are reasonable predictors of risk, not stereotypes or generalizations. A relationship must be demonstrated between the factors chosen and the risk of illegal activity.

3. Passengers should be informed of airlines security procedures and of their right to avoid any search of their person or luggage by electing not to board the aircraft.

4. Searches arising from the use of an automated profiling system should be no more intrusive than search procedures that could be applied to all passengers. Procedures for searching the person or luggage of, or for questioning, a person who is selected by the automated profiling system should be premised on insuring respectful, non-stigmatizing, and efficient treatment of all passengers.

5. Neither the airlines or the government should maintain permanent databases on selectees. Reasonable restrictions on the maintenance of records and strict limitations on the dissemination of records should be developed.

6. Periodic independent reviews of profiling procedures should be made. The Commission considered whether an independent panel be appointed to monitor implementation and recommends at a minimum that the DOJ, in consultation with the DOT and FAA, periodically review the profiling standards and create an outside panel should that, in their judgment, be necessary.

THE 9–11 COMMISSION REPORT

National Commission on Terrorist Attacks Upon the United States, 2004.
Thomas H. Keen, Chair.

We found that as many as 15 of the 19 hijackers were potentially vulnerable to interception by border authorities. Analyzing their characteristic travel documents and travel patterns could have allowed authorities to intercept 4 to 15 hijackers and more effective use of information available in U.S. government databases could have identified up to 3 hijackers.

[S]ince 9/11, significant improvements have been made to create an integrated watchlist that makes terrorist name information available to border and law enforcement authorities. However, in the already difficult process of merging border agencies in the new Department of Homeland

Security—"changing the engine while flying" as one official put it—new insights into terrorist travel have not yet been integrated into the front lines of border security.

[T]here are many databases just in the United States—for terrorist, criminal and immigration history, as well as financial information, for instance. Each is set up for different purposes and stores different kinds of data, under varying rules of access. [T]he development of terrorist indicators has hardly begun, and behavioral cues remain important.

[W]hat are the consequences of finding a suspicious indicator, and who will take action?

One risk is that responses may be ineffective or produce no further information. Four of the 9/11 attackers were pulled into secondary border inspection, but then admitted. More than half of the 19 hijackers were flagged by the Federal Aviation Administration's profiling system when they arrived for their flights, but the consequence was that bags, not people, were checked. Competing risks include "false positives," or the danger that rules may be applied with insufficient training or judgment. Overreactions can impose high costs too-on individuals, our economy, and our beliefs about justice.

A special note on the importance of trusting subjective judgment: One potential hijacker was turned back by an immigration inspector as he tried to enter the United States. The inspector relied on intuitive experience to ask questions more than he relied on any objective factor that could be detected by "scores" or a machine. Good people who have worked in such jobs for a long time understand this phenomenon well. Other evidence we obtained confirmed the importance of letting experienced gate agents or security screeners ask questions and use their judgment. This is not an invitation to arbitrary exclusions. But any effective system has to grant some scope, perhaps in a little extra inspection or one more check, to the instincts and discretion of well trained human beings.

NOTE

1. Subsequent Developments. The "automated profiling system" mentioned in the 1997 Final Report to President Clinton was called the Computer Assisted Passenger Prescreening System (CAPPS I). After the events of September 11, 2001, the newly-created Transportation Security Agency (TSA) commissioned the development of the Computer Assisted Passenger Prescreening System, Second Version (CAPPS II), a program that would use commercial and government databases ("watch lists") in addition to airline data, as called for in the 9–11 Commission Report. CAPPS II was cancelled by TSA in 2004 before being implemented, however, due to widespread privacy concerns. In its place, a third system, called Secure Flight, was developed and scheduled to be implemented in late 2005. However, a Government Accountability Office report, Significant

Management Challenges May Adversely Affect Implementation of the Transportation Security Administration's Secure Flight Program (February 2006), concluded "Secure Flight's system development documentation does not fully explain how passenger privacy protections are to be met, and the TSA has not issued the privacy notices that describe how it will protect passenger data once Secure Flight becomes operational. As a result, it is not possible to assess how TSA is addressing privacy concerns." The implementation of Secure Flight was then suspended.

In October, 2008, the TSA issued the Secure Flight Final Rule, which "shifts pre-departure watch list matching responsibilities from individual aircraft operators to the TSA and carries out a key recommendation of the 9/11 Commission. [A]irlines will be required under Secure Flight to collect a passenger's full name, date of birth, and gender when making an airline reservation. [T]his additional information [w]ill be particularly important for those individuals with names similar to those on the watch list. [D]ata retention for the vast majority of individuals will be no more than seven days." Implementation of Secure Flight began in 2009 and is scheduled to be completed by the end of 2010.

B. ILLEGAL ALIENS

In an effort to control illegal immigration to the United States, the Border Patrol operates permanent "checkpoints" away from the border where all motorists are observed as they drive through. On the basis of this observation, some of the motorists are stopped for questioning and inspection. The empirical foundation for the decision to select certain motorists for closer scrutiny has been the subject of much judicial dispute.

UNITED STATES v. MARTINEZ–FUERTE

Supreme Court of the United States, 1976.
428 U.S. 543, 96 S.Ct. 3074, 49 L.Ed.2d 1116.

■ MR. JUSTICE POWELL delivered the opinion of the Court.

These cases involve criminal prosecutions for offenses relating to the transportation of illegal Mexican aliens. Each defendant was arrested at a permanent checkpoint operated by the Border Patrol away from the international border with Mexico, and each sought the exclusion of certain evidence on the ground that the operation of the checkpoint was incompatible with the Fourth Amendment. In each instance whether the Fourth Amendment was violated turns primarily on whether a vehicle may be stopped at a fixed checkpoint for brief questioning of its occupants even though there is no reason to believe the particular vehicle contains illegal aliens.

[I]n *[United States v.] Brignoni–Ponce,* we recognized that Fourth Amendment analysis in this context also must take into account the overall degree of interference with legitimate traffic. 422 U.S. [873], at 882–883, 95

S.Ct., at 2580–2581 [1975]. We concluded there that random roving-patrol stops could not be tolerated because they "would subject the residents of . . . [border] areas to potentially unlimited interference with their use of the highways, solely at the discretion of Border Patrol officers." [I]bid. There also was a grave danger that such unreviewable discretion would be abused by some officers in the field.

Routine checkpoint stops do not intrude similarly on the motoring public. First, the potential interference with legitimate traffic is minimal. Motorists using these highways are not taken by surprise as they know, or may obtain knowledge of, the location of the checkpoints and will not be stopped elsewhere. Second, checkpoint operations both appear to and actually involve less discretionary enforcement activity. The regularized manner in which established checkpoints are operated is visible evidence, reassuring to law-abiding motorists, that the stops are duly authorized and believed to serve the public interest. [A]nd since field officers may stop only those cars passing the checkpoint, there is less room for abusive or harassing stops of individuals than there was in the case of roving-patrol stops. Moreover, a claim that a particular exercise of discretion in locating or operating a checkpoint is unreasonable is subject to post-stop judicial review.

The defendants arrested at the San Clemente checkpoint suggest that its operation involves a significant extra element of intrusiveness in that only a small percentage of cars are referred to the secondary inspection area, thereby "stigmatizing" those diverted and reducing the assurances provided by equal treatment of all motorists. We think defendants overstate the consequences. Referrals are made for the sole purpose of conducting a routine and limited inquiry into residence status that cannot feasibly be made of every motorist where the traffic is heavy. The objective intrusion of the stop and inquiry thus remains minimal. Selective referral may involve some annoyance, but it remains true that the stops should not be frightening or offensive because of their public and relatively routine nature. Moreover, selective referrals—rather than questioning the occupants of every car—tend to advance some Fourth Amendment interests by minimizing the intrusion on the general motoring public.

[W]e further believe that it is constitutional to refer motorists selectively to the secondary inspection area at the San Clemente checkpoint on the basis of criteria that would not sustain a roving-patrol stop. Thus, even if it be assumed that such referrals are made largely on the basis of apparent Mexican ancestry,[16] we perceive no constitutional violation. As the

---

16. The Government suggests that trained Border Patrol agents rely on factors in addition to apparent Mexican ancestry when selectively diverting motorists. This assertion finds support in the record. Less than 1% of the motorists passing the checkpoint are stopped for questioning, whereas American citizens of Mexican ancestry and legally resident Mexican citizens constitute a significantly larger proportion of the population of southern California. The 1970 census figures, which may not fully reflect illegal aliens, show the population of California to be approximately 19,958,000 of whom some 3,102,-000, or 16%, are Spanish-speaking or of Spanish surname. The equivalent percent-intrusion here is sufficiently minimal that no particularized reason need exist to justify it, we think it follows that the Border Patrol officers must have wide discretion in selecting the motorists to be diverted for the brief questioning involved.[17]

[I]n summary, we hold that stops for brief questioning routinely conducted at permanent checkpoints are consistent with the Fourth Amendment and need not be authorized by warrant. The principal protection of Fourth Amendment rights at checkpoints lies in appropriate limitations on the scope of the stop. We have held that checkpoint searches are constitutional only if justified by consent or probable cause to search. And our holding today is limited to the type of stops described in this opinion. "[A]ny further detention . . . must be based on consent or probable cause." *United States v. Brignoni–Ponce,* supra, at 882.

■ MR. JUSTICE BRENNAN, with whom MR. JUSTICE MARSHALL joins, dissenting.

[I]n abandoning any requirement of a minimum of reasonable suspicion, or even articulable suspicion, the Court in every practical sense renders meaningless, as applied to checkpoint stops, the *Brignoni–Ponce* holding that "standing alone [Mexican appearance] does not justify stopping all Mexican–Americans to ask if they are aliens."[1] 422 U.S., at 887, 95

---

ages for metropolitan San Diego and Los Angeles are 13% and 18% respectively. If the statewide population ratio is applied to the approximately 146,000 vehicles passing through the checkpoint during the eight days surrounding the arrests in No. 74–1560, roughly 23,400 would be expected to contain persons of Spanish or Mexican ancestry, yet only 820 were referred to the secondary area. This appears to refute any suggestion that the Border Patrol relies extensively on apparent Mexican ancestry standing alone in referring motorists to the secondary area.

17. Of the 820 vehicles referred to the secondary inspection area during the eight days surrounding the arrests involved in No. 74–1560, roughly 20% contained illegal aliens. Thus, to the extent that the Border Patrol relies on apparent Mexican ancestry at this checkpoint, see n. 16, supra, that reliance clearly is relevant to the law enforcement need to be reserved. Cf. United States v. Brignoni–Ponce, supra, at 886–887, 95 S.Ct., at 2583, where we noted that "[t]he likelihood that any given person of Mexican ancestry is an alien is high enough to make Mexican appearance a relevant factor . . .," although we held that apparent Mexican ancestry by itself could not create the reasonable suspicion required for a roving-patrol stop. Different considerations would arise if, for example, reliance were put on apparent

Mexican ancestry at a checkpoint operated near the Canadian border.

1. *Brignoni–Ponce,* which involved roving-patrol stops, said:

"[Mexican ancestry] alone would justify neither a reasonable belief that they were aliens, nor a reasonable belief that the car concealed other aliens who were illegally in the country. Large numbers of native-born and naturalized citizens have the physical characteristics identified with Mexican ancestry, and even in the border area a relatively small proportion of them are aliens. The likelihood that any given person of Mexican ancestry is an alien is high enough to make Mexican appearance a relevant factor, but standing alone it does not justify stopping all Mexican–Americans to ask if they are aliens." 422 U.S., at 886–887, 95 S.Ct., at 2583 (footnote omitted).

Today we are told that secondary referrals may be based on criteria that would not sustain a roving-patrol stop, and specifically that such referrals may be based largely on Mexican ancestry. Even if the difference between *Brignoni–Ponce* and this decision is only a matter of degree, we are not told what justifies the different treatment of Mexican appearance or why greater emphasis is permitted in the less demanding circumstances of a checkpoint. That law in this country

S.Ct., at 2583. Since the objective is almost entirely the Mexican illegally in the country, checkpoint officials, uninhibited by any objective standards and therefore free to stop any or all motorists without explanation or excuse, wholly on whim, will perforce target motorists of Mexican appearance. The process will then inescapably discriminate against citizens of Mexican ancestry and Mexican aliens lawfully in this country for no other reason than that they unavoidably possess the same "suspicious" physical and grooming characteristics of illegal Mexican aliens.

Every American citizen of Mexican ancestry and every Mexican alien lawfully in this country must know after today's decision that he travels the fixed checkpoint highways at the risk of being subjected not only to a stop, but also to detention and interrogation, both prolonged and to an extent far more than for non-Mexican appearing motorists. To be singled out for referral and to be detained and interrogated must be upsetting to any motorist. One wonders what actual experience supports my Brethren's conclusion that referrals "should not be frightening or offensive because of their public and relatively routine nature." In point of fact, referrals, viewed in context, are not relatively routine; thousands are otherwise permitted to pass. But for the arbitrarily selected motorists who must suffer the delay and humiliation of detention and interrogation, the experience can obviously be upsetting. And that experience is particularly vexing for the motorist of Mexican ancestry who is selectively referred, knowing that the officers' target is the Mexican alien. That deep resentment will be stirred by a sense of unfair discrimination is not difficult to foresee.[4]

C. Illegal Drugs

By far the most controversial use of social science to provide a context for making law enforcement decisions is the "drug courier profile." At many major American airports, agents of the Drug Enforcement Administration use this screening device to determine which travellers are most

should tolerate use of one's ancestry as probative of possible criminal conduct is repugnant under any circumstances.

4. [E]ven if good faith is assumed, the affront to the dignity of American citizens of Mexican ancestry and Mexican aliens lawfully within the country is in no way diminished. The fact still remains that people of Mexican ancestry are targeted for examination at checkpoints and that the burden of checkpoint intrusions will lie heaviest on them. That, as the Court observes, "[l]ess than 1% of the motorists passing the checkpoint are stopped for questioning," whereas approximately 16% of the population of California is Spanish-speaking or of Spanish surname, has little bearing on this point—or, for that matter, on the integrity of Border Patrol prac-

tices. There is no indication how many of the 16% have physical and grooming characteristics identifiable as Mexican. There is no indication what portion of the motoring public in California is of Spanish or Mexican ancestry. Given the socioeconomic status of this portion, it is likely that the figure is significantly less than 16%. Neither is there any indication that those of Mexican ancestry are not subjected to lengthier initial stops than others, even if they are not secondarily detained. Finally, there is no indication of the ancestral makeup of the 1% who are referred for secondary detention. If, as is quite likely the case, it is overwhelmingly Mexican, the sense of discrimination which will be felt is only enhanced.

likely to be transporting illegal drugs, and thus should receive a disproportionate share of investigatory attention.

———

UNITED STATES v. SOKOLOW

Supreme Court of the United States, 1989.
490 U.S. 1, 109 S.Ct. 1581, 104 L.Ed.2d 1.

■ CHIEF JUSTICE REHNQUIST delivered the opinion of the Court.

Respondent Andrew Sokolow was stopped by Drug Enforcement Administration (DEA) agents upon his arrival at Honolulu International
Airport. The agents found 1,063 grams of cocaine in his carry-on luggage.
When respondent was stopped, the agents knew, *inter alia,* that (1) he paid
$2,100 for two airplane tickets from a roll of $20 bills; (2) he traveled under
a name that did not match the name under which his telephone number
was listed; (3) his original destination was Miami, a source city for illicit
drugs; (4) he stayed in Miami for only 48 hours, even though a round-trip
flight from Honolulu to Miami takes 20 hours; (5) he appeared nervous
during his trip; and (6) he checked none of his luggage.

[T]his case involves a typical attempt to smuggle drugs through one of
the Nation's airports. On a Sunday in July 1984, respondent went to the
United Airlines ticket counter at Honolulu Airport, where he purchased
two round-trip tickets for a flight to Miami leaving later that day. The
tickets were purchased in the names of "Andrew Kray" and "Janet
Norian," and had open return dates. Respondent paid $2,100 for the tickets
from a large roll of $20 bills, which appeared to contain a total of $4,000.
He also gave the ticket agent his home telephone number. The ticket agent
noticed that respondent seemed nervous; he was about 25 years old; he was
dressed in a black jumpsuit and wore gold jewelry; and he was accompanied
by a woman, who turned out to be Janet Norian. Neither respondent nor
his companion checked any of their four pieces of luggage.

After the couple left for their flight, the ticket agent informed Officer
John McCarthy of the Honolulu Police Department of respondent's cash
purchase of tickets to Miami. Officer McCarthy determined that the telephone number respondent gave to the ticket agent was subscribed to a
"Karl Herman," who resided at 348A Royal Hawaiian Avenue in Honolulu.
Unbeknownst to McCarthy (and later to the DEA agents), respondent was
Herman's roommate. The ticket agent identified respondent's voice on the
answering machine at Herman's number. Officer McCarthy was unable to
find any listing under the name "Andrew Kray" in Hawaii. McCarthy
subsequently learned that return reservations from Miami to Honolulu had
been made in the names of Kray and Norian, with their arrival scheduled
for July 25, three days after respondent and his companion had left. He
also learned that Kray and Norian were scheduled to make stopovers in
Denver and Los Angeles.

On July 25, during the stopover in Los Angeles, DEA agents identified respondent. He "appeared to be very nervous and was looking all around the waiting area." App. 43–44. Later that day, at 6:30 p.m., respondent and Norian arrived in Honolulu. As before, they had not checked their luggage. Respondent was still wearing a black jumpsuit and gold jewelry. The couple proceeded directly to the street and tried to hail a cab, where Agent Richard Kempshall and three other DEA agents approached them. Kempshall displayed his credentials, grabbed respondent by the arm and moved him back onto the sidewalk. Kempshall asked respondent for his airline ticket and identification; respondent said that he had neither. He told the agents that his name was "Sokolow," but that he was traveling under his mother's maiden name, "Kray."

Respondent and Norian were escorted to the DEA office at the airport. There, the couple's luggage was examined by "Donker," a narcotics detector dog, which alerted to respondent's brown shoulder bag. The agents arrested respondent. He was advised of his constitutional rights and declined to make any statements. The agents obtained a warrant to search the shoulder bag. They found no illicit drugs, but the bag did contain several suspicious documents indicating respondent's involvement in drug trafficking. The agents had Donker reexamine the remaining luggage, and this time the dog alerted to a medium sized Louis Vuitton bag. By now, it was 9:30 p.m., too late for the agents to obtain a second warrant. They allowed respondent to leave for the night, but kept his luggage. The next morning, after a second dog confirmed Donker's alert, the agents obtained a warrant and found 1,063 grams of cocaine inside the bag.

Respondent was indicted for possession with the intent to distribute cocaine in violation of 21 U.S.C.A. § 841(a)(1). The United States District Court for Hawaii denied his motion to suppress the cocaine and other evidence seized from his luggage, finding that the DEA agents had a reasonable suspicion that he was involved in drug trafficking when they stopped him at the airport. Respondent then entered a conditional plea of guilty to the offense charged.

The United States Court of Appeals for the Ninth Circuit reversed respondent's conviction by a divided vote, holding that the DEA agents did not have a reasonable suspicion to justify the stop. 831 F.2d, at 1423. The majority divided the facts bearing on reasonable suspicion into two categories. In the first category, the majority placed facts describing "ongoing criminal activity," such as the use of an alias or evasive movement through an airport; the majority believed that at least one such factor was always needed to support a finding of reasonable suspicion. Id., at 1419. In the second category, it placed facts describing "personal characteristics" of drug couriers, such as the cash payment for tickets, a short trip to a major source city for drugs, nervousness, type of attire, and unchecked luggage. Id., at 1420. The majority believed that such facts, "shared by drug couriers and the public at large," were only relevant if there was evidence of ongoing criminal behavior and the Government offered "[e]mpirical documentation" that the combination of facts at issue did not describe the behavior of "significant numbers of innocent persons." Ibid. Applying this two-part test to the facts of this case, the majority found that there was no evidence of ongoing criminal behavior, and thus that the agents' stop was impermissible.

[T]he Court of Appeals held that the DEA agents seized respondent when they grabbed him by the arm and moved him back onto the sidewalk. 831 F.2d, at 1416. The Government does not challenge that conclusion, and we assume—without deciding—that a stop occurred here. Our decision, then, turns on whether the agents had a reasonable suspicion that respondent was engaged in wrongdoing when they encountered him on the sidewalk. In Terry v. Ohio, 392 U.S. 1, 30, 88 S.Ct. 1868, 1884–85, 20 L.Ed.2d 889 (1968), we held that the police can stop and briefly detain a person for investigative purposes if the officer has a reasonable suspicion supported by articulable facts that criminal activity "may be afoot," even if the officer lacks probable cause.

The officer, of course, must be able to articulate something more than an "inchoate and unparticularized suspicion or 'hunch'." Id., at 27, 88 S.Ct., at 1883. The Fourth Amendment requires "some minimal level of objective justification" for making the stop. INS v. Delgado, 466 U.S. 210, 217, 104 S.Ct. 1758, 1763, 80 L.Ed.2d 247 (1984). That level of suspicion is considerably less than proof of wrongdoing by a preponderance of the evidence. We have held that probable cause means "a fair probability that contraband or evidence of a crime will be found," Illinois v. Gates, 462 U.S. 213, 238, 103 S.Ct. 2317, 2332, 76 L.Ed.2d 527 (1983), and the level of suspicion required for a *Terry* stop is obviously less demanding than that for probable cause.

The concept of reasonable suspicion, like probable cause, is not "readily, or even usefully, reduced to a neat set of legal rules." Gates, supra, 462 U.S., at 232, 103 S.Ct., at 2329. We think the Court of Appeals' effort to refine and elaborate the requirements of "reasonable suspicion" in this case create unnecessary difficulty in dealing with one of the relatively simple concepts embodied in the Fourth Amendment. In evaluating the validity of a stop such as this, we must consider "the totality of the circumstances—the whole picture." United States v. Cortez, 449 U.S. 411, 417, 101 S.Ct. 690, 695, 66 L.Ed.2d 621 (1981). As we said in *Cortez:*

> "The process does not deal with hard certainties, but with probabilities. Long before the law of probabilities was articulated as such, practical people formulated certain common-sense conclusions about human behavior; jurors as factfinders are permitted to do the same— and so are law enforcement officers." Id., at 418, 101 S.Ct., at 695.

The rule enunciated by the Court of Appeals, in which evidence available to an officer is divided into evidence of "ongoing criminal behavior," on the one hand, and "probabilistic" evidence, on the other, is not in keeping with the quoted statements from our decisions. It also seems to us to draw a sharp line between types of evidence, the probative value of which varies only in degree. The Court of Appeals classified evidence of traveling under an alias, or evidence that the suspect took an evasive or erratic path through an airport, as meeting the test for showing "ongoing criminal activity." But certainly instances are conceivable in which traveling under an alias would not reflect ongoing criminal activity: for example, a person who wished to travel to a hospital or clinic for an operation and wished to conceal that fact. One taking an evasive path through an airport might be seeking to avoid a confrontation with an angry acquaintance or with a creditor. This is not to say that each of these types of evidence is not highly probative, but they do not have the sort of ironclad significance attributed to them by the Court of Appeals.

On the other hand, the factors in this case that the Court of Appeals treated as merely "probabilistic" also have probative significance. Paying $2,100 in cash for two airplane tickets is out of the ordinary, and it is even more out of the ordinary to pay that sum from a roll of $20 bills containing nearly twice that amount of cash. Most business travelers, we feel confident, purchase airline tickets by credit card or check so as to have a record for tax or business purposes, and few vacationers carry with them thousands of dollars in $20 bills. We also think the agents had a reasonable ground to believe that respondent was traveling under an alias; the evidence was by no means conclusive, but it was sufficient to warrant consideration. While a trip from Honolulu to Miami, standing alone, is not a cause for any sort of suspicion, here there was more: surely few residents of Honolulu travel from that city for 20 hours to spend 48 hours in Miami during the month of July.

Any one of these factors is not by itself proof of any illegal conduct and is quite consistent with innocent travel. But we think taken together they amount to reasonable suspicion. We said in Reid v. Georgia, 448 U.S. 438, 100 S.Ct. 2752, 65 L.Ed.2d 890 (1980) (*per curiam*), "there could, of course, be circumstances in which wholly lawful conduct might justify the suspicion that criminal activity was afoot." Id., at 441, 100 S.Ct., at 2754. Indeed, *Terry* itself involved "a series of acts, each of them perhaps innocent" if viewed separately, "but which taken together warranted further investigation." 392 U.S., at 22, 88 S.Ct., at 1881; see also *Cortez,* 449 U.S., at 417–419, 101 S.Ct., at 694–696. We noted in *Gates,* 462 U.S., at 243–244, n. 13, 103 S.Ct., at 2335 n. 13 (1983), that "innocent behavior will frequently provide the basis for a showing of probable cause," and that "[i]n making a determination of probable cause the relevant inquiry is not whether particular conduct is 'innocent' or 'guilty,' but the degree of suspicion that attaches to particular types of noncriminal acts." That principle applies equally well to the reasonable suspicion inquiry.

We do not agree with respondent that our analysis is somehow changed by the agents' belief that his behavior was consistent with one of the DEA's "drug courier profiles."[6] A court sitting to determine the existence of reasonable suspicion must require the agent to articulate the factors leading to that conclusion, but the fact that these factors may be set forth

6. Agent Kempshall testified that respondent's behavior "had all the classic aspects of a drug courier." App. 59. Since 1974, the DEA has trained narcotics officers to identify drug smugglers on the basis of the sort of circumstantial evidence at issue here.

in a "profile" does not somehow detract from their evidentiary significance as seen by a trained agent.

[W]e hold that the agents had a reasonable basis to suspect that respondent was transporting illegal drugs on these facts. The judgment of the Court of Appeals is therefore reversed and the case remanded for further proceedings consistent with our decision.

———

NOTES

1. Experience as "Data." The Supreme Court's original "stop and frisk" case, Terry v. Ohio, 392 U.S. 1, 88 S.Ct. 1868, 20 L.Ed.2d 889 (1968), is an early example of the use of impressionistic data to identify persons in the process of committing crime. Chief Justice Earl Warren described in detail the experience of Officer McFadden, who had stopped and frisked the defendant. "[H]e had been a policeman for 39 years and a detective for 35 and [h]e had been assigned to patrol his vicinity of downtown Cleveland for shoplifters and pickpockets for 30 years. He explained that he had developed routine habits of observation over the years." 392 U.S. at 5, 88 S.Ct. at 1871. Officer McFadden testified that when he noticed Terry, the defendant, and a companion, "they didn't look right to me." He observed the two men standing on a street corner for a lengthy period, taking turns walking down the street to stare into a store window 24 times, and conferring with each other after each trip. The Chief Justice stated that "It would have been poor police work indeed for an officer of 30 years' experience in the detection of thievery from stores in this same neighborhood to have failed to investigate this behavior." Id. at 23, 88 S.Ct. at 1881. Officer McFadden approached the suspects, frisked them for weapons, and found two guns. The Supreme Court ruled that it was constitutionally permissible for Officer McFadden to rely upon his own experience in forming the "reasonable suspicion" necessary to make what is now referred to as a *"Terry*-stop."

2. Research on the Validity of the Drug Courier Profile. The National Institute of Justice conducted an empirical study of the validity of the Drug Enforcement Administration's efforts to identify drug couriers. Zedlewski, The DEA Airport Surveillance Program: An Analysis of Agent Activities (1984). For an eight-week period in the summer of 1982, DEA agents completed an Encounter Report on all passengers they contacted in airports in the United States. In addition, they kept a log on the number of passengers observed on each arriving and departing flight. Of approximately 107,000 passengers observed during this period, 146 were approached by DEA agents, a "contact rate" of 1.3 per thousand passengers. The report stated, id. at 2:

> A preponderance (120 of 146) of the encounters [82 percent] resulted from a combination of behavioral and demographic peculiarities exhibited by the subject which made the agent suspicious (e.g.,

___,[1] etc.). In the opinions of the agents filling out the reports, these behaviors were suspicious but not sufficient to detain the subject.

In 42 of the 146 contacts (29 percent), the agents permitted the passengers to proceed after questioning without searching them. In 81 contacts (55 percent) the passengers consented to being searched. In 15 cases (10 percent) the agents conducted a search either after obtaining a warrant or incident to arrest. There were "other" outcomes, such as "an alert call to the subjects' destination [or] referral to local police" in 8 cases (5 percent).

The study noted that "of the 103 searches conducted, 49 uncovered either contraband or evidence of some other crime. Thus the agent's suspicions were confirmed in nearly half [48 percent] of the occasions in which they sought a search."[2] Id. at 2. In 33 of these 49 cases (67 percent) the evidence discovered consisted of illegal drugs—heroin, cocaine, amphetamines, or "large quantities" of hashish. One case uncovered illegal weapons (and two of the drug discoveries also uncovered firearms). In 25 searches (31 percent) the evidence consisted of "coded payment ledgers," the identification of "known dealers," "large sums of currency" (from $30,000 to $196,000), or "other contraband."

Of the 49 persons whose search uncovered evidence of illegal behavior, 17 (35 percent) had refused a request to consent to the search. The report commented upon this finding, id. at 2:

> The consent to search granted by the other 65 percent has two interpretations: either they were unaware of their rights or they felt that denial was futile. Support for the latter hypothesis can be found in an analysis of those 11 cases[3] where a consent search was denied: agents either obtained a warrant or made an arrest in 9 of those cases. [I]t appears that in certain cases the agent stands ready to arrest or to seek a search warrant if consent is denied.

---

1. Examples of these "profile" characteristics presented in the original report were "deleted in the interest of safeguarding surveillance techniques" in the version that became public information. We would like to thank Charles J. Fanning, Special Assistant to the Assistant Administrator for Operations of the Drug Enforcement Administration, for obtaining the release of this report to the Editors pursuant to the Freedom of Information Act, and Edwin W. Zedlewski, Office of Research and Evaluation Methods, National Institute of Justice, for clarifying several points in the report.

2. The "103 searches" consisted of 81 persons who consented to be searched, 15 persons who were searched with a warrant or incident to arrest and 7 of the persons who experienced "other" outcomes.

3. The discrepancy between the 17 subjects mentioned as refusing a request to consent to being searched and the 11 subjects analyzed here appears to lie in the fact that in 6 of the "other outcomes" cases a search was made, but not by the DEA. For example, the local police may have been called and may have arrested a subject for disorderly conduct and performed a search incident to the arrest.

NEW JERSEY v. SOTO ET AL.

Superior Court of New Jersey, Law Division, 1996.
324 N.J.Super. 66, 734 A.2d 350.

■ ROBERT E. FRANCIS, J.S.C.

These are consolidated motions to suppress under the equal protection and due process clauses of the Fourteenth Amendment. Seventeen defendants of African ancestry claim that their arrests on the New Jersey Turnpike south of exit 3 between 1988 and 1991 result from discriminatory enforcement of the traffic laws by the New Jersey State Police. After a lengthy hearing, I find defendants have established a *prima facie* case of selective enforcement which the State has failed to rebut requiring suppression of all contraband and evidence seized.

Defendants base their claim of institutional racism primarily on statistics. During discovery, each side created a database of all stops and arrests by State Police members patrolling the Turnpike between exits 1 and 7A out of the Moorestown Station for thirty-five randomly selected days between April 1988 and May 1991 from arrest reports, patrol charts, radio logs and traffic tickets.

[T]o establish a standard against which to compare the stop data, the defense conducted a traffic survey and a violator survey. Dr. John Lamberth, Chairman of the Psychology Department at Temple University who I found is qualified as an expert in statistics and social psychology, designed both surveys.

The traffic survey was conducted over twenty-one randomly selected two and one-half hour sessions between June 11 and June 24, 1993 and between 8:00 a.m. and 8:00 p.m. at four sites, two northbound and two southbound, between exits 1 and 3 of the Turnpike. Teams supervised by Fred Last, Esq., of the Office of the Public Defender observed and recorded the number of vehicles that passed them except for large trucks, tractor-trailers, buses and government vehicles, how many contained a ''black'' occupant and the state of origin of each vehicle. Of the 42,706 vehicles counted, 13.5% had a black occupant. Dr. Lamberth testified that this percentage is consistent with the 1990 Census figures.

[T]he violator survey was conducted over ten sessions in four days in July 1993 by Mr. Last traveling between exits 1 and 3 in his vehicle at sixty miles per hour on cruise control after the speedometer had been calibrated and observing and recording the number of vehicles that passed him, the number of vehicles he passed and how many had a black occupant. Mr. Last counted a total of 2096 vehicles other than large trucks, tractortrailers, buses and government vehicles of which 2062 or 98.1% passed him going in excess of sixty miles per hour including 306 with a black occupant equaling about 15% of those vehicles clearly speeding. Multiple violators, that is those violating the speed limit and committing some other moving violation like tailgating, also equaled about 15% black. Dr. Lamberth testified that the difference between the percentage of black violators and the percentage of black travelers from the surveys is statistically insignificant and that there is no evidence traffic patterns changed between the period April 1988 to May 1991 in the databases and June–July 1993 when the surveys were done.

Using 13.5% as the standard or benchmark against which to compare the stop data, Dr. Lamberth found that 127 or 46.2% of the race identified stops between exits 1 and 3 were of blacks constituting an absolute disparity of 32.7%, a comparative disparity of 242% (32.7% divided by 13.5%) and 16.35 standard deviations. By convention, something is considered statistically significant if it would occur by chance fewer than five times in a hundred (over two standard deviations).[3]

[T]he State presented the testimony of Dr. Leonard Cupingood to challenge or refute the statistical evidence offered by the defense. I found Dr. Cupingood is qualified to give expert testimony in the field of statistics. [D]r. Cupingood had no genuine criticism of the defense traffic survey. Rather, he centered his criticism of the defense statistical evidence on the violator survey. Throughout his testimony he maintained that the violator survey failed to capture the relevant data which he opined was the racial mix of those speeders most likely to be stopped or the "tail of the distribution." He even recommended the State authorize him to design a study to collect this data, but the State declined. [I]n any event, his supposition that maybe blacks drive faster than whites above the speed limit was repudiated by all State Police members called by the State who were questioned about it. [M]oreover, Dr. Cupingood acknowledged that he knew of no study indicating that blacks drive worse than whites.

[C]onvinced in his belief that the defense 15% standard or benchmark was open to question, Dr. Cupingood attempted to find the appropriate benchmark to compare with the databases. He did [several] studies of presumedly race-blind stops: night stops versus day stops; [and] radar stops versus non-radar stops.

[I]n his study of night stops versus day stops, he compared the percentage of stops of blacks at night between exits 1 and 7A in the databases with the percentage of stops of blacks during daytime and found that night stops were 37.3% black versus 30.2% for daytime stops. Since he presumed the State Police generally cannot tell race at night, he concluded the higher percentage for night stops of blacks supported a standard well above 15%. His premise that the State Police generally cannot recognize race at night, however, is belied by the evidence. On July 16, 1994 between 9:40 p.m. and 11:00 p.m. Ahmad S. Corbitt, now an assistant deputy public defender, together with Investigator Minor of the Office of the Public Defender drove on the Turnpike at 55 miles per hour for a while and parked perpendicular to the Turnpike at a rest stop for a while to see if

3. Dr. Lamberth erred in using 13.5% as the standard for comparison with the stop data. The violator survey indicates that 14.8%, rounded to 15%, of those observed speeding were black. This percentage is the percentage Dr. Lamberth should have used in making statistical comparisons with the stop data in the databases. Nonetheless, it would appear that whatever the correctly calculated disparities and standard deviations are, they would be nearly equal to those calculated by Dr. Lamberth.

they could make out the races of the occupants of the vehicles they observed. Mr. Corbitt testified that the two could identify blacks versus whites about 80% of the time in the moving mode and close to 100% in the stationary mode.

[N]ext, in his study of radar stops versus non-radar stops, Dr. Cupingood focused on the race identified tickets where radar was used in the databases and found that 28.5% of them were issued to blacks. Since he assumed that radar is race neutral, he suggested 28.5% might be the correct standard. As Dr. Kadane said in rebuttal, this study is fundamentally flawed because it assumes what is in question or that the people stopped are the best measure of who is eligible to be stopped. If racial prejudice were afoot, the standard would be tainted. In addition, although a radar device is race-blind, the operator may not be. Of far more significance is the defense study comparing the traffic tickets issued by the Radar [U]nit which shows again that where radar is used by a unit concerned primarily with speeders [rather than drugs] and acting with little or no discretion like the Radar Unit, the percentage of tickets issued to blacks is consistent with their percentage on the highway.

[T]he right to be free from discrimination is firmly supported by the Fourteenth Amendment to the United States Constitution and the protections of *Article I, paragraphs 1* and *5 of the New Jersey Constitution of 1947*. To be sure, "[t]he eradication of the 'cancer of discrimination' has long been one of our State's highest priorities." *Dixon v. Rutgers, The State University of N.J., 110 N.J. 432, 451, 541 A.2d 1046 (1988)*. It is indisputable, therefore, that the police may not stop a motorist based on race or any other invidious classification. See *State v. Kuhn, 213 N.J.Super. 275, 517 A.2d 162 (1986)*.

[W]here objective evidence establishes "that a police agency has embarked upon an officially sanctioned or *de facto* policy of targeting minorities for investigation and arrest," any evidence seized will be suppressed to deter future insolence in office by those charged with enforcement of the law and to maintain judicial integrity. *State v. Kennedy, 247 N.J.Super. 21, 588 A.2d 834 (App.Div.1991)*.

Statistics may be used to make out a case of targeting minorities for prosecution of traffic offenses provided the comparison is between the racial composition of the motorist population violating the traffic laws and the racial composition of those arrested for traffic infractions on the relevant roadway patrolled by the police agency. *Wards Cove Packing Co. v. Atonio,* [490 U.S. 642 (1989)]. While defendants have the burden of proving "the existence of purposeful discrimination," discriminatory intent may be inferred from statistical proof presenting a stark pattern or an even less extreme pattern in certain limited contexts. *McCleskey v. Kemp, 481 U.S. 279 (1987)*.

[O]nce defendants expose a *prima facie* case of selective enforcement, the State generally cannot rebut it by merely calling attention to possible flaws or unmeasured variables in defendants' statistics. Rather, the State must introduce specific evidence showing that either there actually are defects which bias the results or the missing factors, when properly organized and accounted for, eliminate or explain the disparity.

[H]ere, defendants have proven at least a *de facto* policy on the part of the State Police out of the Moorestown Station of targeting blacks for investigation and arrest between April 1988 and May 1991 both south of exit 3 and between exits 1 and 7A of the Turnpike. Their surveys satisfy *Wards Cove, supra.* The statistical disparities and standard deviations revealed are indeed stark. The discretion devolved upon general road troopers to stop any car they want [e]vinces a selection process that is susceptible of abuse. The utter failure of the State Police hierarchy to monitor and control [its officers] or investigate the many claims of institutional discrimination manifests its indifference if not acceptance. Against all this, the State submits only denials and the conjecture and flawed studies of Dr. Cupingood.

The eradication of illegal drugs from our State is an obviously worthy goal, but not at the expense of individual rights. As Justice Brandeis so wisely said dissenting in *Olmstead v. United States, 277 U.S. 438, 479, 48 S.Ct. 564, 72 L.Ed. 944 (1928)*:

> "Experience should teach us to be most on our guard to protect liberty when the government's purposes are beneficent. Men born to freedom are naturally alert to repel invasion of their liberty by evil-minded rulers. The greatest dangers to liberty lurk in insidious encroachment by men of zeal, well-meaning but without understanding."

Motions granted.

————

UNITED STATES v. NEW JERSEY

United States District Court, District of New Jersey, 1999.
Civil No. 99–5970 (MLC).

JOINT APPLICATION FOR ENTRY OF CONSENT DECREE

Plaintiff, the United States, and Defendants, the State of New Jersey and the Division of State Police of the New Jersey Department of Law and Public Safety, respectfully move this Court for entry of [this] Consent Decree.

The United States has simultaneously filed its Complaint against the Defendants alleging violations of 42 U.S.C. § 14141 and 42 U.S.C. § 3789d(c). The Complaint alleges a pattern or practice of conduct by troopers of the New Jersey State Police that deprives persons of rights, privileges, or immunities secured or protected by the Constitution and the laws of the United States. Defendants deny that the State Police has engaged in a pattern or practice of conduct that deprives persons of rights, privileges,or immunities secured or protected by the Constitution and laws of the United States.

The parties seek to enter into this Decree jointly for the purpose of avoiding the risks and burdens of litigation, and to support vigorous, lawful, and nondiscriminatory traffic enforcement that promotes traffic safety and assists law enforcement to interdict drugs and other contraband, arrest fugitives, and enforce firearms and other criminal statutes.

The United States and the State of New Jersey have agreed upon a proposed Consent Decree that would resolve all claims in the United States' Complaint. The proposed Decree would address the claims in the United States' Complaint by amending certain policies, practices, and procedures relating to the manner in which the State of New Jersey manages and operates the New Jersey State Police.

[T]he proposed Decree includes the following provisions:

1 *Policy Requirements*: State troopers may not rely to any degree on the race or national or ethnic origin of motorists in selecting vehicles for traffic stops and in deciding upon the scope and substance of post-stop actions, except where state troopers are on the look-out for a specific suspect who has been identified in part by his or her race or national or ethnic origin.

[2] *Traffic Stop Documentation*: State troopers engaged in patrol activities will document the race, ethnic origin, and gender of all motor vehicle drivers who are the subject of a traffic stop, and also will record information about the reason for each stop and any post-stop action that is taken (including the issuance of a ticket or warning, asking the vehicle occupants to exit the vehicle and frisking them, consensual and non-consensual vehicle searches, uses of force, and arrests).

3) *Supervisory Review of Individual Traffic Stops*: Supervisors regularly will review trooper reports concerning post-stop enforcement actions and procedures, and patrol car video tapes of traffic stops, to ensure that troopers are employing appropriate practices and procedures.

[4] *Supervisory Review of Patterns of Conduct*: The State will develop and implement an early warning system, called the "Management Awareness Program," that uses computerized information on traffic stops, misconduct investigations, and other matters to assist State Police supervisors to identify and modify potentially problematic behavior.

[5] *Misconduct Allegations*: The State Police will make complaint forms and informational materials available at a variety of locations, will institute a 24–hour toll-free telephone hotline, and will publicize the State Police toll-free number at all State-operated rest stops located on limited access highways.

[6] *Training*: The State Police will continue to implement measures to improve training for recruits and incumbent troopers. The training will address such matters as supervisory issues, communication skills, cultural diversity, and the nondiscrimination requirements of the Decree.

[7] *Auditing by the New Jersey Attorney General's Office*: The State Attorney General's Office will have special responsibility for ensuring

implementation of the Decree. The Office will conduct various audits of State Police performance, which will include contacting samples of persons who were the subject of a State Police traffic stop to evaluate whether the stops were appropriately conducted and documented.

[8] *State Police Public Reports*: The State Police will issue semiannual public reports containing aggregate statistics on certain law enforcement activities, including traffic stop statistics.

9) *Independent Monitor*: An Independent Monitor, who will be an agent of the court, will be selected by the United States and the State of New Jersey to monitor and report on the State's implementation of the Decree.

[10] *Decree Term*: The basic term of the Decree will be five years, however, based on the State's record of compliance, the United States and the Independent Monitor may agree to a request by the State to shorten the term of the Decree if the State has been in substantial compliance for at least two years.

Joint entry of this Decree is in the public interest since it provides for expeditious remedial activity and avoids the diversion of federal and State resources to adversarial actions by the parties.

[F]or the reasons discussed above, entry of the Decree is lawful and appropriate. Therefore, the United States and the State jointly move for entry of the Consent Decree.

SO ORDERED this 30th day of December 30, 1999.

MARY L. COOPER, UNITED
STATES DISTRICT JUDGE

INDEPENDENT MONITORS' SIXTEENTH REPORT, SUBMITTED TO THE UNITED STATES DISTRICT COURT FOR THE DISTRICT OF NEW JERSEY, AND THE UNITED STATES DEPARTMENT OF JUSTICE, CIVIL RIGHTS DIVISION (2007)

The New Jersey State Police appear to have reached a watershed moment during the last two reporting periods [from October 1, 2006, through March 31, 2007]. Ample evidence exists to suggest that the agency has become self-monitoring and self-correcting to a degree not often observed in American law enforcement. [C]ompliance requirements in all areas are now at 100 percent levels. Policy, training, supervision, inspections and audit [a]re fully staffed, fully functioning, and, in the opinion of the monitors, fully capable of self-monitoring and self-adaptation.

NOTE

1. Federal Oversight. Following the Independent Monitor's Sixteenth Report, Governor Corzine formally requested that federal oversight of the New Jersey State Police under the Consent Decree be ended. The request is pending. See http://www.nj.com/south/index.ssf/2007/12/nj_governor_asks_feds_to_end_o.html

SELECTED BIBLIOGRAPHY

Baker, Flying While Arab–Racial Profiling and Air Travel Security, 67 Journal of Air Law and Commerce 1375 (2002).

Gabbidon, Marzette, and Peterson, Racial Profiling and the Courts: An Empirical Analysis of Federal Litigation, 1991 to 2006, 3 Journal of Contemporary Criminal Justice 225 (2007).

Gross, The Rhetoric of Racial Profiling, in Social Consciousness in Legal Decision Making: Psychological Perspectives (R. Weiner, B. Bornstein, R. Schopp, and S. Wilborn eds. 2007).

Kadish, The Drug Courier Profile: In Planes, Trains, and Automobiles; And Now in the Jury Box, 46 American University Law Review 747 (1997).

Harcourt, Rethinking Racial Profiling: A Critique of the Economics, Civil Liberties, and Constitutional Literature, and of Criminal Profiling More Generally, 71 University of Chicago Law Review 1275 (2004).

Michelson, Driving While Black: A Skeptical Note, 44 Jurimetrics 161 (2004).

Slobogin and Schumacher, Rating the Intrusiveness of Law Enforcement Searches and Seizures, 17 Law and Human Behavior 183 (1993).

Slobogin and Schumacher, Reasonable Expectations of Privacy and Autonomy in Fourth Amendment Cases: An Empirical Look at "Understandings Recognized and Permitted by Society," 42 Duke Law Journal 727 (1993).

SECTION IV. CONTEXTS FOR DETERMINING PAST FACTS

The most frequent use of social science to provide a context for determining facts occurs when a fact is alleged to have happened in the past. This use takes place only at trial, the setting in which the legal system formally adjudicates past events. Social science has been used at trial to provide contexts for determining facts concerning defendants, victims, and witnesses.

A. DEFENDANTS

In criminal law, a number of social factors have been brought to bear upon the determination of whether the defendant committed the act in question, and, if so, committed it with the state of mind required by the statute. We here consider the effect of a defendant's culture, subculture, personality, and a variety of what might be called "life events."

1. CULTURE

The question of whether "cultural difference" is a factor that may legitimately be taken into account in reaching decisions about criminal liability and punishment is one that evokes strong opinions. In cases involving recent immigrants to the United States as defendants, anthropologists are increasingly being called as expert witnesses to provide decision makers with a cultural context for making a determination about the defendants' state of mind.

———

PEOPLE v. PODDAR

California Court of Appeal, 1972.
26 Cal.App.3d 438, 103 Cal.Rptr. 84.

■ Devine, Presiding Justice.

Appellant, who was a student at the University of California at Berkeley, killed a young woman, Tanya Tarasoff, with whom he had a romantic interest which, while temporarily and partly reciprocated, later was rejected. He called at her home, asked to speak with her. She refused to converse, and screamed. Thereupon, appellant shot her with a pellet gun, pursued her as she ran from the house, grabbed her and stabbed her many times with a kitchen knife which, with the gun, he had brought with him. He called the police, told them he had stabbed the woman, and asked that he be handcuffed. He was found guilty of second degree murder, and on his plea of not guilty by reason of insanity, he was found sane. On appeal he does not contend that the judgment on the insanity plea should be set aside.

[A]t the trial, appellant offered to present as witness an anthropologist, possessor of a Ph.D. degree in social sciences, who had lived more than twenty years in India. She had particularly studied adjustment and difficulties of Indian students who had come to American universities. Appellant offered to prove that the expert would testify to cultural stresses which would affect the adjustment of appellant in shifting from the simple culture in which he had lived (he was of the Harijan caste, the untouchables) to the sophisticated milieu of an American university. More particularly, she would testify that the cultural strain becomes acute in relationships between men and women because the normal marriage in India is arranged for the parties. Altogether, according to the offer of proof, her testimony would give evidence of diminished capacity.

The judge was of the opinion that the witness was not qualified to testify on the direct consequences to appellant of cultural stresses, but the judge did offer to allow the witness to testify to facts of cross-cultural difficulties, and to allow counsel to ask hypothetical questions of psychiatric experts, the questions to include factual data supplied by the anthropologist. Appellant's counsel declined, on the ground that he wished to use the anthropologist as an independent expert witness on the issue of diminished capacity so that the jury could draw whatever inferences it found proper from this testimony itself and not as filtered through the testimony of psychiatrists.

[W]e conclude that it was proper to exclude the testimony in the form in which it was offered. Diminished capacity is a mental infirmity. To the extent that it is to be evaluated by experts, the experts should be those qualified in the mental sciences. The effect, therefore, of such matters as cultural stress should be assessed by experts in the fields of psychiatry and psychology, and ultimately by the jury with the assistance of the testimony of such experts. We need not consider whether it would have been proper to exclude the anthropologist's testimony completely, because the court was willing, as we have said above, to allow the testimony as furnishing material for the opinions of the psychiatrists. It is desirable to give direction and control to the presentation of expert testimony of such delicate matters as the capacity of a person to deliberate or to entertain malice. To allow independent testimony on sociological, ethnic or like influences, not as reviewed by experts in psychological sciences, but as directly presented to the jury, would be to open the door to a vast amount of argument from various sources, the result of which would often be distraction of the jury and the removing of their deliberation from the essential element of the mental capacity of the accused.

———

NOTE

1. Diminished Capacity. Poddar argued that expert evidence of "cultural stresses" should have been admitted on the issue of diminished capacity. "Diminished capacity" had been explained to the jury as follows: "if you find that [Poddar's] mental capacity was diminished to the extent that you have a reasonable doubt whether he did harbor malice aforethought, you cannot find him guilty of murder of either the first or second degree." 111 Cal.Rptr. at 913 n. 3, 518 P.2d at 345 n. 3.

The California Supreme Court overturned the court of appeal's *Poddar* decision, 10 Cal.3d 750, 111 Cal.Rptr. 910, 518 P.2d 342 (1974), but not on the ground that the anthropologist's testimony was excluded. Rather, the court held that the above jury instructions had been defective because the jurors had not been "specifically told that the evidence of diminished capacity was directly applicable to the questions of whether defendant was both aware that he must act within the law, and that he acted despite such awareness." 111 Cal.Rptr. at 917, 518 P.2d at 349.

The California legislature abolished diminished capacity as a defense to crime in 1982, largely on the basis of the arguments of Professor Stephen

Morse in Diminished Capacity: A Moral and Legal Conundrum, 2 International Journal of Law and Psychiatry 271 (1979).

———

PEOPLE v. APHAYLATH

Court of Appeals of New York, 1986.
68 N.Y.2d 945, 510 N.Y.S.2d 83, 502 N.E.2d 998.

MEMORANDUM

Defendant, a Laotian refugee living in this country for approximately two years, was indicted and tried for the intentional murder of his Laotian wife of one month. At trial, defendant attempted to establish the affirmative defense of extreme emotional disturbance to mitigate the homicide (Penal Law § 125.25[1][a]) on the theory that the stresses resulting from his status of a refugee caused a significant mental trauma, affecting his mind for a substantial period of time, simmering in the unknowing subconscious and then inexplicably coming to the fore. Although the immediate cause for the defendant's loss of control was his jealousy over his wife's apparent preference for an ex-boyfriend, the defense argued that under Laotian culture the conduct of the victim wife in displaying affection for another man and receiving phone calls from an unattached man brought shame on defendant and his family sufficient to trigger defendant's loss of control.

The defense was able to present some evidence of the Laotian culture through the cross-examination of two prosecution witnesses and through the testimony of defendant himself, although he was hampered by his illiteracy in both his native tongue and English. Defendant's ability to adequately establish his defense was impermissibly curtailed by the trial court's exclusion of the proffered testimony of two expert witnesses concerning the stress and disorientation encountered by Laotian refugees in attempting to assimilate into the American culture. It appears from the record before us that the sole basis on which the court excluded the expert testimony was because "neither one * * * was going to be able to testify as to anything specifically relating to this defendant". It is unclear from this ruling whether the Trial Judge determined that she had no discretion to allow the testimony because the experts had no knowledge of this particular defendant or that she declined to exercise her discretion because of the experts' lack of knowledge of the defendant or his individual background and characteristics. Under either interpretation, however, the exclusion of this expert testimony as a matter of law was erroneous because the admissibility of expert testimony that is probative of a fact in issue does not depend on whether the witness has personal knowledge of a defendant or a defendant's particular characteristics. Whether or not such testimony is sufficiently relevant to have probative value is a determination to be made by the Trial Judge in the exercise of her sound discretion.

Accordingly, because the court's ruling was not predicated on the appropriate standard and the defendant may have been deprived of an opportunity to put before the jury information relevant to his defense, a new trial must be ordered.

DANG VANG v. VANG XIONG X. TOYED

United States Court of Appeals, Ninth Circuit, 1991.
944 F.2d 476.

■ BRUNETTI, CIRCUIT JUDGE.

Vang Xiong Toyed ("Xiong") appeals from a judgment entered after a jury verdict against him in a suit pursuant to 42 U.S.C.A. § 1983 (§ 1983). Plaintiffs, along with their spouses, brought this action against Xiong, a Washington State employee, asserting he raped them during the course of his employment.

[T]he parties in this case are Hmong refugees from Laos. Appellee Yia Moua ("Moua") moved with her family to Spokane, Washington in 1979. In 1981 she sought employment and was referred to Xiong who was employed by the Washington State Employment Security office. Xiong was responsible for interviewing and finding refugees suitable employment.

[I]n 1983 Moua contacted Xiong to assist her in learning to drive and in passing the Washington driver's license test. Moua alleged that sometime between January and March 1983 Xiong picked her up and told her he was going to take her some place where she could study for the driver's exam. The two drove to a motel where, Moua charges, Xiong raped her.

In 1983 appellee Maichao Vang ("Vang") moved with her family to the Spokane area from a refugee camp in Thailand. Vang testified she eventually contacted Xiong to assist her in obtaining employment. [O]n one occasion Xiong insisted that she accompany him to Idaho to deliver a letter to a Hmong family. Instead, Xiong drove Vang to a motel where he raped her twice.

[E]ventually each plaintiff revealed the rape to her husband and the couples filed a complaint under § 1983 against Xiong. [T]he trial resulted in a verdict in favor of the plaintiffs for $300,000. [P]rior to trial, Xiong challenged the testimony of Marshall Hurlich, an epidemiologist with the Seattle Department of Public Health. Hurlich described Hmong culture and explained the behavior of the plaintiffs in this case within that cultural context. The trial court granted Xiong's motion in limine in part and denied it in part. Hurlich was permitted to testify "generally as to the Hmong culture, but [he was precluded from testifying] as to his opinion regarding the specifics of this case, such as whether there was a rape or why these particular plaintiffs did not report the rape."

At trial, Hurlich explained that Hmong women are generally submissive, and are raised to respect and obey men. He described the role of

Hmong women in marriage; their attitudes towards sex, discussion of sex, and extramarital affairs. Most significantly, Hurlich explained that upon fleeing from Laos, Hmong refugees were reliant on government officials for their needs and would not survive in the United States without government assistance. Because of this reliance on government assistance, the Hmong have developed an awe of persons in government positions.

[T]he district court in this case did not abuse its discretion in deciding that Hurlich's testimony, which the court limited to a general explanation of Hmong culture and the role of women in that culture, was relevant. In a hearing that preceded the evidentiary ruling the court said "Hurlich is . . . the only expert that either side has located who can explain to the trier of fact who these people are, where they came from, and *why they have responded the way they have in these various functions and various relationships.*" The testimony was relevant to assist the trier of fact to understand certain behavior of the parties here that might otherwise be confusing,[3] and to explain the cause, effect and nature of long term Hmong reliance on governmental agencies for support. The testimony was prejudicial to Xiong because it supported plaintiffs assertions that he raped them. It was not, however, *unduly prejudicial* because of its limited scope and its direct relevance to the issues in the case.

[T]he judgment of the district court is AFFIRMED.

———

PEOPLE v. WU

California Court of Appeal, Fourth District, 1991.
286 Cal.Rptr. 868.*

■ TIMLIN, ACTING PRESIDING JUDGE.

[The defendant, Helen Wu, was convicted by a jury of the second degree murder of her eight year old son, Sidney. Ms. Wu was born and raised in China, where she resided. Sidney lived with his father in the United States. On a visit to California, Ms. Wu learned that her mother-in-law, who had been kind to her son, was dying of cancer. Ms. Wu was also told by Sidney that his father—Ms. Wu's estranged husband—was having an affair with another woman. Upon hearing this, Ms. Wu cut the cord off a window blind and strangled Sidney to death, and then slashed her own wrists. She was discovered several hours later by Sidney's father and revived by paramedics.]

The prosecution's theory seems to have been that defendant killed Sidney because of anger at Sidney's father, and to get revenge. The

---

3. For example, plaintiffs continued to have contact with Xiong after he raped them. Hurlich's testimony regarding the place of Hmong women in that culture was helpful in understanding plaintiffs' actions after Xiong's attacks.

* [Ed. Note: In denying review, the California Supreme Court ordered that this decision be not officially published. See Wu, 286 Cal. Rptr. at 868 n.*. California Rule of Court 977 prohibits its citation as precedent.]

defense's theory was that defendant believed that Sidney [w]as looked down upon and was ill-treated by everyone except his paternal grandmother because he had been borne out of wedlock, and that when she learned that the grandmother was dying of cancer, she felt trapped and, in an intense emotional upheaval, strangled Sidney and then attempted to kill herself so that she could take care of Sidney in the afterlife.

[D]efendant contends that the trial court erred by refusing to give an instruction which pinpointed a significant aspect of her theory of the case, i.e., an instruction which told the jury it could choose to consider the evidence of defendant's cultural background in determining the presence or absence of the various mental states which were elements of the crimes with which she was charged.

[D]efendant requested the following instruction:

"You have received evidence of defendant's cultural background and the relationship of her culture to her mental state. You may, but are not required to, consider that the [sic] evidence in determining the presence or absence of the essential mental states of the crimes defined in these instructions, or in determining any other issue in this case."

At trial, the prosecutor objected to this instruction. ["]I just think we are making law that we simply are not in a position to make. There is no guidance in the appellate courts as far as I know on the issue of cultural jury instructions or cultural defense."

[U]ltimately, the court refused to give the instruction, commenting that it did not want to put the "stamp of approval on [defendant's] actions in the United States, which would have been acceptable in China."

The experts on transcultural psychology specifically testified that, in their opinion, defendant was acting while in an emotional crisis during the time that she obtained the knife and cord, strangled Sidney and then slashed her own wrist, and that her emotional state was intertwined with, and explainable by reference to, her cultural background. Specifically, the following testimony was given:

Dr. Chien testified:

["]In my expertise [in] transcultural psychiatry, in my familiarity [w]ith the Chinese culture, [a]nd from the information [I] obtain from Helen, she thought she was doing that out from the mother's love, mother's responsibility to bring a child together with her when she realized that there was no hope for her or a way for her to survive in this country or in this earth.

"Q Well, are you telling us that the death of Sidney was her act of love?

"A Yes. It's a mother's altruism. This may be very difficult for the Westerner to understand because I have dealt with many other so-called children who are sent to me from the children bureau. Children can be easily taken away from the mother in our agencies' mind. Social worker, when they discovered child abuse case or whatever case, children can be easily taken away from the parents.

"But in the Asian culture when the mother commits suicide and leave the children alone, usually they'll be considered to be a totally irresponsible behavior, and the mother will usually worry what would happen if she died, 'Who is going to take care of the children?'" [B]ecause the requested instruction was, for the most part, a correct statement of the law,[6] and because it was applicable to the evidence and one of defendant's [b]asic defenses in this case, upon retrial defendant is entitled to have the jury instructed that it may consider evidence of defendant's cultural background in determining the existence or nonexistence of the relevant mental states.

Because we have already decided that the judgment must be reversed [on other grounds] and because we only considered defendant's assertion that it was error not to give the cultural background instruction for purposes of guiding the trial court on retrial, we need not consider whether defendant was prejudiced by the failure to give the cultural background instruction.

STATE v. KARGAR

Supreme Judicial Court of Maine, 1996.
679 A.2d 81.

■ DANA, JUSTICE.

Mohammad Kargar, an Afghani refugee, appeals from the judgments entered in the Superior Court convicting him of two counts of gross sexual assault. Kargar contends on appeal that the court erred in denying his motion to dismiss pursuant to the de minimis statute, 17–A M.R.S.A. § 12 (1983).

[O]n June 25, 1993, Kargar and his family, refugees since approximately 1990, were babysitting a young neighbor. While the neighbor was there, she witnessed Kargar kissing his eighteen-month-old son's penis. When she was picked up by her mother, the girl told her mother what she had seen. The mother had previously seen a picture of Kargar kissing his son's penis in the Kargar family photo album. After her daughter told her what she had seen, the mother notified the police.

Peter Wentworth, a sergeant with the Portland Police Department, went to Kargar's apartment to execute a search warrant. [T]he picture of Kargar kissing his son's penis was found in the photograph album. Kargar admitted that it was him in the photograph and that he was kissing his

---

6. The jury should not be instructed that the evidence of defendant's cultural background may be considered in connection with "any issue" in the case as stated in the last portion of the subject instruction; evidence may only be considered if it is relevant, and the evidence of defendant's cultural background was not necessarily relevant to "any issue" in the case. However, upon retrial, the trial court should correct such defects and give the requested instruction as so corrected.

son's penis. Kargar told Wentworth that kissing a young son's penis is accepted as common practice in his culture. Kargar also said it was very possible that his neighbor had seen him kissing his son's penis. Kargar was arrested and taken to the police station.

Prior to the jury-waived trial Kargar moved for a dismissal of the case pursuant to the de minimis statute. With the consent of the parties, the court held the trial phase of the proceedings first, followed by a hearing on the de minimis motion. The de minimis hearing consisted of testimony from many Afghani people who were familiar with the Afghani practice and custom of kissing a young son on all parts of his body.[2] Kargar's witnesses, all relatively recent emigrants from Afghanistan, testified that kissing a son's penis is common in Afghanistan, that it is done to show love for the child, and that it is the same whether the penis is kissed or entirely put into the mouth because there are no sexual feelings involved.[3] The witnesses also testified that pursuant to Islamic law any sexual activity between an adult and a child results in the death penalty for the adult. Kargar also submitted statements from Professor Ludwig Adamec of the University of Arizona's Center for Near Eastern Studies and Saifur Halimi, a religious teacher and Director of the Afghan Mujahideen Information Bureau in New York. Both statements support the testimony of the live witnesses. The State did not present any witnesses during the de minimis hearing. Following the presentation of witnesses the court denied Kargar's motion and found him guilty of two counts of gross sexual assault.

Maine's de minimis statute [Section 12(1)] provides, in pertinent part:

1.   The court may dismiss a prosecution if, ... having regard to the nature of the conduct alleged and the nature of the attendant circumstances, it finds the defendant's conduct:

> A.   Was within a customary license or tolerance, which was not expressly refused by the person whose interest was infringed and which is not inconsistent with the purpose of the law defining the crime; or
>
> B.   Did not actually cause or threaten the harm sought to be prevented by the law defining the crime or did so only to an extent too trivial to warrant the condemnation of conviction; or
>
> C.   Presents such other extenuations that it cannot reasonably be regarded as envisaged by the Legislature in defining the crime.

[O]ur review of the record in the instant case reveals that the court, in its analysis of section 12(1)(C), denied Kargar's motion without considering the full range of relevant factors. The court's interpretation of the subsection, which focused on whether the conduct met the definition of the gross

---

2. Kargar testified during the de minimis hearing that the practice was acceptable until the child was three, four, or five years old.

3. Kargar testified during the de minimis hearing that his culture views the penis of a child as not the holiest or cleanest part of the body because it is from where the child urinates. Kargar testified that kissing his son there shows how much he loves his child precisely because it is not the holiest or cleanest part of the body.

sexual assault statute, operated to nullify the effect of the de minimis analysis called for by the statute. The focus is not on whether the conduct falls within the reach of the statute criminalizing it. If it did not, there would be no need to perform a de minimis analysis. The focus is on whether the admittedly criminal conduct was envisioned by the Legislature when it defined the crime. If the Legislature did not intend that there be an individual, case-specific analysis then there would be no point to the de minimis statute. Subsection 1(C) provides a safety valve for circumstances that could not have been envisioned by the Legislature. It is meant to be applied on a case-by-case basis to unanticipated "extenuations," when application of the criminal code would lead to an "ordered but intolerable" result.

[A]ll of the evidence presented at the de minimis hearing supports the conclusion that there was nothing "sexual" about Kargar's conduct. There is no real dispute that what Kargar did is accepted practice in his culture. The testimony of every witness at the de minimis hearing confirmed that kissing a young son on every part of his body is considered a sign only of love and affection for the child. This is true whether the parent kisses, or as the trial court found, "engulfs" a son's penis. There is nothing sexual about this practice. In fact, the trial justice expressly recognized that if the State were required to prove a purpose of sexual gratification it "wouldn't have been able to have done so."

During its sentencing of Kargar, the court stated: "There is no sexual gratification. There is no victim impact." The court additionally recognized that the conduct for which Kargar was convicted occurred in the open, with his wife present, and noted that the photograph was displayed in the family photo album, available for all to see.[4] The court concluded its sentencing by recognizing that this case is "not at all typical [but instead is] fully the exception.... The conduct was unequivocally criminal, but the circumstances of that conduct and the circumstances of this defendant call for leniency." Although the court responded to this call for leniency by imposing an entirely suspended sentence, the two convictions expose Kargar to severe consequences independent of any period of incarceration, including his required registration as a sex offender [a]nd the possibility of deportation. [T]hese additional consequences emphasize why the factors recognized by the court during the sentencing hearing were also relevant to the de minimis analysis.

Although it may be difficult for us as a society to separate Kargar's conduct from our notions of sexual abuse, that difficulty should not result in a felony conviction in this case. The State concedes that dismissing this case pursuant to the de minimis statute would pose little harm to the community.

[I]n virtually every case the assumption that a physical touching of the mouth of an adult with the genitals of a child under the age of fourteen is

4. Kargar's wife, Shamayel, testified during the sentencing hearing that she took the picture to send to Kargar's mother to show her how much he loved his son.

inherently harmful is correct. This case, however, is the exception that proves the rule. Precisely because the Legislature did not envision the extenuating circumstances present in this case, to avoid an injustice the de minimis analysis set forth in section 12(1)(C) requires that Kargar's convictions be vacated.

———

NOTES

1. Man Bites Dog. Haldane, Culture Clash or Animal Cruelty?, Los Angeles Times, March 13, 1989, Part 2, p. 1, reports the case of two Cambodian refugees who lived in Long Beach, California. A co-worker had given the men a German Shepherd puppy as a pet. Once in their apartment, however, the refugees slashed the dog's throat and began skinning it. Neighbors who heard the dog's yelps called the police, and the two men were arrested for cruelty to animals, an offense that carries a penalty of up to a year in jail.

> The defense [claimed] that the dog was killed humanely in a manner consistent with contemporary slaughterhouse practices, and that the two recent immigrants were following their own national customs with no idea they were offending American sensibilities.

The trial judge ruled that killing a dog for food is not illegal unless done in a cruel way, and that cruelty had not been proven. Accordingly, all charges in the case were dismissed. In the wake of this decision, the Los Angeles Society for the Prevention of Cruelty to Animals began an educational campaign to teach immigrants that American culture does not condone the consumption of domestic pets. The Society began to distribute recipes which substituted other ingredients for dog and cat meat. McMillan, Pets Are Not Food in U.S., SPCA Will Advise Immigrants, Los Angeles Times, March 28, 1989, Part 2, p. 3.

2. Female Genital Mutilation. A Gambian immigrant to Paris was convicted of child mutilation and sentenced to one year in jail for arranging the clitorectomy of her two infants. The practice of "female circumcision" is prevalent in more than 20 nations. "French doctors and social workers described with horror how midwives perform the ritual without anesthetic. Infections and complications that hinder intercourse and childbirth often follow." Simons, Crime or Custom? French Court Jails Mother For Girls' Ritual Mutilation, New York Times, January 17, 1993, p. E–2. One French anthropologist, however, denounced the verdict. "People practice it because they say the mutilation makes a girl more beautiful and cleaner. Girls who are not cut have trouble finding a husband. Parents are under heavy social pressure to do it. They mean no harm to their children. To make this a crime is excessive." Id.

In Mohammed v. Gonzales, 400 F.3d 785 (9th Cir. 2005), a case concerning a Somalian woman's application for asylum, the Ninth Circuit held that "the extremely painful, physically invasive, psychologically damaging and permanently disfiguring process of genital mutilation undoubtedly rises to the level of persecution." Id. at 796. The court "reject[ed] the government's suggestion that female genital mutilation cannot be a basis for a claim of past persecution because it is 'widely-accepted and widely-practiced.' " Id.

3.   Assimilation or Coercion? In England, a Yoruban immigrant was convicted of child abuse for scarring her child's face with a razor. She argued that she was initiating her child into her ethnic group, and that it would have been abusive *not* to have practiced this ritual. The British trial judge refused to recognize a cultural defense, but discharged the mother upon conviction. DeBenedictis, Judges Debate Cultural Defense, American Bar Association Journal, December 1992, p. 28. Professor Alison Dunes Renteln criticized this decision at a meeting of the U.S. National Association of Women Judges.

> A pluralistic society like the United States is "only pretending to accept cultural diversity if it rejects it when it really matters," she said. [R]enteln questioned that judge's assumption that the mother and other Yorubans must assimilate into English society. Requiring or expecting assimilation of minorities into the dominant culture is "potentially coercive," she said. Accommodation of other world views would be better, Renteln argued. Id.

> Others at the conference argued that any cultural defense for immigrants be time-limited, perhaps to be available only during the defendant's first ten years in the new country. It was also argued by a Native American judge that if any cultural defense became available to modern immigrants to the U.S., it should also be made available to Native American ethnic groups. Id. at 29. See Special Issue: The Unique Challenges of Cross–Cultural Justice, 92 Judicature 190 (2009).

2.   SUBCULTURE

Not only foreign cultures, but subcultures within the United States have been argued to influence a criminal defendant's state of mind. The "subculture of poverty" has been the prototypic illustration of this form of social influence.

———

UNITED STATES v. ALEXANDER AND MURDOCK

United States Court of Appeals, District of Columbia Circuit, 1972.
471 F.2d 923.

■ Bazelon, Chief Judge, dissenting.

[Alexander and Murdock, both African–American males, were at a hamburger restaurant when a group of five white male Marine lieutenants and a woman friend of one of the Marines entered and sat at the counter. The two groups exchanged stares. Alexander verbally challenged the Marines, one of whom responded with a racial epithet. Alexander and Murdock then drew guns and began shooting. Two Marines were killed and one other Marine and the woman were wounded. Murdock raised the insanity defense, but was convicted of second-degree murder. Alexander was found guilty of assault with a dangerous weapon.

Numerous issues were raised on appeal, including the claim by Murdock that the instructions given by the trial judge unfairly prejudiced his insanity claim. The instructions included the statement:

> We are not concerned with a question of whether or not a man had a rotten social background. We are concerned with the question of his criminal responsibility. That is to say, whether he had an abnormal condition of the mind that affected his emotional and behavioral processes at the time of the offense.

The majority of the court of appeals did not find this instruction to constitute reversible error.]

The thrust of Murdock's defense was that the environment in which he was raised—his "rotten social background"—conditioned him to respond to certain stimuli in a manner most of us would consider flagrantly inappropriate. Because of his early conditioning, he argued, he was denied any meaningful choice when the racial insult triggered the explosion in the restaurant. He asked the jury to conclude that his "rotten social background," and the resulting impairment of mental or emotional processes and behavior controls, ruled his violent reaction in the same manner that the behavior of a paranoid schizophrenic may be ruled by his "mental condition." Whether this impairment amounted to an "abnormal condition of the mind" is, in my opinion, at best an academic question. But the consequences we predicate on the answer may be very meaningful indeed.

We have never said that an exculpatory mental illness must be reflected in some organic or pathological condition. Nor have we enshrined psychosis as a prerequisite of the defense. But our experience has made it clear that the terms we use—"mental disease or defect" and "abnormal condition of the mind"—carry a distinct flavor of pathology. And they deflect attention from the crucial, functional question—did the defendant lack the ability to make any meaningful choice of action—to an artificial and misleading excursion into the thicket of psychiatric diagnosis and nomenclature.

It does not necessarily follow, however, that we should push the responsibility defense to its logical limits and abandon all of the trappings of the medical or disease model. However illogical and disingenuous, that model arguably serves important interests. Primarily, by offering a rationale for detention of persons who are found not guilty by reason of "insanity," it offers us shelter from a downpour of troublesome questions. If we were to facilitate Murdock's defense, as logic and morality would seem to command, so that a jury might acquit him because of his "rotten social background" rather than any treatable mental illness, the community would have to decide what to do with him.

We are left [w]ith an obligation to choose among four unattractive alternatives:

A.   We can impose narrow and admittedly illogical limitations on the responsibility defense to insure that a defendant like Murdock will not be acquitted on the theory that he lacked responsibility. By confining such a defendant in a penitentiary, we can avoid the difficult questions presented by the effort to hold him in confinement following a successful use of the responsibility defense.

B.   If we remove the practical impediments to Murdock's defense and he is, in fact, acquitted for lack of responsibility, he could be released from custody in spite of his apparent dangerousness. That result would conform with the principle that civil commitment is ordinarily barred where a defendant is dangerous but not mentally ill. And there are even precedents for the acquittal and release of dangerous defendants who have been brought to trial on a criminal charge. The fourth amendment exclusionary rule, for example, effectively precludes conviction of some defendants who appear to be dangerous. But that rule has been subjected to heavy assault even though it serves important, extrinsic interests—the redress and deterrence of unconstitutional action and the preservation of judicial integrity. Acquitting a defendant like Murdock and returning him to the street might also protect our integrity. But it would probably be more difficult to obtain public support for, or even unfriendly acquiescence in, Murdock's release than to defend the operation of the exclusionary rule. It could be said, after all, that acquittal would result not in spite of Murdock's dangerousness, but precisely because of it. Thus, while there may be no reason in logic why Murdock could not be returned to the street, as a practical matter that is probably an unfeasible result.

C.   If the community will not tolerate Murdock's release we can strive to find a vaguely therapeutic purpose for hospitalization. Skinnerian-like techniques may be available to re-program his behavior. We might conclude that they should be used and that their use justifies his confinement. But that will require us to stretch the medical model substantially so that new techniques can be applied to many persons not conventionally considered "sick."

[D.]   Finally, if there are no known or foreseeable techniques for "curing" someone like Murdock (or if we are unwilling to utilize the techniques that may be available), and if the incapacitation of the defendant is a practical imperative, we will have to confine him in exclusive reliance on a prediction of dangerousness. That confinement would be nothing more or less than unadorned preventive detention.

The options that would permit us to acquit Murdock but hold him in custody nonetheless—preventive detention and a stretching of the medical model to permit the use of new techniques—raise profound moral and legal questions. Resolution of those questions would require a prolonged and thorough public debate. But however they are resolved, it is at least clear that each of these options requires an expansion of the boundaries of the civil commitment doctrine. We could strive to limit the expansion by applying the new rationale only to persons who have undergone a criminal trial and been acquitted for lack of responsibility. But as a practical matter it seems very unlikely that the expansion could be so confined. The new rationale would permit—perhaps demand—that all persons who are rendered dangerous by a "rotten social background" should be preventively detained. Or that all persons who exhibit antisocial behavior patterns should have their behavior re-conditioned. We cannot escape the probability, if not absolute certainty, that every effort to diminish the class of persons who can be found criminally responsible will produce a concomitant expansion in the class of persons who can be subjected to involuntary civil commitment. The implications in this context are staggering. The price of permitting Murdock to claim the benefit of a logical aspect of the responsibility doctrine may be the unleashing of a detention device that operates, by hypothesis, at the exclusive expense of the lowest social and economic class.

That result can certainly be avoided—even if we are unwilling to return the defendant to the street—by reading the responsibility doctrine so narrowly that the issue of post-acquittal custody rarely arises. We could, for example, redefine the concept of responsibility so that it would approximate the concept of self-defense. All civil and criminal sanctions on the nonresponsible defendant would be barred, and the test would be reformulated to ask explicitly, which defendants should escape all state-imposed sanctions. Alternatively, we could retain the medical model and acknowledge its illogic as a significant virtue. Psychosis may be an irrational test of criminal responsibility, but it does have a recognizable symptomatology. In the civil commitment context it may provide the only manageable stopping point short of a fullfledged scheme of preventive detention. These limitations on the responsibility defense permit an avoidance—perhaps to the good—of a confrontation with the difficult questions posed by preventive detention and the various forms of behavior control.

On the other hand, we sacrifice a great deal by discouraging Murdock's responsibility defense. If we could remove the practical impediments to the free flow of information we might begin to learn something about the causes of crime. We might discover, for example, that there is a significant causal relationship between violent criminal behavior and a "rotten social background."[122] That realization would require us to consider, for example, whether income redistribution and social reconstruction are indispensable first steps toward solving the problem of violent crime.

---

122. We already know, of course, that there is an enormous *coincidental* relationship between violent street crime and "rotten social backgrounds." And the data plainly suggests that there is a strong *causal* relationship as well. See, e.g., Staff Report to the Nat'l Comm. on the Causes and Prevention of Violence, Vol. 12, Chapter 11: Sociological and Cultural Explanations (1969).

THE TWILIGHT OF WELFARE CRIMINOLOGY

Stephen J. Morse.
49 Southern California Law Review 1247 (1976).

It is helpful to begin this analysis by noting that the probable source of Judge Bazelon's views is "liberal" social science orthodoxy. With the ascent of the social sciences to a position of intellectual respect, it was assumed generally that behavior was "caused" and that the causes of and the cures of crime would be discovered. Sociological thinkers saw the causes of crime in the social order; psychological and psychiatric thinkers saw the causes of crime in the personality disturbances of the criminal—which were usually hypothesized to have been produced by disordered family life. Sick societies and sick individuals were the causes of crime. The traditional criminal justice system was characterized as a band-aid and an ineffective "home remedy." The new scientific approach, however, would cure the underlying causes of crime (e.g., poverty, crowding, slum life, racism, mental illness, broken families) rather than concentrating on the symptom: criminal behavior. [A]s a follower of the liberal social science tradition, Judge Bazelon similarly believes that poverty causes crime and poverty must therefore be eliminated in order to prevent crime.

But does poverty cause crime? It is certainly true that there is a very strong correlation between low socioeconomic status and the sort of violent street crime that worries urban America so much. Further, we must agree with Judge Bazelon that persons of low socioeconomic status probably find it easier than others to turn to violent street crime for money, excitement, or release. Yet it is also true that the majority of poor people are not violent criminals. Judge Bazelon is simply wrong in his belief that poverty "causes" crime. Poverty is neither a sufficient nor a necessary cause of crime. Poverty may make the choice to obey the law more difficult, but the majority choose to obey the law.

Will eradicating poverty eradicate crime? Improvement in the economic conditions of poor persons does not reduce the level of violent crime. Rather, the opposite occurs—there is a rise in crime that accompanies most periods of rising wealth. The "poverty cure" does not work.

———

THE MORALITY OF THE CRIMINAL LAW: A REJOINDER TO PROFESSOR MORSE

David L. Bazelon.
49 Southern California Law Review 1269 (1976).

The crux of his disagreement seems to come in his answer to the question, "Does poverty cause crime?" Professor Morse correctly notes, as I did, that "a rise in crime ... accompanies most periods of rising wealth." From this he concludes that "the 'poverty cure' does not work." But the Professor offers no evidence—and I know of none—suggesting that the increase in crime in periods of economic growth is produced by persons who are no longer poor suddenly turning violent. Rather, it is persons *who remain poor*—who essentially do *not* benefit from the economic growth—who become more violent. The data Professor Morse cites is simply evidence of what de Tocqueville observed long ago, and of what social psychologists have gone to great lengths to explain: violence is born of hope—of rising expectations—not despair. Thus, Professor Morse is simply wrong. For all practical purposes, poverty *is* a necessary cause of violent street crime.

MALIGN NEGLECT—RACE, CRIME, AND PUNISHMENT IN AMERICA (1995)*

Michael Tonry.

The practical objections [to Judge Bazelon's proposal in *Alexander and Murdock*] involve the mechanics of a social adversity defense. Would it apply to all offenses committed by an offender to which it applies? That seems doubly wrong because it would eliminate all incentives to be law-abiding and, as Stephen Morse argues, public safety concerns would inevitably lead to a system of preventive detention to protect the rest of us from offenders who cannot be held legally accountable for crimes.

[T]he overriding objection to a social adversity defense is that there are no groups for which the base expectancy rate for first offenses is 100 percent. No matter how conducive to criminality the circumstances are, there always are people who live law-abiding lives. The reason may be remarkable strength of character, religious convictions, nurturing parents, a friend or coach or employer who provides a positive role model, or sheer good luck. Whatever the reason, the general interests in public safety and in encouraging the development of law-abiding people argue powerfully against a social adversity defense.

The analogy between insanity and social adversity is only partial. In the paradigm case to which the insanity defense applies, there is little question that the defendant is not morally responsible. If we accept that the knife-wielding killer believed that he was slicing bread, [f]ew would argue that he was morally responsible for his actions. He may be dangerous, and we may want to take steps to assess that danger and to prevent future dangerous acts, but he is not responsible.

[T]here are no paradigm cases in which most people agree that a particular disadvantaged offender could not have done otherwise. And if we believe that there are individuals who in specific circumstances may or may not commit an offense, the idea of removing all threat of consequences for making the wrong choice is perverse. As James Fitzjames Stephen, the leading Nineteenth Century scholar of the English criminal law, observed, "it is at the moment when temptation is strongest that the law should speak most clearly and emphatically to the contrary." Put provocatively, a social adversity defense would authorize one or more "free crimes," a policy that public opinion would not tolerate.

————

NOTE

1. Abolition of the Volitional Prong. The test of insanity used in Murdock's trial was that found in the Model Penal Code of the American Law Institute, Section 4.01 (1962):

> A person is not responsible for criminal conduct if at the time of such conduct as a result of mental disease or defect he lacks substantial capacity either to appreciate the criminality [wrongfulness] of his conduct or to conform his conduct to the requirements of the law.

Judge Bazelon stated in *Alexander and Murdock* that "the crucial functional question" in insanity cases is "did the defendant lack the ability to make any meaningful choice of action?," i.e., could he "conform his conduct to the requirements of law?" This is frequently referred to as the "irresistible impulse" or "volitional" prong of the Model Penal Code test.

In the wake of the public outcry over the verdict of not guilty by reason of insanity in the case of John W. Hinckley, Jr., for the attempted assassination of President Ronald Reagan, the American Psychiatric Association issued a Statement on the Insanity Defense, 140 American Journal of Psychiatry 681 (1983). The statement noted that "[s]anity is, of course, a legal issue not a medical one." Id. at 683. It went on to observe, id. at 685, that psychiatry did not have much to offer regarding the assessment of "volition":

> The line between an irresistible impulse and an impulse not resisted is probably no sharper than that between twilight and dusk. Psychiatry is a deterministic discipline that views all human behavior as, to a good extent, "caused." The concept of volition is the subject of some disagreement among psychiatrists. Many psychiatrists therefore believe that psychiatric testimony (particularly that of a conclusory nature) about volition is more likely to produce confusion for jurors than is psychiatric testimony relevant to a defendant's appreciation or understanding [of the wrongfulness of his or her conduct].

The Association then endorsed a proposal by Professor Richard Bonnie for a test of insanity that eliminated the volitional prong of the Model Penal Code. See Bonnie, The Moral Basis of the Insanity Defense, 69 American Bar Association Journal 194 (1983). The American Bar Association also endorsed this test as its official position on the insanity defense. Standing Committee on Association Standards for Criminal Justice, Criminal Justice Mental Health Standards (1984).

In 1984, the "Insanity Defense Reform Act" eliminated the volitional prong of the insanity defense in federal courts. The new federal test (18 U.S.C. § 17) reads:

It is an affirmative defense to a prosecution under any Federal statute that, at the time of the commission of the acts constituting the offense, the defendant, as a result of a severe mental disease or defect, was unable to appreciate the nature and quality or the wrongfulness of his acts. Mental disease or defect does not otherwise constitute a defense.

The act placed the burden of proving insanity on the defendant, by clear and convincing evidence.

3. PERSONALITY

Evidence of an individual's "personality" or "character" is sometimes offered to demonstrate that he or she acted in conformity with established patterns of behavior in the criminal incident at issue. The prosecution attempts to introduce evidence of the defendant's crime-prone personality, and the defense attempts to introduce evidence of the defendant's non-aggressive nature.

———

NEW JERSEY v. CAVALLO

Supreme Court of New Jersey, 1982.
88 N.J. 508, 443 A.2d 1020.

■ PASHMAN, J.

Defendants Michael Cavallo and David Murro were indicted by the Hunterdon County grand jury for abduction, sodomy, private lewdness, and rape. The indictments arose out of an incident on June 16, 1977 involving defendants and S.T., the alleged victim, a married woman who was two months pregnant. S.T. states that she was abducted from a Hunterdon bar and raped by defendants who in turn assert that she willingly accompanied them from the bar to engage in consensual sexual activity. Since there were no witnesses, the trial necessarily focused on the credibility of the conflicting descriptions of those events.

At trial, defendant Cavallo sought to offer the expert testimony of Dr. Kuris, a psychiatrist from the Hunterdon Medical Center. This witness was offered as an expert character witness who would testify that Cavallo does not have the psychological traits of a rapist. The offer of proof, as it appears in the transcript, is as follows:

MR. SKOWRONEK: Your Honor, he is going to testify as to Mr. Cavallo's character which is that he knows right from wrong, that he is a well-meaning individual, he would not wilfully do a wrong, he recognizes the force and violence of rape are wrongful acts, he is a non-violent, non-aggressive person and he will also testify to the fact [that] the characteristics exhibited by rapists in his experience as a psychiatrist are these people are aggressive, violent people and that Mr. Cavallo does not fit within this mold.

The trial judge refused to allow the expert testimony. The sole issue on this appeal is the correctness of that ruling under Evidence Rules 47 and 56.

[D]r. Kuris' testimony is offered as expert opinion evidence of Cavallo's character under Rule 47, which provides:

> Subject to Rules 48 and 55, a trait of character offered for the purpose of drawing inferences as to the conduct of a person on a specified occasion may be proved only by: (a) testimony in the form of opinion, (b) evidence of reputation, or (c) evidence of conviction of a crime which tends to prove the trait. Specific instances of conduct not the subject of a conviction of a crime shall be inadmissible. In a criminal proceeding, evidence offered by the prosecution of a trait of character of the defendant on trial may be admitted only if the judge has admitted evidence of good character offered by the defendant. Character evidence offered by the defendant may not be excluded under Rule 4. The credibility of a character witness testifying on behalf of the defendant may not be impaired by an inquiry into his knowledge of the defendant's alleged criminal conduct not evidenced by a conviction.

This rule, adopted in 1967, amended the prior New Jersey practice by allowing a trait of character to be proved by opinion as well as reputation evidence. This amendment permits both lay and expert opinions. The rule does not exclude expert opinions and the comment explicitly includes them. However, while allowing expert character evidence, Rule 47 clearly contemplates that such testimony must qualify as proper expert evidence:

> This type of evidence is now admissible provided that a proper foundation is laid for the expert's testimony. If the court feels that a witness does not have sufficient expertise to give expert testimony as to character or that the opinion offered does not satisfy the requirements of Rule 56(2), the opinion evidence may be excluded. [State Rules of Court Review Commission, New Jersey Rules of Evidence, Rule 47, comment 4]

[T]he State argues that the proffered evidence is irrelevant, since regardless of whether Cavallo has the characteristics of a "rapist," he may indeed have committed rape on this particular occasion. However, this is not the standard for relevance under our rules. The State's argument would render virtually all character testimony, lay or expert, irrelevant and inadmissible. That argument addresses the weight to be accorded the testimony rather than its relevance.

Rule 1(2) defines relevant evidence as "evidence having any tendency in reason to prove any material fact." New Jersey case law both before and after the promulgation of the rule defines the test to be whether the evidence "renders the desired inference more probable than it would be without the evidence." State v. Deatore, 70 N.J. 100, 116, 358 A.2d 163

(1976). The inquiry is whether knowledge that Cavallo does not possess the traits commonly found in "rapists" increases the likelihood that Cavallo did not commit a rape on the occasion in question. For purposes of determining relevance, we treat the proffered testimony as reliable. Obviously, inaccurate testimony, lay or expert, has no tendency to prove any material fact.

Viewed from that standpoint, the testimony is clearly relevant for the same reason that all character testimony is relevant: favorable evidence of the defendant's character has some tendency to create doubts as to whether the defendant committed the offense charged. Rule 47 assumes the relevance of character evidence "offered for the purpose of drawing inferences as to the conduct of a person on a specified occasion." [T]hat is precisely the inference for which Dr. Kuris' testimony is proffered: the fact that Cavallo has the character of a non-rapist is used to draw an inference that he did not commit rape on this occasion. Assuming the reliability of Dr. Kuris' conclusions, his testimony makes it more likely than otherwise that Cavallo did not rape S.T. Consequently, the proffered evidence is relevant.

Having concluded that the testimony offered is relevant and that expert character testimony is generally permitted under Rule 47, we now determine whether Dr. Kuris' expert testimony satisfies the special limitations placed on expert evidence by Rule 56(2) and by New Jersey case law. Rule 56(2) provides:

> If the witness is testifying as an expert, testimony of the witness in the form of opinions or inferences is limited to such opinions as the judge finds are (a) based primarily on facts, data or other expert opinion established by evidence at the trial and (b) within the scope of the special knowledge, skill, experience or training possessed by the witness.

Under Rule 56(2)(b), expert testimony is admissible only if the expert has sufficient expertise to offer the intended testimony and the testimony itself is sufficiently reliable. No question has been raised as to the general qualification of Dr. Kuris as a psychiatrist. The relevant inquiry therefore is whether the testimony satisfies New Jersey's "standard of acceptability for scientific evidence." State v. Hurd, 86 N.J. 525, 536, 432 A.2d 86 (1981).

Scientific evidence is admissible if the proposed technique or mode of analysis has "sufficient scientific basis to produce uniform and *reasonably reliable* results and will contribute materially to the ascertainment of the truth." State v. Cary, 49 N.J. 343, 352, 230 A.2d 384 (1967), quoted in *Hurd,* 86 N.J. at 536, 432 A.2d 86 (emphasis added). See Frye v. United States, 293 F. 1013 (D.C.Cir.1923) (generally viewed as the seminal case on scientific evidence).

Applying this test to the testimony offered here, the issue becomes whether there exists a "special knowledge, skill, experience or training" by which any expert can determine, with reasonable reliability, whether an individual has a mental makeup rendering him unlikely to have committed rape on a specific occasion.

[I]n this case the psychiatrist sought to testify that Cavallo did not have the characteristics common to all or most rapists. Two assumptions underlie this testimony: (1) there exist particular mental characteristics peculiar to rapists, and (2) psychiatrists, by examining an individual, can determine whether or not he possesses those characteristics. The policy that scientific evidence be reasonably accurate requires us to apply the standards for admission of scientific evidence to Dr. Kuris' testimony. Defendants must therefore demonstrate that these two assumptions satisfy the Rule 56 standard of reliability.

Defendants argue that considerations of reliability should determine the weight accorded to scientific testimony, not its admissibility. Such evidence should be placed before the jury, which can evaluate the evidence as it deems proper, as it traditionally evaluates all evidence before it. However, this Court has previously pointed to substantial countervailing considerations that mandate that there be some assurance of reliability before scientific evidence is admitted.

In *Hurd,* we alluded to the problems of "prejudice, jury confusion, and consumption of time and trial resources." Id. 86 N.J. at 536, 432 A.2d 86. The danger of prejudice through introduction of unreliable expert evidence is clear. While juries would not always accord excessive weight to unreliable expert testimony, there is substantial danger that they would do so, precisely because the evidence is labeled "scientific" and "expert."

Further, if defendants are permitted to introduce psychiatric testimony on their character, "the State will not stand idly by without producing psychiatrists favorable to its cause." State v. Sinnott, 24 N.J. 408, 429, 132 A.2d 298 (1957). The result must necessarily be a "battle of experts" concerning the validity of the expert evidence. This would consume substantial court time and cost both parties much time and expense. Much of the trial would focus on the tangential issue of the reliability of the expert evidence rather than the central issue of what the defendants did or did not do.

The inevitability of a "battle of the experts" in this type of case is clear. In so subjective a field as psychiatry, the experts are bound to differ. The parties will spend untold time and money locating experts and preparing to cross-examine opposing experts. Court time will then be spent presenting the experts. With so much attention paid to the expert testimony, it is likely that the attention of the jury will be similarly diverted. As a result, there is the danger that the trial will turn not on the facts of the case, not on whether the defendant committed the crime of rape, but rather on whether the defendant manifests the characteristics of a "rapist."

[W]here expert testimony is sufficiently reliable to be of assistance to the jury, it should be admitted despite the dangers discussed above. It will then be for the opposing party to discredit the evidence and for the jury ultimately to determine its proper weight. Scientific testimony can be quite useful at trial. However, expert testimony is admissible only if it meets the threshold of reliability required by Rule 56.

[U]nder *Hurd,* scientific evidence is admissible if it possesses a "sufficient scientific basis to produce uniform and reasonably reliable results and will contribute materially to the ascertainment of the truth." 86 N.J. at 536, 432 A.2d 86, quoting *Cary,* 49 N.J. at 352, 230 A.2d 384.

What constitutes reasonable reliability depends in part on the context of the proceedings involved. The policy underlying Rule 56 is to exclude expert evidence when the danger it poses of prejudice, confusion and diversion of attention exceeds its helpfulness to the factfinder because the expertise is not sufficiently reliable. In part, the Rule entails a weighing of reliability against prejudice in light of the context in which the evidence is offered. Expert evidence that poses too great a danger of prejudice in some situations, and for some purposes, may be admissible in other circumstances where it will be more helpful and less prejudicial.

The *Hurd* formulation differs somewhat from the traditional standard set forth in *Frye,* supra, where the D.C. Circuit Court held:

> Just when a scientific principle or discovery crosses the line between the experimental and demonstrable stages is difficult to define. Somewhere in this twilight zone the evidential force of the principle must be recognized, and while courts will go a long way in admitting expert testimony deduced from a well-recognized scientific principle or discovery, *the thing from which the deduction is made must be sufficiently established to have gained general acceptance in the particular field in which it belongs.* [Id. at 1014 (emphasis supplied)]

The *Frye* test recognizes that most judges are experts in few, if any, fields of scientific endeavor. Judges are not well suited to determine the inherent reliability of expert evidence, but they can decide whether the proffered evidence has gained "general acceptance" in the scientific community. The proponent of expert evidence can therefore meet his burden by demonstrating that the testimony has achieved enough acceptance in the scientific community to convince the court that it is reasonably reliable. We need not at this time conclude that this is the only permissible means of demonstrating reliability.

[W]e turn now to the difficult question of how the proponent of scientific evidence can prove its "general acceptance" and thereby its reliability. "Three methods of proof have been recognized by the courts: (1) expert testimony, (2) scientific and legal writings, and (3) judicial opinions." Giannelli, "The Admissibility of Novel Scientific Evidence: Frye v. United States, a Half–Century Later," 80 Colum.L.Rev. 1197, 1215 (1980). All three present problems, but all three may be used in appropriate circumstances. [H]ere, defendants have offered no expert testimony as to the general acceptance, by psychiatrists or any other medical community, of the scientific premises upon which Dr. Kuris based his analysis.[4]

---

4. At oral argument before this Court, counsel for defendants was asked several times whether he was prepared, at trial, to demonstrate the acceptance of those premises in the scientific community. His answers indicated that he was not so prepared.

Evidence of scientific reliability may also be reflected in authoritative scientific and legal writings. [D]efendants did not cite any articles on which we could rely in taking judicial notice of scientific acceptance.

Defendants therefore must rely on precedent from other courts that have considered the matter and have admitted similar evidence. They urge in addition that similar scientific evidence is generally relied on in the law for other purposes.

[T]here is substantial support for the general acceptance of psychiatric witnesses in court. But the issue here is not the reliability of psychiatric testimony relating to an individual's psychiatric condition. Rather, the question is the reliability of psychiatric testimony on the likelihood that an individual behaved in a particular manner on a specific occasion. We must decide here (1) whether psychiatrists agree that rapists share particular mental characteristics and (2) whether psychiatrists can ascertain if an individual possesses those characteristics by examining him.

A review of cases in other jurisdictions does not persuade us that it is generally accepted in the medical or legal communities that psychiatrists possess such knowledge or capabilities.

[S]imilarly, the other areas in which psychiatric or psychological testimony is generally admitted in evidence are inapposite because such evidence there is admitted for different purposes and in different contexts. [For example,] the expert evidence in parole determinations is offered in a quite different context to establish whether there is substantial likelihood that the inmate will commit future crimes. Unlike a jury trial in the parole context, the evidence is heard by the Parole Board, which routinely makes predictions of the sort required and which has substantial experience evaluating psychiatric testimony. Therefore, such testing can be of reasonable assistance to the factfinder there without the concomitant risk of serious confusion, prejudice and diversion of attention that is likely to result from its admission in a jury trial.

Defendants have thus failed to persuade us that the proffered evidence has been accepted as reliable by other jurisdictions, or for other purposes in the New Jersey legal system. Defendants therefore have not met their burden under Rule 56 of showing that Dr. Kuris' testimony is based on reasonably reliable scientific premises.

[W]e conclude that defendants have not met their burden of showing that the scientific community generally accepts the existence of identifiable character traits common to rapists. They also have not demonstrated that psychiatrists possess any special ability to discern whether an individual is likely to be a rapist. Until the scientific reliability of this type of evidence is established, it is not admissible.

The judgment of the Appellate Division excluding the evidence is affirmed.

———

STATE v. HICKMAN

Supreme Court of Iowa, 1983.
337 N.W.2d 512.

■ ULENHOPP, JUSTICE.

[The defendant was charged with first degree murder. The state alleged that he killed a woman after raping her. The defendant admitted stabbing the victim to death, but claimed that the intercourse that preceded the killing had been consensual. This claim, if accepted, would mean that the murder was not in the first degree.]

[R]ebuttal evidence. One of the bases of the State's charge of first-degree murder was murder in the perpetration of sexual abuse. In his defense, defendant testified in substance that the sexual intercourse was consensual.

The State relied of course on its evidence of violence to disprove that the intercourse was consensual. To reinforce that evidence, the State introduced testimony by a psychiatrist who had made a study of the psychology of rapists and had examined defendant and his medical history. The psychiatrist described various kinds of rapists and characterized defendant as of the class of aggressive, antisocial or sociopathic, hatred rapists.

Defendant objected to this testimony as not rebuttal and argues that the trial court should not have admitted it. We agree with the trial court, however, that this testimony was admissible as rebutting defendant's claim of consensual intercourse. See State v. Nelson, 261 Iowa 204, 209, 153 N.W.2d 711, 714 (1967) ("Rebutting evidence is that which explains, repels, controverts, or disproves evidence produced by the other side.").

———

NOTE

1. Character Evidence. The Iowa rules on character evidence are similar to Federal Rule of Evidence 404. There, it is stated that "[e]vidence of a person's character or a trait of character is not admissible for the purpose of proving action in conformity therewith on a particular occasion," but an exception is listed for "[e]vidence of a pertinent trait of character offered by an accused, or by the prosecution to rebut the same." See Appendix A. Given this definition of character evidence, *Hickman* would seem erroneously decided.

———

4.   LIFE EVENTS

Discrete types of "life events"—experiences more circumscribed than culture, subculture, or personality—have also been claimed to influence a criminal defendant's behavior and state of mind in legally relevant ways. Social science research has been used to provide a context for allowing decision makers to better understand the effect on the defendant of having been assaulted, having served in combat, having been kidnapped, and having frequently watched violent television programs.

(a) Assault

The defendant's prior history of having been the victim of assault has been offered by both the prosecution and the defense. The prosecution has attempted to introduce evidence that the defendant fit the "battering parent profile," and the defense has attempted to introduce evidence that the defendant had the "battered woman syndrome" or was a "battered child."

———

MINNESOTA v. LOEBACH

Supreme Court of Minnesota, 1981.
310 N.W.2d 58.

■ Yetka, Justice.

[Appellant Robert Loebach was convicted of the third degree murder of his three-month old son. He was sentenced to a maximum prison term of 15 years. The principal issue raised on appeal was "Whether the trial court erred in admitting testimony as to appellant's background and personality traits used to prove he fit the diagnosis of a 'battering parent.' "]

Dr. Robert ten Bensel, an expert on child abuse, testified concerning the so-called "battered child syndrome." He concluded that it fit this case almost perfectly. [T]he multiple injuries were clearly not caused by accidents of the kind the defendant stated and were not self-inflicted. Dr. ten Bensel was firmly convinced that the baby's death was the final result of nonaccidental physical abuse of the baby over a period of time.

Dr. ten Bensel also was permitted to testify, over a general objection by defense counsel, that battering parents tend to have similar personality traits and personal histories.

Defense counsel objected generally to the state's calling of two witnesses from appellant's past in an attempt to prove appellant fit the pattern of a "battering parent." Judith Carpenter is a former case worker who was assigned to appellant when he was a juvenile in Illinois. She testified that appellant's mother, who raised appellant alone, had abused him until he was old enough to fight back, that his mother expected too much of him, and that appellant was not good at controlling his anger. Charles Nelson, an employee of a school for disturbed adolescent boys which appellant attended for 3 years until he reached age 18, testified that appellant often withdrew from others, had a low frustration level, and was adolescent in behavior. Testimony from other witnesses also aided in showing that appellant fit the "battering parent" profile. There was testimony that appellant and Anna [appellant's wife] were isolated and did not have contact with many people and that in April 1978, appellant had slapped her and broken her nose. Defense counsel did not object to the testimony concerning the broken nose.

The defense strategy for countering this testimony was partly to show that the "battering parent" profile also fit Anna and that it did not necessarily fit appellant. In cross-examining Anna's sister, defense counsel elicited testimony that appellant was proud, confident and not lacking in self-esteem, whereas Anna was hypertense, unable to cope, unable to handle liquor, and was herself a victim of child abuse. Appellant's direct testimony, however, tended to corroborate the state's evidence that he fit the profile. He testified that his mother called him the man of the family and that he developed a bad temper.

Appellant denied abusing the baby. He testified that he did not see anyone else abuse the baby and that he had no explanation for the injuries the doctor found in the autopsy, although he thought he might have broken the baby's ribs when he accidently dropped the baby one day. He also testified that for a period of time, until warned [t]hat it was dangerous, he had playfully thrown the baby high in the air and caught it. He testified that he stopped doing this 1 to 2 months before the baby died. He also testified that while he admitted slapping the baby once, the slap was more like a love pat.

Appellant contends that the state's use of evidence of his character constitutes prejudicial error and warrants reversal. The specific testimony objected to concerns that given by the state's expert, Dr. ten Bensel, and the two prosecution witnesses who knew appellant as an adolescent.

On direct examination, Dr. ten Bensel was asked to state the characteristics of a "battering parent." According to Dr. ten Bensel, the "battering parent" syndrome is an "inner [sic] generational phenomena" in that adults who abuse their children were often abused themselves. The doctor testified that abusing parents frequently experience role reversal and often expect their children to care for them. He also stated that battering parents often exhibit similar characteristics such as low empathy, a short fuse, low temper, short temper, low boiling point, high blood pressure, strict authoritarianism, uncommunicativeness, low self-esteem, isolation and lack of trust. Dr. ten Bensel did not testify that appellant possessed any of these characteristics, but the state's witnesses, Judith Carpenter and Charles Nelson, suggested that he did.

The obvious purpose for the introduction of the Carpenter and Nelson testimony and other character evidence was to demonstrate that appellant fit within the "battering parent" profile. The general rule as to the admission of such character evidence is contained in Minn.R.Evid. 404(a) which provides in relevant part as follows:

> (a) *Character evidence generally.* Evidence of a person's character or a trait of his character is not admissible for the purpose of proving that he acted in conformity therewith on a particular occasion, except:

(1) *Character of accused.* Evidence of a pertinent trait of his character offered by an accused, or by the prosecution to rebut the same;

* * *

Appellant did not put his character in evidence in this case so the cited exception to the rule's general prohibition does not apply.

[T]here are three basic reasons for the exclusion of character evidence used to prove a criminal defendant acted in conformity with such character. First, there is the possibility that the jury will convict a defendant in order to penalize him for his past misdeeds or simply because he is an undesirable person. Second, there is the danger that a jury will overvalue the character evidence in assessing the guilt for the crime charged. Finally, it is unfair to require an accused to be prepared not only to defend against immediate charges, but also to disprove or explain his personality or prior actions.

[T]he state argues that the potential for prejudice to defendants that justifies the rule excluding character evidence is outweighed by the public interest in assuring conviction of persons who batter children. The state's position is that the difficulties involved in prosecuting those who abuse children warrant an exception to the general rule. The victim, as the state's expert testified, is usually an infant and therefore particularly defenseless. Children who are abused are also almost wholly dependent on those who inflict the abuse. The victims' age and dependence act to prevent them from testifying against abusing caretakers. Finally, abuse almost always occurs when the child is in the exclusive care of a battering caretaker. These features of abuse cases make it very difficult to establish a defendant's guilt by means of direct evidence. The state contends, therefore, that an exception to the general rule is necessary to offset these obstacles to the prosecution of battering individuals.

[W]e now hold that in future cases the prosecution will not be permitted to introduce evidence of "battering parent" syndrome or to establish the character of the defendant as a "battering parent" unless the defendant first raises that issue. We feel this finding is required until further evidence of the scientific accuracy and reliability of syndrome or profile diagnoses can be established.

Our determination that the "battering parent" evidence should not have been admitted does not affect the result of this case in the court below. A defendant claiming error in the trial court's reception of evidence has the burden of showing both the error and the prejudice resulting from the error. A reversal is warranted only when the error substantially influences the jury to convict.

The record in this case indicates that the "battering parent" testimony consisted of only a small percentage of the evidence. The record also reveals that there was overwhelming evidence of appellant's guilt even without the "battering parent" testimony.

[I]n light of this substantial evidence to support appellant's conviction, the error in admitting "battering parent" testimony was not prejudicial.

———

NOTE

1. The Effects of Child Abuse. Research on the effects of child abuse on later violent behavior toward one's own children was reviewed in Kaufman and Zigler, Do Abused Children Become Abusive Parents?, 57 American Journal of Orthopsychiatry 186, 190 (1987):

> [T]he best estimate of intergenerational transmission [of abuse] appears to be 30% ± 5%. This suggests that approximately one-third of all individuals who were physically abused, sexually abused, or extremely neglected will subject their offspring to one of these forms of maltreatment, while the remaining two-thirds will provide adequate care for their children. [T]he rate of abuse among individuals with a history of abuse [i]s approximately six times higher than the base rate for abuse in the general population (5%).

In terms of the effects of being victimized as a child on later crime in general (i.e, not limited to crimes victimizing one's own children), Widom and Maxfield, An Update on the "Cycle of Violence," National Institute of Justice Research in Brief, February 2001, reported data following children processed by the courts for having been abused or neglected, and a comparison group of children who had not been abused or neglected. At the time of the follow-up, the subjects' mean age was 32 years.

Of primary interest was the question, "Would arrest histories of those who had been abused or neglected be worse than those with no reported abuse? The answer [w]as evident: Those who had been abused or neglected as children were more likely to be arrested as juveniles (27 percent versus 17 percent), adults (42 percent versus 33 percent), and for violent crime (18 percent versus 14 percent)." Id. at 3.

———

IBN–TAMAS v. UNITED STATES

District of Columbia, Court of Appeals, 1979.
407 A.2d 626.

■ Ferren, Associate Judge.

[Dr. and Mrs. Ibn–Tamas had been married for three and a half years. The marriage "was marred by recurring violent episodes separated by periods of relative harmony." On the morning of his death, Dr. Ibn–Tamas beat his wife. He threatened her with a gun and told her to leave the house. In the ensuing argument, Mrs. Ibn–Tamas picked up the gun and shot him three times, killing him in what she testified was self-defense.

Dr. Ibn–Tamas' secretary, however, testified that between the shots Dr. Ibn–Tamas yelled "don't shoot me any more" and Mrs. Ibn–Tamas said, "I am not going to leave you, I mean it." The prosecution suggested in its closing argument that "Mrs. Ibn–Tamas, threatened with the prospect of being thrown out of her home [h]ad simply decided that she had endured enough of her husband's abuse [and] ambushed him."

Mrs. Ibn–Tamas was convicted of second-degree murder and sentenced to prison for a period of one-to-five years. She raised several issues on appeal, including "the trial court's exclusion of expert testimony offered by the defense on the subject of battered women."]

Appellant claims the trial court erred in excluding the testimony of Dr. Lenore Walker, a clinical psychologist, proffered as a defense expert on the subject of "battered women." Specifically, the defense proffered Dr. Walker for two purposes: to describe the phenomenon of "wife battering," and to give her opinion of the extent to which appellant's personality and behavior corresponded to those of 110 battered women Dr. Walker had studied. The defense claimed the testimony was relevant because it would help the jury appraise the credibility of appellant's contention that she had perceived herself in such imminent danger from her husband that she shot him in self-defense.

The trial court refused to permit this expert testimony on three grounds. First, it would "go [ ] beyond those [prior violent] acts which a jury is entitled to hear about, sift, and try to understand the circumstances under which they arose, and draw conclusions therefrom." Second, it would "invade [ ] the province of the jury, who are the sole judges of the facts and triers of the credibility of the witnesses, including the defendant." Third, Dr. Walker, "of necessity, concludes that the decedent was a batterer. And that is not being tried in this case. It is the defendant who is on trial."

[O]ver the years, appellate courts have applied two levels of analysis to a trial court's ruling on expert testimony. First, there is the question of admissibility, for which a three-fold test is applied. Second, the probative value of the testimony must outweigh its prejudicial impact.

A. *Admissibility*

Of the three grounds given by the trial court for excluding Dr. Walker's testimony, only the second (it would "invade[ ] the province of the jury . . .") goes to admissibility. There are two ways in which an expert can preempt the jury's function. The expert either can speak too directly to the ultimate issue (i.e., guilt or innocence), or can speak to matters in which "the jury is just as competent as the expert to consider and weigh the evidence and draw the necessary conclusions."

1. Here, the expert would not preempt in either fashion. As to the first—the "ultimate facts" or "ultimate issue" rule—Dr. Walker was not going to express an opinion on the ultimate question whether Mrs. Ibn–Tamas actually and reasonably believed she was in danger when she shot her husband. Rather, this expert would have merely supplied background

data to help the jury make that crucial determination. In any event, the ultimate issue rule has, over time, been reduced to a prohibition only against questions to an expert "which, in effect, submit the whole case to an expert witness for decision." There is no such risk here.

2. Even when an expert is not speaking to the ultimate facts or issue, he or she cannot testify to matters which "the jury itself is just as competent" to consider. In order to evaluate this concern, we have adopted a three-fold test for admissibility:

> (1) the subject matter "must be so distinctively related to some science, profession, business or occupation as to be beyond the ken of the average layman"; (2) "the witness must have sufficient skill, knowledge, or experience in that field or calling as to make it appear that his opinion or inference will probably aid the trier in his search for truth"; and (3) expert testimony is inadmissible if "the state of the pertinent art or scientific knowledge does not permit a reasonable opinion to be asserted even by an expert." (Dyas v. United States, [D.C.App., 376 A.2d 827 (1977)] at 832 (quoting McCormick on Evidence § 13 (2d ed. E. Cleary (1972)) (emphasis omitted)).

Thus, the subject of the testimony must lend itself to expertise, the proffered expert must be qualified to give it, and experts must have studied the subject in a manner that will justify an expert opinion.

The substantive element of this test, whether the expert witness' subject matter is "beyond the ken of the average layman," means that Dr. Walker's testimony, to be admissible, must provide a relevant insight which the jury otherwise could not gain in evaluating appellant's self-defense testimony about her relationship with her husband. More specifically, Dr. Walker must purport to shed light on a relevant aspect of their relationship which a layperson, without expert assistance, would not perceive from the evidence itself.

On direct examination, Mrs. Ibn–Tamas had testified that immediately before the shooting Dr. Ibn–Tamas had told her to pack and leave home by 10:00 a.m. When she replied that she could not, he hit her in the head, under the arms, and in the thighs, and kicked her in the stomach even though she was pregnant.

[O]n cross-examination the government attempted to discredit this testimony by suggesting to the jury, through its questions, that Mrs. Ibn–Tamas' account of the relationship with her husband over the years had been greatly overdrawn, and that her testimony about perceiving herself in imminent danger on February 23, was therefore implausible. For example, the government implied to the jury that the logical reaction of a woman who was truly frightened by her husband (let alone regularly brutalized by him) would have been to call the police from time to time or to leave him. In an effort to rebut this line of attack by the government, the defense proffered Dr. Walker's testimony to (1) inform the jury that there is an identifiable class of persons who can be characterized as "battered women," (2) explain why the mentality and behavior of such women are at variance with the ordinary lay perception of how someone would be likely to react to a spouse who is a batterer, and thus (3) provide a basis from which the jury could understand why Mrs. Ibn–Tamas perceived herself in imminent danger at the time of the shooting.

More specifically, Dr. Walker told the trial court, out of the presence of the jury, that she had studied 110 women who had been beaten by their husbands. Her studies revealed three consecutive phases in the relationships: "tension building," when there are small incidents of battering; "acute battering incident," when beatings are severe; and "loving-contrite," when the husband becomes very sorry and caring. Dr. Walker then testified that women in this situation typically are low in self-esteem, feel powerless, and have few close friends, since their husbands commonly "accuse [ ] them of all kinds of things with friends, and they are embarrassed. They don't want to cause their friends problems too." Because there are periods of harmony, battered women tend to believe their husbands are basically loving, caring men; the women assume that they, themselves, are somehow responsible for their husbands' violent behavior. They also believe, however, that their husbands are capable of killing them, and they feel there is no escape. Unless a shelter is available, these women stay with their husbands, not only because they typically lack a means of self-support but also because they fear that if they leave they will be found and hurt even more.

[W]hen asked about appellant, whom she had interviewed, Dr. Walker replied that Mrs. Ibn–Tamas was a "classic case" of the battered wife. Dr. Walker added her belief that on the day of the killing, when Dr. Ibn–Tamas had been beating his wife despite protests that she was pregnant, Mrs. Ibn–Tamas' pregnancy had had a "major impact on the situation.... [T]hat is a particularly crucial time."

Dr. Walker's testimony, therefore, arguably would have served at least two basic functions: (1) it would have enhanced Mrs. Ibn–Tamas' general credibility in responding to cross-examination designed to show that her testimony about the relationship with her husband was implausible; and (2) it would have supported her testimony that on the day of the shooting her husband's actions had provoked a state of fear which led her to believe she was in imminent danger ("I just knew he was going to kill me"), and thus responded in self-defense. Dr. Walker's contribution, accordingly, would have been akin to the psychiatric testimony admitted in the case of Patricia Hearst "to explain the effects kidnapping, prolonged incarceration, and psychological and physical abuse may have had on the defendant's mental state at the time of the robbery, insofar as such mental state is relevant to the asserted defense of coercion or duress." [United States v. Hearst, 412 F.Supp. 889 (N.D.Cal.1976)] at 890. Dr. Walker's testimony would have supplied an interpretation of the facts which differed from the ordinary lay perception ("she could have gotten out, you know") advocated by the government. The substantive element of the *Dyas,* supra, test— "beyond the ken of the average layman"—is accordingly met here.

We conclude, therefore, that as to either substantive basis for ruling that Dr. Walker's testimony would "invade[ ] the province of the jury"—either the "ultimate issue" or the "beyond the ken" basis—the trial court erred as a matter of law.

3. Because *Dyas,* supra, provides a three-fold test, we must consider, next, whether the trial court can be said to have ruled, implicitly, that the expert testimony was inadmissible for failure to meet either the second or third elements of that test.

[W]e therefore confront the question whether the record clearly manifests a trial court ruling that Dr. Walker did not have "sufficient skill, knowledge, or experience" in the field (second *Dyas* criterion), or that "the state of the pertinent art or scientific knowledge" was insufficient for an expert opinion (third *Dyas* criterion).

Dr. Walker testified as to her credentials, her study of battered women, and her diagnosis of Mrs. Ibn–Tamas. The court then inquired whether Dr. Walker was offering a "medical diagnosis" and asked several questions about the 110 women she had interviewed. After reviewing the record, we cannot say that the trial court's ruling was meant to encompass the second or third *Dyas* criterion.

[4.] The question thus becomes whether the trial court, despite its failure to rule on the second or third *Dyas* criterion, had "but one option," [United States v. Green, 548 F.2d 1261, 1268 (6th Cir.1977)]—i.e., whether Dr. Walker's testimony is inadmissible as a matter of law.

[5.] The most we can say from this record is that the second *Dyas* criterion—sufficient skill, knowledge, or experience in the expert's field—may or may not have been satisfied. Although no one has questioned Dr. Walker's qualifications as a clinical psychologist, the expert's credentials must be sufficient for the type of psychological testimony proffered.

[O]n this record, we cannot resolve the question of Dr. Walker's qualifications; but we can say on the basis of her background, that she cannot be disqualified as a matter of law.

6. We turn, finally, to the third *Dyas* criterion: whether "the state of the pertinent art or scientific knowledge" is sufficient to permit an expert opinion. The government argues that the "battered woman" concept is not sufficiently developed, as a matter of commonly accepted scientific knowledge, to warrant testimony under the guise of expertise. The government relies substantially on Frye v. United States, 54 App.D.C. 46, 293 F. 1013 (1923):

> Just when a scientific principle or discovery crosses the line between the experimental and demonstrable stages is difficult to define. Somewhere in this twilight zone the evidential force of the principle must be recognized, and while courts will go a long way in admitting expert testimony deduced from a well-recognized scientific principle or discovery, the thing from which the deduction is made *must be sufficiently established to have gained general acceptance in the*

particular field in which it belongs. [Id. at 47, 293 F. at 1014 (emphasis added).]

The government is mistaken. [I]t is important to note that the third criterion focuses on the general acceptance of a particular methodology in the field, not (as the government would have it) on the subject matter studied. The United States Court of Appeals for the District of Columbia Circuit recently emphasized that *Frye,* supra—which rejected admissibility of lie detector results—dealt with "admissibility of expert testimony based on new methods of scientific measurement." United States v. Addison, 162 U.S.App.D.C. 199, 201, 498 F.2d 741, 743 (1974). Thus, the third criterion is directed to the general acceptance of generic categories of scientific inquiry, such as use of the polygraph, spectrographic identification, psycho-linguistics, tests for marijuana, and even neutron activation analysis, as well as the variety of analyses used by psychiatrists and clinical psychologists.

[I]n summary, satisfaction of the third *Dyas* criterion begins—and ends—with a determination of whether there is general acceptance of a particular scientific methodology, not an acceptance, beyond that, of particular study results based on that methodology. Thus, the relevant question here is whether Dr. Walker's methodology for identifying and studying battered women has such general acceptance—not whether there is, in addition, a general acceptance of the battered woman concept derived from that methodology. Again, on this record, we cannot say, as a matter of law, that Dr. Walker's methodology falls short.

7.   We conclude, therefore, that the trial court erred in ruling Dr. Walker's testimony inadmissible on the ground that it would invade the province of the jury; and, on the record to date, we cannot exclude that testimony as inadmissible on any other ground.

B.   *Probative Value v. Prejudicial Impact*

Because "admissibility" remains an open question, we turn to the second level of inquiry: probative value versus prejudicial impact. The trial court's first and third grounds for excluding Dr. Walker's testimony related to the prejudicial character of the evidence. Specifically, the court stated that the evidence would "go[ ] beyond those [prior violent] acts" which a jury should consider and that, in effect, the testimony put the decedent on trial as "a batterer, [a]nd that is not being tried in this case."

We have stated, apropos of this first ground, that prior acts of violence are admissible in "homicide cases where the defendant raises the claim of self-defense against the decedent as the alleged first aggressor." United States v. Akers, D.C.App., 374 A.2d 874, 877 (1977) (emphasis omitted). The trial court, in fact, admitted a substantial amount of evidence relating to the decedent's earlier attacks on the appellant and other persons. In light of the admission of this evidence, it is apparent that the incremental, prejudicial impact of Dr. Walker's testimony on battered wives, including the labeling of Dr. Ibn–Tamas as a batterer, would have been minimal.

In contrast, as we have previously observed, the testimony on battered wives was highly probative. Because Mrs. Ibn–Tamas' identity as a "battered wife," if established, may have had a substantial bearing on her perceptions and behavior at the time of the killing, it was central to her claim of self-defense. We conclude, accordingly, as a matter of law, that the probative value of this expert testimony would outweigh the risk of "engender[ing] vindictive passions within the jury or ... confus[ing] the issues." [United States v. Green, 548 F.2d 1261, 1268 (6th Cir.1977)]

[A]ccordingly, we must remand the case for a trial court determination of admissibility consistent with this opinion.

■ NEBEKER, ASSOCIATE JUDGE, dissenting.

[A]s to her method for examining or interviewing Mrs. Ibn–Tamas and analyzing her situation, the record reveals only that the expert "had contact" with her. No other indication is made. We learned from the witness that her opinion was going to be based upon a paltry universe of 110 other women who were "researched" by her. We know nothing of these few women other than their apparent claim of being abused. Nothing was said of the techniques for "interviewing," the duration of the interview, the number of times each woman was interviewed or any follow-up. The expert interviewed only the abused women and not their husbands, physicians or family. She even testified that "*we* have talked to" some 60 percent of the abused women referred by others (emphasis added). When questioned by the court, the witness candidly acknowledged that 40 percent of the women apparently were prompted to seek an interview by newspapers, television or radio. No estimated potential margin for error was expressed. The foundation for the testimony is patently inadequate, as there was no indication in the record of what method the expert employed or that the expert's method was generally accepted in the field.

I would affirm the conviction.

IBN–TAMAS v. UNITED STATES

District of Columbia Court of Appeals, 1983.
455 A.2d 893.

This is an appeal from an order entered after remand proceedings. We earlier ordered those proceedings, with discretion whether to hold an evidentiary hearing, for clarification because "we cannot be certain that the record otherwise supports the ruling as a matter of law." Ibn–Tamas v. United States, 407 A.2d 626, 640 n. 29 (D.C.1979). The trial court has stated on remand that it did consider the relevant factors as outlined by this court in its original ruling. It concluded, *inter alia,* "that defendant failed to establish a general acceptance by the expert's colleagues of the methodology used in the expert's study of 'battered women.'" Since the expert's testimony could have been excluded "for failure to meet either the second or third elements of the test," id. at 635, and the trial court did exclude that testimony on one such basis, we are left with deciding whether "the evidence, despite our inability to observe the witness, permits but one interpretation." Id. at 636 n. 17. As the court said in its earlier decision in this case, our scope of review on this issue is "narrow" to the point where manifest error must appear for reversal. Id. at 632. We hold that the trial judge was not compelled, as a matter of law, to admit the evidence. He had discretion whether to admit it and "this court should not substitute its judgment in [such] a discretionary ruling. . . ." Id. at 636 n. 17.

Accordingly, the order appealed from is affirmed.

———

NIXON v. UNITED STATES

District of Columbia Court of Appeals, 1999.
728 A.2d 582.

■ SCHWELB, ASSOCIATE JUDGE:

The principal question presented in this domestic violence case is whether the trial judge committed reversible error by permitting the prosecution to introduce expert testimony on the subject of the battered woman syndrome in order to explain, *inter alia,* the conduct of the complaining witness in response to the alleged battering.

[F]ollowing a lengthy jury trial, [G]regory E. Nixon was convicted of assault with a dangerous weapon, possession of a firearm during a crime of violence, [and] simple assault. [N]ixon's prosecution arose from his relationship with the complainant, Kelita Boyd, who was his live-in girlfriend, and who became the mother of his son, Amore. The evidence against Nixon consisted primarily of the testimony of Ms. Boyd (which was corroborated in part by Ms. Boyd's mother and by several other witnesses) and the expert evidence of Dr. Mary Ann Dutton, a board-certified clinical psychologist. Nixon appeared as a witness on his own behalf and generally denied Ms. Boyd's allegations.

[A]. *The expert testimony.*

Following an *in limine* hearing outside the presence of the jury, the trial judge ruled that Dr. Dutton, the government's expert witness, would be permitted to testify regarding the following topics:

1. myths about domestic violence;

2. common patterns of battering; and

3. common behavior of victims of battering.

At trial, Dr. Dutton addressed these subjects in some detail. She described as a "common myth" regarding domestic violence the widespread belief that the victim can easily leave her abuser. This belief is unfounded, according to Dr. Dutton, because a battered woman will often fear that the batterer will use violence against her or her family if she does attempt to leave. Dr. Dutton also explained that many battered women are economically dependent on their abusers and lack the financial resources to set up households of their own. Moreover, women are often inhibited by personal shame or embarrassment. Dr. Dutton also testified that there is no empirical basis for the notion that battered women stay in abusive relationships because they "enjoy" the abuse.

Focusing on the batterer, Dr. Dutton identified several common patterns of domestic abuse, including, *inter alia:*

1. coercion and threats;

2. emotional abuse, such as degrading or humiliating the victim;

3. intimidation;

4. isolation (*e.g.*, restricting the victim's access to the telephone or to the car, or monitoring her comings and goings); and

5. minimizing the injury, or blaming the victim for being hit.

Dr. Dutton testified that by downplaying the victim's injuries and by isolating her from friends and family, the batterer often reinforces her feelings of helplessness and her tendency to blame herself for her situation.

Dr. Dutton then addressed common patterns of behavior on the part of victims of abuse. According to Dr. Dutton, the relevant studies show that approximately fifty percent of battered women do not report the abuse to the police, and that "[t]here are many women who unfortunately put on one front or one view for the world, even their family and friends, and in private experience the violence." Dr. Dutton stated that the term "cycle of violence" is used to describe the three stages of domestic violence—attention building, acute battering, and contrition. When the abuser appears to be contrite—when there are "apologies, flowers, I'm sorry, it was a mistake, it won't happen again"—and when he pleads for forgiveness, his victim often allows herself to be persuaded that the abuse will not recur. Moreover, abuse is not necessarily constant, for "most abusers aren't battering and mean and abusive one hundred percent of the time." Therefore, according to Dr. Dutton, it is more common than uncommon for a victim to leave the relationship, only to return. In particular, pregnancy and children can intensify the victim's attachment to the abuser and her reluctance to leave or to stay away.

Finally, Dr. Dutton testified that she had not examined either Nixon or Ms. Boyd. She did not know whether Ms. Boyd had been abused at all, or whether Nixon had abused her. Dr. Dutton therefore made it clear that she was not rendering an opinion as to the guilt or innocence of the defendant.

LEGAL DISCUSSION

On appeal from his convictions, Nixon challenges the admission of Dr. Dutton's testimony on several grounds. [B]efore addressing each of Nixon's specific contentions, we first identify the applicable legal standard and the scope of appellate review.

A. *The standard of review.*

The criteria for the admission of expert testimony in the District of Columbia are set forth in a three-part test which was adopted by this court in *Dyas v. United States,* 376 A.2d 827 (D.C.), *cert. denied,* 434 U.S. 973, 98 S.Ct. 529, 54 L.Ed.2d 464 (1977):

> (1) the subject matter must be so distinctively related to some science, profession, business or occupation as to be beyond the ken of the average [juror], (2) the witness must have sufficient skill, knowledge, or experience in that field or calling as to make it appear that his opinion or inference will probably aid the trier in his search for truth, and (3) expert testimony is inadmissible if the state of the pertinent art or scientific knowledge does not permit a reasonable opinion to be asserted even by an expert

Id. at 832. Where an issue is raised for the first time on appeal, we review only for plain error.

[B]. *"General acceptance."*

Nixon [c]ontends that "the admission of Dr. Dutton's expert testimony was reversible error because the methodology behind 'battered woman syndrome' is not generally accepted." He relies on *United States v. Porter,* 618 A.2d 629 (D.C.1992), in which this court reiterated and expanded upon the seminal decision in *Frye v. United States,* 54 App.D.C. 46, 293 F. 1013 (1923):

> [U]nder *Frye,* the proponent of a new technology must demonstrate by a preponderance of the evidence that th[e] technology has been generally accepted in the relevant scientific community.... Given the requirement in *Frye* of general acceptance, [t]he issue is consensus versus controversy over a particular technique, not its validity.... If scientists significant either in number or expertise publicly oppose [a new technique] as unreliable, then that technique does not pass muster under *Frye.*

Porter, 618 A.2d at 633–34.

According to Nixon's appellate counsel, "battered woman syndrome is nothing more than radical political feminism wrapped in the veneer of science, and as such, fails to satisfy the *Frye* test." Counsel cites a number of articles criticizing the methodology used by Dr. Lenore Walker, the author of THE BATTERED WOMAN SYNDROME and by other proponents of BWS, and contends that the consensus contemplated by *Frye* and *Porter* therefore does not exist.

[N]ixon's attorney made no claim in the trial court that there are scientists who dissent from BWS methodology, and the theory on which Nixon now relies is being presented for the first time on appeal. If, under these circumstances, we may consider the contention at all, our review must be for plain error.

The trial judge was not "obviously" wrong in concluding that Dr. Dutton's testimony satisfied the third prong of *Dyas*. Contrary to Nixon's thesis, Dr. Dutton's testimony was not "junk science." A decade ago, the Supreme Court of Washington held that the methodology in the diagnosis and treatment of battered women utilized by an expert witness who relied primarily on Dr. Lenore Walker's work "has received general acceptance in the community of mental health experts." *State v. Ciskie,* 110 Wash.2d 263, 751 P.2d 1165, 1170 (1988). As of 1992, the courts of thirty-two states had allowed the use of expert testimony on the subject of BWS. *See Bechtel [v. State],* 840 P.2d at 7 & n. 5. "The American Psychological Association, representing more than 55,000 psychologists, endorsed expert testimony on the syndrome in its amicus brief [in] *Hawthorne v. State,* 408 So.2d 801 (Fla.Dist.Ct.App.1982). . . ." *Id.* n. 4.

More recently, the Supreme Court of Michigan has recognized that "the majority of jurisdictions favor the admissibility of expert testimony regarding the battered woman syndrome." *People v. Christel,* 449 Mich. 578, 537 N.W.2d 194, 202 n. 26 (1995). The court further stated that "Dr. Walker's premise and understanding of a battering relationship has been widely accepted throughout the United States, and we now join the majority of jurisdictions recognizing the discipline." *Id.* The Supreme Court of Minnesota has likewise stated that "battered woman syndrome has gained sufficient scientific acceptance to warrant admissibility as expert testimony." *State v. Grecinger,* 569 N.W.2d 189, 194 (Minn.1997) (citation omitted). [A]t the very least, in light of [t]he authorities relied on by the courts in those cases, the admission of Dr. Dutton's testimony was not plainly wrong.

[C].   *"Beyond the ken."*

Nixon next contends that "the admission of Dr. Dutton's expert testimony was reversible error because battered woman syndrome is not beyond the ken of the average layperson."

[D]uring the course of the trial, the defense repeatedly attempted to persuade the jury that Ms. Boyd's testimony was not credible. Nixon's counsel argued that for a long period, Ms. Boyd did not report, and even denied, the alleged abuse, and that her allegations were therefore belied by her own conduct. In his opening statement, Nixon's attorney told the jurors that there would be "no medical records . . . no pictures . . . no police reports of my client beating up Miss Boyd." Counsel asked the jurors to ponder why. During his cross-examination of the complainant, Nixon's attorney focused on her failure to report or disclose the abuse. Subsequently, in closing argument, counsel suggested that the failure of Ms. Boyd (or her family) to report the alleged battering to the police "doesn't make sense."

[A]ctions sometimes speak louder than words, and a lay juror might well wonder whether Ms. Boyd's actions (and inaction) at the time of the alleged abuse were consistent with the narrative which she provided in the courtroom long after the events occurred. Dr. Dutton's testimony was designed to apprise the jurors of certain repeated patterns of behavior on the part of many battered women. With that information, the jurors were in a better position to determine whether these patterns of behavior might explain any perceived discrepancy between Ms. Boyd's words and her deeds.

This court and other courts have held that testimony of the type provided by Dr. Dutton may assist the jury in understanding the evidence and is "beyond the ken" of the average lay juror within the meaning of *Dyas. See, e.g., Ibn–Tamas [v. United States]*, 407 A.2d at 635. In *[State v.] Borrelli*, the Supreme Court of Connecticut held that the testimony of the prosecution's expert on battered woman syndrome was "beyond the knowledge and experience of the average juror." 629 A.2d at 1112. The court relied on empirical research indicating that

> potential jurors may hold beliefs and attitudes about abused women at variance with the views of experts who have studied or had experience with abused women. In particular, males are likely to be skeptical about the fear the woman feels in an abusive relationship and about her inability to leave a setting in which abuse is threatened.

Id. (quoting N. Vidmar & R. Schuller, *Juries and Expert Evidence: Social Framework Testimony*, 52 Law & Contemp.Probs. 133, 154 (1989)).

[I]n this case, too, the judge could reasonably conclude, without abusing his discretion, that Dr. Dutton's testimony was beyond the ken of a lay trier of fact and would be helpful to the jurors in their consideration of the evidence.

[D].   *Relevance.*

Nixon also asserts on appeal, as he did in the trial court, that because "Dr. Dutton failed to examine or specifically diagnose Miss Boyd, her opinion regarding 'battered women' generally was irrelevant." The authorities on this issue, however, are uniformly to the contrary. [N]umerous other courts have [h]eld that expert testimony regarding BWS and other aspects of domestic violence is admissible where the expert has not examined the complaining witness and has not testified that she is a battered woman or suffers from BWS. *See, e.g.,* Cynthia Lynn Barnes, J.D., Annotation, *Admissibility of Expert Testimony Concerning Domestic–Violence Syndromes to Assist Jury in Evaluating Victim's Testimony or Behavior*, 57 A.L.R.5th 315 (1998). Indeed, in most of these cases, the courts have held or suggested that testimony by the expert to the effect that the complainant was a battered woman should be excluded as unduly prejudicial and because it would invade the province of the jury. In light of these decisions, any attempt by the prosecution to adduce expert testimony to the effect that Ms. Boyd was a battered woman would have injected into the record a significant possibility of undue prejudice.

[I]n this case, we conclude, as did the trial judge, that Dr. Dutton's testimony was relevant and that the prosecution had laid a sufficient foundation for its admission.

[E]. *Limiting instruction.*

Nixon claims that reversal is required because the trial court failed to give the jury a limiting instruction regarding the purpose for which Dr. Dutton's testimony was received in evidence. [N]ixon argues that in the absence of such an instruction, "the jury may easily mistake the expert's 'general' case-specific testimony as a case-specific diagnosis or as substantive evidence that the defendant is a 'batterer.'" Although a limiting instruction might have been appropriate, Nixon's claim of reversible error is without merit. In the present case, as we have noted, Dr. Dutton testified on direct examination that she had met neither the defendant nor Ms. Boyd and that she therefore had no opinion regarding Nixon's guilt. On cross-examination, Nixon's attorney elicited from Dr. Dutton, even more forcefully, exactly what testimony she did *not* give:

Q. Dr. Dutton, you don't know whether Ms. Kelita Boyd is an abused person, do you?

A. No, I do not.

Q. And, Dr. Dutton, you don't know that my client has ever abused or threatened Ms. Kelita Boyd, do you?

A. No, I do not.

* * *

Q. So, just to conclude, you don't know anything about the specifics of this case; is that correct?

A. That's correct.

Q. Thank you. I have no further questions.

In light of these unequivocal statements on the part of the witness, the jury could not reasonably have understood Dr. Dutton to be testifying that Ms. Boyd was a battered woman or that Nixon was her batterer.

[F]. *Probative value and prejudice.*

Finally, Nixon claims that Dr. Dutton's testimony was more prejudicial than probative, and that it should have been excluded on that ground.

[A] party seeking to override the trial judge's exercise of discretion must show that the probative value of the evidence is *substantially* outweighed by its potential prejudicial effect. Particularly where expert testimony is concerned, reversals on this ground do not abound

In *Ibn–Tamas I,* this court recognized the centrality of Dr. Lenore Walker's testimony regarding BWS when such evidence was offered by a homicide defendant who claimed to have been battered by her late husband, the decedent, whom she was alleged to have murdered. 407 A.2d at 639. The court held, as a matter of law, that the probative value of the proposed testimony outweighed its potential prejudice. *Id.* The issue in the present case is somewhat different, for Ms. Boyd was a prosecution witness, and not the accused. Nevertheless, as the court explained in *Arcoren [v. United States],*

[i]t would seem anomalous to allow a battered woman, where she is a criminal defendant, to offer this type of expert testimony in order to help the jury understand the actions she took, yet deny her that same opportunity when she is the complaining witness and/or victim and her abuser is the criminal defendant.

929 F.2d at 1241 (quoting *State v. Frost,* 242 N.J.Super. 601, 577 A.2d 1282, 1287 (App.Div.1990)).

For the foregoing reasons, Nixon's convictions are hereby *Affirmed.*

STATE v. YUSUF

Appellate Court of Connecticut, 2002.
70 Conn.App. 594, 800 A.2d 590.

■ Healey, J.

The defendant, Asheek Yusuf, appeals from the judgment of conviction, rendered after a jury trial, of kidnapping in the second degree, assault in the second degree, unlawful restraint in the first degree, and cruelty to persons. On appeal, the defendant [c]laims that the court improperly allowed Stark, a sociologist, to testify as an expert witness on battered woman syndrome.

[D]uring his testimony, Stark [w]as asked a number of hypothetical questions that tracked the facts that gave rise to the charges against the defendant.[12] Generally, with respect to each hypothetical question, Stark

---

12. The state's questions and Stark's responses in relevant part were:

"[Prosecutor]: Assume the following facts: A fifteen year old woman becomes romantically involved with a twenty-four year old man who is physically larger and stronger than her. The relationship continues for about a year. During that relationship, the woman is assaulted, punched with fists, kicked with feet, assaulted with inanimate objects, burned with a lighter, verbally degraded with obscenities, all by that same man who's in the relationship with her. She's seriously assaulted perhaps five or six times over the course of this relationship. She never calls the police. She never reports this. She remains in the relationship. Is this behavior on the part of the woman consistent with behavior of a woman suffering from battered woman syndrome?

"[Witness]: Certainly."

[Prosecutor]: Is it consistent with battered women that a woman in that situation, in a relationship wherein she suffered assaults five or six times over the course of that relationship, is it consistent that she may not report these assaults to the police?

"[Witness]: Yes.

"[Prosecutor]: And is there—what role, if any, do minor assaults play based upon your study of women in such situations?

"[Witness]: In our experience ... the vast majority of assaults and battering situations tend to be minor rather than significant in the criminal justice and medical sense. And the effect of those assaults, in addition to the severe assaults which punctuate the history of ongoing minor assaults, is a level of physical intimidation that can create the learned helplessness that we described earlier. There are a variety of reasons why women don't report, but the data is pretty clear that in only a very small minority of instances where history of battering is established are women able or do they call the police or visit the hospital.

"[Prosecutor]: Doctor, assume further that this particular man instructs a woman that was asked to give his expert opinion whether the hypothetical victim's conduct was consistent with that of a woman suffering from battered woman syndrome. In each case, Stark concluded that the victim's conduct

she must call or page him before she goes anywhere, tell him who she'll be seeing, where she'll be going, when she'll return, she has to get [his] permission before she goes out before leaving work, she complies with this order. Is this consistent with a woman suffering battered woman syndrome?

"[Witness]: Yes.

"[Prosecutor]: And why is that?

"[Witness]: In situations—first of all, let me say that the beeper is being used ... more and more frequently in my experience in this area as a way of reporting in and as a form of control. So, that particular thing is certainly consistent in the hypothetical that you offered with what we know about battering, in this area at least.... [I]n addition, because of the isolation and because of the intimidation, the victim often concludes that what is right for her is following the rules. You can get almost a hostage-like situation which creates almost like childlike dependence on the batterer. It's maybe hard for people to understand this....

"The question of why women don't leave in situations like that, or why they don't report, is probably the most perplexing to people who work in the area. And what we've learned ... is that they don't leave because it's more dangerous to leave often than to stay. They don't leave because they love the guy and they hope that things will change even though they fear it won't, and a variety of other reasons associated with that, economic reasons and other dependence. But the main reason they don't leave, seems to be because of the level of control that is not easily observed by people who are outsiders, that he exercises over her every movement and everyday life, in her mind, if not in fact, but usually a combination of both.

"[Prosecutor]: Specifically relating to—continuing from that answer, assume these facts: A man becomes enraged over something because the woman has disobeyed or lied to him. He orders her into his car ... [h]e beats her, assaults her. He then leaves the car momentarily later on, he threatens to kill the woman if she leaves the vehicle, the woman remains in the car. Is it consistent with battered woman syndrome for a woman to comply in this type of situation with a man's

orders even though she may have an opportunity to escape?

"[Witness]: Yeah. I mean, unfortunately it is. What we may think is an opportunity to escape, in her mind may not be. Or she may think, and this is very commonly the case, that if she escapes and she's found, and she believes ... that he can find her anywhere ... that she's even going to be hurt worse; again, as strange as it may sound, there are many women who believe [that] getting the beating over with is better than living with the fear and anxiety and stress of what will happen to them if he does find them and she does escape.... [E]ven people who are mature in years can be reduced to almost childlike dependence in this situation and be paralyzed by the fear of what will happen to them even when to an outsider it seems perfectly reasonable they should open the door, and in the hypothetical you offer, of a car and simply run away." [Prosecutor]: Assume further that the man returns to the car and drives the woman to their apartment, drags her into the apartment, he orders her to remove clothing, orders her to a specific area of the apartment, assaults her ... mandates that she remain there, eats his dinner, goes to sleep, allows her to go to sleep ... the woman sleeps next to him, the man wakes, tells the woman if she leaves the apartment he will kill her, he leaves, the woman falls asleep. Is that a similar situation, similarly consistent with what you just described?

"[Witness]: Yes, it is.

"[Prosecutor]: Despite having a possible method or means or opportunity to escape, does not?

"[Witness]: Well, what you're describing in the hypothetical is what I would call a hostage-like situation, almost. Where, at least, in her mind, these opportunities to escape are not available even though they may be, again, to an outsider....

"[Prosecutor]: The scenario I painted in the last hypothetical ... is it consistent type of behaviors with a woman who is suffering battered woman syndrome?

"[Witness]: It is."

as set out in the hypothetical question was indeed consistent with a woman suffering from battered woman syndrome.

[B]efore expert testimony about battered woman syndrome becomes relevant, an evidentiary foundation must first be established that the victim is a battered woman and that her conduct is such that the jury would be aided by expert testimony providing an explanation therefore. Here, contrary to the defendant's assertions, we conclude that the state presented sufficient evidence of an abusive relationship warranting the testimony on battered woman syndrome.

The state presented evidence that the defendant battered LeJeune [the woman he was living with] on a number of occasions during the course of their relationship. Stark's testimony was offered to assist the jury in understanding whether LeJeune's conduct was consistent with the pattern and profile of a battered woman. His expert testimony provided the jury with a relevant insight into LeJeune's behavior that it might not otherwise bring to its evaluation of her credibility. That insight was made more significant in light of the defendant's extensive cross-examination of Le-Jeune, which focused on her failure to escape from the defendant when she had the opportunity to do so.

Moreover, Stark's testimony was particularly crucial to the jury's determination because although battered woman syndrome has become known to the public more widely than it was in the past, much of the subject still remains beyond the ken of the average juror. Indeed, "[c]ommentators have noted that the research data indicates that potential jurors may hold beliefs and attitudes about abused women at variance with the views of experts who have studied or had experience with abused women. In particular, males are likely to be skeptical about the fear the woman feels in an abusive relationship and about her inability to leave a setting in which abuse is threatened." [State v. Borrelli, 629 A.2d 1105 (1993)]. Reliance, therefore, on an expert such as Stark in a case such as this one was well warranted.

[W]e therefore are not persuaded that the court abused its discretion in admitting Stark's testimony, especially in light of the court's limiting instruction to the jury.[13] [A]ccordingly, the court did not abuse its discretion in admitting Stark's testimony.

[T]he judgment is affirmed.

---

13. In its final charge to the jury, the court instructed in relevant part:

"Dr. Stark's testimony presented a general description of battered woman syndrome, and he then testified as to certain characteristics that are commonly found in relationships involving domestic violence and on general or typical behavior patterns of victims of domestic violence. Dr. Stark, however, did not testify about whether Carissa LeJeune was in fact battered or whether her testimony here in court was truthful and accurate. His testimony was offered instead to help you understand whether Ms. Le-Jeune's conduct was consistent with the pattern and profile of a battered woman to help explain her conduct and thus to aid you in evaluating the credibility of her testimony.

"Expert testimony is presented to you to assist you in your deliberations. No such testimony is binding upon you, however, and you may disregard such testimony either in whole or in part. It's up to you as triers of the facts to determine whether such testimony was credible and whether and how it

SKINNER v. STATE

Supreme Court of Wyoming, 2001.
33 P.3d 758.

■ KITE, JUSTICE.

This is an appeal from Brad Skinner's conviction of aggravated assault and battery. [M]r. Skinner was sentenced to life in prison pursuant to Wyo. Stat. Ann. § 6–10–201, the habitual criminal law.

[I]n its case-in-chief, the state called an expert witness to testify regarding the battered woman syndrome. Mr. Skinner argues a portion of the testimony was inadmissible because the expert referenced patterns in domestic violence situations and how a batterer's anger and violence often escalates. Mr. Skinner complains this testimony implied to the jury that he had acted in conformity with the profile of a batterer and, in fact, held a knife to his wife's throat.

[A]lthough battered-woman-syndrome testimony is admissible and helpful to the jury, it must not run afoul of W.R.E. 404(a) which provides in pertinent part: "Evidence of a person's character or a trait of his character is not admissible for the purpose of proving that he acted in conformity therewith on a particular occasion." When battered-woman-syndrome testimony is raised by the state in its case-in-chief and relates to a defendant, as it did in the instant case, the "testimony 'draws close to commenting directly on what likely happened' and 'looks like character evidence after all.' " *Ryan [v. State]*, 988 P.2d [46] at 55 [Wyo. 1999] (quoting Christopher B. Mueller & Laird C. Kirkpatrick, 3 Federal Evidence § 637 (2d ed.1994)).

[T]he expert in the instant case did not directly reference the particular character traits of Mr. Skinner. He did, however, explore the general cycle of violence, the shortened period of remorse, the escalation of violence, and the patterns of control. The use of profile testimony has been examined in the following way:

> Strictly speaking, the data offered to create a social framework are not "character evidence," since they do not pertain to "*a person's* character or a trait of *his* character." Rather, the research describes the behavior of *groups* or *other* persons. Yet the purpose of offering character evidence is similar to the purpose of introducing social frameworks: to prove—that is, to make "more probable or less probable"—that an individual acted in conformity with an established pattern. By definition, knowledge of the general pattern of an individual's behavior (i.e., his or her character)—like knowledge of the general

applies to the case. It's for you to consider the testimony with the other circumstances in the case and using your best judgment determine whether you will give it any weight and, if so, what weight you will give to it."

pattern of behavior in persons in the groups to which he or she belongs—allows one to recalculate the probabilities that the person acted in a certain way on a given occasion. The policy concern that gave rise to a rule barring the admissibility of evidence of an individual's "characteristic" behavior applies with equal force to the use of information on behavior characteristic of the groups to which he or she belongs: individuals should be accountable for their specific acts and not for their general proclivities.

Laurens Walker & John Monahan, *Social Frameworks: A New Use of Social Science in Law,* 73 Va. L.Rev. 559, 581 (1987). The following aptly describes the most appropriate guideline:

> However firm the libertarian values barring the admission of character evidence, modern evidence law, as exemplified by the Federal Rules, contains several important exceptions allowing the introduction of character evidence. In criminal proceedings, the defendant may offer evidence of his or her own character and, if this occurs, the prosecution may offer character evidence in rebuttal. The defendant also may offer evidence of the victim's character, and if this occurs, the prosecution again may offer character evidence in rebuttal. In either civil or criminal proceedings, any party may offer evidence of the character of a witness. In addition, the prohibition against character evidence operates only when that evidence is used to prove that a person "acted" in conformity with his or her character on a particular occasion. Character evidence may be admissible for many other purposes such as proof of knowledge, intent, or preparation.

> The rule against character evidence, therefore, suggests a bar to some, but by no means all, applications of social frameworks. Where traditional forms of character evidence are prohibited, social frameworks also should be barred; where traditional forms of character evidence are allowed, there is no reason to prohibit social frameworks.

Id. at 581–82. The introduction of the battered woman syndrome should not be a prosecutorial tool to covertly allow expert testimony regarding the dynamics and propensities of batterers intended to show a defendant acted in conformity therewith during the incident at issue.

In this case, the assault itself was undisputed. Mr. Skinner did not first open the door to character testimony, and the testimony did not have an alternate proper evidentiary purpose such as intent or motive. Mr. Skinner argues the only purpose of the expert testimony regarding the behavior of a batterer was to leave the implication that, because he had a history of battering his wife, he had, in fact, threatened his wife with a knife, thus constituting aggravated assault. Under these circumstances, the profile testimony is inadmissible.

Applying the harmless error analysis, we cannot discern from the record a reasonable possibility that the verdict might have been more favorable to Mr. Skinner if the error had never occurred. The expert's testimony, while discussing the pattern of escalating violence, did not suggest the escalation would typically include the use of a deadly weapon, such as a knife. The victim ultimately testified, confirming her initial statement to the police at the time of the assault, that Mr. Skinner had threatened her with a knife. The jury also heard about Mr. Skinner's additional assault on his wife after his arrest and the threats he made against her if she testified at trial that he had used a knife—a fact that most likely persuaded the jury he had done so. The knife was also found in his pocket. There was ample evidence from which the jury could conclude the knife was used without drawing any indirect inference from the expert's profile testimony which covered only seven pages of the more than 530 pages of transcript. In closing argument, the state did not unduly reference the objectionable testimony. [W]e conclude the error did not affect Mr. Skinner's substantial rights and, therefore, was harmless.

––––––

CALIFORNIA EVIDENCE CODE (2005)

§ 1107. Expert Witness Testimony on Intimate Partner Battering and Its Effects.

(a) In a criminal action, expert testimony is admissible by either the prosecution or the defense regarding intimate partner battering and its effects, including the nature and effect of physical, emotional, or mental abuse on the beliefs, perceptions, or behavior of victims of domestic violence, except when offered against a criminal defendant to prove the occurrence of the act or acts of abuse which form the basis of the criminal charge.

(b) The foundation shall be sufficient for admission of this expert testimony if the proponent of the evidence establishes its relevancy and the proper qualifications of the expert witness. Expert opinion testimony on intimate partner battering and its effects shall not be considered a new scientific technique whose reliability is unproven.

––––––

JAHNKE v. WYOMING

Supreme Court of Wyoming, 1984.
682 P.2d 991.

■ THOMAS, JUSTICE.

[On November 16, 1982, Richard John Jahnke, then 16 years old, killed his father with a shotgun as the father was returning home after dinner at a restaurant. Jahnke had prepared for the shooting for an hour and a half. He was charged with first-degree murder. The state did not seek the death penalty. Jahnke pleaded self-defense, arguing that his father had repeatedly beaten him, his sister, and his mother over the course of many years. He was convicted by a jury of the lesser included offense of voluntary manslaughter and sentenced by the trial judge to 5 to 15 years in the state prison. Among the issues raised by the defendant on appeal was the trial judge's exclusion of psychiatric testimony on the issue of "battered youth."]

The essential questions presented in this case arise out of a notion that a victim of abuse has some special justification for patricide.

[P]rior to dealing with the specific issues raised by the appellant his theory of defense should be put in perspective. Appellant has cited to us the case of Buhrle v. State, 627 P.2d 1374 (Wyo.1981), which involved a homicide by a wife who claimed to be a victim of abuse. The cases which are cited in Burhle v. State, supra, lead into a series of cases involving homicides committed by women who were perceived as being victims of the "battered-wife syndrome." While those cases deal with wives as victims of abuse, conceptually there is no reason to distinguish a child who is a victim of abuse. A perusal of those cases leads to a conclusion that the effort which is made on behalf of the defendants is to secure the recognition of a special defense in a homicide case for victims of family abuse. Succinctly stated, the attempt that is made is to establish the concept that one who is a victim of family abuse is justified in killing the abuser.

The departure of this theory from the usual requirements of self-defense is patent. In Garcia v. State, 667 P.2d 1148 (Wyo.1983), the prior decisions of this court with respect to the defense of self-defense were collected. There we said:

> "[T]hat to justify the taking of human life in self-defense, it must appear from the evidence that the defendant not only really, and in good faith, endeavored to decline any conflict with the deceased, and to escape from his assailant, if he had the opportunity to do so, if he was assailed, before he fired the shot in question, but it must also appear that the circumstances were such as to excite the fears of a reasonable person that the deceased intended to take his life, or to inflict upon him great bodily harm, and that the defendant really acted under the influence of such fears, and not in a spirit of revenge.... Ross v. State, supra [8 Wyo. 351, 57 P. 924 (1899)], 8 Wyo. at 383, 57 P. at 931."

It is clear that self-defense is circumscribed by circumstances involving a confrontation, usually encompassing some overt act or acts by the deceased, which would induce a reasonable person to fear that his life was in danger or that at least he was threatened with great bodily harm.

This same circumstantial circumscription is discernible in the line of cases involving abused or battered wives. See Ibn–Tamas v. United States, 407 A.2d 626 (D.C.App.1979); People v. White, 90 Ill.App.3d 1067, 46 Ill.Dec. 474, 414 N.E.2d 196 (1980); and State v. Thomas, 66 Ohio St.2d 518, 20 Ohio Op.3d 424, 423 N.E.2d 137 (1981). [A]lthough many people, and the public media, seem to be prepared to espouse the notion that a victim of abuse is entitled to kill the abuser, that special justification defense is antithetical to the mores of modern civilized society. It is difficult enough to justify capital punishment as an appropriate response of society to criminal acts even after the circumstances have been carefully evaluated by a number of people. To permit capital punishment to be imposed upon the subjective conclusion of the individual that prior acts and conduct of the deceased justified the killing would amount to a leap into the abyss of anarchy.

In People v. White, supra, and State v. Thomas, supra, the courts suggest that the true role of any evidence with respect to family abuse is to assist the jury to determine whether the defendant's belief that he was in danger of his life or serious bodily injury was reasonable under the circumstances. In those cases the courts indicate that expert testimony with respect to such an issue is neither necessary nor relevant and for that reason is best eschewed.

[C]ounsel for the appellant [described] the overall purpose of the testimony of the forensic psychiatrist. It is clear that the psychiatrist had interviewed the appellant on seven separate occasions for a total of twelve hours in preparation for the trial. He also had visited with other people about the appellant. At the trial appellant's counsel advised the court that the psychiatrist would express an opinion as to the appellant's mental or emotional condition, and the assertion was made that the appellant had a right to establish the facts which formed the basis for that opinion. The counter-argument of the State was premised upon Smith v. State, 564 P.2d 1194 (Wyo.1977), and was to the effect that such an opinion was not admissible in the absence of a plea of not guilty by reason of mental illness or deficiency. Reference was made to the psychiatrist's testimony at the time of the hearing on the appellant's motion to transfer the case to the juvenile court. On that occasion the psychiatrist had testified that in his opinion the appellant was a battered youth suffering from a mental disorder which was not defined or recognized under the accepted standards of diagnosis of mental and personality disorders in his field of expertise. At that hearing he related the history of the appellant's abuse at the hands of his father as the appellant had given it to him. He said that the appellant was very much afraid of his father.

[A]s noted, the appellant invokes the theory discussed in Buhrle v. State, supra, and the other cases involving the "battered-wife syndrome." We do not perceive how the offer of proof presented by the appellant was sufficient to satisfy the criteria for admissibility of expert testimony quoted in Buhrle v. State, supra, 627 P.2d 1374 (Wyo.1981) from Dyas v. United States, 376 A.2d 827, 832 (D.C.App.1977), cert. denied 434 U.S. 973, 98 S.Ct. 529, 54 L.Ed.2d 464 (1977). We particularly note that there was no offer to prove that the state of the pertinent art of scientific knowledge permitted a reasonable opinion to be asserted by the expert, and the suggestion of his earlier testimony on the occasion of the motion hearing is to the contrary.

[S]ince there is no error in these proceedings such as that claimed by the appellant, the judgment and sentence of the district court is affirmed.

■ Rose, Justice, dissenting, with whom Cardine, Justice, joins.

This case concerns itself with what happens—or can happen—and did happen when a cruel, ill-tempered, insensitive man roams, gun in hand, through his years of family life as a battering bully—a bully who, since his two children were babies, beat both of them and his wife regularly and unmercifully. Particularly, this appeal has to do with a 16–year–old boy who could stand his father's abuse no longer—who could not find solace or friendship in the public services which had been established for the purpose of providing aid, comfort and advice to abused family members—and who had no place to go or friends to help either him or his sister for whose protection he felt responsible and so—in fear and fright, and with fragmented emotion, Richard Jahnke shot and killed his father one night in November of 1982. In these courts, Richard pleads self-defense and, since the jury was given a self-defense instruction, it must be conceded that the trial judge recognized this as a viable defense theory under the evidence adduced at trial.

In this dissenting opinion, [I] find error in the majority opinion's conclusion that the trial court properly excluded the proffered expert psychiatric witness' testimony from the jury's consideration.

[D]enied the explanatory assistance of a qualified expert witness, it is as though Richard Jahnke had not been permitted to defend himself at all. [H]ow could this young boy structure an understandable defense when—even though the record discloses that since age two he had been bullied, battered, frightened and emotionally traumatized—he was, nevertheless, denied the opportunity to have explained to his jury how abused people reasonably handle their fears and anxieties—what their apprehensions are—how, in the dark moments of their aloneness, they perceive the imminence of danger—and how, in response, they undertake to assert their right of self-defense?

It is my conception that Richard Jahnke properly came to the courts of Wyoming asking—not that he be judged as one who, at the time and place in question, was insanely unreasonable—but that his 14 years of beatings and uncivilized emotional abuse be explained by a qualified expert in order that judgment be passed on the question which asks whether or not his behavior was sanely reasonable. One might wonder why—since our courts admit expert testimony with commendable regularity upon the issue of sanity when that is the ultimate fact—and the plea is insanity—it is not acceptable that a psychiatrist testify about whether behavior such as that with which this case is concerned and which is unlike that which lay jurors would understand to be the expected, is, nevertheless, sanely typical of the behavior of a reasonable person acting in the same or similar circumstances. Richard was not, however, permitted to have the impact of 14 years of abuse upon his alleged self-defensive behavior explained to the jury through the testimony of a psychiatrist even though this is the only way the fallout from brutality can be communicated.

[I]n contemplating the overall problem which brings on my dissent, it is initially necessary to be aware of at least these following facts:

Richard Jahnke, a sensitive boy who had never been in any sort of trouble in his life, had been beaten regularly and unmercifully by his father since he was two years old. On the night of the homicide he had received a severe beating, and when his father and mother left the house to go to dinner that night, his father said:

> "I'm disgusted with the shit you turned out to be. I don't want you to be here when I get back."

The father also said:

> "I don't care what I have to do, I'm going to get rid of you. I don't know how but I'm going to get rid of you, you bastard."

The boy felt he had to protect his sister who was hysterical when the mother and father left for dinner. He did not believe that there was any place or anyone where or to whom they could go for safety. The mother testified that the elder Jahnke always carried a gun, and Richard believed he had one with him that night. Mrs. Jahnke said that when the father said to Richard, "I'm going to get rid of you"?

> "He was trying to frighten him and maybe do something else besides just throwing him out of the house."

When Richard was in the garage after having stationed his father's guns around the house for "backup," he reflected upon past confrontations with his father and he was afraid the father would kill him when he returned and found what Richard had done with the guns. Even as he contemplated these things, the father drove the car into the driveway. Richard said he wanted to go and hug him and tell him he loved him, but he remembered when he had done this before, he had received a beating for his efforts. He knew from past experience that when his father "stomped" after him that he was in for a beating. He testified about how his father approached the garage door that night:

> "A. Yes. I remember he was stomping. When he stomped down the hall when he was really mad and really prepared to beat someone up, beat on one of us. I remember being a little kid, just sitting in my room. My dad stomping after me to hit me, that I could never stop him.

> "This time I stopped him."

[I]n this appeal [w]e do not have defensive behavior with which the lay juror is naturally familiar, and yet a doctor of psychiatric medicine was denied the opportunity to testify that Richard Jahnke's behavior was that of a battered individual whose consequent perception of the imminence of danger is different than the perception of the nonbrutalized person and who would have explained how the battered person responds to danger. Here, the victim was "stomping" up the driveway in a familiarly menacing way into the face of the fears and anxieties of his son whom he had beaten for 14 years and who recognized the "stomping" as a preface to violence. Here, we have a boy who, from long experience, had come to know what to expect from this confrontation—who believed he would be beaten or would be killed by gun—who did not try to escape because he did not believe that he had any place to go and who did not feel that he could leave his sister unprotected—who taught his sister to fire the gun in case his father should kill him—all in what he believed to be his only defense against further savagery which he knew from past experience would surely come. Could a jury understand this behavior as falling within the requirements of the self-defense instruction without help from an expert psychiatric witness? The asking of the question is to answer it.

Therefore, in the ordinary self-defense situation where there are no psychiatric implications and where the jury is permitted to know what the accused knew about the violent character of his victim, there need be no expert testimony touching upon the reasonableness of the defendant's behavior. In normal circumstances, these are things that jurors can fathom for themselves. However, when the beatings of 14 years have—or may have—caused the accused to harbor types of fear, anxiety and apprehension with which the nonbrutalized juror is unfamiliar and which result in the taking of unusual defensive measures which, in the ordinary circumstances, might be thought about as premature, excessive or lacking in escape efforts by those who are uninformed about the fear and anxiety that permeate the world of the brutalized—then expert testimony is necessary to explain the battered-person syndrome and the way these people respond to what they understand to be the imminence of danger and to explain their propensity to employ deadly force in their self-defensive conduct. Given this information, the jury is then qualified to decide the reasonableness of a self-defense defendant's acts at the time and place in question.

[T]HE PROFFERED TESTIMONY OF
THE FORENSIC PSYCHIATRIST

Dr. McDonald, a forensic psychiatrist, was offered by the defendant for the purpose of testifying about the behavior of battered children—that Richard was a battered child—all as an aid to the triers of fact with respect to their obligation to decide whether or not this defendant—as a battered person—behaved reasonably on the night of November 16, 1982, but the court would not permit the jury to hear the testimony.

The defendant suggests that his offer of proof represented that Dr. McDonald would testify that:

1. The doctor had diagnosed Richard Jahnke as a battered child, based on interviews with him and upon other information.

2. Battered children behave differently from other children, and perceive things differently from other children.

3. Because he was a battered child, Jahnke reasonably believed himself to be in immediate danger on the night he shot his father, and perceived himself as acting in self-defense.

[T]his offer says to me that the doctor's testimony would have supplied such underlying psychiatric information as would have permitted the jury to resolve the issue of reasonableness in an intelligent and informed manner. Even if the offer is read to say that the testimony would have touched on the ultimate issue of the reasonableness of the defendant's behavior at the time and place in question, this is no longer prohibited—at least within the context of the law of this case. In Ibn–Tamas v. United States, 407 A.2d 626, 628 (D.C.App.1979), a battered-person self-defense case, the court said:

> "... As to the first—the 'ultimate facts' or 'ultimate issue' rule— Dr. Walker was not going to express an opinion on the ultimate question whether Mrs. Ibn–Tamas actually and reasonably believed she was in danger when she shot her husband. Rather, this expert would have merely supplied background data to help the jury make that crucial determination. See United States v. Hearst, 412 F.Supp. 889 (N.D.Cal.1976) (Hearst I). In any event, the ultimate issue rule has, over time, been reduced to a prohibition only against questions to an expert 'which, in effect, submit the whole case to an expert witness for decision.' n14 Id. There is no such risk here."

[L]astly, the majority opinion takes issue with the fact that the offer of proof does not meet the state-of-the-art criteria for the reception of battered-person expert testimony as set out in Dyas v. United States, 376 A.2d 827, 832 (D.C.App.1977), cert. denied 434 U.S. 973, 98 S.Ct. 529, 54 L.Ed.2d 464 (1977) and adopted by our Buhrle v. State, 627 P.2d 1374 (Wyo.1981). It is urged by the majority that it was not shown by Dr. McDonald's testimony that the battered-person theory had progressed to that place in the scientific scheme of things where a reasonable opinion can be asserted by an expert as to how a battered person perceives the imminence of danger and responds thereto.

[W]ith respect to the state-of-the-art issue, I would hold that the testimony in question is being recognized and admitted in a majority of jurisdictions in this country because it is central to the defense of the battered person who pleads self-defense—as is shown by the numerous citations of authority in this opinion—and therefore it was error as a matter of law to have excluded the testimony for the reason that there was inadequate foundation proof on this subject.

Even if we were to assign the same importance to this issue that the majority does, this court is obligated, in my opinion, to remand the case to the trial court for the purpose of supplementing the record in this regard. Ibn–Tamas v. United States, supra.

———

NOTE

1. Commutation of Sentence. On June 15, 1984, one week after the Wyoming Supreme Court upheld Richard Jahnke's 5–15 year prison sentence, Governor Ed Herschler commuted the sentence to three years at a state reform school. The Governor stated, "I guess I have some compassion for this young individual. I think it's something I had to do." Youth Who Killed Abusive Father Has Term Cut, New York Times, June 16, 1984 at

A6. Deborah Jahnke, Richard Jahnke's younger sister, was convicted at a separate trial and sentenced to 3–8 years in prison, a sentence that was also upheld by the Wyoming Supreme Court. One week after that decision, the Governor commuted her sentence to one year at a home for "troubled women." See A. Prendergast, Poison Tree: A True Story of Family Violence and Revenge (1986).

————

STATE v. NEMETH

Supreme Court of Ohio, 1998.
82 Ohio St.3d 202, 694 N.E.2d 1332.

■ [Moyer, Chief Justice.]

In the early morning hours of January 7, 1995, sixteen-year-old Brian Nemeth took a compound bow and arrows from his room and shot his mother, Suzanne Nemeth, five times in the head and neck. She died eight days later. Brian was tried for aggravated murder.

[A]t his trial, Brian testified that his mother had been abusive toward him for several years. She drank to excess several nights a week and when she was drinking she would become very angry with him—hitting, slapping, and psychologically abusing him.

Brian testified that [on the evening before the killing, his] mother started screaming and cursing at him and threw a full beer can at him, cutting his lip. He ran to his room and locked the door. He testified that his mother's tone had changed and she was cursing him and threatening to beat his face in. He believed that he was in serious danger. She had removed the phone from his room, so he could not call for help. [H]e was crying and shaking. She pounded on his door for several hours. [A]round 4:00 a.m., after hours of sitting there listening to his mother's threats and attempts to get into his room, Brian heard her walk away.

Brian testified, "[S]he walked—I don't know, [s]he kind of—she must have gave up or something. All of a sudden, I just—everything just started coming back to me and I just—the bow was in my room. * * * It was laying on my chair and the way I was facing, I was facing the chair and I was like a robot. I just picked it up and walked out in the hall. * * * I don't even—I don't even know where I was walking to. * * * I just kept on walking out towards the living room and I got to the end of the hall and my mom, she was laying there on the couch. I just started shooting. * * * I only remember the first shot. I blacked out. I found myself on the floor. I went back to my room."

After shooting his mother, Brian called the police and told them what happened. When they did not arrive immediately, he called back and begged the dispatcher to hurry. He cooperated with the paramedics and confessed to the police. His mother had a blood-alcohol level of 0.20 when she was killed.

The Juvenile Court of Jefferson County bound Brian over to the Jefferson County Court of Common Pleas and he was subsequently tried as an adult and convicted of murder. Prior to the bindover hearing, Brian was examined by Dr. James R. Eisenberg, Ph.D. Dr. Eisenberg diagnosed Brian as suffering from "battered child syndrome" and as having "very compatible symptoms as do women in abusive relationships."

[A]t the close of its case, the defense proffered the testimony of Dr. Eisenberg as an expert on battered child syndrome. The proffered testimony would have explained the psychological effects of long-term child abuse, including the effect on a child's perception of danger. The testimony was proffered in support of a self-defense theory. [T]he proffered testimony was not admitted into evidence.

[T]he court of appeals reversed Brian's conviction and remanded the cause for a new trial. The court of appeals held that the defense had put forth sufficient evidence to warrant the admission of expert testimony regarding battered child syndrome, in support of a claim of self-defense, and that preclusion of such testimony was prejudicial.

[T]he defense in this case did not ask that battered child syndrome be recognized as a new defense or an independent justification for the killing of an abusive parent. The proffer made at trial was limited to expert testimony that would explain the psychological effects of long-term child abuse, and was proffered in support of a self-defense theory as well as a charge on voluntary manslaughter. As such, the issue before us is an evidentiary matter and is governed by the Ohio Rules of Evidence.

[I]n this case, the testimony on battered child syndrome, which was proffered by the defense, is relevant for at least four separate purposes, including the determination of whether Brian (1) had acted with prior calculation and design as charged in the indictment, (2) had acted with purpose as required for the lesser included offense of murder, (3) had created the confrontation or initiated the aggression, and (4) had an honest belief that he was in imminent danger, a necessary element in the affirmative defense of self-defense.

[E]xpert testimony on battered child syndrome would, in this case, tend to enhance the probability that Brian's account of the facts leading up to the killing was truthful and would lend credibility to his assertion that he was in a state of rage and dissociation at the time of the killing. A diagnosis of battered child syndrome and an explanation of its effects would therefore be relevant in determining whether the case warranted a jury charge on voluntary manslaughter.

In addition to the requirement of relevancy, expert testimony must meet the criteria of *Evid.R. 702. Rule 702* provides that a witness may testify as an expert if all of the following apply:

"(A) The witness' testimony either relates to matters beyond the knowledge or experience possessed by lay persons or dispels a misconception common among lay persons;

"(B) The witness is qualified as an expert by specialized knowledge, skill, experience, training, or education regarding the subject matter of the testimony;

"(C) The witness' testimony is based on reliable scientific, technical, or other specialized information. * * * "

The first prong of the rule is satisfied in this case. This trial presents precisely the kind of situation in which expert testimony is most necessary. [N]onconfrontational killings do not fit the general pattern of self-defense. Without expert testimony, a trier of fact may not be able to understand that the defendant at the time of the killing could have had an honest belief that he was in imminent danger of death or great bodily harm. Further, it is difficult for the average person to understand the degree of helplessness an abused child may feel.

[E]xpert testimony as to the effects of abuse may also help to counter popular misconceptions about the nonreporting of abuse. Prolonged exposure to abuse results in feelings of powerlessness, embarrassment, fear of reprisal, isolation, and low self-esteem. These effects often prevent a child from seeking help from third parties. The abusive parent also generally becomes adept at concealing the abuse from outsiders. Note, Toffel, Crazy Women, Unharmed Men, and Evil Children: Confronting Myths About Battered People Who Kill Their Abusers, and the Argument for Extending Battering Syndrome Self–Defenses to all Victims of Domestic Violence (1996), *70 S.Cal.L.Rev. 337, 364*. The effects of abuse thereby diminish the likelihood that the defense will be able to present corroborating testimony of third parties.

Absent corroborating evidence, a trier of fact is likely to believe that the abuse allegations are fabricated in response to the charges levied against the child-defendant. The existence and prevalence of such misconceptions are evident in the transcript of this trial. The prosecution repeatedly stressed that Brian could have left the house again, that he could have gone to his father or grandparents, that he was not in actual imminent danger at the time of the killing, and implying that he must have created the allegations of abuse after the fact because, otherwise, more people would have known about it. Even the trial court judge questioned whether there was corroborating evidence of abuse before granting the state's motion *in limine,* excluding testimony on battered child syndrome in connection with a claim of self-defense.

[T]he second prong of the test has not been challenged. The trial court disallowed any testimony as to battered child syndrome and did not specifically challenge the qualifications of Dr. Eisenberg.

The final requirement for the admission of testimony by experts is whether the testimony is based on reliable scientific, technical, or other specialized information. Dr. Eisenberg's testimony was based on scientific, technical, or otherwise specialized information. He is a trained psychologist who has specialized training in the behavioral and psychological effects of child abuse. The only question remaining is whether the information supporting his opinion is sufficiently reliable.

[I]n *Miller [v. Bike Athletic Co., 687 N.E.2d 735 (1998)]*, the court designated the following four factors to be considered in evaluating the reliability of scientific evidence: (1) whether the theory or technique has been tested, (2) whether it has been subjected to peer review, (3) whether there is a known or potential rate of error, and (4) whether the methodology has gained general acceptance. These factors were adopted from *Daubert v. Merrell Dow Pharmaceuticals, Inc. (1993), 509 U.S. 579, 593–594, 113 S.Ct. 2786, 2797, 125 L.Ed.2d 469, 482–483*. Both the United States Supreme Court in *Daubert* and this court in *Miller* were careful to emphasize that none of these factors is a determinative prerequisite to admissibility. *Miller at 612–613, 687 N.E.2d at 741; Daubert at 593, 113 S.Ct. at 2797, 125 L.Ed.2d at 483*.

[T]hough it is not necessary to show general acceptance to pass the threshold of reliability for the admission of expert testimony, the behavioral and psychological effects of prolonged child abuse on the child have been generally accepted in the medical and psychiatric communities and therefore unquestionably meet the requisite level of reliability for admission as the subject of expert testimony.

[T]he behavioral and psychological effects of child abuse, or battered child syndrome, are most often discussed as a form of posttraumatic stress disorder ("PTSD"). PTSD is an anxiety disorder listed in the DSM–IV, which categorizes universally recognized mental disorders. This specific disorder has been recognized in children at least since 1987 when the DSM–III–R was published. The fourth and most recent edition of the manual specifically notes that PTSD can manifest in children. The triggering event for posttraumatic stress disorder can be any traumatic event that involved "actual or threatened death or serious injury, or a threat to the physical integrity of self or others" and where the person's response involved "intense fear, helplessness, or horror." DSM–IV at 427–428.

[T]he psychological effects of abuse suffered by battered children are equivalent to the effects of prolonged abuse experienced by abused women and have been recognized as appropriate for expert testimony in the context of battered women. The psychiatric and legal communities have clearly accepted that despite any minor differences in the degree of power differentials between the batterer and the abused, the psychological effects of family violence are legally indistinguishable whether suffered by children or adults.

Several states have allowed the defendant to present expert testimony of a "battered child" or "battered person" syndrome where a child has killed or attempted to kill an abusive family member. See, *e.g., State v. Janes (1993), 121 Wash.2d 220, 850 P.2d 495 (en banc)*. Still others, while not faced with the issue of expert testimony, have recognized that abused children may exhibit identifiable psychological characteristics that point to a causal connection between the abuse and the killing of the abuser. See, *e.g., People v. Cruickshank (1985), 105 A.D.2d 325, 484 N.Y.S.2d 328*. Six states have enacted statutes that allow the presentation of testimony regarding the psychological effects on victims of domestic violence, including children, in cases where the victim of abuse is on trial for acts of violence against the abuser. [See, e.g.,] *Tex.Code Crim. Pro. Art. 38.36(b)(2) (1997)*.

While specific legislation may be helpful in defining the parameters of a new defense, such legislative action is not necessary in order for us to determine whether expert testimony concerning battered child syndrome meets the evidentiary requirements of *Evid.R. 702* and whether it should therefore be admissible in appropriate cases. Battered child syndrome is not a new defense or justification for murder. We are making no new law with this opinion. Pursuant to well-established Rules of Evidence and case law dealing with the admission of expert testimony, we hold that the proffered expert testimony on battered child syndrome was both relevant and reliable and that the trial court in this case erred in granting the motion prohibiting the testimony. Because the preclusion of such testimony was prejudicial, we affirm the holding of the court of appeals, which vacated the defendant's conviction and remanded the cause for a new trial.

BATTERED CHILD SYNDROME AND OTHER PSYCHOLOGICAL EFFECTS OF SEXUAL AND PHYSICAL ABUSE OF CHILDREN

Regina Schuller and Patricia A. Hastings.
In Modern Scientific Evidence: The Law and Science of Expert Testimony, 2008–2009 ed. (D. L. Faigman, M. J. Saks, J. Sanders, and E. K. Cheng eds. 2008).

Some agreement in the area is found regarding the psychological impact that abuse can have on a child, but as to the existence of a specific syndrome or profile, the literature remains silent. Therefore, attempting to identify agreement and disagreement regarding battered child syndrome in the scientific literature is premature. The parallel between battered child syndrome and battered woman syndrome that has been drawn is, at this point, not based on an empirical body of work. There is a small body of research documenting the existence of some of the symptoms associated with battered woman syndrome in a proportion of abused children, but [t]hese areas are not yet well developed. Further, no studies have attempted to assess what group of symptoms constitute a reliable and valid battered child syndrome and how well it captures the impact of abuse in this population. The heterogeneity of children's responses to abuse suggests, however, that, as is the case with battered women, a single profile is unlikely to adequately capture the impact of abuse on a child.

In summary, the applicability of the research findings on battered women to battered children still needs to be demonstrated. Certainly the impact of the violence on these two populations will result in some similar effects, but generalizing from battered women to battered children, two very different populations, is only speculative until the effects can be demonstrated in the latter population. While there is evidence to suggest that PTSD [post-traumatic stress disorder] is associated with abuse (sexual and physical), there is also considerable variability in children's responses.

(b) Combat

The strain of combat, once known as "shell shock," has long been known to affect human behavior. Only with the advent of the Vietnam War, however, was "post-traumatic stress disorder," with combat being the "stressor," argued as a defense to crime.

STATE v. FELDE

Supreme Court of Louisiana, 1982.
422 So.2d 370.

■ WATSON, JUSTICE.

Defendant, Wayne Robert Felde, was convicted of first degree murder. The jury unanimously recommended a death sentence on the ground of one aggravating circumstance: the victim was a peace officer engaged in his lawful duties. The defendant has appealed.

[F]elde, convicted of manslaughter and assault in Maryland, was serving a twelve year sentence when he escaped from a minimum security job and hitchhiked to his mother's home in Grand Cane, Louisiana. [He] returned to Louisiana because of his mother's terminal cancer. [H]is mother died on October 13, 1978.

On October 20, 1978, Felde's sister, Florence McDonald, told him the police were looking for him. She drove Felde [to] Shreveport where Felde purchased a .357 Magnum gun and a box of shells. [Felde then went] to the Dragon Lounge [where he] drank enough beer to get "pretty loaded." [B]ecause a customer reported there was someone at the Lounge with a gun, two officers arrived. [A]fter being told Felde was the man with the gun, officers Norwood and Thompkins searched him but did not discover the pistol.

[O]fficer Thompkins arrested him as a simple drunk. Felde's hands were handcuffed behind his back and he was placed in the rear seat of Thompkins' police car. While Felde was being driven in the police car, William David Sweet, in another car, observed Felde up close behind the front seat. Felde was leaning forward on the right hand side of the driver. The officer put on his brakes and simultaneously made a motion to push Felde back in the seat. Felde said he was trying to shoot himself when he was pulled forward and pushed back. A shot was fired. There was testimony that the car filled with smoke. Felde did not remember anything after the first explosion. There were three other shots, leaving Felde with at least one bullet in his gun. The vehicle swerved against a guard rail and stopped. Thompkins staggered out of the car across the road before collapsing dead in a ditch.

[T]he defense was insanity at the time of the crime; defendant allegedly suffered a post-traumatic stress syndrome as the result of combat in Vietnam.

[T]here was lay testimony that there was a noticeable difference in Felde's behavior before and after his military duty in Vietnam. Before his service, he was a jovial, happy-go-lucky kid. Afterward, he was moody, depressed, and irritable, with erratic sleeping habits and a low tolerance for alcohol. One of Wayne Felde's sisters, Maria Kristine Krebsbach, testified that she had sent one brother to Vietnam and a different one, a stranger, had returned. This sister, a nurse, and her mother, also a nurse, attempted to get psychiatric help for Felde but were unable to do so.

[D]r. John P. Wilson testified for the defense as an expert psychologist and professor of psychology who has made special studies of the post-traumatic stress disorder in Vietnam veterans. Dr. Wilson examined Felde on August 30, 1979, at the Caddo Parish Jail for four and a half hours. Dr. Wilson concluded unequivocally that Wayne Felde had a chronic form of post-traumatic stress disorder. This is a recognized behavioral disorder or mental defect which is recognized by the American Psychiatric Association. The symptoms are also shared by survivors of atomic attacks, holocausts or natural disasters. Post-traumatic stress response symptoms include: depression; flashbacks to the trauma; inability to control one's impulses; violent, explosive behavior; frequent suicidal thoughts and recurring nightmares. There is often memory impairment and inability to feel close to people, an emotional numbing. There is a great deal of survivor guilt with this disorder. Because of the type of combat required in Vietnam, veterans of that conflict also have moral guilt. The disorder is not new but was only recently recognized by the American Psychiatric Association as a bonafide mental disorder. Sixty percent of Vietnam combat veterans experience post-traumatic stress, a very high percentage. This is because units did not stay together, there was no real war objective, the soldiers were quite young, and drugs were freely available at a low price. Vietnam soldiers averaged 19.2 years, whereas those in World War II and Korea averaged 26½. The units in World War II stayed intact and came home together whereas in Vietnam each veteran came home alone. Vietnam veterans with P.T.S.D., or post-traumatic stress disorder, tend to move from one job to another. Felde's military record showed three AWOLs and a drunk charge, the first AWOL occurring one month after he returned from Vietnam. On one of these occasions, Felde wrecked a brand new car; his behavior was erratic and irrational. These episodes were consistent with his post-traumatic stress syndrome as were his marital difficulties. Part of the syndrome is a hyper alertness, where the person becomes easily irritated and agitated and startles easily. Sleep disturbances are part of the disorder. Twenty-five percent of all men in prison are Vietnam era veterans. The suicide rate of Vietnam veterans is thirty-three to forty percent higher than that of others the same age. The alcoholism rate among Vietnam veterans is sixty percent higher than it was for veterans of World War II or Korea. The Veterans' Administration now recognizes post-traumatic stress disorder as a service connected disability for which treatment can be received. Stress in a person's emotional life, such as the death of a mother, can trigger disassociative reactions. Dr. Wilson said that Felde's Maryland killing sounded like a classic disassociative reaction in which a person uses survival contact tactics because he is not fully aware of what is happening. Many Vietnam veterans suffering from post-traumatic stress disorder are being misdiagnosed as being alcoholics or having other disorders. Felde's prison record in Maryland was exemplary, which is characteristic of Vietnam veterans. The confined, controlled environment helps the post-traumatic stress disorder. Although they suffer tremendously, such inmates tend to behave well while incarcerated. Dr. Wilson testified that, since his father died when Wayne Felde was twelve, he was particularly close to his mother, the most significant support person in his life. After losing his mother and then learning that the police were coming for him, he felt helpless, trapped and scared. He bought the gun as a form of security against an impending threat. Many Vietnam veterans even sleep with their weapons. In the doctor's opinion, Felde bought the gun as part of a decision to kill himself. When Felde pulled the gun in the car, it was Dr. Wilson's opinion that he wanted to kill himself rather than Officer Thompkins. Dr. Wilson recounted Felde's account of the situation beginning at the Dragon Lounge, "they asked me where, where I had the, where the gun was, then they handcuffed me and put me in the police car. I was in the back of the car and I thought I'd blow my brains out. I tried to turn the barrel around towards my face. I remember the jerk going forward then I saw flashes, flashes like incoming round hits, like firecrackers, hearing machine guns, I heard machine guns, I heard rifle fire, I heard more explosions and I couldn't move. I was happy because I knew I was going to die." According to Dr. Wilson, this fragmented memory is totally consistent with a disassociated state and flashback typical of post-traumatic stress disorder. In Dr. Wilson's opinion, "At that time, in that disassociated state, he couldn't discriminate right from wrong and he couldn't conform his conduct to the law. I think he was totally disoriented." (Tr.1806) Dr. Wilson said that Felde needed long term group psychotherapy with other veterans and, if he were put on the street, he would either kill himself or kill someone else.

[I]t is contended that the jury erred in finding Felde guilty of first degree murder and rejecting his defense of insanity at the time of the crime on the basis of the evidence presented.

Defendant is correct in his contention that the expert testimony about Felde's post-traumatic stress syndrome by Dr. Wilson, [and other defense experts], as well as the lay testimony about the effect of the Vietnam combat on Felde, is very persuasive. However, [t]he three members of the sanity commission all testified that defendant was sane at the time of the offense. [Two of these government witnesses] are psychiatrists and a rational jury could have adopted their testimony over that of the defense witnesses.

[T]he conviction and sentence of defendant, Wayne Robert Felde, are affirmed.

DIAGNOSTIC AND STATISTICAL MANUAL OF MENTAL DISORDERS (4TH ED., TEXT REVISION, 2000)*

American Psychiatric Association.

Diagnostic criteria for 309.81 Posttraumatic Stress Disorder

A. The person has been exposed to a traumatic event in which both of the following were present:

(1) the person experienced, witnessed, or was confronted with an event or events that involved actual or threatened death or serious injury, or a threat to the physical integrity of self or others

(2) the person's response involved intense fear, helplessness, or horror. **Note**: In children, this may be expressed instead by disorganized or agitated behavior.

B. The traumatic event is persistently reexperienced in one (or more) of the following ways:

(1) recurrent and intrusive distressing recollections of the event, including images, thoughts, or perceptions. **Note**: In young children, repetitive play may occur in which themes or aspects of the trauma are expressed.

(2) recurrent distressing dreams of the event. **Note**: In children, there may be frightening dreams without recognizable content.

(3) acting or feeling as if the traumatic event were recurring (includes a sense of reliving the experience, illusions, hallucinations, and dissociative flashback episodes, including those that occur on awakening or when intoxicated). **Note**: In young children, trauma-specific reenactment may occur.

(4) intense psychological distress at exposure to internal or external cues that symbolize or resemble an aspect of the traumatic event

(5) physiological reactivity on exposure to internal or external cues that symbolize or resemble an aspect of the traumatic event

C. Persistent avoidance of stimuli associated with the trauma and numbing of general responsiveness (not present before the trauma), as indicated by three (or more) of the following:

(1) efforts to avoid thoughts, feelings, or conversations associated with the trauma

(2) efforts to avoid activities, places, or people that arouse recollections of the trauma

(3) inability to recall an important aspect of the trauma

(4) markedly diminished interest or participation in significant activities

* Reprinted with permission from the Diagnostic and Statistical Manual of Mental Disorders, Fourth Edition, Copyright 2000, American Psychiatric Association.

(5) feeling of detachment or estrangement from others

(6) restricted range of affect (e.g., unable to have loving feelings)

(7) sense of a foreshortened future (e.g., does not expect to have a career, marriage, children, or a normal life span)

D. Persistent symptoms of increased arousal (not present before the trauma), as indicated by two (or more) of the following:

(1) difficulty falling or staying asleep

(2) irritability or outbursts of anger

(3) difficulty concentrating

(4) hypervigilance

(5) exaggerated startle response

E. Duration of the disturbance (symptoms in Criteria B, C, and D) is more than 1 month.

F. The disturbance causes clinically significant distress or impairment in social, occupational, or other important areas of functioning.

———

NOTES

1. Prevalence of the disorder. Hoge, Castro, Messer, McGurk, Cotting, and Koffman, Combat Duty in Iraq and Afghanistan, Mental Health Problems, and Barriers to Care, 351 New England Journal of Medicine 13 (2004), evaluated members of three Army units and one Marine Corps unit either before their deployment to Iraq (n=2,530) or three to four months after their return from combat duty in Iraq or Afghanistan (n=3,671). The percentage of subjects whose responses met the screening criteria for major depression, generalized anxiety disorder, or PTSD was significantly higher after duty in Iraq (16 to 17 percent) than after duty in Afghanistan (11 percent) or before deployment to Iraq (9 percent). Of those whose responses were positive for a mental disorder, only 23 to 40 percent sought mental health care.

2. Veterans Treatment Courts. In 2008, a special court for veterans was established in Buffalo, New York. According to Presiding Judge Robert Russell, Buffalo Establishes First Veterans Treatment Court, 3 National Council Magazine 20 (2008):

> The court seeks to divert eligible veteran defendants with addiction disorders and/or mental illness who are charged with nonviolent criminal offenses to a specialized criminal docket that substitutes treatment and problem solving for traditional court processing. [T]he veterans voluntarily participate in a judicially supervised treatment plan that they help develop, along with a team of court staff, healthcare and mental health professionals, and peer mentors. At regular status hearings, treatment plans and other conditions are reviewed for appropriateness, incentives are offered to reward adherence to court condi-

tions, and sanctions for nonadherence are handed down. Completion of the program is defined according to specific criteria. Many veterans have their charges dismissed, and others are assured of a nonincarcerative sentence on conclusion of treatment.

3. Next edition. The Fifth Edition of the Diagnostic and Statistical Manual of Mental Disorders (DSM–V) is scheduled to be published by the American Psychiatric Association in 2012. Updates on the progress of DSM–V can be found at http://www.dsm5.org.

(c) Kidnapping

While many people have been assaulted and many have served in combat, relatively few have been the victims of kidnappers. In one notorious case, social science research was used to provide an empirical context for decision makers to assess the effects of being kidnapped and held hostage upon the state of mind of the kidnap victim, who later became a criminal defendant.

UNITED STATES v. HEARST

United States District Court, Northern District of California, 1976.
Trial Transcript, Criminal Case 74–374.

[Patricia Hearst was tried for the crimes of armed bank robbery and use of a weapon during the commission of a felony. She pleaded duress as a defense, premised on the fact that approximately 10 weeks prior to the alleged crimes, she had been kidnapped from her apartment in Berkeley, California, by members of a group calling itself the Symbionese Liberation Army and held captive. In support of her defense, Dr. Louis West, a psychiatrist, was called as an expert witness to testify regarding, among other things, the nature of "coercive persuasion."]

Direct Examination by Mr. Bailey:

Q. [Have] you worked together in the past fifteen or twenty years with others who are recognized experts in the field of coercive persuasion?

A. [I] would say that I've joined with others in consulting. Some of the more specific types of laboratory studies to try to reproduce these results, I haven't actually carried out myself. But, when, for example, the Zimbardo experiments at Stanford were published and broadcast last year, they came as no surprise to those of us who were familiar with the old coercive persuasion research, because it was exactly what you would expect. That study done at Stanford University, you may recall, took a group of normal young men, divided them in half, and half of them were assigned the role of prisoners and the other half were assigned the role of captors. And, it was a game. And, they were being paid for this and it was supposed to run two weeks. And, Doctor Zimbardo and his group had to stop the experiment after six days, because by that time fifty percent of those who were supposed to be prisoners in this artificial laboratory game at the university had broken down one way or another and had shown such psychological disturbances that they had to take them out so they couldn't continue it past six days.

[C]ross–Examination by Mr. Bancroft

Q. Doctor, in your direct testimony, you spoke of some studies done by a gentleman down here in Palo Alto by the name of Zimbardo. Do you remember that?

A. Yes.

Q. Those studies, I think to refresh the jury's recollection, had to do with prisoner—a prisoner situation in which students were solicited as volunteers to act as guards and some as prisoners; is that right?

A. Young men were solicited to act as volunteers. I don't think they were students.

Q. And in that study, the volunteers were solicited by a newspaper ad, were they not, calling for them to participate in a psychological study of prison life? Do you remember that?

A. I don't remember the newspaper ad, but I know that Dr. Zimbardo solicited volunteers.

Q. Well, as a matter of fact, you called him down at Stanford a short time ago to ask about his research; didn't you?

A. To ask him about whether there were any other publications on it beyond those that I had already read.

Q. And—

A. Fascinating experiment.

Q. Why?

A. The Zimbardo Study?

Q. Yes.

A. It shows how tremendously people can be caught up in a role even to the point of getting sick in it in a very short period of time.

Q. Do you think that that's what that study represents, Doctor?

A. That's a very important part of what it represents.

Q. Well, real prison guards and real prisoners aren't sick, are they, and they are assigned their roles in a prison?

A. [I]t's been my observation that people commonly do get sick in prisons, especially under conditions of the type that were simulated in the Zimbardo experiment.

[Q.] Doctor, does the Zimbardo study really prove anything more than when people are assigned certain tasks, they tend to solidify themselves and do it with some vigor?

A. They weren't assigned the task of having nervous breakdowns.

Q. No, and therefore, isn't that study peculiar for that very reason?

A. Well, I didn't consider it peculiar. The thing that differentiated the Zimbardo study and made it especially interesting was that it was done under such relatively benign conditions and results were so disastrous so fast; in six days, 50 percent of the prisoners were sick. Now, that's a significant result.

Q. Do you think comparing that to the general prison situation, real prisoners put in real prisons, 50 percent of them get mentally sick?

A. No, I wouldn't say that.

[Q.] Wasn't it—don't you think, Doctor, it was because they thought it was a game and not even though they thought it was a game [that the subjects became sick]?

A. Mr. Bancroft, I assure you people do not deliberately develop the kind of psychiatric disturbances that these young men did in the course of a game.

UNITED STATES v. HEARST

United States District Court, Northern District of California, 1976.
412 F.Supp. 889.

MEMORANDUM AND ORDER DENYING PLAINTIFF'S MOTIONS TO BAR DEFENDANT'S PROFFERED PSYCHIATRIC TESTIMONY AND MOTION TO STRIKE EXPERT TESTIMONY

■ Oliver J. Carter, Chief Judge.

The Government has filed extensive points and authorities in support of its motion to bar the introduction of testimony by expert witnesses on the defendant's mental state at the time of the bank robbery for which she is now on trial.

[A]s the Court understands the purpose of psychiatric expert testimony offered here by the defense, it is to explain the effects kidnapping, prolonged incarceration, and psychological and physical abuse may have had on the defendant's mental state at the time of the robbery, insofar as such mental state is relevant to the asserted defense of coercion or duress. The jury, of course, are free to accept or reject the defendant's own account of her experiences with her captors. If they choose, however, to believe her testimony, then they may be served by the testimony of the experts called by both sides in determining whether or not the defendant was coerced into committing the offenses charged in the indictment.

[T]he Court is of the opinion that the peculiar question to which the experts here will address themselves—whether the defendant's initial status as a kidnap victim and the subsequent treatment of her by her captors could have deprived her of the requisite general intent to commit the offense charged—is not only relevant to the asserted defense of coercion but also beyond the common experience of most jurors and within the special competence of the experts. The jury need not concur with the expert opinions expressed on this matter, but this Court will not deprive them of the opportunity to consider the testimony that will be offered and make whatever use of it they deem advisable.

Accordingly, IT IS ORDERED that plaintiff's motion to bar admission of expert psychiatric testimony on the issue of coercion and general intent be, and the same is hereby, denied.

IT IS FURTHER ORDERED that plaintiff's motion to strike the testimony of Dr. Louis J. West be, and the same is hereby, denied.

INTERPERSONAL DYNAMICS IN A SIMULATED PRISON

Craig Haney, Curtis Banks, and Philip Zimbardo.
1 International Journal of Criminology and Penology 69 (1973).

The effects of playing the role of "guard" or "prisoner" were studied in the context of an experimental simulation of a prison environment. The research design was a relatively simple one, involving as it did only a single treatment variable, the random assignment to either a "guard" or "prisoner" condition. These roles were enacted over an extended period of time (nearly one week) within an environment which was physically constructed to resemble a prison. Central to the methodology of creating and maintaining a psychological state of imprisonment was the functional simulation of significant properties of "real prison life" (established through information from former inmates, correctional personnel and texts).

The "guards" were free with certain limits to implement the procedures of induction into the prison setting and maintenance of custodial retention of the "prisoners". These inmates, having voluntarily submitted to the conditions of this total institution in which they now lived, coped in various ways with its stresses and its challenges. The behaviour of both groups of subjects was observed, recorded and analyzed. The dependent measures were of two general types: transactions between and within each group of subjects, recorded on video and audio tape as well as directly observed; individual reactions on questionnaires, mood inventories, personality tests, daily guard shift reports, and post experimental interviews.

Subjects

The 21 subjects who participated in the experiment were selected from an initial pool of 75 respondents, who answered a newspaper advertisement asking for male volunteers to participate in a psychological study of "prison life" in return for payment of $15 per day. Those who responded to the notice completed an extensive questionnaire concerning their family background, physical and mental health history, prior experience and attitudinal propensities with respect to sources of psychopathology (including their involvement in crime). Each respondent who completed the background questionnaire was interviewed by one of two experimenters. Finally, the 24 subjects who were judged to be most stable (physically and mentally), most mature, and least involved in anti-social behaviour were selected to participate in the study. On a random basis, half of the subjects were assigned the role of "guard", half to the role of "prisoner."

The subjects were normal, healthy males attending colleges throughout the United States who were in the Stanford area during the summer. They were largely of middle class socio-economic status, Caucasians (with the exception of one Oriental subject). Initially they were strangers to each other, a selection precaution taken to avoid the disruption of any pre-existing friendship patterns and to mitigate against any transfer into the experimental situation of previously established relationships or patterns of behaviour.

[P]rocedure

Physical aspects of the prison

The prison was built in a 35–ft section of a basement corridor in the psychology building at Stanford University. It was partitioned by two fabricated walls, one of which was fitted with the only entrance door to the cell block, the other contained a small observation screen. Three small cells (6 x 9 ft) were made from converted laboratory rooms by replacing the usual doors with steel barred, black painted ones, and removing all furniture.

A cot (with mattress, sheet and pillow) for each prisoner was the only furniture in the cells. A small closet across from the cells served as a solitary confinement facility; its dimensions were extremely small (2 x 2 x 7 ft) and it was unlit.

[R]ole instruction

All subjects had been told that they would be assigned either the guard or the prisoner role on a completely random basis and all had voluntarily agreed to play either role for $15.00 per day for up to two weeks. They signed a contract guaranteeing a minimally adequate diet, clothing, housing and medical care as well as the financial remuneration in return for their stated "intention" of serving in the assigned role for the duration of the study.

It was made explicit in the contract that those assigned to be prisoners should expect to be under surveillance (have little or no privacy) and to have some of their basic civil rights suspended during their imprisonment, excluding physical abuse. They were given no other information about what to expect nor instructions about behaviour appropriate for a prisoner role. Those actually assigned to this treatment were informed by phone to be available at their place of residence on a given Sunday when we would start the experiment.

The subjects assigned to be guards attended an orientation meeting on the day prior to the induction of the prisoners. At this time they were introduced to the principal investigators, the "Superintendent" of the prison (P.G.Z.) and an undergraduate research assistant who assumed the administrative role of "Warden". They were told that we wanted to try to simulate a prison environment within the limits imposed by pragmatic and ethical considerations. Their assigned task was to "maintain the reasonable degree of order within the prison necessary for its effective functioning", although the specifics of how this duty might be implemented were not explicitly detailed.

[U]pon arrival at our experimental prison, each prisoner was stripped, sprayed with a delousing preparation (a deodorant spray) and made to stand alone naked for a while in the cell yard. After being given the uniform described previously and having an I.D. picture taken ("mug shot"), the prisoner was put in his cell and ordered to remain silent.

Administrative routine

When all the cells were occupied, the warden greeted the prisoners and read them the rules of the institution (developed by the guards and the warden). They were to be memorized and to be followed. Prisoners were to be referred to only by the number on their uniforms, also in an effort to depersonalize them.

The prisoners were to be served three bland meals per day, were allowed three supervised toilet visits, and given two hours daily for the privilege of reading or letterwriting. Work assignments were issued for which the prisoners were to receive an hourly wage to constitute their $15 daily payment. Two visiting periods per week were scheduled, as were movie rights and exercise periods. Three times a day all prisoners were lined up for a "count" (one on each guard work-shift). The initial purpose of the "count" was to ascertain that all prisoners were present, and to test them on their knowledge of the rules and their I.D. numbers. The first perfunctory counts lasted only about 10 minutes, but on each successive day (or night) they were spontaneously increased in duration until some lasted several hours. Many of the pre-established features of administrative routine were modified or abandoned by the guards, and some were forgotten by the staff over the course of the study.

[R]esults

Although it is difficult to anticipate exactly what the influence of incarceration will be upon the individuals who are subjected to it and those charged with its maintenance (especially in a simulated reproduction), the results of the present experiment support many commonly held conceptions of prison life and validate anecdotal evidence supplied by articulate ex-convicts. The environment of arbitrary custody had great impact upon the affective states of both guards and prisoners as well as upon the interpersonal processes taking place between and within those role-groups.

In general, guards and prisoners showed a marked tendency toward increased negativity of affect and their overall outlook became increasingly negative. As the experiment progressed, prisoners expressed intentions to do harm to others more frequently. For both prisoners and guards, self-evaluations were more deprecating as the experience of the prison environment became internalized.

Overt behaviour was generally consistent with the subjective self-reports and affective expressions of the subjects. Despite the fact that guards and prisoners were essentially free to engage in any form of interaction (positive or negative, supportive or affrontive, etc.), the characteristic nature of their encounters tended to be negative, hostile, affrontive and dehumanising. Prisoners immediately adopted a generally passive response mode while guards assumed a very active initiating role in all interactions. Throughout the experiment commands were the most frequent form of verbal behaviour and, generally verbal exchanges were strikingly impersonal, with few references to individual identity. Although it was clear to all subjects that the experimenters would not permit physical violence to take place, varieties of less direct aggressive behaviour were observed frequently (especially on the part of guards). In lieu of physical violence, verbal affronts were used as one of the most frequent forms of interpersonal contact between guards and prisoners.

The most dramatic evidence of the impact of this situation upon the participants was seen in the gross reactions of five prisoners who had to be released because of extreme emotional depression, crying, rage and acute anxiety. The pattern of symptoms was quite similar in four of the subjects and began as early as the second day of imprisonment. The fifth subject was released after being treated for a psychosomatic rash which covered portions of his body. Of the remaining prisoners, only two said they were not willing to forfeit the money they had earned in return for being "paroled". When the experiment was terminated prematurely after only six days, all the remaining prisoners were delighted by their unexpected good fortune. In contrast, most of the guards seemed to be distressed by the decision to stop the experiment and it appeared to us they had become sufficiently involved in their roles so that they now enjoyed the extreme control and power which they exercised and were reluctant to give it up. One guard did report being personally upset at the suffering of the prisoners and claimed to have considered asking to change his role to become one of them—but never did so. None of the guards ever failed to come to work on time for their shift, and indeed, on several occasions guards remained on duty voluntarily and uncomplaining for extra hours—without additional pay.

The extremely pathological reactions which emerged in both groups of subjects testify to the power of the social forces operating, but still there were individual differences seen in styles of coping with this novel experience and in degrees of successful adaptation to it. Half the prisoners did endure the oppressive atmosphere, and not all the guards resorted to hostility. Some guards were tough but fair ("played by the rules"), some went far beyond their roles to engage in creative cruelty and harassment, while a few were passive and rarely instigated any coercive control over the prisoners.

[C]onclusions and Discussion

It should be apparent that the elaborate procedures (and staging) employed by the experimenters to insure a high degree of mundane realism in this mock prison contributed to its effective functional simulation of the psychological dynamics operating in "real" prisons. We observed empirical relationships in the simulated prison environment which were strikingly isomorphic to the internal relations of real prisons, corroborating many of the documented reports of what occurs behind prison walls.

The conferring of differential power on the status of "guard" and "prisoner" constituted, in effect, the institutional validation of those roles. But further, many of the subjects ceased distinguishing between prison role and their prior self-identities. When this occurred, within what was a surprisingly short period of time, we witnessed a sample of normal, healthy American college students fractionate into a group of prison guards who seemed to derive pleasure from insulting, threatening, humiliating and dehumanizing their peers—those who by chance selection had been as-signed to the "prisoner" role. The typical prisoner syndrome was one of passivity, dependency, depression, helplessness and self-deprecation. Pris-oner participation in the social reality which the guards had structured for them lent increasing validity to it and, as the prisoners became resigned to their treatment over time, many acted in ways to justify their fate at the hands of the guards, adopting attitudes and behaviour which helped to sanction their victimization. Most dramatic and distressing to us was the observation of the ease with which sadistic behaviour could be elicited in individuals who were not "sadistic types" and the frequency with which acute emotional breakdowns could occur in men selected precisely for their emotional stability.

———

NOTES

1. External validity. The most frequent criticism of this study is that it lacked external validity, i.e., that its findings cannot be generalized to "real" prisoners and guards. This was the contention of the prosecution in *Hearst* and also of Banuazizi and Movahedi, Interpersonal Dynamics in a Simulated Prison: A Methodological Analysis, 30 American Psychologist 151, 156 (1975), who offered the following alternative explanation to account for the findings of the Haney et al. study:

> (a) The subjects entered the experiment carrying strong social stereotypes of how guards and prisoners act and relate to one another in a real prison; (b) in the experimental context itself, there were numerous cues pointing to the experimental hypothesis, the experi-menters' expectations, and possibly, the experimenter's ideological

commitment; and thus (c) complying with the actual or perceived demands in the experimental situation, and acting on the basis of their own role-related expectancies, the subjects produced data highly in accord with the experimental hypothesis.

To evaluate whether Haney, Banks, and Zimbardo's subjects had pre-existing stereotypic expectations of the prisoner and guard roles, Banuazizi and Movahedi sent a questionnaire to 185 undergraduate students in the Boston area (who had not heard of the Stanford study) describing its methodology. They asked their respondents to identify the purpose of the Stanford study and to predict the subjects' behavior. "[T]he overwhelming majority of the respondents (81%) were able to articulate quite accurately the intent of the experiment [and] 89.9% predicted that the behavior of guards toward prisoners would be oppressive, hostile, aggressive, etc." Id. at 157–8.

2. **Website.** Material related to the Stanford Prison Experiment, including a slide show, can be found at http://www.prisonexp.org.

———

FINAL REPORT OF THE INDEPENDENT PANEL TO REVIEW DEPARTMENT OF DEFENSE DETENTION OPERATIONS, 2004.

James R. Schlesinger, Chair.

The potential for abusive treatment of detainees during the Global War on Terrorism was entirely predictable based on a fundamental understanding of the principle of social psychology principles coupled with an awareness of numerous known environmental risk factors. Most leaders were unacquainted with these known risk factors, and therefore failed to take steps to mitigate the likelihood that abuses of some type would occur during detainee operations. While certain conditions heightened the possibility of abusive treatment, such conditions neither excuse nor absolve the individuals who engaged in deliberate immoral or illegal behaviors.

The abuse the detainees endured at various places and times raises a number of questions about the likely psychological aspects of inflicting such abuses. Findings from the field of social psychology suggest that the conditions of war and the dynamics of detainee operations carry inherent risks for human mistreatment, and therefore must be approached with great caution and careful planning and training.

The Stanford Prison Experiment

In 1973, Haney, Banks and Zimbardo published their landmark Stanford study, "Interpersonal Dynamics in a Simulated Prison." Their study provides a cautionary tale for all military detention operations. The Stanford Experiment used a set of tested, psychologically sound college students in a benign environment. In contrast, in military detention operations, soldiers work under stressful combat conditions that are far from benign.

The Stanford Prison Experiment attempted to "create a prison-like situation" and then observe the behavior of those involved. The researchers randomly assigned 24 young men to either the "prison" or "guard" group. Psychological testing was used to eliminate participants with overt psychopathology, and extensive efforts were made to simulate actual prison conditions. The experiment, scheduled to last two weeks, was cancelled after only six days due to the ethical concerns raised by the behaviors of the participants. The study notes that while guards and prisoners were free to engage in any form of interpersonal interactions, the "characteristic nature of their encounters tended to be negative, hostile, affrontive and dehumanizing."

The researchers found that both prisoners and guards exhibited "pathological reactions" during the course of the experiment. Guards fell into three categories: (1) those who were "tough but fair," (2) those who were passive and reluctant to use coercive control and, of special interests, (3) those who "went far beyond their roles to engage in creative cruelty and harassment." With each passing day, guards "were observed to generally escalate their harassment of the prisoners." The researchers reported: "We witnessed a sample of normal, healthy American college students fractionate into a group of prison guards who seemed to derive pleasure from insulting, threatening, humiliating, and dehumanizing their peers."

Because of the random assignment of subjects, the study concluded the observed behaviors were the result of situational rather than personality factors:

> The negative, anti-social reactions observed were not the product of an environment created by combining a collection of deviant personalities, but rather, the result of an intrinsically pathological situation which could distort and rechannel the behaviour of essentially normal individuals. The abnormality here resided in the psychological nature of the situation and not in those who passed through it.

The authors discussed how prisoner-guard interactions shaped the evolution of power use by the guards:

> The use of power was self-aggrandizing and self-perpetuating. The guard power, derived initially from an arbitrary label, was intensified whenever there was any perceived threat by the prisoners and this new level subsequently became the baseline from which further hostility and harassment would begin. The most hostile guards on each shift moved spontaneously into the leadership roles of giving orders and deciding on punishments. They became role models whose behaviour was emulated by other members of the shift. Despite minimal contact between the three separate guard shifts and nearly 16 hours a day spent away from the prison, the absolute level of aggression as well as the more subtle and "creative" forms of aggression manifested, increased in a spiraling function. Not to be tough and arrogant was to be seen as a sign of weakness by the guards and even those "good" guards who did not get as drawn into the power syndrome as the others

respected the implicit norm of never contradicting or even interfering with an action of a more hostile guard on their shift.

In an article published 25 years after the Stanford Prison Experiment, Haney and Zimbardo noted their initial study "underscored the degree to which institutional settings can develop a life of their own, independent of the wishes, intentions, and purposes of those who run them." They highlighted the need for those outside the culture to offer external perspectives on process and procedures. [Haney and Zimbardo, The Past and Future of U.S. Prison Policy, Twenty–Five Years After the Stanford Prison Study, 53 American Psychologist 709 (1998).]

UNITED STATES v. FREDERICK

Victory Base, Bagdad, Iraq, 2004.

[Professor Zimbardo testified at the General Court Marshall of Staff Sergeant Ivan Frederick II, who was a guard at the Abu Ghraib prison in Iraq. Frederick was charged with taking part in a highly-publicized incident in which a prisoner had wires attached to his hands and was forced to stand on a box, after having been told that he would be electrocuted if he stepped off the box. Frederick was also charged with forcing nude prisoners into a pyramid, forcing a prisoner to masturbate in front of other prisoners and guards, and forcing a prisoner to place his face into the pubic region of another prisoner, simulating oral sex.]

Dr. Philip Zimbardo, civilian, was called as a witness for the defense, was sworn, and testified via video teleconference as follows:

DIRECT EXAMINATION

Q. You mentioned that you have done studies with respect to abuse. I believe that you have done a study at Stanford that gained significant scientific recognition. Could you describe to the military judge what that study was?

A. This was the study conducted 32 years ago in which I created a prison-like environment at the university in which we put ordinary young men, college students from all over the United States who were in the San Francisco area that summer. [The Stanford Prison Experiment, excerpted above, was then described in detail].

[Q]. Can you differentiate for me in your own studies and for circumstances at Abu Ghraib night versus dayshift? You found some interesting things, didn't you?

A. It was really eerie. I mean, my study is a little experiment done many years ago. The parallels between my study at the Stanford University basement and Abu Ghraib are eerily eerie. Most of the abuse in my study took place on the nightshift, just as at Abu Ghraib. Our guards stripped prisoners naked for any reason to humiliate them. Our guards put bags over prisoners' heads to confuse them. Our guards, the escalation of abuse went from cleaning toilet bowls out with their bare hands to simulating sexual behavior among the prisoners. That was just in 5 days, and so we saw this still study, microcosm of what could have happened had we kept our study going to months at a time or had we had guards at high levels of stress. So all I mean to say is that, and actually, the Schlesinger report [excerpted above] says that research should have been a [w]arning to the military about the importance of adequate training, adequate preparation to all the people in a prison of that kind.

[Q].   Would you suggest, Doctor, that given all the factors that you know of with respect to this sort of circumstance and given the actual circumstances that existed at Abu Ghraib, that irrespective of who occupied the role of nightshift guard, that there was a certain inevitably to abuse, given all the factors that existed?

A.   [N]ot every single individual in a setting like that gets out of control. What we have found not only in my prison study, but many other studies, is that the majority, that the typical reaction of someone in that study is to give in to the situational forces. And it's the exceptional person, the heroic person who can somehow resist. But it's impossible to do so when you're encouraged to soften up the detainees for interrogation. [S]o the question is, you know, did he bring some pathology into the situation, or did that situation bring out pathology in this good, young American soldier who I would be willing to have him take care of my kids at any time. Because in the experience that I had with him, he is a wonderful young man who did these horrible things.

CROSS–EXAMINATION

[Q].   Now, you listed a number of ways that you believe the situation at Abu Ghraib paralleled the experiment you conducted at Stanford. Is that correct?

A.   Yes, I did.

[Q].   One of those parallels would be hooding and the chaining and sexual humiliation, is that correct?

A.   Yes, it is.

Q.   Now, the guards in your experiment were young college students, right?

A.   Yes, they were all between 18 and 23 or 4.

Q.   And they had no experience or training whatsoever in being prison guards.

A.   Correct.

Q.   And Staff Sergeant Frederick is 38 years old, right?

A.   Correct, yes.

Q.   With 7 years of experience as a correctional officer?

A.   Yes.

[Q].   With the hooding of the inmates in your experiment, that was not the idea of the guards. That was actually yours and your staff's idea, correct?

A.   Yes. It was our idea when the prisoners left the yard to go to the toilet, the guards then escalated using the hoods on their own to increase the confusion of the prisoners at various other times.

[Q].   It was yours and your staff's idea of what the inmates would wear during your experiment, correct?

A.   Correct.

Q.   And it was yours and your staff who picked smocks and insisted that the inmates not wear any underclothes in order to sexually humiliate and emasculate them, correct?

A.   Correct.

Q.   So the parallels you see between Abu Ghraib and your experiment, specifically hooding and chaining and sexual humiliating were not abuse that your guards originally came up with, but were actually research controls of your own experiment.

A.   No, not completely, because what the guards did was use the prisoners as playthings. They had prisoners bend over and had other prisoners simulate sodomy. That's not anything that we encouraged, anything that we allowed. All we did was put prisoners in smocks because we wanted to emasculate them, essentially, so you would want to minimize their masculinity. And this is what happens in many, many prisons. But the guards went way beyond that simple fact of having prisoners would leapfrog over one another so their testicles would bang on their other prisoner's heads, to have them, again, simulate sodomy. That has nothing to do with me or the staff. This was the invention of the guards on the nightshift.

REDIRECT EXAMINATION

[Q].   You're not here to excuse [the defendant's] conduct, are you?

A.   Oh, I don't excuse his conduct. Again, the situational approach is not excuseology. It's not saying, oh, we're going to blame the situation and take the person off the hook. It simply says in trying to understand why Sergeant Frederick suddenly did these terrible things to which he has nothing in his history, nothing in his personal background, nothing in any psychological test that would have predicted that he did these terrible things, that what we have to put on trial is both the situation and also the system of—on trial has to be all of the officers who should have prevented it, all the officers who should have given adequate training for him and the other soldiers, who should have given adequate oversight that would have prevented this. [S]o I think that the military is on trial, particularly all of the officers who are above Sergeant Frederick who should have knew what was going on, should have prevented it, should have stopped it, should have challenged it. They are the ones who should be on trial. Or if Sergeant

Frederick is responsible to some extent, whatever his sentence is has to be, I think, mitigated by the responsibility of the whole chain of command.

NOTE

1. Outcome of the General Court Marshall. In exchange for other charges being dropped, Staff Sgt. Ivan Frederick pled guilty to conspiracy, dereliction of duty, maltreatment of detainees, assault, and committing an indecent act. He was sentenced to eight years in prison, forfeiture of pay, a dishonorable discharge, and a reduction in rank to private. He was paroled from prison in 2007, after serving three years of his sentence.

(d) Television

The effects of televised violence on the behavior of children and adolescents has been the subject of a great deal of research. In one case, that research was brought to bear on the criminal responsibility of an adolescent for murder.

FLORIDA v. ZAMORA

Circuit Court, Dade County, Florida, 1977.
Trial Transcript, Case No. 77–2566.

[Ronney Albert Zamora was tried for the first degree murder of Elinor Haggart, his next door neighbor in Miami Beach. Zamora was 15. Mrs. Haggart was 82. Zamora admitted that he shot her with a pistol he found in her house when she returned home and found him in the process of burglary. Zamora and an accomplice stole $400 after having shot Mrs. Haggart. Due to Zamora's age, the state did not ask for the death penalty.

Zamora's attorney, Ellis Rubin, pleaded him not guilty by reason of insanity. Rubin argued that Zamora was a "television addict," that he was "a sociopathic personality who could not refrain from doing wrong," and that because of the "thousands and thousands and thousands of murders that he has seen [on television], this was a reaction that he imitated or a conditioned reflex."

Rubin attempted to introduce expert witnesses to present empirical studies on the association between watching violent television programs and later violent behavior.

The first such witness was Dr. Margaret Thomas. The prosecutor was Thomas Headley. The trial judge was H. Paul Baker. In an innovative program, the trial was videotaped and shown on public television in the Miami area for nine nights.]

ELLIS RUBIN: Your Honor, this witness is a Doctor of Psychology, currently the Assistant Dean of Academic Affairs of Florida Technological University, Orlando, Florida. She has a B.A. from Vanderbilt, an M.A. from Vanderbilt, a Ph.D. from Tulane. She has fellowships and awards, several teaching positions, psychological testing and evaluation experience, and she has had published—how many papers, round figures?

DR. THOMAS: Around fifteen. I'm not sure.

RUBIN: Around fifteen.

JUDGE BAKER: Okay, Now, that qualifies her as an expert in something. Now, what's she going to testify to?

RUBIN: Well, here are some of the titles of some of the papers that she has published: "Does Media Violence Increase Children's Toleration of Real Life Aggression?" "Toleration of Real Life Aggression as a Function of Exposure to Televised Violence and Age of Subject;" "Desensitization to Portrayals of Real Life Aggression as a Function of Exposure to Television Violence;" "Effects of Television Violence on Expectation of Other's Aggressions."

Doctor Thomas is an expert on behavior and the social ramifications of certain types of behavior. Since 1969, she has specialized in the field of what effect, if any, does television violence have on the viewer, and, specifically, young children, adolescents, and adults. We will confine her testimony to adolescents. She is. . . .

JUDGE BAKER: That goes beyond the scope of what the Court's instructions were at the pretrial conference.

RUBIN: No, Your Honor . . .

JUDGE BAKER: She will have to be confined to Ronney Zamora.

RUBIN: It *is* confined to Ronney Zamora. Your Honor, if I may, I would like to make this presentation.

JUDGE BAKER: All right. Go ahead.

RUBIN: It's the heart of my defense. Your Honor, this is similar to a defense of intoxication by alcohol, intoxication by hypnosis, or any other defense. The jury has nothing to compare Ronney Zamora's conduct with, if they do not hear that there have been studies on children his age, relating what the effect of X amount of hours of violence on television has shown by experiments with children. It's the same as if I brought an expert in here, if I were defending on the grounds of not guilty by involuntary intoxication. I certainly would have a right to bring in an expert on what are the properties of alcohol, how much alcohol is required to give a 1.0 reading on the drunkometer, unless the Court wished to take judicial notice that 1.0 is drunk. Your Honor, how can the jury understand what the effect of television is on Ronney Zamora if there is no one from the defense to show, through expert experiments and testimony, what the effect has been on other youngsters his age? All that we're doing is establishing a standard. The defense of involuntary television intoxication is new, but so was insanity at one time a new defense. So was involuntary intoxication by alcohol at some stage in our civilization, a new defense. But there are expert....

JUDGE BAKER: But let's stop right there. The first word you've mentioned to me is "involuntary." I haven't heard one bit of testimony throughout this trial that anything that happened to this defendant was involuntary.

RUBIN: Well, here we . . .

JUDGE BAKER: Now how do we get over that hurdle?

RUBIN: Right. This is the lady who's going to get over that hurdle.

JUDGE BAKER: How can she do that? She's never seen the defendant.

RUBIN: She doesn't have to see the defendant, Your Honor. If I may make myself . . .

JUDGE BAKER: Go ahead.

RUBIN: I'm trying to make myself understood. And I realize that it may be a difficult premise.

This expert on the effects of television violence is prepared to testify, and we have others who will testify likewise, that what comes out of television on the programs that are produced by the networks and the sponsors contain an inordinate amount of violence. Young children— but especially, Your Honor, the studies will show that sociopaths and emotionally disturbed children are more affected by violence on television than any other category of human beings. And that what comes out of that television tube is not controlled by the viewer and the viewer doesn't realize that he is being desensitized to violence by seeing so much of it. Involuntarily, he is seeing all of these heroes and bad guys, the black hats and the white hats using guns, stabbing people, abnormal behavior, bizarre situations, robberies, burglaries, killings of old ladies. And this is coming to him and going into his brain and is desensitizing this child to the normal regard for violence, the normal standards of right and wrong for killing, because this boy is a classic example. And we have laid the predicate that he is an addict, that his viewing hours were more than ordinary, and his type of programs . . .

Your Honor, what's the difference in bringing in somebody who's an expert on alcohol, a chemist, and who can testify that by experiments over the years, we find that a certain amount of alcohol will cause a loss of control? Well, that's what I want to do with television. This witness is prepared to say that television does affect the viewer, did affect Ronney Zamora. She doesn't have to interview Ronney Zamora. I have other people who have interviewed Ronney Zamora. The jury has already heard the testimony of his mother. Certainly television, if the jury believes Mrs. Zamora—and that's a jury question. Not to allow me to present an expert who will say, well, there have been so many studies, and here is what has been found, and it's uncontradicted—and she has done papers that have been accepted for publication by the scientific journals, and she has to be quizzed on those, and there has to be verification of them, and that has been done.

Your Honor, don't deny me the right to present everything to the jury that they should have for this defense, and that is this doctor who is an expert on what are the effects of television on children. Then, let the jury say does it affect Ronney Zamora—and we will have other witnesses who will so say. This is the premise for our whole defense.

JUDGE BAKER: Mr. Headley?

THOMAS HEADLEY: Your Honor, I thought that we had argued this at the pretrial conference. Your Honor, the State's position is quite clearly that this testimony is completely irrelevant and immaterial.

Now, the example given of the alcohol—it doesn't apply here, Your Honor. When you come in with a machine reading of a certain amount of alcohol in your blood, then possibly, a doctor can come in and say what effect that has, because that has an organic or a biological effect on the body that influences or affects everyone the same way. This isn't true, Judge. We're not dealing with an intoxicant. There's been nothing to establish that television is an intoxicant. There's nothing to show that the viewing of television reacts or treats everyone the same way. This doesn't have anything to do with this defendant, Judge, and it would be totally irrelevant and immaterial.

RUBIN: Television does affect everybody the same way, when they are a sociopathic personality. Those are the studies—that these people copy and imitate what they see on television and it arouses them to unusual actions. That's just like—how did the alcohol expert establish that .10 was the point of drunkenness? There had to be tests made. There had to be scientific studies. We're giving that to the jury through this witness. What is the standard for television being too much or not enough? Somebody has to start from somewhere.

JUDGE BAKER: All right. The rule in Capelin, which is adopted in Rodriguez is very simple: where the evidence is based solely upon scientific tests and experiments, it is essential that the reliability of the tests and results thereof shall be recognized and accepted by scientists, or that the demonstration shall have passed from the stage of experimentation and uncertainty to that of reasonable demonstrability. And I do not see that in this defense.

HEADLEY: Judge, excuse me . . .

RUBIN: May I make the proffer, then? May I put the doctor through the testimony?

JUDGE BAKER: Yes.

RUBIN: And then we'll see. (to Dr. Thomas) What is your name and address?

DR. THOMAS: Margaret Hanratty Thomas. (She states her address)

RUBIN: What is your occupation or profession?

DR. THOMAS: Psychologist and college professor.

RUBIN: Are you prepared to say that an excessive amount of television viewing would have an effect on an emotionally disturbed fifteen-year-old male child from a middle class, poor economic background?

DR. THOMAS: It's very possible.

RUBIN: Very possible? Can you say it within a reasonable psychological certainty?

DR. THOMAS: I would feel fairly confident that, given that type of background, an excessive amount of television violence would—well, it has an effect on everyone. It would be much more likely to have an unusual or extreme effect on such a child, in my opinion.

RUBIN: (to Judge Baker) You may inquire.

JUDGE BAKER: Let me ask you this. Can you state, within reasonable psychological certainty, under the set of facts that Mr. Rubin just gave you, that such an amount of television on the type of child could produce . . .

RUBIN: Your Honor, I should have added six to eight hours a day, as has been testified. I'm sorry. I didn't put that in.

JUDGE BAKER: Whatever—could produce a state of mind where he did not know right from wrong and could not appreciate the nature and consequences of his acts?

DR. THOMAS: Watching that much television over a long period of time, in my opinion, is at least one of the important factors as to how a person acquires a sense of right and wrong.

JUDGE BAKER: That's not the question. The question is can you state, with reasonable psychological certainty, in any of the tests that you've conducted, in any of the tests that you have referred to, in any of the papers that you've published—not that it could—that it has—had that effect on any individual tested, to the extent that they did not know right from wrong?

DR. THOMAS: Would studies that show that children who tend to watch a lot of violent television tend to be more approving . . .

JUDGE BAKER: No. Not approving. Would they be so affected that they would not know right from wrong and appreciate the nature and consequences of their act—in other words, have absolutely no idea of right or wrong, couldn't appreciate the nature and consequences of their act? In other words, are you familiar with the rule of M'Naghten's case?

DR. THOMAS: Well, I learned of it last evening when Mr. Headley was taking my deposition, and I guess I'm a little confused.

HEADLEY: Judge, excuse me.

DR. THOMAS: What I'm saying is . . .

HEADLEY: May I ask a question, Your Honor?

JUDGE BAKER: Please.

RUBIN: Your Honor, she's answering your questions.

JUDGE BAKER: Let her answer mine. Then you can ask one. But just please let me finish. Go ahead.

HEADLEY: I'm sorry.

DR. THOMAS: The distinction that I'm having trouble with is that, yes, I would feel comfortable saying that exposure to television violence can shape a child's conceptions of what is right and wrong—that is such that a very heavy television viewer, perhaps, who comes up in an atmosphere where there are not other restraints built in can—could develop such an attitude that what society in general sees as right and wrong is not his reality, is not his sense of right and wrong. You see what I mean, that it's all—for example, there are studies that show that children tend to think of aggression as more ordinary, more commonplace, and approve of it more as a result of exposure to television violence. Their sense of right and wrong then, is a little different than that of a child who watches very little television. They do have it, I mean, I guess those values are different.

JUDGE BAKER: I'll accept that values are different. But we're talking about the legal definition of insanity, which—go ahead, Mr. Headley. Ask your question. Maybe it'll clear it up.

HEADLEY: Dr. Thomas, can you advise the Court of one study or one experiment or any number that have linked the viewing of television violence with insanity?

DR. THOMAS: You mean use the term "insanity"?

HEADLEY: Yes.

DR. THOMAS: Legal insanity—of course not.

HEADLEY: I think that's all we're resolving here, Your Honor.

JUDGE BAKER: That's it.

RUBIN: One more chance. They're comparing apples and oranges. How can you relate, Your Honor, psychological, medical, scientific experiments of proof with the legal definition of the word "insanity"? This is not her field. Our field is the legal definition of a defense. Her field is what are the effects of television violence on children. Your Honor will instruct the jury on the law of insanity. I want to show the jury the facts that went into this child's concept of right and wrong. Your Honor, she's prepared to—I have psychiatrists who will use this testimony, subject to cross examination, who will testify as to what you asked this young doctor. She can't testify that there's ever been a case where insanity has been found to result from too much television, because they don't have the word "insanity" in her field. They don't have it even in the field of psychiatry, as you know.

JUDGE BAKER: I understand that.

RUBIN: Let the scientists come—let the psychiatrists, Your Honor, come in. And let Your Honor voir dire the psychiatrists and say, "Has there ever been a case where too much television has caused insanity?" And they will answer, "Yes." And the victim is Ronney Zamora. And let the jury hear that. Please.

JUDGE BAKER: Let me ask you this, Ma'am. Let's forget the word "insanity." In any of your tests, in any scientific journal that you have read, have you ever conclusively linked any particular television program or amount of television violence directly to a homicide?

DR. THOMAS: Well, those are not scientific studies. There are cases . . .

JUDGE BAKER: Or any crime?

DR. THOMAS: No, because they're always after the fact. You can't . . .

JUDGE BAKER: Thank you. The testimony is excluded.

ZAMORA v. STATE

District Court of Appeal of Florida, Third District, 1978.
361 So.2d 776.

■ HENDRY, JUDGE.

At trial, Zamora's insanity defense was based upon "involuntary subliminal television intoxication." On appeal, Zamora contends that certain rulings of the trial judge limiting the scope of defense counsel's inquiry into the area of television's effect upon sociopathic children effectively frustrated his insanity defense. In particular, appellant argues that the trial judge committed reversible error by failing to allow psychologist Dr. Margaret Hanratty Thomas to testify at trial on the effect of television violence upon adolescent viewers. We are not of the opinion that the court erred in granting the state's motion in limine thereby limiting inquiry into television and its effects on children.

[B]ased upon the law of insanity, as established in this state, the trial judge correctly limited the evidence of insanity to the M'Naghten standard. *Sub judice,* as brought out through proffer, Dr. Thomas' testimony would have been directed to the effect of television on adolescents, generally. She would have been, however, unable to testify that watching violent television programs to excess affects an individual to the extent that said individual would not be able to distinguish between right and wrong under the M'Naghten test. Her testimony, therefore, would not have been relevant to the proceedings. [A]s Dr. Thomas' testimony was not relevant as to the issue of insanity, it was properly excluded.

[O]ne final comment need be made. In the concluding pages of defense counsel's lengthy brief the following language appears: "In the case at bar, television was on trial . . . and the trial was on television." Such was simply not the case. While the proceedings were televised (and much covered by the media, generally), television was not on trial; Ronney Zamora was on trial. Zamora was on trial for the senseless slaying of an elderly woman. His defense was not guilty by reason of insanity induced by "involuntary subliminal television intoxication" and a jury, failing to accept that defense, found Zamora guilty on all charges. The proceedings below in no way represented a forum for the discussion of the relative pros and cons of the television media. Stated simply, this was a murder trial, and it is to the trial judge's credit that he confined the testimony and evidence to the relevant issues. Anyone failing to comprehend the true nature and purpose of these proceedings suffers from a total misconception of our criminal justice system.

ZAMORA v. DUGGER

United States Court of Appeals, Eleventh Circuit, 1987.
834 F.2d 956.

■ Johnson, Circuit Judge.

This case involves an appeal from the district court's denial of Appellant's petition for a writ of habeas corpus.

[Z]amora contends that his trial counsel was ineffective. [Z]amora argues that Rubin made a mockery of his insanity defense by alleging that it was caused by "television intoxication" even though the cause of insanity is irrelevant to the defense itself. [However,] Rubin's attempt to explain Zamora's alleged insanity by claiming it was caused by subliminal "television intoxication" does not render his assistance ineffective.

On the issue of preparation for trial, Rubin testified [t]hat he read many studies linking violence to television viewing. He also interviewed many psychologists regarding television violence, but he was unsuccessful in attempting to introduce their testimony. The evidence suggests that counsel was prepared and that he attempted to develop a defense in a weak case. In addition, the magistrate and district court determined that by focusing on television violence Rubin was able to introduce evidence of Zamora's unfortunate background, to the defendant's advantage.

[A]ccordingly, we affirm the district court's denial of habeas corpus.

NOTE

1. The Status of Research on Television Violence. In 1972, the Scientific Advisory Committee on Television and Social Behavior, appointed by the Surgeon General at the request of Congress, issued a report, Television and Growing Up: The Impact of Televised Violence. The major conclusion of that report was:

> There is a convergence of the fairly substantial experimental evidence for a short-run causation of aggression among some children

by viewing violence on the screen and much less certain evidence from field studies that extensive violence viewing precedes some long-run manifestations of aggressive behavior. The convergence of the two types of evidence constitutes some preliminary indication of a causal relationship, but a good deal of research remains to be done before one can have confidence in these conclusions.

A review of subsequent research in this area, Felson, Mass Media Effects on Violent Behavior, 22 Annual Review of Sociology 103 (1996), concluded that "exposure to television violence probably does have a small effect on violent behavior for some viewers, possibly because the media directs viewer's attention to novel forms of violent behavior that they would not otherwise consider." Id. at 103. The most recent review, Huesmann and Taylor, The Role of Media Violence In Violent Behavior, 27 Annual Review of Public Health 393 (2006), concluded:

> Research shows that fictional television and film violence contribute to both a short-term and a long-term increase in aggression and violence in young viewers. [T]he relationship between media violence and real-world violence and aggression is moderated by the nature of the media content and characteristics of and social influences on the individual exposed to that content. Still, the average overall size of the effect is large enough to place it in the category of known threats to public health.

B.   VICTIMS

In addition to providing a context for decision makers to reach judgments on facts that pertain to criminal defendants, social science research has also been used to provide decision makers with a context for determining facts relating to victims. The principal application of victim-oriented frameworks has been in the "rape trauma syndrome."

———

PEOPLE v. TAYLOR

Court of Appeals of New York, 1990.
75 N.Y.2d 277, 552 N.Y.S.2d 883, 552 N.E.2d 131.

■ WACHTLER, CHIEF JUDGE.

In these two cases, we consider whether expert testimony that a complaining witness has exhibited behavior consistent with "rape trauma syndrome" is admissible at the criminal trial of the person accused of the rape.

[I.]   People v. Taylor

On July 29, 1984, the complainant, a 19–year–old Long Island resident, reported to the town police that she had been raped and sodomized at gunpoint on a deserted beach near her home.

[T]he complainant arrived home around 11:00 P.M., woke her mother and told her about the attack. Her mother then called the police. Sometime between 11:30 P.M. and midnight, the police arrived at the complainant's house. At that time, the complainant told the police she did not know who her attacker was. She was taken to the police station where she described the events leading up to the attack and again repeated that she did not know who her attacker was. At the conclusion of the interview, the complainant was asked to step into a private room to remove the clothes that she had been wearing at the time of the attack so that they could be examined for forensic evidence. While she was alone with her mother, the complainant told her that the defendant John Taylor, had been her attacker. The time was approximately 1:15 A.M. The complainant had known the defendant for years.

[H]er mother summoned one of the detectives and the complainant repeated that the defendant had been the person who attacked her.

[T]he defendant's first trial ended without the jury being able to reach a verdict. At his second trial, the Judge permitted Eileen Treacy, an instructor at the City University of New York, Herbert Lehman College, with experience in counseling sexual assault victims, to testify about rape trauma syndrome. The prosecutor introduced this testimony for two separate purposes. First, Treacy's testimony on the specifics of rape trauma syndrome explained why the complainant might have been unwilling during the first few hours after the attack to name the defendant as her attacker where she had known the defendant prior to the incident. Second, Treacy's testimony that it was common for a rape victim to appear quiet and controlled following an attack, responded to evidence that the complainant had appeared calm after the attack and tended to rebut the inference that because she was not excited and upset after the attack, it had not been a rape. At the close of the second trial, the defendant was convicted.

[II.]   People v. Banks

On July 7, 1986, the defendant Ronnie Banks approached the 11–year–old complainant, who was playing with her friends in the City of Rochester. The complainant testified that the defendant told her to come to him and when she did not, he grabbed her by the arm and pulled her down the street. According to the complainant, the defendant took her into a neighborhood garage where he sexually assaulted her. The complainant returned to her grandmother's house, where she was living at the time. The next morning, she told her grandmother about the incident and the police were contacted. The defendant was arrested and charged with [several sex offenses].

At trial, the complainant testified that the defendant had raped and sodomized her. In addition, she and her grandmother both testified about the complainant's behavior following the attack. Their testimony revealed that the complainant had been suffering from nightmares, had been waking up in the middle of the night in a cold sweat, had been afraid to return to school in the fall, had become generally more fearful and had been running and staying away from home. Following the introduction of this evidence, the prosecution sought to introduce expert testimony about the symptoms associated with rape trauma syndrome.

Clearly, the prosecution, in an effort to establish that forcible sexual contact had in fact occurred, wanted to introduce this evidence to show that the complainant was demonstrating behavior that was consistent with patterns of response exhibited by rape victims. The prosecutor does not appear to have introduced this evidence to counter the inference that the complainant consented to the incident, since the 11–year–old complainant is legally incapable of consent (Penal Law § 130.05[3][a]). Unlike *Taylor,* the evidence was not offered to explain behavior exhibited by the victim that the jury might not understand; instead, it was offered to show that the behavior that the complainant had exhibited after the incident was consistent with a set of symptoms commonly associated with women who had been forcibly attacked. The clear implication of such testimony would be that because the complainant exhibited these symptoms, it was more likely than not that she had been forcibly raped.

The Judge permitted David Gandell, an obstetrician-gynecologist on the faculty of the University of Rochester, Strong Memorial Hospital, with special training in treating victims of sexual assault, to testify as to the symptoms commonly associated with rape trauma syndrome. After Gandell had described rape trauma syndrome he testified hypothetically that the kind of symptoms demonstrated by the complainant were consistent with a diagnosis of rape trauma syndrome. At the close of the trial, the defendant was [c]onvicted.

[III.] *Rape Trauma Syndrome*

In a 1974 study rape trauma syndrome was described as "the acute phase and long-term reorganization process that occurs as a result of forcible rape or attempted forcible rape. This syndrome of behavioral, somatic, and psychological reactions is an acute stress reaction to a life-threatening situation" (Burgess & Holmstrom, *Rape Trauma Syndrome,* 131 Am.J.Psychiatry 981, 982 [1974]). Although others had studied the reactions of rape victims prior to this publication (see, e.g., Sutherland & Scherl, *Patterns of Response Among Victims of Rape,* 40 Am.J.Orthopsychiatry 503 [1970]), the Burgess and Holmstrom identification of two separate phases in a rape victim's recovery has proven enormously influential.

According to Burgess and Holmstrom, the rape victim will go through an acute phase immediately following the incident. The behavior exhibited by a rape victim after the attack can vary. While some women will express their fear, anger and anxiety openly, an equal number of women will appear controlled, calm, and subdued (Burgess & Holmstrom, op. cit., at 982). Women in the acute phase will also experience a number of physical reactions. These reactions include the actual physical trauma that resulted from the attack, muscle tension that could manifest itself in tension headaches, fatigue, or disturbed sleep patterns, gastrointestinal irritability and genitourinary disturbance (id.). Emotional reactions in the acute phase generally take the form of fear, humiliation, embarrassment, fear of violence and death, and self-blame (id., at 983).

As part of the long-term reorganizational phase, the victim will often decide to make a change in her life, such as a change of residence. At this point, the woman will often turn to her family for support (id.). Other symptoms that are seen in this phase are the occurrence of nightmares and the development of phobias that relate to the circumstances of the rape (id., at 984). For instance, women attacked in their beds will often develop a fear of being indoors, while women attacked on the street will develop a fear of being outdoors (id.).

While some researchers have criticized the methodology of the early studies of rape trauma syndrome, Burgess and Holmstrom's model has nonetheless generated considerable interest in the response and recovery of rape victims and has contributed to the emergence of a substantial body of scholarship in this area (see, e.g., Nadelson, Notman, Zackson & Gornick, *A Follow-up Study of Rape Victims,* 139 Am.J.Psychiatry 1266 [1982]; Ruch, Chandler & Harter, *Life Change and Rape Impact,* 21 J.Health & Social Behavior 248 [1980]; Kilpatrick, Veronen & Resick, *The Aftermath of Rape: Recent Empirical Findings,* 49 Am.J.Orthopsychiatry 658 [1979]; Notman & Nadelson, *The Rape Victim: Psychodynamic Considerations,* 133 Am.J.Psychiatry 408 [1976]; *see generally,* Symonds, *Victims of Violence: Psychological Effects and Aftereffects,* 35 Am.J.Psychoanalysis 19 [1975]; Note, *Checking the Allure of Increased Conviction Rates: The Admissibility of Expert Testimony on Rape Trauma Syndrome in Criminal Proceedings,* 70 Va.L.Rev. 1657, 1667–1680 [summarizing the research in the field and criticizing the reliability of rape trauma syndrome studies]). The question before us today, then, is whether the syndrome, which has been the subject of study and discussion for the past 16 years, can be introduced before a lay jury as relevant evidence in these two rape trials.

We realize that rape trauma syndrome encompasses a broad range of symptoms and varied patterns of recovery. Some women are better able to cope with the aftermath of sexual assault than other women (see, e.g., Ruch, Chandler & Harter, op. cit., at 253). It is also apparent that there is no single typical profile of a rape victim and that different victims express themselves and come to terms with the experience of rape in different ways. We are satisfied, however, that the relevant scientific community has generally accepted that rape is a highly traumatic event that will in many women trigger the onset of certain identifiable symptoms (see, Frye v. United States, 293 F. 1013 (D.C.Cir.); People v. Hughes, 59 N.Y.2d 523, 537, 466 N.Y.S.2d 255, 453 N.E.2d 484).

We note that the American Psychiatric Association has listed rape as one of the stressors that can lead to posttraumatic stress disorder (American Psychiatric Association, Diagnostic & Statistical Manual of Mental Disorders 247, 248 [3d ed. rev. 1987] [DSM III–R]). According to DSM III–R, there is an identifiable pattern of responses that can follow an intensely stressful event. The victim who suffers from posttraumatic stress disorder will persistently reexperience the traumatic event in a number of ways, as through dreams, flashbacks, hallucinations, or intense distress at exposure to events that resemble or symbolize the traumatic event (id., at 250). The victim will also avoid stimuli that he or she associates with the trauma (id.). Finally, the victim will experience "persistent symptoms of increased arousal," which could include difficulty in falling or staying asleep, sudden outbursts of anger, or difficulty concentrating (id.). While the diagnostic criteria for posttraumatic stress disorder that are contained in DSM III–R have convinced us that the scientific community has accepted that rape as a stressor can have marked, identifiable effects on a victim's behavior, we would further note that although rape trauma syndrome can be conceptualized as a posttraumatic stress disorder (see, Nadelson, Notman, Zackson & Gornick, *op. cit.,* at 1267), victims of rape will often exhibit peculiar symptoms—like a fear of men—that are not commonly exhibited by victims of other sorts of trauma (see generally, Massaro, *Experts, Psychology, Credibility, and Rape: The Rape Trauma Syndrome Issue and Its Implications for Expert Psychological Testimony,* 69 Minn.L.Rev. 395, 447).

We are aware that rape trauma syndrome is a therapeutic and not a legal concept. Physicians and rape counselors who treat victims of sexual assault are not charged with the responsibility of ascertaining whether the victim is telling the truth when she says that a rape occurred. That is part of the truth-finding process implicated in a criminal trial. We do not believe, however, that the therapeutic origin of the syndrome renders it unreliable for trial purposes. Thus, although we acknowledge that evidence of rape trauma syndrome does not by itself prove that the complainant was raped, we believe that this should not preclude its admissibility into evidence at trial when relevance to a particular disputed issue has been demonstrated.

IV.   The Law

Having concluded that evidence of rape trauma syndrome is generally accepted within the relevant scientific community, we must now decide whether expert testimony in this area would aid a lay jury in reaching a verdict. "[E]xpert opinion is proper when it would help to clarify an issue calling for professional or technical knowledge, possessed by the expert and beyond the ken of the typical juror" (De Long v. County of Erie, 60 N.Y.2d 296, 307, 469 N.Y.S.2d 611, 457 N.E.2d 717). [R]ape is a crime that is permeated by misconceptions (*see generally,* Brownmiller, Against Our Will: Men, Women and Rape, at 343–350; Estrich, *Rape,* 95 Yale L.J. 1087). [S]tudies have shown that one of the most popular misconceptions about rape is that the victim by behaving in a certain way brought it on herself (see, Massaro, op. cit., at 404). For that reason, studies have demonstrated that jurors will under certain circumstances blame the victim for the attack and will refuse to convict the man accused (id.). Studies have also shown that jurors will infer consent where the victim has engaged in certain types of behavior prior to the incident (id., at 405–406).

[B]ecause cultural myths still affect common understanding of rape and rape victims and because experts have been studying the effects of rape upon its victims only since the 1970's, we believe that patterns of response among rape victims are not within the ordinary understanding of the lay juror. For that reason, we conclude that introduction of expert testimony describing rape trauma syndrome may under certain circumstances assist a lay jury in deciding issues in a rape trial.

In reaching our conclusions in this area, we note that an extensive body of case law has developed concerning the admissibility of this type of evidence. There is no uniform approach to the admission of evidence of rape trauma syndrome among the States that have considered the question. The Minnesota Supreme Court in one of the earliest rape trauma syndrome cases held such evidence inadmissible (State v. Saldana, 324 N.W.2d 227).

[C]alifornia has similarly held that evidence of rape trauma syndrome is inadmissible to prove that a rape occurred (People v. Bledsoe, 36 Cal.3d 236, 203 Cal.Rptr. 450, 681 P.2d 291). The court noted in dicta, however, that where evidence of rape trauma syndrome was offered not to prove that a rape had occurred, but to explain conduct of the victim after the incident that may appear inconsistent with a claim of rape, "expert testimony on rape trauma syndrome may play a particularly useful role by disabusing the jury of some widely held misconceptions about rape and rape victims, so that it may evaluate the evidence free of the constraints of popular myths" (36 Cal.3d at 247–48, 203 Cal.Rptr. at 457, 681 P.2d at 298).

Among those States that have allowed such testimony to be admitted, the purpose for which the testimony was offered has proven crucial.

In the two cases now before us, testimony regarding rape trauma syndrome was offered for entirely different purposes. We conclude that its admission at the trial of John Taylor was proper, but that its admission at the trial of Ronnie Banks was not.

As noted above, the complaining witness in *Taylor* had initially told the police that she could not identify her assailant. Approximately two hours after she first told her mother that she had been raped and sodomized, she told her mother that she knew the defendant had done it. The complainant had known the defendant for years and had seen him the night before the assault. We hold that under the circumstances present in this case, expert testimony explaining that a rape victim who knows her assailant is more fearful of disclosing his name to the police and is in fact less likely to report the rape at all was relevant to explain why the complainant may have been initially unwilling to report that the defendant had been the man who attacked her. Behavior of this type is not within the ordinary understanding of the jury and testimony explaining this behavior assists the jury in determining what effect to give to the complainant's initial failure to identify the defendant. This evidence provides a possible explanation for the complainant's behavior that is consistent with her claim that she was raped. As such, it is relevant.

Rape trauma syndrome evidence was also introduced in *Taylor* in response to evidence that revealed the complainant had not seemed upset following the attack. We note again in this context that the reaction of a rape victim in the hours following her attack is not something within the common understanding of the average lay juror. Indeed, the defense would clearly want the jury to infer that because the victim was not upset following the attack, she must not have been raped. This inference runs contrary to the studies cited earlier, which suggest that half of all women who have been forcibly raped are controlled and subdued following the attack (Burgess & Holmstrom, op. cit., at 982). Thus, we conclude that evidence of this type is relevant to dispel misconceptions that jurors might possess regarding the ordinary responses of rape victims in the first hours after their attack. We do not believe that evidence of rape trauma syndrome, when admitted for that express purpose, is unduly prejudicial.

The admission of expert testimony describing rape trauma syndrome in *Banks,* however, was clearly error. As we noted earlier, this evidence was not offered to explain behavior that might appear unusual to a lay juror not ordinarily familiar with the patterns of response exhibited by rape victims. We conclude that evidence of rape trauma syndrome is inadmissible when it inescapably bears solely on proving that a rape occurred, as was the case here.

Although we have accepted that rape produces identifiable symptoms in rape victims, we do not believe that evidence of the presence, or indeed of the absence, of those symptoms necessarily indicates that the incident did or did not occur. Because introduction of rape trauma syndrome evidence by an expert might create such an inference in the minds of lay jurors, we find that the defendant would be unacceptably prejudiced by the introduction of rape trauma syndrome evidence for that purpose alone. We emphasize again that the therapeutic nature of the syndrome does not preclude its admission into evidence under all circumstances. We believe, however, that its usefulness as a fact-finding device is limited and that where it is introduced to prove the crime took place, its helpfulness is outweighed by the possibility of undue prejudice. Therefore, the trial court erred in permitting the admission of expert testimony regarding rape trauma syndrome under the facts present in *Banks.*

On this record, we cannot conclude that the introduction of the evidence of rape trauma syndrome evidence in *People v. Banks* was harmless error. Accordingly, in *People v. Banks,* the order of the Appellate Division should be reversed and a new trial ordered.

We have considered defendant John Taylor's other arguments and we conclude that they are without merit. The order of the Appellate Division in *People v. Taylor* should therefore be affirmed.

———

STATE v. KINNEY

Supreme Court of Vermont, 2000.
171 Vt. 239, 762 A.2d 833.

■ DOOLEY, J.

Defendant Steven Kinney was convicted by a jury on charges of kidnapping, aggravated sexual assault, and lewd and lascivious behavior.

He was sentenced to two concurrent terms of forty-years-to-life imprisonment and one concurrent term of four-to-five-years imprisonment. On appeal he argues that the trial court erred [i]n admitting expert testimony about rape trauma syndrome.

[A]ccording to defendant's testimony, [h]e and the victim got into bed, where "one thing led to another," and they had consensual sex. The victim, on the other hand, testified that when they got to defendant's house, he took her to his room and raped her. Afterwards, she fell asleep. In the morning when she woke up, she asked to be taken home, and he arranged for a friend to give her a ride.

[T]he State called Dr. Jan Tyler to testify about rape trauma syndrome and the characteristics and conduct of rape victims. The admissibility of this testimony was first contested in pretrial proceedings when the State made an offer of proof indicating Dr. Tyler would testify about rape trauma syndrome and "the behavioral patterns of victims of sexual assault." The State noted that the expert witness would have no contact with the victim and would not offer an opinion on whether the victim was raped by defendant. Defendant challenged the evidence as inadmissible under *Daubert v. Merrell Dow Pharmaceuticals, Inc., 509 U.S. 579, 113 S.Ct. 2786, 125 L.Ed.2d 469 (1993)*.

Dr. Tyler testified that rape trauma syndrome is associated with post-traumatic stress disorder—that is, it is a set of behaviors and symptoms experienced by victims of trauma. She explained that victims of severe trauma commonly experience symptoms such as nightmares, anxiety, and fear as a result of the trauma. Victims of rape, in particular, may experience symptoms such as difficulty in interpersonal relationships, guilt, shame, and sexual dysfunction. [F]urthermore, she said that it is not unusual for victims to delay in reporting a rape, especially if the attacker is an acquaintance, and that a rape victim may be more likely to report to a friend first, rather than to someone with whom she is having an intimate relationship. This delay in reporting is related to the feelings of guilt and shame experienced due to the trauma of the rape. Dr. Tyler then testified to statistics regarding the rate of false reporting of rape. Finally, she testified that, although she had no statistics, she thought it would not be unusual for a victim of rape to fall asleep immediately after the assault, due to the physical exertion and psychological responses to the trauma such as denial and withdrawal.

[I]n this Court, defendant makes three arguments: (1) the court failed to conduct a proper *Daubert* inquiry; (2) the expert's evidence was not admissible under *Daubert*; and (3) the expert's testimony on the rate of false reporting improperly bolstered the credibility of the victim.

[W]e recognize that *Daubert,* and the more recent decision in *Kumho Tire Co. v. Carmichael, 526 U.S. 137, 119 S.Ct. 1167, 143 L.Ed.2d 238 (1999),* emphasized the gatekeeper function of the trial court to determine that novel scientific or technical evidence is sufficiently reliable and relevant before it is admissible. [T]he gatekeeper can perform this function in a number of ways. In many cases, like this one, [t]he issue is whether a certain category of evidence is admissible, often in particular types of cases that are recurring. In some cases, both the trial court and this Court can fully evaluate the reliability and relevance of the evidence generally based on the decisions of other appellate courts. In this way, we can avoid conducting our own lengthy and expensive evidentiary hearing aimed at establishing, or attacking, the foundation for the disputed expert testimony.

We are not suggesting that the new standard for admissibility has somehow become general acceptance among appellate courts. Irrespective of the decisions of other courts, the responsibility for determining the admissibility of evidence in Vermont courts remains with our trial judges, and on appeal with this Court. However, scientific or technical evidence which is novel to us is frequently not novel to many other state and federal courts. To the extent the evaluation of these courts is complete and persuasive, we can affirmatively rely upon it in reaching our own decision.

[M]uch of defendant's argument is that the trial court in this case failed to comply with the procedural requirements of *Daubert*—that is, that it failed to exercise its gatekeeping function by determining the reliability and relevance of Dr. Tyler's testimony based on foundational evidence presented to the court in this case. We acknowledge that we have never explicitly ruled upon the admissibility of evidence of rape trauma syndrome and the common behavior of adult rape victims. [T]hus, the trial court was required to evaluate the admissibility of Dr. Tyler's testimony, beyond her qualifications to provide such testimony, and the result of this evaluation was not clearly dictated by a decision of this Court. This does not mean, however, that the State was obligated in this case to present independent evidence that Dr. Tyler's methodology could be tested, was subject to peer review and publication, had a known and measurable error rate, and was generally accepted in the relevant scientific community, the factors suggested in *Daubert*. Nor was the trial court required to make findings on each of these factors. It could find the evidence admissible because its reliability equals that of other technical evidence we have given trial courts the discretion to admit and the evaluation of other courts allowing admission of the evidence is complete and persuasive.

We concur with the trial court that expert evidence of rape trauma syndrome and the associated typical behavior of adult rape victims is admissible to assist the jury in evaluating the evidence, and frequently to respond to defense claims that the victim's behavior after the alleged rape was inconsistent with the claim that the rape occurred. [F]or example, the defense made much of the fact [t]hat the victim appeared to be sleeping peacefully in defendant's bed the next morning, and that she failed to immediately tell her boyfriend she had been raped. Dr. Tyler's testimony explained why a rape victim might exhibit these behaviors. [A]s the trial court noted in this case, Dr. Tyler was prepared to address some of the studies that formed the bases for her opinions if the defendant raised them in cross-examination.

We note that the evidence here was of a type that the danger of improper usage or excessive prejudice was at a minimum. The expert never interviewed the victim and offered no opinion whether the victim suffered from rape trauma syndrome or exhibited any of the behavior of a rape victim. Thus, there was little risk that Dr. Tyler would be seen as a truth detector

We do not, however, have the same view of the expert's testimony about the incidence of false reporting by rape victims. The prosecutor asked Dr. Tyler whether "there are any data on the issue of false reporting that you are aware of?" She answered:

> False reporting, the percentages are very low. About two percent. That's about the same as any other crime that's committed. In other words, the number of people who would report a burglary that didn't happen is about the same as people who would report a rape, with one difference. The statistics for the rape include those reports that are made and then either withdrawn by the victim for whatever reason, either they were false or there's a fear of going through the legal system, or they're being pressured by other persons. Those also include reports that the police will not arrest on because they don't feel they have enough evidence. And they also include those that don't get to trial because the prosecutor feels it's not a winnable case. So when you get down to literal false reporting of this really never happened, it's very small.

In short, Dr. Tyler testified that at least 98% of the rapes reported actually occurred.

[D]r. Tyler's testimony on the rate of false reporting clearly went over the line. [T]he jury could infer from her testimony that scientific studies have shown that almost no woman falsely claims to have been raped and convict defendant on that basis.

[A]lthough the evidence of the incidence of false reporting of rape accusations was inadmissible and prejudicial, the State argues that its admission is not grounds for reversal. [D]r. Tyler never testified about the story or credibility of the victim because she had never interviewed, or even met, the victim. Her testimony was entirely theoretical. Further, defense counsel was able to reduce the prejudicial effect of the testimony of the low incidence of false reporting by cross-examination. Finally, the prosecutor did not highlight this testimony in closing argument.

We cannot conclude that failure to exclude the inadmissible expert testimony caused a miscarriage of justice in this case. Accordingly, we find no plain error. Affirmed.

———

RAPE TRAUMA SYNDROME

Patricia A. Frazier.
In Modern Scientific Evidence: The Law and Science of Expert Testimony, 2008–2009 ed. (D. L. Faigman, M. J. Saks, J. Sanders, and E. K. Cheng eds. 2008).

[I]t is important to acknowledge some of the difficulties of doing research in this area. One such difficulty concerns recruiting victims to participate in the research. Several different methods have been used and each has its strengths and limitations. One method is to recruit participants from clients seen at rape crisis centers. Investigators that recruit victims through rape crisis centers are able to assess immediate reactions and assess symptoms longitudinally over time. However, because many women do not seek help at such centers, those that do may not be representative of most victims.[5] To further compound the problem, of the minority that do report, often a small percentage participate in the research. Another recruitment method is to advertise for research participants who have been sexually assaulted. Sample representativeness also is a concern in studies that rely on this method because research volunteers may differ in various ways from other victims. A third method is to identify rape victims through screening questions in surveys of larger samples. The validity of studies that identify victims in this manner depends in large part on the screening questions used to assess sexual assault. Because many women do not define experiences as "rape," even if they meet the legal definition, many victims will be undetected if that terminology is used. Questions that describe rape in behavioral terms are much more likely to identify victimization experiences.

———

NOTE

1. Sexual Assault and Posttraumatic Stress Disorder. Tolin and Foa, Sex Differences in Trauma and Posttraumatic Stress Disorder: A Quantitative Review of 25 Years of Research, 132 Psychological Bulletin 959 (2006), reviewed 290 studies of PTSD and concluded

> Although male participants are more likely to report an overall PTE [Potentially Traumatic Event] history than are female participants, we wondered whether female participants were more likely to experience certain kinds of PTEs that might be associated with a greater vulnerability to develop PTSD. Results indicated that male participants are more likely than female participants to report experiencing accidents, nonsexual assault, combat or war, disaster or fire, or serious illness or unspecified injury and witnessing death or injury. Female participants, on the other hand, are more likely than male participants to report experiencing sexual assault and child sexual abuse, which may be more likely to contribute to the development of PTSD. Thus, one possible

5. Women who seek help at rape crisis centers may, however, be representative of victims whose cases go to trial because both groups have sought help.

interpretation of the higher frequency of PTSD among women and girls is that they are more likely than their male counterparts to experience sexual assault and abuse. Id. at 977.

————

CHECKING THE ALLURE OF INCREASED CONVICTION RATES: THE ADMISSIBILITY OF EXPERT TESTIMONY ON RAPE TRAUMA SYNDROME IN CRIMINAL PROCEEDINGS

Robert Lawrence.
70 Virginia Law Review 1657 (1984).

The systematic use of RTS [Rape Trauma Syndrome] in the criminal process may [e]ventually undermine important accomplishments of the rape law reform movement. If courts consistently permit the introduction of expert testimony on RTS, defendants will seek, under their sixth amendment rights, to introduce this evidence on their own behalf. The confrontation and compulsory process clauses of the sixth amendment are read together to guarantee the criminal defendant the right to present all probative evidence in his defense. If the RTS evidence is admitted to assist the state in making its case, the defendant must be allowed to introduce it to the extent that it may demonstrate innocence.

In exercising this right, the defendant may seek to have a court appointed psychiatrist examine the complainant. If the doctor concludes that the complainant does not suffer from RTS, the defendant may introduce testimony to that effect as evidence of consent. Although rape reform advocates have denounced compulsory psychiatric examinations of rape victims, the admissibility of expert testimony on RTS could reinstitute that practice. Rape trials once again would focus not on the defendant's conduct but on the psychological state of the victim. The dispositive issue in most rape trials could become whether the alleged victim exhibited symptoms of RTS. Unless the complainant suffered clinically observable signs of a PTSD, the state would be unable to secure a conviction. Because not all rape victims experience RTS as a result of the attack, the defendant's use of RTS testimony might lead to acquittals of guilty defendants.

[E]xpert testimony on RTS would also have implications with respect to the rape shield statutes. Most rape shield statutes allow inquiries into the complainant's sexual history only when it is relevant to an issue in controversy. For example, if the victim is pregnant or has venereal disease and claims this resulted from the alleged rape, the defendant may offer evidence that the pregnancy or venereal disease resulted from sexual intercourse with another. The sixth amendment guarantees the defendant this right. Similarly, if the state introduces evidence that the victim suffers from RTS, the door is open for the defendant to probe the complainant's sexual or psychological history in attempting to establish another cause of the PTSD. Courts once again would focus on the victim's character and conduct rather than the defendant's. This focus would eviscerate the goal of the rape reform movement of treating rape like other violent crimes.

————

HENSON v. STATE

Supreme Court of Indiana, 1989.
535 N.E.2d 1189.

■ DeBruler, Justice.

Defendant Rickey J. Henson was convicted in a jury trial of Rape as a Class B Felony, Criminal Deviate Conduct as a Class A Felony, Criminal Confinement, and Battery in Howard Circuit Court. He was sentenced to [65 years in prison.]

[O]n appeal, Henson argues that [t]he trial court erred by not allowing the testimony of an expert witness that the victim's conduct after the alleged rape was inconsistent with that of a person who had suffered a traumatic forcible rape.

[T]he facts which tend to support the conviction are as follows: Henson was at a crowded bar in Kokomo and asked J.O., who was sitting alone, if he could join her. She consented and the two exchanged names, but otherwise did not speak. Two other men joined them at the table and J.O. danced with them during the course of the evening but not with Henson. J.O. stayed at the bar until it closed and then left to have more drinks at the home of one of the bar's waitresses. After she got in her car, but before she could shut the door, Henson approached her with a knife, pushed her over to the passenger's seat, got in the car and drove to a secluded place. He then forced her to have sexual intercourse with him as well as oral sex. He also attempted to cut her blouse off with the knife and J.O. received superficial lacerations as a result. The next evening, J.O. returned to the same bar where she stayed for two hours and drank.

At trial, one witness testified that J.O. was drinking as well as dancing on the evening after the rape allegedly occurred. Defendant then called a psychologist, Dr. David Gover, and established that the witness was an expert in the study and treatment of post-traumatic stress syndrome. Defendant's counsel then asked the following question:

> Q. Doctor, in your professional opinion, a person who has allegedly suffered a traumatic, forcible rape, would it be consistent in your experience that a person who had gone through a situation such as that would go back to the same place the act allegedly occurred and socialize, drink, dance, on the same day of the alleged act?

After establishing that Dr. Gover had never consulted with J.O. personally and that he had no firsthand knowledge of the incident in question, the prosecution objected to the question. The objection was sustained on the grounds that the testimony was not relevant and that a proper foundation had not been laid. There followed a lengthy offer to prove, out of the jury's presence, in which the objection was again sustained on the grounds that the testimony was too speculative.

The testimony of Dr. Gover would clearly have been relevant to the issues at trial. Evidence is relevant if it is material and has probative value. Evidence is material if it is offered to prove a matter in issue. Evidence has probative value if it has any tendency to make the existence of any fact that is of consequence to the determination of the action (i.e., any material fact) more or less probable than it would be without the evidence. Here, Dr. Gover's testimony would have tended to prove that J.O.'s behavior after the incident was inconsistent with that of a victim who had suffered a traumatic rape such as that which J.O. recounted. The evidence therefore would have a tendency to make it less probable that a rape in fact occurred, clearly a matter in issue at trial, and was therefore relevant.

Still, where an expert is to give opinion testimony in the form of an answer to a hypothetical question, more than mere relevance is required to make the evidence admissible. A proper foundation must be laid which is two-fold. First, the expert's ability to give such an opinion must be established through testimony showing he has the requisite knowledge, skill, education or experience on which to base the opinion. However, firsthand knowledge of the facts are not required. It is well established in our state that an expert may give opinion testimony even though he does not have personal knowledge of the facts on which his opinion is based.

Second, there must be a proper evidentiary foundation supporting the facts that are included in the hypothetical question. That is to say, a hypothetical question is proper if it embraces facts that have been placed into evidence. However, it is not necessary that a hypothetical question include all pertinent facts that are in evidence. If the opposing counsel feels the facts included do not fairly include all the pertinent facts as presented in the record, the remedy is not exclusion of the expert's testimony but to include such facts in questions on cross-examination.

[H]ere both foundations were met. The record indicates that, once counsel for the defendant had fully explored Dr. Gover's credentials, the trial court was fully satisfied with the psychologist's ability to testify. The evidence shows Dr. Gover had worked extensively with patients who had suffered from post-traumatic stress syndrome and these included patients with rape in their backgrounds. Moreover, there was ample evidence to support the facts embraced by the hypothetical question posed to Dr. Gover by defendant's counsel. One witness for the prosecution had testified that J.O. had returned to the bar on the evening after the alleged rape and was drinking and dancing; and J.O. herself admitted she was drinking at the same bar that evening. If the State did not think the hypothetical embraced facts favorable to its version of the events, its remedy was to bring these inconsistencies out on cross-examination of the witness.

[T]he State also argues that the testimony was too speculative.

[However,] the record clearly reflects Dr. Gover's competence to give an opinion as to behavior of the victim without having interviewed her. On cross-examination, he stated that it would not have been particularly helpful to talk with the victim since he was merely making a general observation that certain behavior, of which there was evidence from previous testimony, was inconsistent with post-traumatic stress syndrome. To argue that evidence is too speculative is to say merely that it is lacking in probative value. There is little doubt that an alleged rape victim's conduct after the fact is probative of whether a rape in fact occurred. The prosecution in this case was clearly aware of this as they introduced testimony regarding J.O.'s behavior after the rape was reported: she was upset, had difficulty sleeping and was shaking when she identified the defendant in a photo lineup. It cannot be said, therefore, that the testimony of Dr. Gover was lacking in probative value. That the expert did not personally interview the victim bears on the weight of the evidence not on its admissibility; and such facts may be brought out by opposing counsel on cross-examination just as any perceived deficiencies in the facts underlying the hypothetical question are brought out.

[M]oreover, this Court has already recognized the admissibility of rape trauma syndrome evidence in *Simmons*. It would be fundamentally unfair to allow the use of such testimony by the State, as was the case in *Simmons*, and then deny its use by a defendant here. In so holding, we are not unmindful of the considerable body of literature in this area and recent case law in other jurisdictions. See, e.g., State v. Marks (1982), 231 Kan. 645, 647 P.2d 1292; People v. Bledsoe (1984), 36 Cal.3d 236, 203 Cal.Rptr. 450, 681 P.2d 291; Kruse v. State (Fla.App.1986), 483 So.2d 1383; Massaro, Experts, Psychology, Credibility, and Rape; The Rape Trauma Syndrome Issue and Its Implications for Expert Psychological Testimony, 69 Minn. L.R. 395 (1985); McCord, The Admissibility of Expert Testimony Regarding Rape Trauma Syndrome in Rape Prosecutions, 26 B.C.L.Rev. 1143 (1985); Annot., 42 A.L.R.4th 879 (1985). The commentators and case law address, for the most part, whether evidence of post-traumatic stress syndrome in the form of rape trauma syndrome should be admissible at all. A large part of the discussion has centered on the reliability of such evidence under the familiar *Frye* rule that expert scientific testimony is only admissible if the phenomenon testified to is generally accepted in the relevant scientific community. Frye v. United States, 293 F. 1013 (D.C.Cir.1923). Since we have already crossed that hurdle in *Simmons*, our decision here is focused more on the issue above: whether, having allowed a trial court to admit such testimony when offered by the State to prove a rape was committed, we can say it is not an abuse of discretion to exclude it when offered by a defendant to prove that one was not. We conclude, in light of our decision in *Simmons*, that to bar the defendant from presenting such evidence exceeds the discretion of the trial court; and, in this case, the trial court's ruling impinged upon the substantial rights of appellant to present a defense and was reversible error.

[T]he judgment of the trial court is accordingly vacated and this case is remanded for a new trial.

———

RAPE TRAUMA SYNDROME

Particia A. Frazier.
In Modern Scientific Evidence: The Law and Science of Expert Testimony, 2008–2009 ed. (D. L. Faigman, M. J. Saks, J. Sanders, and E. K. Cheng eds. 2008).

[T]he legal framework [presented in Henson v. State, above] is somewhat more complicated than any simple *quid pro quo* approach would suggest. Most evidence codes today provide special protection for alleged victims of sexual assault in what are commonly called "rape shield statutes." These provisions, enacted to remedy the historical abuses surrounding the examination of complainants, severely restrict defense inquiries into the personal histories of alleged victims. To the extent that defense use of RTS raises the possibility that the alleged victim's personal history will be put in issue, contrary to a rape shield statute, some control over defense use should be exerted. Otherwise, unrestricted defense use of RTS could lead to the evisceration of the safeguards enacted in rape shield statutes.

How courts strike the balance regarding defense use of RTS depends on both the values embodied in evidence codes and the Constitution, together with the validity of the science associated with testimony on RTS. Unrestricted prosecutorial use of this evidence while, at the same time, complete foreclosure of defense use, would violate basic precepts of fairness. This is particularly true given the criminal justice system's commitment to guaranteeing defendants due process. At the same time, most jurisdictions are committed to protecting alleged victims from the kinds of abuse that were commonplace prior to enactment of protective legislation. These considerations might lead courts to strike a balance whereby defense use of RTS is limited to rebuttal of prosecution use of this evidence. In particular cases, therefore, if the state opens the door to the "psychological state" of the alleged victim, the defense would be permitted to rigorously test and rebut this claim.

———

NOTES

1. Prosecution Use of Defense Expert. In State v. Jackson, 97 N.M. 467, 641 P.2d 498 (1982), a defendant charged with rape requested a mental health examination of the complainant to ascertain whether she experienced the rape trauma syndrome. The prosecution had not first raised the issue of rape trauma. The trial judge ordered the complainant to submit to the examination. Contrary to the expectations of the defense, however, the examining psychologist "reported that this was one of the worst cases of rape trauma syndrome he had ever seen." Id. at 499. Accordingly, the defense did not seek to introduce the expert. The prosecution then attempted to call the psychologist as an expert witness of its own, and the defense objected. The New Mexico Supreme Court held that the prosecution could make use of the expert witness originally retained by the defense.

2. Male Victims. In People v. Yates, 168 Misc.2d 101, 637 N.Y.S.2d 625 (N.Y. Sup.1995), the issue arose as to whether expert testimony on the rape trauma syndrome was admissible when applied to male complainants alleging homosexual assault. The Court concluded as follows:

> [L]egal authorities, scientific writings, constitutional doctrine and logic all favor acceptance of the principle that expert testimony concerning rape trauma syndrome as applied to male victims is scientifically reliable and may, when appropriate, be admitted to aid a jury in understanding the sequelae of sexual assault against a man. Id. at 630.

C.   WITNESSES

Finally, in addition to its use in determining facts pertaining to defendants and victims, social science research is often offered to provide a context for decisionmakers in evaluating the testimony of witnesses. Research on eyewitness identification has been the primary witness-oriented framework that has been offered at trial.

———

ARIZONA v. CHAPPLE

Supreme Court of Arizona, 1983.
135 Ariz. 281, 660 P.2d 1208.

■ FELDMAN, JUSTICE.

[Three persons were murdered in the process of transacting the sale of 300 pounds of marijuana. Malcolm Scott and his sister, Pamela Buck, both of whom were parties to the transaction, identified Dolan Chapple as the murderer in a police photo line-up and in the courtroom. Chapple was convicted of first degree murder and sentenced to life imprisonment without the possibility of parole for twenty-five years.]

With identification the one issue on which the guilt or innocence of [the] defendant hinged, [d]efense counsel offered the testimony of an expert on eyewitness identification in order to rebut the testimony of Malcolm Scott and his sister, Pamela Buck. The witness called by the defense was Dr. Elizabeth Loftus, a professor of psychology at the University of Washington. Dr. Loftus specializes in an area of experimental and clinical psychology dealing with perception, memory retention and recall. Her qualifications are unquestioned, and it may fairly be said that she "wrote the book" on the subject. The trial court granted the State's motion to suppress Dr. Loftus' testimony. Acknowledging that rulings on admissibility of expert testimony are within the discretion of the trial court, defendant contends that the court erred and abused its discretion in granting the motion to suppress Dr. Loftus' testimony.

The admissibility of expert testimony is governed by Rule 702, Ariz.R. of Evid. That rule states:

If scientific, technical, or other specialized knowledge will assist the trier of fact to understand the evidence or to determine a fact in issue, a witness qualified as an expert by knowledge, skill, experience, training, or education, may testify thereto in the form of an opinion or otherwise.

In what is probably the leading case on the subject, the Ninth Circuit affirmed the trial court's preclusion of expert evidence on eyewitness identification in United States v. Amaral, 488 F.2d 1148 (9th Cir.1973). In its analysis, however, the court set out four criteria which should be applied in order to determine the admissibility of such testimony. These are: (1) qualified expert; (2) proper subject; (3) conformity to a generally accepted explanatory theory; and (4) probative value compared to prejudicial effect. Id. at 1153. We approve this test and find that the case at bar meets these criteria.

We recognize that the cases that have considered the subject have uniformly affirmed trial court rulings denying admission of this type of testimony. However, a careful reading of these cases reveals that many of them contain fact situations which fail to meet the *Amaral* criteria or are decided on legal principles which differ from those we follow in Arizona.

[A]pplying the *Amaral* test to the case at bench, we find from the record that the State has conceded that the expert was qualified and that the question of conformity to generally accepted explanatory theory is not raised and appears not to be a question in this case. The two criteria which must therefore be considered are (1) determination of whether the probative value of the testimony outweighs its possible prejudicial effect and (2) determination of whether the testimony was a proper subject.

(1) PROBATIVE VALUE vs. PREJUDICE

The State argues that there would have been little probative value to the witness' testimony and great danger of unfair prejudice. The latter problem is claimed to arise from the fact that Loftus' qualifications were so impressive that the jury might have given improper weight to her testimony. We do not believe that this raises the issue of *unfair* prejudice. The contention of lack of probative value is based on the premise that the offer of proof showed that the witness would testify to general factors which were applicable to this case and affect the reliability of identification, but would not express any opinion with regard to the accuracy of the specific identification made by Scott and Buck and would not express an opinion regarding the accuracy percentage of eyewitness identification in general.

We believe that the "generality" of the testimony is a factor which favors admission. Witnesses are permitted to express opinions on ultimate issues but are not required to testify to an opinion on the precise questions before the trier of fact.

(2) PROPER SUBJECT

[T]he remaining criterion at issue is whether the offered evidence was a proper subject for expert testimony. Ariz.R. of Evid. 702 allows expert testimony if it "will assist the trier of fact to understand the evidence or to determine a fact in issue." Put conversely, the test "is whether the subject of inquiry is one of such common knowledge that people of ordinary education could reach a conclusion as intelligently as the witness...." State v. Owens, 112 Ariz. 223, 227, 540 P.2d 695, 699 (1975). Furthermore, the test is not whether the jury could reach some conclusion in the absence of the expert evidence, but whether the jury is qualified without such testimony "to determine intelligently and to the best possible degree the particular issue without enlightenment from those having a specialized understanding of the subject...." Fed.R.Evid. 702 advisory committee note (quoting Ladd, Expert Testimony, 5 Vand.L.Rev. 414, 418 (1952)).

In excluding the evidence in the case at bench, the trial judge stated:

> I don't find anything that's been presented in the extensive discussions that I have read in your memorandum with regard to the fact that this expert is going to testify to anything that isn't within the common experience of the people on the jury, that couldn't really be covered in cross-examination of the witnesses who made the identification, and probably will be excessively argued in closing arguments to the jury.

This basis for the view that eyewitness identification is not a proper subject for expert testimony is the same as that adopted in United States v. Amaral, supra, and in the great majority of cases which have routinely followed *Amaral*.

However, after a careful review of these cases and the record before us, we have concluded that although the reasons cited by the trial judge would correctly permit preclusion of such testimony in the great majority of cases, it was error to refuse the testimony in the case at bench. In reaching this conclusion, we have carefully considered the offer of proof made by the defense in light of the basic concept of "proper subject" underlying Rule 702.

We note at the outset that the law has long recognized the inherent danger in eyewitness testimony. Of course, it is difficult to tell whether the ordinary juror shares the law's inherent caution of eyewitness identification. Experimental data indicates that many jurors "may reach intuitive conclusions about the reliability of [such] testimony that psychological research would show are misguided." Note, Did Your Eyes Deceive You? Expert Psychological Testimony on the Unreliability of Eyewitness Identification, 29 Stan.L.Rev. 969, 1017 (1977).

Even assuming that jurors of ordinary education need no expert testimony to enlighten them to the danger of eyewitness identification, the offer of proof indicated that Dr. Loftus' testimony would have informed the jury that there are many specific variables which affect the accuracy of identification and which apply to the facts of this case. For instance, while most jurors would no doubt realize that memory dims as time passes, Dr. Loftus presented data from experiments which showed that the "forgetting curve" is not uniform. Forgetting occurs very rapidly and then tends to level out; immediate identification is much more trustworthy than long-delayed identification. Thus, Scott's recognition [of another suspect as the murderer when the other suspect's photograph was shown] at the inception of the investigation is probably a more reliable identification than Scott's identification of Chapple's photograph in the photographic lineup thirteen months later. By the same token, Scott's failure to identify Chapple's photograph when it was first shown to him on March 26, 1978 (four months after the crime) and when Scott's ability to identify would have been far greater, is of key importance.

Another variable in the case is the effect of stress upon perception. Dr. Loftus indicated that research shows that most laymen believe that stressful events cause people to remember "better" so that what is seen in periods of stress is more accurately related later. However, experimental evidence indicates that stress causes inaccuracy of perception with subsequent distortion of recall.

Dr. Loftus would also have testified about the problems of "unconscious transfer," a phenomenon which occurs when the witness confuses a person seen in one situation with a person seen in a different situation. Dr. Loftus would have pointed out that a witness who takes part in a photo identification session without identifying any of the photographs and who then later sees a photograph of one of those persons may relate his or her familiarity with the picture to the crime rather than to the previous identification session.

Another variable involves assimilation of post-event information. Experimental evidence, shown by Dr. Loftus, confirms that witnesses frequently incorporate into their identifications inaccurate information gained subsequent to the event and confused with the event. An additional problem is the "feedback factor." We deal here with two witnesses who were related and who, according to Loftus' interview, engaged in discussions with each other about the identification of [the defendant]. Dr. Loftus, who interviewed them, emphasized that their independent descriptions of [the defendant] at times utilized identical language. Dr. Loftus would have explained that through such discussions identification witnesses can reinforce their individual identifications. Such reinforcement will often tend to heighten the certainty of identification. The same may be said of the continual sessions that each witness had with the police in poring over large groups of photographs.

The last variable in this case concerns the question of confidence and its relationship to accuracy. Dr. Loftus' testimony and some experimental data indicate that there is no relationship between the confidence which a witness has in his or her identification and the actual accuracy of that identification. Again, this factor was specifically tied to the evidence in the case before us since both Scott and Buck indicated in their testimony that they were absolutely sure of their identification. Evidently their demeanor on the witness stand showed absolute confidence.

We cannot assume that the average juror would be aware of the variables concerning identification and memory about which Dr. Loftus was qualified to testify. [T]hus, considering the standard of Rule 702, supra,—whether the expert testimony will assist the jury in determining an issue before them—and the unusual facts in this case, we believe that Dr. Loftus' offered evidence was a proper subject for expert testimony and should have been admitted. [T]here were a number of substantive issues of ultimate fact on which the expert's testimony would have been of significant assistance. Accordingly, we hold that the order precluding the testimony was legally incorrect and was unsupported by the record. It was, therefore, an abuse of discretion.

In reaching this conclusion, we do not intend to "open the gates" to a flood of expert evidence on the subject. We reach the conclusion that Dr. Loftus should have been permitted to testify on the peculiar facts of this case and have no quarrel with the result reached in the vast majority of cases which we have cited above. The rule in Arizona will continue to be that in the usual case we will support the trial court's discretionary ruling on admissibility of expert testimony on eyewitness identification. Nor do we invite opinion testimony in even the most extraordinary case on the likelihood that a particular witness is correct or mistaken in identification or that eyewitness identification in general has a certain percentage of accuracy or inaccuracy.

[T]he judgment below is reversed and the case remanded for a new trial.

■ HAYS, JUSTICE, concurring in part and dissenting in part.

I cannot agree with the majority's position that the trial court abused its discretion in excluding the testimony of an expert witness on eyewitness identification. With a view to preserving the integrity of the jury as finders of fact, I dissent in part.

[M]y concern here goes beyond the borders of this case. Once we have opened the door to this sort of impeaching testimony, what is to prevent experts from attacking any real or supposed deficiency in every other mental faculty? The peculiar risk of expert testimony with its scientific aura of trustworthiness and the possibility of undue prejudice should be respected. I have great reluctance to permit academia to take over the fact-finding function of the jury. Although clothed in other guise, that will be the practical effect. With little to distinguish this case from the general rule against admitting expert testimony on eyewitness identification, we are left with no guidelines to decide the deluge of similar issues which are sure to result.

———

NOTES

1. Common Experience. It was the position of the trial court in *Chapple* that the subject of eyewitness identification is within the "common experience"—that is, it is not "beyond the ken"—of the jury and therefore not a proper subject for expert testimony about empirical research. However, a survey of a random sample of jury-eligible persons in one jurisdiction described the methodology of several published eyewitness identification studies and asked the prospective jurors to estimate the percentage of accurate identifications that were made in the studies described. For one study, in which the actual percent of correct identification was 12.5, the prospective jurors estimated the accuracy rate at 70.6 percent. For another study, in which the actual accuracy rate was 31.3 percent, the prospective jurors estimated that 68.9 percent of the subjects made an accurate identification. According to the authors, "the present data refute the claim that expert psychological testimony on eyewitness identifications would not tell the jury members anything they do not already know. [The] data indicate that the testimony of an expert on these matters would not invade the province of the jury." Brigham and Bothwell, The Ability of Prospective Jurors to Estimate the Accuracy of Eyewitness Identification, 7 Law and Human Behavior 19, 29 (1983).

2. Widespread Consensus. Kassin, Tubb, Hosch, and Memon, On the "General Acceptance" of Eyewitness Testimony Research: A New Survey of the Experts, 56 American Psychologist 4–5 (2001), surveyed a "blue-ribbon" sample of 64 psychological experts on the topic of eyewitness testimony. They summarized their conclusions as follows:

> By an agreement rate of at least 80%, there was a strong consensus that the following phenomena are sufficiently reliable to present in court: the wording of questions, lineup instructions, confidence malleability, mug-shot-induced bias, postevent information, child witness suggestibility, alcohol intoxication, the cross-race bias, weapon focus, the accuracy-confidence correlation, the forgetting curve, exposure time, presentation format, and unconscious transference. Id. at 405.

3. The Whole Truth. At a conference on eyewitness identification, Professor Loftus described an expert testimony issue that she "felt a little uneasy about":

> What if the psychologist [testifying for the defense] is quite sure that the prosecuting attorney doesn't know enough about the research to raise damaging questions? Should the psychologist mention the one or two studies whose results contradict the gist of numerous other studies? Should she mention how the length of time since the crime can affect memory, but leave out that the length of time with the assailant is also a factor? The current ethical standards that govern psychologists, such as the [American Psychological Association's] Ethical Principals of Psychologists, offer little guidance in defining the degree of advocacy to be taken in court.

Cunningham, Scientific Expert Witnesses Cross–Examine Own Value, 14 American Psychological Association Monitor 6 (1983).

———

WEATHERRED v. STATE

Court of Appeals of Texas, Beaumont, 1998.
963 S.W.2d 115.

■ WALKER, CHIEF JUSTICE.

A jury convicted appellant of Capital Murder. [Appellant] complains of the trial court's refusal to allow appellant to call Dr. Kenneth Deffenbacher as an expert witness on the issue of photo bias and eyewitness misidentification.

[T]he State contends that appellant failed to carry his burden to show that the testimony was admissible by failing to show that the testimony was reliable and that it was relevant. The leading Texas cases on the issue at present are Kelly v. State, *824 S.W.2d 568 (Tex.Crim.App.1992)*, which was available at the time of the trial of the instant case, and Jordan v. State, *928 S.W.2d 550 (Tex.Crim.App.1996)*, which was not available. Both cases discuss, and rely heavily upon, the United States Supreme Court case of Daubert v. Merrell Dow Pharmaceuticals, Inc., *509 U.S. 579, 113 S.Ct. 2786, 125 L.Ed.2d 469 (1993)*.

We [present] pertinent portions of the testimony of Dr. Deffenbacher as it appears in the record:

[Q]. Are there specific variables that can, at least according to your research, alter or vary the reliability of eyewitness identification?

A. Yes.

[Q]. What do these variables do or what effect do they have upon the credibility of eyewitness identification?

A. [Y]ou [h]ave to be concerned about the fidelity or faithfulness of human memory. That's the most important factor. But one thing— well, one of the variables I mentioned is forgetting. We all have common sense intuitions about forgetting and these are approximately true. The strength of a trace or a representation in our brain of whatever circumstances we have been exposed to rarely gets stronger over time and it ordinarily over time and circumstances gets weaker.

[I]f you ask most laypersons, and studies have done this, they will agree that memory gets worse over time, memory traces get weaker. What is not always—in fact, frequently isn't clear to the layperson is just how fast they get weaker over time. And that is where cognitive psychologists with the aid of mathematics and a lot of research on live human subjects are able to provide some more specificity as to how strong a memory representation might be in hours, days, weeks after a person's been exposed to a situation.

[Q]. Okay. And I believe you also, when you were talking to me, mentioned something about the relationship of eyewitness confidence to eyewitness accuracy?

A. Yes. This was a somewhat surprising finding. I don't think I was the first to find it, but there was one previous finding out there. The finding I am referring to is a somewhat counter-intuitive one. We all have the common sense intuition that the more confident that somebody appears to be, the more likely they are accurate in what they are representing to us. The less confident they appear to be, the less accurate they are.

That had been my assumption prior to conducting a study that was published in 1977. And it isn't—this particular finding is not one we set out to find, but we had the data. We not only asked people are—is—are each of these people in these photographs or in this live line-up, are they the person that you saw in a particular situation or doing a particular thing. And we also asked them on a five-point rating scale how confident are you when they made their decision, yes or no. And we decided we had this information so we would just check to see how closely the ratings, their own ratings of how confident they felt, how well those related or correlated with their accuracy.

And we were somewhat startled to find out in several different calculations we did in this series of studies that the relationship was virtually zero, that is, given the one piece of information confidence, the subjective ratings that they made of their confidence, an observer could not use that information to predict at all the actual accuracy. In other words, a highly confident person could just as easily be inaccurate. A low confidence, a person who did not feel very confident could just as likely be making the correct decision in each case.

[Q]. One other area that we have touched on just briefly a few minutes ago and that is a variable that you have labeled, called photo bias; is that correct?

A. Yes.

Q. And, in your opinion, having reviewed this testimony and seen the pictures and so forth that have been admitted into evidence, is this a variable that you feel would be significant in this particular case?

A. Yes.

Q. [W]ould you tell the Judge just a little short summary or synopsis of what photo biases is as you view it or as you use it in connection with your research?

A. Well, this is the situation where an eyewitness confronts some kind of situation that involves them encountering a stranger and sometime later prior to them viewing any sort of [live] line-up or photo line-up, they are exposed to one or more photographs that also include the presence of an image of a person who later turns out to be a suspect and at that time or at those times, they don't make a positive identification, but later at a line-up they do make a positive identification of the suspect who turns out to have been in one or more previous photo viewings. Sometimes these can be photo spreads and/or they may be a picture somebody saw in the paper, on TV or whatever. But these represent additional encounterings of an image of a person in different circumstances than the presumably original circumstances.

[Q].   The principles that we have been discussing the last 15 or 20 minutes and the findings that have resulted from your scientific studies and review of other scientific data, do you feel that they apply to the specific facts of this case?

A.   Yes.

Q.   Would you tell us how they apply to the facts of this case?

A.   Taking each of those three factors I mentioned?

Q.   Yes.

A.   Well, starting with the forgetting of a stranger's face, as I have been given to understand the facts in this case, the time between the ultimate memory test and that—and the original exposure to the incident or the circumstances of their encountering, of the witness encountering the stranger was, I understand, on the order of 12 to 13 weeks. And our studies and those of others show that if one has, let's say, a five to ten-second glimpse of a stranger, that on average, it depends on how distinctive the face is and there are some individual differences in how good—we don't understand how they exist, but there are some individual differences on how good people are at recognition memory of stranger faces.

[But] in general the degree of strength of a person's memory representation after around 90 days or three months could easily been down to maybe 30 percent accuracy.

Q.   There was [another] area you said applied in this specific case?

A.   Well, [o]ne was the operation of photo biasing of line-ups.

[Q].   How does it apply specifically to this case?

A.   Well, you have the circumstances of eyewitnesses getting a brief look at the face of a stranger or no look at the face of a stranger and then subsequently days or a few weeks later they are shown two different— well, two different sets of photographic images that both contain the image of the suspect. And then I believe in the case of one witness whose testimony I heard this morning that witness apparently was exposed to a newspaper photo as well which included the image also of the suspect.

So what we have here then are two or three subsequent encounters with, presumably under good viewing circumstances when you get to look at the photograph of the image or the suspect. So the question then becomes can an eyewitness base their identification only on the image of the face of the stranger they saw at the scene of the crime or is their memory based wholly or in part on the subsequent images they have seen.

And from what cognitive psychologists [know] about human memory, it especially—when the glimpse wasn't that long or the viewing circumstances weren't that good, the possibility of photo bias becomes stronger and there is no way for the individual involved or for any of us to know for certain how much the identification would be based on the subsequent images.

Q. The third area, the third variable you mentioned a little earlier that you felt would apply to this case, I believe you called it eyewitness confidence to eyewitness accuracy?

A. Yes.

Q. And how would that variable apply to the specific facts of this case?

A. Well, given, as I mentioned earlier, that it is common sense intuition that highly confident people ought to be accurate and less confident people are less likely to be accurate, the assumption of most laypersons including triers of fact would be that that is what is operating in the case of human [eyewitnesses].

[But] what tends to happen over time is as a person goes over their memory for an event, as they tell others about it, they get more confident, and sometimes more confident for reasons that have little to do with accuracy.

Meanwhile, the memory representation that is the only basis for an eyewitness' accuracy of report, that never gets stronger and generally over time and circumstances gets weaker. So what you have is individuals who are moderate to highly confident and that may increase over time for reasons unrelated to accuracy and you have accuracy going the other way. And in that way confidence, an eyewitness' confidence and their actual accuracy can kind of get unhinged or unhooked and that may explain why confidence is typically not all that highly related to actual accuracy.

[I]n addition to the above testimony, appellant included in his bill of exceptions articles taken from a variety of publications describing scientifically-conducted experiments and the results of said experiments; all related to the accuracy of eyewitness identification.

[T]he testimony of Dr. Deffenbacher taken together with the scientific articles lead us to conclude that appellant proved, by clear and convincing evidence, the reliability prong of Daubert and Kelly. [T]he trial court abused its discretion in refusing to admit said evidence before the jury. [T]he erroneous refusal to permit Dr. Deffenbacher's evidence, which would have called into question the accuracy of the State's only *direct,* as opposed to circumstantial, witnesses, in the light of the entire record before us, affected appellant's substantial rights to the extent that had the evidence in question been admitted, it could have had a substantial influence on the jury.

[T]he judgment of the trial court is reversed, and the cause remanded to said court for a new trial on the merits.

———

NOTE

1. Historic Precedent. While the use of empirical data at trial to question the accuracy of an eyewitness' identification has become frequent only in recent years, the practice has a distinguished precedent. Shortly after his debate with Stephen Douglas, Abraham Lincoln was asked by a friend to assist in defending her son against the charge of having murdered a man during a fight on the evening of August 29, 1857. According to F. Hill, Lincoln the Lawyer, 232–233 (1906):

> [At trial] no very damaging testimony was elicited until a man by the name of Allen took the stand. This witness, however, swore that he actually saw the defendant strike the fatal blow with a slungshot [sic] or some such weapon; and Lincoln, pressing him closely, forced him to locate the hour of the assault as about eleven at night, and then demanded that he inform the jury how he had managed to see so clearly at that time of night. "By the moonlight," answered the witness promptly. "Well, was there light enough to see everything that happened?" persisted the examiner. The witness responded that "the moon was about in the same place that the sun would be at ten o'clock in the morning and was almost full," and the moment the words were out of his mouth the cross-examiner confronted him with a calendar showing that the moon, which at its best was only slightly past its first quarter on August 29, had afforded practically no light at eleven o'clock and that it had absolutely set at seven minutes after midnight. This was the turning-point in the case, and from that moment Lincoln carried everything before him, securing an acquittal of the defendant after a powerful address to the jury.

STATE v. VIA

Supreme Court of Arizona, 1985.
146 Ariz. 108, 704 P.2d 238.

■ CAMERON, JUSTICE.

Defendant, William Dabney Via, Jr., was convicted by a jury of first degree murder. [D]efendant raises [an issue] on appeal:

> [W]as the testimony of an expert witness on eyewitness identification improperly limited?

[D]efendant presented the testimony of an authority on eyewitness identification, Dr. Elizabeth Loftus. She testified as to the variables affecting the accuracy of eyewitness identifications and to the empirical studies done in the field. The trial court, however, precluded her from testifying as to an informal test she had conducted. She performed the test at airports and on board a plane en route to Phoenix to testify. The test involved providing fifteen persons with a photograph of the live lineup and a description of defendant. Dr. Loftus would have testified that fourteen of those tested picked defendant as the person described to them.

Defendant maintains that the trial court's ruling violated our holding in State v. Chapple, 135 Ariz. 281, 660 P.2d 1208 (1983). [O]n the contrary, one of the factors we emphasized in *Chapple* was that:

> The testimony offered was carefully limited to an exposition of the factors affecting reliability, with experimental data supporting the witness' testimony and *no attempt was made to have the witness render opinions on the actual credibility or accuracy of the identification witnesses. Issues of ultimate fact may be the subject of expert testimony, but witnesses are not "permitted as experts on how juries should decide cases."* Ariz.R. of Evid. 704 comment.

Id. at 295, 660 P.2d at 1222 (emphasis added).

We have also examined the progeny of *Chapple* and have been unable to find a case mandating admissibility of the type of testimony proffered by defendant. Rather, these cases stand for the proposition that general testimony as to the variables affecting eyewitness identification is permissible, but within the discretion of the trial court.

NEWSOME v. McCABE

United States Court of Appeals, Seventh Circuit, 2003.
319 F.3d 301.

■ EASTERBROOK, CIRCUIT JUDGE.

Fifteen years after his conviction for killing Edward Cohen, James Newsome was pardoned on the ground of innocence: fingerprints and other information strongly imply that Dennis Emerson committed the crime. Newsome filed this suit under 42 U.S.C. § 1983, seeking damages from police officers who, he contends, induced three witnesses to identify him as the killer. Two years ago we held that officers McCabe and McNally are not entitled to qualified immunity if, as Newsome alleges, they not only induced witnesses to accuse him falsely but also concealed their improper activities. *Newsome v. McCabe*, 256 F.3d 747, rehearing denied, 260 F.3d 824 (7th Cir.2001). On remand the City of Chicago, which has a financial stake in the outcome as a potential indemnitor of the officers, intervened to protect its interests. A jury found that, by concealing evidence favorable to the defense, McCabe and McNally had violated Newsome's constitutional right to due process of law and awarded him $15 million in damages, to which the district judge (after denying all post-trial motions) added some $850,000 in attorneys' fees and costs. In this appeal Chicago [c]ontests some of the district judge's evidentiary decisions at trial.

[A]nthony Rounds, Josie Nash, and John Williams supplied the principal evidence at Newsome's criminal trial. Rounds and Nash, who had been in Cohen's grocery store when the murder occurred, positively identified Newsome as the killer; Williams, who had been outside, testified that he saw Newsome flee.

[M]ost persons have difficulty remembering or describing the features of strangers. A person who sees a criminal for only a brief time takes away a vague sense of appearance and behavior—and that sense may be focused by a sketch, photograph, showup, or lineup after the events. Sometimes the witness zeroes in on the correct person, sometimes not; there is an element of chance and an opportunity for manipulation. Once the witness decides that "X is it" the view may be unshakable. Psychological research has established that the witness's faith is equally strong whether or not the identification is correct. We described these findings in *Krist v. Eli Lilly & Co.,* 897 F.2d 293 (7th Cir.1990): "An important body of psychological research undermines the lay intuition that confident memories of salient experiences ... are accurate and do not fade with time unless a person's memory has some pathological impairment.... The basic problem about testimony from memory is that most of our recollections are not verifiable. The only warrant for them is our certitude, and certitude is not a reliable test of certainty.... [T]he mere fact that we remember something with great confidence is not a powerful warrant for thinking it true." 897 F.2d at 296–97 (citations to the scholarly literature omitted). See Elizabeth F. Loftus & James M. Doyle, *Eyewitness Testimony: Civil and Criminal* (3d ed.1997); Elizabeth F. Loftus, *Eyewitness Testimony* (1979; rev. ed.1996); Daniel L. Schacter, *The Seven Sins of Memory: How the Mind Forgets and Remembers* 112–37 (2001). Jurors, however, tend to think that witnesses' memories are reliable (because jurors are confident of their own), and this gap between the actual error rate and the jurors' heavy reliance on eyewitness testimony sets the stage for erroneous convictions when (as in Newsome's prosecution) everything depends on uncorroborated eyewitness testimony by people who do not know the accused.

[B]ecause recollection is suggestible, it was important in this civil case to explore the question whether the testimony of Rounds, Nash, and Williams identifying Newsome at the criminal trial was attributable to deliberate manipulation or instead to chance. For if chance errors are to blame, and the witnesses would have identified Newsome no matter how the officers prompted them during the lineups, then defendants' conduct did not cause the wrongful conviction and an award of damages would be improper. To explore this issue Newsome presented the testimony of Gary Wells, a professor of psychology who has performed experiments and written scholarly works in this field. See, e.g., Gary L. Wells & Elizabeth A. Olson, *Eyewitness Identification,* 54 Ann. Rev. Psych. 277 (2003); Gary L. Wells, *Eyewitness Identification: A System Handbook* (1988). Wells conducted an experiment to determine the likelihood that three persons who saw Emerson nonetheless would identify Newsome. He showed two panels of subjects different pictures of Emerson for 15 seconds then, after some time had passed, showed them pictures of the men in the lineup and asked them to choose the one they had seen in the initial photograph. Of 50 members on the first panel, none selected Newsome's photo; of 500 members on the second panel (which was shown a different photo of Emerson), 15 chose Newsome's photo. Performing a chi-square test, Wells calculated that the probability of all three eyewitnesses independently picking Newsome out of a lineup by chance error was substantially less than one in 1,000, implying that the officers must have manipulated their identifications.

Chicago asked the district judge to exclude Wells' testimony under Fed.R.Evid. 702, which as amended in 2000 codifies (with some variation) the holding of *Daubert v. Merrell Dow Pharmaceuticals, Inc.,* 509 U.S. 579, 113 S.Ct. 2786, 125 L.Ed.2d 469 (1993). The district judge concluded that Wells is an expert on the subject of identification, that his testimony was based on sufficient data, that his methods were reliable by the standards of the field, and that he applied these methods reliably to the facts of Newsome's case. Experiments of the kind that Wells performed are the norm in this branch of science and have met the standard for scholarly publication and acceptance. There were of course potential problems. For example, Wells assumed that Emerson is the killer, so that the witnesses saw him; if anyone other than Emerson committed the murder, the test is invalid. Wells was candid about this vital assumption, which was open to probing and argument by the defendants. Wells also assumed that two-dimensional images (pictures) yield the same effects on memory as three-dimensional views (live action in the victim's grocery store; lineups in the police station; identifications in open court). This may or may not hold, but the claim of equivalence was open to exploration at trial, and it is hard to see what else Wells could have done. Even if he could have conscripted Emerson and the lineup participants for an experiment, time has so altered their appearance since the events of October 1979 that the results would have been unreliable. Chicago does not contend that there was a better way to find out whether Rounds, Nash, and Williams would have identified Newsome without the coaching. Instead it insists that Wells' testimony was irrelevant because he did not determine *how* the witnesses had been induced to believe that they saw Newsome commit the murder. Yet testimony need not prove everything in order to be useful. As we have said, the jury had to consider the possibility that unhappy chance rather than malfeasance led to the mistaken conviction. Wells provided information valuable in this endeavor. Appellate review of the district judge's decision is deferential, *General Electric Co. v. Joiner,* 522 U.S. 136, 118 S.Ct. 512, 139 L.Ed.2d 508 (1997), and there was no abuse here; indeed, we would have acted precisely as did the district judge.

———

EYEWITNESS IDENTIFICATION PROCEDURES: RECOMMENDATIONS FOR LINEUPS AND PHOTOSPREADS*

Gary Wells, Mark Small, Steven Penrod, Roy Malpass, Solomon Fulero, and C. Brimacombe.
22 Law and Human Behavior 603 (1998).

The evidence [from psychological research] makes a strong case that some lineup identification procedures lead to increased risk of false identifi-

* With kind permission of Springer Science and Business Media.

cation or inflated confidence. These procedures are under the control of the criminal justice system. Hence, any role of these procedures in contributing to false identification or false confidence could be eliminated by controlling the procedures in critical ways. In the present section, we describe four simple rules of procedure that follow from the scientific literature that we argue could largely relieve the criminal justice system of its role in contributing to eyewitness identification problems.

[R]ule 1. Who Conducts the Lineup

The person who conducts the lineup or photospread should not be aware of which member of the lineup or photospread is the suspect.

[R]ule 2. Instructions on Viewing

Eyewitnesses should be told explicitly that the person in question might not be in the lineup or photospread and therefore should not feel that they must make an identification. They should also be told that the person administering the lineup does not know which person is the suspect in the case.

[R]ule 3. Structure of Lineup or Photospread

The suspect should not stand out in the lineup or photospread as being different from the distractors based on the eyewitness's previous description of the culprit or based on other factors that would draw extra attention to the suspect.

[R]ule 4. Obtaining Confidence Statements

A clear statement should be taken from the eyewitness at the time of the identification and prior to any feedback as to his or her confidence that the identified person is the actual culprit.

[A] main reason why we are proposing only these four rules at this time is [b]ecause we think that proposing too many rules would produce resistance by police and legal policy makers and perhaps dilute the import of the four primary rules. There are, however, two potential recommendations that are particularly important, [n]amely a recommendation that lineups be sequential rather than simultaneous and a recommendation that lineups be videotaped. We recognize that there are many eyewitness scholars who believe that the sequential idea and the videotaping idea should be among the rules recommended in this article.

[T]he extensive scientific literature in eyewitness identification has led to a good understanding of the fact that eyewitness identification errors can arise out of the procedures that are used for obtaining those identifications. The psychological processes involved in eyewitness identifications from lineups and photospreads, especially the relative judgment process, require that eyewitnesses be warned that the actual culprit might not be in the lineup and that all members of the lineup fit the verbal description that the eyewitness had given of the perpetrator. The dynamic interaction between the person administering the lineup and the eyewitness, in conjunction with what we know about interpersonal influence, necessitates that the administering agent not know which person in the lineup is the suspect. In addition, the primary role played by eyewitness confidence in the legal system's assessment of the credibility of the identification, in conjunction with clear empirical evidence of confidence malleability, demands that confidence statements be obtained at the time of the identification (before other variables begin to exert their influence on the eyewitness). The adoption of these four rules into lineup practices can remove a great deal of the contribution that the justice system itself contributes to the problem of mistaken identification.

EYEWITNESS EVIDENCE: A GUIDE FOR LAW ENFORCEMENT

National Institute of Justice, 1999.

In an effort to bring together the perspectives of law enforcement, lawyers, and researchers, the National Institute of Justice convened the Technical Working Group for Eyewitness Evidence. The purpose of this group was to recommend uniform practices for the collection and preservation of eyewitness evidence. [T]his *Guide* is supported by social science research. During the past 20 years, research psychologists have produced a substantial body of findings regarding eyewitness evidence. These findings offer the legal system a valuable body of empirical knowledge in the area of eyewitness evidence. This *Guide* makes use of psychological findings, either by including them in the procedures themselves or by using them to point the way to the design and development of further improvements in procedures and practices for possible inclusion in future amendments or revision to this document.

[A]dvances in social science and technology will, over time, affect procedures used to gather and preserve eyewitness evidence. The following examples illustrate areas of potential change. Scientific research indicates that identification procedures such as lineups and photo arrays produce more reliable evidence when the individual lineup members or photographs are shown to the witness sequentially—one at a time—rather than simultaneously. Although some police agencies currently use sequential methods of presentation, there is not a consensus on any particular method or methods of sequential presentation that can be recommended as a *preferred* procedure; although sequential procedures are included in the *Guide*, it does not indicate a preference for sequential procedures.

Similarly, investigators' unintentional cues (e.g., body language, tone of voice) may negatively impact the reliability of eyewitness evidence. Psychology researchers have noted that such influences could be avoided if "blind" identification procedures were employed (i.e., procedures conducted by investigators who do not know the identity of the actual suspect). However, blind procedures, which are used in science to prevent inadvertent contamination of research results, may be impractical for some jurisdictions to implement. Blind procedures are not included in the *Guide* but are identified as a direction for future exploration and field testing. In the interim, an enhanced awareness on the part of investigators of the subtle impact they may have on witnesses will result in more professional identification procedures.

Procedures for Eyewitness Identification of Suspects

A.   Composing Lineups

Live Lineup: In composing a live lineup, the investigator should:

1.   Include only one suspect in each identification procedure.

2.   Select fillers who generally fit the witness' description of the perpetrator. When there is a limited/inadequate description of the perpetrator provided by the witness, or when the description of the perpetrator differs significantly from the appearance of the suspect, fillers should resemble the suspect in significant features.

3.   Consider placing suspects in different positions in each lineup, both across cases and with multiple witnesses in the same case. Position the suspect randomly unless, where local practice allows, the suspect or the suspect's attorney requests a particular position.

4.   Include a *minimum* of four fillers (nonsuspects) per identification procedure.

5.   When showing a new suspect, avoid reusing fillers in lineups shown to the same witness.

6. Consider that complete uniformity of features is not required. Avoid using fillers who so closely resemble the suspect that a person familiar with the suspect might find it difficult to distinguish the suspect from the fillers.

7.   Create a consistent appearance between the suspect and fillers with respect to any unique or unusual feature (e.g., scars, tattoos) used to describe the perpetrator by artificially adding or concealing that feature.

B.   Instructing the Witness Prior to Viewing a Lineup

Live Lineup: Prior to presenting a live lineup, the investigator should:

1.   Instruct the witness that he/she will be asked to view a group of individuals.

2.   Instruct the witness that it is just as important to clear innocent persons from suspicion as to identify guilty parties.

3.   Instruct the witness that individuals present in the lineup may not appear exactly as they did on the date of the incident because features such as head and facial hair are subject to change.

4.   Instruct the witness that the person who committed the crime may or may not be present in the group of individuals.

5.   Assure the witness that regardless of whether an identification is made, the police will continue to investigate the incident.

6. Instruct the witness that the procedure requires the investigator to ask the witness to state, in his/her own words, how certain he/she is of any identification.

C. Conducting the Identification Procedure

Live Lineup: When presenting a sequential live lineup, the lineup administrator/investigator should:

1. Provide viewing instructions to the witness as outlined in subsection B, "Instructing the Witness Prior to Viewing a Lineup."

2. Provide the following *additional* viewing instructions to the witness:

   a. Individuals will be viewed *one at a time*.

   b. The individuals will be presented in random order.

   c. Take as much time as needed in making a decision about each individual before moving to the next one.

   d. If the person who committed the crime is present, identify him/her.

   e. All individuals will be presented, even if an identification is made; *or* the procedure will be stopped at the point of an identification (consistent with jurisdictional/departmental procedures).

3. Begin with all lineup participants out of the view of the witness.

4. Instruct all those present at the lineup not to suggest in any way the position or identity of the suspect in the lineup.

5. Present each individual to the witness separately, in a previously determined order, removing those previously shown.

6. Ensure that any identification actions (e.g., speaking, moving) are performed by all members of the lineup.

7. Avoid saying anything to the witness that may influence the witness' selection.

8. If an identification is made, avoid reporting to the witness any information regarding the individual he/she has selected prior to obtaining the witness' statement of certainty.

9. Record any identification results and witness' statement of certainty.

[F]urther Reading: Wells, Small, Penrod, Malpass, Fulero, and Brimacombe, Eyewitness Identification Procedures: Recommendations for Lineups and Photospreads, 22 Law and Human Behavior 603 (1998).

————

REPORT OF THE TASK FORCE ON EYEWITNESS EVIDENCE

Office of the Suffolk County District Attorney and the Boston Police Commissioner, 2004.

On March 8, 2004, the Suffolk County District Attorney, Daniel F. Conley and the Boston Police Commissioner, Kathleen M. O'Toole, announced the formation of a Task Force on Eyewitness Evidence. The Task Force was charged with reviewing the investigative process for cases in which eyewitness identification was a significant issue, and recommending any appropriate changes in the means and manner of investigation. The Task Force was born of the concern, as evidenced by a series of recently overturned convictions, that better practices in such cases would yield more reliable results and significantly reduce the potential for error.

The Task Force offers 25 separate recommendations. A number of these are, to our knowledge, without precedent in any major city police department and prosecutor's office. Taken together, these 25 recommendations represent a dramatic leap forward in the manner in which police and prosecutors investigate and prosecute cases and would place Boston and Suffolk County in the forefront in comprehensively addressing an issue of both local and national concern.

[I]dentification Procedures.

The Task Force recommends adoption of the identification protocols described in the Department of Justice's Eyewitness Evidence Guide [excerpted above]. Using the DOJ protocols is an important step forward for fair and reliable identification procedures, but the Task Force concluded that there were significant steps that go beyond the DOJ Guide that need to be taken to insure the highest standards for Boston. Scientific research strongly supports sequential identification procedures and blind administration procedures as the best tools available to combat misidentifications. Historically, law enforcement in this country has not used either sequential or blind administration procedures. Research conducted in the 1980s and 1990s built academic support among psychological scientists for these new procedures. Despite the best efforts of some of its members, the DOJ national working group that produced the DOJ Guide could not agree to recommend the two biggest changes: sequential and blind administration procedures. After reviewing the scientific evidence, the Task Force concluded that sequential and blind administration procedures should, in conjunction with the DOJ protocols, be used in Boston as the most effective way to reduce misidentifications.

The following list [i]ncludes each specific recommendation made by the Task Force.

1. Adopt in full the recommendations on eyewitness evidence set forth by the United States Department of Justice.
2. Use sequential presentation of photographs in photo lineups.
3. Use sequential presentation of persons in live lineups.
4. Blind administration of photo lineups, which requires that the photo lineup be shown by an investigator who has no knowledge of which photograph is the suspect's.
5. Blind administration of live lineups, which requires that the live lineup be administered by an investigator who does not know which person is the suspect.

6. Use a standard printed form which provides eyewitnesses essential instructions for viewing a photo lineup or a live lineup.

7. Require detailed documentation, by means of a separate report, of every identification procedure conducted by the Boston Police.

8. Adopt as policy that every photo lineup shall consist of 8 photographs (7 fillers and 1 suspect) and that every live lineup shall consist of 6 persons (5 fillers and 1 suspect).

9. Use a live lineup subsequent to a photographic array in certain cases where testing the witness' ability to make an in-person identification could be of significant evidentiary value.

10. Use booking photograph compilations ("mug books") of scores of people as a possible source of identification only when all other investigative leads have been exhausted.

[T]he Scientific Approach to Eyewitness Evidence

In studying eyewitness evidence, Professor [Gary] Wells [, a member of the Task Force,] uses an analogy that assisted the Task Force in its analysis and recommendations. Professor Wells likens eyewitness evidence to physical trace evidence. Physical trace evidence, such as fingerprints, fibers or blood, can help determine the facts of a crime and the identity of the perpetrator. The observations of an eyewitness are items of trace evidence contained in the witness' memory. Like physical evidence, memory trace evidence can be contaminated, lost, destroyed or otherwise made to produce inaccurate results. Like physical trace evidence, the manner in which memory trace evidence is collected can have important consequences for the accuracy of the results. The Task Force concluded that a more scientific approach to collecting and analyzing eyewitness evidence should be the guiding principle for our recommendations.

———

UNITED STATES v. SMITH

United States District Court, Middle District of Alabama, Northern Division, 2009.
621 F.Supp.2d 1207.

■ MYRON H. THOMPSON, DISTRICT JUDGE.

On June 22, 2007, Montgomery Police responded to a report of a bank robbery at Compass Bank. After several weeks, police identified the robber as [Andreas JeJuan] Smith and a warrant was issued for his arrest. [A] jury found Smith guilty of bank robbery.

Dr. [Sol] Fulero's expert testimony [at trial, which the prosecution had moved to exclude] went principally to the reliability of witness identifications of Smith as the bank robber. While Smith was found guilty of the robbery after the court allowed Fulero's expert testimony, the court believes that an opinion setting forth its reasoning for allowing the testimony is still warranted.

DISCUSSION

The issue before the court is a pressing one. Eyewitness testimony has long been recognized as one of the most persuasive forms of evidence in criminal cases. "[T]here is almost nothing more convincing than a live human being who takes the stand, points a finger at the defendant, and says 'That's the one!' " *Watkins v. Sowders,* 449 U.S. 341, 352 (1981) (Brennan, J., dissenting).

Despite eyewitness testimony's persuasive nature, mounting evidence has suggested that it is not as reliable as has often been assumed. By some estimates, roughly 84% of convicts who have been exonerated by DNA testing were convicted on the basis of mistaken eyewitness testimony. Barry Scheck, et al., *Actual Innocence Five Days To Execution, and Other Dispatches From the Wrongly Convicted* (2000). There is, then, a vast lacuna between jurors' perceptions of the power of eyewitness testimony and this testimony's accuracy.

Still, despite this gap, courts have sometimes looked askance at expert testimony on the factors that can influence eyewitnesses' perceptions. In *United States v. Amaral,* 488 F.2d 1148, 1152–54 (9th Cir.1973), the Ninth Circuit Court of Appeals upheld a district court's decision to exclude eyewitness-identification expert testimony, reasoning that cross-examination would unveil any weaknesses in identifications.

[Y]et, as the body of evidence has grown showing the unreliability of some eyewitness testimony, courts have gradually recognized the potential value of expert testimony on this subject. *United States v. Mathis,* 264 F.3d 321, 339–40 (3rd Cir.2001) (examining an eyewitness expert's methods and "welcom[ing]" such testimony). It has been over a decade since the Eleventh Circuit last addressed the admissibility of eyewitness-identification expert testimony in a published opinion. In *United States v. Smith,* 122 F.3d 1355, 1358 (11th Cir.1997), the Eleventh Circuit held that "a district court does not abuse its discretion when it excludes expert testimony on eyewitness identification." Before that decision, the "established rule" of the Eleventh Circuit was apparently that such testimony was not admissible. *[United States v.] Holloway,* 971 F.2d [675] at 679 [(11th Cir. 1992)].

While *Smith* acknowledged that eyewitness-identification expert testimony has been looked upon "unfavorably" in the Eleventh Circuit, 122 F.3d at 1357, the court explicitly declined to decide at that time whether the "per se inadmissibility rule" remained in effect. *Id.* at 1358. The court also emphasized that the decision whether to admit expert testimony rests within the discretion of the trial court. *Id.* at 1359.

A per se proscription against all eyewitness-identification expert testimony is irreconcilable with the United States Supreme Court's decision in *Daubert v. Merrell Dow Pharms., Inc.,* 509 U.S. 579 (1993). There, the Court eschewed such categorical prohibitions of entire classes of expert *conclusions;* in determining whether to admit testimony, the Court stated, the focus "must be solely on principles and methodology, not on the conclusions that they generate." *Daubert,* 509 U.S. at 595. [H]eeding the

Supreme Court's command, this court at trial examined whether the proposed expert testimony complied with the strictures outlined in *Daubert.*

A.   Rule 702

[I]n *Daubert,* the Supreme Court urged lower courts, first, to examine whether reliable methodology undergirds proposed expert testimony. That is, courts are to consider: whether the theory or technique "can be (and has been) tested," "whether the theory or technique has been subjected to peer review and publication," whether there is a known or potential error rate in the scientific technique, and whether the theory or technique has achieved general acceptance in the particular scientific community. 509 U.S. at 593–94. Second, if the opinion testimony is reliable, the court must determine whether the testimony would aid the trier of fact. *Id.* at 589.This, essentially, is nothing more than a restatement of the general rule that the trial judge ensure the evidence is "relevant to the task at hand."*Id.* at 597.To answer this second question, courts should look to whether the reliable scientific methods "fit" the case before a court, *id.* at 591, an inquiry that typically involves scrutinizing the particular testimony offered and matching that testimony to the specific factual context of a case. The government challenges the admission of Fulero's testimony at each of these stages.

1.   Reliability

The government argues that Dr. Fulero's opinion does not constitute reliable scientific or technical knowledge. [T]his court [c]oncluded that Fulero's methods satisfied the reliability prong of *Daubert.* In compliance with *Daubert,* the theories underlying Fulero's testimony have been well-tested in peer-reviewed publications, including in articles authored by Fulero. *See, e.g.,* Nancy Stebay, Jennifer Dysart, Sol Fulero, & R.C.L. Lindsay, *A Meta–Analytic Comparison of Showup and Lineup Identification Accuracy,* 27 Law & Hum. Behav. 523 (2003).

Furthermore, Fulero testified that the methods he relies upon are generally accepted, and this representation accords with this court's own findings. Numerous studies have been done under controlled conditions assessing the factors that influence eyewitnesses "in accordance with generally accepted practice in the behavioral science community" done independent of any litigation. Hon. Robert P. Murrian, *The Admissibility of Expert Eyewitness Testimony Under the Federal Rules,* 29 Cumb. L.Rev. 379, 384–85 (1999) (collecting studies). As the Department of Justice recognized in a 1999 guide, "research psychologists have produced a substantial body of findings regarding eyewitness evidence. These findings offer the legal system a valuable body of empirical knowledge in the area of eyewitness evidence." U.S. Dept. of Justice, *Eyewitness Evidence: A Guide for Law Enforcement* 1 (1999), *available at* http://www.ncjrs.gov/pdffiles1/nij/178240.pdf (last visited Mar. 28, 2008). The Department of Justice guide relied in part on an article co-authored by the proffered expert in this case. U.S. Dept. of Justice, 42 (citing Gary L. Wells, Mark Small, Steven D. Penrod, Roy S. Malpass, Sol M. Fulero, & Elizabeth Brimacombe, *Eyewit-*

ness Identification Procedures: Recommendations for Lineups and Photo-spreads, 22 Law and Human Behavior 603 (1998)). [T]hese facts satisfied the court that Fulero is qualified in the field and equipped to provide the jury with reliable expert testimony on eyewitness identifications.

2. *Assistance to the Jury*

The United States contended that Fulero's proposed testimony would not aid the jury because Fulero's proffered testimony presented no analysis from Fulero tailored to this case. *See Daubert,* 509 U.S. at 591 (stating that testimony must "fit" the facts of a case to satisfy Fed.R.Evid. 702). Instead, Fulero's testimony would discuss only general problems associated with eyewitness identifications. Such testimony, the government argued, would not aid the jury because problems with eyewitness identification are within the "ordinary knowledge of most lay jurors." In addition to the lack of support for the proposition that juries commonly understand the unnamed (but likely myriad) problems with eyewitness testimony or the ways in which those problems interact with each other and in different factual settings, a further problem with the government's argument was that Fulero's expert testimony actually fitted quite well to Smith's case. This is precisely the type of case in which eyewitness-identification expert testimony would be of particular use. The strongest evidence that Smith committed the armed bank robbery was two eyewitness identifications by individuals who had had little contact with him.

Importantly, Fulero was not permitted to testify about what weight the jury should give the testimony in this case. Rather, he was allowed to supply jurors with information about some specific factors that, according to well-established social science-research, impact witness accuracy and, as a result, might assist them in their own determination of the facts. Chief among these factors is the information concerning cross-racial eyewitness identifications; the evidence concerning the reliability of such identification is stunning and robust and, of crucial importance here, not likely well understood by juries. In addition, the expert evidence also indicates that the accuracy of identifications, including cross-racial identifications, is impacted by whether the witness perceived the event in a high-stress environment and whether the witness has subsequently been exposed to facts that potentially altered his or her memory of an event.

The jury's decision-making process can be enhanced by learning how these factors combine to impact perception and memory. For example, here, one of the government's eyewitnesses is white, and the defendant is black. Research shows that cross-racial identifications are less accurate than same-race identifications. Brandon L. Garrett, *Judging Innocence,* 108 Colum. L.Rev. 55, 79 (2008) ("Social science studies have long shown that cross-racial identifications are particularly error prone."); Gary L. Wells & Elizabeth A. Olson, *The Other–Race Effect in Eyewitness Identification: What Do We Do About It?,* 7 Psychol. Pub. Pol'y & L. 230, 231 (2001) ("[A] Black innocent suspect has a 56% greater chance of being misidentified by a White eyewitness than by a Black eyewitness."). [T]he potential inaccuracies of cross-racial identifications are not necessarily within the common knowledge of the average juror or, for that matter, the average judge. The Supreme Court of New Jersey, in fact, requires jury instructions on the potential unreliability of cross-racial identifications for that reason. *State v. Cromedy,* 158 N.J. 112, 128, 727 A.2d 457 (1999).

Fulero also testified about how stress can impair a witness's perceptions and memories. One of the government's eyewitnesses testified that the bank robbery was the most traumatic experience of her life. Particularly in combination with the evidence about cross-racial identification, the jurors' judgment could be enhanced by learning that trauma and fear can cause a sincere person to wrongly recall an event. C. Neil Macrae et al., *Creating Memory Illusions: Expectancy–Based Processing and the Generation of False Memories,* 10 Memory 63, 72, 76–77 (2002) (finding that stress impairs an individuals perception and ability to accurately recall an event). This court will not assume that this psychological phenomenon is within the common knowledge of jurors.

Also of assistance to the jury was Fulero's expert testimony regarding how "post-event information" can influence an eyewitness. Research regarding post-event information shows that access to facts after an occurrence can, under some circumstances, "change a witness's memory and even cause nonexistent details to become incorporated into a previously acquired memory." Cohen, 16 Pace L.Rev. [237] at 246 [(1996)]. In this case, the two eyewitnesses to the bank robbery conversed with each other prior to providing testimony, and they acknowledged that they may have discussed what the robber looked like. Under such circumstances, testimony about post-event information could be of use to the jury. *See* Fiona Gabbert, et al, *Memory Conformity: Can Eyewitnesses Influence Each Other's Memories For An Event?,* 17 Applied Cogn. Psychol. 533 (2003) (finding that when witnesses discuss events with one another, shared false recollections sometimes result). And because "jurors tend to be unduly receptive to, rather than skeptical of, eyewitness testimony," *[United States v.] Smithers,* 212 F.3d [306] at 315 [6th Cir. 2000], the jury's factfinding ability [w]ill be enhanced by learning about the effects of post-event information.

Another useful aspect of Fulero's testimony was his discussion of the factors that impact the reliability of [p]hotograph identifications. For example, research shows that a photo identification works best when neither the person conducting the photo array, nor the eyewitness, knows who the targeted suspect is. *See* Fradella, 2006 Fed. Cts. L.Rev. [3] at 17. Further, eyewitnesses exhibit greater accuracy when they are explicitly informed that "a suspect may or may not be" in a photo array. *Id.* Yet another factor that affects accuracy is whether an eyewitness is shown photographs one after another, rather than being shown multiple photographs at the same time; eyewitnesses who are shown photographs sequentially show greater reliability than those who view photographs simultaneously. *Id.*

The evidence was that, in this case, the eyewitnesses were shown photographs simultaneously; and there was no evidence that these witnesses were told that the suspect "may or may not be" present in the photo array. The research revealing the potential consequences of these facts is likely not within the ken of the average juror. Indeed, exposure to this research proved of great assistance to this court during an earlier phase of this case, as it considered a motion to exclude the photo identifications as unduly suggestive under *Neil v. Biggers,* 409 U.S. 188, 93 S.Ct. 375, 34 L.Ed.2d 401 (1972); this court ultimately concluded that the photo identifications should not be excluded. If social-science research regarding eyewitness identifications aided this court's ability to understand the evidence as it considered this motion, it would be curious to assume that this same research would be of no aid to the jury.

Finally, Fulero testified to the highly counter-intuitive, but well-founded, theory that the amount of confidence a person has in a recollection does not correlate well with the accuracy of that recollection. In other words, just because a witness says she is 100% sure of an identification does not mean that the witness's identification is correct. As the Seventh Circuit Court of Appeals has observed, "Sometimes the witness zeroes in on the correct person, sometimes not; there is an element of chance and an opportunity for manipulation. Once the witness decides that 'X is it' the view may be unshakable." *Newsome v. McCabe,* 319 F.3d 301, 305 (7th Cir.2003). Social-science research "has established that the witness's faith is equally strong whether or not the identification is correct." *Id.* The appellate court in *Newsome* collected an array of publications documenting this phenomenon, *id.*

In the present case, one witness testified that he was 70% to 80% sure of his identification of the defendant. Another testified on the stand without equivocation that the defendant committed the bank robbery. Jurors often believe that a witness who testifies with such confidence should be accorded stronger weight than a witness who does not. In an instance such as this, where intuition is belied by scientific research, testimony from an expert may be of great assistance to a jury. Particularly in light of the implications of cross-racial identification, all of this information, particularly to the extent it is not common knowledge or intuition, could assist the jury in reaching a fair and accurate determination of the factual issues before it.

It bears reiterating that the expert was not permitted to testify about the credibility and believability of the witnesses in this case. Fulero was not permitted to discuss witnesses in this case at all; nor was Smith allowed to ask Fulero about the credibility or believability of witnesses in this case. Fulero was instead allowed to educate the jury about the psychological literature regarding: cross-racial identifications; how stress impacts identifications; post-event information; and the weak correlation between a witness's confidence and his or her accuracy because these issues are specifically implicated by the factual context of this case. The advisory committee notes to Fed.R.Evid. 702 expressly contemplate that sometimes experts will have this limited role. The notes explain that it is wrong to conclude "that experts testify only in the form of opinions." *Id.* Rather, "an expert on the stand may give a dissertation or exposition of scientific or other principles relevant to the case, leaving the trier of fact to apply them to the facts." *Id.*

The court was convinced at trial that the psychological research supporting the above four subjects is both reliable and helpful and that the constantly increasing knowledge social scientists are obtaining about the inner workings of the human animal are likely not commonly understood or obviously apparent to jurors (or, for that matter, judges). Therefore, educating the jury about this research does not (and, in this case, did not) run afoul of Rule 702, and, indeed, it is an important step along the road to using improved scientific knowledge to create more accurate and fair legal proceedings. It would be anachronistic to categorically bar courts from employing the latest reliable scientific evidence in their effort to make sure that the trials that they administer resemble as closely as possible a search for truth; such a search requires diligently pursuing better understandings of human decisionmaking, including the flaws, weaknesses, and biases that characterize human life. Particularly for cases like this one, in which the reliability of eyewitness testimony is so important and so linked to well-established flaws in human perception and memory, such testimony may be crucial to fair, thorough, informed, and rigorous decisionmaking. It can only help to make factfinders more informed. Applying this research to the facts of this case, however, is within the sole province of the jury.

B.   Rule 403

The United States argued that Dr. Fulero's testimony transgressed Fed.R.Evid. 403. [A]ccording [to] the government, admitting Fulero's testimony would incite unfair prejudice because his assertions would confuse and mislead jurors about their role as the ultimate arbiters of eyewitnesses' credibility. [T]his court appreciates the especial risk that accompanies expert testimony; despite jury instructions advising jurors not to embrace expert testimony uncritically, *Eleventh Circuit Pattern Jury Instructions (Criminal Cases),* Basic Instruction 7, courts have long expressed concern that jurors may still do exactly that. [T]his risk was present in Smith's case because unfettered expert testimony could have been construed as direct commentary on other witnesses' credibility. [B]ut the critical point here is, instead, that this kind of expert testimony can, in some specific circumstances, be helpful, and even essential, to assisting the jury in its exercise of the exclusive power to determine witness credibility. With respect to many other factual determinations which are also within the sole province of the jury, expert testimony can help the jury find the relevant facts in a more informed way. Eyewitness-identification expert testimony, as a category, is no different.

The parameters this court placed on Fulero's testimony, moreover, significantly allayed the concern that he would improperly invade the jury's role. Because he was *not* permitted to testify about specific witnesses in this case and instead was allowed only to educate the jury about empirical evidence regarding the previously specified areas of eyewitness-identification research, his testimony did not mislead the jury about its role as the sole factfinder in a criminal jury trial.

[I]ndeed, it is difficult to see how it could possibly be prejudicial to provide scientifically robust evidence that seeks to correct misguided intuitions and thereby prevent jurors from making common errors in judgment simply by giving them more accurate information about issues directly relevant to the case. The court's restricted approach, which presented little risk of unfair, targeted, and prejudicial attacks on specific witnesses, maximizes the important values that underlie our legal system's reliance on criminal trials, including the role the jury plays as a factfinder to be trusted and a defendant's right "to have compulsory process for obtaining witnesses in his favor." U.S. Const. Amend VI.

* * *

In conclusion, [this Court has three observations regarding] how the admission of the eyewitness-identification expert testimony actually played out at Smith's trial. First, the admission of the testimony did not pose any unusual or especially difficult problems for the parties or the court. Each side was able to examine the expert adequately and, using the expert's testimony, present to the jury in an orderly way a picture of the evidence that was more fully developed and reliable than it would otherwise have been. Second, the jury, in assessing the evidence and reaching its verdict, had important and practical information that it would otherwise not have been [able] to use in [a]ssessing the evidence and engaging in fair, thorough, informed, and rigorous decisionmaking. Finally, as a result, not only did Smith receive a fairer trial, but the jury, the court, and the entire judicial system can rest much more comfortably that Smith's robbery conviction is a reliable outcome because the conviction is much less likely to have been infected by the flaws uncovered by recent empirical studies on eyewitness-identifications. While the court cannot, and does not, say that the admission of eyewitness-identification expert testimony is essential to a fair trial, its admission can, most certainly, be quite helpful in some cases.

SELECTED BIBLIOGRAPHY

A. Defendants

Anderson, Berkowitz, Donnerstein, Huesmann, Johnson, Linz, Malamuth, and Wartella, The Influence of Media Violence on Youth, 4 Psychological Science in the Public Interest 81 (2003).

Coughlin, Excusing Women, 82 California Law Review 1 (1994).

Dixon and Dixon, Gender–Specific Clinical Syndromes and Their Admissibility Under the Federal Rules of Evidence, 27 American Journal of Trial Advocacy 25 (2003).

Faigman, Discerning Justice When Battered Women Kill, 39 Hastings Law Journal 207 (1987).

Faigman, Struggling to Stop the Flood of Unreliable Expert Testimony, 76 Minnesota Law Review 877 (1992).

Faigman, The Battered Woman Syndrome and Self–Defense: A Legal and Empirical Dissent, 72 Virginia Law Review 619 (1986).

Faigman and Wright, The Battered Woman Syndrome in the Age of Science, 39 Arizona Law Review 67 (1997).

Gatowski, Dobbin, Richardson, and Ginsburg, The Globalization of Behavioral Science Evidence About Battered Women: A Theory of Production and Diffusion, 15 Behavioral Sciences and the Law 285 (1997).

Giardino, Combat Veterans, Mental Health Issues, and the Death Penalty: Addressing the Impact of Post–Traumatic Stress Disorder and Traumatic Brian Injury, 77 Fordham Law Review 2955 (2009).

Glymour, Glymour, and Glymour, Watching Social Science: The Debate About the Effects of Exposure to Televised Violence on Aggressive Behavior, 51 American Behavioral Scientist 1231 (2008).

Greenawalt, The Cultural Defense: Reflections in Light of the Model Penal Code and the Religious Freedom Restoration Act, 6 Ohio State Journal of Criminal Law 299 (2008).

T. Grisso and R. Schwartz, Youth on Trial: A Developmental Perspective on Juvenile Justice (2000).

Heilbrun, DeMatteo, Marczyk, Finello, Smith, and Mack–Allen, Applying Principles of Forensic Mental Health Assessment to Capital Sentencing, 11 Widener Law Review 93 (2005).

Heilbrun, Poythress, Slobogin, and Stevens, Insanity and Diminished Capacity, in Modern Scientific Evidence: The Law and Science of Expert Testimony, 2008–2009 ed. (D. Faigman, M. Saks, J. Sanders, and E. Cheng eds. 2008).

Held and Fontaine, On the Boundaries of Culture as an Affirmative Defense, 51 Arizona Law Review 237 (2009).

Hoge, Auchterlonie, and Milliken, Mental Health Problems, Use of Mental Health Services, and Attrition From Military Service After Returning From Deployment to Iraq or Afghanistan, 295 Journal of the American Medical Association 1023 (2006).

Huesmann and Taylor, The Role of Media Violence in Violent Behavior, 27 Annual Review of Public Health 393 (2006).

Huss, Tomkins, Garbin, Schopp, and Kilian, Battered Women Who Kill Their Abusers: An Examination of Commonsense Notions, Cognitions, and Judgments, 21 Journal of Interpersonal Violence 1063 (2006).

Jayaraman, Rotten Social Background Revisited, 14 Capital Defense Journal 327 (2002).

Johnson, Cohen, Smailes, Kasen, and Brook, Television Viewing and Aggressive Behavior During Adolescence and Adulthood, 295 Science 2468 (2002).

Koch, O'Neill, and Douglas, Empirical Limits for the Forensic Assessment of PTSD Litigants, 29 Law and Human Behavior 121 (2005).

Lam, Culture as Defense: Preventing Judicial Bias Against Asians and Pacific Islanders, 1 UCLA Asian American Pacific Islands Law Journal 49 (1993).

Levine, Negotiating the Boundaries of Crime and Culture: A Sociolegal Perspective on Cultural Defense Strategies, 28 Law and Social Inquiry 39 (2003).

G. Melton, J. Petrila, N. Poythress, and C. Slobogin, Psychological Evaluations for the Courts (3d ed. 2007).

Morse, Excusing and the "New" Excuses, in Crime and Justice: An Annual Review of Research (M. Tonry ed. 1997).

Morse, Deprivation and Desert, in From Social Justice to Criminal Justice: Poverty and the Administration of Criminal Law (W. Heffernan and J. Kleinig eds. 2000).

Morse, Rationality and Responsibility, 74 Southern California Law Review 251 (2000).

Multicultural Jurisprudence: Comparative Perspectives on the Cultural Defense (M. Foblets and A. Renteln eds. 2009).

North, Suris, Davis, and Smith, Toward Validation of the Diagnosis of Posttraumatic Stress Disorder, 166 American Journal of Psychiatry 34 (2009).

Note, A Place for Consideration of Culture in the American Criminal Justice System: Japanese Law and the Kimura Case, 4 Journal of International Law and Practice 507 (1995).

Savage, Does Viewing Violent Media Really Cause Criminal Violence? A Methodological Review, 10 Aggression and Violent Behavior 99 (2004).

Schuller and Rzepa, Expert Testimony Pertaining to Battered Woman Syndrome: Its Impact on Jurors' Decisions, 26 Law and Human Behavior 655 (2002).

Scott, Reppucci, and Woolard, Evaluating Adolescent Decision Making in Legal Contexts, 19 Law and Human Behavior 221 (1995).

Seal, Metzler, Gima, Bertenthal, Maguen, and Marmar, Trends and Risk Factors for Mental Health Diagnoses Among Iraq and Afghanistan Veterans Using Department of Veterans Affairs Health Care, 2002–2008, 99 American Journal of Public Health 1 (2009).

R. Shweder, Why Do Men Barbecue? Recipes for Cultural Psychology (2003).

Slobogin, A Jurisprudence of Dangerousness, 98 Northwestern University Law Review 1 (2003).

Veinsreideris, The Prospective Effects of Modifying Existing Law to Accommodate Preemptive Self-defense by Battered Women, 149 University of Pennsylvania Law Review 613 (2000).

Wanderer and Connors, Culture and Crime: *Kargar* and the Existing Framework for a Cultural Defense, 47 Buffalo Law Review 829 (1999).

Wang, Battered Asian American Women: Community Responses from the Battered Women's Movement and the Asian American Community, 3 Asian Law Journal 151 (1996).

B. Victims

Dobbin and Gatowski, The Social Production of Rape Trauma Syndrome as Science and as Evidence, in Science in Court (M. Freeman and H. Reece eds. 1998).

Ellison and Munro, Turning Mirrors Into Windows: Assessing the Impact of (Mock) Juror Education in Rape Trials, 49 British Journal of Criminology 363 (2009).

Frazier and Borgida, Rape Trauma Syndrome: A Review of Case Law and Psychological Research, 16 Law and Human Behavior 293 (1992).

Orenstein, No Bad Men! A Feminist Analysis of Character Evidence in Rape Trials, 49 Hastings Law Journal 663 (1998).

Posttraumatic Stress Disorder: Acute and Long–Term Responses to Trauma and Disaster (C. Fullerton and R. Ursano eds. 1997).

Posttraumatic Stress Disorder in Litigation: Guidelines for Forensic Assessment (R. Simon ed. 1995).

Stefan, The Protection Racket: Rape Trauma Syndrome, Psychiatric Labeling, and the Law, 88 Northwestern University Law Review 1271 (1994).

C. Witnesses

Abshire and Bornstein, Juror Sensitivity to the Cross–Race Effect, 27 Law and Human Behavior 471 (2003).

Deffenbacher, Bornstein, Penrod and McGorty, A Meta–Analytic Review of the Effects of High Stress on Eyewitness Memory, 28 Law and Human Behavior 687 (2004).

Devenport and Cutler, Impact of Defense–Only and Opposing Eyewitness Experts on Juror Judgments, 28 Law and Human Behavior 569 (2004).

Gerrie, Garry, and Loftus, False Memories, in Psychology and Law: An Empirical Perspective (N. Brewer and K. Williams eds. 2005).

Goodman, Bottoms, Rudy, Davis, and Schwartz–Kenney, Effects of Past Abuse Experiences on Children's Eyewitness Memory, 25 Law and Human Behavior 269 (2001).

Leach, Cutler, and Van Wallendael, Lineups and Eyewitness Identification, 5 Annual Review of Law and Social Science (in press).

E. Loftus, Eyewitness Testimony (1979; reissued 1996).

McAuliff and Kovera, Estimating the Effects of Misleading Information on Witness Accuracy: Can Experts Tell Jurors Something They Don't Already Know?, 21 Applied Cognitive Psychology 849 (2006).

Meissner and Brigham, Thirty Years of Investigating the Own—Race Bias in Memory for Faces, 7 Psychology, Public Policy, and Law 3 (2001).

Schmechel, O'Toole, Easterly, and Loftus, Beyond the Ken? Testing Jurors' Understanding of Eyewitness Reliability Evidence, 46 Jurimetrics 177 (2006).

Steblay, Dysart, Fulero, and Lindsay, Eyewitness Accuracy Rates in Police Showup and Lineup Presentations: A Meta–Analytic Comparison, 27 Law and Human Behavior 523 (2003).

Wells, Eyewitness Identifications, in Modern Scientific Evidence: The Law and Science of Expert Testimony, 2008–2009 ed. (D. Faigman, M. Saks, J. Sanders, and E. Cheng eds. 2008).

Wells, Memon, and Penrod, Eyewitness Evidence: Improving Its Probative Value, 7 Psychological Science in the Public Interest 46 (2006).

Wells and Quinlivan, Suggestive Eyewitness Identification Procedures and the Supreme Court's Reliability Test in Light of Eyewitness Science: 30 Years Later, 33 Law and Human Behavior 1 (2009).

SECTION V.   SOCIAL FRAMEWORKS

We began this chapter by stating that social frameworks have some of the characteristics of social facts and some of the characteristics of social authority. We end it by drawing upon both of these primary uses of social science to develop—and to revise—a heuristic theory for providing decision makers with frameworks for determining facts in court.

———

SOCIAL FRAMEWORKS: A NEW USE OF SOCIAL SCIENCE IN LAW

Laurens Walker and John Monahan.
73 Virginia Law Review 559 (1987).

PROCEDURES FOR USING SOCIAL FRAMEWORKS IN COURT

A.   The Traditional "Fact" Perspective

Social science used as a social framework is now almost always introduced in court precisely as is social science used as an "adjudicative fact"—by expert testimony before a jury or other factfinder. This customary procedure has two significant liabilities. First, it is an inefficient use of court time. The same testimony about the same research studies must be heard in case after case, whenever a framework for a given type of factual determination is sought. Second, the current method of introducing empirical frameworks is expensive. The pool of expert witnesses is limited to a small group of basic researchers in each topical area and these researchers must be transported and paid to repeat their testimony in each new case. Access to expert testimony on empirical research is effectively precluded in a large number of cases in which the introduction of a framework would seem justified.

One source of proposals for improving the introduction of social frameworks might derive from the recognition that frameworks resemble legislative facts as much as they resemble adjudicative facts. Social frameworks possess a legislative fact "generality" based on the research from which they are derived and an adjudicative fact "specificity" which currently controls the procedures for their introduction. Pursuing this insight, one might consider formulating a two-stage process for introducing social frameworks: first, attention should focus on the legislative fact "generality" of the framework; and then, attention should shift to the adjudicative fact "specificity" of its application to the given case.

The practical difficulty of this seemingly plausible tack, however, [is that] recognizing the legislative fact aspect of social frameworks does not yield a coherent set of procedural ideas for introducing those frameworks in court.

B.   The Social Authority Perspective

A heuristic concept is needed that reflects the generality of the basic research data used in a framework and at the same time provides a richer source of procedural ideas than the concept of legislative fact. One such concept may be "social authority." Under this view, courts would treat social science research, when used to create a rule of law, as a source of authority rather than as a type of fact. Accordingly, courts would deal with empirical research much as they now deal with legal precedent in a common-law system.

[C.]   Social Frameworks as a Mix of Social Authority and Fact

Reconceptualizing social frameworks as a mix of social authority and fact yields a two-stage process with clear procedural ramifications. First we consider how courts should obtain and evaluate frameworks, recognizing the dominance of the social authority classification at this stage; then we specify communication techniques that follow from the factual aspect of social frameworks.

1.   Obtaining and Evaluating Social Frameworks

The social authority aspect of frameworks suggests two corollary propositions regarding how a court should obtain empirical research: parties should present empirical research to the court in briefs rather than by testimony; and the court may locate social science studies through its own research.

Under this view, when the attorney for one of the parties determines that providing an empirical context or framework for a factual issue in the case would be useful [t]he attorney would begin a search for relevant empirical information. If such information were found, it would be presented to the court in a written brief, the purpose of which, as described below, would be to propose and justify a set of jury instructions incorporating a social framework.

[2.] Communicating Social Frameworks

Considering social frameworks as part social authority and part fact leads to radically different roles for the jury and the court than exist under current practice. [W]hat we call social frameworks are now presented to the jury by expert testimony, and it is the jury's responsibility to evaluate what they have heard and to apply it to the facts of the case at bar. The court's role is a passive one, limited to ruling on whether given expert testimony is admissible as evidence for the jury's consideration. Under the mixed social authority-fact view, in contrast, the court is much more active. The research is presented directly to the court by brief, or the court may independently locate the research. Most importantly, just as it is the responsibility of the court, rather than the jury, to evaluate case precedent, so it is the responsibility of the court, rather than the jury, to evaluate the social science research.

If the evaluating judge finds both that the research supports the introduction of a social framework and that no policy issues—for example, the prohibition against some forms of character evidence—bar a framework's application, then the final procedural implication of the social authority view is clear: the result of the court's evaluation of the applicable research should be communicated to the jury in the same manner that the court's evaluation of the applicable statutes and case law is communicated to the jury, that is, by instruction. The role of the jury is thus limited to applying the social framework given by the court to the specific facts of the case, just as the role of the jury is traditionally limited to applying the law given by the court to the specific facts of the case.

[A]s social science is repeatedly brought to bear in framing a given type of factual determination, attention should be given to establishing standard instructions on a variety of topics. This could be done either through the common law process of taking instructions from prior cases, or by an appellate court using its supervisory powers to endorse "pattern" instructions, perhaps drafted by a committee composed of lawyers and social scientists. Whichever the means of their creation, establishing pattern instructions and providing for their periodic review and revisions hold great promise for standardizing the third use of social science in law.

———

EMPIRICAL QUESTIONS WITHOUT EMPIRICAL ANSWERS

John Monahan and Laurens Walker.
1991 Wisconsin Law Review 569 (1991).

The question [i]s what courts should do when a party requests "social framework" instructions but presents no social science research, or only inadequate social science research, to support the request. The answer is to be found by turning to the standard for framing jury instructions. That standard is clear: courts must give only instructions that state the law "correctly" or "accurately." As was the case with judicial review of state legislation, general principles for obtaining and evaluating research can be employed: correctness, accuracy, or what a social scientist would term "validity"—rather than the "relevancy" or "Frye" rules used to test scientific evidence of social facts. If the research comprising the framework is valid in the court's estimation, and relevant to the facts of the case, the instruction should be given. If the research is invalid, or nonexistent, it would follow from the law regarding jury instructions that no instruction would be forthcoming. An instruction would be unnecessary to decide the case: lacking valid research, a jury is as well equipped as a judge to speculate on the effect of social context in determining the facts at issue in the case.

—————

DUKES v. WAL–MART, INC.

United States Court of Appeals, Ninth Circuit, 2007.*
509 F.3d 1168.

■ Pregerson, Circuit Judge.

[The facts of this case are described on page 186].

Rule 23(a)(2) [specifying, in part, when a district court can certify a class] requires that "there are questions of law or fact common to the class." Fed.R.Civ.P. 23(a)(2). Commonality focuses on the relationship of common facts and legal issues among class members. [T]he commonality test is qualitative rather than quantitative—one significant issue common to the class may be sufficient to warrant certification.

[T]he district court found that Plaintiffs had provided evidence sufficient to support their contention that significant factual and legal questions are common to all class members. After analyzing Plaintiffs' evidence, the district court stated:

> Plaintiffs have exceeded the permissive and minimal burden of establishing commonality by providing [s]ignificant evidence of company-wide corporate practices and policies...

Plaintiffs presented evidence from Dr. William Bielby, a sociologist, to interpret and explain the facts that suggest that Wal–Mart has and promotes a strong corporate culture-a culture that may include gender stereotyping. Dr. Bielby based his opinion on, among other things, Wal–Mart managers' deposition testimony; organizational charts; correspondence, memos, reports, and presentations relating to personnel policy and practice,

—————

* [Ed. Note: On February 13, 2009, the Ninth Circuit ordered that Dukes v. Wal–Mart be reheard en banc. "The three-judge panel opinion shall not be cited as precedent by or to any court of the Ninth Circuit." The case was reargued on March 24, 2009.]

diversity, and equal employment opportunity issues; documents describing the culture and history of the company; and a large body of social science research on organizational policy and practice and on workplace bias.

Dr. Bielby testified that by employing a "social framework analysis,"[1] he examined the distinctive features of Wal–Mart's policies and practices and evaluated them "against what social science shows to be factors that create and sustain bias and those that minimize bias." In Dr. Bielby's opinion, "social science research demonstrates that gender stereotypes are especially likely to influence personnel decisions when they are based on subjective factors, because substantial decision-maker discretion tends to allow people to 'seek out and retain stereotyping-confirming information and ignore or minimize information that defies stereotypes.' " *Dukes I, 222* F.R.D. [137] at 154 [(N.D. Cal. 2004)]. Dr. Bielby concluded: (1) that Wal–Mart's centralized coordination, reinforced by a strong organizational culture, sustains uniformity in personnel policy and practice; (2) that there are significant deficiencies in Wal–Mart's equal employment policies and practices; and (3) that Wal–Mart's personnel policies and practices make pay and promotion decisions vulnerable to gender bias. *See id.*

Wal–Mart challenges Dr. Bielby's third conclusion as vague and imprecise because he concluded that Wal–Mart is "vulnerable" to bias or gender stereotyping but failed to identify a specific discriminatory policy at Wal–Mart. Specifically, Wal–Mart contends that Dr. Bielby's testimony does not meet the standards for expert testimony set forth in Federal Rule of Evidence 702 and *Daubert v. Merrell Dow Pharm., Inc.* ("*Daubert I*"), 509 U.S. 579 (1993), which held that a trial court must act as a "gatekeeper" in determining whether to admit or exclude expert evidence.

Wal–Mart [d]oes not challenge Dr. Bielby's methodology or contend that his findings lack relevance because they "do[ ] not relate to any issue in the case," *Daubert,* 509 U.S. at 591, but challenges *only* whether certain inferences can be persuasively drawn from his data. Because *Daubert* does not require a court to admit or exclude evidence based on its persuasiveness, but rather, requires a court to admit or exclude evidence based on its scientific reliability and relevance, *id.* at 587–90 (evidence is relevant if it has " 'any tendency to make the existence of any fact that is of consequence to the determination of the action more probable or less probable than it would be without the evidence'" (citing Fed.R.Evid. 401), and relevance standard "is a liberal one"), testing Dr. Bielby's testimony for "*Daubert* reliability" would not have addressed Wal–Mart's objections. It would have simply revealed what Wal–Mart itself has admitted and courts have long accepted: that properly analyzed social science data, like that offered by Dr. Bielby, may add probative value to plaintiffs' class action claims. *See Price Waterhouse v. Hopkins,* 490 U.S. 228, 235–36, 255, 109 S.Ct. 1775, 104 L.Ed.2d 268 (1989) (considering similar evidence offered by expert social psychologist).

1. For a description of the "social framework analysis," see John Monahan and Larry Walker, *Social Science in the Law: Cases and Materials* (4th ed.1998).

Accordingly, Wal–Mart's contention that the district court was required to subject Dr. Bielby's testimony to the *Daubert* test, simply because the conclusion he reached seemed unpersuasive absent certain corroborating evidence, is misplaced. *See Daubert,* 490 U.S. at 595 ("The focus, of course, must be solely on principles and methodology, not on the conclusions that they generate."). While a *jury* may ultimately agree with Wal–Mart that, in the absence of a specific discriminatory policy promulgated by Wal–Mart, it is hard to believe, based solely on Dr. Bielby's social science analysis, that Wal–Mart engaged in actual gender discrimination, that question must be left to the merits stage of the litigation. At the class certification stage, it is enough that Dr. Bielby presented properly-analyzed, scientifically reliable evidence tending to show that a common question of fact—i.e., "Does Wal–Mart's policy of decentralized, subjective employment decision making operate to discriminate against female employees?"— exists with respect to all members of the class. This he did and, thus, we find no error in the district court's acceptance of Dr. Bielby's evidence to support its finding of commonality.

CONTEXTUAL EVIDENCE OF GENDER DISCRIMINATION: THE ASCENDANCE OF "SOCIAL FRAMEWORKS"

John Monahan, Laurens Walker, and Gregory Mitchell.
94 Virginia Law Review 1715 (2008).

In *Dukes v. Wal–Mart, Inc.,* the U.S. Court of Appeals for the Ninth Circuit upheld the certification of a gender discrimination class action seeking over $1.5 billion on behalf of more than 1.5 million current and former female employees of Wal–Mart's 3,400 stores across the United States. A crucial piece of the evidence supporting class certification came from a sociologist who performed what he called a "social framework analysis" of Wal–Mart. [D]r. Bielby's analysis [f]igured prominently in the district court's decision to certify the largest employment discrimination class in history and the appellate court's decision to uphold this certification.

As authority for the propriety of social framework analysis, Dr. Bielby relied on the work of the first two authors of this Essay. [T]he ascendance of social frameworks in the context of landmark civil rights litigation provides occasion to revisit the substance and procedures associated with that concept.

[W]hile acceptance of social framework as a concept that captured a new and important development in courts' use of social science research was immediate and widespread, the procedure that we advocated for communicating social framework information to the jury—namely, judicial instruction—has rarely been endorsed by scholars or implemented by courts. From the beginning, others have argued that expert testimony is a "higher quality" procedure for communicating social framework information than is jury instruction, because juries can understand live testimony from an expert better than they can understand instructions that are read to them by a judge.

[P]erhaps partially as a result of widespread scholarly misgivings about the effectiveness of jury instructions—as compared with expert testimony—in conveying social framework information to fact-finders, courts have been exceedingly reluctant to order that instructions be used.

[I]. Social Framework: A Revised Proposal

Although we remain committed to social framework as a valuable concept to describe general findings from social science research used to provide context to determine specific factual issues at trial, we are no longer committed to our proposal that frameworks be delivered to the jury only by instruction. Some judges may prefer the use of instructions, and we continue to view instruction as an acceptable method. Generally, however, we view the criticism of the commentators as well taken and the practical judgment of the courts as persuasive. Both sources suggest that expert testimony is often the most effective mechanism for informing the jury about relevant general research that would be helpful in carrying out its fact-finding responsibilities. Since those responsibilities are a ubiquitous aspect of our system of justice, the best possible mode of communicating frameworks is clearly desirable. Often, as our critics have convinced us, communicating social frameworks by means of the testimony of expert witnesses will be more effective than communicating frameworks via instruction. For example, [c]ross-examination of experts may help explain methodological aspects of the research, and, in some jurisdictions, jurors can submit clarifying questions to be asked of the witness.

However, using experts to communicate social frameworks to juries leads to an important question, and one that did not arise when we proposed that social frameworks be communicated by means of judicial instruction: what, if anything, can the expert testify to by way of linking the general research to the specific facts of the case before the jury?

[W]e believe that [e]xperts presenting social frameworks should be prohibited from providing any linkage to the case at hand, leaving application (or not) of the general research findings entirely to the fact-finder. We continue to believe that "[t]he role of the jury is ... to apply[ ] the social framework ... to the specific facts of the case," and "[i]n applying a framework ..., the jury is free to determine that the general research findings are inapposite to the facts of the specific case before it."[54]

[II]. Social Framework in Dukes v. Wal-Mart

[I]f experts in [employment discrimination class actions] simply described social science findings on the circumstances under which gender

---

54. [Walker and Monahan, Social Frameworks: A New Use of Social Science in   Law, 73 Virginia Law Review 559 (1987)], at 594 n. 117.

stereotyping is more or less likely to occur within the research settings, leaving it to the fact-finder to determine the applicability of this research to the circumstances of a particular employer, such testimony would be entirely consistent with both our original argument—that social frameworks provide valuable contextual information to assist in understanding the facts of a particular case—and the argument here that experts be allowed to communicate the social framework to jurors but not make case-specific applications. In many cases, however, experts have not been content to provide a description of the general research to create a context for the facts of the case, and judges have not required such circumspection.

For instance, Dr. Bielby, the sociologist testifying for the plaintiffs in *Dukes*, went well beyond a description of general research findings on the operation and prevalence of stereotypes and the conditions under which persons are more or less likely to rely on particular stereotypes. Dr. Bielby expressly linked general research on gender stereotyping to conditions across all Wal–Mart locations, concluding (1) that "[s]ubjective and discretionary features of the company's personnel policy and practice make decisions about compensation and promotion vulnerable to gender bias" and (2) that "there are significant deficiencies in the company's policies and practices for identifying and eliminating barriers to equal employment opportunity at Wal–Mart."[81] Dr. Bielby then linked his opinions about conditions at Wal–Mart to another expert's statistical analysis of the pay and promotion disparities between female and male employees at Wal–Mart, purporting to identify specific "personnel policies and practices that contribute to those disparities."[82]

Dr. Bielby's testimony in *Dukes* departs from our conception of a social framework and exceeds the limits on expert framework testimony proposed above. The very idea of a social framework is to supply fact-finders with information about general social science research to provide a context or "framework" for the *fact-finder* to use when evaluating the evidence in a particular case. Thus, a social framework necessarily contains only general statements about reliable patterns of relations among variables as discovered within social scientific research, whether communicated via jury instructions or testimony of a qualified expert, and goes no further.

[W]e believe it essential that courts limit expert testimony to a description of the findings of relevant and reliable research and of the methodologies that produced those findings, and preclude the witness from speculatively linking the general research findings to alleged policies and practices of a specific firm. *[D]ukes v. Wal–Mart* represents a high-water mark in the influence of social frameworks, but unfortunately this influence extends well beyond what is warranted by the underlying social science.

81. [Declaration of William T. Bielby, Ph.D. in Support of Plaintiffs' Motion for Class Certification, Dukes v. Wal–Mart Stores, Inc., 222 F.R.D. 137 (N.D. Cal. 2004)] at 5–6.

82. Id. at 15.

SELECTED BIBLIOGRAPHY

Fiske and Borgida, Divergent Paths: Providing Expert Knowledge in an Adversarial Context: Social Cognitive Science in Employment Discrimination Cases, 4 Annual Review of Law and Social Science 123 (2008).

Goodman and Croyle, Social Framework Testimony in Employment Discrimination Cases, 7 Behavioral Sciences and the Law 227 (1989).

Hart and Secunda, A Matter of Context: Social Framework Evidence in Employment Discrimination Class Actions, 78 Fordham Law Review (in press).

King and Amin, Social Framework Analysis as Inadmissible "Character" Evidence, 32 Law and Psychology Review 1 (2008).

Monahan, Walker, and Mitchell, The Limits of Social Framework Evidence, Law, Probability, and Risk (in press).

Mosteller, Legal Doctrines Governing the Admissibility of Expert Testimony Concerning Social Framework Evidence, 52 Law and Contemporary Problems 85 (1989).

Nagareda, Class Certification in the Age of Aggregate Proof, 84 New York University Law Review 97 (2009).

Paluck and Green, Prejudice Reduction: What Works? A Review and Assessment of Research and Practice, 60 Annual Review of Psychology 339 (2009).

Nelson, Berrey, and Nielsen, Divergent Paths: Conflicting Conceptions of Employment Discrimination in Law and the Social Sciences, 4 Annual Review of Law and Social Science 103 (2008).

Saks and Koehler, The Individualization Fallacy in Forensic Science Evidence, 61 Vanderbilt Law Review 199 (2008).

Vidmar and Schuller, Social Framework Evidence and Jury Decision Making Processes, 52 Law and Contemporary Problems 133 (1989).

CHAPTER SIX

SOCIAL SCIENCE AND LITIGATION STRATEGY

It is now common for attorneys to employ social scientists to assist in the preparation of a case for trial and during trial. The contributions of these social scientists have been quite varied, but issues involving the place of trial, the selection of jurors, and the instruction of jurors have dominated. This work began during the early 1970's when conditions of social unrest generated much controversial criminal litigation. Recently, the techniques have been increasingly applied in important civil cases.

SECTION I.   CHOOSING A VENUE

Both state and federal courts recognize the occasional need to change the place of trial because local public opinion may render a fair jury unlikely. For example, Federal Rule of Criminal Procedure 21(a) provides that "The court upon motion of the defendant shall transfer the proceeding ... if the court is satisfied that there exists in the district where the prosecution is pending so great a prejudice against the defendant that the defendant cannot obtain a fair and impartial trial." Proof that this situation exists is made to the trial judge, and now often involves the use of social science research.

————

PRETRIAL PUBLICITY, CHANGE OF VENUE, PUBLIC OPINION POLLS—A THEORY OF PROCEDURAL JUSTICE

Peter D. O'Connell.*
65 University of Detroit Law Review 169 (1988).

The excitement that a sensational case causes in a small community is a phenomena that one must observe in order to fully understand its impact on the community. During morning coffee breaks, over backyard fences, while obtaining gas, while getting a haircut or purchasing a newspaper, each citizen becomes an expert on the facts of the case.

* [Judge, 76th District Court, Mt. Pleasant, Michigan].

The existence of the news media has left only the hermit uninformed as to the details of the case. As a result of this publicity, most citizens consciously or subconsciously develop an attitude concerning defendant's guilt or innocence. This attitude is embedded into each juror's subconscious.

The court must determine if prospective jurors are capable of rendering a fair and impartial verdict when they are called for jury duty. This is an awesome responsibility. It is critical to the fair administration of justice. It is also an area where trial judges receive little formal education. In the interest of efficiency, some judges tend to qualify jurors who have expressed doubts about their biases and prejudices.

Bias and prejudice are attitudes. They are not something you can see, feel, or touch. They are discovered through the use of wisdom, knowledge, and an understanding of human nature. In this regard, they are similar to the concepts of truth, beauty, goodness, and justice. The senses cannot experience these notions. Only the mind can capture these concepts because they are incapable of absolute definition. They exist in degrees. The best we can do is to define the characteristics of bias and prejudice and search for a methodology that will facilitate discovery of these characteristics.

[T]he favorite tool of the trial judge is to ask the jurors a series of questions. The answers to the questions lead to the discovery of a juror's attitude on any given subject. This attitude can be discovered if the proper questions are asked. However, the answers can be suppressed if the wrong questions are asked or if the voir dire examination places too much pressure on the juror.

The pressure of the voir dire examination sometimes causes jurors to temporarily forget their own names. In fact, when novices attempt to probe a juror's psyche, some jurors are offended. The result is juror repression of the attitude rather than juror exposure of the attitude.

Generally, the last question the trial judge asks is whether the juror can render a fair and impartial verdict. If the juror answers "yes," he or she is usually qualified to sit as a juror:

This methodology is a little like asking a practicing alcoholic if he has his drinking under control; we are asking the person who has the prejudice to determine if the prejudice will affect his decision. This method of determining prejudice has been approved by the Supreme Court. No one can be certain that jurors will render a fair and impartial verdict and no better system has been developed.

[T]he public opinion poll is conducted in an atmosphere free from the pressure and regimentation of the jury selection process. The answers to the poll's questions are an indication of what the juror's attitudes may be on a given subject. Their answers may or may not be an accurate assessment of a juror's true feeling, but these answers combined with the responses of other individuals in the community create the atmosphere of the community. These responses assist the court in determining if the pretrial publicity is inherently prejudicial.

PENNSYLVANIA v. COHEN

Supreme Court of Pennsylvania, 1980.
489 Pa. 167, 413 A.2d 1066.

■ Roberts, Justice.

On November 14, 1974, a man walking along a fire trail in Reading's Egelman Park discovered the body of Steven Warunek, a sixteen year-old Reading youth. Warunek had been shot to death. On November 18, police arrested three eighteen year-old suspects [a]nd charged all three with murder. Police also charged appellant with conspiracy to commit murder. Police investigation revealed that appellant hired the other two to kill Warunek in retaliation for threats Warunek made on appellant's life. Warunek allegedly told his fiancé, Kerry Young, he would kill appellant, Young's former boyfriend.

[A]ppellant filed a number of pre-trial applications, including [o]ne for a change of venue. [T]he trial court [h]eld a hearing on appellant's application for a change of venue. At the hearing, appellant presented copies of Berks County newspaper articles and transcripts of local radio broadcasts which discussed appellant's case. Appellant also presented Dr. Jay Schulman, a professor at Columbia University and member of the National Jury Project, who is an expert on the impact of publicized criminal proceedings on public opinion. Dr. Schulman testified on the results of a public opinion poll he conducted which tested Berks County residents' views on appellant's guilt. Dr. Schulman, four other expert witnesses, and six lay witnesses all expressed an opinion that appellant could not receive a fair trial in Berks County. The Commonwealth opposed the application for a change of venue, but offered no evidence. The court denied appellant's application without opinion or other explanation of record.

[O]n September 2, 1975, before the scheduled date of trial, appellant filed a "Re–Application For Change of Venue." In support of his "Re–Application," appellant presented the results of a second public opinion survey. This survey was conducted on August 22 and 23 by Dr. Robert Buckhout, another member of the National Jury Project. Once again, the Commonwealth, opposing the motion, presented no contrary evidence. The court denied appellant's "Re–Application," again without explanation. Appellant immediately applied for and was denied another continuance. Trial was set for September 8.

Voir dire began Monday, September 8 and lasted two full weeks, through Friday, September 19. In all, 180 persons were called in order to select a twelve-member jury and two alternates. The court ordered each juror immediately sequestered upon selection. At the close of voir dire, appellant for the third time requested a change of venue. The trial court denied this request, again without explanation. Trial began the following Monday, September 22.

[T]he case went to the jury on Wednesday, October 1. That Friday, October 3, the jury returned verdicts of guilty of murder of the third degree and conspiracy to commit murder.

Appellant then filed written post-verdict motions for a new trial and in arrest of judgment, which included appellant's claim that the trial court erred in denying a change of venue.

[J]udge Edenharter, however, denied all of appellant's post-verdict motions. In his accompanying opinion, Judge Edenharter for the first time sought to explain his orders denying appellant's three pre-trial applications for a change of venue. The court summarily dismissed appellant's principal contention that the pre-trial publicity was "inherently prejudicial," concluding that [t]here is insufficient evidence that any inflammatory information was widely disseminated at the time of trial. The court also concluded that the jury appellant did select was not affected by the pre-trial publicity.

On July 15, 1977, the court imposed sentence of ten to twenty years imprisonment, costs, and a fine of $15,000 on the murder conviction, as well as a concurrent sentence of five to ten years, costs, and a fine of $10,000 on the conspiracy conviction. These appeals followed.

[F]rom appellant's arrest in mid-November, 1974 until hearings in May of 1975 on appellant's first application for a change of venue, Reading's two newspapers the "Times" and the "Eagle," as well as Reading radio stations WRAW and WEEU, extensively covered every aspect of this case. The record contains thirty-seven newspaper articles, including sixteen front-page stories, and thirty-eight radio broadcasts which directly feature aspects of this case.

Most extensively publicized is the allegation of a "contract killing." The front page of the December 13 Eagle reported Assistant District Attorney Murphy's disclosure that the Commonwealth "may seek the death penalty which, he said, is allowed for premeditated contract killings." The December 14 Times and radio station WRAW also immediately gave similar coverage. Forty-one subsequent newspaper stories, reporting through the May hearings on appellant's application for a change of venue, carried what became standard-reference to the fact that a "contract killing" was involved.

[A]lso well-publicized were allegations that appellant and the co-conspirators made plans to kill Warunek while "high" on drugs and alcohol. A front-stage story of the January Times 25 entitled "Cohen murder hearing begun," accompanied by a 6½ inch by 6¾ inch photograph of appellant and his attorney, summarizes witnesses' allegations that

> "a conspiracy to 'mess up' the 16–year–old Steve E. Warunek was made during a dope and booze party in an apartment at 111 S. 8th St. when the alleged conspirators were 'high.'"

The same day the Eagle also carried a story entitled "Killing Linked To Lover's Spat." Accompanying this story, like the story in the Times, is a 5 inch by 6 inch photograph of appellant and his attorney. The story begins:

> "The November slaying of 16–year–old Steve E. Warunek in Egelman Park was depicted Friday as a contract murder, carried out amidst fear of reprisal in a heated lovers' triangle with the conspirators discussing plans during smoke-filled pot and alcohol parties."

[B]erks County media also gave great attention to appellant's pre-trial application for a change of venue. The court began to hear testimony on appellant's application on May 1. The May 2 Times carried a lengthy story entitled "Court ponders trial site plea" which set forth testimony on the qualifications of appellant's expert witness Dr. Jay Schulman. The same day's Eagle carried another extensive story entitled "Survey Allowed in Cohen Case," which discussed the court's ruling allowing appellant to introduce Schulman's expert testimony. Both the May 3 Times and Eagle carried related, extensive stories.

Eight more stories appeared between May 5 to May 9, all of which discussed testimony at the hearing on appellant's application for a change of venue, including "Consultant Queried on Survey Errors," "Jury researcher calls Berks biased," " 'Prejudice' Is Probed At Hearing," "Prejudice Is Estimated," and "4 rule out fairness."

[T]he record clearly establishes that the repeatedly-disseminated prejudicial material was widespread throughout Berks County at the time of trial. Thus inapposite are those cases in which the allegedly objectionable reports were not particularly widespread. Equally distinguishable are those cases in which the claimed objectionable reports so long preceded jury selection as to allow for a period of "cooling off."

Here in the months between arrest and trial Berks County residents became increasingly aware of this case. So too an ever-growing number of residents formed an opinion on the merits. The public opinion poll conducted by Dr. Schulman in March and April of 1975 and admitted into evidence at the May hearing on appellant's first application for a change of venue revealed that, of 804 randomly-selected Berks County registered voters, 65% then were aware of the case. Of those polled, 30%, or 242 out of 804 people, expressly conceded they had prejudged appellant guilty. Dr. Buckhout's survey, conducted approximately four months later in late August, revealed a still greater public awareness of this case. Of the 250 people randomly interviewed, 79% were aware of this case, an increase of approximately 15% from the level of awareness found four months earlier. Dr. Buckhout's survey also revealed that 57% of all persons interviewed, or 143 out of 250 people, attributed guilt to appellant.[34] This figure is nearly twice as great as the figure found in the previous poll. These results, unchal-

---

34. Dr. Buckhout asked persons polled to rate their belief of appellant's guilt on a scale of "zero" to "ten." One hundred forty-three ascribed more than "zero" guilt. One hundred thirty-eight of the 143, or 55% of all persons interviewed, ascribed to appellant guilt of "five" or greater.

lenged and undisturbed by the trial court, demonstrate with unquestionable clarity the substantial extent to which pretrial publicity had reached the local population and had influenced its judgment.[35]

Voir dire, conducted in September, about two weeks after Dr. Buckhout's August survey, confirmed the results of Dr. Buckhout's poll. Of the 180 prospective jurors called, eleven were excused on various grounds of hardship and not questioned concerning the merits. Of the 169 persons questioned, 105 stated they held an opinion concerning the merits. Indeed, of these 105 prospective jurors, eighty-nine were excused on the ground that they admitted a "fixed," irrevocable opinion on guilt. Thus, 53% of the prospective jurors questioned were excused because of prejudgment.

These percentages of persons expressing an opinion on an accused's guilt are unprecedented in our cases.

[I]t therefore must be concluded that the prejudicial material was widespread at the time of trial and that the court abused its discretion in refusing on this record to grant a change of venue.

————

NOTE

1. **Oklahoma City**. In United States v. McVeigh, 918 F.Supp. 1467 (W.D. Okl. 1996), the court considered an application by defendants for a change of venue. The defendants, Timothy McVeigh and Terry Nichols, were charged with building a "truck bomb" and using the bomb on April 19, 1995, to destroy the Murrah Federal Building in Oklahoma City, Oklahoma, resulting in the deaths of 168 men, women, and children, injuries to hundreds, and costs estimated at $651,594,000. "Dramatic pictures of the Murrah Federal Building were shown nationwide immediately after the explosion. There was intensive coverage of the rescue efforts. The immediate reactions of the President, the Attorney General and an FBI spokesman were broadcast across the nation. There were extensive interviews with injured victims, members of the families of the dead and missing persons, rescue and relief workers, and residents of Oklahoma City." Id. at 1470–1471. After his arrest, McVeigh was shown on television "in restraints and clad in bright orange jail clothing being led into a van while surrounded by a very vocal and angry crowd. Some bystanders could be heard shouting 'murderer' and 'baby killer'." Id. at 1471. The question before the Court was whether trial could be held anywhere in Oklahoma. All parties had agreed that trial could not be held in Oklahoma City, and Lawton had been designated by the Court as the trial site. The defendants supported their motion with a public opinion survey. The opinion poll showed that almost

---

35. The trial court here in no respect questioned the basic results of the surveys relied upon in text. Instead, the trial court merely questioned Dr. Schulman's estimation based upon the results of the survey that as many as 75% to 80% of Berks County residents prejudged appellant guilty. (Nowhere in its opinion does the trial court in any respect dispute either the evidence or conclusions of Dr. Buckhout.)

half of the respondents in the Lawton area had formed an opinion about the guilt of McVeigh and ninety six percent of those respondents believed McVeigh was guilty. Jones and Hillelman, McVeigh, McJustice, McMedia, 1998 University of Chicago Legal Forum 53. The Court ordered that the venue be changed to Denver, Colorado. Both McVeigh and Nichols were convicted in the Colorado trial which followed, and McVeigh was sentenced to death and executed June 11, 2001.

———

THE PSYCHOLOGY OF THE AMERICAN JURY (1987)

Jeffrey T. Frederick.

In view of the impact of prejudicial pretrial publicity, the question arises as to how one can assess the exposure of jurors to pretrial publicity and the detrimental effects produced, if any. Social sciences can provide valuable information regarding the possibility of prejudice in the community where a trial is to be held and, therefore, are of great assistance in determining the need for and/or the validity of change of venue motions. Such assistance can come in several areas. Expert evaluation can be provided regarding the impact of the content of the media coverage on community opinions. Affidavits from members of the community attesting to levels of prejudice present in the community can be presented to the court. Probably the best tool at the disposal of the social scientist is the use of surveys or polls of the community to reveal the *actual* level of prejudice, not simply the inferred level. At least 12 years ago the courts began to find this kind of information relevant and useful. It is therefore, worthwhile to look more closely at the methods used by social scientists to determine the presence or absence of prejudice.

In conducting an attitudinal survey for support of a change of venue motion, random samples of jury-eligible persons must be drawn from at least two communities or districts. The use of a random sample ensures a valid representation of the range and distribution of community attitudes and provides a basis for valid statistical tests. The use of two or more communities reflects the relative nature of social science statements, e.g., County "X" has a higher level of prejudice than County "Y." The use of a comparison community helps to eliminate the ambiguity in interpreting an absolute figure (a measurement of one county only). For example, suppose a community poll reveals that approximately 40% of the community believes that the defendant is guilty. Should the venue be changed? Obviously, the establishment of an acceptable absolute level of bias in the community is difficult, if not impossible. The question of change of venue is difficult to answer without a meaningful standard of comparison. If a poll of an adjacent community revealed that 15% of its population was biased, this fact would obviously make the need for a change of venue clear. This conclusion would be impossible to come to without comparative data. The use of comparison communities provides the necessary ground on which to make a decision about the need for a change of venue. That is, using one or more comparison communities or districts provides a way of assessing whether a fair trial could be gained by such a move. It is always possible that a move could place the trial in a more prejudiced community, thus worsening the plight of the defendant.

The questionnaire used in assessing a change of venue motion should contain questions concerning level of publicity, case-specific issues, and general attitudes. In support of a change of venue motion based upon prejudicial pretrial publicity, information is needed about how much exposure to publicity the residents have had. A question such as "How much have you heard about the _____ case?" with response categories of "none," "a little," "somewhat," and "a lot," is generally appropriate. In the event that a particular news story is at issue, it may be necessary to ask specifically how they have heard about the case in order to determine if they have been exposed to the prejudicial publicity.

Questions concerning case-specific issues are included in the venue questionnaire in order to determine the level of prejudice in the community. A question such as "Do you believe that the defendant, X, is guilty?" is necessary to detect any preconceptions of the defendant's guilt in the community. However, additional questions regarding other issues (e.g., opinions about insanity defense or a defendant's prior criminal record) may be asked in order to support an assertion of a specific prejudice against the defendant. Finally, general attitudinal questions should be asked (e.g., about racial attitudes, attitudes toward crime, bias against defendants, or sex and political biases) in order to determine if a general prejudice against the defendant exists. While this latter information may not by itself support a change of venue motion, it can buttress the assertions of specific prejudice.

ABA STANDARDS FOR CRIMINAL JUSTICE (3D ED. 1992)

Standard 8–3.3. Change of venue or continuance

The following standards govern the consideration and disposition of a motion in a criminal case for change of venue or continuance based on a claim of threatened interference with the right to a fair trial:

(a) Except as federal or state constitutional or statutory provisions otherwise require, a change of venue or continuance may be granted on motion of either the prosecution or the defense.

(b) A motion for change of venue or continuance should be granted whenever it is determined that, because of the dissemination of potentially prejudicial material, there is a substantial likelihood that, in the absence of such relief, a fair trial by an impartial jury cannot be had. This determination may be based on such evidence as qualified public opinion surveys or opinion testimony offered by individuals, or on the court's own evaluation of the nature, frequency, and timing of the material involved. A showing of actual prejudice shall not be required.

————

NOTES

1. Prosecution Requests. The opportunity of the prosecution to request a change of venue is severely limited. In federal court, the language of Criminal Rule 21(a) does not permit a prosecution motion, and prosecution motions are also barred by the Sixth Amendment of the Constitution which guarantees to criminal defendants the right to trial in the district where the offense was committed. Of course, a defendant's request for change constitutes a waiver of this right. Changes within the district where the offense was committed are not barred by the Rule or the Constitution, so presumably the prosecution could request such a limited move. See Wright, 2 Federal Practice and Procedure 3d Sec. 341 (2000). In state courts, similar statutory and state constitutional limits would also constrain such requests. Thus, the use of social science to change venue in criminal trials is largely reserved for defendants.

2. Discovery. In federal court, and in states which have adopted the Federal Rules model, discovery of research materials produced in an effort to secure a change of venue motion would generally not be permitted. Criminal Rule 16(b)(1)(B), limits prosecution discovery of "scientific tests or experiments" to situations where the defendant has first requested discovery of similar materials from the government. Discovery by a defendant of prosecution research would likely be permitted by Criminal Rule 16(a)(1)(D). Of course, a defendant requesting prosecution research materials might be required to exchange similar materials. Contrary to this situation, Moskitis, The Constitutional Need for Discovery of Pre–Voir Dire Jury Studies, 49 Southern California Law Review 597 (1976), argues in favor of widespread discovery of juror studies as a solution for potential constitutional issues. Richardson, Swain, Codega and Bazzell, Forensic Sociology: Some Cautions and Recommendations, 18 The American Sociologist 385 (1987), report a successful prosecution effort to obtain research materials developed for a defendant's change of venue motion.

————

FIRESTONE v. CROWN CENTER REDEVELOPMENT CORP.

Supreme Court of Missouri, 1985.
693 S.W.2d 99.

■ Higgins, Judge.

Plaintiff obtained a jury verdict of $15,000,000 damages for injuries suffered when suspended balconies in the Hyatt Regency Kansas City Hotel fell on July 17, 1981.

[A]ppellants assert that the trial court erred in denying their application for a change of venue. The publicity surrounding the tragic collapse of the Hyatt Regency skyways, causing the deaths of 114 people and severe injuries to scores of others; the pretrial publicity about plaintiff's case; and publicity about the lawsuits of three other Hyatt Regency victims which had been tried in the three months preceding plaintiff's case, had, according to defendants' argument, caused the residents of Jackson County to be prejudiced against defendants so that they could not receive a fair trial there.

The granting of a change of venue in Jackson County, a county of over 75,000 population, is discretionary with the trial court, Rule 51.04, subject to review for abuse of discretion.

In an evidentiary hearing upon defendant's application, the defendants produced evidence of newspaper and television publicity about the Hyatt Regency disaster and the ensuing litigation over a period beginning with the disaster itself and continuing up to the time of trial. The Kansas City Star and the Kansas City Times, reaching half the households of Jackson County on a daily basis, published over 1,000 articles on the subject. The television coverage was no less intense.

The news media featured stories about the purported causes of the collapse, and the persons responsible. Another favorite topic was possible criminal penalties and disciplinary proceedings against persons participating in the design and construction of the hotel. There were newspaper articles and television pieces reporting on the commencement of investigations by the Jackson County Prosecutor, the U.S. District Attorney, a Jackson County Grand Jury, and the Missouri board licensing architects and engineers. Also reported and highlighted after the commencement of litigation were allegations (from whatever source) of misconduct on the part of defendants and their counsel in the conduct of litigation.

[A]ppellants do not claim that the publicity necessarily caused adverse community reaction, but acknowledge that they must show such prejudice. The disaster occurred July 17, 1981; this trial took place September 13, 1983. The intensity of the publicity had considerably abated several months before trial. If, as appellants argue, the publicity had incited public passion and prejudice against them, the passage of time had done its healing work. The trial judge noted in overruling the change of venue on September 6, 1983: "Generally speaking, in the past nine to twelve months the publicity involved has been substantially reduced and consisted mainly of reporting on the three trials that have been conducted."

To show the public hostility toward themselves, defendants produced the results of a telephone survey of 1,000 randomly selected Jackson County residents. The findings of this survey were conditionally admitted by the trial judge, but were ultimately excluded by him. The exclusion of this survey is said to be erroneous. Appellants say that if the survey had been admitted and been given proper weight, it would have supported their application for change of venue.

The survey consisted of two questions. The first question was: "Have you heard, or read or seen any news coverage about the Hyatt Hotel skywalk collapse?" Ninety-eight percent of the respondents said they had.

The next question was, to those who answered the first question in the affirmative: "Based on what you have heard, read or seen, do you believe that in the current compensatory damage trials, the defendants, such as the contractors, designers, owners, and operators of the Hyatt Hotel, should be punished?" Five hundred thirty-six of the respondents, or 54 percent, answered yes. One hundred thirty-five, or 14 percent, answered no. One hundred one, or 10 percent, refused to comment; and two hundred twelve, or 22 percent, were reported as unable to comment.

One of the requirements for the admissibility of a survey is that it be trustworthy. This does not mean merely that it be honestly conducted, but that it be designed to yield an accurate assessment of the relevant public opinion, belief or attitude under investigation.

[W]hat is the public opinion, belief or attitude being inquired into upon an application for change of venue? The reason for the change of venue provisions of Rule 51 is that a party is entitled to an impartial jury to hear and decide his case. If there is in the venue from which the jury is to be drawn a pervasive hostility toward a party, or a pervasive prejudgment of the case, it will be difficult or impossible to select an impartial jury. It is assumed that the jury panel members, and ultimately the jury, will reflect the prevailing opinion of the community from which they are drawn. In such a case the party is entitled to a change of venue.

The question becomes whether the survey rejected by the trial court gave a reliable reading of whether there was in Jackson County a pervasive hostility toward defendants or a pervasive prejudgment of Sally Firestone's case. On this question, this Court cannot condemn the trial court's rejection of the survey. The responses to the critical question were not an index to the true sentiments of the community. The fault is in the design of the question. A layman's answer to the critical question (i.e., "[D]o you believe that ... the defendants ... should be punished?"), having no more background than the generalized information gained from newspaper and television accounts, will reveal nothing at all about his ability to deal fairly with a specific case upon the basis of specific evidence, guided by the court's instructions and the argument of counsel. In admitting the results of a survey in Zippo Manufacturing Company v. Rogers Imports, Inc., 216 F.Supp. 670 (S.D.N.Y.1963), the court noted: "The developmental phase of the project involved preparation of questions that could be handled properly by an interviewer, correctly understood by respondents [i.e., those persons interviewed in the survey] and easily answered by them. This required several drafts of questionnaires and some pretesting." Id. at 681.

The question asked of the interviewees in this case did not measure up to the standard of the *Zippo* questions. The question used in this survey could neither be "correctly understood" nor "easily answered" by them. The phrase "compensatory damages" summons to the lawyer's mind a certain well-defined concept. The concept includes the idea of focusing upon the plaintiff's loss, and determining the amount of money which will make him whole; the concept excludes the idea of focusing upon the quality of defendant's fault to determine what if any penalty he should pay, above the amount which will make plaintiff whole, to make the defendant smart. All this is assumed by the lawyer, but not by the layman. The ideas of compensatory as opposed to punitive damages do not spring to his mind with the term "compensatory damages."

The word "punished" is another confusing word in this context. "Punished" how? Would the answers have been the same had the persons interviewed known (as the jury was instructed in the trial of this case) that defendants had paid $20,000,000 punitive damages to be distributed among the persons injured in the disaster?

It is doubtful whether any single "yes" or "no" question could be designed which could be relied upon to test the kind of prejudice which would disqualify a person as an impartial juror. This is not such a question. Among those who answered "yes," that the defendants should be "punished," was the belief a deep-seated one, one which could not be laid aside if he were selected as a juror, or was it shallow and tentative? Did it take into account the good will which some of the defendants enjoyed in the community? It is noted that none of the defendants was named in the survey.

Appellants say the survey, even with its deficiencies, should have been admitted by the court and given such weight as it deserved. This was, perhaps, an option for the court. If evidence is remotely relevant to prove an issue under investigation, an appellate court can approve the trial court's discretionary ruling in admitting it, saying that its weight is for the trier of fact.

[T]he defendants filed a motion to reconsider the court's denial of their motion for a change of venue, to which motion was appended a second survey. The second survey contained the following prefatory explanation: "Some of the cases resulting from the skywalk collapse are now coming to trial. The jurors are being asked to determine the amounts of money those bringing suit should receive as compensation for the injuries, pain incurred, medical costs and other losses they have suffered."

There followed the question: "Do you feel that the defendants such as the contractors, designers, owners and operators of the Hyatt Hotel should be required to pay damages to those bringing suit in addition to the compensation I have mentioned?"

Over one-half of the total number of interviewees answered in the affirmative.

This question, with the prefatory explanation, was more easily understood by the layman than the question submitted in the first survey; still, the survey could not really plumb the attitudes of the respondents. If the respondents had a fixed opinion that the defendants "should be required to pay damages to those bringing suit in addition to the compensation," that would not have disqualified them as jurors in this case. That the defendants would pay punitive damages was agreed, as the jurors in the trial were expressly told by the court's instructions.

[The jury verdict is affirmed.]

NOTES

1. Federal Cases. The *Firestone* case shows that change of venue can be an issue in state court civil litigation. In federal civil cases similar issues would arise under a statute, 28 U.S.C. § 1404(a), which suggests that social science methods might be used to change the place of trial, based on a claim of local prejudice. The statute includes "in the interest of justice" as one reason for change, and some courts have cited this language in considering motions based on local prejudice. See Wright, Miller and Cooper, 15 Federal Practice and Procedure Sec. 3854 (1986). At least in federal court, the motion for change may be made by either plaintiff, defendant, or by a party added to the litigation after the beginning of suit. Id. at Sec. 3844. Of course plaintiffs, who choose the place to begin suit, will typically be satisfied with their choices. The availability of the motion in civil cases should be about the same in most state courts, though plaintiffs requesting a change might sometimes face the effective argument that the initial choice of a forum constituted a waiver of any request for change.

2. Discovery. In federal court and in states following the federal model, discovery of research done to support a change of venue motion would likely be governed by Civil Rule 26 (a) and (b). In the case of an expert expected to be called at trial, as would ordinarily be the case in a change of venue situation, the rule requires disclosure of the identity of and a written report signed by the expert, including the substance of facts and opinions which the expert will discuss in court. The Rule also provides that such an expert's deposition may be taken by any party.

SELECTED BIBLIOGRAPHY

Brodsky, Change of Venue Assessments in Civil Litigation: Methodologies for a Comprehensive Evaluation, 28 Journal of Law and Psychiatry 335 (2000).

Jones and Hillerman, McVeigh, McJustice, McMedia, 1998 University of Chicago Legal Forum 53.

Kovera, The Effects of General Pretrial Publicity on Juror Decisions: An Examination of Moderators and Mediating Mechanisms, 26 Law and Human Behavior 43 (2002).

M. Nietzel and R. Dillehay, Psychological Consultation in the Courtroom (1986).

O'Connell, Pretrial Publicity, Change of Venue, Public Opinion Polls—A Theory of Procedural Justice, 65 University of Detroit Law Review 169 (1988).

Ogloff and Vidmar, The Impact of Pretrial Publicity on Jurors: A Study to Compare the Relative Effects of Television and Print Media in a Child Sex Abuse Case, 18 Law and Human Behavior 507 (1994).

Otto, Penrod and Dexter, The Biasing Impact of Pretrial Publicity on Juror Judgments, 18 Law and Human Behavior 453 (1994).

Posey and Dahl, Beyond Pretrial Publicity: Legal and Ethical Issues Associated With Change of Venue Surveys, 26 Law and Human Behavior 107 (2002).

Steblay, Besirevic, Fulero, and Jimenez–Lorente, The Effects of Pretrial Publicity on Juror Verdicts: A Meta–Analytic Review, 23 Law and Human Behavior 219 (1999).

Studebaker, Robbennolt, Pathak–Sharma, and Penrod, Assessing Pretrial Publicity Effects: Integrating Content Analytic Results, 24 Law and Human Behavior 317 (2000).

Studebaker, Robbennolt, Penrod, Pathak–Sharma, Groscup, and Devenport, Studying Pretrial Publicity Effects: New Methods for Improving Ecological Validity and Testing External Validity, 26 Law and Human Behavior 19 (2002).

SECTION II.   CHOOSING A JURY

A traditional aspect of the jury trial is the opportunity, during the voir dire phase, for parties and their attorneys to participate in the selection of members of the jury. In recent years social scientists have been asked to assist in this part of the process. Typically, these social scientists have furnished advice concerning the best use of peremptory challenges to prospective jurors, the right to eliminate a limited number of prospective jurors without stating a reason. For example, in federal court, in criminal cases, Rule 24(b) provides that in capital cases each side has 20 peremptory challenges, and lesser numbers are provided to each side as the potential punishment diminishes. In federal civil cases, 28 U.S.C. § 1870 provides that each side will have 3 peremptory challenges. According to that statute, if there are several plaintiffs or defendants, the court may allow additional challenges. The same general pattern can be found in state courts.

From the beginning, this use of social science has been controversial, in large part (and ironically) because lawyers and judges seem to believe these practices are highly effective. Even the title of an early description of this work, Schulman, Shaver, Coleman, Emrich and Christie, Recipe for a Jury, 7 Psychology Today 34 (1973), has evoked consternation. The image of social scientists concocting a "recipe" for a jury and passing that along to the lawyers that retain them has surely troubled many members of the legal community.

———

ATTORNEY FOR THE DEFENSE

Clarence Darrow.
5 Esquire Magazine 36 (May 1936).*

[L]et us assume that we represent one of "the underdogs" because of injuries received, or because of an indictment brought by what the prosecutors name themselves, "the state." Then what sort of men will we seek? An Irishman is called into the box for examination. There is no reason for asking about his religion; he is Irish; that is enough. We may not agree with his religion, but it matters not; his feelings go deeper than any religion. You should be aware that he is emotional, kindly and sympathetic. If he is chosen as a juror, his imagination will place him in the dock; really, he is trying himself. You would be guilty of malpractice if you got rid of him, except for the strongest reasons.

An Englishman is not so good as an Irishman, but still, he has come through a long tradition of individual rights, and is not afraid to stand alone; in fact, he is never sure that he is right unless the great majority is against him. The German is not so keen about individual rights except where they concern his own way of life; liberty is not a theory, it is a way of living. Still, he wants to do what is right, and he is not afraid. He has not been among us long, his ways are fixed by his race, his habits are still in the making. We need inquire no further. If he is a Catholic, then he loves music and art; he must be emotional, and will want to help you; give him a chance.

If a Presbyterian enters the jury box and carefully rolls up his umbrella, and calmly and critically sits down, let him go. He is cold as the grave; he knows right from wrong, although he seldom finds anything right. He believes in John Calvin and eternal punishment. Get rid of him with the fewest possible words before he contaminates the others.

[N]ever take a wealthy man on a jury. He will convict, unless the defendant is accused of violating the anti-trust law, selling worthless stocks or bonds, or something of that kind. Next to the Board of Trade, for him, the penitentiary is the most important of all public buildings. These imposing structures stand for capitalism. Civilization could not possibly exist without them. Don't take a man because he is a "good" man; this means nothing. You should find out what he is good *for*. Neither should a man be accepted because he is a bad sort. There are too many ways of being good or bad. If you are defending, you want imaginative individuals. You are not interested in the morals of the juror. If a man is instinctively kind and sympathetic, take him.

————

MODERN TRIALS (2D ED. 1982)

Melvin Belli, Sr.

CONSIDERATIONS IN SELECTING A JURY— RACIAL CONSIDERATIONS

[A]s a rule of thumb, if plaintiff is an Irishman or a Swede, prospective juror Olsen or O'Brien in the several cases will not be excused by plaintiff's lawyer. On the other hand, rule of thumb would lead to a plaintiff's peremptory challenge of an Italian juror when defendant is an Italian and particularly if a vigorous cross-examination is to be contemplated of the Italian defendant.

[C]ONSIDERATIONS IN SELECTING A JURY—ACCOUNTANTS, STATISTICIANS AND BANK CLERKS

The author believes that a plaintiff does better on the amount of verdict by peremptorily challenging the accountant, statistician and bank and insurance clerks. [H]e will be the first to think, and even argue, that "this amount of money that plaintiff is asking is more than he would ever have earned in his lifetime and certainly more than he would need presently."

[C]ONSIDERATIONS IN SELECTING A JURY—ARTISTS, MUSICIANS, WRITERS AND ACTORS

The rule of thumb here: artists, writers, musicians, actors and public figures generally make good plaintiff jurors on the civil side, and good defendant's jurors in the criminal case. As plaintiff's counsel and a criminal defendant's lawyer, I love this type of juror. They are philosophically tuned in to my side of the case and will vote for me substantively, and will usually give a substantial award.

[C]ONSIDERATIONS IN SELECTING A JURY—FARMERS

If I had my choice I would not want a jury of farmers. I do not mean to be disrespectful of those who make it possible for me to survive, but in the dealings I've had with farmers, their concept of law is different from mine as is their concept of the adequacy of awards—to others, not themselves.

What then do you do as a plaintiff's lawyer when you find yourself in a farming community? I think your time would be better spent picking corn than arguing to this type of jury!

————

THE EFFECT OF PEREMPTORY CHALLENGES ON JURY AND VERDICT: AN EXPERIMENT IN A FEDERAL DISTRICT COURT*

Hans Zeisel and Shari Seidman Diamond.
30 Stanford Law Review 491 (1978).

Trial lawyers tell us that they occasionally win their cases at voir dire by the shrewd use of their peremptory challenges. This is the report of an experiment designed to discover whether they really do. Normally, this question cannot be answered with precision: Because the excused jurors do not attend the trial, there is no way of knowing how they would have voted had they not been removed. Our experiment attempted to secure this missing information by asking the peremptorily excused jurors to remain as shadow jurors in the courtroom and to reveal at the end of the trial how they would have voted in the case. This allowed us to become retrospectively clairvoyant—to see how well the prosecutor and defense counsel performed in their attempts to eliminate hostile jurors. More important, by combining this knowledge with posttrial interviews of the real jurors, we reconstructed the vote of the jury that would have decided the case had there been no peremptory challenges—that is, if the first 12 jurors in the venire, not excused for cause, had formed the jury. By comparing what the reconstructed "jury without peremptory challenges" would have done with what the real jury did, we were able to gauge the effect, if any, of the peremptory challenges on the composition of the jury and its verdict.

[T]he experiment was conducted in 12 criminal trials before three judges of the United States District Court for the Northern District of Illinois. Financial considerations limited the number and size of the cases, and we selected only trials that were expected to last no longer than 2 weeks. Within these bounds, the willingness of the judge, prosecutor and defense attorney to cooperate in the experiment dictated the actual selection of cases. We initially planned to look at both criminal and civil cases, but while the parties to the criminal trials generally gave their consent to the experiment, we managed to obtain consent in only three civil cases, too small a sample to integrate into our experimental design. In retrospect, the overwhelming refusal rate in civil cases was a blessing, for it gave us a more homogeneous sample of exclusively criminal cases.

Because of these constraints on their selection, the 12 cases that formed the basis of our study are not a probability sample of anything: They are 12 modestly sized criminal jury cases. Therefore, our experiment should be regarded as only the first step toward an understanding of the effect of peremptory challenges on jury verdicts.

[O]ur data gave us some idea of how well the attorneys used their allotted challenges to excuse jurors who, had they been allowed to sit on the jury, would have voted against their side. We designed a rough performance index that evaluated the extent to which counsel employed peremptory challenges to dismiss hostile or friendly jurors. [The nature of the index is illustrated by calculating, as follows, the prosecutor's performance in one of the 12 cases.]

The original venire consisted of 28 potential jurors, of whom 22.2 would have voted guilty and 5.8 not guilty.[43] The prosecutor's "best performance," therefore, would have used the allotted 6 peremptory challenges to eliminate all 5.8 jurors voting not guilty; 100% of the remaining jurors would have voted guilty. In formulating our attorney performance index, we would have assigned this optimal performance a score of +100. The prosecutor's "worst performance" would have excluded 6 guilty-voting jurors, leaving the proportion of guilty votes at 16.2 out of 22, or 73.6%; this worst possible performance would have been assigned a score of −100. A zero score would represent a performance leaving unchanged the original distribution of the venire, estimated at 79% guilty votes.

In the actual case (Case 10), the prosecutor selected his jurors so as to leave a voting constellation of 91.1% guilty votes. We therefore computed this prosecutor's score as follows: (1) because the prosecutor increased the proportion of favorable jurors, the score was given a positive value; (2) the absolute value then was measured by calculating the difference between the percentage of guilty votes in the original venire (79) and the percentage of guilty votes after the prosecutor's challenges (91.1), a score of 12.1; (3) this value then was normalized by dividing by the maximum possible improvement (the difference between the guilty percentage at a zero score, 79, and the guilty percentage at a +100 score, 100). The resulting ratio, +12.1/21, expressed as a percentage, +58, became the prosecutor's performance score.

To complete the attorney performance index, we performed parallel computations for the prosecution and defense counsel in each of the 12 cases.

[T]he collective performance of the attorneys is not impressive. The prosecutors' average score is close to zero (0.5). Thus, in the aggregate, the prosecutors made about as many good challenges as bad ones. The defense counsel's average performance score (+17.0) is slightly better, which suggests that, on the average, defense attorneys shifted in their favor the proportion of not guilty votes in the venire. These averages are misleading, however, because the fluctuations around them are so large. The prosecutors' scores fluctuate between +62 (Case 11) and 61 (Cases 6 and 12); the defense counsel's scores fluctuate between +48 (Case 5) and 62 (Case 8). The average fluctuations around the mean scores are ±38 for the prosecutor and ±25 for the defense, suggesting that in this limited sample of 12 cases, attorney performance was highly erratic. As a result, even though

---

43. We established this distribution of first ballot votes in the standardized 28-person venire by determining the proportion of guilty votes among the potential jurors questioned during voir dire.

attorneys' scores on the average were around zero, in some cases the attorneys performed very poorly, and in others very well. And if, in a case, one side performs poorly while the other side performs well, such disparity may have interesting results.

THE USE OF SOCIAL SCIENCE IN TRIALS WITH POLITICAL AND RACIAL OVERTONES: THE TRIAL OF JOAN LITTLE

John B. McConahay, Courtney J. Mullin, and Jeffrey Frederick.
41 Law and Contemporary Problems 205 (Winter 1977).

The Joan Little case began in Washington, North Carolina. Early on the morning of August 27, 1974, Clarence Alligood, the night jailer for the Beaufort County jail, was found dead in a locked cell in the women's section of the jail. Alligood, a sixty-four-year-old white male, had ice pick punctures in his body and semen on his leg; and his pants and shoes were outside the cell. The person incarcerated in the cell during the preceding weeks was Joan Little, a twenty-year-old black female. Both Ms. Little and the keys to the cell and jail were missing. Over the next few days, there was an extensive search for Ms. Little in Beaufort and adjacent counties. She was on the verge of being declared an outlaw when, accompanied by her attorney, Jerry Paul, she turned herself in to the authorities in Raleigh. She was immediately charged with first degree murder. On April 28, 1975, her trial was moved from Beaufort to Wake County (Raleigh), North Carolina. And on August 15, after a trial of five weeks, she was acquitted of all charges.

[I]n the trial of Joan Little, the judge asked potential jurors, in groups of twelve, general questions—largely regarding their ability to serve for the expected four-to six-week period. Then they were examined individually out of the sight and hearing of other jurors. The prosecution questioned them first and, if they were not excused for cause, made a decision to accept or peremptorily challenge the juror. Once it had passed a juror, the prosecution could not change its decision. At this point, the potential juror was examined by the defense and, if the person was not excused for cause, the defense had to decide to accept or use one of its peremptory challenges. If the defense accepted a juror, he or she was immediately sequestered in the jury room. This process continued until sixteen jurors (twelve regular jurors and four alternates) were seated. The process of jury selection took ten working days during which over two hundred potential jurors were interviewed.

[S]treams of data were combined in the defense's decision to accept or reject a potential juror. First, on the basis of a random sample survey of Wake County, we had developed a mathematical model of the juror who would be ideal for the defense. Second, we observed the behavior of the potential juror during the voir dire and rated him or her on a psychological characteristic known as authoritarianism. Third, we observed the "body language" including both kinesic and paralinguistic behavior in order to determine the degree to which a potential juror was defense or prosecution oriented. Fourth, the attorneys drew upon their voir dire experience and common sense. [F]inally, Ms. Little was asked how she felt about any juror whom we were seriously considering accepting.

[A.]   The Survey and Mathematical Model

Although it was expensive to construct (about $35 thousand), the most important scientific tool we had was the mathematical model of the defense's ideal juror based upon a random sample survey of Wake County. Its effectiveness rested upon two assumptions which, fortunately, proved to be justified. First, we assumed that the jury pool would be close to a random sample of the citizens of Wake County eligible for jury service. Second, we assumed that those characteristics of the survey respondents which enabled us to predict opinions regarding Joan Little's guilt or innocence in the sample survey would also enable us to predict them in the jury pool.

In order to facilitate a general understanding of the mathematical model by readers unfamiliar with statistical methods, it will be described in a brief, nontechnical fashion. The basic idea behind this approach is that individuals who are predisposed to believe that the defendant in question is guilty will differ from other individuals with respect to a number of observable characteristics. Once these characteristics have been identified for the population as a whole, they can be used to predict the predispositions of each potential juror.

Before the model can be employed, a survey of attitudes in the particular geographical area of interest must be undertaken. This provides an assessment of the attitudinal composition of that area from which the mathematical model will then generate its predictions. The mathematical model itself is a predictive hybrid of several statistical techniques. First, we chose an appropriate measure of the attitudes or opinions we wished to predict, i.e., belief in the guilt or innocence of the accused. Next, a series of statistical techniques was employed to determine what demographic characteristics of the respondents in the sample would act as predictors of these important opinions. Demographic characteristics might include age, race, sex, political and religious affiliations.

In the first phase of the procedure, an attempt was made to divide the sample into groups possessing similar opinions. That is, if those of higher ages and lower ages differed in their opinions regarding the guilt or innocence of the accused, it would be helpful to divide the sample into younger and older age groups before an attempt was made to formulate predictions of their important opinions. This was accomplished by using a modified version of a statistical computer program known as AID (Automatic Interaction Detection).

The AID program searched the survey data until it had successfully divided the sample into as many groups as possible based upon the homogeneity of the sample members' opinions. Membership in any one homogeneous group was often defined by several demographic characteristics—for example, young democrats with at least a college education. As a result of this first phase, our ability to predict opinions was increased by decreasing the variability of our sample.

After the sample was divided into groups of individuals with fairly similar opinions, each group was examined to establish which of their social and psychological characteristics were important with respect to our ability to predict a potential juror's opinions. In more technical terms, this phase was concerned with the formulation of predictive equations for jurors' opinions. In order to do this, we used a [statistical] technique [w]hich enabled us to develop a mathematical model of the opinions of potential jurors based upon a series of characteristics that differed from one demographic group to another. An example of this would be the case where one group produced by phase I consisted of young democrats with at least a college education. For members of this group we may need to know the sex, religious attitudes, and income characteristics of the individuals. In another group from phase I, e.g., democrats over forty-five years old with a high school education, the terms in the predictive equation might be the type of magazines read, sex, and preferred presidential candidate.

Though the social and psychological factors used to predict opinions varied from group to group, they combined to form the same thing: a prediction of the likelihood that a potential juror would be willing to vote Joan Little not guilty before hearing any of the evidence.

One of the advantages of this procedure is obvious. Regardless of what a juror might say during the voir dire, by observing or obtaining his or her demographic characteristics (age, education, etc.) and social-psychological characteristics (politics, reading habits, etc.), the mathematical model enabled us to predict how predisposed he or she was to side with the prosecution or defense. Potential jurors might lie about their preconceptions of guilt or innocence, but they were much less likely to lie about their age or education.

A second advantage is not so obvious. Because the judge permitted both prosecution and defense to send out with the jury summons a questionnaire concerning the jurors' demographic characteristics, we were able to get a preliminary estimate of what proportion of the jury pool would be predisposed to be "pro-defense" or "pro-defendant" before the voir dire began and before we had seen a single juror. The advantage here is that in the early part of the voir dire we could afford to let some promising jurors go because we knew that better potential jurors would appear later. Many of the news reporters failed to see how important this was. Informally, if not in print or on the air, they expressed the opinion that the mathematical model and the other scientific procedures were not necessary because anyone would have known we wanted health food waitresses (the final jury had two of them) and a former drama major turned record store manager. What they failed to notice was that we got these persons as jurors because we had not already filled the slots with secretaries and IBM engineers.

B. Authoritarianism

Although we expected the math model to be between 85 per cent and 95 per cent accurate, we supplemented it with courtroom observations of authoritarianism and body language. Our observations of authoritarianism were based upon the theory of the authoritarian personality developed in the 1950s by researchers at the University of California at Berkeley.

According to this theory, which is supported by mountains of empirical research, extreme authoritarians are rigid, racist, anti-semitic, sexually repressed, politically conservative, highly punitive individuals who will accept the word of an authority figure over that of a lesser person. The authoritarian is servile and obsequious in a subordinate position, but takes out all of his or her pent-up hostility and frustration upon those perceived to be in violation of the conventional norms of society.

It is obvious that no defense attorney would want a jury loaded with extreme authoritarians. However, people vary in the degree to which they exhibit authoritarian personality traits. To the extent that potential jurors are more or less authoritarian, we would expect them to be more or less desirable from the viewpoint of the defense as jurors in trials involving minority persons, political and social nonconformists, or other controversial defendants. It is possible that the juror's level of authoritarianism might be something of a factor in all criminal trials. In the adversary system, the juror must weigh the evidence and arguments presented by the prosecution on behalf of the state or society and by the defense attorney on behalf of someone accused of a crime and therefore of lower status than the prosecutor.

[T]he authoritarianism rating scale we used in the courtroom ranged from a low of zero which represented minimum authoritarianism to a high of thirty which represented maximum authoritarianism. The neutral point between high authoritarian and low authoritarian behavior was fifteen. [The psychologists believed] that the average American rated about twenty on this scale of authoritarianism. By observing the authoritarianism-related behavior of potential jurors—their rigidity, their sexual prudery, their introspectiveness, and so on—three social psychologists were able to rate reliably the person's level of authoritarianism. When a decision was made to accept or reject a potential juror, these independently made, written ratings were combined to feed an authoritarianism rating into the decision making process.

The average rating assigned by our observers to all persons who were interviewed for Ms. Little's jury was 21.02, which is not very different from the general American population. On the other hand, the average for the sixteen seated jurors was 14.03. For the twelve who made the final decision to acquit her, the average authoritarianism rating was 12.95. Thus, we were able to pick a jury which was significantly less authoritarian than the jury pool as a whole.

C. Body Language

In a highly publicized case such as Ms. Little's, there were some people who actively desired to be on the jury. These people might have said whatever was necessary to insure that they were picked for the jury. Some of them could be expected to be pro-defense, some to be pro-prosecution. It was crucial for the defense to determine in some way the truthfulness of the jurors being selected. To do this, we called upon the newly emerging science of kinesics and paralinguistics, i.e. body language.

Although people frequently communicate their true feelings in the words they speak, it is now clear that we can also communicate a great deal of information by means of our body movements, gestures, positions, vocal intonations, pauses and the like. In other words, it is not what we say but the way we say it. We are perfectly capable of expressing one type of attitude with our language and a diametrically opposed attitude with our body language, for example, by unduly long pauses when speaking or by loudness or softness of the voice.

Our approach was to measure the levels of anxiety expressed by the individuals being questioned. We employed five variables to determine the kinesic response (body movement, body orientation, body posture, eye contact, and hand movement). We also employed two paralinguistic measures (vocal intonation and vocal hesitancy).

No single kinesic or paralinguistic response determined the acceptance or rejection of any juror. We were looking for patterns of behavior. Human communication is extremely complex and one must look at the whole in order to make any determination as to the attitudes being expressed. Some popular writers on the subject would have one believe that a single gesture is indicative of an overall attitude. In truth, the single gesture must be deeply incorporated into a pattern of response expressed throughout the body and by the voice.

[O]bservers [n]oted each prospective juror's pattern of [b]ehavior [a]nd rated the juror on a scale ranging from one point, least favorable to the defense, to five points, most favorable to the defense. These preliminary ratings were written down independently by each observer and then combined to form a final five-point rating of the juror's attitude toward the defense (a high score indicating maximum favorableness).

To assess the relationship between the measures made on the basis of authoritarianism and body language, we correlated the two scales. The overall correlation was .79. This correlation was high and indicated that authoritarianism was associated with being least favorable toward the defense. The correlation was not so high, however, as to indicate that the two scales were simply measuring the same phenomena. Each measure both reinforced and added to the other. The use of both approaches insured more complete knowledge of the attitudes of the potential jurors than the use of either alone.

D. The Final Decision

When, in the course of the voir dire, a member of the defense team thought that a decision should be made on the potential juror under consideration, a conference was called. At this point, the members of the team put their heads together in a fashion that resembled a football huddle. Each social scientist read to the team from a written estimate of the potential juror based upon the juror's demographic rating, authoritarianism, or body language. In this way we minimized the influence upon an estimate from one technique (e.g., body language) by another technique (e.g., authoritarianism). The attorneys [a]nd Ms. Little also indicated their opinions of the potential juror in this "huddle." One of three decisions was made: accept, reject, or obtain more information.

[A]t the close of the five week trial, the jury took seventy-eight minutes to find Ms. Little not guilty of all charges.

————

NOTES

1. Prosecution Use. Virtually all of the reported instances of the use of social science research to choose a jury in criminal cases have involved use by defendants. Whether the prosecution could use these methods remains an open question, though apparently no specific statutory or constitutional provision seems, on its face, to bar such action. Indeed, in State v. Banks, 295 N.C. 399, 245 S.E.2d 743 (1978) the court refused to rule that the trial judge abused his discretion in permitting a student psychologist "to consult with the district attorney during the *voir dire* of the jury." Id. at 749. On the other hand, in United States v. Collins, 972 F.2d 1385 (5th Cir.1992), the prosecution commissioned a survey intended to aid in jury selection. The defendants found out about the survey and reported it to the trial judge, who ordered the government to terminate the survey and turn over the results to the court. For some, prosecution use of social science in choosing a jury would seem only prudent trial preparation by government attorneys; for others, it would seem an unfair advantage for an already advantaged party. The later view might be translated into arguments that a defendant's due process rights under the Fifth and Fourteenth Amendments of the United States Constitution would be infringed or that the Sixth Amendment right to trial by an impartial jury would be impaired. See Moskitis, The Constitutional Need for Discovery of Pre–Voir Dire Jury Studies, 49 Southern California Law Review 597, 607–621 (1976). Indeed, Moskitis even contends that constitutional principles might prevent defense use of scientific jury selection, a view not likely to be supported and contrary now to long practice. Id. at 621–24. These issues do not, of course, arise in civil cases where two private parties are typically involved and, presumably, either is free to use social science research in choosing a jury.

2. Discrimination. In Batson v. Kentucky, 476 U.S. 79, 106 S.Ct. 1712, 90 L.Ed.2d 69 (1986), the Supreme Court, in an opinion by Justice Powell, held that the Constitution "forbids the prosecutor to challenge potential jurors solely on account of their race or on the assumption that black jurors as a group will be unable impartially to consider the State's case against a black defendant." 476 U.S. at 89, 106 S.Ct. at 1719. The Court listed several elements that defendants must show to establish a prima facie case of discrimination, then recognized the possibility that a prosecutor might "come forward with a neutral explanation for challenging black jurors." Id. at 97, 106 S.Ct. at 1723. The role, if any, of social science research in providing such a "neutral explanation" was not discussed by Justice Powell in his opinion.

3. Discovery. Where social science research is used to assist in jury selection, the research would be generally protected from discovery in federal court and in states adopting federal rules. In criminal cases, the reciprocal limitation of Federal Rule 16(b)(1)(B) would protect defendant research unless defendant sought similar prosecution studies, an unlikely situation. In civil cases, Federal Rule 26(b)(4)(B) would permit discovery only upon a showing of "exceptional circumstances under which it is impracticable for the party seeking discovery to obtain facts or opinions on the same subject by other means." This very restrictive requirement applies to experts who are employed to prepare for trial but who will not testify, the invariable situation in scientific jury selection.

———

THE LIMITS OF SCIENTIFIC JURY SELECTION: ETHICAL AND EMPIRICAL

Michael Saks.
17 Jurimetrics Journal 3 (1976).

[T]he defense of scientific jury selection might begin by pointing out that it is thoroughly legal. Prospective jurors are not themselves approached or tampered with. They are merely compared to statistical profiles of the population from which they were drawn. They are questioned only during *voir dire,* and only to the extent permitted by the trial judge, as has been the way for generations. All that has changed is that lawyers can now know the hidden meaning of the answers and of jurors' background characteristics.

The practice of *voir dire* and of challenging jurors was not invented by [social scientists]. [I]t has been part of the jury system for centuries. And for those centuries lawyers have sought to impanel the most favorable possible juries for their clients. This has always been widely regarded as a proper goal for the lawyer. Why should the fact that he has finally been given the means to achieve that goal be so objectionable? If the goal was good, why has the ability to actually achieve it become bad?

[T]he goal of jury selection is not, I think, an unwise one. The intent is to impanel an impartial jury, that is, a jury whose members do not have biases that would make them unable to fairly weigh the evidence. Jurors are supposed to reach a verdict shaped by the weight of the evidence and not by the decision-makers' biases. The strategy for achieving that goal—allowing both advocates some opportunity to exclude from the jury persons thought to be biased against their side—also seems to me a wise and workable one. Scientific jury selection can add substantially to the achievement of that goal. Instead of guessing at who will be biased and will therefore not respond impartially to the evidence, lawyers can make informed judgments. If both sides have social science help, each will more effectively exclude jurors favorable to the other side, and the final panel will consist of the neutral jurors, the very ones who will be most able to do what a jury is intended to do. Thus, juror attitudes and personality would play a minimal role in determining the outcome of the trial. Evidence would be permitted to play the greatest possible role, which is how it was always supposed to be. Thus, scientific jury selection would make the goal of impartial jury decisions more attainable than has ever before been possible.

But, the critics would interject, the presence of such expertise on both sides is a fantasy which ignores the realities of justice in America. Today only the wealthy and celebrated have such help, and tomorrow the only additional people to have it will be prosecutors, and they will use it routinely. And this criticism is probably entirely true. But it does not demonstrate some evil inherent in scientific jury selection. It points instead to a fundamental inequity in our courts. *All* resources will be unevenly distributed in a system where those with wealth or the right friends can obtain services unavailable to the average citizen. This is not the fault of the resources or their inventors.

[E]very material and service commodity is systematically more available to one side than it is to the other. And every new invention of social scientists, legal service providers, or anyone else will be too. The problem lies not in each service and invention but in the system in which these things are used. The critics of scientific jury selection, to keep existing inequities from becoming more pronounced, would keep this new technology out of the courtroom or restructure court proceedings to minimize its potential impact. But next year or decade they will have to rally again to ban yet another innovation and then another and another after that. I suggest that these energies would be more efficiently directed at reforming the system which fosters all of these inequities. To do so would eliminate long standing inequities and make future innovations welcome for the benefits they may offer. The alternative is to live with existing imbalances and eternally eschew new developments.

[I] have saved for last what is perhaps the most interesting reason for not worrying excessively about scientific jury selection: the empirical reason. No evidence exists to support the apparently widely held belief that scientific jury selection is a powerful tool. What has most people upset about the technique is the fact that no one who has used it has lost a case. By the usual standards for evaluating empirical evidence, the same standards used by the social and behavioral scientists who developed the basic principles for the technique, this seemingly impressive evidence is really no evidence at all. The venerated scientific method usually calls for a control group, that is, a comparison group to tell you what an observation really means. To elucidate, suppose there were a control group. Suppose each of the cases had been tried before two juries—one selected the scientific way and one selected the old way. We could then compare the verdicts delivered by the scientific juries with those delivered by the conventional juries (the control juries.) We know that all of the scientifically selected juries refused to convict. What would the conventionally selected juries have done? The answer to this question is absolutely essential to an assessment of how effective scientific jury selection is or even whether it works at all. Without such comparisons it simply is impossible to know. If a significant number of control juries convicted we would know that the use of scientific jury selection techniques helped the defense effort.

If all of the conventional juries also refused to convict, we would know that scientific jury selection offered no help to the defense in those cases.

[A] balanced assessment of the effectiveness of scientific jury selection, based on what is generally known about human decision-making and on the data offered by the studies that have been done is, I believe, the following. It is safe to say that scientific jury selection "works;" juror characteristics do influence the decisions they make. But it is evidence that most determines the outcome of trials, rather than the characteristics of the jurors. If the evidence against a defendant is very strong or very weak, it isn't going to matter who is on the jury. If the evidence is close, then the jury selection could make the difference. One wouldn't be wasting money or time if he employed scientific jury selection, but if he did so at the expense of building a strong case out of evidence, he would be making a mistake. In cases where the evidence is close or ambiguous, scientific jury selection would be especially helpful.

———

SOCIAL SCIENCE INVOLVEMENT IN VOIR DIRE: PRELIMINARY DATA ON THE EFFECTIVENESS OF "SCIENTIFIC JURY SELECTION"*

Jeffrey T. Frederick.
2 Behavioral Sciences and the Law 375 (1984).

[The author examined data from an important civil case to answer the question of whether the survey technique of scientific jury selection is an effective litigation device.]

This case involved a suit for breach of contract between Shell Oil Company and Newport News Shipbuilding, Inc., concerning the late delivery of Ultra Large Crude Carriers (large oil tankers) to Shell. The plaintiff claimed that the over two year delay in delivery had cost it approximately $100 million. The defendant claimed that the delays (allegedly resulting from facility construction delays, subcontractor delays, and governmental priorities on other projects, among others) were justified under the contract signed by the parties. In conjunction with its litigation efforts, the defendant sought assistance in evidence preparation and persuasion and jury selection. Two projects were conducted which have a bearing on the present discussion of systematic jury selection, community survey and mock jury projects.

Methods

The first project conducted was an attitudinal survey of the Fourth Federal Judicial District, the jurisdiction in which the trial was to be held. A random sample of 967 registered voters were interviewed by telephone.[8] The questionnaire employed in this survey explored a variety of content areas. These areas included items addressing contracts, delays in delivery of products, buyer mitigation of losses, and defense contractor issues, among others. The general perceptions of the two litigants outside the scope of the case were assessed. The questionnaire also examined attitudes regarding equity, victim compensation, and authoritarianism. In addition, over 15 demographic questions were asked.

A critical component of the questionnaire was the introduction of a hypothetical case (concerning an aircraft manufacturer) that mirrored the basic facts and issues in the case. Respondents were given the basic facts and asked to decide whether the plaintiff should be awarded full compensation, partial compensation, or no compensation at all. Following this decision, respondents were presented with a series of seven independent informational items.

[A]fter each informational item, respondents again decided whether to provide the plaintiff with full, partial, or no compensation.

A mock jury project was also conducted for the defendant. While this project was aimed at testing evidentiary and persuasive aspects of the case, data from this project are also relevant to jury selection. A one hour and 35 minute videotape of a mock trial involving the litigants was developed using attorneys and law faculty as the actors in the case.

[J]urors viewed the videotape, rendered a preliminary verdict, participated in deliberations, rendered a final verdict, and answered special interrogatories.

[Based on the survey results, a model or profile of juror favorability was constructed.] A four variable predictive equation consisting of belief concerning the responsibility of manufacturer for delays beyond its control, race of respondent, prior military service, and education of the respondent proved to be the best predictors of the dependent measure.

---

8. The total sample had an approximately 30% refusal rate which yielded the present sample size.

[T]he question now becomes how effective was this model in predicting individual juror decisions in this case. The case settled the day before the trial was to begin and, therefore, any actual verdict data in this case do not exist. However, relevant data are available from the mock jury project. The voir dire for that project included all the questions necessary to fit these individuals to the profiles developed from the survey. Thus, a comparison can be made between jurors' predicted orientation and their preliminary verdicts.

The individual jurors were assigned a party specific orientation score by fitting these individuals to the predictive equation. Because of the complex nature of the verdict questionnaire, the preliminary verdicts were classified into four categories: $20 million to $50 million award for the plaintiff equals *1*, $1 million to $19 million award for the plaintiff equals *2*, no award for the plaintiff equals *3*, and $1 to $12 million award for the defendant equals *4*.[11] The party specific orientation score was then correlated with the verdict scale.

[T]o further examine how effective the party specific orientation scores were in predicting the verdicts of jurors these scores were used to classify jurors into one of three categories, pro-plaintiff, undifferentiated, and pro-defense. The classification was based on approximately equal representation in each of the groups. This yielded a distribution of the seven lowest scores classified as pro-plaintiff, the five middle scores classified as undifferentiated, and the seven highest scores classified as pro-defense. In view of the small sample size, verdict scores were classified as either a plaintiff's verdict (1 or 2) or a defense verdict (3 or 4). The overall distribution of verdicts was 42% favoring the plaintiff and 58% favoring the defense.

[A]nalysis of these classifications reveal that they tended to correctly predict verdict preference. Seventy-one percent of those classified as pro-plaintiff rendered verdicts in favor of the plaintiff. Of those classified as undifferentiated, 40% found for the plaintiff. Finally, only 14% of those classified as pro-defense returned a verdict for the plaintiff. In other words, 86% of those classified as pro-defense found for the defendant.

[T]hese results reveal several important points. First, they show that individual differences in party specific orientation could be established in survey respondents' decision preferences using a case relevant hypothetical situation. Second, this orientation could be estimated by the use of a predictive equation. Third, these estimates could accurately predict verdicts in an analogous trial situation using an independent sample (mock jurors).

SELECTED BIBLIOGRAPHY

Cramer, Adams, and Brodsky, Jury Selection in Child Sex Abuse Trials: A Case Analysis, 18 Journal of Child Sexual Abuse 190 (2009).

---

11. The jurors could award money to the defendant because of a cross-claim in this case being brought by the defendant.

Diamond, Scientific Jury Selection: What Social Scientists Know and Do Not Know, 73 Judicature 178 (1990).

J. Frederick, Mastering Voir Dire and Jury Selection: Gain an Edge in Questioning and Selecting Your Jury (2d ed. 2005).

J. Lieberman and B. Sales, Scientific Jury Selection (2007).

Saks, What Do Jury Experiments Tell Us About How Juries (Should) Make Decisions? 6 Southern California Interdisciplinary Law Journal 1 (1997).

Sommers and Norton, Race and Jury Selection: Psychological Perspectives on the Peremptory Challenge Debate, 63 American Psychologist 527 (2008).

SECTION III. CHOOSING INSTRUCTIONS

A third use of social science has involved the preparation of jury instructions. In federal court, the instruction practice is controlled by Criminal Rule 30 and by Civil Rule 51. Both rules provide that the parties may request particular instructions to the jury. Commentators have long speculated that the traditional jargon-laden jury instruction is often little help to jurors, and sometimes is actually misleading, and researchers have demonstrated the truth of these speculations. Happily, they have also demonstrated that the effectiveness of a particular instruction can be enhanced by following a series of relatively simple drafting rules. This research has already been used in drafting "pattern instructions," standard suggestions for trial judges. Recently, courts have begun to use research about jury instructions to determine the adequacy of these instructions.

PATTERN JURY INSTRUCTIONS: THE APPLICATION OF SOCIAL SCIENCE RESEARCH

Harvey S. Perlman.
65 Nebraska Law Review 520 (1986).

Since 1970 a series of empirical studies have documented first, that pattern jury instructions are not completely understood by the jurors to whom they are addressed, and second, that the use of certain techniques of drafting and organization improve juror comprehension.

In 1976 Strawn and Buchanan examined juror comprehension of Florida's criminal pattern jury instructions.[35] Randomly selected Florida jurors were shown videotaped jury instructions and were then tested by a multiple choice, true/false test to measure their comprehension. A control

---

35. Strawn & Buchanan, Jury Confusion: A Threat to Justice, 59 Judicature 478 (1976).

group was given the test without viewing any instructions. Jurors who had received instructions knew more than those who had not, but the instructed jurors still missed thirty percent of the test items, and on four issues regarded by the study's authors as critical, including an understanding of the concept of "reasonable doubt," the instructed jurors showed no better understanding than the control group.[36]

In 1977, Elwork, Sales, and Alfini published the first results of a large study they conducted utilizing the Michigan civil pattern instructions.[37] Again, random subjects viewed videotaped instructions and were then compared against a control group that had been given no instructions. In one study the subjects watched an entire videotaped trial to provide a factual context. Again, the authors found that traditional pattern jury instructions did not provide a significant measure of comprehension beyond that of the control group. They found, in fact, a nearly forty-percent rate of misunderstanding among those who viewed the traditional pattern instructions.

However, Elwork, Sales, and Alfini went further. Utilizing psycholinguistic literature, and, I think they will admit, a substantial measure of common sense, they redrafted the traditional instructions to improve juror comprehension. The literature they employed and the techniques they adopted focused on vocabulary, grammar, and organization. They replaced legal jargon with common words, abstract words with concrete words, and negative words with positive words. Homonyms—words with multiple meanings—were avoided.

Their revised instructions were sensitive to grammatical construction that had been shown empirically to improve comprehension. They avoided, where possible, embedded and compound sentences and the passive voice. They adopted what some social scientists termed a hierarchical and algorithmic organization scheme which breaks down general concepts into component parts such that concepts flow from previously explained concepts. Empirical tests demonstrated that their revised instructions heightened comprehension by lay jurors.

In 1982 the same authors published a book-length treatment of the subject entitled *Making Jury Instructions Understandable,* which reports on a wider test sample, refines the linguistic rules that demonstrably improve comprehension, and then sets out a step-by-step process through which lawyers (or others) may both rewrite instructions to improve understanding and empirically test their efforts.

36. Id. at 480–83. Although I disclaim any expertise in empirical validity, as a lawyer I am uncomfortable with these findings. The jurors did not deliberate, they did not have a context within which to understand or apply the instructions as they did not see a trial, and they were not asked to apply the instructions. They were, in fact, given a test much like students in a classroom. Judged in that context a 73% on a test is by any normal measure a passing grade. This study, although not conclusive, did encourage more sophisticated efforts.

37. [Elwork, Sales & Alfini, Juridic Decisions: In Ignorance of the Law or In Light Of It, 1 L. & Human Behav. 167 (1977).]

A similar project was conducted by Charrow and Charrow and published in the Columbia Law Review in 1979.[41] In their study subjects listened to instructions and were then asked to paraphrase what they had heard. Comparing the traditional to the linguistically revised instructions, they concluded again that much could be done to improve juror comprehension.

In two more recent studies,[44] Severance, Green, and Loftus carried the empirical observations a step further. To find sources of misunderstanding, they surveyed those cases in which juries had asked the judge questions during deliberations. They isolated three particularly bothersome instructions—those dealing with intent, reasonable doubt, and the use of evidence of prior convictions.

In the first study, jury-eligible college students viewed an hour-long videotape of a burglary trial and were then divided into six groups. One group received no instructions, one received a general instruction telling it what its duties were, and one received specific pattern instructions on the three areas to be studied. Half of each of these groups deliberated, the other half did not.

The authors examined the "jurors" through a questionnaire to determine whether they could distinguish between correct and incorrect expressions of the relevant law. In a separate test to determine whether jurors could apply the instructions to novel fact situations, the jurors were given ten hypothetical situations and asked to evaluate the outcome.

Comprehension measures replicated the earlier studies. Subjects receiving no instructions missed 35.6% of the questions on comprehension, subjects receiving the general instruction only missed 34.7%, and subjects receiving the specific instructions erred 29.6% of the time.

In measuring the subject's ability to apply the law to new situations, subjects receiving specific instructions did apply the law correctly more often, but the specific instruction on intent actually diminished that ability.

The authors then redrafted the specific instructions using the psycholinguistic techniques developed by the Charrows and Elwork groups and obtained consistently more accurate responses. Jurors receiving the redrafted specific instructions had an error in comprehension of 20.3%.[50]

In a second, more detailed study, the same authors used both ex-jurors and persons who had been called for jury duty. They discovered that the more experienced jurors had greater accuracy of comprehension. They also replicated the finding that their revised instructions aided comprehension, particularly when jurors were able to deliberate. They also used the

41. Charrow & Charrow, Making Legal Language Understandable: A Psycholinguistic Study of Jury Instructions, 79 Col.L.Rev. 1306 (1979).

44. Severance, Greene & Loftus, Toward Criminal Jury Instructions that Jurors can Understand, 75 J.Crim.L. & Criminology 198 (1984); Severance & Loftus, Improving the Ability of Jurors to Comprehend and Apply Criminal Jury Instructions, 17 L. & Soc'y R. 153 (1982).

50. Id. at 213. By comparison, jurors receiving the pattern instruction had a 24.3% error rate, and jurors receiving no instruction had an error rate of 29.3%. The difference was statistically significant.

Charrow technique of asking jurors to paraphrase instructions and again found their revised instructions were better understood.

The Severance group also surveyed trial judges throughout the country to determine whether the group's set of revised instructions were regarded as correct statements of the law. They concluded that judges would accept as accurate their revised instructions.

———

THE LAW AND PSYCHOLOGY OF JURY INSTRUCTIONS

J. Alexander Tanford.
69 Nebraska Law Review 71 (1990).

Much of the empirical research [about jury instructions] has focused on how to improve [c]omprehension. [P]sycholinguists suggest that comprehension would be improved if instructions were written along the following guidelines:

1. Eliminate nominalizations (making nouns out of verbs) and substitute verb forms; e.g., changing "an *offer* of evidence" to "items *were offered* into evidence."

2. Replace the prepositional phrase "as to" with "about;" e.g., changing "you must not speculate *as to* what the answer might have been" to "you must not speculate *about* what the answer might have been."

3. Relocate prepositional phrases so they do not interrupt a sentence; e.g., avoiding sentences such as "proximate cause is a cause which, *in a natural and continuous sequence,* produces the injury."

4. Replace words that are difficult to understand with simple ones; e.g., changing "agent's negligence is *imputed* to plaintiff" to "agent's negligence *transfers* to plaintiff."

5. Avoid multiple negatives in a sentence; e.g., "innocent *mis*recollection is *not un*common."

6. Use the active rather than passive voice; e.g., changing "no emphasis is intended by me" to "I do not intend to emphasize."

7. Avoid "whiz" deletions (omitting words "which is"); e.g., by changing "statements of counsel" to "statements *which are* made by counsel."

8. Reduce long lists of words with similar meanings to only one or two; e.g., shortening "knowledge, skill, experience, training, or education" to "training or experience."

9. Organize instructions into meaningful discourse structures that avoid connecting unrelated ideas in ways that make them seem related.[63]

63. ([E.]g., change "If in these instructions any rule is repeated, no emphasis there-on is intended; for that reason, you must consider these instructions as a whole; the

10. Avoid embedding subordinate clauses in sentences; e.g., "you must not speculate *to be true* any insinuation *suggested by a question asked a witness.*"

MITCHELL v. GONZALES

Supreme Court of California, 1991.
54 Cal.3d 1041, 1 Cal.Rptr.2d 913, 819 P.2d 872.

■ Lucas, Chief Justice.

In this case we decide whether BAJI No. 3.75,[1] the so-called proximate cause instruction, which contains a "but for" test of cause in fact, should continue to be given in this state, or whether it should be disapproved in favor of BAJI No. 3.76, the so-called legal cause instruction, which employs the "substantial factor" test of cause in fact.[2]

Plaintiffs James and Joyce Mitchell, the parents of 12–year–old Damechie Mitchell, who drowned in Lake Gregory on July 4, 1985, sued defendants Jose L. Gonzales, Matilde Gonzales, and Mrs. Gonzales's son Luis (hereafter defendants) for damages, claiming defendants' negligence caused Damechie's death. By special verdict, the jury found that defendants were negligent, i.e., they had breached a duty, but that the negligence was not a proximate cause of the death.

The Court of Appeal concluded that, under the facts, the trial court erred when it denied plaintiffs' request to instruct the jury pursuant to BAJI No. 3.76 and instead instructed under BAJI No. 3.75. After reviewing both instructions, the Court of Appeal concluded that BAJI No. 3.75 is potentially misleading and should not have been given, and that the trial court committed prejudicial error when it refused to give BAJI No. 3.76.

We granted review in this case to determine whether courts should continue to instruct juries on cause in fact using BAJI No. 3.75 in light of the frequent criticism of that instruction.

order in which they are given has no significance" to "There are three things you must keep in mind: first, repetition of an instruction does not mean I am emphasizing it; second, you must consider all the instructions together; and third, the order has no significance.")

1. All BAJI [Book of Approved Jury Instructions] instructions referred to are from the bound volume of the seventh edition (1986) unless otherwise noted.

2. BAJI No. 3.75, requested by defendants and given by the trial court, provides: "A proximate cause of [injury] [damage] [loss] [or] [harm] is a cause which, in natural and continuous sequence, produces the [injury] [damage] [loss] [or] [harm] and without which the [injury] [damage] [loss] [or] [harm] would not have occurred." Because of the "without which" language, courts often refer to this instruction as the "but for" instruction of causation.

BAJI No. 3.76, requested by plaintiffs and refused by the trial court, provides: "A legal cause of [injury] [damage] [loss] [or] [harm] is a cause which is a substantial factor in bringing about the [injury] [damage] [loss] [or] [harm]."

[A]lleged Instructional Error

As Dean Prosser observed over 40 years ago, "Proximate cause remains a tangle and a jungle, a palace of mirrors and a maze...." Cases "indicate that 'proximate cause' covers a multitude of sins, that it is a complex term of highly uncertain meaning under which other rules, doctrines and reasons lie buried...." (Prosser, Proximate Cause in California (1950) 38 Cal.L.Rev. 369, 375.)

[T]he misunderstanding engendered by the term "proximate cause" has been documented. In a scholarly study of 14 jury instructions, BAJI No. 3.75 produced proportionally the most misunderstanding among laypersons. (Charrow, *Making Legal Language Understandable: A Psycholinguistic Study of Jury Instructions* (1979) 79 Colum.L.Rev. 1306, 1353 (hereafter *Psycholinguistic Study).*) The study noted two significant problems with BAJI No. 3.75. First, because the phrase "natural and continuous sequence" precedes "the verb it is intended to modify, the construction leaves the listener with the impression that the cause itself is in a natural and continuous sequence. Inasmuch as a single 'cause' cannot be in a continuous sequence, the listener is befuddled." (*Psycholinguistic Study,* supra, 79 Colum.L.Rev. at p. 1323.) Second, in one experiment, "the term 'proximate cause' was misunderstood by 23% of the subjects.... They interpreted it as 'approximate cause,' 'estimated cause,' or some fabrication." (Id., at p. 1353.)

[W]e recognize that BAJI No. 3.76 is not perfectly phrased. The term "legal cause" may be confusing. As part of the psycholinguistic study referred to above, the experimenters rewrote BAJI No. 3.75 to include the term "legal cause."[8] The study found that "25% of the subjects who heard 'legal cause' misinterpreted it as the opposite of an 'illegal cause.' We would therefore recommend that the term 'legal cause' not be used in jury instructions; instead, the simple term 'cause' should be used, with the explanation that the law defines 'cause' in its own particular way."[9] (*Psycholinguistic Study,* supra, 79 Colum.L.Rev. at p. 1353.)

[T]he continued use of BAJI No. 3.75 as an instruction on cause in fact is unwise. The foregoing amply demonstrates that BAJI No. 3.75 is grammatically confusing and conceptually misleading. Continued use of this instruction will likely cause needless appellate litigation regarding the propriety of the instructions in particular cases. Use of BAJI No. 3.76 will avoid much of the confusion inherent in BAJI No. 3.75. It is intelligible and easily applied. We therefore conclude that BAJI No. 3.75, the so-called proximate cause instruction, should be disapproved and that the court

---

8. The modified instruction read, "A legal cause of an injury is something that triggers a natural chain of events that ultimately produces the injury. [ ] Without the legal cause, the injury would not occur." (*Psycholinguistic Study,* supra, 79 Colum.L.Rev. at p. 1352.)

9. Although we need not decide whether BAJI No. 3.76 should be rewritten to eliminate the term "legal cause," we do suggest that the Committee on Standard Jury Instructions consider whether the instruction could be improved by adopting the suggestion of the *Psycholinguistic Study* or by otherwise modifying the instruction.

erred when it refused to give BAJI No. 3.76 and instead gave BAJI No. 3.75. [A]ccordingly, the decision of the Court of Appeal reversing the judgment in favor of defendants is affirmed.

————

DECIDING ON DEATH: REVISING JURY INSTRUCTIONS TO IMPROVE JUROR COMPREHENSION OF THE LAW

7 Researching Law: An ABF Update 1 (1996).

In 1972 the Supreme Court, in *Furman v. Georgia*, invalidated the death penalty statutes of thirty-five states on the grounds that the broad discretion under which juries operated in imposing the death penalty was producing arbitrary and inconsistent decisions in violation of the Eighth and Fourteenth Amendments. In setting forth a new standard of guided discretion, the Court held in later cases that states could constitutionally execute offenders if jurors were told what factors to consider and how they should be weighed. But a study* conducted by [American Bar Foundation] Research Fellow Shari Diamond, in collaboration with Professor Judith Levi, has found that the instructions jurors receive in some capital cases do not provide sufficient guidance and that jury deliberations cannot be relied on to reduce the high level of miscomprehension. In an experiment with jury-eligible citizens, Diamond and Levi found that a revised set of instructions that addressed sources of juror confusion did increase comprehension substantially.

Incorrect Interpretations

It was not until 1991 that a court was persuaded by scientific evidence that jury instructions in a capital case were unconstitutional because "they failed to provide jurors with a clear understanding of the law," the researchers note. The issue arose in a hearing on the capital habeas corpus petition of James Free, an Illinois death row inmate. A magistrate judge recommended that the petition be granted on the ground that survey evidence had "raised serious questions about the ability of Illinois capital jury instructions to provide the constitutionally requisite guidance to the jury."

The survey had been conducted by the late Professor Hans Zeisel. Jurors in a Chicago courthouse were asked to hear and read both a description of the evidence from a trial and capital sentencing hearing and the jury instructions used in the sentencing hearing. They then read a series of juror decisions and were asked whether the hypothetical juror had correctly followed the judge's instruction.

———

* [Ed note: Diamond and Levi, Improving Decisions on Death by Revising and Test- ing Jury Instructions, 79 Judicature 224 (1996)].

The sixteen questions on the survey were designed to test understanding of several key legal issues, including:

- Unenumerated Mitigators—whether jurors understand that they may consider any reason supported by the evidence as a possible mitigator, not just those enumerated in the instructions or comparable to them.

- Nonunanimity in Mitigation—whether jurors understand that one juror can identify a factor (like age) as a mitigator even if other jurors do not agree that it should be considered.

- Weighing—whether jurors understand that the law asks jurors to weigh the aggravating and mitigating factors, rather than to assume that death is the appropriate sentence unless mitigating factors are sufficient to overcome that presumption.

Respondents did not perform well on the Zeisel survey, the authors note. A majority of the respondents gave the correct answer on only three of the sixteen questions. On eleven of the sixteen questions, "the majority explicitly gave the incorrect answer (rather than the correct answer or 'do not know.')"

After extensive hearings on the quality of evidence, the magistrate judge concluded that the instructions were not "intelligible and definite enough to provide even a majority of jurors hearing them with a clear understanding of how they are to go about deciding whether the defendant lives or dies." He then found that the jury instructions violated the Eighth and Fourteenth amendments because they permitted arbitrary and unguided imposition of the death penalty. The Federal District Court judge accepted the magistrate's recommendation and vacated the death sentence pending a resentencing. But later, the Seventh Circuit voted two to one to reinstate Free's death sentence "on the ground that it was offered as the basis for a new rule and was produced after the judgment in *Free* had become final." However, Judge Posner, writing for the majority, did not reject the position "that an instruction in a death penalty case could be constitutionally defective if empirical evidence indicated that jurors were confused by it." But Posner had two concerns about the Zeisel survey. He noted first that "jurors simply might not be good test takers" but still might be able to perform effectively in the juryroom. Posner also considered the absence of a control group to be "fatal" because the study could not demonstrate that "performance would be better if the instructions were rewritten." Joining the opinion, Judge Bauer raised a third issue—the survey did not capture the effect of deliberations. That is, initial misunderstanding might be cured after a juror has a chance to discuss the instructions with fellow jurors.

Experimenting With Revised Instructions

Diamond and Levi designed their study to respond to some of the issues raised by the Seventh Circuit in *Free*. They preserved the basic format of the Zeisel study but made two changes in the research design:

- The jury instructions were rewritten so that "we could see whether the responses of jury-eligible citizens to the original and the revised instructions would differ." Adding a "control" group would test whether the revised instructions provided clear guidance to jurors and whether the poor juror performance in the original survey "was attributable merely to the test-taking ability of jurors."

- To test whether deliberations improved juror comprehension of instructions, half the participants in the new study were given the opportunity to deliberate as jurors.

Participants in the study were 170 jury-eligible persons. Of this number, 21 were excluded from the study because their responses to a questionnaire indicated either that they would always favor the death penalty for anyone convicted of a capital crime or that [their attitude against the death penalty would substantially impair their ability to find a defendant guilty or] to vote as a juror for the death penalty. The remaining 149 death-qualified jurors, in groups of 12 to 16, listened to an audiotaped description of the evidence in the guilt phase and the sentencing phase of James Free's trial, and to an audiotape of jury instructions, either the Illinois Pattern Jury Instructions for capital cases or the researchers' revised version of those instructions.

One group of six jurors from each session was then randomly selected to deliberate. The remaining jurors individually answered written questions "designed to elicit their understanding of what these instructions told them about how jurors should apply the law." At the end of the questions, the jurors were asked "whether they were leaning toward or against a death sentence." The deliberating jurors also answered the same set of questions when they finished their discussion.

The revised instructions addressed general linguistic problems, such as ambiguous vocabulary, but also attempted to clarify the three major legal points that appeared to confuse jurors in the Zeisel survey.

- Unenumerated mitigators, which were treated tersely in the pattern instructions, were placed in a more prominent position in the revised instructions, and the instruction was expanded considerably to provide "more detailed guidance on identifying mitigating factors beyond the enumerated ones."

- The text on mitigating factors in the pattern instructions "obscures or simply fails to express" the fact that decisions on mitigators need not be unanimous and that jurors have individual discretion. The revised instructions expanded the text and state explicitly, "Illinois law permits each juror to decide for himself or herself whether one or more mitigating factors exist. . . . [T]he jury does NOT need to reach a unanimous decision about what counts as a mitigating factor."

- The pattern instructions simply tell the jurors to consider the aggravating and mitigating factors. There is no mention of weighing or balancing. Further, the researchers note, "the wording of the pattern instructions suggested that the default sentence is death." The revised instructions have a more balanced vocabulary. "In references to the penalty ..., the word *death* occurs only 57% of the time (rather than 100%), while the word *imprisonment* appears 33% of the time (rather than never). The words *weigh, weight,* or *outweigh* appear seventeen times in the revised instructions but never in the pattern instructions." Further, a revised instructions include a section on weighing aggravating and mitigating factors that "explains in detail which decisions are to be made by individual jurors, which decisions by the jury as a whole, and the relation between those two kinds of decisions."

Improved Comprehension

In analyzing the responses, Diamond and Levi found that the revised jury instructions increased juror comprehension levels significantly. The percentage of correct responses increased on average from 50% to 65%; incorrect responses dropped from an average of 45% to 30%. The revised instructions also produced substantial improvement in comprehension of the three issues raised in *Free*:

- The greatest improvement occurred on the issue of Unenumerated Mitigators, moving from an average of 41% correct to an average of 58% correct. Percent correct on questions about Weighing increased from 51% to 66%. However, the opportunity to deliberate did not further increase comprehension levels on these two issues.

- Comprehension also increased significantly on questions related to Nonunamity on Mitigators with the revised instructions. Moreover, deliberation was found to increase comprehension on this issue: nondeliberators averaged 67% correct while jurors who deliberated averaged 79% correct. The isolated positive effect of deliberation on this issue also "suggests why earlier studies have shown little or no effect of deliberation on comprehension," the authors note. Their findings indicate, "that deliberation can be depended upon to improve comprehension only when a substantial majority of the members of a jury begin deliberations with a correct understanding of the information at issue."

- Using the deliberating jurors as a basis for comparison, revising the instructions (a single rewrite in this case) was found to increase the performance of deliberating jurors on average from 52% to 67%. Agreeing on an acceptable level of comprehension is a policy issue, not a research question, the authors note, but the results indicate "that a comprehension level of 52% is a cost that neither the legal system as a whole, nor capital defendants in particular, need pay in capital sentencing hearings."

Diamond and Levi reviewed the content of juror discussions during deliberations to determine how the revised instructions "produced greater clarity." They found that "the revised instructions encouraged jurors to consider unenumerated mitigating factors, to determine individually what mitigators are worthy of consideration, and to apply a weighing standard in reaching a decision on the appropriate penalty."

Since the revised instructions gave more attention to mitigation and the weighing standard, it was expected that jurors who received them would be less likely to favor the death penalty than those receiving the pattern instructions, and this was confirmed by the data. However, the authors state, the difference was of only borderline statistical significance. Because the sample was small and the analysis based on one question, the researchers note that further research is needed to determine if this finding holds up. Some additional supporting evidence, however, could be gleaned from this study: Jurors who understood the instructions better were significantly less likely to lean toward a sentence of death.

The research findings support "the District Court's original conclusion that James Free was sentenced to death by a jury that received unnecessarily confusing instructions," the authors argue, "but they came too late for Mr. Free. He was executed on March 22, 1995."

Their experience in this research suggested to Diamond and Levi that the best way to identify and remedy comprehension problems in jury instructions, such as discrepancies between legal terminology and common usage, is through collaborations among attorneys and/or judges, psychologists, and linguists. Further, they say, obtaining input from jurors in posttrial interviews or in simulations can identify "sources of miscomprehension and unintended meanings." Finally, the researchers note, revising instructions is not sufficient. They must be tested to determine when "an acceptable level of performance has been achieved" and to identify areas for further improvement. And the revision and testing process should begin in sentencing hearings, they maintain. "In view of the constitutionally-mandated guidance required in capital cases, improving the clarity of death penalty instructions would appear to be an appropriate and indeed a necessary place to institute reform."

UNITED STATES v. I. LEWIS LIBBY

United States District Court, District of Columbia, 2006.
461 F.Supp.2d 3.

■ REGGIE B. WALTON, DISTRICT JUDGE.

On October 26, 2006, this Court heard extensive testimony and argument on the defendant's motion to admit the expert testimony of Dr. Robert A. Bjork. Specifically, the defendant opines that he should be permitted to introduce the testimony of Dr. Bjork "regarding [what he characterizes as] the widely-accepted findings from the science of memory."

[T]he defendant is charged in a five-count indictment with obstruction of justice in violation of 18 U.S.C. § 1503 (2000), two counts of false statements in violation of 18 U.S.C. § 1001(a)(2) (2000), and two counts of perjury in violation of 18 U.S.C. § 1623 (2000). All of these charges arise from a criminal investigation into the possible unauthorized disclosure of classified information—Valerie Plame Wilson's affiliation with the Central

Intelligence Agency ("CIA")—to several journalists. [T]he alleged false statements occurred when the defendant recounted conversations he had in June and July 2003, with news reporters Tim Russert, Judith Miller, and Matthew Cooper to the FBI Agents and to the grand jury.

The defendant has made clear that in his effort to rebut these charges he will argue, in part, (1) that it is the government's witnesses, and not him, who misremembered the facts and the substance of the various conversations detailed in the indictment and (2) that any errors he may have made in describing the events were occasioned by confusion or faulty memory, not any wilful intent to misrepresent the truth. This Court has acknowledged that this "faulty memory defense" is a viable defense to the charges.

[T]o support his faulty memory defense, the defendant seeks to introduce at trial the testimony of Dr. Bjork "to show that it is entirely plausible, given how memory has been found to function, that Mr. Libby or the government witnesses-or both-have innocently confused or misremembered the conversations on which this case turns." Specifically, Dr. Bjork would testify about thirteen scientific principles concerning human memory, including the process by which memory is encoded, stored, retained, and retrieved and various scientific bases for memory errors including "content borrowing," source misattribution, subsequent recall, divided attention, and "retroactive interference." According to the defendant, Dr. Bjork's expert testimony "will assist the jury by providing information about the findings of memory research that are not already known to the jurors." It is the admissibility of Dr. Bjork's testimony under Federal Rule of Evidence 702 that is the subject of this opinion.

[C]entral to the court's determination of whether expert testimony is admissible under Rule 702, and consistent with the Rule's purpose, is the two-prong test enunciated by the Supreme Court in *Daubert v. Merrell Dow Pharm.,* 509 U.S. 579 (1993). Under this test, a court determining the admissibility of purported expert testimony must first determine "[1] whether the reasoning or methodology underlying the testimony is scientifically valid and [2] whether that reasoning or methodology properly can be applied to the facts in issue." *Id.* at 592–93.

The government does not challenge the proposed testimony of Dr. Bjork on the grounds that his testimony fails to satisfy the first prong of *Daubert,* noting that it "does not quibble with Dr. Bjork's expertise concerning research into memory, particularly with respect to the reliability of eyewitness identification."[6] Rather, the government contends that the

---

6. Although a former member of this Court concluded almost twenty years ago that the "psychodynamics of memory and perception" are not sufficiently scientifically reliable to permit an expert to testify on the subject, *Robertson v. McCloskey,* 676 F.Supp. 351, 355 (D.D.C.1988), this conclusion hardly remains good law. [B]ased upon a review of the scientific literature provided to the Court, there can be little doubt that today (as opposed to twenty years ago) the science of memory is well established and accepted in the scientific community, and the subject of Dr. Bjork's testimony has been well tested and subjected to peer review. Moreover, Dr. Bjork's curriculum vitae and a review of his defendant "cannot meet his burden as the proponent of the evidence of establishing that the testimony will assist the jury in understanding or determining any of the facts at issue in this case." Thus, this is the only question the Court must resolve.

[T]o support his argument that Dr. Bjork's testimony will be helpful to the jury, the defendant relies on various studies, which he avers stand for the proposition that "jurors are generally unaware of the frequency and causes of honest errors of recollection, and that they underestimate the fallibility of memory." As further support for his position, the defendant offered the testimony of Dr. Elizabeth Loftus, who detailed her belief, based upon her research and the research of others, that many of the principles which Dr. Bjork would testify to are not commonly understood by jurors.

[T]he studies relied upon by the defendant were based upon research that examined prospective juror understanding of factors that could impact the reliability of eyewitness identifications. *See, e.g.,* R. Schmechel, T. O'Toole, C. Easterly, & E. Loftus, *Beyond the Ken? Testing Jurors' Understanding of Eyewitness Reliability Evidence,* 46 Jurimetrics J. 177–214 (2006) (*"Beyond the Ken"*) (noting that this survey "would discern what potential District of Columbia jurors understood about memory in general and *the reliability of eyewitness identification evidence in particular."*) (emphasis added). This Court cannot accept the proposition that the research findings concerning juror knowledge of factors impacting the reliability of eyewitness identification applies equally to juror knowledge of the factors that impact memory and cognition in other contexts, such as the memory and recall of conversations. Thus, while the defendant has proffered numerous scientific studies describing how memory functions, the research showing that jurors do not understand these concepts is limited to the application of the concepts in the discrete area of eyewitness identification and its findings have limited, if any, applicability in other respects.[9]

[T]here can be little doubt that the average juror is not regularly, if at all, presented with issues of eyewitness identification of an alleged perpetrator of a criminal offense. Thus, it is highly probable that the average juror would be less familiar with concepts that may impact a witness's identification such as weapons focus, mug-shot-induced bias, or lineup format. However, on a daily basis the average juror is personally faced with innumerable questions of memory and cognition, as everyone in their daily lives is called upon to store, encode, and retrieve information he or she has been subjected to. Although the average juror may not understand the scientific basis and labels attached to causes for memory errors, jurors

research demonstrates that he is eminently qualified to testify on the subject of memory and perception. Thus, even if the government had raised an objection on this point, it could not be sustained.

9. In addition, this Court has difficulty placing significant weight on this study because it is quite clear from reading this article that it is more an article of advocacy than a piece of scientific literature. First, the principal authors of *Beyond the Ken* are attorneys (public defenders), not psychologists. And, Dr. Loftus noted during her testimony that these attorneys contacted her to participate in this research, thereby acknowledging that the attorneys (as opposed to the researcher) were the driving force behind this study.

inevitably encounter the frailties of memory as a commonplace matter of course. *See, e.g., United States v. Welch,* 368 F.3d 970, 973–75 (7th Cir.2004) ("[a]lthough the average person may not know what the term 'clothing bias' means, it is common knowledge that one may mistake a person for someone else who is similarly dressed. Moreover, the typical juror would know that two people who are structurally similar are more likely to be confused for each other than are dissimilar individuals. Finally, it does not require an expert witness to point out that memory decreases over time."); *United States v. Labansat,* 94 F.3d 527, 530 (9th Cir.1996) ("[i]t is common knowledge that memory fades with time"). Thus, this Court has no doubt that the average juror understands that if, for example, A learns from B that B had been on vacation in Hawaii and then later learns from C that she spent her vacation in Jamaica, that A could later misremember where each spent their vacations because he was consumed with pressing matters, either when he acquired this information, when he was asked to recall it, and possibly at any time in between. Accordingly, the jury does not need a tutorial on the science of "content borrowing," "memory conjunction," or "source misattribution" errors to appreciate that people sometimes experience mistaken memories. [A]nd as the Court has already indicated, it is prepared to provide the jury with an instruction that will remind them of the factors they may consider in accessing the accuracy of memory.

Based on the foregoing, the Court cannot conclude that the defendant has satisfied his burden of establishing that the expert testimony of Dr. Bjork will be helpful to the jury. Not only are the studies offered by the defendant inapposite to the situation here, but the theories upon which Dr. Bjork would testify are not beyond the ken of the average juror. And as the facts of this case unfold during the trial, the Court has no doubt that aided by the normal trial processes, and the assistance of very capable legal counsel, the jurors will have the ability to collectively draw upon their common-sense understanding of memory and render a fair and just verdict. [T]he defendant's motion to present the testimony of Dr. Bjork must therefore be denied.

———

UNITED STATES v. I. LEWIS LIBBY

United States District Court, District of Columbia.
Defendant's Proposed Jury Instruction, Filed November 13, 2006.*

Findings from the Science of Memory

As you have heard, the defense contends that Mr. Libby confused, forgot, or misremembered all or parts of some of the conversations that you

* [Ed. Note: After Judge Walton denied the defendant's motion to introduce Dr. Bjork as an expert witness, above, defense counsel for Mr. Libby proposed that these instructions be given to the jury.]

have heard about during the trial. In considering this argument, it is appropriate for you to take into account the following:

1.   Human memory does not function like a tape recorder, with memories recorded, retained and played back verbatim. Stored memories may not remain in the same form over time and can be altered by memories of events and information already stored in a person's brain or by the person's later experiences.

2.   People can create inaccurate memories of real events or even seemingly real memories of events that did not occur. A person may unintentionally combine memories of two distinct events to form a composite memory that seems real but is not. To give a simple example, a person who has read the sentences "I went to the dance with Susan" and "I went skating with Alice" might incorrectly recall seeing the sentence "I went to the dance with Alice" or "I went skating with Susan."

3.   People sometimes recall accurately the substance of information but attribute the information to an incorrect source. Thus, a person may recall correctly what was said during a conversation but misidentify the individual with whom he had that conversation. A person might also misidentify the source of information if he is paying attention to several things at once when he attempts to retrieve the memory.

4.   A person is less likely to remember information accurately if he is paying attention to several things at once at the same time he receives the information.

5.   A person is more likely to remember accurately information that is important to him than information that is unimportant to him.

6.   If a person remembers an event incorrectly the first time he tries to recall it, his later recollections of the event are likely to repeat that error.

7.   A person's confidence in the accuracy of his recollection of an event has little, if any, relation to the accuracy of the person's recollection. In other words, a person may be very confident that his memory of an event is accurate when in fact it is inaccurate.

8.   Also, just as people can forget events, people can forget that they once recalled an event. This is especially likely to occur when a person attempts to recall an event that he has previously been able to recall, but under different conditions or in a different context.

9.   Further, a person's ability to recall precisely what was said during a conversation, as well as the gist of the conversation, may drop significantly after a period of even a few days. The decline in one's ability to remember the details of a conversation occurs faster than the drop in one's ability to recall the gist of a conversation. Moreover, a person who only hears a conversation is less likely to recall the substance of the conversation accurately, and is more likely to recall information that was not part of the conversation, than a person who both hears and observes the conversation.

10.   Finally, providing a person with clues that certain information is out of date or otherwise not important hastens the forgetting of that informa-

tion and increases the possibility that any later attempt to recall that information will be faulty.

————

UNITED STATES v. I. LEWIS LIBBY

United States District Court, District of Columbia.
Transcript of Proceedings, February 21, 2007.

Jury Instructions by the Honorable Reggie B. Walton.*

In considering Mr. Libby's position and the testimony of any other witness whose memory is at issue, it is appropriate for you to take into account the following:

One, your assessment, based on your life experiences, of the capacity of human beings to remember things they said and were told when asked to recall those matters at a later point in time;

Two, the amount of time between when a person said or heard something and the impact the passage of time had on the person's memory to accurately recall those events;

Three, the circumstances that existed when the person was exposed to the events he or she is asked to recall;

Four, the nature of the information or the event the person is called upon to remember;

Five, the circumstances that existed when the person was asked to recall the earlier event;

Six, the circumstances that existed during the time between when the person was exposed to an event he or she is asked to recall and when that person was asked to recall the earlier event;

Seven, your assessment of the memory capacity of the person whose memory is in question; and

Eight, any evidence that was presented during this trial that shed light on any issues related to the memory of the individuals you have to assess in this trial.

————

NOTE

1. Outcome of the Libby Case. Mr. Libby was convicted by the jury of four of the five charges against him on March 6, 2007. He was sentenced by Judge Walton to 30 months' imprisonment, two years' supervised release,

———

* [Ed. Note: These are the actual instructions given by Judge Walton to the jury in the Libby case.]

and a fine of $250,000. On July 2, 2007, President G.W. Bush commuted the prison component of Libby's sentence.

SELECTED BIBLIOGRAPHY

Diamond, Instructing on Death, 48 American Psychologist 423 (1993).

Diamond and Levi, Improving Decisions on Death by Revising and Testing Jury Instructions, 79 Judicature 224 (1996).

Ellsworth and Reifman, Juror Comprehension and Public Policy: Perceived Problems and Proposed Solutions, 6 Psychology, Public Policy, and Law 788 (2000).

Haney and Lynch, Comprehending Life and Death Matters: A Preliminary Study of California's Capital Penalty Instructions, 18 Law and Human Behavior 411 (1994).

Hannaford, Hans, and Munsterman, Permitting Jury Discussion During Trial: Impact on the Arizona Reform, 24 Law and Human Behavior 359 (2000).

Kassam, Gilbert, Swencionis, and Wilson, Misconceptions of Memory: The Scooter Libby Effect, 20 Psychological Science 551 (2009).

Otto, Applegate, and Davis, Improving Comprehension of Capital Sentencing Instructions: Debunking Juror Misconceptions, 53 Crime & Delinquency 502 (2007).

Paglia and Schuller, Jurors' Use of Hearsay Evidence: The Effects of Type and Timing of Instructions, 22 Law and Human Behavior 501 (1998).

Rose and Ogloff, Evaluating the Comprehensibility of Jury Instructions: A Method and an Example, 25 Law and Human Behavior 409 (2001).

Saks, Flying Blind In The Courtroom: Trying Cases Without Knowing What Works or Why, 101 Yale Law Journal 1177 (1992).

Stoffelmayr and Diamond, The Conflict Between Precision and Flexibility in Explaining "Beyond a Reasonable Doubt," 6 Psychology, Public Policy, and Law 769 (2000).

Terrance, Matheson, and Spanos, Effects of Judicial Instructions and Case Characteristics in a Mock Jury Trial of Battered Women Who Kill, 24 Law and Human Behavior 207 (2000).

Vidmar and Wolfe, Fairness Through Guidance: Jury Instruction on Punitive Damages After *Phillip Morris v. Williams*, 2 Charleston Law Review 307 (2008).

Wissler, Kuehn, and Saks, Instructing Jurors on General Damages in Personal Injury Cases: Problems and Possibilities, 6 Psychology, Public Policy, and Law 712 (2000).

Wissler, Rector and Saks, The Impact of Jury Instructions on the Fusion of Liability and Compensatory Damages, 25 Law and Human Behavior 125 (2001).

*

APPENDIX A

FEDERAL RULES OF EVIDENCE

Rule 104. Preliminary Questions

(a) **Questions of admissibility generally.** Preliminary questions concerning the qualification of a person to be a witness, the existence of a privilege, or the admissibility of evidence shall be determined by the court, subject to the provisions of subdivision (b). In making its determination it is not bound by the rules of evidence except those with respect to privileges.

(b) **Relevancy conditioned on fact.** When the relevancy of evidence depends upon the fulfillment of a condition of fact, the court shall admit it upon, or subject to, the introduction of evidence sufficient to support a finding of the fulfillment of the condition.

(c) **Hearing of jury.** Hearings on the admissibility of confessions shall in all cases be conducted out of the hearing of the jury. Hearings on other preliminary matters shall be so conducted when the interests of justice require, or when an accused is a witness and so requests.

(d) **Testimony by accused.** The accused does not, by testifying upon a preliminary matter, become subject to cross-examination as to other issues in the case.

(e) **Weight and credibility.** This rule does not limit the right of a party to introduce before the jury evidence relevant to weight or credibility.

Rule 201. Judicial Notice of Adjudicative Facts*

(a) **Scope of rule.** This rule governs only judicial notice of adjudicative facts.

(b) **Kinds of facts.** A judicially noticed fact must be one not subject to reasonable dispute in that it is either (1) generally known within the territorial jurisdiction of the trial court or (2) capable of accurate and ready determination by resort to sources whose accuracy cannot reasonably be questioned.

---

* Advisory Committee's Note

56 F.R.D. 183, 201

Subdivision (a). This is the only evidence rule on the subject of judicial notice. It deals only with judicial notice of "adjudicative" facts. No rule deals with judicial notice of "legislative" facts. Judicial notice of matters of foreign law is treated in Rule 44.1 of the Federal Rules of Civil Procedure and Rule 26.1 of the Federal Rules of Criminal Procedure.

The omission of any treatment of legislative facts results from fundamental differences between adjudicative facts and legislative facts. Adjudicative facts are simply the facts of the particular case. Legislative facts, on the other hand, are those which have relevance to legal reasoning and the lawmaking process, whether in the formulation of a legal principle or ruling by a judge or court or in the enactment of a legislative body. The terminology was coined by Professor Kenneth Davis in his article An Approach to Problems of Evidence in the Administrative Process, 55 Harv.L.Rev. 364, 404–407 (1942).

(c) When discretionary. A court may take judicial notice, whether requested or not.

(d) When mandatory. A court shall take judicial notice if requested by a party and supplied with the necessary information.

(e) Opportunity to be heard. A party is entitled upon timely request to an opportunity to be heard as to the propriety of taking judicial notice and the tenor of the matter noticed. In the absence of prior notification, the request may be made after judicial notice has been taken.

(f) Time of taking notice. Judicial notice may be taken at any stage of the proceeding.

(g) Instructing jury. In a civil action or proceeding, the court shall instruct the jury to accept as conclusive any fact judicially noticed. In a criminal case, the court shall instruct the jury that it may, but is not required to, accept as conclusive any fact judicially noticed.

Rule 401.   Definition of "Relevant Evidence"

"Relevant evidence" means evidence having any tendency to make the existence of any fact that is of consequence to the determination of the action more probable or less probable than it would be without the evidence.

Rule 402.   Relevant Evidence Generally Admissible; Irrelevant Evidence Inadmissible

All relevant evidence is admissible, except as otherwise provided by the Constitution of the United States, by Act of Congress, by these rules, or by other rules prescribed by the Supreme Court pursuant to statutory authority. Evidence which is not relevant is not admissible.

Rule 403.   Exclusion of Relevant Evidence on Grounds of Prejudice, Confusion, or Waste of Time

Although relevant, evidence may be excluded if its probative value is substantially outweighed by the danger of unfair prejudice, confusion of the issues, or misleading the jury, or by considerations of undue delay, waste of time, or needless presentation of cumulative evidence.

Rule 404.   Character Evidence Not Admissible to Prove Conduct; Exceptions; Other Crimes

(a) Character evidence generally. Evidence of a person's character or a trait of character is not admissible for the purpose of proving action in conformity therewith on a particular occasion, except:

(1) Character of accused. In a criminal case, evidence of a pertinent trait of character offered by an accused, or by the prosecution to rebut the same, or if evidence of a trait of character of the alleged victim of the crime is offered by an accused and admitted under Rule 404 (a)(2), evidence of the same trait of character of the accused offered by the prosecution;

(2) Character of alleged victim. In a criminal case, and subject to the limitations imposed by Rule 412, evidence of a pertinent trait of character of the alleged victim of the crime offered by an accused, or by the prosecution to rebut the same, or evidence of a character trait of peacefulness of the alleged victim offered by the prosecution in a homicide case to rebut evidence that the alleged victim was the first aggressor;

[(b)] Other crimes, wrongs, or acts. Evidence of other crimes, wrongs, or acts is not admissible to prove the character of a person in order to show action in conformity therewith. It may, however, be admissible for other purposes, such as proof of motive, opportunity, intent, preparation, plan, knowledge, identity, or absence of mistake or accident.

Rule 412. Sex Offense Cases; Relevance of Alleged Victim's Past Sexual Behavior or Alleged Sexual Predisposition

(a) Evidence generally inadmissible. The following evidence is not admissible in any civil or criminal proceeding involving alleged sexual misconduct except as provided in subdivisions (b) and (c):

(1) Evidence offered to prove that any alleged victim engaged in other sexual behavior.

(2) Evidence offered to prove any alleged victim's sexual predisposition.

(b) Exceptions.

(1) In a criminal case, the following evidence is admissible, if otherwise admissible under these rules:

(A) evidence of specific instances of sexual behavior by the alleged victim offered to prove that a person other than the accused was the source of semen, injury, or other physical evidence;

(B) evidence of specific instances of sexual behavior by the alleged victim with respect to the person accused of the sexual misconduct offered by the accused to prove consent or by the prosecution; and

(C) evidence the exclusion of which would violate the constitutional rights of the defendant.

(2) In a civil case, evidence offered to prove the sexual behavior or sexual predisposition of any alleged victim is admissible if it is otherwise admissible under these rules and its probative value substantially outweighs the danger of harm to any victim and of unfair prejudice to any party. Evidence of an alleged victim's reputation is admissible only if it has been placed in controversy by the alleged victim.

(c) Procedure to determine admissibility.

(1) A party intending to offer evidence under subdivision (b) must—

(A) file a written motion at least 14 days before trial specifically describing the evidence and stating the purpose for which it is offered unless the court, for good cause requires a different time for filing or permits filing during trial; and

(B) serve the motion on all parties and notify the alleged victim or, when appropriate, the alleged victim's guardian or representative.

(2) Before admitting evidence under this rule the court must conduct a hearing in camera and afford the victim and parties a right to attend and be heard. The motion, related papers, and the record of the hearing must be sealed and remain under seal unless the court orders otherwise.

Rule 701. Opinion Testimony by Lay Witnesses

If the witness is not testifying as an expert, the witness' testimony in the form of opinions or inferences is limited to those opinions or inferences which are (a) rationally based on the perception of the witness, and (b) helpful to a clear understanding of the witness' testimony or the determination of a fact in issue, and (c) not based on scientific, technical, or other specialized knowledge within the scope of Rule 702.

Rule 702. Testimony by Experts

If scientific, technical, or other specialized knowledge will assist the trier of fact to understand the evidence or to determine a fact in issue, a witness qualified as an expert by knowledge, skill, experience, training, or education, may testify thereto in the form of an opinion or otherwise, if (1) the testimony is based upon sufficient facts or data, (2) the testimony is the product of reliable principles and methods, and (3) the witness has applied the principles and methods reliably to the facts of the case.

Rule 703. Bases of Opinion Testimony by Experts

The facts or data in the particular case upon which an expert bases an opinion or inference may be those perceived by or made known to the expert at or before the hearing. If of a type reasonably relied upon by experts in the particular field in forming opinions or inferences upon the subject, the facts or data need not be admissible in evidence in order for the opinion or inference to be admitted. Facts or data that are otherwise inadmissible shall not be disclosed to the jury by the proponent of the opinion or inference unless the court determines that their probative value in assisting the jury to evaluate the expert's opinion substantially outweighs their prejudicial effect.

Rule 704. Opinion on Ultimate Issue

(a) Except as provided in subdivision (b), testimony in the form of an opinion or inference otherwise admissible is not objectionable because it embraces an ultimate issue to be decided by the trier of fact.

(b) No expert witness testifying with respect to the mental state or condition of a defendant in a criminal case may state an opinion or inference as to whether the defendant did or did not have the mental state or condition constituting an element of the crime charged or of a defense thereto. Such ultimate issues are matters for the trier of fact alone.

Rule 705. Disclosure of Facts or Data Underlying Expert Opinion

The expert may testify in terms of opinion or inference and give reasons therefor without first testifying to the underlying facts or data, unless the court requires otherwise. The expert may in any event be required to disclose the underlying facts or data on cross-examination.

Rule 706. Court Appointed Experts

(a) Appointment. The court may on its own motion or on the motion of any party enter an order to show cause why expert witnesses should not be appointed, and may request the parties to submit nominations. The court may appoint any expert witnesses agreed upon by the parties, and may appoint expert witnesses of its own selection. An expert witness shall not be appointed by the court unless the witness consents to act. A witness so appointed shall be informed of the witness' duties by the court in writing, a copy of which shall be filed with the clerk, or at a conference in which the parties shall have opportunity to participate. A witness so appointed shall advise the parties of the witness' findings, if any; the witness' deposition may be taken by any party; and the witness may be called to testify by the court or any party. The witness shall be subject to cross-examination by each party, including a party calling the witness.

(b) Compensation. Expert witnesses so appointed are entitled to reasonable compensation in whatever sum the court may allow. The compensation thus fixed is payable from funds which may be provided by law in criminal cases and civil actions and proceedings involving just compensation under the fifth amendment. In other civil actions and proceedings the compensation shall be paid by the parties in such proportion and at such time as the court directs, and thereafter charged in like manner as other costs.

(c) Disclosure of appointment. In the exercise of its discretion, the court may authorize disclosure to the jury of the fact that the court appointed the expert witness.

(d) Parties' experts of own selection. Nothing in this rule limits the parties in calling expert witnesses of their own selection.

Rule 801. Definitions

The following definitions apply under this article:

(a) Statement. A "statement" is (1) an oral or written assertion or (2) nonverbal conduct of a person, if it is intended by the person as an assertion.

(b) Declarant. A "declarant" is a person who makes a statement.

(c) Hearsay. "Hearsay" is a statement, other than one made by the declarant while testifying at the trial or hearing, offered in evidence to prove the truth of the matter asserted.

Rule 802.   Hearsay Rule

Hearsay is not admissible except as provided by these rules or by other rules prescribed by the Supreme Court pursuant to statutory authority or by Act of Congress.

Rule 803.   Hearsay Exceptions; Availability of Declarant Immaterial

The following are not excluded by the hearsay rule, even though the declarant is available as a witness:

(1) Present sense impression. A statement describing or explaining an event or condition made while the declarant was perceiving the event or condition, or immediately thereafter.

[18]   Learned treaties. To the extent called to the attention of an expert witness upon cross-examination or relied upon by the expert witness in direct examination, statements contained in published treatises, periodicals, or pamphlets on a subject of history, medicine, or other science or art, established as a reliable authority by the testimony or admission of the witness or by other expert testimony or by judicial notice. If admitted, the statements may be read into evidence but may not be received as exhibits.

FOR LAWYERS: HOW TO FIND SOCIAL SCIENCE

When beginning a search for social science materials, it is often useful to get a broad perspective on the topic of interest. Just as casebooks and treatises provide summary overviews of the law, recent social science textbooks contain brief surveys and key references relevant to various topics. Textbook often cite recent articles, and the bibliographies of these articles will lead to many useful sources.

Familiarity with the following resources will aid more comprehensive efforts to find social science materials. While there is some overlap among these resources, many emphasize the publications of a specific discipline such as psychology or sociology. Since legal questions frequently cross social science disciplinary boundaries, it is often necessary to consult resources from more than one discipline.

Encyclopedias. A social sciences encyclopedia can provide a comprehensive overview of a topic, define and explain terminology, describe the issues that have been of most concern to social scientists, and provide references to leading texts and articles. The most comprehensive such work is the *International Encyclopedia of the Social & Behavioral Sciences* (26 vols., 2001), which covers fields ranging from anthropology to political science as well as general methods of social science research and scholarship. Several major encyclopedias are also published in more specific areas, such as *Encyclopedia of Psychology* (8 vols., 2000), and *Encyclopedia of Sociology* (5 vols., 2d ed. 2000). Some encyclopedias are particularly useful for interdisciplinary research because they provide both legal and social science perspectives. These include *Encyclopedia of Crime and Justice* (4 vols., 2d ed. 2002), *Encyclopedia of Law and Society* (3 vols., 2007), and *Encyclopedia of Psychology and Law* (2 vols., 2008). Some encyclopedias are available online through library websites as well as in print.

Journal Articles. Just as much of legal analysis is found in academic law reviews, scholarly journals in other disciplines are the places to track developments and find in-depth discussion of specific issues. Several resources for finding journal articles are available to students at most law schools. A few resources are available free on the Internet, such as Google Scholar <http://scholar.google.com> and PubMed <http://www.pubmed.gov>, the National Library of Medicine's comprehensive index of biomedical journals. Most, however, are accessible by subscription only, and a first research step should be consulting a library's website or talking to a librarian to learn what databases are available.

---

* Ed. Note: Appendix B and Appendix C were updated for this edition by Kent C. Olson of the University of Virginia School of Law.

JSTOR. One of the most useful multidisciplinary sources for journal articles is the subscription database JSTOR <http://www.jstor.org>, which provides full-text access to articles in hundreds of journals in several dozen fields of study. Articles can be found through keyword searches and retrieved in PDF format. A JSTOR search for the words "deterrent" and "capital punishment" in the titles of articles, for example, finds more than twenty articles in journals such as the *American Journal of Sociology*, *Journal of Political Economy*, and *Journal of the American Statistical Association*. JSTOR coverage is retrospective to the first volume of each journal but does not include very recent issues, so other databases or indexes must be used to find current articles.

IngentaConnect. One of the most comprehensive indexes to journal literature, IngentaConnect <http://www.ingentaconnect.com> provides access to some 21 million articles from over 31,000 publications. Only some of these are available online in full text, but abstracts are provided for many of the others. An IngentaConnect search for "deterrent and capital punishment" finds several articles, including one from a 2006 issue of the *American Journal of Economics and Sociology*.

ISI Web of Knowledge. Another multidisciplinary database, Web of Knowledge <http://www.isiknowledge.com> indexes more than 1,950 journals in its Social Science Citation Index component, as well as thousands of journals in the sciences and humanities. Web of Knowledge provides abstracts, rather than full text of articles, but one of its great strengths is a "Cited Reference Search" that can be used like KeyCite or Shepard's to find recent articles that cite an older work. You can then see in turn where *those* articles are cited, bringing research up to the most recent published scholarship.

SSRN. The Social Science Research Network <http://www.ssrn.com> is a way to expand research beyond published journals into working papers and other sources that have not yet been published. Papers can be found through title and abstract keyword searches, and most can be retrieved in PDF without charge.

Specialized Resources. Social science scholarship can also be found in abstract services covering publications of specific disciplines. One advantage of these more specialized services is that they may cover not just journal articles but a broader range of sources in the discipline, such as book chapters, conference proceedings, and dissertations. Two of the most important of these services for our purposes are PsycINFO and Sociological Abstracts.

PsycINFO <http://www.apa.org/psycinfo/> (available by subscription through one of several database vendors) is the most comprehensive index of the literature in psychology, and also covers selected material from related fields such as psychiatry, medicine, biology, education, and social work. It provides abstracts of articles in more than 2,100 journals, as well as dissertations, book chapters, books, and book reviews. A search for "deterrence" in article titles finds works in sources such as *Deviant*

Behavior, Journal of Applied Social Psychology, and *Journal of Personality & Social Psychology* as well as criminology and law/psychology journals.

Sociological Abstracts <http://www.csa.com/factsheets/socioabs-set-c. php> (like PsycINFO, generally available through a login link from a library site) is the principal index for articles relating to sociology. Such disciplines as political science, anthropology, economics and the humanities are also reviewed. More than 2,600 journals are covered. Here a search for "capital punishment and deterrence" finds sources such as dissertations, books, and articles in the *Journal of Social Issues*, *Punishment & Society*, and *Social Justice Research*.

Statistics. Finding statistics can be an important part of establishing social baselines or identifying social trends. The best starting point for finding statistics is often the Bureau of the Census's annual *Statistical Abstract of the United States* <http://www.census.gov/compendia/statab/>, which covers a wide range of demographic, economic, and social information. It gives source references for each of its nearly 1,400 tables, making it a convenient lead to other resources with more extensive coverage of specific areas. The FedStats website <http://www.fedstats.gov> is another major resource for links to numerous federal statistical sources.

Criminal statistics are published each year by the U.S. Department of Justice in two major sources. The Federal Bureau of Investigation's *Uniform Crime Reports* (also known as *Crime in the United States*) <http:// www.fbi.gov/ucr/ucr.htm> focuses on criminal activities, and the Bureau of Justice Statistics' *Sourcebook of Criminal Justice Statistics* <http://www. albany.edu/sourcebook/> provides a broader survey of the social and economic impacts of crime. *Uniform Crime Reports* has statistics on homicides, for example, while the *Sourcebook* covers capital punishment topics such as the demographics of death row prisoners and public attitudes on the deterrent effect.

Dissertations. Doctoral dissertations are often overlooked by legal scholars but contain an enormous body of scholarly research. Access to dissertations once required borrowing or purchasing a print or microform copy, but ProQuest Dissertations & Theses: Full Text <http://www. proquest.com> now provides online access in PDF to most dissertations since 1997 as well as selected earlier works. Most dissertations not only have extensive original research but also review the relevant literature and include thorough bibliographies.

*

FOR SOCIAL SCIENTISTS: HOW TO FIND THE LAW

While at first blush it may appear daunting, the way in which American law is published and organized is actually quite systematic. This appendix provides a brief roadmap to help students without legal training to locate the original legal material cited in this book, to update it over time, and to find the law on other topics of interest.

Law students generally do most of their research using the online database systems Westlaw <http://www.westlaw.com> and Lexis <http://www.lexis.com>. These may not be readily available to researchers outside law schools but many Lexis databases are also available through LexisNexis Academic <http://web.lexis-nexis.com/universe>, to which many college university libraries subscribe. Some legal information is accessible for free on the Internet (in particular recent cases and current statutes), but comprehensive legal research usually requires resources available only in a law library or from a major subscription database such as Westlaw or Lexis.

Legal Citation Form. Legal citations can be confusing at first, because they generally use very concise abbreviations and leave out any information considered superfluous. Their basic format was developed over the centuries to allow lawyers and judges to provide long lists of supporting authorities in as little space as possible. The volume number usually goes before the name of the publication, rather than after, and only the first page of a case or article is given. If a second page number appears, it refers to the specific page within a case or article that is quoted or cited. A typical article citation might read Laurens Walker & John Monahan, *Sampling Evidence at the Crossroads*, 80 S. CAL. L. REV. 969, 990 (2007). This cites an article beginning on page 969 of the 80th volume of the *Southern California Law Review*, with a reference specifically to material appearing on page 990.

The format for case citations is similar. A citation to the case reprinted on page 578 in Chapter Five, for example, would read: *Newsome v. McCabe*, 319 F.3d 301 (7th Cir. 2003). This citation conveys who the parties were, where the case can be found, what court issued the decision, and when it was decided. The lead parties to this civil action were James Newsome and Helen McCabe. The text of the decision can be found in volume 319 of the third series of the *Federal Reporter*, beginning on page 301. The abbreviation "7th Cir." informs lawyers that the case was decided by the U.S. Court of Appeals for the Seventh Circuit, the federal appellate court covering Illinois, Indiana, and Wisconsin.

Statutory citations generally indicate the jurisdiction, a specific section, and the year in which the statutory volume was published. Some statutory citations, including those for federal laws, also include a title number designating a specific subject area. 42 U.S.C. § 1983 (2006), for example, refers to section 1983 of title 42 (Public Health and Welfare) in the 2006 edition of the United States Code. Citation form varies somewhat from state to state, but all state statutory citations indicate the name of the source, the section, and the year of publication.

Primary Sources. While American law includes a broad range of authoritative sources (including constitutional provisions, administrative regulations, and presidential executive orders), this brief discussion is limited to the most frequently used—cases and statutes.

Cases. Much of case research is done online these days, but court decisions are still generally cited to the published court reports found in most law libraries. The opinions of the U.S. Supreme Court are published officially in *United States Reports* (abbreviated in citations as U.S.), and in two unofficial series, *Supreme Court Reporter* (abbreviated as S. Ct.) and *United States Supreme Court Reports, Lawyers' Edition* (cited as L. Ed. or L. Ed. 2d). All three reporters provide the full text of the same court opinions. One difference is that the *Supreme Court Reporter* contains numbered headnotes summarizing the points of law in the case, with a classified *key number* assigned to each headnote; the same classification system is also used for reporters covering the lower federal courts and state appellate courts.

Cases from the lower federal courts are found in the *Federal Reporter* (abbreviated as F., F.2d, or F.3d, depending on the series), which publishes decisions of the U.S. Courts of Appeals, and *Federal Supplement* (abbreviated as F. Supp. or F. Supp. 2d), which publishes important decisions of the U.S. District Courts (the main trial courts in the federal system). All state appellate court cases appear in one of several *regional reporters* that cover state courts from the entire country. The *Atlantic Reporter*, for example, covers New Jersey, Pennsylvania, and several other northeastern states.

Most official court websites have the court's opinions for the past several years, and free resources such as FindLaw <http://www.findlaw.com> may provide links to other sources of court decisions. All Supreme Court cases and U.S. Courts of Appeals cases back to 1950 are available free from several online sites, including AltLaw <http://www.altlaw.org> and Public Library of Law <http:/www./plol.org>. Most state court cases before the mid–1990s, however, are only available in print or through the subscription databases.

There are many ways to find cases. Searching online resources for specific keywords is the most common approach, but there are so many thousands of cases that it is easy to be overwhelmed by the results. Some resources rank retrieved documents by relevance, and others permit advanced search approaches such as proximity connectors and they ability to limit a search to specific fields such as headnotes.

When beginning a search for relevant cases, it is often most productive to begin in the secondary sources such as treatises and law reviews to be discussed below. These provide background information as well as citations to major court decisions. Other research approaches that take advantage of case law's extensive classification and indexing systems can also be useful:

Digests. A digest is a subject index to cases, with summaries of decisions arranged by topic and assigned to specific sections or "key numbers." A digest listing consists of a short paragraph summarizing a statement of law from an opinion, followed by a citation to the case. The issue in *Newsome* on the admissibility of expert testimony, for example, is classified as Evidence key number 557, Opinion Evidence— Examination of Experts—Experiments and Results Thereof. Searching in a digest (or on Westlaw) under this key number will find other cases on similar issues. West publishes digests for individual states, for most of its regional reporters (e.g., *Atlantic Digest*), for the federal court system (*Federal Practice Digest*), and for comprehensive coverage of state and federal courts (the *Decennial Digest* series). Relevant key numbers can be found in case headnotes or in the Descriptive Word Index at the beginning or end of each digest set.

American Law Reports. Another source helpful when beginning research is *American Law Reports* (A.L.R.), which publishes legal essays, called *annotations*, that analyze the legal issues involved in various topical areas and describe relevant cases. Someone researching eyewitness testimony issues, for example, might be particularly interested in the annotation "Admissibility, at Criminal Prosecution, of Expert Testimony on Reliability of Eyewitness Testimony, 46 A.L.R.4th 1047 (1986). Even though this annotation was first published more than twenty years ago, it is kept current through an annual supplement (the "pocket part") in the back of the volume. One way to find relevant annotations is to use the multivolume *A.L.R. Index* accompanying the set.

KeyCite and Shepard's Citations. Another way to find relevant cases, as well as law review articles and other documents, is to use a service that lists documents citing a given case. The two major services are KeyCite (available through Westlaw) and Shepard's Citations (available through Lexis and LexisNexis Academic). For lawyers this is an essential part of legal research, because KeyCite and Shepard's also indicate if a case has been overruled or is otherwise no longer good law. For researchers without access to these online resources, sets of *Shepard's Citations* can also be found in print form in many law libraries.

Statutes. In many research situations, the first place to look for controlling authority is in the statutes rather than the case law. A statute governing a situation may be dispositive, although it is necessary to read not only the text of the statute but also court decisions that have applied its provisions. The language of a statute is often subject to varying interpretations, and it is essential to review cases to see how it has been construed by the courts.

Federal laws are published in the official *United States Code* (U.S.C.), which is arranged by subject into numbered titles and sections. Two commercial versions, the *United States Code Annotated* (U.S.C.A.) and *United States Code Service* (U.S.C.S), contain not only the text of the law but also summaries of court decisions under the statute. State statutes are published in similar annotated codes, with each section accompanied by notes of any relevant court decisions. The index volumes at the end of any of these codes can be used to find appropriate sections, and supplements in the back of each annotated code volume provide information on statutory amendments and court decisions issued since the publication of the volume.

Federal and state statutes are also available online through Westlaw and Lexis. LexisNexis Academic includes the U.S.C.S. and annotated state codes. Unannotated codes, without notes of court decisions, are available free online from official federal and state government websites. Resources such as FindLaw <http://www.findlaw.com> can be used to find these sites, but researchers should be aware that most free sites do not provide information about the cases that may be needed to understand statutory provisions.

Secondary Sources. While court decisions and legislative acts determine what the law is, it is usually easiest and most productive to begin legal research in a secondary source, one that reviews the cases and statutes and attempts to fit them together into a cohesive structure. The two major genres of secondary legal material are texts such as treatises and encyclopedias, and articles in law reviews and other legal journals.

Treatises and Encyclopedias. Legal treatises are usually written by respected scholars and explain specific areas of law. Some of these, such as *Nimmer on Copyright* or Larson's *Employment Discrimination*, are massive works spanning ten volumes or more. Others are comprehensive one-volume works sometimes known as *hornbooks*, such as Dobbs's *The Law of Torts* (2000) or LaFave, Israel & King, *Criminal Procedure* (4th ed. 2004). Treatises and hornbooks summarize legal doctrine, provide references to major cases and statutes, and are often good sources of policy arguments for or against various legal rules.

Legal encyclopedias are similar to treatises but much broader, in that they attempt to cover the entire field of American law. They are often the first resource novices consult when researching a topic. Like treatises, they summarize particular topics and provide extensive references to cases and other material that can aid in research. There are two national encyclopedias, *American Jurisprudence 2d* (Am. Jur. 2d) and *Corpus Juris Secundum* (C.J.S.), and most large states have their own encyclopedias summarizing state law. Each encyclopedia has an extensive multivolume index and annual pocket parts to provide updated information.

Law Reviews. Unlike the journals of other professions, most scholarly legal journals (usually known as law reviews) are edited entirely by students. Law review articles can be excellent sources of information on and analysis of legal developments. They contain both *articles* written by law professors, judges or practitioners; and *notes or comments* written by law students.

More than 500 law reviews are published at American law schools, many focusing on specific subject areas. Almost all of these law reviews are available online through Westlaw and Lexis, including LexisNexis Academic. Older issues may be available through other subscription services, such as HeinOnline <http://www.heinonline.org> and (to a more limited extent) JSTOR <http://www.jstor.org>. Many law reviews also make recent issues available on their websites. When using a full-text database of articles, limiting a search to words in the titles of articles (e.g., "title(eyewitness)" rather than simply "eyewitness and reliability") may retrieve articles more directly focusing on a research topic.

Not all law reviews are available online in full text, and another way to find articles is through periodical indexes. An index can even be more effective than a full-text search, because subject headings such as "Eyewitness identification" or "Evidence, expert" can be used to find relevant articles. The two major indexes are *Index of Legal Periodicals and Books* (ILP) and *Current Law Index* (or LegalTrac). Both of these are available in law libraries in printed volumes, and many libraries subscribe to online versions through H.W. Wilson <http://hwwilsonweb.com> (ILP) or the InfoTrac system <http://infotrac.galegroup.com> (LegalTrac).

Other Legal Resources. Another highly respected source of information and analysis is the American Law Institute's (ALI) *Restatements of the Law*. ALI is composed of leading professionals who review the state of the law in a subject area and attempt to articulate its basic principles. Some of the areas covered by *Restatements* include torts (injuries to persons or property), property, contracts, and conflict of laws (choice among different laws). The *Restatements* are authoritative summaries of what the law is and, sometimes, what the ALI members think the law should be. They are available in law libraries and through Westlaw and Lexis (but are not included in LexisNexis Academic).

Finally, be aware that legal research has many nuances that cannot be adequately covered in this brief appendix. An important first step may be to consult a more comprehensive guide such as Morris L. Cohen & Kent C. Olson, *Legal Research in a Nutshell* (9th ed. 2007). Reference librarians at law libraries can also provide assistance.

INDEX

References are to pages.

†